IRIS MURDOC

Iris Murdoch was born in Dublin in 1919. She read Classics at Somerville College, Oxford, and after working in the Treasury and abroad, was awarded a research studentship in philosophy at Newnham College, Cambridge. In 1948 she returned to Oxford as fellow and tutor at St Anne's College and later taught at the Royal College of Art. Until her death in 1999, she lived in Oxford with her husband, the academic and critic, John Bayley. She was made a Dame of the British Empire in 1987 and in the 1997 PEN Awards received the Gold Pen for Distinguished Service to Literature.

Iris Murdoch made her writing debut in 1954 with *Under the Net*. Her twenty-six novels include the Booker Prize-winning *The Sea, The Sea* (1978), the James Tait Black Memorial Prize-winning *The Black Prince* (1973) and the Whitbread Prize-winning *The Sacred and Profane Love Machine* (1974). Her philosophy includes *Sartre: Romantic Rationalist* (1953) and *Metaphysics as a Guide to Morals* (1992); other philosophical writings, including *The Sovereignty of Good* (1970), are collected in *Existentialists and Mystics* (1997).

AVRIL HORNER

Avril Horner is Emeritus Professor of English at Kingston University, London. She writes on women authors and Gothic fiction; her publications include co-authored books on Daphne du Maurier and Edith Wharton. With Anne Rowe she co-edited *Iris Murdoch and Morality* (2010) and *Iris Murdoch: Texts and Contexts* (2012).

ANNE ROWE

Anne Rowe is Associate Professor of English Literature and Director of the Iris Murdoch Archive Project at Kingston University. She is Lead Editor of the *Iris Murdoch Review* and has published widely on Iris Murdoch including *The Visual Arts and Iris Murdoch* (2002) and, with Priscilla Martin, *Iris Murdoch: A Literary Life* (2011).

IRIS MURDOCH

Living on Paper

Letters From Iris Murdoch 1934–1995

Edited by Avril Horner
and Anne Rowe

VINTAGE

1 3 5 7 9 10 8 6 4 2

Vintage
20 Vauxhall Bridge Road,
London SW1V 2SA

Vintage is part of the Penguin Random House group of companies whose addresses can be found at global.penguinrandomhouse.com

Penguin
Random House
UK

Ed Victor Ltd are the agents for the Iris Murdoch estate and handle publication rights to all other works. They can be contacted at info@edvictor.com

United Agents are the agents for film, television and dramatic rights. They can be contacted at gsmart@unitedagents.co.uk

First published by Vintage in 2016
First published in Great Britain in 2015 by Chatto and Windus

penguin.co.uk/vintage

A CIP catalogue record for this book is available from the British Library

ISBN 9780099570158

Printed and bound in Great Britain by Clays Ltd, St Ives PLC

Penguin Random House is committed to a sustainable future for our business, our readers and our planet. This book is made from Forest Stewardship Council® certified paper.

MIX
Paper from
responsible sources
FSC
www.fsc.org   FSC® C018179

For our grandchildren: Rhiannon, Ffion, Owain,
Iestyn, Eirian and Huw Rowe

and

Samuel, Felix, Lulu, Elise and Dexter Horner

Yet words are so damned important now that we're living on paper again. I shall want words from you – and words and words! Write all that you think, sweetheart, including the doubts and terrors. Write all that you think and feel.

Iris Murdoch to David Hicks, 5 January 1946

I can live in letters.

Iris Murdoch to Philippa Foot, June 1968

CONTENTS

LIST OF ILLUSTRATIONS

First Plate Section

Iris Murdoch with Ann Leech and another friend at Badminton School. *From the private collection of Ann Leech by kind permission of Chetham's Library, Manchester.*

Iris Murdoch, 1936. *From the Conradi Archive in the Murdoch Archives at Kingston University.*

Iris Murdoch's Matriculation at Somerville, Oxford, 1938. *By kind permission of Somerville College, Oxford.*

Eduard Fraenkel. *By kind permission of the British Academy; copyright by kind permission of Corpus Christi College, Oxford.*

Donald MacKinnon. *By kind permission of the British Academy.*

Lucy Klatschko taken from 1936 matriculation photograph at Somerville. *By kind permission of Somerville College, Oxford.*

Philippa Foot, 1943.

Frank Thompson, photograph from the Conradi Archive at Kingston University. *Photographer Jean Weinberg.*

Hal Lidderdale, 1943. *Kindly provided by Mary Lidderdale. Photographer Jean Weinberg.*

Leo Pliatzky. *Kindly provided by Jean Harris. Photographer: Jean Weinberg.*

Iris Murdoch in UNRRA Uniform. *From the Conradi Archive in the Murdoch Archives at Kingston University.*

David Hicks. *By kind permission of Tom Hicks.*

Raymond Queneau. *By kind permission of Éditions Gallimard, Paris.*

Wallace Robson. *By kind permission of Mrs Anne Robson.*

Franz Steiner. *Reproduced by kind permission of the Deutsches Literatur Archiv, Marbach; copyright by kind permission of Jeremy Adler.*

Peter Ady. *By kind permission of St Anne's College, Oxford.*

Margaret Hubbard. *By kind permission of St Anne's College, Oxford.*

Iris Murdoch studio portrait. *By Bennett, 117 Oxford Street W1, in the Murdoch Archives at Kingston University.*

Second Plate Section

Cedar Lodge, Steeple Aston. *From the Iris Murdoch Archives at Kingston University.*

Iris Murdoch and John Bayley in the garden of Cedar Lodge, Steeple Aston. *From the Iris Murdoch Archives at Kingston University.*

Michael Oakeshott. *By kind permission of the London School of Economics & Political Science (LSE/IMAGELIBRARY/578).*

Brigid Brophy. *Copyright by kind permission of Topham Picturepoint, 2000.*

Iris Murdoch photographed by Brigid Brophy at Brophy's flat in 1963. *From the Murdoch Archives at Kingston University; copyright by kind permission of Kate Levey.*

Brigid Brophy photographed by Iris Murdoch at Brophy's flat in 1963. *From the Murdoch Archives at Kingston University; copyright by kind permission of Ed Victor Ltd.*

David Morgan. *By kind permission of David Morgan.*

Rachel Fenner. *By kind permission of Rachel Fenner.*

Norah Smallwood. *By kind permission of Ed Victor.*

Elias Canetti, 1963. *By kind permission of Helen Craig.*

Iris Murdoch, 1970. *By Jerry Bauer in Chatto & Windus Archives with kind permission of Chatto & Windus.*

Iris Murdoch taking tea in the garden at Litton Cheney. *By Janet Stone with kind permission of the Reynolds and Janet Stone Estate.*

Iris Murdoch accepting the Booker Prize for *The Sea, The Sea* in 1978, with A. J. Ayer and Booker director Michael Caine. *Permission to reproduce by Oxford Brookes University.*

Roly Cochrane. *By kind permission of Judy Shane.*

Harry Weinberger. *By kind permission of Joanna Garber.*

Josephine Hart. *By kind permission of Lord Maurice Saatchi.*

Iris Murdoch swimming. *By Janet Stone, with kind permission of the Reynolds and Janet Stone Estate.*

Philippa Foot. *By kind permission of Somerville College, Oxford.*

John Bayley, Iris Murdoch, Peter Conradi and Cloudy (Anax in *The Green Knight*). *By kind permission of Peter Conradi.*

Iris Murdoch at her desk at Charlbury Road, Oxford.

Objects in Iris Murdoch's study in Charlbury Road, Oxford. *By Chris Thomas, from the Iris Murdoch Archives at Kingston University.*

Iris Murdoch's desk in Charlbury Road, Oxford. *By Chris Thomas, from the Iris Murdoch Archives at Kingston University.*

Every effort has been made to trace and contact all copyright holders. If there are any inadvertent omissions or errors we will be pleased to correct them at the earliest opportunity.

INTRODUCTION

Iris Murdoch had two studies in her final home, a house in Charlbury Road, Oxford; one was tucked quietly away upstairs at the back, the other was downstairs at the front and was lighter and more accessible. In the small, cluttered upstairs study, Murdoch worked from early in the morning on her philosophical writings and her novels, surrounded by more than a thousand books of philosophy, theology, fiction, poetry and travel. Later, in the afternoons, she retired to the lighter downstairs study where, sitting near the window at a roll-top desk that once belonged to J. R. R. Tolkien, she settled to write her letters. During the course of her life she wrote thousands of letters and was to be remembered fondly by her many friends, her students, would-be writers, interviewers, fans and the most casual of acquaintances, for being so generous with her time. She answered every letter she received, responding even to complete strangers with the utmost courtesy and grace.

All Murdoch's letters were written by hand, many with her Montblanc fountain pen. She would spend up to four hours a day on her correspondence, often responding immediately to friends or lovers who were currently in her thoughts. Her official biographer, Peter J. Conradi, has suggested that 'pen-friendship offered her cost-free intimacy, a point of entry into the imaginative worlds of others, and a stage on which to try out her own personae'[i] – and both the role-playing involved in writing letters, and the information elicited through them, fed into Murdoch's fiction. Unlike biographies, which usually offer coherent portraits of their subjects, letters provide a kaleidoscopic picture, their authors sometimes responding in remarkably different ways to different correspondents, even on the same day. Murdoch's life (1919–99) spanned most of the twentieth century, and her letters give us not only the story of a life lived to capacity by an extraordinary woman, but also a sense of the zeitgeist of both England and Europe during the mid to late twentieth century.

Living on Paper: Letters from Iris Murdoch opens with correspondence from 1934–41, formative years full of raw intellectual excitement and political intensity. These letters written in her youth already demonstrate serious thinking about morality and the human condition. However, pitted against the privileged future almost guaranteed by her Oxford education, loomed the shadow of the Second World War and by 1941 her life was taking turns she had never envisaged. Letters between 1942 and 1944 catalogue both the tedium of her conscripted work at the Treasury and her frustration at being excluded from the war effort. By contrast, letters written when she had been transferred by the United Nations Relief and Rehabilitation Administration (UNRRA) to work in Europe convey both her satisfaction at being able to help displaced persons in Austria and her intoxicated delight with European philosophy and culture. She became enthralled by the intellectualism of café life in Paris and Brussels where, in October 1945, she met Jean-Paul Sartre. By this time she was committed to philosophy and determined to become a writer. The increasing complexity of the love relationships that characterise the letters of these years formed a pattern that would mark her life and her fiction for years to come.

Having resigned from UNRRA in 1946, in 1947 Murdoch became a post-graduate student for a year at Cambridge University, where she found the philosophical climate both stimulating and frustrating. In 1948 she took up a post as fellow and tutor in philosophy at St Anne's in Oxford and letters written between this date and 1954 suggest her pleasure in teaching and learning and her enjoyment of college social life. More poignantly, they catalogue both her unrequited longing for the French writer Raymond Queneau – whom she had met in Innsbruck in 1946 and regarded as her intellectual soulmate – and her final dignified settling for his friendship. The years between 1955 and 1962 saw her fame as a writer rise dramatically and she became an important figure in British culture. Her letters to friends are nevertheless full of humility and empathy, although her compassion occasionally shades into a voyeuristic interest in their private lives. Her marriage in 1956 to John Bayley, that was to prove strong and enduring, ensured a reputable public image. However, her personal life was complicated, each of her many correspondents unaware of either the many others to whom Murdoch also wrote, or how often her life came perilously close to scandal. Even more complex and unwise emotional imbroglios, most notably with two of her students, dominate the letters from the Royal College of Art years (1963–7). Letters written during the extraordinarily productive years between 1968 and 1978, when she wrote a book almost every year, predominantly record intense relationships with two female friends, Philippa Foot and Brigid Brophy. The decade between 1979 and 1989 brought emotional calm, marital security and new enduring friendships that allowed a freer engagement with the politics and the cultural concerns of her time, most evident perhaps in her letters to the American lawyer Albert Lebowitz and his wife, Naomi Lebowitz, a professor of English and comparative literature at Washington University in St Louis. *Living on Paper* ends in 1995, a year in which her letters begin to evidence the onset of the memory loss that was to worsen before her death from Alzheimer's disease in 1999.

Iris Murdoch was a remarkably prolific author. She produced twenty-six novels, a body of philosophical writing which included a study of Sartre, two Platonic dialogues, over thirty essays and two seminal philosophical tracts, *The Sovereignty of Good* (1970) and *Metaphysics as a Guide to Morals* (1992). She also wrote six plays, three of which were adaptations of her novels, a radio play and some poetry, of which only a small proportion has been published. Murdoch's fame, though, came largely from her fiction. Although her novels have been accused of being patrician and socially narrow, they appeal to a wide range of readers. They manage to combine challenging highbrow intellectualism with gripping realism while the powerful passions and paralysing obsessions of her characters drive plots that are both fantastic and compelling. Her characters experience common moral and emotional dilemmas but many also undergo greater extremes of suffering, such as the anguish of male homosexual desire (at a time when it was illegal to act on it), or the transgressive pleasures and horrors of sadomasochism and incest. Above all, she was superb at portraying the madness of love and the way it can transform ordinary people into crazed and possessive beings. The reading public eagerly awaited the latest best-seller while scholars welcomed her fresh engagement with the works of philosophers such as Plato, Sartre and Simone Weil.

Despite her own reputation as a significant philosopher, Murdoch never wavered from her belief in the paramount importance of literature: 'For both the collective and the individual salvation of the human race, art is doubtlessly more important than philosophy, and literature most important of all'.[ii] If the point of philosophy is to 'clarify', then the point of literature is to 'mystify' – or make her readers *think*. She believed that literature could touch people's lives profoundly; philosophy less so because of its esoteric nature. Indeed, her artistic ambition was to construct a 'moral psychology' within her fiction that would enchant and challenge her readers intellectually and morally. While this intellectual rigour gave her novels originality and English fiction a distinctive new voice, Murdoch's spellbinding narratives – which combine psychological complexity with humour, tolerance and a deep understanding of human frailty – ensured her continuing popularity with the general reader.

Murdoch's versatility makes her fiction hard to categorise neatly, even in retrospect. She has been described variously as a surrealist, a magical realist and a fabulist. The theologian Don Cupitt remembers how, to those who read her novels as they appeared from the 1950s onwards, the most obvious comparison was not with the realists but 'with the great Swedish film director Ingmar Bergman'.[iii] Her extensive and complex dialogues with other art forms, in particular painting, challenge the definition of Murdoch as a realist writer in the conventional sense. Despite her claim to be working in the nineteenth-century tradition and her admiration for novelists such as Tolstoy, Dostoevsky and Henry James, she strongly asserted that she was driving the novel forward, not backward. 'One can't go back', she said. 'One's consciousness is different; I mean our whole narrative technique is something completely different'.[iv] Her early novel, *The Sandcastle* (1957), alludes to Henry James's short story 'The Figure in the Carpet' and thus implicitly chides critics who fail to see that aesthetics and form are as important to a story's meaning as its plot and characters. The point of this reference was to alert readers to the experimentalism in her own writing: 'there is a great deal of experimentation in the work, but I don't want it to be too evident', she once said.[v] The wording of a novel's title often hints at the complex use of a symbol – a net, a bell, the sea, a dream, a severed head, a rose, a unicorn – that the reader will find within it. Titles also sometimes refer to groups whose meaning outstrips their superficial significance: angels, enchanters, philosophers, nuns, soldiers. Even simple words can carry huge symbolic weight in Murdoch's work, marking her out as both a modern and a highly poetic novelist.

Many prizes for fiction came her way, including the James Tait Black Memorial Prize for *The Black Prince* (1973) and the Booker Prize for *The Sea, The Sea* (1978). Nonetheless, she fell out of fashion, both as a novelist and a philosopher, during the 1980s and 1990s. This partial eclipse occurred perhaps because her reputation became dogged by some reviewers' dismissive claims that her novels deal only with the bourgeois sorrows of highly educated characters obsessed by their overcomplicated love lives. In academia, fired by structuralism and postmodernism, university departments were adopting a rigorously theoretical approach to the analysis of literary works, looking for evidence of Derridean wordplay and a desire to deconstruct absolutes while dismissing the idea that a literary text can have intrinsic and stable meaning. Murdoch's novels – which uphold absolutes such as love and the Good and which promote the moral worth of art as a path to truth – were seen to fail such tests and were sidelined. It is true that she was suspicious of fashionable literary theories, in particular structuralism and deconstruction, which seem to privilege the linguistic system over the will and freedom of the individual, but in fact she engaged closely with contemporary philosophy, including Jacques Derrida's work.

Murdoch's eclipse lasted less than twenty years: since the late 1990s her writing has been internationally celebrated and her reputation revived. Her fiction is now hailed by many as a paradigm for morally responsible art and her philosophy is seen as important matter for debate in the field of virtue ethics. Since 2000 a raft of new publications on her work has emerged from the UK, Europe, Japan and the USA. This global response is redefining Iris Murdoch as an eminent philosopher of the twentieth century and has triggered fresh interest in her fiction.

Recent research into Murdoch's life has, however, revealed a number of enigmas and contradictions and these have occasioned both perplexity and fierce debate among her critics. Revelations about her personal life since the publication of Peter J. Conradi's official biography in 2001 have sometimes been used to challenge the previously held image of her as a somewhat saintly puritanical figure. Bran Nicol, a subtle reader of her fiction, has described her as 'a complex, sexualised being, capable of cruelty and deception as much as kindness and wit'.[vi] Even Conradi, whose biography is both comprehensive and compassionate, has more recently observed that her letters to Frank Thompson, a contemporary at Oxford to whom she became close and who was killed in the Second World War, can seem 'arch and irritating'. He notes that Thompson was deeply hurt by Murdoch's promiscuity and by her casual frankness about it in letters to him (in particular her taking M. R. D. Foot, a fellow Oxford student, and Thomas Balogh, an Oxford tutor, as lovers during the summer of 1943). Conradi even speculates that Thompson's fateful decision to enter Bulgaria might have been in part prompted by the 'unwelcome news' received when he was in Serbia in 1944 about Murdoch's affair with Foot: 'was [Thompson's] reckless disregard for his survival a peevish reprisal for her troubled love life?'.[vii] Martha Nussbaum, a careful interpreter of Murdoch's philosophy, has claimed that Murdoch was unable to live up to her own definitions of moral goodness and that she was self-absorbed, controlling and predatory.[viii] In a measured epilogue to her most recent book on Iris Murdoch, Maria Antonaccio defends the author in the face of Nussbaum's claims and warns against reading the work alongside the life in any simple way.[ix]

Perhaps the same caveat needs to be made in relation to reading Murdoch's life through her letters. Effusive and emotionally weighted language in Murdoch's correspondence can be misleading. Indeed her language frequently blurs the boundaries between platonic and sexual liaisons so that deciphering accurately the extent of intimacy is challenging. Her vocabulary is often of the kind most usually reserved for sexually intimate relationships: 'I love you deeply' or 'I embrace you with much love' are refrains throughout. But such language in Murdoch's letters does not necessarily imply sexual intimacy and/or a desire for total commitment to one person. She was progressive, both in her advocacy of complete emotional and sexual freedom in relationships and in her sense of gender as something fluid rather than fixed.

For Murdoch, however, the highest form of love 'is the perception of individuals. Love is the extremely difficult realisation that something other than oneself is real'.[x] Such deep attention to the Other also occasions precisely that emotional generosity and lack of possessiveness that her letters display, making room for the possibility of complete freedom. The person one loves should not be entrapped in one's own fantasy world, as so often happens with Murdoch's fictional characters. (The emotionally and sexually rapacious Charles Arrowby in *The Sea, The Sea* comes to mind here.)

Murdoch's 'love' in this sense is enabling and not restricting, and sexual encounters in her fiction are often part of a healing process that allows characters to move on from debilitating obsessions (as, for example, in *The Green Knight* when the young, wounded Harvey Blackett and Sefton Anderson make love briefly and therapeutically). However, her best novels also portray the tension between freedom and obsession that she experienced herself; this tension is what makes her novels compulsive reading. She was well aware that love could enslave as well as liberate, and many letters in *Living on Paper* demonstrate Murdoch's own obsessive desire for, or obsessive interest in, certain people at various points in her life. David Hicks, an Oxford contemporary, is replaced by Raymond Queneau, the French experimental writer, who is followed by the political philosopher Michael Oakeshott, the author Elias Canetti and the writer and activist Brigid Brophy as individuals with whom she cultivated intense and passionate liaisons. This pattern in her life has influenced the structure of *Living on Paper*; letters to specific people often appear in 'blocks', indicating periods of emotional obsession.

Such real-life experience undoubtedly flows into her portrayal of obsessive desire in her fiction, as do her own sexual relationships (which often took the form of 'diffused eroticisms'[xi] – erotically charged relationships that were deliberately not fully sexually consummated). And here we have another puzzle: in a letter to David Morgan written in mid-January 1972, Murdoch notes, 'I disapprove of promiscuity'. The apparent contradiction between this statement and the fact that Murdoch had many lovers herself – and that she encouraged others to engage in such free relationships – is perhaps illuminated by the remark that follows: 'To be oneself, free, whole, is partly a matter of escape from obsession, neurosis, fear, compulsions etc.' Sexual freedom was for Murdoch just one aspect of a wider freedom – social and political – that is paradoxically and inevitably tied up with other people and their difference from oneself. For Murdoch, freedom is always defined within a relationship or a social context and so 'love' for her is 'the imaginative recognition of, that is respect for, this otherness'.[xii] This is not to say that she was blind to the potential damage to others that such sexual freedom could bring in its wake, and this ambivalence is expressed in the novels repeatedly.

The reader is, then, faced with a choice: whether to see Murdoch's many intimate relationships as an attempt to live out a liberal forward-thinking moral philosophy, or whether to see that philosophy as a convenient legitimation of a personal freedom that, it could be argued, included a rather casual attitude to sexual relations and some emotional exploitation. In the end, it is for the reader to decide; *Living on Paper* adds another piece to the jigsaw of biographical information that helps us put together a picture of this complex and enigmatic personality.[xiii] In trying to understand Murdoch's chameleon nature, perhaps we would do well to remember her fondness for the myth of Proteus, who was able to change himself into any shape he wished, a myth that she used to assuage John Bayley's occasional anxiety about their marriage:

> It was in reply to my despairing comment that I couldn't understand her, or the different person she became for the many others with whom she seemed, in my view, helplessly entangled. 'Remember Proteus', she used to say. 'Just keep tight hold of me and it will be all right.' [. . .] When Hercules held tightly on to him throughout all these transformations he was compelled in the end to surrender, and to resume his proper shape as the man he was.[xiv]

Living on Paper tells Murdoch's life story in her own words and provides a rather different portrait from those currently available. Her letters vividly convey her wonderful sense of humour and her sometimes wicked irreverence – thereby providing a sharp contrast to the almost austere and serious tone of many formal interviews and some previous accounts of her life. Moreover, her relationships with Michael Oakeshott and Brigid Brophy, to name but two of her correspondents, are fully documented for the first time in this volume. Her letters also give unique glimpses into the minutiae that made up her everyday life and they record her frequent travels, mostly omitted from biographical accounts; she was deeply interested in and stimulated by other cultures and traditions and eager to communicate her experiences on paper to lovers and friends. Her love of painting and languages and her desire to understand them better are displayed in many letters, as is her constant openness to new writers and new ideas. She was not intellectually or emotionally closed in any way and this openness contributed to the development of both her fiction and her philosophy. She was not closed, either, to the difficulties facing others and her letters are full of many small and sometimes extravagant acts of kindness and offers of help. Her lifelong insecurity about her own abilities is often painfully evident, as is her modesty about her achievements (she rarely used the title of 'Dame'). Although *Living on Paper* paints a picture of immense energy and commitment, we should remember that it represents only a fragment of the activity that produced a remarkable body of work.

Finally, the great value of Murdoch's letters – which are often direct and very intimate – is that they give the reader a strong and lively sense of what

Iris Murdoch was like, not only as a novelist or philosopher, but also as a woman living out her daily life. If Murdoch's philosophy gives us a picture of a gifted intellectual and her novels convey her abiding interest in moral psychology and the contingency of life, Murdoch's letters show us a warm and complicated woman who loved life but who also frequently struggled with a sense of her own frailty and who endured dark episodes. Surprisingly, perhaps, few letters engage with philosophical ideas and theories in any depth; readers must turn back to her philosophy for that. Instead, they give us a portrait of a woman who lived unconventionally and according to her own moral code; of a complex individual whose reactions to others and world events were often intense and frequently irreverent; of a woman whose ideas and values changed profoundly over the years. However, the young Communist does not simply follow the predictable pattern of metamorphosing into the old conservative as the years pass: reactionary thoughts often jostle with radical ideas, even during the last phase of her life. Because they document so vividly the complexity of their author, Murdoch's letters constitute a distinct aspect of her writing persona: they are not merely an addition to her *oeuvre*, but an integral part of it, both illuminating and complicating our understanding of her philosophy and her fiction.

Editorial Matters

The 3,200 or so letters written by Iris Murdoch and held in the Iris Murdoch Archives at Kingston University, London, were the first inspiration for *Living on Paper*. Of the sixty runs held there, we selected letters from Murdoch to Marjorie Boulton, Brigid Brophy, Elias Canetti (copies), Roly Cochrane, Peter Conradi, Scott Dunbar, Rachel Fenner, Philippa Foot, Lucy Klatschko (Sister Marian), Georg Kreisel (copies), Michael Levey, Hal Lidderdale, Leo Pliatzky, Raymond Queneau, Suguna Ramanathan, Wallace Robson and Harry Weinberger. We have also accessed letters from many other archives in the UK and abroad, and read in excess of 5,000 when making our selection for this volume.

Five letters to Frank Thompson and eighteen to David Hicks that are held in the Bodleian Library, Oxford, have previously been published in Peter J. Conradi's *A Writer at War: Letters and Diaries 1938–46*.[xv] They are included here because they document how important both these relationships were to Murdoch's emotional development, and because they are historically and biographically relevant.

We have also chosen to include information about Murdoch's relationships with certain individuals who are not represented by any letters in this volume but who were important to her. They include her two Oxford colleagues, Peter Ady and Margaret Hubbard, and her lover Franz Steiner, letters to whom have either been destroyed or were not accessible when we compiled

Living on Paper. Also, two disproportionately short letter runs from the Conradi Archive[xvi] at Kingston University serve only fleetingly to represent Murdoch's love for two highly significant figures in her life, Elias Canetti[xvii] and Sister Marian of Stanbrook Abbey. These relationships were profoundly important to Murdoch and to omit them from the overview of her life would be to diminish it; they therefore feature in our narrative despite the paucity or absence of letters. Sadly, we could not locate any letters to John Bayley.

Living on Paper is not an exhaustive account of Murdoch's epistolary history. Letters to some significant figures in her life (such as Vladimir Bukovsky, A. S. Byatt, Honor Tracy and Richard Wollheim) are not included, either because they have been destroyed or because they were unavailable at the time of writing. Nor have we included letters from two other recently published collections of letters: Geoffrey Meyers's *Remembering Iris Murdoch* and Gillian Dooley and Graham Nerlich's edited correspondence between Iris Murdoch and the Australian philosopher Brian Medlin.[xviii] While both collections are noteworthy in relation to Murdoch's friendships, readers can easily access these volumes independently.

Limitations of space have meant that some fascinating letter runs that are held in the Iris Murdoch Archives at Kingston University, or that have been loaned to us, have been omitted, for example letters to the architect Stephen Gardiner, to Murdoch's former student Julian Chrysostomides, to her philosopher friend Denis Paul and to the painter Barbara Dorf. Other important runs held at Kingston that are only minimally represented here include letters to Roly Cochrane, an American fan of her work, and her painter friend, Harry Weinberger. Reading these letter runs, however, helped us to understand more fully Murdoch's personality and the way her mind worked – and therefore aided us in the selection and editing of the letters that are included.

To cut down on distracting apparatus in the letters, readers will find biographical profiles of all correspondents, close friends and other significant figures in the Directory of Names and Terms at the end of *Living on Paper*. Other names, of less significance and perhaps mentioned only once or twice in the letters, are explained in footnotes. The Directory also includes brief explanations of important philosophical movements, and profiles of certain philosophers and writers whose work influenced Murdoch.

For the ease of the reader – and to save space – we have occasionally removed from letters: detailed information concerning arrangements for future meetings; repetition of information from one letter to another; some cryptic comments that are so esoteric as to be impenetrable or meaningless; references to people or events that are either insignificant or that we cannot account for or explain adequately. Such omissions are indicated in the usual way with ellipses. There are a handful of individuals whose identities we have been unable to explain, despite our best efforts; as these are minor characters in the tapestry of Murdoch's life we hope readers will not be too distracted by them. In order to protect the privacy of certain individuals we have anonymised them by using names that are not their own.

Dating Murdoch's letters has been largely a process of sleuthing. While her early letters do usually include day and month (e.g. 4 October), she often omits the year. Later letters are sometimes not dated at all. Fortunately many of the letters were kept in their original envelopes by her correspondents and have been dated from postmarks where these are legible. Other letters have been dated from content or by liaising with still living correspondents. Any date, or part of date, that appears in square brackets signifies either date of posting (rather than date of writing) or is a date that has been deduced by us. Where we have had to guess a date, or part of it, we have included a question mark. All letters selected for inclusion were checked by more than one transcriber and sustained attempts were made to decipher any remaining illegible words; there are therefore very few gaps within letters due to illegibility.

Despite our best efforts, *Living on Paper* might still contain errors; these are our responsibility alone and we would be pleased to hear from readers with any relevant information and corrections. We would also be pleased to hear from anyone possessing, or knowing of, any letters written by Iris Murdoch that are not already in the public domain.

PART ONE:

Schoolgirl and Student

August 1934 to December 1941

Iris Murdoch was born on 15 July 1919 at 59 Blessington Street, North Dublin, her mother's home town. She and her mother soon moved to 12 Caithness Road, Hammersmith in London to join her father, Hughes Murdoch, who had taken the post of second-class clerk at the Ministry of Health in 1919 after having served as second lieutenant in the 1st King Edward's Horse regiment during the First World War. In 1926 the Murdochs moved to 4 Eastbourne Road, Chiswick where the family of three, remembered with great fondness by Murdoch as 'a perfect trinity of love',[i] was to live for many years. Although they lived in London, they returned to Ireland most years for holidays. At the age of five, Murdoch was sent to the Froebel Demonstration School at Colet Gardens, Hammersmith where she was very happy, later recalling those years as a time of 'light, of freedom' during which she enjoyed 'the great greedy pleasures of learning, the calm kindly authority of teachers, the instant amiability of the children'.[ii] Excelling at all aspects of her learning, she was made head girl in her final year. In 1932, Murdoch won one of the two open scholarships to Badminton School, Bristol, a small, 'internationally minded', 'forward-looking', tolerant and liberal institution with only 163 girls, of whom ninety-six were boarders.[iii] After an unhappy and homesick start, she soon settled in and began to thrive on its atmosphere of rigorous learning and left-wing politics. In 1938 she was awarded an Open Exhibition to read English at Somerville College, Oxford. She quickly changed direction, however, moving to Classics in order to study 'Mods' (Greek and Latin language and literature) and 'Greats' (philosophy and ancient history). Here she met Mary Scrutton (later to become Mary Midgley), Philippa Bosanquet (later to become Philippa Foot), David Hicks, Frank Thompson, M. R. D. Foot, Hal Lidderdale and Leo Pliatzky, who would all feature significantly in her life.

The short run of eleven early letters that comprise this section spans the years from 1934, when Murdoch was a fifteen-year-old at Badminton School, to the end of 1941, when she was in her final year at Oxford. A number are to her school friend, Ann Leech, the youngest daughter of a Manchester doctor, whom she met on her first day at Badminton and who was to become a lifelong friend. Murdoch's future talents and interests are already evident: the teenager's excited recording of a dramatic incident on a family holiday in Ireland presages more mature impulses to transform life into narrative. An early love of the visual arts, as well as a determination to paint, foreshadows her courting the company of painters and the inclusion of favourite paintings in her novels. Her enthusiastic reading of Gorki and Mallarmé anticipates her subsequent intoxication with European philosophy and literature.

The zeitgeist of the late 1930s generated a fierce left-wing political idealism, and Murdoch became heavily involved in Labour Club activities and joined the Communist Party soon after arriving at Oxford. On the one hand she loathed politics, much preferring the study of Classics; on the other she believed that in such times no one had any choice but to be politically engaged. Her radical leanings are expressed in her letters to Ann Leech and include an animated account of 'The Festival of Music for the People' at the Royal Albert Hall in 1939. Her Communist sympathies had stripped her of the Protestantism of her youth and she defined her religion at this point in her life as a passionate belief in the beautiful and a faith in the ultimate triumph of the people. In 1939 she shared the common anxiety that Britain might be overrun by Nazis in the near future; indeed, in March of that year some of her Oxford contemporaries, including Frank Thompson and Leo Pliatzky, acted in and produced their own play, *It Can Happen Here*, which imagined Britain as a fascist state.[iv] Later that year Murdoch performed with an acting troupe, the Magpie Players, a travelling theatre comprising young men and women from Oxford who toured the West Country from 28 August to 16 September 1939, performing in small theatres, village halls, schools and in the open air. All proceeds were donated to various humanitarian organisations. Murdoch became fully aware of the privileged life she led during the war years that followed, when so many were suffering and dying, and in 1940 confessed to Eduard Fraenkel, her tutor, that she felt guilty about her inability to participate in the war effort. One of the central tenets of her philosophy, that morally improving the self is a fundamental prerequisite for a healthy society, is seen to emerge during these years, as does persistent insecurity about her intellectual abilities. In a more intimate vein, Murdoch confides to Ann Leech that she already has the capacity to be in love with six men at once. Such 'complications and distresses' will continue well into her adult life and will also feature in the fictional lives of her characters.

To Ann Leech, written from Ireland where Murdoch was on holiday with her parents.

15 Mellifont Av
Kingstown
Co. Dublin
29 August 1934

Dear Ann,

Hello! A grey and relentless sky has been pouring rain on us for the last week, and the sun has forgotten how to shine.

I will come to Manchester on September 4th, Tuesday, by the train arriving at London Road station at 2.10 p.m., 10.30 from Euston. Will that be all right? Please write to 4 Eastbourne Rd and say if it is.

Great excitement here! Last Sunday week night (that sounds queer) a terrible storm got up, and on Monday morning about 8 a.m. the first maroon[1] went for the lifeboat. I was in the bathroom at the time. I never got washed so quick as I did then. I was dressed and doing my hair when the second maroon went. Then I flew out of the house. Doors were banging all the way down the street, and the entire population of Dun Laoghaire[2] seemed to be running to the harbour. Doodle (Daddy) and my cousin had already left with the first maroon.

The lifeboat was in the harbour mouth when I arrived. I asked a man what was up. A yacht had evidently broke its moorings and drifted out of the harbour or something, anyway we could just see it on the horizon. A high sea was running and I was glad to have my mackintosh with me. I dashed down the pier – which by the way is a mile long – and was drenched by the spray and the waves breaking over the pier. The sand whipped up by the wind, drove in clouds and I got some in my eye, which hurt like anything.

The lifeboat had an awful job, it was pitching and tossing, and once we thought it was going down, but it got to the yacht, which turned out to be empty, and towed it back amid the enthusiastic cheers of the populace. Three

---

1 A firework intended to imitate the noise of a cannon, used especially as a warning.
2 Town on the east coast of Ireland, about seven miles (11 km) south of Dublin.

other yachts broke their moorings in the harbour, of these, two went down, and the other was saved and towed to calmer waters just as it was dashing itself to pieces against the pier. That was a great thrill. The next excitement was a huge German liner – three times as big as the mail boat – that anchored in the bay. It was too big to get into the harbour. Launches took the passengers ashore and the officers conversed in German, much to everyone's delight. The ship was touring Ireland and the tourists were taken in buses round the Wicklow Mountains. Today they are raising one of the yachts that sunk.

We go back to England tomorrow, and I hope we have a better crossing this time. Goodbye Ann.

See you on Tuesday.

Lots of love

From

Iris

To Ann Leech.

Badminton School
Bristol
17 July 1938

Dear Ann,

You angel! Thanks ever so much. Your present was *Lust for Life* by Irving Stone – a novel about Van Gogh. I read it most of Friday, finished it about 6.30 – 500 large pages, not bad going – and shall probably change it tomorrow! I may add 2s 6d and get Herbert Read's *Art Now*.[1] I haven't quite decided. *Lust*

---

1 Published in 1933. Read was a champion of modern British artists such as Paul Nash, Ben Nicholson, Henry Moore and Barbara Hepworth. Between 1933 and 1938 he was editor of the trendsetting *Burlington Magazine*.

for Life was terrific. It just knocked me off my feet – I had no idea Van Gogh was such a wonderful, passionate, dramatic sort of person. He began as a clerk in an art dealer's, where he was not successful, as he refused to humour customers who had bad taste. Then he tried teaching, tried to go to a university, went as an Evangelist to the worst Belgian mining districts. Here he lost his job because the heads of his missionary society, coming round unexpectedly, found him conducting a service in a filthy hut, all covered with coal dust and dressed in sacking, as he had given all his clothes away. This, they thought, was a most shameful degradation of the dignity of the church!

He was heartbroken – and one day, sitting outside the mine, he began to sketch the miners as they came out – and that was the beginning. During his whole life he only sold *one* picture – and had to be supported by his brother Theo, a Paris art dealer and one of the salt of the earth. He went to Arles eventually and lived with Gaugin [*sic*], painting passionately, wildly all day in the terrific heat, quarrelling about art with Gaugin all night, and living on absinthe. This couldn't last long – he began to have epileptic fits, and finally shot himself lest he should become permanently mad and be a burden on Theo. Theo was heartbroken and died a few months later.

I am now, consequently, consumed with the desire to paint all day and all night – and am making a start this morning with an oil painting of Maria. If only I were about six times as good as I am, I'd chuck up Oxford and go to an art school. I'd sell every faculty I have to paint one good picture.

Sorry – I hope all this hasn't bored you.

Yesterday Architecture Club and me went to Montacute House, near Yeovil – my God it was glorious. It's a *huge* Elizabethan house, in perfect preservation inside and out, full of the most exquisite carving, and surrounded by the most perfect Elizabethan gardens. It's just the place Bacon[1] would have loved – square velvety lawns, lily ponds, yew trees centuries old, and two 'gazebos'. (Bet you don't know what they are!) There were white fantail doves flying about it all the while, and there *were* peacocks to walk on the terraces, but apparently the ungrateful birds spend all their time roosting in the depths of the wood! I wonder what they think they're kept for?

Good luck for Sweden – I expect you are feeling thrilled. [. . .] Some people have all the luck! We shall probably go to Ireland and join in the family quarrel – ugh.

I hope you have a marvellous time – and thanks awfully for the present.
Lots of love
Iris

Finished the painting – it's frightful!

---

1 Francis Bacon (1561–1626), English philosopher, statesman, scientist, essayist and author.

To Ann Leech.

4 Eastbourne Rd
Chiswick
London
W4
27 September 1938

Dear Ann,

Thank the gods for one piece of good news – I am most terribly glad –
only sad that I shan't be with you. I was going to write you today anyhow,
as I heard your news from Orpen[1] – or was it Ysobel? Dulci[2] has just been
staying with me, and I haven't been to bed before 1 for about a week. She
is very gloomy, that is she believes the worst will happen, but is taking it
calmly. I too believe that the worst will happen – but I don't feel at all afraid
yet – only sad and strangely amused. I don't want to leave London – I love
the city, and if it's going to be smashed up, I want to be there.

I can see nothing beyond Saturday[3] – so I am treasuring these last few days
of peace, and perhaps of life – reading poetry, and enjoying pictures and
music. Of course this is just melodramatic rot – the chances are that you and
I will be alive and healthy this time next year, and the world certainly won't
end on Saturday – but I feel the sword of Damocles over me all the same.

We are storing food, my father is helping the man next door to build an
air raid shelter in his garden, and tonight we get our gas-masks – 'Oh brave
new world . . .'[4]

Singularly enough I feel happier now, in spite of my sadness, than I have
ever felt for years. This isn't *real* you know – the real things will go on,
whether we are blown to pieces or not – I am very close to reality now –
something infinitely calm and still and beautiful.

Sorry to have become mystical – Dulci and I went into Westminster Abbey
yesterday, and prayed with many other people beside the grave of the
Unknown Warrior – the atmosphere was indescribable.

I was to go to lunch with an MP tomorrow, but Parliament is meeting,
so I wrote to ask him to get me a ticket instead. It will be exciting if he
managed to get me one.

1 Margaret Orpen, who was later to become Lady Margaret Lintott. The headmistress of Badminton
  School, Beatrice May Baker ('BMB'), had asked Margaret Orpen to keep an eye on the young Iris who
  felt homesick on joining the school. 'Ysobel' was presumably another school friend.
2 Dulcibel Broderick, another Badminton friend who later became Dulcibel MacKenzie, author of *Steps
  to the Bar*.
3 Neville Chamberlain's eagerly awaited return from Munich on Saturday 1 October 1938. Chamberlain
  returned triumphantly to Britain claiming to have negotiated 'peace in our time' but this act of
  appeasement failed: almost a year later, Hitler invaded Poland.
4 Miranda's exclamation in Shakespeare's *The Tempest*.

I am happy that you are going to Cambridge as you wished – the best of all luck to you. Do you remember in *Julius Caesar*, where Brutus and Cassius take leave of each other before Philippi? 'And if we meet again, why then we'll smile – If not, this parting is well taken . . .'[1]

Forgive me – it's not often I get such a grand opportunity for melodrama.

Auf Wiedersehen

Love

Iris

To David Hicks, an Oxford contemporary three years older than Murdoch, who graduated in PPE (philosophy, politics and economics) at Worcester College in the summer of 1938 and who had recently embarked on a Diploma of Education course. Murdoch, now in her first year at Somerville College, met Hicks through the university branch of the Communist Party.[v] Zuzzanna Przeworska, mentioned in the letter, was a Polish undergraduate at Somerville in the year above Murdoch and an enthusiastic member of the Communist Party.[vi]

Somerville

20 November 1938

Dear David,

Zuzzanah is in a raging fury – Gaetulian lions[2] are as sucking doves beside her – so I think on the whole it would be a good thing to return her typewriter *quam celerrime*.[3]

I have just returned from having a rather embarrassed tea with the principal[4] – it consisted of a series of nerve-wracking pauses strung together by desperate attempts at conversation, the chief topic being Siamese cats! – What a waste, to go to tea with a really intelligent woman and talk about Siamese cats. I have now come back to the more imperial company of Aeschylus, whom you no doubt consider to be on an equal level of futility – and I admit his plays have no great bearing on surplus value[5] and bills of exchange.

I hope you have sustained no fresh damage since last we met in fights

1 Murdoch misquotes Brutus's words: 'If we do meet again, why, we shall smile; / If not, why then this parting was well made'.

2 The Gaetulian lion was an African lion of fierce reputation, described in both Horace's *Odes* and Pliny's *Natural History*. Gaetulia, in the ancient world, was the land of the Gaetuli, a warlike Berber Libyan tribe.

3 as quickly as possible.

4 Helen Darbishire, principal of Somerville between 1931 and 1945.

5 'Surplus value', a concept developed by Karl Marx, refers to the value produced by workers in excess of their own labour-cost. This profit is appropriated by the capitalist owner and forms the basis of capital accumulation.

with fascists or pseudo-fascists[1] – I feel like having a fight with somebody right now – Siamese cats! What a charming world we live in.

Well, goodbye, give my love to the deadheads,[2] and don't forget Zuzzanah's typewriter.

Iris

To David Hicks.

4 Eastbourne Rd
29 December 1938

Dear David,

Thank you very much indeed for your charming letter. The weather didn't hurt me in the least and as for feeling 'fooled' – well, I didn't come all that way to see any refugees, Czech or otherwise, or any number of other Davids – I came to see you and your family. May I say how very much I liked your family – and how much pleasure it gave me to see *you* in your natural habitat.

I didn't realise you wouldn't be coming back to Oxford and I certainly didn't know you were going to start teaching so soon – you should have told me. I won't pretend I'm not sorry about it. A very short while now I have 'delighted in your company',[3] but long enough to know that you have something I want and that I've not hitherto found and I think I have something you want. I am, to use your words, 'a seeker after my own species'.

I shall write when there is time from Oxford and tell you of Zuzzanah's latest *affaire* and what sort of ties Peter Shinnie[4] is wearing and why I think my philosophy of life is better than yours – and in return I should appreciate an occasional dissertation on the universe in general and young Hampstead in particular. Next vac – well, the animals at the zoo will still invite us with their interesting curves, and I should like extremely to improve my acquaintance with your family.

And now I wish you all the luck and happiness in the world. Believe in yourself. You're *not* so 'bloody mediocre'.

Love from

Iris

---

1 Minor altercations between Communist Party student members and other political groups occasionally took place in Oxford.

2 Boring or unenterprising people.

3 From the late sixteenth-century song 'Greensleeves'.

4 Peter Shinnie (1915–2007) was active in the Communist Party club at Oxford. He later became one of the founders of African archaeology and held professorial posts in Ghana and Canada.

PS And pray cease considering me as a child. I am in many ways considerably more mature than you are.

To Ann Leech.

                                                        4 Eastbourne Rd
                                                   [early April 1939[vii]]

Dear Ann,
    Hello, Hello, Hello! I'm terribly sorry too that I didn't write all last term,
but for reasons similar to yours I have been cutting down everything, and
correspondence was one of the first to go.
    I'm terribly glad you are enjoying Cambridge now – I was sure you would
soon. Gosh! I was glad to hear from you – going to write to you very soon.
But you haven't joined CUSC[1] yet! Shades of Marx and Engels!! Of course
it's sensible from an academic point of view. You will get a first and I shall
get a third or a *satisfecit* (*quod avertant dei!*).[2] Still, there are days in which I
think every intelligent man and woman has a definite duty to study politics.
Next year it may all be too late.
    Yes, I've been thinking things over lately, and certain facts are becoming
painfully clear. If I chucked politics (which I loathe) and devoted myself to
Classics (which I love) I *might* just get a first, and I *might*, not impossibly, get
some sort of research or archaeological job, and spend the rest of my life
in a museum (which I am beginning to believe is my natural habitat) delving
into the origins of Greek religion and pursuing the labyrinthine paths of
comparative mythology. That would be – paradise. And I'd write a few
poems, and publish a modest little novel now and then (maybe). But you
see I can't. I can't go and be happy while the world goes to hell. I saw that
dimly when I joined the party, and I see it clearer now. And anyway it all
concerns me personally – if England goes fascist (a not improbable contingency if we don't do something damn quick) I shan't be able to write what
I please or study what I please. In fact I shall be in a concentration camp or
some other even less desirable spot. So I've got to be a political worker. If
I can be a great Hellenic scholar as well, so much the better, but I'm not a
genius – and I'm even doubting whether I have much talent. My faith in my
intellectual ability has been shaken in the last few months. I can feel, I can
appreciate art and understand symbolism perhaps better than average, but
I haven't a clear mind. You see, Ann, to return to the point, my job is not

1 Cambridge University Society of Communists.
2 Satisfactory degree (God forbid!).

to go and dig at Knossos, it is to see that the next generation even hears of Knossos – it is not to write fine poems, it is to work for a world in which man will read and write fine poems. O Christ! If only I'd been born into the world we're trying to build, instead of this damnable place!

Sorry. Excuse all these heroics, but I am in earnest. I thank God that I have the party to direct and discipline my previously vague and ineffective idealism. I feel now that I am doing *some* good, and that life has a purpose and that the history of civilisation is not just an interesting series of unconnected muddles, but a comprehensible development towards the highest stage of society, the Soviet world state. Ann, you *must* see, that this is the only way – it's no use dabbling about on the surface, as a Labour government would do, with always the risk that the Conservatives will come in at the next election and undo all their work. We've got to reorganise society from top to bottom – it's *rotten*, it's inefficient, it's fundamentally unjust, and it must be radically changed, even at the expense of some bloodshed. Remember, a Bolshevik revolution is not a wild emotional business of random bomb-throwing – it's a carefully planned, scientific affair, which occurs at a moment when there will be a minimum of people to be dealt with violently. And the ring of financiers who control every state in the world except one will never, *never* let go their hold unless they are forced to. And better a little violence than the physical, mental and spiritual starvation and depredation of millions of men and women.

On Saturday I went with some nice Oxford reds to the Festival of Music for the People at the Albert Hall. You would have loved it – it was a pageant tracing the relation of music to the class struggle right from feudal times to the present day. In fact a Marxist line on music, which was quite new to me. Parry Jones and Robeson sang – Robeson was, O magnificent, and the house went wild with enthusiasm.[1] Near the end they played the Spanish national anthem, and everyone stood, which pleased us.[2] And at the very end Tom Mann[3] and Fred Coperman[4] and the dean of Canterbury[5] spoke. The dean was a glorious surprise to me – I knew he was that way inclined, but never dreamt he dared to come out so openly. To see him standing there in his red robes, calling us all 'comrades' and talking in a voice like thunder

---

1 Gwynn Parry Jones (1891–1963), famous Welsh tenor. Paul Robeson (1898–1976), American singer and actor who was a political activist for the civil rights movement.
2 The Spanish Civil War (1936–9) had stirred great passion in Oxford and elsewhere. Many idealistic British students and intellectuals of the time supported the Republican left.
3 A noted British trade unionist.
4 An English volunteer in the International Brigades during the Spanish Civil War who had commanded the British Battalion.
5 Hewlett Johnson (1874–1966) was an avowed Christian – Marxist and in 1931 became dean of Canterbury, where he acquired his nickname 'The Red Dean of Canterbury' for his support for the Soviet Union and its allies.

about the 'fullness of life in the Soviet Union' was simply wonderful. And God! the house was enthusiastic! A great sense of comradeship with all sorts of people one gets from being a communist.

About Christianity – I'm glad you are finding it good and a help to you. And I hope that it will lead you to what I consider its only logical conclusion – communism. I have finally decided that I cannot accept it as a religion, though of course I accept fully most of the teaching. My religion, if I have one, at the moment is a passionate belief in the beautiful, and a faith in the ultimate triumph of the people, the workers of the world. And in a longing for the civilisation in which every worker shall possess and love beauty lies the mainspring of all my political ideals.

I enjoyed this last term – though perhaps it wasn't such unalloyed heaven as my first term. I saw more of the seamy side of Oxford – and it's certainly a pretty vicious place in some ways. Also I had *much* too much to do and nearly had a nervous breakdown a few weeks before the end of term. However I stayed up a week and worked in the Ashmolean library – a well of silence – and recovered. My emotional life gives me trouble too – I find myself quite astonishingly interested in the opposite sex, and capable of being in love with about six men all at once – which gives rise to complications and distresses. And too many people are in love with me just at present – which though pleasing to my vanity, is also liable to be annoying and difficult.

But on the whole I find life, if not a sweet flower garden with endless vistas of roses, at any rate a very rich, lively, interesting place, and not without hope and promise, though not for me as an individual.

And now Ann dear, please pardon me for talking so loftily about myself for all these pages. I do wish you were here and we could discuss things – will you by any chance be in London this vac? Anyhow, write to me soon and say how all this strikes you.

I am going to Ireland tomorrow for four days – Oh joyous thought! After so long a time in the land of the Sassenachs without one ray of Celtic twilight to relieve the gloom! I am travelling on the Ulster Express, so if you hear the IRA have blown it up, weep a tear for me, won't you.

Now I really must put a period to my talk. The very best of luck for next term, if I don't see you before – and anyway I'll see you at the Old Badmintonian Association.

Ever so much love.

Iris

PS I must just add a note to the effect that Chamberlain must go, and that forthwith because:

1.) He is gradually introducing fascism into this country – he takes action without consulting the Cabinet, conveniently 'forgets' vitally important proposals, and deliberately misleads the country by withholding information e.g. the Cabinet knew five days before it happened that Czechoslovakia was to be invaded.

2.) He has consistently betrayed the working class movement and played into the hands of H and M[1] e.g. in Spain by 'non-intervention' and the recognition of F[2] and in Czechoslovakia by the Munich concessions.

3.) He is now betraying Poland by refusing to make a definite alliance with USSR and by making vague promises and talking about 'negotiations' – i.e. leaving Hitler a free hand.

This is my last piece of paper and I must stop. Good thing too. Love I.

To Ann Leech, written after Germany had invaded Poland on 1 September and Britain and France had declared war on 3 September.

4 Eastbourne Road
9 September 1939

Dear Ann – how is it with you? I hope you are not feeling too sad about the way the world's going. It's a beastly miserable business, yes, but maybe we can make something good out of it. After all it *is* a war against fascism, though undertaken for imperialist reasons, and if we play our cards properly we can make it into a war for socialism. But first, we've got to get rid of Chamberlain. Our government would infinitely prefer a Hitler-ruled Germany to a free and possibly socialist Germany. But Hitler threatens the British Empire, ergo, Hitler must go. But they will do their level best to prevent the German people from working out their own destiny afterwards. So we *must* get a decent government in this country that will really fight to *free* Germany and not merely to defend British interests.

I shall go back to Oxford. There will be plenty of party work and war work for me to do there. Funny, I thought once I was going to a university to study the classics. It must have been a dream. I'm sorry about my academic career – but really at the moment it seems to me that the only thing to do is to fight for a world in which it will be worthwhile having an academic career at all. O God, how I loathe politics . . . But, believing as I do, I have no choice.

1 Hitler and Mussolini.
2 General Franco, leader of the Nationalist military rebellion in the Spanish Civil War.

What will you do? I hope you will go back to Cambridge and carry on. We are so lucky not to have the whole tenor of our lives upset. Also, we've had a fine year of university life. When I think of Maria and Lalage I could weep.

Also, I had a grand finale in the Magpie Tour, when we acted plays all over the Cotswolds for the Oxford Refugee Fund.[viii] Hitler curtailed it by two days, which proved rather disastrous financially, but we had such tremendous fun for our money, and had not a moment to brood over the international situation. Questions of lighting, and props, and interpretation and how many two shilling seats were sold, were of much greater importance.

On the whole, I feel optimistic now – perhaps unduly so. At any rate, full of fire and fighting spirit, thank God. Really, I think any sort of hell, with a fighting chance of heaven beyond, is preferable to the limbo we've been drifting through for the last five years. (Easy words, of course, from a non-combatant.) And if a socialist Germany comes out of this, any sort of sacrifice will have been worth it. But the bitterest fight will be at home . . .

Do write and tell me how you are feeling and what you are doing. And will you ever be in London? I shall be here until I go up (I refer to my return to Oxford, not to a possible air raid) and I'm just longing to see you and talk and talk and talk.

Goodbye my dear, I wish you all possible peace of mind. Love Iris.

To Margaret Orpen, Murdoch's school friend at Badminton, who was unhappy in love and also missing her brother, a British Army cadet being trained at Dartford.

4 Eastbourne Road.
20 September 1939

My dear – I'm terribly sorry – I do hope you are feeling happier now than you were when you wrote that letter. After all we are young – and we aren't really going to be cheated. We shall have our chances surely, if not to be happy, at any rate to live, to experience, to do – and life even at its most hellish can still be interesting. Yet I do cherish a possibly irrational belief that there *is* a good time coming.

But forgive me for this vague optimism – I know you have such great reason to be unhappy, and my God I wish I could do something for you – I must see you when you come to London – I shall be here probably till mid October.

I don't know whether you have these two books or whether they interest you or whether they will cheer you up at all – I hope they may. My apologies that they aren't new.[1]

I'll see you soon.

Meanwhile, look up, dear lass.

Love

Iris

To David Hicks, who had abandoned his Diploma of Education course in order to work for the British Council in Egypt.

Somerville College
29 April 1940

Dear David,

My greetings. How is it with you? I think of you decorating the skyline on a camel and taking your well-earned siesta in the shade of a pyramid. Or is Egypt not romantic? Yes, I know. I had an aunt once who used to teach the young Egyptians to love God. What do you teach them? I hope it's something with an equally good moral. And altogether, how wags the world in your region of it?

You and your pyramids seem almost as fabulous and mythical to me as Oxford and I must seem to you now. I expect an act of faith is necessary to persuade yourself you ever were here. (But you were, I remember you quite distinctly.)

Everything here seems curiously the same – and yet I don't know why it should, for every month batches of men fade away into khaki, and Balliol is full of glossy civil servants from Whitehall. Worcester is still largely academic – I go there twice a week to hear Pickard-Cambridge[2] talking about moral philosophy. Lectures and all the clubs proceed as before, and the only difference it all makes to me is that I have ten times as much organisational work to do as I would normally, owing to the increasing man-shortage.

I have just done Mods, and got the distinguished second which you once so kindly predicted for me. (Damn you. I held that against you for a long time. I suppose it would be unreasonable to bear the grudge any longer) and now I am doing Greats. The philosophy is not as philosophical as one would wish, but the ancient history is very ancient (especially in the matter of the dons appertaining thereto) and I find them both pretty good mental exercise.

---

1 A note about these books at the end of this letter, possibly written later by Margaret Lintott (née Orpen) reads, 'Donne's love poems; *Rubáiyát of Omar Khayyám* translated by Fitzgerald'.

2 Arthur Wallace Pickard-Cambridge (1873–1952), an authority on the theatre of ancient Greece.

The *personelle* of the university has changed tremendously. Freeling and Lucy[1] are vanished as though they had never been. Carol[2] I hear of spasmodically achieving great things in the Ministry of Economic Warfare. A few old-timers like Jack Dawes and Denis Healey[3] are still here and active. Peter Shinnie is in the air force and getting incredibly tough – others of them are in the artillery and fleet air arm. None of the women whom you knew, I'm glad to say, has joined the ATS.[4]

Myself, I am incredibly busy this term with committees [. . .] and with acting. You see I have achieved one of my ambitions, to play the chorus leader in *Murder in the Cathedral*.[5] Christ Church dramatic society is doing it and our stage is the cloister quad at Christ Church with the cathedral as a backcloth. Also I am bringing out a revised version – an *editio maior*[6] rather – of your song sheet. (Remember?)

The world – yes. It's a pretty interesting and fast-moving little world these days. There's a lot to be depressed about certainly, but I can't say I feel very fundamentally downhearted. In fact I've never felt so full of hope and new life as I do now. We're not doing so badly.

Meanwhile this place is raving wild with spring. I met a calf this morning that looked like Michelangelo's Moses[7] – and the calf's mother was like Epstein's Madonna.[8] I won't tell you about the cherry trees or how green the Cherwell banks are, or you'll be homesick. How homesick are you? Don't be too. Though indeed there's nothing much wrong with the flora and fauna. As I think Browning observed.[9]

I hope very much life isn't boring or unhappy or lonely or any of the things it shouldn't be but so often is. How many English people are there with you? Are they interesting? How hard do you work? What is the work like? Do you still paint? Have you written anything? I tell you one thing you

1 Lucy Klatschko, a half-Latvian and Jewish senior scholar, had read modern languages at Somerville between 1936 and 1939. She was later to become Sister Marian.
2 Carol Stewart, an Oxford contemporary two years older than Murdoch, who later translated Canetti's *Masse und Macht* into English with the title *Crowds and Power*. On marrying, she became Carol Graham-Harrison.
3 Denis Healey (1917–), who was reading Greats at Balliol, met Murdoch through the Communist Party but left it in the summer of 1940 when France fell to the Germans. Murdoch read his copy of Samuel Beckett's *Murphy*, a book that influenced her considerably.
4 The Auxiliary Territorial Service, formed in September 1938, was the women's branch of the British Army.
5 This production of T. S. Eliot's play at Oxford in 1940 allowed male and female students to act together for the first time; previously dons' wives had acted the female roles.
6 A jocular reference – 'major edition'.
7 A sculpture that depicts Moses with horns on his head.
8 Jacob Epstein's *Madonna and Child* (1927).
9 Oblique reference to Robert Browning's poem 'Home Thoughts, from Abroad' which opens 'Oh, to be in England / Now that April's there'.

might write, and that's a letter to me, if you feel like it, and if you have anything of note to say about a) Egypt, b) David.

The best of luck to you.

Love

Iris

PS John Willett,[1] from whom I got your address, sends his love and says he misses you a lot – but as he said all this some time ago I expect he has conveyed it himself by now.

I

To Eduard Fraenkel, professor of Latin at Corpus Christi College, Oxford, whose famous seminars on Aeschylus's Agamemnon *Murdoch had been attending and from whom she was – unusually for an undergraduate – also receiving private tuition. The Ministry of Health (Murdoch's father's employer at this time) relocated to Blackpool in 1939, necessitating her parents' move. They lived in Cavendish Road, Blackpool in 1940 and then in Waller Avenue, Blackpool from 1941, returning to London after the war.*[ix]

196 Cavendish Road

Bispham

Blackpool

[October 1940]

Dear Professor Fraenkel,

Greetings. How is it with you? I hope you're having a very peaceful and unanxious vacation. As for me, my exile will produce no *tristitia*[2] after all – I left London for here about a month ago, and haven't regretted it yet for a moment. Never before have I been able to come out of my front door and see *mountains* – I can't see them every day, but when it's clear there are the sharp Lake District peaks in the North. And I love the wideness and freedom of the land here so different from the closeness of London – I'm so used to having my horizon 300 yards off.

There *are* crowds of people, yes, and they all talk like Gracie Fields[3] and rush madly from one variety show to another – but they have a ballet-like quality of gaiety and colour and one can't help liking them. Anyway they

---

1 John Willett (1917–2002) read PPE at Christ Church 1936–9, and went on to translate and publish on the work of Bertold Brecht. He managed the stage lighting for *It Can Happen Here*.

2 Sadness, melancholy.

3 The actress, singer and comedienne Gracie Fields (1898–1979) was born over a fish and chip shop in Rochdale, Lancashire.

stay in the centre of the town, and we live a little way out. No one bathes – they all seem quite oblivious of the sea, though they often sit on the sands just to keep up appearances – so from here I can bathe or walk for miles along the shore and hardly meet anyone. And on a windy sunny blue and white day full of seagulls and wave crests that is well worth doing. I've also made several cycling expeditions to the Pennines, some fifteen or twenty miles off, and had days full of heather and butterflies and no people.

One of the best things about being here is that I am quite cut off from the endless acquaintances who used to be always passing through London and calling on me. I have time to read, thank God. I've almost finished *The Republic*. I find Plato at times a vile casuist, and almost always a reactionary. But he does write exquisite Greek. (Don't take this for my verdict on *The Republic*! But he does make me very angry now and then.) I've read Farrington's *Science and Politics* which you were so harsh on last term. I see the reasons for your hard opinions and I agree he does in many cases rush at his conclusions without a satisfying array of evidence. But in general I think (in all humility) that his view of the situation deserves to be considered. His remarks on Lucretius particularly seem to me to be pretty sane. And frankly, after being brought up in an atmosphere of mystical and irrational adoration of Plato, I found him refreshing. I do want to think honestly and clearly about this period and come to some coherent conclusions and I'm not at all sure I'm prepared to accept a lot of the things that are taken for granted by the historians. But I realise that with the small quantity of knowledge I possess at present I ought to be keeping my mouth shut, and that I have an obligation to reserve judgement till after the fullest consideration of the evidence – which will take a long time. So, enough!

My form of National Service at present (though I doubt if Churchill would appreciate it) is running a Left Book Club[1] group (on strictly Marxist lines) and selling the *Daily Worker*[2] in the street. But don't worry, as I don't 'waste' a great deal of time on these activities. I've met a lot of fine people, for which I am chiefly thankful. Altogether my days are full to the brim and I have little time to reflect on what a miserable world it is. I have various friends in internment camps for whom I feel a dull misery whenever I think of them – and others, far worse . . . Happiness can only be reckoned in individuals now. Living this easy pleasant life I have a perpetual sense of guilt and desire to hurt myself or something. I feel myself a rather opinionated

1 Presumably in imitation of the Left Book Club, a venture founded in the UK in May 1936, set up by Stafford Cripps, Victor Gollancz and John Strachey in order to revitalise and educate the British left. The club's aim was to encourage the struggle for peace and the fight against fascism; it closed in 1948.
2 The *Daily Worker* newspaper, the voice of the Communist Party of Great Britain, was founded in 1930. It was renamed the *Morning Star* in 1966.

fool with very little knowledge of suffering and life – (I stick to the opinions nevertheless!) and I wish for a time of trial and a chance to strip my spirit to its essentials. One wish at any rate which is sure to come true in an age like this.

Forgive this soliloquising letter so full of me. I hope you and all your family are well and happy – as happy as may be.

Best wishes to you for the rest of the vacation. I hope there will be a next term.

Yours affectionately

Iris

To Frank Thompson, a fellow student at Oxford. He first saw Murdoch in November 1938 at a political meeting and was attracted to her, but did not manage to speak to her until the following term. A gifted poet and an intense idealist, he left New College in 1939, where he had been reading Mods and Greats, to volunteer for the army. On becoming a member of both 'Phantom', a small communications intelligence unit, and later the Special Operations Executive (SOE), he served in North Africa, Syria, Iraq, Sicily, Serbia and Bulgaria. He was posted to the Middle East in March 1941 and there contracted septicaemia, spending two months in hospital in Damascus; by November 1941 he was back in Cairo. Murdoch's pacifism had strengthened after she joined the Communist Party in 1938; however, by the time she wrote this letter she could see the necessity for military action in Europe.[x]

9 Waller Avenue
Bispham
Blackpool
24 December 1941

Frank Me darlin'

It is Christmas eve and I in Blackpool. There is the hell of a wind blowing over the house and I feel a bit withered away already. I have just received a box of expensive Turkish cigarettes from Michael.[1] Dear old Michael. A lost soul too. (The trouble is, I have been reading Virginia Woolf, the darling dangerous woman, and am in a state of extremely nervous self-consciousness. The most selfish of all states to be in.)

The most important thing of course is that the Russians are winning at last thank God.[2] May they go on winning. I feel ashamed of my defeatist

---

1 M. R. D. Foot (1919–2012), a school friend of Frank's from Winchester College who was reading PPE at New College, Oxford.
2 Nazi Germany had invaded the Soviet Union on 22 June 1941.

mood of a month ago – then it seemed that nothing could halt the Germans this side of Moscow – now I feel that nothing can halt the Russians this side of Berlin. An equally false optimism of course. The war begins to affect me emotionally far more than it did – possibly because my watertight rationalism has broken down. It's all damn complex and confusing. I don't have a clear line on it any more. I feel myself approaching the state of ἀπορία[1] which I imagined only Liberals and the *New Statesman* suffered from – it couldn't happen to me, this pathetic confusion and suspension of judgement. But it has. Actually in a way I'm quite pleased, because such a condition contrasts favourably with the suspension of thought which preceded it. And of course the foundations are as sound as ever. It's only a lot of the fancy superstructure that's been blown away.

Last term was good. I got face to face with my work for the first time since Mods – and the results weren't too depressing. I was beginning to be afraid that my brain had decomposed in the interim. It's too late I'm afraid as far as Schools[2] is concerned – but I've got a lot of satisfaction out of doing philosophy and getting my mind clear on one or two questions. This man MacKinnon[3] is a jewel, it's bucked me up a lot meeting him. He's a moral being as well as a good philosopher. I had almost given up thinking of people and actions in terms of value – meeting him has made it a significant way of thinking again. (Obscure. Sorry.)

Soon my charming American lassy and her kid (now two years old) are coming to stay. That will be good. I'm feeling a bit vampirish and want to have my friends around. Her husband is in the ME[4] (in artillery – one William Holland, in case you ever meet him). She's upset about her country too. I'm afraid I can't muster much emotion about the Philippines[5] – except that it's bloody that all these people are killing each other – but that's probably because I'm no strategist.

What is important is whether you are in on this Libyan business.[6] It's very hard, sitting here and looking out at the cabbages and the semi-detached villas, to imagine you in a war – killing people maybe – you and Leo and

1 Aporia: doubt, perplexity.
2 Final examinations.
3 Donald MacKinnon (1913–1994), Murdoch's philosophy tutor at Oxford; like Eduard Fraenkel, he was a charismatic, intellectually demanding individual and greatly influenced Murdoch. Many years later, criticising Sartre's introduction to a work by Jean Genet, Murdoch described it as 'the sort of thing I would throw back at a clever and favourite pupil with a few sharp words. "Attractive slapdash stuff" as MacKinnon said to me, tossing my essay on the table and searing my soul, sometime back in 1941'. (Letter to Brigid Brophy postmarked 21 March 1965.)
4 Military Engineers.
5 The Philippines were invaded by Japan between December 1941 and May 1942.
6 The Allies' Western Desert Campaign in what is now south-east Libya.

Hal[1] – I can't imagine it at all. Whereas I *can* imagine you at the Coptic monastery, swimming in the cistern. God. I do feel bloody, sitting here writing self-conscious letters.

I wish June were over and I were (even) in the ATS. I don't care how tough the job is so long as I can use what mind I have. The primrose path is getting me down a bit. It's unsettling looking forward into a blank, though. A sort of queer interregnum has set in. I feel I've outgrown my old personality and not yet acquired a new one. I guess I shan't get a new one till after June. Then I shall learn some things.

I've read Gorki's *Mother* – yes a darling book. My Czech lassy is more like Sonya than anything I've ever met. As for being simple and warm-hearted – fine, grand – but unfortunately we aren't peasants with a straightforward line on life, we're just bemused intellectual misfits – or at least I am. I think. I'll know for certain after June and I'll tell you.

I'm reading Mallarmé who suits my mood again – exotic, restless, obscure. He passes me, *laissant toujours de ses mains mal fermées / Neiger de blancs bouquets d'étoiles parfumées.*[2] But Gorki is better. Of course – if only one could and were. I must go to America after the war.

I'm writing a little poetry again. It has its moments. I hope you are safe, dear Frank. Good luck.

Love I

---

1 Leo Pliatzky was awarded a first in Classical Mods at Corpus Christi, Oxford in 1939. He then served with the Royal Army Ordnance Corps and the Royal Electrical and Mechanical Engineers for the next five years. His friend, Hal Lidderdale, read Greats at Magdalen College, Oxford before joining the Royal Scots Fusiliers.

2 From an early poem entitled 'Apparitions' (1862), in which the poet's feelings for his beloved evoke memories of his mother who 'would hover above me sprinkling from her gentle hands / Snow-white clusters of perfumed stars'.

PART TWO:

Work and War

July 1942 to October 1947

Murdoch graduated with a first in Greats in 1942 and was conscripted to work in London as an assistant principal in the Treasury in June of that year. She stayed until 1944, becoming an expert in the tedious task of assessing notional pay rises and promotions for civil servants who had joined the armed forces, so that their careers would not be disadvantaged by wartime service. In September 1942 she took a lease on 5 Seaforth Place, Buckingham Gate, a studio flat half a mile from the Treasury Office. In October 1943 her friend from Somerville College, Philippa Bosanquet, who had recently been appointed as an economics research assistant at Chatham House in St James's Square, moved in and stayed with Murdoch until the spring of 1945. Under her married name of Philippa Foot, Philippa Bosanquet was later to become an outstanding philosopher in the field of virtue ethics and an important figure in Murdoch's life. Murdoch relished London's bohemian culture, giving parties and drinking in Soho pubs such as the Wheatsheaf and the Pillars of Hercules in Greek Street where she mingled with writers and artists. The two women often had to cope with blackout and wartime bombing, frequently waking up to find that nearby buildings had been demolished in the night. Although Murdoch probably resigned her formal membership of the Communist Party on joining the Treasury in 1942, she spied during the war for the party, copying Treasury papers then leaving them in a tree that was a dead-letter drop[i] in Kensington Gardens.[i] Later she was to become disillusioned with the Communist Party and gradually detached herself from its politics although she retained a deep interest in Communist ideology for many years.

---

i An espionage arrangement whereby items pass between two individuals using a secret location so that they never have to meet face to face.

In June 1944 Murdoch applied successfully to join the United Nations Relief and Rehabilitation Administration (UNRRA), a large international agency founded in 1943 and representing forty-four nations. Its European HQ, where Murdoch worked, was in Portland Place, London. UNRRA's purpose was to help and provide sustenance for victims of war in any area under the control of the United Nations. It had a major role in helping displaced persons (DPs) return to their home countries in Europe in 1945–6 and Murdoch played her part in this venture for two years. She was posted to Brussels and subsequently transferred to Innsbruck in late 1945; from there she was sent in March 1946 to Graz in south-east Austria. Here she worked in the Hochsteingasse Displaced Persons camp, set up by the British Allied Military Government for students who had been accepted at the University of Graz.[ii] She also spent brief periods in Vienna and in Holland. She resigned from UNRRA in July 1946, remaining unemployed until she was offered a place in 1947 at Newnham College, Cambridge as a postgraduate researcher.

Already thrilled by modern French literature, Murdoch's travels in Europe introduced her to the excitement of existentialism. In a letter from Brussels to David Hicks, dated November 1945, she vividly expresses her delight at hearing Jean-Paul Sartre lecture: 'his writing and talking on morals – will, liberty, choice – is hard and lucid and invigorating. It's the *real thing* [. . .] after [. . .] the shallow stupid milk and water "ethics" of English "moralists" like Ross and Prichard'.[1] In 1945 she discovered the work of Simone de Beauvoir, whose novels greatly impressed her. She was also intoxicated by the intellectual fervour of European café culture. She wrote to her Oxford friend Marjorie Boulton in November 1945: 'The mixture is perfect – philosophy ("existentialism", the new philosophy of France, which is catching the Belgian intellectuals as well) novels (Sartre, Queneau, Simone de Beauvoir) poetry (André Breton, Verhaeren, Valéry[2]), chaps and girls (writers, philosophers, miscellaneous intellectuals), cafés (for talking in for hours and hours on end, open indefinitely) [. . .] I get a *frisson* of joy to think that I am of *this* age, *this* Europe – saved or damned with it'. Given the dominance in English philosophy at this time of logical positivism – which held that truth and knowledge derive solely from verifiable scientific observation – Murdoch's immersion in European fiction and philosophy was unusual.

In her spare time during these hectic years Murdoch was learning German, Russian, Italian and Turkish. She was also reading voraciously in literature and philosophy, preparing for a possible career as an author and philosopher.

1 W. D. Ross (1877–1971), Scottish philosopher who worked in the field of ethics; H. A. Prichard (1871–1947), English philosopher best known for his work on ethical intuition.
2 André Breton (1896–1966), poet and novelist, founder and leader of the French surrealist movement; Emile Verhaeren (1855– 1916), Belgian poet who wrote in French and one of the chief founders of the school of symbolism; Paul Valéry (1871–1945), French poet, essayist and philosopher.

While many young British would-be philosophers were following the path of logical positivism, Murdoch was avidly devouring the work of Hegel, Kierkegaard, Gabriel Marcel, Wittgenstein, Heidegger, Kant and Sartre. The work of the Danish philosopher Søren Kierkegaard (1813–55) in particular influenced her and she was to draw on it later when formulating her ideas about individual choice. She committed her energies to the Labour Party in 1944 but expressed disappointment with its leaders, complaining to David Hicks in May of 'the usual lack of unity and intelligent leadership on the left'. To her surprise and delight, however, the Labour Party swept to victory in July 1945.

No longer a Communist, she was also able to engage more freely with the matters of faith that were beginning to preoccupy her. In 1946 she wrote to the French author, Raymond Queneau, whom she had met in February of that year in Innsbruck when she heard him speak on 'The Crisis in French Literature', 'I started life as a political animal thinking my soul didn't matter – now I am almost a religious animal, thinking it matters vitally. In the swing between those two attitudes lie all the philosophical problems that interest me'.[iii] While expressing scepticism about the Christian faith, she confided to Queneau three weeks later that she wished she 'could be Christian. There is such worth there – and values which are *real* to one – but the rest remains a fairy tale to me [. . .] Van Eyckish light on white wimples and jewelled crosses, the beautiful unwearying plainsong, speaking though a grille [. . .] Life is very strange isn't it?'[iv]

Murdoch now began writing fiction seriously, producing three novels that were either unfinished or discarded.[v] She submitted her second completed novel in the autumn of 1944 to Faber & Faber where it was rejected by T. S. Eliot. Looking for inspiration for a new way of writing, she turned to French experimentalism: her letters to Queneau express deep admiration for his work and her desire for a mentor. He, in turn, saw her as *'une fille épatante'* ('a striking young woman'), confiding to his journal after their first meeting that *'Je suis tout de suite séduit. Longue conversation. Nous nous entendons parfaitement'* ('I am immediately captivated. Long conversation. We understand each other perfectly').[vi] Queneau was to be a strong influence on Murdoch's development as an author and, enchanted by his writing, she spent much time during 1946 translating his novel, *Pierrot mon ami*, into English. In April of that year she wrote to him, 'I can't tell you how good it makes me feel to read anything written by you. You're like a principle of hardness and dryness in the marshland where I'm lost! And I believe you are the only writer who has this effect on me'.[vii] As a token of her esteem, Murdoch later dedicated her first published novel, *Under the Net* (1954), to Queneau.

Several crises in Murdoch's personal life occurred during these years and her letters portray a dizzying range of emotions from elation to despair.

There were a number of lovers and a few casual sexual liaisons: Murdoch's tendency to fall quickly in and out of love is illustrated by her letters to David Hicks and Raymond Queneau, to whom she wrote obsessively in turn. While thriving on a complicated love life, she occasionally felt uneasy about the emotional entanglements into which she was so easily drawn. Confiding in Marjorie Boulton in 1943 she wrote, 'I have all my life made terrible mistakes with people. I say this with real agony and remorse [. . .] I have shirked the exacting effort of being consistently and completely sincere'.[viii] She was also beginning to recognise her own neediness and insecurity; in the same letter she acknowledges that 'I am, like you, an extremely emotional and sentimental person, with most extravagant cravings for affection'. Such insights did not, however, prevent future complications with friends and lovers. The painful rift with Philippa Bosanquet that resulted from Murdoch's appropriation of one of Philippa's lovers, the Balliol economics tutor Thomas Balogh, in 1944 – and her simultaneously cruel treatment of M. R. D. Foot (whom Murdoch had left for Balogh, and whom Philippa married in 1945) – had only partially healed by 1946. In Murdoch's confessional letter to David Hicks, dated 6 November 1945, she describes the imbroglio as 'a quadrilateral tale that would make rather a good psychological novel'. The rift with her Oxford tutor, Donald MacKinnon – caused possibly by his intense feelings for her (to which his wife took exception) – brought more misery. In relation to this upset she wrote to Philippa Foot in August 1947, 'I'm sick at heart and can't work. Life's been disintegrated in a nightmarish way for so long now, one almost forgets what it would be like to feel normal and secure and loved'. In early 1947 she had written to Queneau: 'As for "happiness", *mon dieu*, I have dropped that word from my vocabulary. A sort of force and *integritas* is what I yearn towards, and the *felicitas*, a sort of by-product, scarcely enters my head now!'[ix] While such inner turbulence was obviously painful, it provided rich experience for the emotional complications of her fictional worlds.

To Philippa Bosanquet, congratulating her on her first-class degree. Having returned to London from Blackpool, Murdoch wrote this letter from a house a street away from her parents' home in Eastbourne Road, which had suffered bomb damage a year or so before.[x]

55 Barrowgate Rd
Chiswick
W4
[early July 1942]

Pip, that was splendid – I'm terribly glad – my joy is now complete. It was a certainty of course – and I'm so pleased you were spared the miseries of a viva. You and Mary[1] have provided such wonderful instances of Mind triumphing over Matter – I feel myself to be quite fugitive and cloistered by contrast – not of such fine metal! Now there is *nothing* for you to worry about, and you can lie in a dreamy coma and rest that back. And *don't* read Virginia Woolf. [. . .]

I have been a servant of His Majesty now for two weeks. Life is all rather dreamlike – I live in a fantastic world, ringing with telephone voices, and peopled by strange fictional personalities such as the Lords Commissioners of His Majesty's Treasury . . . (Oxford has nothing on the Treasury as far as tradition goes.) I can't believe that it's *me* writing these peremptory letters and telling people over the phone where they get off. I don't think I shall feel real again till I acquire a flat and start on some serious occupation, such as making a verse translation of Sophocles – all I do at present feels like play acting.

The flat is still a problem – most likely seems a single room in Gerrard Place – with a wonderful view of the Blitz and practically no plumbing. I hope you won't mind that when you come and stay.

I feel a bit Tchekov at the moment. Questions such as 'What is the Significance of Life?' which I know to be strictly meaningless assume a sort of 'expressive meaning'. I have a great many friends in London – I have lunch or dinner with a different person every day – but I get no satisfaction or consolation from them, and our relations seem superficial and even chilly. I feel like going out and picking up the first man I meet that's willing, simply for the sake of a more intense relationship of any description with another human being.

All of which is nonsense of course and just means that it's raining and I have indigestion. [. . .]

Very few of the people I knew at Oxford seem real to me now, even after this short interval – and I don't want to lose touch with the ones that still retain their flesh and blood!

I'm really delighted about your first Pip – take care of that back.

I hope I shall see you before too long.

Love

Iris

---

1 Mary Scrutton (1919–), who had studied Mods and Greats at Somerville College alongside Iris Murdoch.

To Marjorie Boulton, who was at this time reading English at Somerville College. She was later to become an author, poet, college principal and an expert on Esperanto, a constructed and politically neutral language designed to foster international under-standing and peace which – not surprisingly – enjoyed a revival during and after the war years.

55 Barrowgate Road
Chiswick
London W4
16 August 1942

Dear Marjorie,

For a long time I have been intending to reply to your charming letter – but life has been full of a Number of Things, and no letter-writing got done. This seems to be the first breathing space I've had since the beginning of July, what with the new work, flat-hunting, and wild dashes into the country every weekend.

I was very interested in what you said about your poetry – and I liked the remarks of Treece[1] which you quoted. He is right, you know, about the big things being composed of small units. Of course one *must* be conscious of the rhythm of the whole – the 'movement of history' – whatever one understands by these vague and rather dangerous phrases. But such things make themselves intelligible in a concrete day-to-day manner. It has been one of the mistakes of modern left-wing poets to try, at times, to get too much onto their canvas – to evoke an indeterminate cloudy notion of Something or Other – and in the end get nothing across. Inevitable perhaps when our poets live an insulated life, away from the blood tears toil and sweat of real political activity. So beware. Avoid the sugar. But avoid the Political Apocalypse stuff too. James Joyce used always to ask of some new writer 'Is he trying to express something he has understood?'

Forgive the didactic tone. I have made all these mistakes myself and still make them. And above all, *do* go on writing. For you have a real feeling for words and something to say – *and* sufficient power to drive the whole machine (which people frequently lack, even when they have all the rest).

I haven't written anything at all since Schools – or even read very much, except a little Proust and some poetry (my latest pastime is reading Homer aloud in the Underground. There is such a racket that no one can hear you – and the hexameter goes very well with the rhythm of the train). Life has been rather strange and feverish. I like my work on the whole, though I'm not at all good at it to date. It's not the sort of work I ever imagined myself

---

1 Henry Treece (1911–66), poet, editor and writer of historical novels.

enjoying – pure administration – dealing with laws and regulations, applying them, amending them where necessary, coping with the unusual cases, and in general oiling the amazing machine of which I find myself part. I feel a certain humility towards this set-up – for in spite of all the Red Tape Legends, it's a remarkably efficient and businesslike organisation, and I am beginning to value such efficiency very highly. I want to become a full working partner as soon as possible.

I have felt very restless though, chiefly for want of a place to lay my head. I've felt no inclination, in these rather unsatisfactory digs, to settle down and work or read in the evenings – and I've been tempted to stay up in town till late and rush around breathlessly with various friends. Now however I see a level lagoon beyond the breakers, as I have at last acquired a flat. This is a flat of quite indescribable charm – it's what is called, in house agent language, a 'studio flat', and is situated over an empty garage and amid various disused warehouses. Its disadvantages are many, the chief being a three-year lease, the District Railway as a next door neighbour, and some six square miles of window to guard in Blitz and blackout. Its advantages are its position (fifty yards from Victoria Street and 300 yards from Whitehall), its rent (£60 p.a. unfurnished) and its utterly irresistible personality. The address is 5 Seaforth Place, Buckingham Gate, SW1, and I move in in September.[1]

All this has filled my mind for the moment – which is well in a way. The news is so incredibly bloody.[2]

I must go now. (I am going to the zoo this afternoon, chiefly to see the zebras – I have an intense occult passion for zebras.) Write when you feel inclined and let me know how life treats you. When you are in London you must come and stay at my studio – this is a permanent invitation.

I'll probably see you next term in Oxford. Good luck.

Love

Iris

---

1 In her 2005 memoir *The Owl of Minerva*, Mary Midgley comments '[Iris] had got this flat [. . .] cheap because it had been bombed, and at first it looked much like a stage set for a school performance of something by Dostoevsky. It was an attic with cracks in the roof revealing the sky and cracks in the floor revealing no ceiling below, so that nothing blocked the alarming rumble of the underground trains passing beneath us. What furniture she had then was mainly orange-boxes.'

2 In July 1942 Soviet troops had been encircled in Millerovo by German forces and taken into captivity.

To Frank Thompson, stationed in Iraq.

5 Seaforth Place
Buckingham Gate
London SWI
24 November [1942]

Frank, my brave and beloved, your letter dated Oct. 7th has only just arrived – in which you record your linguistic failure with a Ukrainian truck driver. Yes, a fascinating language – not, so far, as difficult as I had expected – but I daresay fearful pitfalls and craggy *arrêts*[1] await me. Nor can I yet quite realise what poetry in such a language must be like. Our ambitious teacher[xi] has already made us learn a little poem by Pushkin (called 'Utro') – but I can't pretend I feel breathless on a peak in Darien as a result.[2] That will come, that will come.

As I write this the world has woken up with a vengeance and all sorts of encouraging and interesting things are happening in Russia and in North Africa – may it still be so when you receive this.[3] This ingrained inferiority complex must be shaken off – one had got too much into the habit of thinking that the only people who can beat the Germans are the Russians – and they can't do it all the year round. But now, thank God . . . In a way of course it seems terrible to rejoice at anything which must total up to such a sum of human anguish when considered in detail – especially when one is snug in Whitehall oneself – lord, lord. I get so damnably restless from time to time. I would volunteer for *anything* that would be certain to take me abroad. Unfortunately, there is no guarantee given one when one joins the women's forces! – and anyway the Treasury would never let me go; for, inefficient as I am, I am filling a very necessary post in a semi-skilled sort of way. Sometimes I think it's quite bloody being a woman. So much of one's life has to consist of having an attitude. (I hope you follow this, which is a little condensed.)

I trust *you* are as far from the firing line as ever? I was amazed to observe that your latest letter contained no references to tamarisk or swiftly flowing brooks – however, 'PAI Force'[4] seems to indicate that you have not yet left

---

1 Halts or stops.
2 The title of Pushkin's poem, published in 1829, means 'Winter Morning'. The phrase 'breathless on a peak in Darien' echoes the words 'Silent, upon a peak in Darien', the last line of Keats's sonnet 'On First Looking into Chapman's Homer'.
3 In late 1942 the Russians began to recapture various cities taken by the Germans; on 19 November the Red Army cut off and surrounded the German 6th Army in Stalingrad. On 8 November an Anglo-American force, led by Eisenhower, had invaded French North Africa. An armistice was arranged on 11 November and the Anglo-American forces assumed control of French North Africa and West Africa.
4 Persia and Iraq Force; members of the forces were not allowed to reveal their whereabouts when writing home.

the company of such delicious flora. Long may you stay. I should, of course, like you to be a hero – but I doubt if I could accept the risk – and I am quite certain you have all the qualities of a stout fella, without the necessity of a vulgar display.

News of our friends at this end I have little. What of Leo and Hal and any others that I know out your way? I miss you all, you know – I miss that unanxious society in which we trusted each other and were gentle as well as gay. I miss your burly self especially. Like all sensible people, I am searching out substitutes. The Treasury yields a number of pleasant men and women who, besides being very intelligent (and some of them very beautiful) are good company over a glass of beer or whisky. But they lack withal a certain redness of the blood – a certain human gentleness and sensitiveness. On the other hand, my Soho Bloomsbury and Chelsea acquaintanceship is widening also. The Swiss in Old Compton Street, the Wellington in Wardour Street, and the Lord Nelson in King's Road are the clubs which I frequent in search of the Ultimate Human Beings – and knowledge and experience and freedom. A strange society – composed of restless incomplete ambitious people who live in a chaotic and random way, never caring about the next five minutes, drunk every night without exception from six o'clock onwards, homeless and unfamilied, living in pubs and copulating upon the floors of other people's flats. Poetry is perhaps the only thing taken seriously by them all – and the only name they all respect is that of T. S. Eliot. Politics they do not understand or care about. Their thought and their poetry is concerned with subtleties of personal relations – with the creation of the unexpected in words – 'dredging the horrible from unseen places behind cloaks and mirrors'.[1]

Perhaps it is a betrayal to make friends with these people while our armies are fighting in North Africa. But I cannot help finding these offscourings of *Horizon*[2] a goodly company in some ways – they seem, indefinably, to be better human beings than these smiling Treasury people who drink, but never too much, and who never in any sense give themselves away. They are queer and unreliable, many of them – but they meet you in a level human sort of way, without the miles and miles of frigid protective atmosphere in between. They have a sort of freedom too, which I envy. I think it arises from a complete lack of any sense of responsibility – (so of course my envy is not wholehearted. I may be flying blind at present, but I would not cast *all* the instruments overboard. Why, I don't know. A person with a moral sense but no moral axioms is a ship crowded with canvas which has lost its rudder. Failing another rudder, one should strike sail, I suppose).

1 From Terence Tiller's 'The Singers' in his *Poems* (1941).
2 *Horizon: A Review of Literature and Art*, an influential literary magazine published in London between 1940 and 1949 and edited by Cyril Connolly.

In the intervals of my Soho adventures and my grapplings with Russian verbs and rules for the use of the genitive, I do a large number of things. Seaforth still needs much attention in the way of scrubbing floors and spreading coats of spotless paint over variegated surfaces. I write a bit. I read a lot – am having an orgy of Edmund Wilson[1] at the moment – (good on literature, superficial on history) and lately I reread *Seven Pillars of Wisdom*.[2] I feel a sort of reverence for that book – for that man – which it is hard to describe.[xii] To live such a swift life of action, and yet *not* simplify everything to the point of inhumanity – to let the agonising complexities of situations twist your heart instead of tying your hands – that is real human greatness – it is that sort of person I would leave anything to follow. Also I've read much poetry – various moderns, Wilfred Owen (a magnificent poet) – and Pindar (who always brings you to my mind!).

It is good to write to you, my brother, and try to disentangle for your benefit the strands of my far from satisfactory life. I feel in a peculiar sort of way that I mustn't let you down – yet don't quite know how to set about it. I don't think I believe any more in clean hands and a pure heart. Ignorance I know – 'innocence' I imagine is just a word. What one *must* have is a simple plan of action.

So what so what so what.

I am on First Aid Duty tonight at the Treasury – an oasis of peace in a far too full life. I must go down to bed pretty soon. (We had one casualty tonight. Great excitement. A man with a cut finger. Christ.)

I think of you often. May the gods guard you.

Goodnight, my gentle Frank –

Much love to you.

Iris

To Frank Thompson.

5 Seaforth Place
22 January [1943]

Darling the mice have been eating your letters (not indeed that that is my excuse for not writing for so long, my excuse for that is everything or nothing, whichever way you like to look at it). I am very angry about this, chiefly because your letters are rather precious documents, but also because I am not on very good terms with the mice, and the fact that I have been careless enough to leave valuables around where they could get at them can be

---

1 American writer, editor and literary critic (1895–1972).
2 By T. E. Lawrence.

chalked up as a point to them. One day I shall declare serious war on the mice in a combined trap-poison operation. At present I am just sentimental with a fringe of annoyance. I meet them every now and then, on the stairs, or underneath the gas stove, and they have such nice long tails.

Look here, though. I don't seem to have heard from you for some time. How are things? Are you still in a land of incredible shrubs and amazing mountains having unsuccessful conversations with Ukrainian truck drivers? Your silence I think portends action. I hope it has been, is being, effective – and not I do hope too dangerous – at any rate in its outcome. I don't mind how many dangers you face, so long as I don't know at the time, and you emerge in good condition – and don't suffer miseries en route of course. All the better – you will have more tales to tell when you come home – you will have the tales anyway, I guess. You are obviously designed by the universe to be a teller of tales! We must write a novel in collaboration when you return. You can write the action part and I'll do the psychological interludes.

Oh I chafe at this inaction. I'd take on any job now – *any* job – if it would get me out of England and into some part of the world where things are moving. You will say 'Baloney – things are moving in very few places (and there they're going *too* damn fast) and everywhere else you'd be just as browned off as you are in England'. Maybe – but then at least I'd know two ways of getting browned off, instead of one.

Not that I'm unhappy. All things considered, life is OK. I like my job on the whole. It's not strenuous. I have a pleasant flat near St James's Park (the park is thinking about spring already – soon *you* will be thinking about fritillaries, no doubt), which (the flat, not the park) is rapidly becoming so full of volumes of poetry of all eras and languages that I shall have to go and camp on the railway line (or feed 'em all to the mice, after they've finished their present strict diet of Airgraphs[1]). I read a good deal – but not as much as I'd like. I write a little – but Oh Christ not one bit as much as I'd like. That's part of the trouble at present. I have just so many very tiring and quite *unavoidable* activities that I have just no time to live my own life – at a time when my own life feels of intense value and interest to me. Jesus God how I want to write. I want to write a long long and exceedingly obscure novel objectifying the queer conflicts I find within myself and observe in the characters of others. Like Proust I want to escape from the eternal push and rattle of time into the coolness and poise of a work of art. (Agreeing with Huxley for once, I think it is not what one has experienced, but what one *does* with what one has experienced that matters. The only possible

1 In 1941 the General Post Office introduced the Airgraph Service for correspondence between service people and civilians. Letters were photographed onto microfilm and sent to their destinations where they were developed into full-size prints and posted to the recipients.

doctrine of course for one who has experienced remarkably little of the big world!) But all this requires peace and calm and time time time which I haven't got oh blazing hell I haven't got it. [. . .]

Frank, I wish you would come home (a simple wish, often reiterated). You and the others. You offered me – and still may it please the Gods offer me – a friendship I'm finding it harder and harder to attain these days. I'm hellishly lonely in my great and beautiful and exciting London, and in my cushy job – Oh I know tens and hundreds of people some wild some tame and all interesting, and most kindly but so few my friends. I feel more independent actually than ever before – no longer at all anxious to seek the mob's approbation, to be admired or impress my intellect upon the chance gathering. But oh so much in need of intellectual intimacy. The patient mind which is prepared to comprehend my own and toss me back the ball of my thought. (This sounds a bit intellectual snob. Maybe. I'd believe almost anything of myself these days. I'm becoming the Compleat Cynick[1] where I. Murdoch is concerned.)

I should tell you that I have parted company with my virginity. This I regard as in every way a very good thing. I feel calmer and freer – relieved from something which was obsessing me, and made free of a new field of experience. There have been two men. I don't think I love either of them – but I like them and I know that no damage has been done. I wonder how you react to this – if at all? Don't be angry with me – deep down in your heart. (I know you are far too Emancipated to be angry on the surface.) I am not just going wild. In spite of a certain amount of wild talk I still live my life with deliberation.

Ersatz? Well, yes, a bit – but then all life is rather ersatz now, since the genuine articles have been separated from us and he is a fool who does not go ahead on the basis of what he has.

News of our friends I have little. Noel Martin[2] I saw the other day when he was in town for a medical exam. (He passed A1.) He's volunteering for a special air observer job which sounds rather suicide squaddish to me. He's been driven crazy with boredom in his searchlight racket. He's in love with an ATS subaltern age thirty and may soon propose to her. The gods speed his suit. She sounds rather nice. Leonie[3] I hope before long to have staying with me, complete with infant. (I haven't yet seen the latter.)

---

1 *The Compleat Cynic*, a play written by Alaric Jacob (1909–95) who was a war correspondent for the *Daily Express*. He was based in Teheran and Cairo during the early 1940s where he might possibly have met Frank Thompson and/or David Hicks.

2 An Oxford contemporary and friend of Leo Pliatzky. In 1940 Martin had asked Murdoch to marry him.

3 Leonie Marsh, an Oxford friend and a member of the Communist Party. During her first year at Oxford she fell in love with Frank Thompson (who loved Murdoch) and was loved by M. R. D. Foot. She married Tony Platt in 1941.

People are getting awfully damn complacent about the war. I wish they wouldn't. We're hardly beginning to see the way out of the wood yet. Beveridge[1] is a good thing though – *that's* all right, so long as people don't start relaxing with a sigh of relief. (I've just been reading Bev. – a fine piece of work – thorough and equitable – and it will be a good fight, trying to get it put into operation – doomed to failure I surmise, but instructive.)

Poetry (said she slipping around in a random manner from subject to subject, please forgive this) obsesses me more and more – it is a great sea which, whenever I can escape from my detestable duties, even for ten minutes, I slip into with a sign of relief. Poets I have discovered lately – Louis Aragon[2] – *Le crève-coeur* – the first real war poems I have read that *are* poems. *Dunkirk* at last seen by an artist – a handful of real jewels – a limited edition in France, all confiscated. One or two copies escaped to England and have been reprinted here. Then – a favourite of your father's evidently – archy the cockroach![3] And (rediscovered) Wilfred Owen. And Ann Ridler.[4] And innumerable moderns.

Do you ever read now? Or write? Oh you should have that civilisation you could take part in so richly – too. For the mountains and the truck drivers are very good also. And I *do* agree with you about the Russian language!

Write to me you frightful cad and say what you are feeling about our pretty baffling universe.

> you write so many things
> About me which are not true
> Complained the universe.
>
> There are so many things
> About you which you seem to be
> Unconscious of yourself said archy[5]

---

1 The Report on Social Insurance and Allied Services, known as the Beveridge Report (1942), was produced by a committee chaired by the economist William Beveridge (1879–1963). It formed the basis for the post-war reforms in the UK and resulted in the creation of the welfare state and the National Health Service.

2 French poet, novelist and essayist (1897–1982), a founder of the surrealist movement and a member of both the Communist Party and the French Resistance movement.

3 *archy and mehitabel* (1927), by Don Marquis, originated in a series of satirical newspaper columns in the 1910s and 1920s; archy is a fictional cockroach who has been a free-verse poet in a former life; mehitabel is an alley cat.

4 English poet (1912–2001) and an editor at Faber & Faber.

5 From *archy and mehitabel*.

Out in the kitchen I can hear the mice eating something or other. Better go
and see what.

Look after yourself.
Much love
Iris

*To Frank Thompson who, having landed in Sicily on 10 July, was now being shuttled
back and forth between countries, including Malta and Libya; his squadron finally
reassembled in Egypt in mid-August. Murdoch's decision to learn Turkish was perhaps
a gesture of sympathy and identification with Frank, who was required to learn the
language in preparation for the possible invasion of the Dodecanese Islands.*[xiii]

5 Seaforth Place
15 August [1943]

Old campaigner, you preserve a stubborn (and no doubt prudent and correct)
silence about your martial activities, and it is only from Hal that I have learnt
where you have been lately. Yes, I daresay it is all just so much more sweat
and hotness and sordid scenery for you – but at least you are in the big river
– and we at home can't help envying you. I can imagine your comments on
that – but Christ, can you imagine how it feels to fulfil a serene daily routine,
having to make greater and greater imaginative efforts to believe that a war
is on at all, as the memory of the Blitzes fades – and yet knowing intellectually all the time that humanity's future is being fought out, and that one's
own friends are out there and may get hurt in the process?

Pardon my tiresomeness – just this old restless feeling, annoyance against
the easy stay-at-home life.

I'm glad you see Hal now and then. Hal is a very good guy, and as you say,
has a special brand of wisdom. Re your suggestion that a photograph of me
be forwarded, I have to inform you that action has been taken. Viz. I have
made an appointment with Polyfoto[1] for their next free date, viz. the end of
August. So you may expect the radiant thing to arrive about Christmastime.

You don't mention old Leo. Hal tells me – and indeed I had a letter
recently from the old cynic himself – that he is shortly to be commissioned.
Your army takes a long time to recognise a good proposition.

The leaves are falling portentously all over St James's Park. I am rereading
large sections of the Bible and wondering about Man. I am getting on capitally
with my Turkish teacher, except that he will call me 'Mudrock' in spite of

1 Popular brand of national photographic studios.

frequent reproaches.¹ ('What you must never forget, Bayan Mudrock . . .'
'*Murdoch*, efendim!' 'Ah yes – now as I [was] saying Bayan Mudrock . . .').²
But – and this, the only conclusion of importance I have come to of late is
that if (I say if, and cannot give the word too horrid an emphasis) I have any
métier it is to be a writer.

Writing is the only activity which makes me feel 'Only I could produce
this'. Whether or not 'this' is any use is of course the crucial question to
which I know not, and may not ever know, the answer. Meanwhile I am
writing fairly regularly, both poetry and prose.

The autumn brings melancholy. Will this war never end – will it always
be you battening on Chianti and cakeshops, I on Burtons and the ABC³ – and
never a united celebration? Soon I shall break into a lament and compare
our inconvenienced youth with the fall of leaves in high summer – as they
are falling now. What bosh. And the Red Army advancing too.⁴

Later I will write a more virile letter and prove to you that I am not
fundamentally downcast.

Do thou, oh my brother, prosper.

Love I

*To Frank Thompson, written from Blackpool where Murdoch was convalescing
following a bout of jaundice. Although this appears to be Murdoch's last letter
to Thompson, he continued writing to her until the spring of 1944; Murdoch's
letters written in response have been lost but it is clear from Thompson's replies
(held in the Bodleian) that they chronicled her 'disaster-prone love-life', including
her affairs with M. R. D. Foot and Thomas Balogh.*ˣⁱᵛ *In Thompson's last letter
to her, dated 21 April 1944, he wrote: 'I can honestly say I've never been in
love. When I pined for you I was too young to know what I was doing
– no offence meant. [. . .] All the same, I don't think you should fall for
"emotional fascists" – Try to avoid that . . .'*ˣᵛ *Thompson probably had Thomas
Balogh in mind when using the phrase 'emotional fascists'. In November 1944,
Philippa Foot was to bring Murdoch the news that Thompson was 'Missing
Believed Killed'.*

Blackpool
12 November [1943]

1 Murdoch had persuaded the secretary to the Turkish Embassy to teach her the language.
2 'Bayan' is Turkish, in this context, for 'Miss'; 'efendim' means 'sir'.
3 Burton's jam teacakes; ABC (Aerated Bread Company Ltd) was famous for its self-service tea shops.
4 The Soviet summer campaign of 1943 saw the Russians defeating the Germans in the air and recapturing Russian cities.

Dearly beloved, thank you for Прыг *and* Скок,[1] who have just arrived! Yes, it pleases me too to think that these people of blood and iron have their human moments – perhaps after all we are wrong in thinking of them as somewhat barbarous Asiatics fundamentally differing from ourselves. Viva the confraternity of Peter Rabbits.

I am delighted too to hear that a Mayakovsky[2] may be en route. [. . .] When I get back to London I shall send you some of the stuff that is being written now by the Younger School – our contemporaries, God help us – the New Apocalyptics, the *Poetry (London)* gang, the sensibility boys who think with their stomach.[3] You probably won't approve – you may nevertheless enjoy. Just occasionally some of these folks produce an exquisite lyric – and a good lyric is a good lyric, and infinitely to be preferred to the barren political jargonising that even real poets spent so much time on in the play-time of the '30s when we were all conscience-ridden spectators. [. . .]

I am reading another Henry James called *The Ambassadors* – the man is uncanny the way he unravels a psychological situation. He writes in about five dimensions – and in that gorgeous convoluted style which, if you give it your closest attention, is nevertheless not obscure. He is the only novelist I know who really says *everything* – and gets away with it. To write like that is self-evidently one of the greatest activities of the human mind. I hope the New World Order will agree! [. . .]

I'd love to know what you're up to – (though of course I know you can't tell me). Still, if the Russians, God bless 'em, continue to hare along like this maybe you'll all be home before too long. Au revoir then.

Con amore, devotissima
I

To Leo Pliatzky.

5 Seaforth Place
17 June 1944

1 Russian children's book *Skip and Jump*, about small animals such as frogs and rabbits, that Frank had sent in order to help her improve her Russian.
2 Vladimir Mayakovsky (1893–1930), Russian poet and playwright.
3 Murdoch describes three groups here: the Apocalyptic Movement, or the New Apocalypse, was a group of Scottish, Welsh and English poets of the late 1930s and early 1940s, including G. S. Fraser, Norman MacCaig, Edwin Morgan, Vernon Watkins, Kathleen Raine, David Gascoyne, George Barker, Henry Treece and Herbert Read, who drew on myth to convey the idea that European civilisation was destined to collapse. The second group comprised those who published in the magazine *Poetry (London)*, which ran from February 1939 until January 1951. The third group was probably the New Romantics, poets who were reacting against the intellectualism and realism of 1940s poetry and whose most famous member was Dylan Thomas.

Old Leo, hello, I was so glad to get your letter and to know you were safe and secluded, though irked at being so. I have so far avoided bombs, torpedoes, pilotless planes and other such. I have changed my job, without however attaining any great spiritual satisfaction thereby. I have escaped from the Treasury into UNRRA. There I wander, amid the chaos of what may one day be an organisation, trying to persuade myself and others that I am doing a job. Actually I just read odd memoranda, learn people's names, and try to decide what the word 'rehabilitation' means.

The Second Front, as I write is proceeding nicely.[1] How good it is to hear these French names! How charming to be freeing a place called St Mère Église. (Not so charming, no doubt, if one is on the spot.) I hope this is no false dawn for all these people. Perhaps they will see to it that it is not. Morale at home (of course) is fine, to judge from conversations in trains, applause in cinemas and so on! (Tito[2] got such a rousing reception at a cinema the other day, I was quite surprised.) Even pilotless planes do not depress unduly. They provide such fascinating material for the uninstructed theorist. Everyone in London has his little idea.

I suppose this business will end. It looks as if it might. Any ideas yet of what you'll do thereafter? It's a queer prospect. I feel tired, myself, of the vague administrative task. If I saw a chance I'd bolt for the academic ticket – but I doubt the appearance of a chance. Otherwise, to be a hander out of cocoa and Fry's chocolate to the savage tribes of Europe might be sufficiently perplexing and preoccupying and pity and terror inspiring to divert the attention from the self.

Write again oh my dear Leo. I will do the same, I will.

As always my love to you

I

To David Hicks who had just left his post in Cairo to work in Teheran. Although Persia had become Iran in 1935, its old name seems to have stuck.

5 Seaforth Place
4 September 1944

David my dear, your letter, thanks. But oh Lord what a picture of deserts and bad Persians and awful Englishmen. It hurts that one can't *really* imagine the cockroaches or the heat or the fever. I can a little imagine the hatred. I

1 6 June 1944 – D-Day – had seen the beginning of the Second Front, the Allied invasion of France which lasted for eleven months and ended in Berlin.
2 Josip Tito (1892–1980), Yugoslav revolutionary and statesman.

was moved – but it remains all too vague this picture of you and of Teheran. Or else a little too mythological, with Black Girls and Leopards and so on. And your voice, still sounding familiar, in the background. I hope you haven't been ill again. And have your chiefs turned decent and is life reasonably calm and sane? The main thing is obviously that you must come home pretty soon – but you've thought of that yourself. [. . .]

You ask about UNRRA. UNRRA, to be brief, is a pretty unstable show at the moment. It's rather too full of inept British civil servants (whom their departments could well spare; me for instance), uncoordinated foreigners with Special Ideas and an imperfect command of English and go-getting Americans and Canadians. The result is pretty fair chaos. There are a few able people here and there and very many noble-hearted good-intentioned people – but they drown in the general flood of mediocrity and muddle. Yet maybe I paint too black a picture. The machinery for repatriating 'displaced persons' (the one job UNRRA certainly *will* have to do) is being planned with a fair amount of sense and energy – and if we do the right thing by these 8,000,000 we shan't have lived altogether in vain. My own part in this great show is small. A sort of jungle life prevails at my level (survival of the fittest etc.) and I have to spend much of my energy preventing myself being (quite genuinely) mistaken for a clerk or girl messenger by newcomers from Washington. The nervous strain is pretty considerable; I'm certainly not enough of a go-getter for that sort of existence. Prospects of going abroad are nil at the moment. (I nearly got a job the other day on a 'flying squad' in connection with repatriation, but was rejected because I can't ride a motor bicycle! What a useless character I am.) Altogether gloom and obscurity prevails about the future. I might try to get some academic job – but that mightn't be too easy and anyway would I make the grade? Heigh ho. I suppose the trouble is I have a little too good an opinion of my intellect – thus I easily get fed up with mediocre jobs, and imagine I'm being victimised while all the time (maybe) I'm just not rising to occasions. A problem. Well, I shall learn. I still cherish the illusion that I can write, though that too is getting a little battered by the waves of time. *Eh bien*. Meanwhile, most of the people at UNRRA are perfectly charming (especially the Czechs – I like next best the French, Dutch, Belgians, Poles, British, Americans and Canadians in that order!) and so one is not perpetually in a state of (righteous/unrighteous) indignation. (It's revolting to observe the extent to which a little social success relieves and rehabilitates one's vanity.)

On other fronts change goes forward at its usually breakneck speed. Shortly after I wrote to you last I tore myself away, with agonies which I could not even have conceived of a year ago, from the utterly adorable but wicked Hungarian with whom I'd been living.[1] Now that I'm no longer bleeding at every artery I see this was a very good move. At present I'm having a rather decorous *affaire* with a French diplomat,[2] which is at any rate good for my French. Nothing very world- or soul-shaking I must say, though, I am rather in love with France. *La lointaine princesse*[3] maybe. (London shewed considerable restrained enthusiasm about the liberation of Paris,[4] and one sees a suitable number of tricolours about.) My own passion grows and grows. A large percentage of sheer romanticism of course. Yet too the feeling that if France lives Europe will live – meaning that there will be something left not Russianised or Americanised. Meaning too that France is likely to be a decent progressive force and will be useful to have around. And oh, all the rest – French people, French films, French songs, Baudelaire and Mauriac and the dangerous intellects of the Church and Giraudoux[5] and Aragon and Jeanne d'Arc and what have you. (I got very vividly your picture of the French women who wished they hadn't married Persians.) [. . .]

How nice it would be to be Catholic and to be able to light candles for people and feel it was some use. (Today Sunday and the angelus from Westminster Cathedral, which is 200 yards from here, has just ceased ringing.) Anyhow, keep well, my dear, and get that home leave. [. . .]

Much love to you, David

Iris

To David Hicks, in which Murdoch mentions briefly Frank Thompson's death. In charge of a Special Operations Executive mission, Thompson had been executed in Bulgaria in June 1944 with some partisans and villagers who had helped the SOE team. However, he was not officially to be declared dead until 1945.[xvi]

5 Seaforth Place

12 December 1944

Dear David, a long time ago, as I may or may not have mentioned, I sent you off some Eliot and some Aragon. [. . .] Anyhow that was a long time ago. If those chaps are to be seen on every bookstall in Teheran, my apologies. I cannot stop imagining your city as consisting of three mud huts and a bazaar.

1 Thomas Balogh.
2 Olivier Wormser, an acquaintance of Thomas Balogh.
3 The 'distant princess' is a stock figure in medieval romance literature.
4 On 25 August 1944.
5 Hippolyte Giraudoux (1882–1944): French novelist, essayist, playwright and diplomat.

Since then, I have a feeling all sorts of things have happened. I heard the news of the death of my old friend Frank Thompson – you may have met him in Cairo. He used to be at New College. He was a brilliant and full-blooded creature, one of the best I ever knew. I suppose only now I'm beginning to realise the war isn't just a short interval after which one resumes – something. There's nothing to resume. Oh it was all very golden and beautiful and pure-hearted, all that time – but now one is quite different and wants different things. A very obvious conclusion, but I hadn't up till now felt it so violently, that severance from the golden lads and lasses period.[1] What the present period should be called, I really don't know. What does it consist of? Oh whirls of charming people, and much hard work directed to no very clear end (and which anyway will probably all have to be scrapped when we finally clear up our relations with the military!), and loads of Henry James and Kierkegaard and lots of French things – French books and French conversations and Frenchmen. At last there's a reasonable flow of news from Paris, and one begins to feel that that's a city, after all, in the same universe as one's own, and which one might even conceivably visit. One's friends go off there for a week and come back. A few books come across. All that's very refreshing and exciting. [. . .]

Send me a photograph of yourself. And write, old dear, about the wicked Persians and your black girl and the loathsomeness of officialdom and what you yourself are thinking and doing in the midst. I hope you are well and not miserably prostrated with real or imagined illnesses. Somehow or other, I thirst for news.

My love to you.

Iris

To Leo Pliatzky.

5 Seaforth Place
[5 April 1945]

Leo, dear, it was good to hear from you. You still sound rather sandy – I hope life isn't being too arid. I didn't know the people you mentioned – but I know of plenty like cases. *Mon dieu.* Friends? I suppose I have been lucky – I've made about four really good friends in the last year or two – and, lord, that makes all the difference between the desert and the rose gardens of Shiraz and Ispahan.[2] (Have been reading Rilke into the bargain.)

1 Echoing Shakespeare's *Cymbeline*: 'Golden lads and girls all must, / As chimney-sweepers, come to dust'.
2 Ancient cities in Iran.

Hal Lidderdale is due home tomorrow on seven days' leave. It will be queer to see him again after four or five years, and now that it comes to it I don't altogether want to. In a way you know, I'm savagely jealous of you people who have been out of England during the war – even granted all your cares about only seeing the world from inside the military machine. What I've been seeing is the dirty depressing muddled insides of offices – consoled of course by friends and poems and novels and soaring scintillating ideas and the rest of that paraphernalia. I suppose you will be home too before long – it's odd to think of it.

The usual caucus race goes on in my mind about what to do after the war: university, WEA,[1] British Council, BBC, journalism, League of Nations (or whatever), Allied Control Commission – anything, anywhere, heaven only knows. What about you Leo? Any plans?

Have just been reading Henry Miller's torrential book about Greece.[2] His lyrical enthusiasm about people and places is infectious. I suppose it's not such a bad old world – for people like us, anyway. It has possibilities – and I imagine, with the war ending, one should be thinking more and more about how good life might be. Yet of course one isn't. Yet indeed the daffo-dils are now 9d a dozen in London.

See you soon, old Leo. I can remember nothing except the long eyelashes. Good luck and write again and so will I.

Love
I

To David Hicks.

5 Seaforth Place
13 May 1945

Hello. It is extremely hot and I am sobering down after the uneasy excesses of VE.[3] We did all the right things in London, such as dancing in Piccadilly at 2 a.m. Now I suppose one will cool down, think about poor old Europe, and wonder if our rulers have learnt a great deal from this. Yet to hell with such gloomy reasonings! Thank God part of the damned war is over. I did thank God very earnestly in the RC Cathedral on Tuesday where the emotion was as thick as incense and the cardinal (or is he a cardinal) made a dreadful speech which was happily soon

1 The Workers' Educational Association, founded in 1903 to provide access to education and lifelong learning for adults in the UK and Northern Ireland.
2 *The Colossus of Maroussi* (1941).
3 Victory in Europe Day, 8 May 1945.

drowned in the Hallelujah Chorus. After that I went and got drunk, which was good too.

I hope you reached the Caspian all right with your mule and got back again safely and met many charming Russians on the road. When are you coming home on leave? Do these extraordinary events make any immediate difference to your life?

Sometime or other you will receive *The Brothers Karamazov* which I at last managed to get sent off. When I next remember and am in Charing Cross Road I will send you some French books. I am getting some fascinating stuff over from France at the moment. As a result of late repercussions from Kierkegaard and Kafka the French novelist seems to be in a dilemma, wondering whether to write a philosophical essay or a novel. Some, like Albert Camus, write first the one and then the other. Maybe the French have been that way for some time (Gide . . . Mauriac . . .) but the malady is certainly intensified now. Poets too are getting philosophical about the nature of language. The Silence of Rimbaud is becoming a great subject for meta-physical speculation. Out of this hurly-burly a lot of exciting and maybe good literature seems to be getting written. I'm quite intoxicated by all this. The intellectual fumes are strangely mixed, very strong, overpowering.

I saw Hal Lidderdale, home on leave, a few weeks ago. I like Hal a lot. (He looks much less like Chatterton[1] than when last I saw him.) I like his warmth and humanness, his lazy pleasure in life's good things, and his lack of petty vanities and meannesses. A good chap. He's now in Germany. He's had a fairly peaceful time throughout the war, and didn't in the last phase discover any Germans who wanted to fight.

Now I am going out into St James's Park to look at the tufted ducks.

Au revoir.

Love, I

To David Hicks, now working in Prague.

5 Seaforth Place
1 June 1945

David dear,

Your fine epic *did* arrive, a few days after I sent off my last letter. Maybe it was too heavy, and that delayed it. Heavy or not, I consumed it with joy. I envy you these flirtations with a Nature wilder than anything I've ever seen.

---

1 Thomas Chatterton (1752–70), early Romantic poet, who died by taking arsenic at the age of seventeen and who is famously commemorated in Henry Wallis's painting *The Death of Chatterton* (1856).

I've never met with this Monk Lewis sort of Nature.[1] Sorry about the snow – however you were both so thoroughly British and determined about it.

Czechoslovakia? Good God. What shuttling to and fro you chaps seem to do. I can't think at the moment whether I'm glad or not. Of course I'm *very* glad you're getting out of the backwoods – you were due for that anyway. But I wish you were coming a bit nearer home than Czecho. I feel an occasional dash to Prague will probably be beyond my income. I hope you'll be coming to England en route? Well, yes, I think I *am* glad. I like to think of you in Prague. There seems to be an obscure suitability about it. Maybe that's because of a dim pre-war memory of your telling me how you stood with some Czech on some balcony looking down on the fair city with him saying sadly *'für Hitler's Bomben'* – or did I dream that? It must have got shelled, I suppose, at the end – perhaps it's not too bad.[2] Baroque, baroque – what else? Not much else I can connect with the picture of Prague. Never mind. Maybe you'll be in Bratislava after all. Know any Czech?

Yes, I liked your epic: pondering now over the preludium. I was amused by your stuff about our Master Raceness. I suppose you get stuck right up against this problem. For me, I just don't see it at all. I suppose simply because of staying put here in England and not ever having to think about putting anything across. I feel *now* that I'm not of any particular country. There's Ireland, there's England – but if I have a fatherland, it would be something like the literature of England perhaps – and so, one escapes from chauvinism. Or does one? Yes, I know I will change some of this after I have lived outside England for a while. Even a few months in UNRRA have shewn me that universal brotherhood is not a condition that comes naturally to people. (Canadians. Grrr!) I wonder will you hate Prague too? I can't believe that. But oh Teheran – I shudder in sympathy. Come out of it, David, soon.

Peace, and all that. They have brought back about fifty pictures to the National Gallery. Oh heavenly bliss! Sir Kenneth Clark's favourites, I suppose.[3] Well, they're all right. The Van Eyck man and pregnant wife. Bellini and Mantegna Agonies. Titian *Noli me tangere*. Rubens' *Bacchus and Ariadne*. El Greco *Agony*, Rembrandt portraits of self and of an old lady. His small *Woman Bathing* (lovely!). A delicious Claude fading into blue blue blue – blue lake, mountains, sky. Incredible distances to breathe. Two Vermeers, so blue and lemon, honey stuff, girls at the Virginals. And then oh more Bellini and Rubens, and then the Ruisdaels, the Hobbemas, and chaps like Cuyp that

---

1 Wild, sublime landscapes as described in the Gothic novels of Matthew ('Monk') Lewis (1775–1818).
2 In fact, Prague had been bombed on 14 February 1945, when the US Army Air Forces carried out an air raid on Dresden and (possibly accidentally) hit the Czech city as well.
3 Kenneth Clark was director of the National Gallery from 1933 until 1946. All paintings were sent to Wales during the ten days preceding the declaration of war on 3 September 1939. For further safety, in 1941 the paintings were housed in converted slate mines near Blaenau Ffestiniog.

one had forgotten about. I still feel delirious with the first shock. It felt *really* like peace. And all the people wandering round looked dazed.

The UNRRA wheels are really turning at last and I have far, far too much to do. I'm liking it though. Just now and then one can, for a moment, grasp the whole tiresome chain of causes and effects and realise that what one does in one's office has some remote connection with someone or other over there being fed, clothed, calmed, who wouldn't otherwise be. Outside office hours, this damned election is taking my time. I spent last weekend sitting on an interviewing board to look at chaps who had the effrontery to offer themselves as possible Labour candidates in Westminster. They were uniformly frightful (ignorant, opinionated, careerist, insensitive . . .) – well, I suppose we shall have to choose one of them. [. . .] Heigh ho, Russian exam on July 2nd, general election on July 5th, and UNRRA Council opens in London on July 12. In June, however, I'm going to Scotland and will stay at the gayest hotel in Edinburgh. In August maybe, Ireland . . . island of spells, provincial pigsty. ('Little brittle magic nation dim of mind'. Joyce, of course.)[1]

The other day I came up the steps on one side at St James's Park station, and up the other side, meeting at the top, came Denis Healey. He was with Edna Edmonds. Remember those characters? D. is Labour candidate for Pudsey,[2] his home region. He looked bronze and sleek and rough and handsome and very pleased with himself. I was glad to see him.

Am just reading [Arthur] Koestler's *The Yogi and the Commissar* (shall I send you this, or can you get it out there?). Why am I convinced Koestler is Satan? He's so well aware of so much that no one else notices or can comment on. He sees what are the real moral problems of now. He's a better moralist than Sir David bloody Ross and all the Oxford and Cambridge chaps rolled together. Well, just for those reasons. He makes the left self-conscious – good – but he administers no corrective, no antidote . . . It's the same old dreary cynical undertone. There's No Solution – let's just be conscious of the problems – fine subtle intellectual chaps seeing the problems and understanding our neuroses. He quotes Pascal 'Man is neither an angel nor a brute – but in trying to be an angel he becomes a brute'.[3] We'll never find Koestler trying to be an angel. Oh what tangles, what circles . . . Seductive whirlpools. The best moralists are the most satanic.

How fantastic to think of you back in Europe. Give me news of that soon. If I think of it when I'm shutting the envelope I'll put some stamps in. Whistle if you want that Koestler. It will annoy you. There's a lot of

1 *Finnegans Wake* (1939).
2 Denis Healey narrowly failed to win Otley and Pudsey (a constituency near Bradford) but went on to hold several important positions in the Labour Party, including Chancellor of the Exchequer (1974–9) and deputy leader (1980–3).
3 Blaise Pascal (1623–62), *Pensées*, Section VI, No. 358.

potboiling stuff in it too – written for Yankee magazines. God! And any
other books you want. I'll raid Charing Cross Road for you soon.
   Au revoir chéri.
   I

To David Hicks.

5 Seaforth Place
21 July 1945

My dear, as you see I am still *in situ* – and likely to remain so for quite a
time, as things look at present.[1] I may even still be here on September 1st.
But God knows. Hell blast this damned Administration, nothing ever remains
the same for two days together. There is now a plot that I should go to
Frankfurt. In any case, my departure to anywhere looks like being indefinitely
delayed. The nervous strain is frightful. I always guessed that international
organisations needed employees with iron nerves. At least at Geneva one
could go swimming or drown oneself in the lake or go and contemplate the
Dents du Midi and feel that it would all be the same in a thousand years.
Not that this is an international organisation actually. Your picture of mouse-
lets on office stools is quite wrong. You have no *idea* how we live. We are
not run by quiet bowler hats from Ealing and Dagenham, who at least
behave approximately like gentlemen, but by the citizens of Milwaukee and
Cincinnati and New Haven, Conn., let loose in their myriads to deal a death
blow to tottering Europe. They do not sit on office stools but lounge, with
cellulose belts and nylon braces, behind enormous desks and chew gum and
call their fellow citizens by their Christian names. Oh God. However, I must
admit (and this spoils my race theory) that I have got quite fond of a number
of these *Herrenvolk*[2] – these are mainly disgruntled intellectuals from Cornell,
Ithaca, who have found in UNRRA the means of having a long holiday from
the Ithacans: Odyssey in reverse.
   Oh David I feel so tired and angry these days. I wish you were coming
home earlier than September blast you. As for seeing you I feel quite confident that I shall manage that, once you're in Europe, even if it means hitch-
hiking 500 miles in jeeps or unofficially chartering a Lancaster. I have some
leave left which I could take in England *if* by any chance I am gone before
you arrive.

1 In a letter written on 6 July, Murdoch had told David Hicks that she expected to be sent to Brussels
   soon.
2 Master race.

We shall all freeze next winter in our respective capital cities. But I shall see you before then. I will write again soon when I am feeling a little less enraged. My rude beloved David with vine leaves in your hair, my love to you.

I

To David Hicks, following the Labour Party's definitive victory in the general election. This gave Labour its first majority government and a mandate to implement reforms, including those outlined in the Beveridge Report.

5 Seaforth Place
27 July 1945

Oh wonderful people of Britain! After all the ballyhoo and the eyewash, they've had the guts to vote against Winston! I feel really proud of them, and ashamed at not having believed in them. I thought they would be fooled. But they have sense, they can think! I feel proud to be British! This *is* the beginning of the new world.

My own affairs are damnably delayed and God knows when I shall get away. It looks as if I shall be going, for a while at any rate, to Frankfurt. Dismal but educative.

Oh David, what a time this is! I know they will make endless mistakes and it will be bloody hard. All the same I can't help feeling that to be young is very heaven![1]

Much love

I

To Leo Pliatzky, written when Murdoch was expecting to be posted to Brussels at any moment.

4 Eastbourne Road
11 August 1945

Leo darling, hello, thank God that other war is over too or seems to be. I know a lot of Naval and other mothers, brothers and sweethearts who are pretty damned relieved.

I am still *in situ*, as you see, but likely to be gone before the end of August.

---

1 'Bliss was it in that dawn to be alive/But to be young was very heaven!' William Wordsworth, *The Prelude*, Book XI.

When are you coming on leave? I saw a newsreel last week of you Italian chaps coming on lorries through most of Europe in order to get home, but I didn't see you. Write soon, please, whatever the news.

London and I are feeling faintly hysterical at present. The great game is to shower torn paper out of the top windows on main thoroughfares *à la* New York. I am out of my old life and not yet into my new. I can't dream of settling down to universities or anything else in England that would have me till I've had a good sniff at Europe and listened to the French tongue for a while. After that I shall probably be too restless to settle down at all!

And you? Any plans yet? When do you get out? Will you be coming to the BLA[1] before you do? If so, come via Brussels or come there on leave. And if you should get to England before the end of August, ring up or call at once. *Write*, anyway, immediately. Love to you.

Iris

To Leo Pliatzky.

UNNRA
c/o British Military Mission to Belgium
FPO [Field Post Office]
BAOR [British Army of the Rhine]
4 September 1945
Home address in Brussels:
c/o Agence Continentale et Anglaise, 32 Rue Picard

Dear Leo, greetings. I am most sorry I missed you. *This* is where I am now. [. . .]

Of course I think Brussels is glorious. It has a wild feminine charm. Even the 19th century here was sufficiently baroque to be delightful. I haven't had much time yet to explore the old Flemish quarters fully – but, oh, it's all delightful to me: the French voices, ridiculous little dogs, the little clanging trams, and the way everyone rides on the running boards and never pays their fare –

More of all this anon. Write me how England strikes you after these years. Where do you go next with the army? And what will you do after? Have you decided yet? Au revoir.

Love I

1 The 21st Army Group, known also as the British Liberation Army, which operated in several European countries, including Belgium, from June 1944 until the end of the war.

To David Hicks, who was at this time on leave in the UK.

UNRRA
c/o British Military Mission to Belgium
4 October 1945

Dearest David, your letter written in the Flying Scotsman[1] is now with me. It's strange to think of you wandering round all my old haunts in London – and many other haunts, I daresay, that I never dreamed of. You are probably able to get infinitely more out of the literary pub life than I ever got. I just ran away from it in the end. One of the many disadvantages of femininity, of course, is that it's more difficult to cope with that sort of society and appear neither a whore nor a bluestocking. Also, in the end, it seemed to me that the percentage of really intelligent conversation was rather small. Soho is so damnably full of people with some talent and sensibility, but not much solid ferro-concrete intelligence – and (bluestocking after all, perhaps) I find as I grow older that I do require from people, if I'm really to enjoy their company, plenty of the good old Oxford and Cambridge clearness of thought and expression. And oh the nauseating vanity of so many of those bohemians! I liked a lot of them very well. Tambi,[2] for instance, is a darling and has beautiful hair. But relationships were always stormy. People turned out so often to be childish and malicious. Finally I decided I was wasting my time and ceased frequenting the pubs and started staying at home and reading or else chatting with colder more civilised sort of chaps and was much happier. But maybe I was just unlucky in the individuals I met, and as I say it's all more tricky for a woman. What a croaking raven I am, enough of this! [. . .]

I'm amused to hear that your new boss is Edwin Muir.[3] I connect him, though not very clearly, with all sorts of things – literature, and some Polish friends of mine in London, and Kafka's mistress.[4] I forget exactly what the latter story was – that the Muirs took her in after Kafka's death, or something. What would there be left to do in the world after having been Kafka's mistress?

Which reminds me that I have discovered a *wonderful* novelist – more or less everything that the modern novelist should be, and a woman, bless her!

1 London to Edinburgh express train service.
2 Meary James Thurairajah Tambimuttu ('Tambi') came to London in 1938 from Sri Lanka (then Ceylon). In 1939, with Anthony Dickins, he set up *Poetry (London)* which became the leading poetry magazine of the 1940s.
3 Scottish poet and translator who was director of the British Council in Prague and Rome between 1945 and 1949.
4 Probably Dora Diamant, Kafka's last love.

Simone de Beauvoir, Jean-Paul Sartre's mistress and full of his philosophy. However, I'll tell you no more about her now, as you must be fed up with these cries of enthusiasm about the French.

I can't think why the British Council should send you to Scotland. A consolation prize, after Iran, so that you could tell the Czechs about the Scots? More talk later, when I'm in a more coherent mood.

Au revoir, chéri.

I

PS I can't place the Black Horse.[1] Where is it?

To Leo Pliatzky.

c/o British Military Mission to Belgium
30 October 1945

Dear Leo,

I was delighted to get your letter. I had been wondering what had happened to you, and was cursing you for not writing! I'm so glad you've escaped from the army. A year of Oxford will be an odd fantasia, but can do no harm. How I envy you, with *time* before you to think and wonder and decide! Your remarks about people gave me very strange sensations. It is eerie, this business of meeting people again, and meeting all one's previous selves – melancholy and desolating in a vaguely pleasant sort of way! What will you *do* in PPE in your one year? If you're doing any philosophy *insist* on MacKinnon! Anyway, do go to all his lectures, and let me know what he's talking about now. [. . .] Please let me know lots more about all the chaps and girls we used to know. What is Stuart Schultz[2] doing now? Is Denis Healey back? How is the Lehmann–Alastine Bell[3] marriage turning out? Give my greetings to dear Fraenkel! All that, and London too, seems so infinitely far away now.

Of course I absolutely love being here. I forget if you ever touched Brussels on your many voyages? If you did, you will remember the Grand Place and its perfection and its rich Flemish buildings and the gilded statuettes high on the roofs, and the tower of the Hôtel de Ville, and the churches, old

1 The Black Horse, Rathbone Place in north Soho (now called Fitzrovia), a pub that was to feature in *The Black Prince*.

2 An Oxford contemporary who spent the war serving in the Royal Army Education Corps but who never progressed beyond the rank of private because he was thought too Bolshevik to promote.

3 Alastine Bell was a former girlfriend of David Hicks. She had married Andrew George Lehmann in January 1942.

Flemish, and the churches, Romanesque – and also (not less amazing to my innocent uncontinental eye) the thousand and one cafés and the insane tramway system. Just being here and breathing the air and walking on the cobbles and reading the advertisements and hearing the soft twitter of French and the harsher music of Flemish fills one with a crazy joy.

What you say about the curse of military life is probably truer of UNRRA, Germany, than of UNRRA Brussels. There *is* all the military paraphernalia – I get a certain kick out of that too. It's rather bizarre, now the war is over, to be masquerading as a British officer, drinking cheap drinks in the clubs, and being cared for by NAAFI and ENSA.[1] However, I have managed to get to know a number of Belgians as well and that is much more important – mainly literary chaps and university people. The intellectuals of Brussels are insanely *francophil* (naturally) and that suits me very well. So there are long conversations in cafés about Jean-Paul Sartre, and Simone de Beauvoir, and Albert Camus and Raymond Queneau, and all the boys that we were just beginning to get excited about in London when the first French literature filtered across after the Liberation. My God, Leo, there is some very interesting stuff being written in France at present on the philosophical and literary front. I begin to get some glimmering too about 'existentialism' the latest philosophy of France – Sartre, out of Husserl, Heidegger and Kierkegaard. Last week I had a very great experience. Jean-Paul Sartre came to Brussels to give a lecture on existentialism, and I met him after the lecture, and on the following day during an interminable café séance. He is small, squints appallingly, is very simple and charming in manner and extremely attractive. What versatility! Philosophy, novels, plays, cinema, journalism! No wonder the stuffy professional philosophers are suspicious. I don't make much yet of his phenomenology, but his theories on morals, which derive from Kierkegaard, seem to me first rate and just what English philosophy needs to have injected into its veins, to expel the loathsome humours of Ross and Prichard.

UNRRA is as crazy as ever. A recent reorganisation has completely crippled my job, which I was very attached to, and left me with very little to do. I'm afraid the magic carpet will soon call for me and translate me to Bad Oeynhausen or Wiesbaden or Spenge or London or some other outlandish place for the winter. If I *am* translated back to England I will of course shoot straight down to Oxford to see you.

I still can't think what to do with my Life, which still remains oddly unstarted. Brussels is putting all sorts of foolish intoxicating ideas into my

---

1 NAAFI: Navy, Army and Air Force Institutes, set up in 1921 to provide goods and leisure facilities for servicemen and their families. ENSA: Entertainments National Service Association, created in 1939 to provide entertainment for British armed forces personnel during the Second World War.

head. The Importance of Living in Paris is becoming more and more evident. My French improves slowly. It's odd how few even of the intelligent people here can talk English.

Dear Leo, please write again *soon* and give me more news of yourself. Hal Lidderdale, who passed through Brussels recently, asked after you.

Love

Iris

PS Tonight *Charles Trenet*[1] sings in Brussels and I shall be there. What joy! Any news of Noel Martin?

To David Hicks.

UNRRA
c/o British Mil. Mission to Belgium
6 November 1945

Your letter of November 2 has at last arrived. I was beginning to be really very angry with you, my dear, for not replying – and rather angry with myself for minding so much. You will have received by now another short lecture on Jean-Paul Sartre (what a bore I am) and a letter expressing panic which I now kick myself for having written. Reflecting on my other letter I thought afterwards I'd said one or two foolish things. Anyway, never mind. Thank you for the photo. I find I'd quite forgotten what you looked like. My 'pleasantly selective memory', to which you once referred me, retained only a general impression of black hair and mockery. Here, you look as if you were attending a lecture on the Right and the Good.[2] You look a nice sort of chap though and I wish I could meet you. Have you any inside information on how soon the general public might be able to visit Prague? I've always wanted to study those baroque styles.

I'm glad you saw Alastine. I'm sorry it hit you like that, but of course it would. It was far better to see her. Re her feelings, I don't see why you should imagine that you are the only one who can behave how you don't feel. I hope the pain has worn off a bit by now.

This point you asked me to elaborate – I find it rather difficult. Vague generalisations don't help much, and the various illustrative stories would take a long time to tell, and would probably sound just like penny dreadfuls[3]

1 French singer and prolific songwriter.
2 An allusion to *The Right and the Good* (1930) by W. D. Ross.
3 Popular lurid serial stories printed on cheap paper during the nineteenth century, each part costing one (old) penny.

at the end of it all. There are certain subtle treasons which are hard to describe. In general I notice a tendency to want to be loved, and not engage myself in return – that, plus a really dangerous lack of decision and will-power where other people's feelings are concerned. A sort of paralysis, maybe, before the picture of myself which I see in someone who loves me. Mortal sin; hell, not purgatory. The real crash as far as my self-esteem and general psychological security was concerned was this Hungarian story, which I think I mentioned to you in a letter at the time. Recently I tried to tell you the whole of this story on paper, but I was so sickened at the results that I tore it up. It was all rather dramatic and the mixture of *s'accuse* and *s'excuse* was nauseating. It's a quadrilateral tale that would make rather a good psychological novel. The outline, it won't make sense in outline, but anyway, it started when I went to live with a young man whom I didn't love but whom I was sorry for because he was in love with me, and because he has a complex about women (because of a homosexual past) and because he was likely to be sent abroad any moment. This was one Michael Foot[1] of Oxford, whom you may remember. In the midst of this, the brilliant and darling Pip Bosanquet came to lodge at Seaforth, who was then breaking off her relations with an economics don at Balliol, called Thomas Balogh, a horribly clever Hungarian Jew. I met Thomas, fell terribly in love, and he with me, and thus involved Michael in some rather hideous sufferings – in the course of which I somehow managed to avert my eyes and be, most of the time, insanely happy with Thomas. That is until I began to realise that Thomas was the devil incarnate and that I must tear myself away, although I adored him more and more madly every day. Pip, whom I love too, more than I ever thought I could love any woman, fell in love with Michael, most successfully salvaged what was left after my behaviour and married him, and they are now living happily at Oxford. She has the philosophy post at Somerville[2] which I was after too, but she deserves it anyway, as she is much better at philosophy than I am, and will be a real Sue Stebbing[3] one day. Thomas and I continued to tear each other's guts out for some six months and then parted. The whole process took about eighteen months and left me in a state of utter despair and self-hatred. I can't really describe what happened without explaining the characters of the people concerned – and it would take too long. Michael – terribly tense and tangled emotionally, very intelligent, honest and good. Pip – very tender and adorable, yet morally tough and subtle, and with lots of will and self-control – Thomas, well Thomas is hard to describe – age thirty-eight, very brilliant

---

1 M. R. D. Foot, not to be confused with the Labour politician, Michael Foot.
2 The Rosa Hovey graduate scholarship.
3 British analytical philosopher and key figure in the 1930s in the Cambridge School of Analysis.

and attractive and (without really realising it himself) quite unscrupulous. Self-deception to infinity. Myself – oh insanely in love and utterly devoid of willpower. It was my first introduction to complete passionate love. It was also my first introduction to hate. Michael hated me for deceiving him and then for seeming indifferent. Pip hated for me making Michael suffer. I hated Michael because he spoilt my celestial relation with Thomas. Later, I hated Thomas diabolically because he was the devil and was making me into a devil too. Above all I loathed and despised myself for being what I was and not being able to end a situation which was torture for all of us. Pip and I continued to live together at Seaforth almost till the end – it was fantastic – we wept almost continually. I saw my relation to her gradually being destroyed, by my own fault, yet I did nothing to save it. She behaved wonderfully throughout. My God, I did love her. Since then Thomas has married a hunting and shooting woman with lots of money,[1] who is thoroughly extroverted and probably will never realise that he is Satan. I am told they are very happy. Pip still writes me long affectionate letters – but there are some things which no friendship can survive. I still feel sick when I think of her and Michael – and they must feel the same when they think of me.

I seem to have written something down after all. There are two other men I should mention, not because they come into the story directly, but because I rather loved, and lost them both, about the same time, when I was looking round for support. One was Frank Thompson, whom I mentioned to you, who was British liaison officer with the partisans in Bulgaria and whom the Germans captured and shot. The other is Donald MacKinnon, whose name you may know, who was my philosophy tutor, also Pip's. Donald is rather like Bernanos' country priest[2] – he carried his love for people and his mistrust of himself almost to the end of insanity. Yet he is lucid and unsentimental and tough and really good in the strong brave way which is real goodness, and not self-love with a twist. He's also, incidentally, a philosopher of the first quality. I think I'll always be a bit in love with Donald, in a Mary Magdalen–Christ sort of way. After meeting him one really understands how the impact of one personality could change one's entire view of the universe, and how those people at Galilee got up and followed without any hesitation. I learnt all sorts of things from Donald. Then a moment came when his wife began to imagine (wrongly, I am sure) that he was falling in love with me. As a result, he broke off our relationship. Suddenly and completely – and since then (two years ago) I haven't seen or

1 Pen Gatty (née Tower); Balogh was her second husband.
2 Georges Bernanos (1888–1948), author of *Journal d'un curé de campagne* (1936) translated into English and published in 1937 as *Diary of a Country Priest*.

heard from him, except for one note asking me not to come to a philosophical meeting which he was going to attend. He must have known from Pip
and from things I had told him before about Michael, the outline of the
events that followed – but during all that hideous time, he didn't say one
word or make one gesture – which, for someone like him must have needed
a great strength and courage, for which I admire and love him. I hope this
makes some sense to you. Not I mean because he's in love with me – he
isn't – but because he must have known his intervention could have been
decisive.

I didn't mean to say this sort of thing when I started, but now I'm glad
I've said it – for these people and these events are part of me. There are lots
of other people, of course, and lots of other men, before and since, and
some of them important, but not so much. Your existence helped a good
deal in an odd way. Yet everything was so poisoned at that time that I had
the feeling that I was deceiving you too. I remember once sitting down to
write you in Thomas's cottage at Dorchester where we used to spend idyllic
weekends, and feeling somehow a bloody imposter and wishing I could
really talk to you, and not being able to. Not that I have any 'duty' to tell
you about my love *affaires* – but I would like you to know me. [. . .]

Brussels is as lovely as ever, but I've very little work to do and with the
winter coming on I've a bad conscience. It might be better to get into
Germany where, even if there's no work, I shall be a lot colder and more
uncomfortable, which may ease my conscience! I evidently have a strain of
nemisism,[1] as a result of my parents being too lenient in early youth. Looking
at that photograph of you makes me remember my childhood and how I
used to feel weak at the knees. What a fantastic frightening irrational world
one lives in. Be patient with me always, David. I do love you rather a lot.
I'll write again soon and bore you with more observations on Sartre and
Camus and Jouhandeau.[2] I'll also tell you about a novel which I've begun to
write. Let me know your moves. It's pouring with rain and I must go out
to tea with some Belgians. Damn.

Love I

---

1 The word 'nemisism' is coined by Murdoch from 'nemesis', meaning the inescapable agent of someone's downfall. She is aware that her own nature is often the cause of her suffering.
2 Marcel Jouhandeau (1888–1979), French writer whose villages chronicles, based on his life in Guéret,
   near Limoges in the Creuse, brought him fame.

To Hal Lidderdale.

UNRRA
c/o British Mission to Belgium
6 November 1945

Hello. News please. Where are you now, in what distant deeps or skies?[1] *Me voici encore à Bruxelles*[2] but I still don't know for how long. Brock[3] has been supplanted, our contract with Agence Continentale is to end this month, several people have disappeared, rumours circulate that UNRRA is bankrupt, no one bothers about *me*. I have practically nothing to do and am cynically enjoying myself with the *jeunesse dorée*,[4] or rather I should say, the *jeunesse sartrienne*. Since seeing you *I have met Jean-Paul Sartre*! He came here to give a lecture on existentialism, and I was introduced to him at a select gathering after the lecture, and saw him again at a long café séance the following day. He is small, simple in manner, squints alarmingly and talks exquisitely. At present I am busily reading everything of his I can lay my hands on. This excitement – I remember nothing like it since the days of discovering Keats and Shelley and Coleridge when I was very young!

Dear Hal, I hope all is well with you. Write soon with news. It was very good to see you in Brussels.

Much love to you
I

To David Hicks, written on Murdoch's return to Brussels after she had spent ten days in London with him, having not seen him since 1938. On their second day together they had decided to marry.

UNRRA
c/o British Military Mission to Belgium
1 December 1945

Dear Heart, here I am in Brussels, after the usual travel horrors. I eventually got on a boat about five o'clock yesterday, and reached Brussels at 2 p.m. today. Since then I have been turned out of my hotel, got myself into another and better one, and called at UNRRA HQ to talk about my future (where

1 From William Blake, 'The Tyger'.
2 Here I am still in Brussels.
3 Possibly Brock Chisholm, who was to become the first director general of the World Health Organization in 1948.
4 Gilded youth.

I found awaiting me alas only one out of date letter from you containing your brief observations on Nietzsche!). The idea at the moment seems to be that I should go to an UNRRA transit camp in Holland till I am reassigned to Germany or Austria. But all that may be changed on Monday when I go to Antwerp to see my proper chief. God knows.

I feel happy go lucky about it. Anywhere, in dear bad Europe, so long as there is a postal service to Prague. (And I can take Être et le néant[1] with me!) I feel quite unprecedentedly autonomous (which is odd, as I'm now engaged to surrender my autonomy, in certain respects at least. Paradox! Ho! Hunt it down! 'Whose service is perfect freedom'[2] etc.).

Let me say, quick, now, and get it over, that of course, if you meet someone else in Prague, or if you decide you like the Jewesses too much, or if you just decide I am not quite right for you after all, don't feel yourself tied up, dearest, but speak at once, which will be much better and avoid miseries later. I fully realise how we have, in a way, been 'framed' – just by circumstances. It would have been so dreadful if we had not fallen in love, after that build-up. But don't let the heavy hand of Destiny push you etc. unless you really want etc. Sorry, darling, to talk thus too much, but I must just say this and then shut up. Realising that perhaps with e.g. Lucy there was a sort of joy – and not with me – I don't know. I want to be perfect for you. Yet one must first face all the puzzles and paradoxes, not to brood on them, but to choose firmly with them all in sight and knowing what one is doing. And let *me* say that I think I have the general idea of what a curious sort of bastard you are, but that I *do* want to marry you (fully realising how often we should annoy each other) and I want to bear your children.

Which things having been said, let us change the subject. (God! How much I want a letter from you. This letter business is going to be ghastly, with me trailing round the continent, and you shut in behind those Bohemian mountains or whatever and letters taking months. And that photograph, which isn't at all like you and just mocks me with its powerful non-resemblance!) This man William Faulkner is excellent. Bless the Belgians for having told me about him! Whatever minor deity it is that is allowed to do me minor good turns arranged that, amid the dozen or so detective stories on the shelf in the Purfleet transit camp there should be a copy of Faulkner's *Sanctuary*! This I read, after I'd finished *Absalom*. A very nasty powerful tragic pathetic piece, with fewer purple patches. Faulkner has it in for chaste college girls with short skirts. (Quite right too!) He sharpens my zest for writing, that man. (Which reminds me of another thing for which *je t'en veux*![3] You

1 *L'être et le néant: Essai d'ontologie phénoménologique* by Jean-Paul Sartre (1943), translated into English as *Being and Nothingness: An Essay on Phenomenological Ontology*.
2 From 'A Collect for Peace', Book of Common Prayer.
3 I'm annoyed with you.

let me go away without telling you *anything* about what I've been writing and what I'm intending to write. Even where there was a large typescript under your nose you refused to rise. Of course I wanted to show you, imbecile, I just wanted you to press me!) [. . .]

I must stop talking now, for the moment.

Write to me, you blue-eyed David, and if you can find a photo of another of your faces, do send it. Oh darling, good night, all my love to you.

I

To David Hicks, written from Austria, where Murdoch had been sent in mid-December.

UNRRA USFA
Salzburg
APO 777 US Army
15 December 1945

Darling, this is an experiment to see if these airmail letters arrive quicker. An APO[1] chap told me it made no difference at all, but maybe he was wrong. God knows however when I'll ever get your reply with the information. On Monday I see the UNRRA personnel department here, who will probably push me on to some other part of Austria. I don't mind. I breathe this wonderful air and look at the sun on mountain peaks behind mountain peaks – and what does it matter, so long as I stay in Austria and can go on looking at mountains or walking along their edges? Oh David, what a gem of a city Salzburg is though. It's bedraggled and poor and dirty with the war and the melting snow – but so lovely, with the swift river in the centre, and the medieval castle up above, and the dozens of fine arrogant baroque churches, and the ecclesiastical squares with ironwork doorways, and the chaps wearing Tyrolean hats and carrying rucksacks, and the endless sun-slashed mountains all around. I'm just drunk with it. One well-placed bomb has blasted the cathedral, but there's hardly any other war damage. My German is dreadful I find. I must work at it. Oh darling darling what an odd life. When ever shall I see you again? Keep on writing (and so will I) – we shall get the letters some day!

Much love
I

1 Army Post Office.

To David Hicks.

UNRRA
Salzburg
17 December 1945

Dearest, I would give Gross Glockner and the Koenigsee[1] just now for a letter from you – but alas it will probably be weeks before I get one.

Yesterday I went skiing, 6,000 feet up over Zell am See – henceforth you may consider me a convert to mountains, snow, exercise and the open-air life. I shall take every chance I can to ski. Oh David, what a sensation! What a lot of things in earth and heaven were never dreamt of in my philosophy![2] The blazing sun on the snow, the air, the sunburnt faces, the sounds that carry for miles, the sea of mountain peaks all round . . . Yes. How far shall we be in Prague from such things, and please may we go to winter sports next winter?

Today was fantastic. I went with four UNRRA chaps and a guide to Hitler's house at Berchtesgaden. There is this huge wonderful villa, with its incredibly lovely view over the mountains, and near it the chalets of Goering, and of Mussolini, and the enormous SS barracks that housed the 2,000 troops that guarded Hitler. The whole place wrecked and blasted, since the raids of last February – and the whole place entirely desolate and deserted. We saw only one American soldier in the distance while we were there. We wandered about by ourselves and explored the houses. The whole region was completely silent. The only sound we heard all the time we were there was the bells of a wood sleigh passing along the road. All completely silent and deserted and covered in snow and marked with the names of Yankee soldiers. It was such a fitting and beautiful anticlimax!

Tomorrow I am going on a tour of the lakes near Salzburg. And on Wednesday, my darling, I am going to *Innsbruck*, where I shall be stationed. I'm to be communications officer there – liaison with the French Army. (Innsbruck is in the French zone.) It will be tricky and I hope amusing. Food is dreadful I gather – but mountains will make up for vitamin deficiencies. [. . .]

David, this is bloody, isn't it, this separation. Not a word from you since you left England. Where are all those letters? Keep on writing darling, and the dam will break somewhere. I will do the same.

My dearest, I miss you constantly, with a sort of physical pain. I love you,

---

1 Grossglockner: the highest mountain in Austria; Königssee: Germany's deepest lake.
2 Echoes Hamlet's words: 'There are more things in heaven and earth, Horatio, / Than are dreamt of in your philosophy'.

and I'm conscious of you all the time. I long for next year, and for the trials and the high winds of our life together! In expectation of that, I greet you joyously!

Darling, farewell for the moment, and my love, my love –

To E. P. Thompson, Frank Thompson's brother, who was collecting material for There is a Spirit in Europe, *the family's memorial to Frank, which was published in 1947.*

Winter 1945

Dear Palmer,

I was very glad to hear from you, and very moved to read again those extracts from Frank's letters – certainly there is nothing there that I would think it unwise to print. The letters speak best for him. How can one 'describe' a personality of such richness? About Oxford – there's little I'd like to add to the few facts you mention. It wasn't *all* politics. He loved his work – remember his wild rather romantic enthusiasms for Pindar. (That was one of his not quite serious ambitions at one time, to be a great authority on Pindar.) Then there was the big joyous world of his friends, not only political ones. The first time I ever saw him he was very drunk and lying flat on his back in the entrance hall of the Union with his head inside the telephone box. That was some sort of theatrical do, I think. Then his joy in New College garden in the summer, exuberant quotings of Theocritus, Bion and Moschus,[1] his very untidy room with Liddell and Scott[2] always open on the table, and a large teddy bear and a top hat on the mantelpiece and '*voi che sapete*'[3] on the gramophone. And stories, such as his leaping fully dressed into the Cherwell after a lost paddle and returning triumphantly with it crying 'Comrades we have saved the Soviet Fatherland'. Leo Pliatzky, writing lately, reminded me of that. Very little recoverable fact in all this. It was a period of transition of course, but it was full of the real Frank, the things he breathed and was later – it's all of a piece. Not as with so many of the rest of us. He joined the Party, as I remember, about February or March 1939.

All very fragmentary; and he is so much more than the odd collection of things one remembers. One gets rather mixed up too with the feeling of sickness about not having loved him enough – which was true at the start, though not later. And the sheer sickness of loss. You have a difficult job.

1 Theocritus: third-century BC Greek poet who wrote pastoral poetry and epics; Bion of Smyrna and Moschus were also bucolic poets of ancient Greece.
2 Probably Liddell and Scott's *Greek–English Lexicon* (1843 and many later editions).
3 An aria ('Tell me what love is') from Mozart's opera *The Marriage of Figaro* (1786).

Then his opinions, his splendid positive uncompromising faith in the world's people. Oneself, one goes on changing, and can't argue out with him one's shifts of opinion on the USSR, one's compromises with life. It's not easy to write about him, even a few paragraphs of a letter, he was pure gold.

He often spoke about you, and for very long I've wanted to meet you. At present I'm in Innsbruck, in the beautiful Tyrol, dealing with the touchy French and the sullen but courteous Austrians, and the thousands of tragic displaced persons who are collected in this pocket between Italy and Switzerland – bad hats many of them by now, after so much survival of the fittest discipline, and hard to do anything for. A curious desert island life with a few people and a few books and very many mountains.

I shall probably come home on leave in the summer and I'll seek you out wherever you are. I hope you are enjoying Cambridge and making [*rest of letter lost*]

To David Hicks.

c/o UNRRA Central HQ
Vienna CMF
25 January 1946

Darling, after a day which seems to have been interminable I sit down (4 a.m.) to write to you, once again under the influence of drink, I regret to say.

Much emotion in this last day or two. On Wednesday I was involved in a midnight dash to the Brenner in pursuit of a DP Yugoslav driver who, having smashed up an UNRRA truck, was afraid to return to HQ and tried to make a dash for Italy via the Brenner, carrying a loaded pistol with him, the poor fool. The French arrested him at the frontier and I, being the only French-speaker in the office when the crisis occurred, had to cope with complicated phone calls and eventually go up to investigate in a jeep. We brought him back to Innsbruck and he sat behind us in the jeep and cried all the way. Thereafter, a great battle with the hard cynical swine at HQ whose only reaction was 'put him in the cooler' and a cynical laugh. God! So few people in this great relief organisation can make any imaginative effort to understand what the displaced person problem really is. *All* these DPs are either apathetic or inclined to be thugs or crooks – they've had to be to survive. This boy – age twenty-four – a King Peter partisan[1] – God knows how he's lived these last five years. And when he does something

---

1 A supporter of Peter II (1923–70), king of Yugoslavia, who had been overthrown in 1940. He fled abroad and was formally deposed by Yugoslavia's Communist Constituency in 1945.

hysterical all our HQ gentleman can think of is getting him the maximum penalty, just because they're riled at an UNRRA truck being smashed! I haven't felt such misery and fury for a long time. The charge of 'stealing a car' (quite false) was eventually dropped, and he is now in jug,[1] awaiting trial on charge of carrying firearms – and will probably end up being shot willy-nilly back to Yugoslavia to be slaughtered by Tito's men. What a sickening world. These sort of incidents suddenly make one realise how *irrevocably* broken so many lives have been by this war. Nothing nothing nothing ahead for these people. What can one do?

I went dancing tonight, with some of the worst HQ offenders, and got thoroughly drunk on slivovitz, the local beverage. A contradictory paradoxical life. Yet self-mutilation does no good. If it did I'd gladly cut off a few fingers in the mood I am now.

Oh darling, be there and steady me. You must understand.

And I do love you, in the depths as in the heights.

I

To David Hicks.

c/o UNRRA Central HQ
Vienna CMF
9 February 1946

Sweetheart, still no letter from you since one dated in December! Sorry to harp on this, but it does make a difference to life. Not your fault I know – but oh, do do what you can to push those letters round by the quickest way. I still have no news of Bratislava or your job or the Danube or you or anything. [. . .]

My greatest consolation here is a pair of Parisian boys, age about twenty-four, who speak only French (and lovely argot[2] at that), who spent most of their war in the Maquis[3] (having escaped from POW camps), *croix de guerre,*[4] very wild and mad and bad, and regarded by the English and Yanks here as a damn nuisance – which they probably are. Oh David, how can I describe these two to you? I wish I could 'photograph' them – their gestures, their voices, their expressions. They give me the same sort of joy that one gets from watching squirrels or birds at play – a pure ecstatic tenderness! Their devotion to each other is so charming too. (Do you remember the two Arab

1 Slang for jail.
2 Slang.
3 The French Resistance.
4 French medal awarded for bravery.

boys in *The Seven Pillars*, who were such a nuisance to everyone?) They are always exceedingly gay, yet very human and gentle. (I am now coming back to my old way of dividing humanity into the people who have hearts and the people who are heartless. These two are definitely of the warm-hearted.) There is also with us a girl, a French typist, very correct French *Jeune Fille*, but very gay and charming (also + heart), and I spend a lot of time with these three, just chattering, or learning songs. (André and Pierre know more French songs than anyone I've yet met. Hélène and I coax these songs out of them at the rate of one or two a week.)

Such things are very important. The balance of people is easily upset. A fresh personality can put us all off our feed for days. God! David, how much I need *tendresse* from people, and gentleness, the possibility of liking and being liked with real warmth. [. . .]

Au revoir, chéri – je t'aime – je t'embrasse.[1]

To David Hicks.

c/o UNRRA Central HQ
Vienna CMF
12 February 1946

Dearest, a letter from you *did* arrive yesterday – dated December 14th! It came with a batch, all dated about that time, that had gone astray, probably sent to the China Mission or UNRRA Iceland. I nearly wept, it was almost worse than nothing. Darling, where *are* all your letters going to? You must have written to me once or twice since December 28th!

I feel very cut off from people at present, *y compris* you. Many *ennuis*[2] at the office. You remember the two French boys I spoke of in a previous letter? To my intense sorrow and desolation, they have decided to quit – they say the English (apart from me) don't like them and that they're stifling here – too much sitting, not enough rolling. All true. I see they *have* to go. Like caged birds, one must free them – but oh how sad when they fly away forever. These two have such *joie de vivre*, they've been very good for me. I'd better confess too that I have been to bed once with André – he is the more beautiful Italianate one, the younger of the two. A fully conscious act, which I do not regret at all, unless it upsets you, and please don't let it.

Everyone here is in a nervous condition at present. Whenever I enter the dining room now I have a nervous crisis about where I'm to sit for fear of

1 Goodbye, darling – I love you – I send kisses.
2 . . . including you. Many troubles . . .

hurting someone's feelings! I dare say your little communities suffer the same electrical storms from time to time. Shifts in the emotional balance of power upset the whole office for days. I find myself less and less in sympathy with the upper strata and more and more with the lower. My main pals now are not the assistant directors, but the drivers and the telephonist and the transport officer, who are a little (only a little) less useful point of view[1] culture, but oh so much more satisfactory point of view humanity. There's no one here at all anyway who has any sort of intellectual finish or even general knowledge. I am reading Brod's[2] book on Kafka, and almost everyone has seen me reading it and asked 'Who is Kafka?' and that goes for the directors and assistant directors too, the ignorant bastards. Au revoir, my dear, my dear – I long for your letters –

My love, I

To David Hicks, written after he had abruptly broken off their engagement by letter.

c/o UNRRA Central HQ
Vienna CMF
18 February 1946

My dear, your letter of 21st January has just come. A shock, yes. It's hard to know what to say. It's frightening how people can deceive themselves and how quickly their moods can change, from very deep too. Yet it did seem stable, in spite of our panics. Thank you for having had the guts to write so frankly (even lyrically, if I may say so). What do I suggest? Well, I suggest we quietly call it off as far as you and I are concerned. There seems little choice – and in my saner moments I do see that it would have been risky. I don't seem to have a real gift for making you happy, and others have it, that's that. Further, I'd suggest that you *don't* marry this Dornford Yates[3] heroine without considerable reflection and lapse of time. For heaven's sake don't tie yourself up in a moment of exaltation to someone you'll gradually find out to be not intelligent enough or not profound enough for you. Remember that you've just nearly made one mistake – don't go and make

1 Murdoch frequently uses the phrase 'point of view' in this rather odd way, presumably as a contraction of the more usual English construction 'from the point of view of', although it also seems to echo the phrase '*d'un point de vue*', often used in French.

2 Max Brod (1884–1968), a German-speaking Czech who was a close friend of Franz Kafka and became his literary executor. After Kafka's death in 1924, Brod did not burn his friend's manuscripts, as Kafka had requested, but instead published them. He also published a biography of Kafka in 1937.

3 Pseudonym of the British novelist Cecil William Mercer (1885–1960), whose novels and short stories were best-sellers in the period between the First and Second World Wars. All his heroines are rather similar, having dancing eyes, glorious hair, slim ankles, small hands and a quick wit.

another. Take it coolly and gently. If you do *so* much want to get married, why not consider old Muluk[1] who *would* be faithful to you and *did* make you happy? I feel afraid for you, miserable in Bratislava and being pressed for decisions. Don't make them. Also, don't fret at all about me. I see the wisdom of our conclusion and I'm not shattered by it.

I hope you got my letters addressed to British Council Bratislava – not that it matters, since letters from me must be simply an occasion of embarrassment now. You must have been miserable in this interval waiting for my answer. Well, darling don't be miserable any more. Concentrate on being *prudent*. Do write to me please and tell me what's happening and be as frank as you can. And don't worry about me because I am perfectly all right and only wishing you not to be a fool and wreck your chances of happiness. You are a splendid creature David and lots of splendid women will want to marry you, so don't throw yourself away on someone unworthy.

I care very much about your being happy.

All my love, and write soon.

In a later letter, written 28 May 1947 from Bratislava – in which he explained his decision to marry someone else – Hicks tried to explain why he had called off the engagement: 'I did like you enormously, better than anyone I can think of. But was much worried at the thought of being married to you. Probably the same with anyone else, but it seemed more terrifying in your case. Brain, will and womb, you are formidable: you used to write, you wanted to be subdued, but I couldn't picture it somehow. I believed you, of course, my girl, I believed you wanted it. But didn't fancy myself being chap enough to do it. We see the world very differently'.[xvii]

To Hal Lidderdale.

c/o UNRRA Central HQ
Vienna
28 February 1946

Hal my dear, WHERE are you, and WHAT are you doing now? Please write. Here, I sit in my office, looking out onto a range of mountains and hearing the warm wind from Italy roaring about the house and the melted snow falling from the roof in a series of shattering crashes.

Maintenant je vais vous raconter une histoire de fous.[2] I went on leave in

---

1 A young Iranian woman with whom Hicks once had a relationship.
2 Now I'm going to tell you something quite mad.

November, or maybe I told you, in order to see David Hicks. It was a tornado. Ten days that positively shook the world. I suppose I had expected something, but not a great soul-rending drama such as we actually met. On the second day we decided that we would get married. There was just no other answer. We would have completed the bargain straight away, only there wasn't enough time. We made definite plans to get married in the spring, or in the summer at latest – as soon as David could make arrangements for me to come to Prague. Then he went off to Czecho, and I to Holland, eventually to Austria. I got letters from him regularly up to the middle of January, all full of plans for the future. Then there was a gap of several weeks – and about ten days ago I get a long lyrical letter saying that he has met in Prague a WONDERFUL (whom however he describes as a 'Dornford Yates heroine') and English girl incidentally, and that he is very much in love with her, and suggesting in a final line or two that maybe we'd better call our arrangements off. I wrote back at once, saying yes, call them off, but don't be in *too* much of a hurry to marry the DY heroine. After the initial shock, my main feeling is extreme relief, and amazement at this period of temporary insanity. The doubts and reluctances which I had all the time, but suppressed, are now released and I can look at the whole affair with a dazed surprise. You will ask why the hell I never told you about this – a grave *suppressio veri*.[1] Well, partly because I doubted whether David would in fact remain loyal – and partly because of a grain of doubt about my own feelings. I'm sorry, Hal. It was an odd business altogether. A *very* narrow escape. However, it was necessary – otherwise I would have been fretting about David for years. Now the spell is completely and finally broken and I feel thoroughly happy and integrated and free, only with an increased horror of all ties, especially marital.

I am sorry to hurl this story at you, old dear. I've been feeling guilty for some time because I hadn't told you. I suppose I didn't really believe in the thing myself. Now I feel much better and restored, rather shamefacedly, to my real and good friends. I hope I shall not again give rein to this dangerous facility for choosing the second rate.

Here, there is beautiful spring beginning, with masses of catkins, heavy snowfalls and then strong sun and wind to melt the snow. I haven't done much skiing lately – more reading and writing. Through a charming ex-surrealist in the French Army here I have discovered that remarkable American writer Erskine Caldwell.[2] Know him? Famous in France, unknown in England (*vive la France*). Also I've read Max Brod's life of Kafka. Odd, to find that Kafka has a whole particular history and background, and didn't

1 Suppression of the truth.
2 Author (1903–87) whose novels about poverty and racism in the South made him famous.

just fall from heaven. Brod is narrow, devoted, pedantic and hopelessly below Kafka but does his best to 'explain'.

   Write to me, lad Lidderdale.

   Iris

To Raymond Queneau (1903–76), French poet, novelist and lyricist whom Murdoch had met on 16 February 1946 in Innsbruck. Drawn to each other, they spent a great deal of time together that weekend, climbing Mount Igls and the Patscherkofel. Ernest Collet, a well-known bookseller in Brussels who had befriended Murdoch, had nego-tiated rights for her to translate Queneau's fiction. This letter, like many of her early letters to Queneau, was written in French and contains a few minor errors of expres-sion and some missing and misplaced accents. It appears in French and then is translated into English below; all subsequent letters written in French are translated into English.

SP 50310

Armée Française[1]

28 February 1946

Cher M. Queneau,

   Votre letter de samedi est arrivée hier et m'a rendu très heureuse. Maintenant j'attends avec impatience et inquiétude l'arrivée de *Pierrot* et les autres. Je suis un peu effrayée quand j'y pense. Je sais à tel point vous avez créé en français une langue nouvelle pour des buts assez definis, et je me demande si je suis bien capable de faire autant en anglais. En tout cas, je vais essayer (c'est toujours un plaisir de tenter quelque chose de difficile comme ça) et je vous prie de juger les resultats rigoureusement et de me dire toute de suite s'ils ne vous conviennent pas. La chose la plus importante est de presenter *Pierrot* (et les autres) aux anglais avec, si c'est possible, la même force et durété et lustre qu'ils ont en français. Si je ne me trompe pas, ça a d'importance pour le roman anglais, qui est aussi en ce fameux état de crise, mais plus tranquillement et avec moins de fracas intellectuel que le roman français.

   C'est difficile à vous expliquer comment ça m'a boulversé et ravi et delivré à la fois, de vous avoir rencontré – une recontre assez bizarre, comme vous avez dit. Avant votre miraculeux coup de telephone j'étais dans une humeur vraiment triste et deroutée. Décéptions emotionelles. Désillusion avec mes efforts à penser et à écrire. (On se demande quelquefois qu'est ce qu'on fait, muni d'une telle opinion de soi même, luttant comme ça avec on ne sais

---

1   Murdoch was at this time in the French sector of Allied-occupied Austria, hence the notepaper heading.

exactement quoi pour on ne sais exactement quoi.) Vous m'avez fait tellement du bien et donné du poids et des couleurs à tout un univers que je
commençais à croire irréel. Aussi tout simplement (et à part la question de
chercher un 'maître' – problème important et dangereux!) je tiens à vous et
je voudrai tant meriter et garder et jouir de votre amitié. (Je veux dire pas
seulement vous-auteur-de-*Pierrot* etc. mais aussi vous-avec-telle-façon-de-
sourire etc.)

Je ne m'exprime pas bien en français. Est ce que ça ne vous fait rien si
j'écris quelquefois en anglais? Pardonnez les fautes dans cette lettre – et
permettez moi de dire encore comment j'aime et admire vos oeuvres. Il ya
tant de choses que je voudrai discuter avec vous. J'espère que nous aurons
du temps plus tard, à Paris, peut-être. Merci pour toutes vos bontés.

I am most devotedly and affectionately yours
Iris Murdoch

SP 50310
Armée Française
28 February 1946

Dear Mr Queneau,

Your letter of Saturday arrived yesterday and made me very happy. I'm
waiting anxiously and impatiently now for the arrival of *Pierrot* and the other
books.[1] I feel rather alarmed when I think about it. I know that you have
invented a new language in French for quite specific purposes, and I wonder
if I will be capable of doing the same thing in English. Anyway, I shall try
(it will be a joy to attempt something difficult like this), and I beg you to
judge the results rigorously and to tell me immediately if it doesn't please
you. The most important thing is to present *Pierrot* (and the others) to
English readers with, if it's possible, the same strength and hardness and
radiance that they have in French. If I'm not mistaken, this is important for
the English novel, which is also in a state of crisis, but less obviously so and
with less intellectual din than the French novel.

It is difficult to explain to you how overwhelmed and delighted and liber-
ated I felt all at the same time when meeting you – a rather odd meeting,
as you said. Before your wonderful phone call I was in a really sad and
somewhat dispirited mood. Emotional disappointments. Disillusion with my
efforts to think and write. (I sometimes ask myself what I'm doing, saddled
with such an opinion of myself, battling like this for I don't know exactly
what, or for what reason.) You have done me so much good and given
substance and colour to a world that I was beginning to believe unreal. So,

---

1 Murdoch was to spend much of 1946 trying to translate into English Queneau's novel *Pierrot mon ami*,
published in 1942 and written in colloquial and slangy French.

to put it simply (and apart from the question of searching for a 'master' – something important and possibly dangerous!) I care about you and would like so much to be worthy of and to keep and enjoy your friendship. (I mean not only you-as-author-of-*Pierrot* etc. but also you-with-that-special-way-of-smiling etc.)

I don't express myself well in French. Would you mind if I sometimes wrote in English? Excuse my mistakes in these letters – and allow me to tell you once again how much I like and admire your work. There are so many things I would like to discuss with you. I hope we shall have time to do so later, perhaps in Paris. Thank you for all your kindness.

I am most devotedly and affectionately yours
Iris Murdoch

To Raymond Queneau, written in French.

SP 50310
Armée Française
11 April 1946

I've translated the first twenty-five pages of *Pierrot*. There's plenty not quite right yet and I'll need to revise the thing two, three, ten times. I'll send it to you within maybe fifteen days. I'm not rushing anything – (and anyway I'm short of time). A mixture of joy and despair. The former results from your style, and its reflection (even when poorly done) in English (yes, translation is exciting work indeed). But it's not easy. It's not so much your greatness or your poetry – I think I can follow you to those heights of verbal felicity full of Latin polysyllables – that's easy enough. It's some of the slang that I find difficult. First, I can't quite catch the meaning of some words and phrases and secondly (more seriously) I think my knowledge of English slang is not rich enough to do you justice. [. . .]

Oxford has written suggesting I apply for a studentship in philosophy at Newnham College Cambridge (to do a DPhil). There was also the possibility of a scholarship at Vassar University,[1] and a post in the department of philosophy at Sheffield University. Without much hope, but feeling carefree, I wrote to all three. It's hopeless, but I have to do it – after that I won't bother about the academic life (or at least that's what I think now!). The studentship at Newnham tempts me the most; I'd like to write a thesis on Kierkegaard. I wrote a rather indiscreet letter to the illustrious masters, in which I talked

---

1 The Durant Drake Fellowship at Vassar College, an exclusive private college in the state of New York that, until 1969, took women students only.

of Nietzsche, Dostoevsky, Buber, Dilthey,[1] Kierkegaard and Sartre, instead of discussing Plato, Hume, Kant, Moore[2] and Ross. But no, in any case I lack the required discipline at the moment – I can't think clearly, things get drowned in emotions. I'm not up to these masters and their world.

At the moment there is absolutely no one here to talk to. Result: I work, which is a good thing. But from time to time . . .

The lake becomes more and more splendid – unbelievable blues – and there are also gentians of an absolutely striking blue-black colour. Incredible scenery.

I don't feel at all confident in myself at the moment. Compared to Newnham and to you I feel too weak an instrument for what I want to achieve. But things will work out. I'm beginning to sound gloomy! I'll write to you again, very dear Queneau, within a few days. Write to me and tell me about yourself. Sometimes I die of thirst here. Now for *Pierrot*. Well!

Your affectionate pupil,

IM

[*Added in English*] Since writing this, *Gueule de Pierre* and *Temps mêlés* and *Chêne et chien* have arrived![3] Thank you my extremely slangy but poetic friend! Verdicts later.

To Hal Lidderdale.

c/o UNRRA Central HQ
Vienna
17 April 1946

Hal old darling, your letter of 28th March reached me at last and how *very* glad I was to hear from you. I have been all over the place lately, including Vienna, where I met Eric Stenton, who told me Akiba is in Cazerta, and asked most tenderly after you. Now I am at Klagenfurt down near Yugoslavia. A few days ago I met a Royal Scots Fusilier lieutenant *very* drunk in the local officer's club who swore to me that the second battalion had moved to Trieste! Elated beyond words by this joyous news I sent off to you (addressed CMF) a picture postcard of the Vienna opera house, giving you my telephone number! (Trieste is a short hop from here.) But alas your letter arrived a day

1 Martin Buber (1878–1965), Austrian-born Jewish theologian; Wilhelm Dilthey (1833–1911), German historian, psychologist, sociologist and philosopher much influenced by Kant.
2 G. E. Moore (1873–1958), influential Cambridge philosopher.
3 *Gueule de Pierre* and *Les temps mêlés*: novels by Queneau published in 1934 and 1941 respectively. *Chêne et chien*: a volume of poetry by Queneau published in 1937.

or two later, saying you are still up in the harsh North! I will not be had again by a drunken Scot.

Vienna was extraordinary – very golden and ruined and magnificent, under an intense sun. Lots of music and a fair amount of life, though one still has to climb over mountains of debris in the streets. A gorgeous picture exhibition, lots of the best Brueghels and five first-rate Rembrandts, five ditto Velázquez, the Vermeer *Artist's Studio* (*magical* picture – remember?) and rooms full of other excellent stuff. Inebriating.

Here life is a mixture of intense boredom (office hours) and the Earthly Paradise[1] (other hours). We live on the bank of the most exquisite lake – the Wörthersee – with violets and gentians and anemones rioting up to the door, and, and forests and mountains and flowering orchards reflected in the waters, and deer skipping on the hillside 'Stumbling on melons as I pass'[2] and so on, only the melons aren't quite ripe yet. I lead an existence of unprecedented peace. In the evening, drinking a pre-prandial beer on the terrace in the sun, and looking away across the lake I feel a most ecstatic stillness within and without. (Our billet is a fashionable guesthouse, 10 km from Klagenfurt, and literally on the verge of the lake.) I am writing quite a lot. The office work has reached its nadir, but I dream through the day somehow. Immoral, but there it is.

Yugoslavia interests me a lot. This region is full of anti-Tito Yugoslavs[3] who are waiting for the anti-Soviet crusade to begin (heralded in no doubt by Franco's atom bombs) – and meanwhile are making fortunes in the local black market. (Latest prices quoted are astronomical. UNRRA types are not guiltless in this respect either – all a bad show.) I would like to find out what really is happening though, down in those Slav souls in Serbia and Dalmatia. Contradictory reports as usual.

Thank you for your moralising, dearest Hal. I wish I could express how highly I value you and the goodness of your friendship for me. I would give a whole lot for a talk with you now – that damned RSF drunk made me really joyous with his false report!

I got a letter from David a few days ago (the first since his lyrical outburst about the Dornford Yates heroine, who recited short stories by Daudet[4] in bed, did I mention that last detail?) in which he does not mention the DY heroine, but complains about his bronchitis and shows tentative indications

1 Possibly a reference to William Morris's *The Earthly Paradise* (1868–70).
2 From Andrew Marvell, 'The Garden' (1681).
3 In a letter to Marjorie Boulton dated 14 April 1946 Murdoch described Tito as 'the local ogre for half the population and Joan of Arc for the other'. Tito, who had led his Communist pro-republican People's Front party to victory in the election of 1945, was seen by many as the liberator of his country. However, monarchists and nationalists saw him as betraying their nation.
4 Alphonse Daudet (1840–97), French writer.

to re-establish relations. I have written saying no thank you. He is really a weak and troublesome character and egocentric to an almost incredible degree. It all seems very faint and far away now.

What are you going to do in June? I too will soon be shot onto the labour market, as UNRRA is shutting up shop. What are the British Council prospects? I can't bear the thought of settling down in England either! What a difficult life. If only someone would leave me a steady income of £400 a year I would be quite happy! (Not true in fact, but it would leave me to concentrate on loftier sources of misery.)

Write to me – Leo Pliatzky writes lengthily from Oxford, where many of our old pals are living in a rather superior seclusion from undergraduate affairs.

Write to me, I say again.

Much love to you –

I

By the way, congratulations on your promotion!

To Raymond Queneau, written in English.

SP 50310
Armée Française
2 June 1946

I am now at Graz working at the Studentenheim. I *love* this camp. Why didn't I come here months ago instead of hanging around in HQs waiting to be promoted? As I cross the 'quad' at evening to check on the accommodation in Barrack V I meet the two Jančars,[1] just back from the university. They are studying medicine. Under the trees is Pardanjač, one of the *philosophes* (but not the *Pierrot* kind) deep in a book. Here comes Elfriede Petek who is an art student and always exquisite though she lives in an overcrowded room with ten other girls. Kamnetsky lounges on the horizon, a problem child, but remember he was in a concentration camp. There is so much *life* here – quite mysterious to me still, like fishes in a dark aquarium, but very moving and obscurely significant. Most of the students are Yugoslavs, but there are also lots of Poles and Ukrainians and some Albanians, White Russians, Lithuanians, Jews various and others. About 300 in all. German is

---

1 Jože Jančar and his wife, Marija, from Slovenia. They managed to get to England in 1948 and Murdoch helped Jože pursue his medical studies; he later became vice president of the Royal College of Psychiatrists.

the main mode of communication; I find I can talk it enough for practical purposes, *aber Schrecklich*,[1] but as their German is dreadful too we understand each other very well in a happy indifference to tenses, genders and cases. Some of them talk French so horribly I can't bear it and we soon fall again to murdering German cheerfully together. The main factor in our lives though is the *food*. The camp is now on a real starvation diet and my God how can those children study on 200 grammes of bread and one plate of stew and some coffee per day? Improvements soon I hope – but meanwhile heartbreaking – [. . .]

We recently had delivered to us a batch of letters addressed to people in Nairobi, so maybe by now your letters to me are being urgently flown across the Sahara. Forgive me by the way for talking English now. Talking French, though I enjoy it, puts me one remove farther away. (As seen from my side anyway.) Not that English, very often, is other than a complicated barrier, however much one wants to approach the other person –

I have abandoned my own writing for the present. The novel on Carrington's telepathy theory[2] has reached a sort of airy witty flashing perfection in my head which I should undoubtedly spoil by putting pen to paper, and there I think I shall leave it. I have also abandoned, for the moment, *Pierrot*. Silence (mine) on this subject does not mean indifference; the reverse. I am concentrating on *Être et le néant* in a sort of panic feeling that some ghastly zero hour will soon strike and I shall not have understood. A *femme savante*,[3] once a fellow student, now teaching philosophy at Oxford, writes me that the Bodleian Library copy has been six weeks at the binders but anyway she is told that only one person in France has understood *E. et le n.* and that was the anonymous hero who noticed that page 258 had been transposed with page 366 in the first edition or some such tale! I don't find it so hard going now. At the level at which I understand it I am quite unruffled. I find myself saying *yes*, *yes*, on every other page. I am carried along by his superb technique for saying subtle (and I think unsaid-before unless by Heidegger and those boys) things about the human consciousness. I *recognise* what he describes. But oh the way he throws his terms about (as if *everyone* knows 'what a *néant* is') would make Oxford hair stand on end and mine too sometimes. My cold critical judgement has not yet caught up with my emotional assent. (Now and then I think let it go to hell anyway why not read philosophy just for the emotional kick if you can get it – *vive* Kierkegaard.)

Also this stuff about being a perpetual '*manque*'.[4] Fine. (*Very* fine and fascinating.) But a lot of the time one feels the reverse. Positively *overfull* –

1 But dreadfully.
2 Hereward Carrington (1880–1958), British investigator of psychic phenomena and the paranormal.
3 A learned woman; perhaps also an oblique reference to *Les femmes savantes* (1672) by Molière.
4 Emptiness (of being).

and not straining toward the future but expanding in the present. (Sartre undoubtedly deals with this later. *Ignosco. Mea culpa.*[1]) E.g. when enjoying art, when creating, when thinking about someone loved.

You know I have not had a *conversation* with anyone since before I left Innsbruck – only indifferent chatter about UNRRA or what's for dinner. Just at this moment I feel bad about this, though often too I don't mind. Always it does me good to think of certain people whom I care about – there are various chaps and girls in England whom I'm very grateful to for existing though they rarely write to me the cads. Also e.g. you. On these occasions I feel a sort of I-and-Thouish[2] warmth and am no longer in the desert. I can't live without giving and receiving affection, oh lots of it I suppose – and the cool dignity of not expressing it is also far from me.

Pierrot and les Kougards[3] and the rest have been a wonderful mythology to me. (Poet, joker, myth-maker. Alas my impossible possibles!) To know their creator has made me very happy too. Or rather, to have met, not to know. (My remarks on *Chêne et chien*, which I have now reread, were gauche. I'm sorry.) Why this gratuitous display of feeling? *Faut me pardoner: la solitude.*[4] Anyway why should one hoard one's sentiments, however little they may be valuable or important? In a year or two we may all be blown up in some grand atomic experiment and then you would never know, in case it should amuse you at all, that one hot Sunday evening in Graz I was thinking about you. It's odd. Here I sit, the time being approximately 7.50, writing you this letter and having the illusion of talking to you. When you get the letter weeks later, opening it hastily as you step into the metro to go to some writers' conference or racing chez Gallimard[5] or to the radio HQ or something and stuff the sheets back into your pocket you probably won't at all have the illusion of being talked to. All of which illustrates some profound fact about *das Leben*[6] but I'm not sure what.

UNRRA's time here is short so I expect I'll be flashing through Paris one of these days on my way home and I hope you won't be in New York by then (whither I see Camus has gone.[7] What has England done?).

If you are in any sort of difficulties in Paris please forgive me for so much foolish talk and know that I wish you in all things well. If there is ever anything I can do for you –

1 Apologies. My mistake. (Meaning presumably that Murdoch acknowledges that the fault in under-standing is hers, rather than Sartre's.)
2 Oblique reference to *Ich und Du* (*I and Thou*) (1923) by Martin Buber.
3 Characters in Queneau's novels.
4 Forgive me: [it's because of] the loneliness.
5 Prestigious French publishing house where Queneau worked and where Murdoch sent her letters.
6 Life.
7 At this time the French novelist Albert Camus was lecturing on French thought in the United States.

The jeep is coming soon to take me to the camp where there is a dance and cabaret show tonight, I am getting quite good at understanding low jokes in German. And it will take everyone's mind off the food. [. . .]

Look after yourself.

I am your most devoted reader

IM

To Raymond Queneau, written in French and sent immediately after he and Murdoch had spent some time together in Paris. Having resigned from UNRAA on 1 July 1946, Murdoch had stopped there briefly en route for England.

London

5 July 1946

I was absolutely miserable to leave you – and miserable to think of your anguish and that there is nothing I can do. I was deeply touched that you confided in me – I thank you and I hope that you don't regret it. I listened while feeling so helpless – all my tenderness for you rendered dumb and ineffectual. I just couldn't find the words. I wish for you – oh, happiness, peace – the strength to find a solution – and an end to all your miseries. I hope that you will find, now and always, the real friendship and love for which you are searching. I know very well the feeling of wanting to die – but one doesn't die, one survives, and one is happy once more, people are good. The miracle happens. Meanwhile, my dear, take it all gently and patiently.

Forgive me if I talk and talk and seem to say nothing. I have such tender feelings for you that I can't express. I want to be simple and direct with you. We all depend, of course, on circumstances and distances and people. But in the end what I feel for you is something so strong and simple. You have given me such joy – as a supreme creator, and as yourself, Raymond, with your curious voice and your conversation and your laugh and all that is you. Oh I have delighted in your company – I say it with humility. I feel real sadness at your sadness – but also, I feel deep joy because you exist.

I beg you, work. It's terrible that you are wasting time. You must write. The Good God created you to do that, right? And also to be such a good man –

It's late. I arrived at Victoria station two hours ago. I'm in my Westminster flat. The girl who shares it is away on holiday. I am alone. I'm thinking of you and wishing hard for a solution to your problems. You have become, very strangely considering how little we know each other, one of the most important people in my life.

Tomorrow I shall go to Chiswick. Write to me there. I'll write to you again in two or three days. Very dear Raymond, don't torment yourself too much. I kiss you very tenderly –

Iris

To Raymond Queneau, written in English.

4 Eastbourne Road

14 July 1946

Well now (your letter of 10th July) – I am truly *very* sorry to have been, even for a moment, a further problem and embarrassment for you. Thank you however for writing frankly. Please don't think that I 'expect' anything of you – beyond, I hope, your continued friendship. We have expressed to each other our sincere '*sympathie*'[1] – that remains, I think? For the rest, our ways lie pretty far apart and I see no reason why our relationship should be a problem for either. Please, please don't distress yourself about it. I realise of course that your moral and emotional situation must be most unhappy – I sympathise very profoundly. I *will not be* a complicating factor. You know that I care about all this; I *have* become very attached to you and shall certainly remain so, but I don't think there is any cause for agitation in that.

I am trying to work, but London is more nerve rending than ever. I have finished *Être et le néant*, thank God, with much admiration and some flutters of criticism. It stops just where I want to begin; I suppose I shall now have to do some thinking for myself. (Or shall I just wait until Sartre publishes his Ethics?) MacKinnon at Oxford seems to be going through some sort of spiritual crisis and can't see me. A bunch of goddamn neurotics I have for friends. I have continued a little with *Pierrot* and find this the one soothing occupation in a somewhat ragged world.

Thank you very much for *Les ziaux*,[2] which I have not yet had time to read. Work well at Avignon and don't worry yourself to death.

I wish you most heartily the strength to solve your problems.

Now and always I remain your calm tender devoted reader and friend

Iris

PS My surname ends with an H not a K. *Pax tecum.*[3]

---

1 Warm affinity, deep liking.
2 A collection of poems by Queneau published in 1943.
3 Peace be with you.

To Raymond Queneau, written in French, at a time when Murdoch was preparing to take up a one-year fellowship at Vassar College. Her application for a visa would, however, be turned down because she declared to the American Embassy that she had been a member of the Communist Party.

4 Eastbourne Road
7 August 1946

Dear Raymond,

Your charming letter of 31st July, with its usual apologies for all the 'I's', has just reached me – but why do you apologise when it is that very cosmic and unbounded 'I' capable of being a dozen different people at the same time who can thereby completely smash the elementary rules of language and logic? You correct your proofs, you work on *Gueule de Pierre III*,[1] you read books on Hegel and Joyce, you continue (stubbornly) with *Exercices de style*[2] and (enthusiastically) a drawing course, you visit Romanesque churches and (my God) you even have time for plenty of sleep! I laughed a lot, forgive me, on seeing this picture (which I find absolutely convincing) of the life Queneauesque. Of all your various activities what you told me about *G. de P.* pleased me most, and the pictograms greatly amused me. Is this the first time you've tried your hand at drawing – and painting –? (What a landscape must surround you down there[3] – quite apart from the rather surreal mixture of Petrarch and de Sade. I think I can see it in Van Gogh's canvases, burning and violent and as mad as he was.[4]) [. . .]

No, I haven't seen the article on Sartre in *Life*. I haven't yet been able to get hold of this exalted manifestation of the American spirit. I'd really like to see it. I'm sure it's much more entertaining than Freddy Ayer's[5] rants in *Horizon*. Ayer is a 'logical positivist' of the most scholarly kind. He has come up with some accurate and damaging critiques of Sartre – but he reads his work with an absolute lack of imagination. He is a rattle of dry bones. However, Sartre is actually quite vulnerable on the linguistic side.

---

1 A sequel to his earlier novels *Gueule de Pierre* and *Les temps mêlés*.
2 Queneau's popular and funny book tells, in ninety-nine different ways, the story of a man seeing the same stranger twice in one day, thereby demonstrating the number of ways in which a tale can be told.
3 Queneau had recently left Paris to stay in the Vaucluse region of Provence for a while in order to devote himself to writing.
4 Petrarch travelled to Provence, famously climbing Mont Ventoux in April 1336; the Marquis de Sade owned a castle, the Château de Lacoste, in Provence; and Van Gogh spent time in Provence during the last two years of his life, producing some of his most vivid paintings there.
5 A. J. Ayer, British philosopher, at this time Grote Professor of the Philosophy of Mind and Logic at University College London, had strongly promoted logical positivism in his book *Language, Truth, and Logic* (1936).

As for me, since reading his analysis of love I've become quite disenchanted! (He is seductive and captivating, isn't he – for me *Être et néant* unwound like a spell.) But that apart, I find this mechanics of nothingness very metaphysical (in a pejorative sense), I don't want to concede that all awareness is self-awareness, and I find his concept of freedom vague and transcendental. (It seems there is a freedom-precondition of experience in an almost Kantian sense – and another, our choice in the world, in the more usual sense.) But I'll look again at all this. However, as psychological studies his analyses of *'mauvaise foi'* (bad faith) and *être-pour-autrui* (being for others) are very profound. I'm also very drawn to the Sartrean concept of anguish and to the portrait of man alone in the universe faced by choice, architect of his own values. What do you make of Sartre's philosophy? [. . .]

I wait impatiently for the notes on Hegel,[1] a philosopher about whom I know, *horresco referens*,[2] very little. Your continuing neglect of Kierkegaard is disgraceful. I think this man has almost all the virtues – profound and spiritual and writes like an angel. (One could if one had time build an interesting theory of humour out of his works, where the humourist is just below the religious man in the Kierkegaardian hierarchy. 'Recklessness and frivolity as productive energies produce the loud laughter of indeterminacy and sensuous irritability, which is extremely different from the laughter that accompanies the great translucency of the comical'.[xviii] *Translucency*. Aristophanes, Shakespeare, Laurence Sterne – yes – and the Marx brothers and Queneau and Beckett.)

How's the eternal struggle with *Finnegans Wake* going? I find it rather hard going, that sort of book! Life is too short . . . these days I begin to feel my mortality – the influence of Sartre perhaps. By the way, I've seen *Huis clos*[3] here, in an English translation – *wonderful*. (Most of the critics were disgusted by it. Alas my country.) Oh wonderful. I wasn't surprised however to hear Marcel's declaration: *'Les autres, c'est le ciel!'*[4] If love exists (not the Sartrien sort) it is a vital aspect of the study of freedom – and that too one must study. And so back to the cosmos which claims our attention. There is no stopping . . .

I continue with *Pierrot*, a lively arabesque between my philosophical preoccupations. (Philosophical reasoning is like following the arabesque patterns on a carpet.) I'm still having real problems getting a visa and

---

1 *Introduction à la lecture de Hegel* (1947), edited by Raymond Queneau.
2 'I shudder as I tell the story' – or, more colloquially, 'I'm ashamed to admit'.
3 *No Exit*, existentialist play by Sartre written in 1944.
4 'Heaven is other people': presumably in response to the famous line from Sartre's play: *'L'enfer, c'est les autres'* ('Hell is other people'). Although Gabriel Marcel (1889–1973), the French philosopher, was sometimes described as a Christian existentialist, he dissociated himself from writers such as Jean-Paul Sartre, preferring the term 'Philosophy of Existence' to define his own thought.

organising my passage to America. I'm beginning to doubt whether I'll be able to arrive in time. It seems that even very important people are having to wait some weeks or months to get a ship. ("*Sed deis aliter visa*"[1] as Jupiter wittily remarked as he walked invisibly up the gangway' writes a friend this morning trying to console me.) [. . .]

I wanted to send you a couple of books (for example, the incomparable *Murphy* by Samuel Beckett that I've just reread for the nth time) but they're sold out for the time being. But if I can send you anything or do anything for you over here, you know . . .

I'm impatient to begin the *Journal métaphysique*[2] but I'm unable to live six parallel lives (like you!). Actually I'm rereading Kant's *Metaphysics of Morals* and I'm feeling a bit bloated (not to mention bogged down! Now *there's* some vocabulary for you!).

I'd love to see your pictograms. Write to me when you have time and tell me (please) what you think of Sartre's work. I hope you're now finding life more peaceful and simple and that you're pleased with your work – I get much pleasure from imagining you so busy in so many different ways!

Very dear Raymond, I am forever your affectionate friend,

I

To Raymond Queneau, written in French.

4 Eastbourne Rd
25 August 1946

Dear Raymond,

Life on Sartre, oh my God. People in the Midwest who aren't bleak or pessimistic or mystical themselves have a clear eye for European crazies. (But have you seen the news about the atomic bomb?[3] Like a painting by Salvador Dali. A real American madness and much greater than our little European 'isms'.) I was delighted to see at last a photograph of the intellectual heavyweight Simone de Beauvoir who is exactly as I'd imagined her.

I'm sad that you don't share my feelings for *Murphy*. At first I thought: have I made a mistake? But no. It's you who are wrong. Shame. Don't bother to read it again – it's not worth arguing about!

---

1 A play on the Latin phrase '*dis aliter visum*' ('it is seen otherwise by the gods', i.e. the gods arrange things for their own purposes). Here the word '*visum*' has been put into the plural – '*visa*' – making the phrase jokingly readable also as 'But a visa is obtained – or required – otherwise by the gods.'

2 In 1927 Marcel published his philosophical notebooks, which covered the period 1914–23, as *Journal métaphysique*.

3 The Bikini Atoll test on 1 July 1946.

I finally managed to talk to my philosophy tutor, Donald MacKinnon, who pinched (for a short time) the *Journal métaphysique* (that I haven't yet had time to read) and he's going to devour it this week in the countryside. He is very interested in French philosophy at the moment, has read Sartre but not yet Marcel. MacKinnon is Anglo-Catholic and linked with Catholic groups in France – he has told me about Maydieu,[1] a young Dominican philosopher (do you know of him?), confessor to Mauriac, who will soon be in England. Also he (MacKinnon) will probably visit France in the autumn to give some lectures. I hope that perhaps you'll meet him in Paris – he is (I believe) one of our best young English philosophers and a rare being in every way.

Thank you for your comments on Sartre. I'm beginning to realise that I need to understand the Germans. (Not yet translated. Alas.) I was in Oxford where I talked to lots of people. It seems that everyone there is a logical positivist. Linguistic analysis has reached such a point of perfection that one or two young people have abandoned philosophy (since most problems can be so easily resolved!) and others imagine a grand semantics laboratory where the English language can be examined word by word! Sartre? A joke. Kierkegaard? Unreadable. It's interesting that this linguistic approach is much less popular in France. Does the Church have something to do with it?

I feel rather discouraged these days. I absolutely must read or reread all of Plato-Aristotle-Descartes-Spinoza-Hume-Berkeley-Kant-Bradley and Wittgenstein. At the moment I know nothing. Not in the Socratic sense. My thoughts, like flies stuck in honey, stay glued to Jean-Paul Sartre whom I like so much.

I hope that all goes well with your books, dancing, bridge and poker, and that you're attending the fête days organised by the aggressively charming local population and taking part in the general festivities. Lots of wine no doubt. Oh how lucky you are! Here one is lucky to find a bottle of British sherry or Australian wine, exorbitantly priced, awful home-grown products of the British Empire.

I would really like to talk to you this evening. It's a shame you don't live in Chelsea. I'm so thirsty – I'm in one of those moods when one feels alone with one's own personal mythology – God – if only one could believe in this convenient being – no, we have instead a pantheon of little gods and devils – above all devils. Or the desert where one passes one's time among the grotesque shapes of cactuses. Beethoven's piano concerto number 3 is

---

1 Probably Jean-Pierre Maydieu, a Dominican priest-intellectual who died in 1955 and who edited *La vie intellectuelle*, a Catholic journal, from 1945. He had been imprisoned during the Occupation for participating in the French Resistance.

playing on the TSF[1] and seems so sad it brings tears to my eyes. I think I'm feeling sick tonight. Forgive this horribly nauseating letter. Don't forget about G. *de p. III* between all the card games and music and drawing. (Shut up! You are annoying the man. He knows well enough what he wants to do.)

I am, devotedly, your most contingent but always most faithful friend,
Iris

To Leo Pliatzky, who had succeeded for a brief moment in reviving the romantic relationship he had with Murdoch during their Oxford days.

4 Eastbourne Road
30 August 1946

After thinking over the decision we came to when we last met – I'm afraid I must go back on it. You will think me a tiresome nervy devil and so I am. I am really in a hell of an emotional mess at present. Various factors which I haven't explained to you. I can't face any more complications of any kind. Also, I am beginning to feel, in general, that these casual friendly liaisons are wrong. Forgive me. I don't undervalue your friendship – I do prize it very much and it has helped me a lot. Please go on being patient and gentle with me if you can. I think it would be better, if for the present, we don't meet. I'll write you news of my progress or regress with visas and passages.

I'm sorry to behave in this irritating manner. But I don't want to hurt you or complicate your life – or to entangle my own any more. I am feeling very desperate and hating myself and must get these things straight alone. Thank you, dear Leo, for caring about me – I am ever and always your friend –
I

To Hal Lidderdale.

Chiswick
6 September 1946

Hal dear, thank you for your charming letter and the deep emotion of your anti-weather tirade! It cheered me a lot.

---

1 *Télégraphie sans fil*: the radio.

Yesterday, I must say, I felt that the only practical problem now remaining to me was: can one rely on a hundred aspirins, or is a tube train safer? Today I think perhaps there are alternatives to instant death, though I'm not at all sure what they are.

I'll ring you Monday as you suggest –

Love to you

I

To Hal Lidderdale, who had just taken the examination for entrance to the Civil Service.

4 Eastbourne Road
7 September 1946

Hal old dear, if I wrote you a horrid letter yesterday, and I think I did, please forgive me. Sheer gloom. I was offered (did I tell you?) a passage for Friday but couldn't accept because the goddamn visa isn't ready. No passage now till October. All infuriating.

Let me know at once when you hear about your exam. I send herewith Geoffrey's pamphlet to aid your speech on 'literature as a career'!

Hope your cold is better. Thanks for returning the Sartre article. Never mind about disclosures to Pippa, *no* importance. Write news of progress in due course.

Love to you I

To David Hicks.

4 Eastbourne Rd
14 September 1946

David old dear, I was glad to hear from you. I'm sorry I didn't write earlier – I meant to write wishing you luck and so on. Not overtime, but a series of crises of one kind and another delayed me. Let me know however most heartily wish you all happiness and the peace which you so much need. I think Molly looks *delightful*.[1] I'm sure her technique for dealing with your moods is far better than mine would ever have been. The more I reflect, the more I think it a good thing that we (you and I) did not marry – it would have been disastrous. We are (you were right) basically such very

---

1 Molly Purchase, the 'Dornford Yates heroine' whom David Hicks had married in July 1946.

different types of chaps. Superficially we seem to be at the same 'stage' – but our presuppositions, and the things we really want in the end, are not the same. I'm very glad you have married Molly and I hope you'll both be very happy.

How is the environment taking you? How is your Czech, and do you like Bratislava more than you did the last time I heard you on that subject?

Myself, I have been getting onto some philosophical stuff lately which excites me a lot (Sartre, Unamuno,[1] Heidegger etc.) and I shall probably work on it till next year (possibly with Prof. Hodges at Reading) and then try to get an academic job. I had some plans for going to USA, but they have now, I think definitely, fallen through. I'm sorry in some ways, though not in others. Oxford is more 'logical positivist' than ever, and anyone inter- ested in psychology, history or religions is regarded as 'romantic' and ergo unsound. Sartre is mentioned only with derision and no one reads Kierkegaard. At present I am struggling with Kant and Hegel and trying to get a hard intellectual grip on certain problems which I only grasp imaginatively and emotionally. I'm still not at all sure whether I can really *think* philosophically at all! However I have rarely felt more *insouciante*[2] and generally more serene. [. . .]

I shall probably push off to Paris for a while – or maybe I'll wait till next spring. Winter in Paris would be *no* fun.

Let me know when you're likely to be on home leave, and we can go boozing together. I shall be very glad to meet Molly. I do most sincerely want you to be happy.

Pax vobiscum[3]
and love from
I

To Hal Lidderdale.

4 Eastbourne Road
[September 1946]

Thanks for nice note. Everything here is bloody. The American visa office is unspeakable and the difficulties put in the way of those wishing visas interminable. Am very fed up. Mind not working. I begin vaguely to feel I disagree with Sartre about this and that, but can't work out quite what. The

1 Miguel de Unamuno (1864–1936), Spanish essayist, novelist, poet, playwright and philosopher.
2 Carefree.
3 Peace be with you; a more formal version of '*Pax tecum*', used in a previous letter to Raymond Queneau.

only pleasant thing lately has been the Marx brothers which I have betrayed you by seeing. Have seen innumerable people lately, mostly tiresome. Had Delacroix to Dufy[1] spoiled by meeting John Russell[2] there.

What day are you coming? [. . .]

> I am told that
> Humperdinck
> Was fond of plumpuddink
> Which kept him in fine fettle
> For writing *Hansel and Gretel*.

Heigh ho life is hard
Much love I

To Philippa Bosanquet, now Philippa Foot, who was a Rosa Hovey Graduate Scholar at Somerville College, Oxford between 1945 and 1947. She had married M. R. D. Foot in 1945. Some distance naturally arose between the two women, possibly because Murdoch felt some remorse and embarrassment about the way she had treated Michael Foot in 1944. In this letter she seeks to re-establish her friendship with Philippa.

4 Eastbourne Road
10 October [1946]

Dear, I expect you have heard tell of my recent misadventures. Our efforts in London to get the Yanks to relent have drawn a blank – and altogether I conclude I've had the USA. Never mind –

Look, Pippa – it does occur to me that you and Michael may have been worrying about me – in general, I mean. I should be sorry if that were so. One doesn't – as I know you realise – get over an *histoire* like that of 1944 very quickly. When one has behaved as I then behaved to two people one loves the hurt and the sense of guilt go very deep. In a way it's only since I came home from Austria that I've realised those events *fully* as things that I did, as apart from things that I suffered. You understand. I have lived through them again, seeing my own responsibility. This has not been pleasant, but was necessary. Forgive me for intruding this into your happiness with M. I am *truly* glad that you and M have found this happiness together. It

---

1 Exhibition at the Lefevre Gallery.
2 John Russell (1919–2008) was an unpaid intern at the Tate Gallery before working in Naval Intelligence during the Second World War. He then became an art critic for the *Sunday Times* and later for the *New York Times*.

seems perhaps a foolish useless gesture after so long to say – I'm sorry I caused you both to suffer – but I do say it, most humbly, and believe me I do *feel* it. I have been very deep in the pit over this affair, but I think that that time has passed now. You are *not* to worry about me, either of you, for there is no cause any more.

Pippa, you know without my telling you that my love for you remains as deep and as tender as ever – and always will remain, it is so deep in me and so much a part of me. I cannot imagine that anyone will ever take your place. I think of you very often. My dear heart, I love you –

Yes, all goes well with me now. I am working very peacefully and begin even to understand one or two things. (E.g. about Kant, who I now realise was a complete mystery to me at Oxford!) I'll let you have news of my movements when I have any movements.

Be tolerant to this perhaps tiresome letter.

My love and blessings on you both –

I

To Hal Lidderdale, after hearing he had failed the examination for entrance into the Civil Service.

4 Eastbourne Road
[October 1946]

Old dear, my condolences to you on joining the band of really *distinguished* people who have failed that exam! I think I should congratulate you too on being *out* of the Civil Service. The British Council will probably be much more fun. I hope very much it materialises. [. . .]

Thank you VERY MUCH for *Le sang des autres*[1] which I've been wanting to get for a long time and searched Paris in vain – I'm delighted you got it. *Les chemins de la liberté* is well worth getting for yourself.[2] I possess the first two vols (*L'age de raison* and *Le sursis*) – if the third vol. is out, you might pick that up for me. I'm *most* grateful. (I doubt if it's out yet though.)

Have been feeling rather despairing over intellectual and other matters lately.

[...]

à bientôt –

I

---

1 1945 novel by Simone de Beauvoir.
2 A series of novels by Jean-Paul Sartre, translated as *The Roads to Freedom*. It remained unfinished, with only three of the planned four volumes published.

To Philippa Foot.

Chiswick
[mid–late October 1946]

Darling – thank you – your letter gave me such joy. The fact that you do, after all *that*, still care for me, gives me great hope that the past will fall away and this good thing between us will grow and be stronger than ever. Love can work miracles. Dear, there have been times when I have felt lacerated and broken beyond repair. But that does pass – and the fact that this precious central thing in my life, my friendship with you, does remain gives me such courage and calm of mind. My love for you has never *at any time* wavered or diminished by an iota – well, you know this – and it seems now greater than it ever was.

I was glad too of what you said about there being no opposition between your love for Michael and for me. Not that I really doubted it. I know that I have been – and deserved to be – hateful in M's eyes. I hope that may change. I think that the part of me which hurt him so is dead and cut away. Now that I am out of the despair and frenzy I feel the strength to change myself. I have learnt a lot from these horrors.

Dear, at times I have felt that the kindest thing that I could do for you and M would be to fade out of your lives entirely. But my love for you is so deep, my need for you so profound – so I dare to 'hang on', and hope that our love and our strength may hold us so that what is good may grow, and what is bad may die – as indeed I think most of it has now died –

My darling, be patient with me – it is a long way back and I have still far to go and many knots to untie. That you still care for me makes an infinite difference – be patient and don't let go your hold – all shall be well.

I do long to see you, and I'll come to Oxford later on. We now have a 'phone (Chiswick 1913) so please ring if you're in London.

All my love to you
I

To Hal Lidderdale.

4 Eastbourne Road
[late October/early November 1946]

Visa refused: reason, ex-member of CP! My opinion of USA, always low, now reaches a new low! More news later.

Love I

To Philippa Foot.

4 Eastbourne Rd
11 November 1946

Dearest – thank you. I can't tell you how very much it warmed my heart to be with you at the weekend. I feel so much relieved and calmed and can think peace and joy are possible for me again. Oh, full of doubts and pains still, but I believe they will pass. I was truly glad too to see Michael and talk with him – I do indeed care so deeply for him and I hope we may be able to rebuild something. For that, I would be endlessly patient and come any distance.

It's very late and I seem to have no words – Pip, seeing you again was really freedom and life to me, after being entombed for so long – I can't express this.

I suppose the time of sheer frenzy passes anyway – and I did feel sure of *wanting* new things – and being to that extent different. But there was no joy at all. But I did find with you – oh my dear, that deep joy in our constant love and in our whole world of thought and feeling together. There is no one who can be to me what you are.

I hope that Michael did not find it a strain to meet me. I care very much – I love you both dearly –

Sorry, I'm quite inarticulate this evening. Darling, my love to you

I

To Raymond Queneau, written during a visit to St Ives in Cornwall where Murdoch was immersing herself in philosophy as preparation for applying to Newnham College, Cambridge, for the Sarah Smithson Studentship in philosophy. Murdoch wrote the first, third, fourth and seventh paragraphs in English and the second, fifth and sixth in French. After this letter Murdoch wrote to Queneau in English only.

Larissa
The Belyars
St Ives
Cornwall
15 February 1947

Dear Raymond,

I am very sorry to hear you are still feeling sad and finding life tiresome. I hope things get better – I do most sincerely wish you all good things.

Concerning *Pierrot mon ami*, don't worry about it.[1] Of course I'm sad – but there it is. I'm aware that perhaps I'm not such a great mistress of slang – that you might be better off with a man as translator. I'll await the translation with great interest and some sympathy! I hope that Lehmann has found someone good.

I am spending a few weeks here, working, watching the cormorants and this most improbable blue and green sea.

I begin to see my way a little with the philosophy – find Marcel most profound and suggestive – continue my struggles with Kant – in a complete haze about Hegel. (Hope still for your Hegel notes one day. Yes?)

These exercises in disappointment do one good in the end, so one likes to imagine (see Marcel on *épreuves!*[2]). Anyway, how adaptable one is! (I find), like those newt embryos that biologists like to torment. I must try another novel soon.[3] Anything I shall ever write will owe so much, so much, to you. I wish I knew if I could write – shall find out by trying no doubt.

I haven't yet seen *Les temps modernes*[4] but I'll try to find it in Oxford (where I'll be for a few days) – in order to see what state of mind you're in, however sad that may be! I'll be in Paris in the spring (I think) and I hope I'll see you.

Life continues to be, *inter alia*, very *odd*. I wish I could meet you this evening, *pour prendre un verre.*[5] I feel so much like talking. One day perhaps. You are very much in my thoughts. Write now and then when you have a moment – I shall much want to hear your news. Dear Raymond, all my love to you – your devoted friend and reader –

I

To Raymond Queneau.

Manor Farm
Farleigh Wallop
Basingstoke
Hampshire
17 July 1947

1 Murdoch's translation of *Pierrot mon ami* had recently been rejected by the publisher John Lehmann.
2 Ordeals.
3 This novel is described briefly in the following letter to Queneau. It was never published.
4 A Paris-based literary journal first published in October 1945, the editorial board of which included Sartre, de Beauvoir and Maurice Merleau-Ponty; Queneau was one of its contributors. The journal filled the void left by the loss of the pre-war literary magazine, *La nouvelle revue française*, which had been shut down after the liberation of France because of its collaboration with the Occupation.
5 For a drink.

Très cher Raymond, just a hasty note to put on record one piece of luck, which is that I've got a scholarship for a year to Newnham College, Cambridge – to research on modern metaphysics (or what I please). Supervised, *horresco referens*, by Prof. Broad,[1] who I'm sure doesn't care for metaphysics, except the mathematical kind. *Mais on verra.*[2] Thank God for Cambridge, anyway.

I got back from Ireland a day or two ago (Dublin was *beautiful* – and so luxurious) – and am now down here helping some friends out of a house-keeper crisis.

When in Ireland I read Bosco's *Hyacinthe*[3] with much interest and admiration – and reflected much on Roman *mythologiques* in general – confirmed my supreme admiration for you as *mythologue*. There's a sort of funny ambiguous vertiginous absurdity – oh dear!

I have started writing the novel about the Bogus Scholar and the Archaic Goddess[4] which has been in my head so long, but doubt if I'll finish it before the autumn. I'll shew it you, if it ever gets done. In idea at least, it's a bit Queneau-esque. In execution – I don't know. [. . .]

Write, my dear friend, when you have time. I'll write a proper letter when I get back to London.

Always affectionately, your

Iris

To Philippa Foot.

4 Eastbourne Road
[end July 1947[xix]]

Old darling, it was wonderful, wonderful, to see you last week. Let it be again before long.

I'm in a frightful haste – off to an Old Girls Reunion at Bristol. This ghastly thing (which I attend solely to please Miss Baker[5]) is inter alia a dress parade, so I am ironing all my most smashing robes.

I have just finished *Prak. Vernunft.*[6] I am *much* excited by it – but of that

---

1 C. D. Broad, Knightbridge Professor of Moral Philosophy at Cambridge University at this time. The title of Murdoch's thesis was initially formalised as 'The concept of "Dialogue" in relation especially to existentialism and the linguistic approach'.

2 But we shall see.

3 Henri Bosco (1888–1976), French writer whose novels, including *Hyacinthe* (1940), evoked life in Provence.

4 Probably a reference to an unpublished novel entitled *Our Lady of the Bosky Gates* which featured a bogus spiritual seeker and a statue of a Greek goddess that comes to life.

5 Beatrice May Baker ('BMB'), headmistress of Badminton School, Bristol between 1911 and 1946, and an educational pioneer in many ways.

6 Immanuel Kant, *Kritik der praktischen Vernunft* (*Critique of Practical Reason*) (1788).

more later. [. . .] I've bought Paton's new book,[1] by the way, and hope it's a good investment! (Am now reading the Berdyaev *Met. Eschat.*[2] – most thrilling stuff!)

Talking of money, I'm applying to the Ministry of Education for an additional £50 or £100 to eke out Newnham's cash – no idea if I'm eligible. I've named Donald as a referee – you might tell him – I hope he won't mind. Another news item you might tell him, point of view general interest, is that I'm to be supervised by Broad. I'm not *sure* if this is a Good Thing or not! I haven't seen the great man yet. (When is D going permanently north – is that finally known yet?)[3]

Did you hear *Les mouches*[4] on the Third Programme on Tuesday? I was impressed by it – (a good piece of propaganda for violent resistance – played in Paris under Germans' noses I believe!) – and a good speech from Orestes about yesterday having a thousand roads, all other people's – today only one, his own. Interesting how everyone can have a go at the Orestes story and produce something different. Lying awake last night I imagined how I would treat that tale and produced something very different from Sartre (and highly autobiographical). Myths. What is it to invent a *new* myth?

Mustn't *start* writing this letter – more anon – must return to sewing on of hooks and eyes.

Darling Pippa – so much love to you,

I

To Raymond Queneau, written immediately after a trip to Paris with Mary Scrutton and Tom Greeves, both friends from her Oxford days, during which Murdoch managed to spend some time alone with Queneau.[xx]

4 Eastbourne Road
[21 September 1947]

My dear, I am back in London, God help me. There is the usual collection of nerve-rending letters waiting. Inter alia, a manuscript of mine (a novel written in '44) politely rejected by a publisher – and a request from a learned body that I should lecture on existentialism in London in the autumn. (Marcel

---

1 *The Categorical Imperative: A Study in Kant's Moral Philosophy* by Herbert Paton.
2 *The Beginning and the End: Essay on Eschatological Metaphysics* (1947) by Nikolai Alexandrovich Berdyaev, Russian religious and political philosopher, whose philosophy is sometimes described as Christian existentialist.
3 In 1947 Donald MacKinnon ('D') took up the post of Regius Professor of Moral Philosophy at Aberdeen University, where he taught until 1960.
4 *The Flies*, a play by Jean-Paul Sartre.

is to lecture in the same series.) I feel alarm at this – sometimes I think my playing the philosopher is a great hoax and one day someone will denounce me. You see already I'm fretting about these trifles. But not all trifles – some distressing letters too from sad friends –

You said that love between a man and a woman made always some sort of basis for life. Yes. Yet how rarely it occurs without hurt to one or both parties – or rather both, for if one is hurt both are hurt. Yet I don't know – I can't tell for other people really, only for myself.

I meant all I said last night – but don't be distressed – very simply and loyally. I hope and pray we won't ever harm each other. I'm very tired at the moment – sort of drunk with tiredness and nothing to eat, you know the way one can be. My parents are out playing cards. It's late. I can't help wishing for simple things, simple solutions. I wish I could see you often and get to know you. Maybe I will get to know you better in time.

I'll write again in a few days when I'm feeling less feverish. Thank you, for very many things. I'm happy that I know you and happy that I love you.

I'm so glad you like Prince Myshkin.[1]

I hope all goes very well with all your projects.

Most tenderly

I am your

I

To Raymond Queneau.

From tomorrow: NEWNHAM COLLEGE, CAMBRIDGE

4 Eastbourne Road
5 October [1947]

I can't decide whether or not I'm very depressed this evening. I suppose I'd better decide not to be. I've sketched out my two lectures on Sartre, which has been amusing, though revelatory of my ignorance. Capacity for the wild statement. Sartre is exciting though – demonic. A sort of *vertige* (vertigo) overcomes me, as if S were repeating a spell: Be like me, be like me. I'm almost ready to say: yes, dammit, I am – But I'm not quite spellbound.

Sometimes though I do see my philosophical pursuits as a process of intoxication. Some subtlety can be so voluptuous. Sartre has it. (Though such blind spots too.) When one has refined to a certain degree upon the

---

1 From Dostoevsky's *The Idiot.*

notion of truth and verification . . . Marcel realises this. But then he became a Catholic. Heigh ho.

I wish I could put my learning into novels, as you do. Sea-changed of course into the rich and strange.[1] (I visited the stick insects by the way in the Jardin des Plantes[2] while waiting for a train.)

Actually I don't care a hang this evening about anything theoretical. I care so much more about people, indeed I always do. I am so grateful, when I think about it, to the people I love for being so loveable. Today when I'd finished with Sartre I began to think about various people. I thought a lot about you and felt most happy that we are friends. But oh this formal statement doesn't at all express the warmth with which I thought it and think it! This is a rotten letter. I just want to talk to you, to open my mind to you, my heart to you, as if they were a couple of boxes, and yet I can't do this. Never mind. You understand. *Cher* Raymond, I'll write later from Cambridge. The gods go with you.

Your friend,

I

1 Echoes Ariel's song in Shakespeare's *The Tempest*.
2 Botanical garden in Paris.

PART THREE:

Academic and Author

October 1947 to September 1954

Murdoch was now pursuing her interest in European thought and literature with enthusiasm. As a research student at Newnham College between 1947 and 1948 she found Cambridge both stimulating and frustrating: 'There is a gang of about ten young philosophers, disciples of Wisdom[1] and Wittgenstein, whom I meet every day at classes and lectures, and there is much passionate argument. Wisdom himself I like very much', she wrote to Queneau in 1947.[i] Indeed, having arrived with the intention of writing on Husserl, who had broken with positivism and established the school of phenomenology – the study of subjective experience – she soon found she was more interested in the work of Wittgenstein. However, the intellectual insularity of Cambridge was disappointing: 'No one is interested in ethics – except as a sort of butt for philosophical jokes! [. . .] The result is I begin already to feel that I am a dreadful obscurantist'.[ii] Her enduring antipathy to psychoanalysis also emerged at this time; she wrote to Queneau: 'Another feature of the land-scape that worries me is the prevalence of half-baked Freudians. Most people know a little psychology and are metaphysically conditioned accordingly. ("But *of course* other people know you better than you know yourself – that's axiomatic" said a young man from Nebraska to me yesterday)'.[iii]

On leaving Cambridge in 1948 Murdoch took a post as tutor in philosophy at St Anne's Society, Oxford, becoming a fellow in 1952 when it became St Anne's College. Here she taught moral and political philosophy through the work of Aristotle, Kant, Descartes, Hobbes, Berkeley, Locke and Hume –

---

1 John Wisdom, British philosopher influenced by G. E. Moore, Wittgenstein and Freud, and based at Trinity College, Cambridge for most of his career. In the 1940s his work was one of the few published sources of information about Wittgenstein's later philosophy. He replaced C. D. Broad as Murdoch's supervisor.

though she often departed from what most of her colleagues would have been teaching by introducing her students to the work of Kierkegaard, Sartre and de Beauvoir. She returned to Christianity in 1948, much to the surprise of her friends. However, by 1953 she was no longer a practising Christian: Elias Canetti, whom Murdoch certainly knew by 1952, had persuaded her to rethink her religious views.[iv]

She now embarked on numerous professional activities, including speaking at various universities and to philosophical societies, taking part in BBC discussion programmes and publishing essays and book reviews. In early 1950 she gave two radio talks on the BBC Third Programme, 'The Novelist as Metaphysician' and 'The Existentialist Hero'. Her first academic papers, 'Thinking and Language' (1951) and 'Nostalgia for the Particular' (1952), which show the influence of Wittgenstein, question the limits of behaviourism (which draws its conclusions from the observable behaviour of people and animals) and, instead, champion the value of the 'inner life' (including emotions) and the importance of mental events (the way we construct the world we see). When writing her book *Sartre: Romantic Rationalist*, which was published in 1953 in Bowes & Bowes's series 'Studies of Modern European Literature and Thought', Murdoch focused mainly on Sartre's fiction, finally laying to rest the 'spell' the French author and philosopher had cast on her. While acknowledging the rush of excitement and intellectual challenge that existentialism brought to philosophy, she was by now able to see its limitations more clearly. Having previously admired Sartre's emphasis on the individual as a free responsible agent who determines development through conscious acts of will, she now questioned his portrayal of modern man as inevitably alienated and solipsistic. She also rejected Sartre's embrace of the absurd, characterised by the doomed effort to find inherent meaning in a world so full of information and the unknown that the task becomes impossible and results in nausea. Instead, drawing on Marcel, she argued that the particularity and contingency of the world can be seen as glorious riches, rather than as emblematic of the absurd. Sartre's fictional world, she claimed, lacked mystery and poetry; his heroes, in failing to value and pay attention to the Other, forfeit goodness and love. Murdoch's love affair with existentialism was approaching its end.

Her first novel, *Under the Net*, was published in 1954 by Chatto & Windus in the UK and by Viking Press in the United States. Stylistically, it looked to French experimental writing and owes something to both Raymond Queneau's *Pierrot mon ami* (1942) and Beckett's *Murphy* (1938); philosophically, it engages ambitiously with Plato, Sartre, Wittgenstein and Simone Weil. Set in post-war London, the novel tells the story of a struggling young writer, Jake Donaghue. Taking individual freedom as her theme, a topic that also preoccupied her philosophically at this time, Murdoch tests existential ideas within a fictional world. Plato's analogy of the cave (which illustrates the attempt to understand the true nature of reality and reach a greater degree of self-knowledge) is as fundamental to this book as it is to later novels. The 'net' of the title refers to the net of language that Wittgenstein had identified in the *Tractatus*[1] as a barrier both to the expression of truth and to the adequate translation of thought into language. Here Murdoch acknowledges the legitimacy of his attack on language but defends it against him. *Under the Net* also documents the effects of alienation caused by physical and psychological displacement, something Murdoch had witnessed when working with refugees during the war and was later to find explored philosophically in the work of Simone Weil. In *The Need for Roots* (1949), Weil diagnoses rootlessness as a sickness of modern life, and in *Under the Net* it is a cause of alienation but also opportunity. A first novel by a serious author, the book is consciously self-reflexive and meditates on what qualities make a good writer and good art, simultaneously telling the funny and engaging story of its own birth. It was a tour de force that established a new kind of fiction in English and put Iris Murdoch's name on the literary map; its mixture of wit, intellectual flair and the picaresque made it instantly popular and it was generally well reviewed and seen by many (including Mary Warnock[2]) as a brilliant debut.[v] Still regarded as one of her finest books, *Under the Net* won second prize at the Cheltenham Literature Festival in 1954 (first prize went to Brigid Brophy's *Hackenfeller's Ape*).

Murdoch's personal life between 1947 and 1954 was complicated. There were many friendships, old and new. Ex-Oxford friends included David Hicks, Mary Midgley, Elizabeth Anscombe, Philippa Foot (all three women later to become important philosophers of virtue ethics) and Lucy Klatschko, who took the veil and became Sister Marian at Stanbrook Abbey in 1954. Although initially dismayed by her friend's decision to renounce the world, Murdoch was to remain fascinated by, and rather envious of, Sister Marian's ability to devote herself to God. When Murdoch took up her post at St Anne's, she stayed with Philippa Foot and her husband Michael in their Oxford home for over a year. Despite the two women's optimism that this would work well, it introduced some tension into the Foot marriage. Michael's earlier love for Murdoch and her shabby treatment of him then made it difficult for them to be together in the house when Philippa was absent: 'relations were constrained: intimacy had lapsed'.[vi] When Murdoch moved into her own flat in the autumn of 1949, she reassured Philippa that they would stay close – 'Dear darling lunatic,

1 Wittgenstein's *Logisch-Philosophische Abhandlung* (1921) was translated into English and published in 1922 as *Tractatus Logico-Philosophicus*.
2 At this time a fellow and tutor in philosophy at St Hugh's College, Oxford, Warnock was later to become a distinguished philosopher whose work focused on existentialism, ethics and education.

how could you possibly lose me?' – but in fact their correspondence diminished over the next ten years and their friendship waned until the Foots separated in 1959.

New friends included her editor at Chatto & Windus, Norah Smallwood, who was charmed by Murdoch, and Brigid Brophy, whom Murdoch met at the Cheltenham Literary Festival in 1954. Brophy, wife of the art historian Michael Levey, was beautiful, unconventional, politically active, and a gifted writer; Murdoch found her fascinating and they were to become very close over the next few years. Many affairs were played out with male academics and intellectuals – three of them European Jews. It is perhaps no coincidence that the main characters of *The Flight from the Enchanter* – written between 1953 and 1955 and dedicated to Elias Canetti – are refugees. Murdoch met Wallace Robson, a fellow in English at Lincoln College, Oxford, with whom she was to have a rather volatile relationship, in February 1950. In the autumn of that year she had a brief affair with Michael Oakeshott, professor of political science at the London School of Economics, thereby causing Robson much pain.[vii] Oakeshott ended the affair in early December 1950 and by October 1951 Murdoch and Robson had recommitted to each other and became unofficially engaged in January 1952. They parted in April, however, Murdoch having decided that the relationship should end. She had become wary of Robson's mercurial personality and was now attracted to Franz Baermann Steiner, a Czech émigré and lecturer in social anthropology at the Anthropological Institute in Oxford, whom she had met in May 1951. By March 1952 they were in a romantic relationship. He was a sensitive, mystical, highly intelligent Jew, whose parents had died in the concentration camp at Treblinka. Although he earned his living as an academic social anthropologist, his passion was literature (especially the work of Kafka) and he and Murdoch shared both a love of languages and a deep desire to write.[viii]

In June 1952 she found herself drawn to Asa Briggs,[1] whom she had met at a fancy-dress party in Oxfordshire; at about the same time she began an intense relationship with Peter Ady, a female colleague and fellow in economics at St Anne's. Also during 1952 she became involved with Arnaldo Momigliano, who had recently been appointed professor of ancient history at University College London, and whom she had probably met when an undergraduate (Momigliano was close to Murdoch's tutor Isobel Henderson). He would travel to Oxford every Saturday to work at the Ashmolean or Bodleian libraries until late afternoon and then spent time with Murdoch in her flat. They read the *Divine Comedy* in Italian together

---

1 Educated at Cambridge, Briggs went on to have a distinguished academic career as a historian, becoming a leading specialist on the Victorian era.

and Murdoch would make him a light supper; he would leave at 11.30 to return to his hotel on the Banbury Road. Murdoch's love of Dante grew out of these meetings and she regarded Momigliano as one of her great teachers.[ix] By August 1952 they were lovers and they travelled to Italy together during that month and again in 1953 and 1955. Married to a wife who tolerated his liaisons with other women, in April 1953 Momigliano wrote to Murdoch describing her as 'his life', and declaring that he 'lived in fullness only when with her'.[x] A possessive man, he was deeply upset by Murdoch's relationships with other men; her marriage to John Bayley in 1956 was to result in a bitter rift between them. They were not fully reconciled until 1979; Murdoch later dedicated *The Philosopher's Pupil* (1983) to him – perhaps as an act of contrition. Throughout these years she still wrote frequently to Queneau, her intellectual soulmate, and in August 1952 wrote confessing her deep love for him. To her acute disappointment, her feelings were still not reciprocated.

Murdoch was greatly distressed by Steiner's sudden death from heart failure on 27 November 1952, her grief exacerbated by feelings of guilt for the emotional pain she had caused him. Like Frank Thompson, he was to become idealised in her memory. At Steiner's funeral on 28 November, his close friend Elias Canetti renewed his acquaintance with Murdoch; in December 1952 she recorded in her journal 'that the only one person' she wanted to see at that time was Canetti.[xi] They began a love affair in January 1953, despite the fact Canetti was married and already had mistresses, including Friedl Benedikt. Already ill at this time, Benedikt died of Hodgkin's disease in April 1953. Just as Canetti replaced Steiner in Murdoch's life, so she was to replace Canetti's writer-mistress.[xii] Murdoch recorded in her journal on 10 January 1953 that Canetti filled her 'with wonder and delight and fear [. . .] He is a bull, a lion, an angel. [. . .] I gave him one of my fossil stones shaped like a heart'.[xiii] Canetti was to have an important emotional and intellectual impact on Murdoch and her work; through him, and her feelings for him, she learnt much about the workings of power within sexual relationships. They kept their affair, which lasted several years, so secret that even close friends remained unaware of it throughout Murdoch's life. Haunted by Canetti, Murdoch met her future husband, John Bayley, then a tutor at St Antony's (a graduate college of Oxford University), at a party in January 1954. She was immediately attracted to him, associating him with gentleness, laughter and 'a sense of joyous carnival'; in May of that year Murdoch noted in her journal that she had fallen deeply in love.[xiv] Despite Canetti's decree that Murdoch and Bayley should not have sexual relations, they became lovers during 1954 although what Murdoch called her 'endless capacity for new loves'[xv] made her cautious about committing herself to one person.

To Raymond Queneau.

Newnham College, Cambridge
8 October 1947

This is all very curious. It's all so like my first year at Oxford, and yet so unlike. When I wake in the morning, I imagine I'm at Oxford – and when I wander in the town I get confused and look for shops and streets which are really in Oxford. Sense of repetition is very strong.

I'm living in a (most luxurious) college hostel, peopled by the college steward, two other research students (students of *botany* from Auckland, New Zealand my God. Very nice girls, but talking to each other all the time about fungi), and the French *lectrice*, not yet come, called Mme Magny,[1] alleged to be a writer – sounds familiar to me but I daresay there are many? Any *renseignements?*[2]

I am reading with the utmost enthusiasm devotion and passion of humility Camus' *La peste. Chapeau bas.*[3] This seems to me really a great novel. What do you think of it? A visionary and a *writer*. How he can be so ambiguous and yet so positive!

This ban on import of foreign books is a great *embêtement*[4] to me.[5] Later I may perhaps ask you to send me one or two books of philosophy. I shall keep *compte*[6] and pay you when next we meet. I hope you won't mind this.

This is an interim bulletin. More anon about lovely Cam and dangerous Broad and wild Wisdom and Wittgenstein. I have hopes too of the *inconnue*[7] Magny.

All my love to you, most dear Raymond
Ever your
I

To Raymond Queneau.

Newnham College, Cambridge
17 October 1947

1 Claude-Edmonde Magny.
2 Any information?
3 Hats off.
4 Irritation.
5 During and immediately after the Second World War, about 10,000 staff were employed in the UK to censor or withhold suspicious mail, which sometimes included foreign books.
6 An account.
7 Unknown.

I was most interested to get your letter about Mme Magny! She arrived yesterday, but so far I haven't even seen her. I shall wait a while, and if I don't meet her in the normal course of events, I shall introduce myself. I'm delighted by what you say about her, and much look forward to meeting her. My God, Raymond, the landscape here is pretty barren, point of view people. Newnham is full of estimable and learned women with whom, so far as I can see, I shall be quite unable to communicate, except about the simplest banalities. Cambridge philosophers are mainly sportive logicians and mathematicians, letting off logical fireworks. Except for Wisdom, who is at least a solid human being with blood in his veins and some gift of seriousness and imagination. Maybe it's just because I'm so bad at these logical sports that I talk this way. But Christ! The need of someone with whom I can *communicate* is an anguish sometimes. (I was in Oxford yesterday and had some philosophical talk there, which did me good.) I shall, also in a little while, look up your Kahnweiler[1] friends. *Thank you.* Of botanists and logicians I have, for the moment, enough. [. . .]

I was interested too in your reactions to *La peste*. Now that I've finished it, I'm not sure that my admiration is so unqualified, though I do still admire. The man, after all, can *write*. I should say *orgueil* was the word, if at all, not *vanité*.[2] There is a sincerity there for which one forgives much. But indeed it raises problems, that book. There are regions where one commits the sin against the Holy Ghost as soon as one opens one's mouth. Those of no faith will speak. And those of great faith?

Much gloom and doubt about my own work. I find the Ministry of Education is willing to give me *some* sort of grant for three years, so I could do a Doctor of Philosophy thesis if I cared to. The question is, can I really exploit the *advantages* (instead of as hitherto simply suffer from the disadvantages) of having a mind on the borders of philosophy, literature and politics – all bloody doubtful. Every time I open a newspaper I wonder bitterly what on earth I'm up to.

I'll report again when I've met Mme Magny. If she tells me any horrors about you, I'll discount them as not being fair play. (May I quote Marcel whom you hate so? *'L'amour porte sur l'être, pas sur l'idée de l'être.'*[3] Relevant perhaps?)

Much love to you, as always, from

I

1   Daniel-Henry Kahnweiler, German-born art historian and art collector based in Paris. He was one of the leading French art dealers of the twentieth century and an early champion of Pablo Picasso, Georges Braque and cubism.

2   In a previous letter Queneau had declared of Camus's novel: *'Je trouve que c'est un acte d'orgueil. Je ne suis pas assez dur pour dire: an acte de vanité.'* ('I see it as an act of pride. I'm not quite harsh enough to say: an act of vanity.')

3   Love is realised through being, not through the idea of being.

To Raymond Queneau.

Newnham College, Cambridge
6 November 1947

Thank you, most dear R, for your letter. I'm very sorry your bad luck continues – I hope by now the tide's turned – that you're not upset about your father, that your son is better.

As for symbolic logic, I wish you were here and I in Paris. I don't care for the stuff. As between Wisdom's young men (linguistic analysts) and Russell's young men (symbolic logicians) (the two factions in our School) I prefer the former, who tend to have more imagination. Truth is, I can't do symbolic logic and probably don't know what it is.

I haven't seen much of Mme Magny in the last week (I've been in London and very busy when in Cambridge) but I shall seek her out at the weekend. I much admire her erudition, enjoy talking to her, but have got no sort of clear impression of her as a person yet.

My own orientation? I become schizophrenic, trying to understand the later Wittgenstein and logically tame the 'I-Thou' at the same time. The Wittgenstein stuff digs very deep indeed I begin to see. I wish I could send you some, but there's a limited number of typescript copies, and one has to have the Master's personal permission etc. etc. All rather esoteric and emotional. But the stuff itself is miles away from crude logical positivism. I don't know why you should think I am less Marcelian – though I think this is so maybe. I still find the *Journal métaphysique* full of gems, but I'm out of patience with his later writings. I like the old bird himself though – I saw him yesterday in London and we looked at the ducks in St James's Park. I learnt with regret (but no surprise) that he is, if not Gaullist, at least 'Gaullisant'. In the evening he gave a talk on his plays, which was received with enthusiasm but not much comprehension. (I gave two lectures earlier in the same series on Sartre. Spurious, as all 'popular philosophy' is.) Afterwards we had a sort of party in his honour, attended by various bourgeois, ecclesiastical, reactionary and learned notables. Conversation turned on Camus' *La peste* which everyone, including Marcel, found admirable. I pondered your words and wondered what I really thought and why. What is it (so beautifully) that's been said that can't be said? Can't liberalism have its saints? Apparently not.

Much political and religious tension (in me I mean) at the moment. A feeling of dishonesty and divided loyalties. I expect I shall have to become a Christian sooner or later. All my thought drives in that direction. Ecclesia Anglicana though, not Romana. Another compromise. [. . .]

Since you ask, yes I suppose I am (almost) happy. The first time in years.

I love my work and I like the community I belong to. No, I'm not in love, thank God. *Amoureuse/heureuse*[1] are contradictions in my universe of discourse.

I'd like to talk to you this evening. This letter feels a bit off the mark. Not quite what I want to say. There are better things, honester, deeper maybe, that don't get said. (Mirage, Wittgenstein would say.)

I hope all goes well again and that you're not deeply distressed by any of your difficulties.

I miss you often. Let me know if I can help you e.g. in the book line, or any other line. With sincere expressions of solidarity, and, my dear, with all my love –

I

To Raymond Queneau.

Newnham College
15 November 1947

[. . .] Wittgenstein *alas* is leaving Cambridge on Tuesday forever; leaving two or three honest and reliable disciples, and lots of unreliable imitators. My own master, John Wisdom, is a Wittgensteinian, how reliable I'm not sure, less good (but then so is everyone) but with lots of imagination. He's a somewhat fantastic personage whom I've come to like a lot – a mixture of the magician and the great clown. I wish you could meet him – you would appreciate him I think (and he you!). His French is very bad I fear – which is not surprising as he reads no books in any tongue. (No Cambridge philosopher reads.) 'You can't learn philosophy as you learn chemistry – you learn it as you learn to play tennis' – dictum of John Wisdom. And clearly one doesn't learn tennis out of a book. (An excellent principle up to a point.) He did struggle through a bit of the *Journal métaphysique* apropos of some point I tried to make, and absolutely hated it. (And I can well imagine why!)

I'm writing this letter lying down, which may explain why the lines don't go straight. I am very tired after spending the entire day checking (at publisher's request) a translation by some person unknown of Paul Foulquié's[2] little book *L'existentialisme* – a work which didn't inspire me with anything but a distaste for Louis Lavelle,[3] whom the author seems to admire. (Though I

1 In love/happy.
2 Jesuit philosopher.
3 Prominent French philosopher.

know one can't judge a philosopher from quotes even chosen by admirers.)
Is Lavelle a great institution in French philosophy?

Anyway I feel a bit weary of existentialismus and even wish I could do
some symbolic logic for a change. No, I'm not acquainted with the Instituto
Galois, or 'T. C. Mitts'.[1] (What mysterious names!) I doubt if I know enough
mathematics really to appreciate wit on that subject. (Alas, indeed! Claude-
Edmonde [Magny] tells me I was never properly taught it, which I'm sure
is true. It's not well taught in this country.)

The other day I reread some notes I made in 1945 on Sartre's *L'imaginaire*,[2]
and it struck me what a fascinating and brilliant book that was. Is there
anything like a 'school' of 'phenomenological psychologists' – or was Sartre's
essay just a lovely flash?

I could go on for pages talking to you (whereas there are lots of worthy
people to whom I've owed letters for weeks, and I put off writing to them
with perfect *mauvaise foi*[3] because I tell myself I haven't time!), there's a lot
more I want to say. But on second thoughts perhaps I'll stop and go to bed.

Political news as gloomy as ever (I'm amazed by the way how *un*political
most of the undergraduates I've met here are. Indifferent or *plutôt*[4] Tory).

Au revoir then, dearest Raymond, and *thank you*. Tell me though, who is
this Jeanson?[5] (Piaget[6] I know by repute.)

My dear, as always, most affectionately, most faithfully –
your
I

*To Raymond Queneau, sent during the Christmas vacation from Murdoch's parents'
home in Chiswick.*

4 Eastbourne Road
2 January 1948

1 Instituto Galois: a college specialising in mathematics in Oaxaca, Mexico; *The Education of T. C. Mitts*,
   a witty book about mathematical thinking in which Lillian Rosanoff Lieber tried to convey the idea
   that mathematics can be understood by anyone. Queneau was very interested in mathematics; one
   of the main characters in his novel *Odile* is a mathematics student.
2 Sartre published *L'imaginaire: psychologie phénoménologique de l'imagination* in 1940. It was later translated
   into English as *The Imaginary: A Phenomenological Psychology of the Imagination*.
3 Bad faith, an existential concept used by Sartre and de Beauvoir to describe the situation when someone
   under pressure from social forces adopts false values and forfeits his or her innate freedom to act
   authentically.
4 Rather.
5 Presumably Henri Jeanson, French writer and journalist.
6 Jean Piaget, French child psychologist.

Thank you *very* much for your letter and for the magnificent edition of *Bouvard et Pécuchet*,[1] received with much joy! I've never read that work, but I shall now easily be persuaded by your introduction to do so. Much thanks!

London has been just impossible this vacation. Feverish. I've seen dozens and dozens of people without much pleasure (Why does one?) – and only a couple of days ago settled down to some work: the writing of a paper on psychology and metaphysics for a group of psychologists. These latter are I suspect pretty bogus and so is my paper I suspect too. What anguish it is really to *think*. I do almost anything to avoid it.

What news and impressions of your political situation? Were you persuaded to make any moves? Do these things in any way persuade you towards an '*engagement*'?[2]

Oh damn it, I wish I could talk with you now and then. Are space and time really necessary? For instance at Cambridge the two people I like best are an Arab and an Indian.[3] What's the use of making friends with people domiciled some 1,000 miles away? It seems ridiculous enough that I see you only once a year. Mortality one might accept more easily than these absurd separations.

Further news: that I have become a Christian (of the English Church). I am most glad of this move, which I should have made long ago. I can't 'explain' it nor expect it to be 'understood'. Only be patient with me a little –!

I'll write again soon. (I go back to Cambridge on the 13th.)

A very happy New Year to you. Thank you extremely for the book.

I think of you very often and love you always.

Most faithfully

Your

I

To Raymond Queneau.

Newnham College
11 February 1948

I was very glad to get (*enfin*) your letter. I had been trying to think of devices to make you write (since writing you letters didn't seem to work) and all I could think of was to send you a copy of Wittgenstein's *Tractatus*. This work

1 A satirical and unfinished novel by Gustave Flaubert (1821–80), published posthumously. Queneau had written the introduction for the edition published in 1947.
2 An author *engagé* is a politically committed writer.
3 Wasfi Hijab, a Palestinian postgraduate, and Kanti Shah, from south India – both research students at Cambridge with whom Murdoch frequently discussed Wittgenstein's work.

(if it's still in print in the London shop I ordered it from) you'll shortly receive, and if you already possess a copy you can give it away to the deserving poor. In future if you don't write to me you shall receive: Broad, *Mind and its Place in Nature*; Moore, *Principia ethica*; Russell, *Our Knowledge of the External World*, and other works by Cambridge philosophers of increasing degrees of boringness.

Wittgenstein, actually, doesn't enter this series since (of course) he's not boring. I am more and more astonished at the *Tractatus* (of which I understand only parts). This, and everything he writes, has a terribly disturbing transparent quality. It seems to manage in some purely *intellectual* way to be great prose. I was much struck by a remark of his that someone quoted to me lately, about the book he's writing now. He said: 'This stuff is no good. If this was *philosophy* one could learn it by heart.'

I wasn't surprised at your reactions to my Christianising move. I can't offer any explanations or justifications – and indeed I can imagine well how you see the thing. (Vide Kierkegaard on this situation, and on the importance of the 'secret' categories.[1]) ('*Quelle nervosité.*'[2]) I see it so myself in a way and probably feel as antireligious and anticlerical as you do. Indeed I'm not unmoved by the disgust of my friends (and many of my English friends have been much more violent on the subject than you) which I suppose shows I still have doubts (of course, hosts of them). But there it is. There are times when one must move, even in the dark. And to explain is impossible. 'Whereof one cannot speak, thereof one must be silent.' *Tractatus* p. 189.

I'm *delighted* to hear you are going on with *Gueule de Pierre*[3] – I long to see what you'll make of that. (Though I can't grasp your title – it has the same odd look as some chapter headings of Kierkegaard: 'Dread as Original Sin Progressively' etc.[4])

I think your telepathy experiments are most significant; you certainly have the right principle for producing positive results. (I see Trinity College here are advertising a studentship in psychical research, which shows how obscurantist our old universities are becoming. Any moment now Oxford may be recognising psychology as a science.)

I hope to bring my parents to France in the summer – one of the many advantages of this plan being that they will probably then pay my expenses, as I shall by then have no money whatsoever.

---

1 Possibly a reference to Kierkegaard's belief that God comes to each individual mysteriously and to his late work in which he attacks the State and the Church for lulling people into a false sense of Christianity.
2 Such anxiety.
3 Queneau's envisaged second sequel (the first sequel having been *Les temps mêlés*) to his earlier book of the same title; the word '*gueule*' is slang for 'mouth' so the title could be translated as *Pierre's Gob*.
4 The title of Chapter 2 in Kierkegaard's *Begrebet Angest* (1844).

I miss you dreadfully (a ridiculous statement. How can you miss what you've never had?) – as I say, I miss you dreadfully, think of you very often, and send you, as always, dear Raymond, my love –

I

To Philippa Foot.

4 Eastbourne Road
18 March 1948

Darling, I'm *so* glad you're coming to London! Yes, please, see you both days if you can. I already owe you £1 by the way, and I mustn't borrow more, and of course you can't start paying my fares! I'll rustle up some money from somewhere and come to Oxford after Easter. Sorry, I meant to tell you I'd been shanghaied into opening an account at Parkers[1] and had given you as a reference! I'm glad you told them my *intentions* would be good!

About GEN,[2] yes, I think I like this word. It's much a matter of habit. I've used it so much, it seems like an ordinary English word to me now – and I think it does play a certain convenient role. I prefer it to 'the dope', or 'the low-down' which are the only alternatives which spring to mind, and which I shall have to use henceforth when writing to you! (I'm surprised at this purism from you!) [. . .]

I hope you are well out of your Melancholy – I'm sure you need rest. Don't talk of giving up philosophy! If you gave it up completely for say three weeks (and you can do that in the summer) that would surely do the trick. I know how sick one can get – I hope you have less teaching next term. Take it gently, old sweetheart – carry on with Nothing if possible. (Not meaning *néant*[3] of course which is a *serious* matter, but just old-fashioned Nothing.) I do long to see you. Let me know about time on the 31st. I'm quite free either day and will fit in with your moves.

Meanwhile, please rest – so much love, darling, as always and always,
From
I

1 Bookshop in Oxford.
2 American slang for 'general information'.
3 'Nothingness' as in Sartre's *L'être et le néant*.

To Raymond Queneau.

4 Eastbourne Road, W4
31 March 1948

Dear Raymond, thank you very much for your letter of sometime ago which I've *thought* but not written several answers to! – and also for Hippolyte on Hegel which has just come.¹ This looks most interesting and will make a good foil to Kojève² (quite a different kettle of fish I imagine). Many thanks!

At the moment actually I am in bed with some nameless illness (psychological I expect) and not in any frame of mind to be introduced to Hegel ('Thank you, this gentleman and I have met before') and generally feeling that I shall never think again. But I know from experience that this state soon passes. Till yesterday I was reading with admiration and confused disagreements Merleau-Ponty's admirable *Phénoménologie.*³ Today, thank heavens, someone has lent me *Le chiendent*⁴ so I shall read that instead.

I was very pleased to have your news of *Gueule de Pierre*. I very much look forward to seeing this, like an astronomer waiting for a new planet. I'm glad you are rewriting the other two a bit – particularly *Temps mêlés*. *G. de P. I* was such an imaginative explosion – I wonder much how you will bind them together and enlarge your universe – and finish the story!

Oh dear! I would so much rather have written *Gueule de Pierre* than have written the *Tractatus*! I wish the spirits of metaphysics didn't demand *so much* of one's blood before they speak.

(Which reminds me by the way I hope you received the two Neurath⁵ books, sent off soon after the *Tractatus*.)

I am working on Alexandre's⁶ play and find it a very pleasant task. I find it deeply disturbing and moving, though obscure and almost over-weighted with a sort of poetry. Having decided it's not either Zionist or anti-Christian

1 *Genèse et structure de la phénoménologie de l'esprit de Hegel* by Jean Hippolyte, French philosopher who translated and championed the work of Hegel in France.
2 Alexandre Kojève, who introduced Hegel into twentieth-century French philosophy and influenced the many leading French intellectuals who attended his lecture series entitled 'The Phenomenology of Spirit' in Paris in the 1930s. Queneau was the editor of Kojève's *Introduction à la lecture de Hegel*, the published version of these lectures, a copy of which he had sent to Murdoch in September 1947.
3 *Phénoménologie de la perception* by Maurice Merleau-Ponty, French phenomenological philosopher, strongly influenced by Husserl and Heidegger, whose work focused on the vital role perception plays in understanding the world.
4 A novel by Queneau.
5 Otto Neurath, Austrian philosopher of science and a political economist. Since he was so prolific, it is difficult to know which works are being referred to here.
6 Maxime Alexandre, French surrealist writer, whom Murdoch had met through Queneau in Innsbruck in February 1946.

I'm still not sure *to whom* it speaks. (Well, it speaks to me.) It's anti-Pharisee – I wish there were some position where one could be against *all* Pharisees – so often one finds oneself with some against the others –

I'm glad you've met Dotremont.[1] What do you think of this nice enthusiast?

I'd give a lot for a quiet talk with you sometime tomorrow in some café not too far from the Seine. How horribly time and space interfere with one's friendships.

Best of luck to *G. de P.* much love to you, Raymond

from

I

To Philippa Foot, who had sent Murdoch the advertisement for a 'Tutor to teach Philosophy' at St Anne's from the Oxford University Gazette *on 21 April 1948.*

Newnham College

[24 April 1948]

My dear, thanks so much for the further St Anne's details. I feel very sick at the idea of competing with Mary [Scrutton]. But I think I shall apply all the same. She is much more likely to get it – has teaching experience, is a Latinist etc. – so I shall try not to think too much about the job. But I find myself wanting it very much indeed. (Another reason why I shan't get it, is that I was once secretary to an UNRRA committee of which Miss Plumer[2] was chairman – and this tried both our tempers!) If you or Michael are writing to Donald [MacKinnon], please thank him very much for sending me the testimonial. But tell him that as St Anne's say 'Don't send formal testimonials' I *shan't* send it to them, but will just mention his name as a reference – and they'll presumably write to him direct. And give D *all my love.*

At the moment actually I am quite drunk with someone else's joy – the delight of one José Jančar, Slovene 'head boy' at the camp at Graz,[3] who has just come to England on the Ministry of Labour scheme. His wife, labelled fiancée, is coming separately! (Married couples not being eligible!) After many years of the camp, and more lately having TB and then being put in prison, Jančar (who arrived in England on Thursday!) feels this is the start of the new life. He suddenly walked into my room yesterday – and I've never seen anyone so completely intoxicated with happiness and freedom

1 Christian Dotremont, Belgian poet and energetic cultural figure who was influenced by late 1930s Belgian surrealism.

2 Eleanor Plumer, principal of St Anne's between 1940 and 1953.

3 The UNRRA camp for displaced persons in south-east Austria where Murdoch had worked in 1946.

and hope! Thank God for such people. He's a fine chap – you must meet him. (Medical student. He hopes to get some humble job in a hospital, and finish his studies later.)

My other concern is cooking meals for Shah and Hijab, who think this is a good way of saving money! (They hope I will learn quickly!) Shah being a vegetarian, this poses many moral problems, such as should I mix the meat fat with the vegetable fat, or keep them scrupulously separate? Such things are much more important than philosophy.

Very much love, old darling

From I

To Hal Lidderdale, now working for the British Council in Afghanistan.

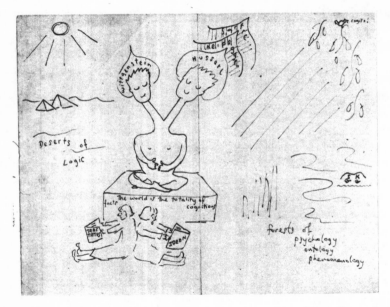

Newnham College
[late spring 1948]

So glad to get your letter (late and at last, like Odysseus coming to the surface). I have been wondering how you had been getting on with the excitable Arab world. I hope it has calmed down since you wrote? Take care of yourself. And, oh, get yourself to Europe soon!

Not that the outlook is so hot in Europe. I feel sick and confused, reading the paper lately.[1] But determined not to be flurried into any simplistic anti-Soviet attitudes. Most people here *are* though. Everything's topsy-turvy –

I loved your letter. I hope Eng. Lit. goes well. Does all this amuse you? It seems to. But oh, get soon to a country you can love –

Philosophically speaking, fertile confusions are developing. I recently realised with a shock that Wittgenstein's *Tractatus* and Husserl's *Ideen*[2] are trying to do much the same thing, though in different ways. My schizophrenia now takes a new and more hopeful form. Sartre, I gather, has no time to write his great book on morals, and has delegated it to Simone de Beauvoir, who has bungled it thoroughly (so I'm told) under the title of *Une morale de l'ambiguité*.[3] Heigh ho. The rapprochement effected via Husserl is only by courtesy (so far) extended to Heidegger and Sartre. (*Sein und Zeit* will be published here in the summer and after that All will be New.[4]) John Wisdom (petulantly) 'I want to take the excitement out of philosophy.' Sartre remains impenitently exciting. Wisdom on another day: 'Anyway I'd much rather go fox hunting than do philosophy.'

Gabriel Marcel, lately in England (I went over to Oxford to hear him speak there) is to give the Gifford Lectures.[5]

That concludes my philosophical gossip column I think. Except that I have been reading (via Elizabeth Anscombe[6]) part of Wittgenstein's new book (in German) and it is like nothing on sea or land. Except perhaps the 'pointing finger' in Leonardo's pictures. Significant gesture beautifully indicating – what?

When are you coming on leave? Where are you spending your summer? Write soon (better than your last effort please!) and let me have all the news. Love to you, Hal old darling from I

1 Probably refers to the Berlin blockade during which Soviet occupation forces in eastern Germany began a blockade of all rail, road and water communications between Berlin and the West.
2 *Ideen zu einer reinen Phänomenologie und phänomenologischen Philosophie. Erstes Buch: Allgemeine Einführung in die reine Phänomenologie* (1913) was translated into English as *Ideas: General Introduction to Pure Phenomenology*.
3 Simone de Beauvoir's response to Sartre's *Being and Nothingness*, entitled *Pour une morale de l'ambiguité*, was published first in instalments in *Les temps modernes*, then as a book in November 1947.
4 *Being and Time* by Martin Heidegger was published in 1927 but not translated into English until 1962. It was dedicated to Edmund Husserl and deeply influenced twentieth-century philosophy, particularly existentialism, hermeneutics and deconstruction.
5 A series of lectures given in Scotland at one of its major universities and delivered annually by a distinguished scholar.
6 Anscombe was an expert on, and translator of, Wittgenstein's work.

To Philippa Foot, on holiday in Cahors, France during the summer of 1948. Murdoch's application for the post at St Anne's had been successful. This meant a return to Oxford and also a return to some of the previous emotional complications of her life there.

4 Eastbourne Rd
8 July 1948

My dear, thank you so much for your two cards! I am so glad you and Michael are having a lovely time. You so much needed a holiday and lots of sun and wine! Beakers full of the warm south and all that![1]

Here it is cold and raining and I am reading the *Social Contract*[2] and must soon read Tacitus' *Germania*, set book for next year! (Someone railing against the Romans lately said if they had to be damned imperialists they might at least have done the job properly and civilised the Germans!) Not much happening. I work a little and lengthen my skirts.[3] When will you be in England again? Hijab has left for Palestine and Shah goes in a few weeks. I wish they'd left together and one didn't have this twice over. It breaks the heart.

I'll probably go to France in August with the Lidderdales. I shall write a Touching Letter to the Income Tax people! Still not quite sure when.

Dear, I feel so very glad at coming back to Oxford, though frightened too.

Dear heart, I do love you – *ça continue, ça reste, ça me donne de la paix.*[4] Give my love to Michael.

Always, my darling, ever and always,

Yours

I

To Raymond Queneau.

4 Eastbourne Road
20 July 1948

I was so delighted to get the *Saint-Glinglin*[5] which arrived today from Newnham – though so far I haven't had time to read more than the (irresistible

1 'O for a beaker full of the warm South' from Keats's 'Ode to a Nightingale'.
2 *The Social Contract, Or Principles of Political Right* (1762) by Jean-Jacques Rousseau.
3 Dior's 'New Look' for 1948 featured long swirling skirts.
4 This continues, this remains, this gives me peace.
5 A novel published by Queneau in 1948.

d'ailleurs!)[1] remarks on the yellow paper. Thank you, and in general three cheers, I'm very pleased! *Impressions plus tard.*[2]

Yugoslavia, and the world, in short, your goddam country too I see from today's paper, fill me with gloom and confusion.[3] *Que penser, que faire, je n'y comprends rien.*[4]

Yes, yes, I'm pleased about Oxford but displeased (as usual) about other things, apart even from the fairly certain prospect of an early death by atom bomb, such as there being no time to finish my novel about that goddess which has been waiting for so long.[5] At the moment I am reading the basic chaps, Berkeley, Hume, Locke, Descartes, in preparation for becoming a teaching hack next term. Hume *actuellement* whom I enjoy a lot. *Au moins celui là est un homme.*[6] I look forward to seeing 'Philosophes et Voyous'[7] – though the *principium divisionis*[8] is still not clear to me. Is Hume a *philosophe* or a *voyou*?

Oh Raymond, how bloody it is that I never see you. I'm eternally short of real people – and you remain always so real to me. *Mais voilà* – I leave for France on August 9, but go straight to Avignon, and will be returning via Paris toward the end of August. Would you be in Paris then I wonder?

Sorry about the *prix de la vie.*[9] My own (simpler no doubt) finances are now so hopeless after much borrowing that I cease to worry. And now of course I have a Good Job (hell!) in prospect.

There are lots of things I want to say to you, but they can wait and just at this instant I must go. I'll write again. The chief thing to be said is the usual thing, *que je ne vous oublie pas, que vous m'êtes cher, ce que vous savez bien d'ailleurs.*[10] Some rude remarks I want to make about your language (French in general I mean) will be reserved for later. (I heard two *jeunes filles* conversing, *avec beaucoup de franchise*[11] because they thought the natives wouldn't understand, in a Lyons tea shop the other day and was struck by the number of curious formal clichés they used. But I must reflect more on the English equivalents.)

1 By the way.
2 Impressions to follow.
3 Probably refers to the expulsion of Yugoslavia from Cominform (for hostility to the Soviet Union) and to a recent crisis in the government of France.
4 What to think, what to do, I don't understand any of it.
5 *Our Lady of the Bosky Gates* featured a much-travelled character called the Guardian who discovers he can communicate with the statue of a Greek goddess, possibly Aphrodite, which then comes to life. It was never completed.
6 At least he's a real man.
7 'Philosophers and Hoodlums', an article Queneau was writing for the journal *Les temps modernes*.
8 A term used in psychology and philosophy meaning the manner in which a thing is identified as different from other things.
9 Cost of living.
10 That I'm always thinking of you, that you are dear to me, that you know all this anyway.
11 I heard two young women conversing very openly.

I want very much to see you, sometime, somewhere, this summer. Write soon, even if briefly. So glad to have *Saint-Glinglin!* Much love to you, as always, *cher voyou*
 from Iris

To Philippa Foot, who had invited Murdoch – soon to take up her post at St Anne's – to stay with her and her husband Michael at their home, 16 Park Town in Oxford. Murdoch lodged with them for over a year.

4 Eastbourne Rd
20 July 1948

My dear, sorry I didn't write earlier. I hope I catch you now before you go North. I was so glad to hear your voice on the 'phone the other day.

About the flat – thank you so much! I suspect you're grossly undercharging me and I shall have to go the Rent Tribunal about it, but we'll see!

I felt, as you can imagine, some terror about this, but now I feel better about the idea which is from almost every point of view a *wonderful* one. I hope that truly truly in the depths of his heart Michael won't be offended by my presence in the house. Forgive this. If I could be utterly sure of *this* I should be *so happy* about the whole plan. Sorry. I expect I have much more of a 'complex' here than either you or M. And anyway I feel nervous about coming back to Oxford – forgive the nerves. This is rather 'daring' this notion of living with you, and I think perhaps *enfin de compte*[1] it is a good and right daring, I hope so. Thank you anyway so much and so much, both of you.

Hijab has gone back to Palestine, as I think I told you, and Shah goes soon.

Darling, write to me soon. The thought of you, as always, comforts and warms my heart. I love you so much –
 I

PS Dear, you know I want *so much* to come and live chez toi. I shall get over the nerves – in fact they've almost gone already. Just a last fit or two. Be patient with me!
 Very much love
 I

1 After all.

To Philippa Foot.

4 Eastbourne Road
22 July 1948

Dear, thank you so much for the book on Marcel! It's been recommended to me by a number of people (including Marcel!) and I've much wanted to have it. Thank you even more for your lovely letter. I'm sorry I wrote you such a nervy one yesterday. I feel honestly better and better about this matter – it flows away in time – and I feel such *absolute* confidence and trust in you and M. And, yes, I have too that feeling that you so excellently describe! It will be pure joy to be so near to you. Please don't be worried by my letter of yesterday. I must say the thing and be rid of it – I feel less and less fear and more and more joy. [. . .]

May you all have a lovely time in Yorkshire. I'll write again soon. Very much love to you darling
      from I

To Philippa Foot, written just before Murdoch left for a holiday in France.

Chiswick
9 August 1948

My dear, just a note before I go. I'm so very glad you will be seeing Donald. Take care of him – but I know you will. Give him my very best and most faithful love. Tell him I didn't see the abbess when I was at Malling – she was too ill – but I had a very very good stay there. So peaceful and moving that place.[1]

Take care of yourself, sweetheart. What a sick world – oh God –
I'll write again soon –
Very much love
I

1 Murdoch first went to Malling Abbey in Kent to see its abbess, Dame Magdalene Mary Euan-Smith, in October 1946 during a period of personal crisis. (In a letter to Philippa Foot, dated October 1946, she expressed remorse and a sense of responsibility for the fracture of their friendship in 1942.) She visited the Benedictine community and abbey again in August 1948 (the visit referred to here) and in August 1949. Murdoch was to draw on her knowledge of Malling Abbey when writing *The Bell*.

To Raymond Queneau, sent after meeting him in Paris in early September.

London Underground
18 September 1948

Well, I am back in this delightful sober country again, where politicians are fairly honest and there is no inflation and people behave in a quiet and sensible manner. I am not very pleased, but I shall be happy when I have done some work, which will be about next Friday. I am going to Oxford on Wednesday as working in London is impossible, and I want to get settled down. (Address by the way is 16 Park Town, Oxford.) I wonder where you are? I can't find General Post Office in my grammar book, which is a scholarly edition designed for people who want to talk about Dante and Garibaldi and not enquire: Where is the General Post Office, please, I am expecting some letters poste restante. Anyway you will probably have left Venezia by now (how did you like it?) – so I shall address this to *nrf*[1] and hope you get it.

I'm sorry about the state I was in in Paris. I could offer several explanations, but what the hell. You are such an old friend now and such a dear one that I shall expect you to put up with such things from time to time and take it as all in the day's work. I'm sorry though. I felt such despair suddenly at the way one brushes past people in life and never really knows them. That maybe one will pass one's whole life without ever having known this person properly, done that thing, been to that place, written the novel one wanted to write – very mortal I felt all of a sudden in Paris. (The *quartier* St Germain is hard on the nerves anyway, don't you think? I found that chance encounters with people would upset me there in a way I can't remember being upset in since Oxford days.)

I'll probably be in Paris in the spring with my mother, who is Romantic, and has never been to France. I want to show her Paris some day. I shall be very sensible then though. Some fever has been stilled or at least transformed. Since I have been to Rome and have wept on your shoulder nothing will ever be the same again. Have you been to Rome? I hope at any rate you got to Florence.

I must start work, then all will be well. Write to me soon, please, and tell me how you liked Italy. Very much love to you, Raymond –

from

I

1 Having tried unsuccessfully to work out how to send a letter to Queneau while he was in Venice, Murdoch wrote to him at the office of Gallimard, previously known as *Les Éditions de la Nouvelle Revue Française* (nrf).

To Raymond Queneau.

16 Park Town, Oxford
22 October 1948

Oh I was glad to get your letter. I was beginning to think that I'd put you quite out of patience with me by being so tiresome in Paris! I was so glad to hear your voice again.

I hope you are no longer *gâteux* and *abruti?*[1] Such a picture of gloom you paint in your letter, I see you through a green haze, like some absinthe drinker painted by some impressionist. (What a vocabulary, one way and another, I have picked up from you!) May you emerge from the *marasme*,[2] full of joy and penicillin –

Here all goes well – I haven't been found out yet. I've got far too goddamn much to do – teaching Plato, Aristotle, Kant, Descartes, Berkeley, Hume, moral philosophy and some accursed Latin. But I do love the stuff (except the Latin and even that is fun in a quiet pedestrian way) and I enjoy the teaching. It's a perpetual race with time as I have to do all the work I set my pupils to do, being so rusty on much of these chaps. No chance to teach Hegel and Husserl – and as for Sartre! My pupils are beautiful young women with new-look skirts and red fingernails and it seems almost a shame to drag them through the horrors of the Transcendental Deduction.

Altogether, I like being back in this precious enclosed community again, with all its pedantry and its intellectual jokes, yes, yes, I do love this place.

Paris is real to me now, it occurs to me, thinking of it at this moment – and picturing you as you were that day in the rain, wandering so sadly on the Boulevard St Germain – as never before. There's really a part of me in Paris, something of me that I must go there to join. I can *believe* – looking out of my window onto trees and a north Oxford Gregorian facade – that Paris exists!

Don't be sorry about *ce soir là*.[3] My fault altogether. It was indeed that you were *bien renfermé comme une huitre*,[4] but why not – I felt such a desire to come close to you, and at the same time that this couldn't be. I suppose I love you a lot, and somehow I wanted you and needed you that evening. But please believe that I am after all a sensible person! For I am indeed *en fin de compte* so sensible and calm and full of the English virtues!

Heigh ho, I must go now and consider whether Socrates was a utilitarian,

1 Feeling dazed and stupid.
2 Gloom.
3 The other evening.
4 Shut tight like an oyster.

before my pupils start telling me whether he was or not. More news soon.
I do hope you are well again. Dearest Raymond, all my love

I

To Raymond Queneau.

4 Eastbourne Road, Chiswick W4
18 December 1948

Thank you for your nice letter. It made me hear your curious voice very
clearly. [. . .]

I can't think why you should find it *drôle* that I give parties. *Est ce que je
vous semble un individu tellement mélancolique?*[1] Teaching philosophy, yes maybe
that is *drôle*. I find it odd myself sometimes, as if it were all a great deception
and I should be unmasked any moment. I enjoy Oxford, I enjoy teaching, I
adore philosophy, but somehow the whole ambiance gets me down because
it is so *intellectual.* I am not an intellectual and I don't think I like intellectuals.
(En masse anyway.) I find myself feeling much solider, slower, warmer, more
imaginative and less *spirituelle* than most of the people around me. Not that
I don't get on delightfully with them. But I am not good at the sort of talk
which is a facade and not communication. And yet to speak more directly
can seem like a dull foolishness or sheer seduction.

I am rather in revolt at the moment, end-of-term weariness and so on.
Imagining my life will begin when I chuck philosophy and just write novels and
poetry. Philosophy takes all my life blood at present, and I'm not brilliant at it.
(I am intensely involved with Wittgenstein's stuff just now, which isn't my natural
line – 'naturally' I should spend ten years or so thinking about Hegel.)

Did I say to you how much pleasure your poems gave me, the ones you
sent just lately?[2] I don't read much poetry now except Rilke and Shakespeare's
sonnets and some Yeats, always reading the same poems – and your stuff,
when put under my nose, I took with great delight. (I've written some poetry
again lately myself, the first for some years. Lousy of course. But I feel full
of vague power at the moment.) Yes, I sometimes see *Temps modernes* about
the place and shall watch out for your work, good.

Much tempted, yes, to come to Paris (a permanent state) and shall come
in spring or summer, *plutôt pour voir mes amis.*[3] (I must *work* this summer.
Leap the gap from prehistory into history.) My novel is where it was a year

1 Do I strike you as such a melancholy person?
2 Queneau's collection *L'instant fatal.*
3 Mainly to see my friends.

ago; I daren't even think about it, it has such a siren voice. (What one wants is a *rich patron*, sorry Gallimard aren't much good in that role.)

I'm very sorry you've been (and are?) ill – this can be so damn depressing. May you get better and stay well. (I should think Paris must be a killing place to live in, even if you *don't* go to parties. Take it gently.) Don't let beastly Gallimard overwork you.

Paris, yes – am reading Rilke's *Malte Laurids Brigge* – an odd scattered work though it has good things in it – other people's 'dream Parises' are always touching – Miller's, James's. Reading it in French which is maybe a pity, it sounds so like Camus or something, oddly up-to-date.

Dear Raymond, I must close this letter. I wish you all that's good for Christmas and the New Year. May all go truly well with you. As ever and always,

    love to you
    from
    I

To Raymond Queneau.

4 Eastbourne Rd
18 March 1949

Back at Chiswick (term over thank heavens) have been reading Fisson's *Voyage aux horizons.*[1] Can't think why it was advertised as 'not literature' *pointe de vue du style*[2] anyway it seems to me pure post-Hemingway literature. It's rather rambling and formless though, so perhaps that's what was meant. (I've only read half of it.) Don't care for it much so far – there's a sort of smell of unreflective human comradeship that comes out of it which is vaguely pleasant. But I think I shall forget all these people very rapidly. It's politically zeitgeistically interesting in a way I suppose. Have you read it? (Perhaps you gave it the Prix Goncourt?) What do you think? Maybe I'm becoming incapable of reading novels.

Have got hold of *Sein und Zeit* at last and it lies in my room like an unexploded bomb.[3] Hope my German will make it. Best way to learn a language is to assume you know it and start reading – this has worked before with German, but never with *this* sort.

---

1 A novel by Pierre Fisson.
2 As far as the style is concerned.
3 Gilbert Ryle, philosophy professor at Magdalen College, Oxford – whose behaviourist viewpoint Murdoch would attack in *Sartre: Romantic Rationalist* – had lent her his copy of *Sein und Zeit*. She liked the man, if not his philosophy.

I *may* be in Paris for a few days, end of March or beginning of April with my parents. I hope you'll be around and we have time to take a glass (no vodka). But we may not come, I don't know. Love to you from

I

To Raymond Queneau, written after Murdoch had moved out of the Foots' home and into a flat nearby.

58 Park Town, Oxford
16 October 1949

Today, a state of depression, *à cause de*:

1. *la mort inattendue de Mathieu.*[1] He made a good end, could hardly have been better – but I shall miss him, and there are other characters that seemed mainly interesting *en fonction de lui. Je ne me passione plus tellement que ça pour Bovis et Ivich.* Though I begin to know all the moves very well –
2. I never met your son when he was in England (I presume he must have returned to Paris by now?). My own fault, I should have got hold of his address and organised something earlier in the summer, only I was so immersed in my own affairs. No excuse.
3. I can't (at the moment) do philosophy. I ought soon to start writing a thesis. This shall be on *Meaning*. But I find that I can't think. It's like turning a billiard ball in one's hands and trying to tear it open. I can't get started.
4. You haven't written to me for so long that I begin to suspect that you are offended.
5. La solitude.

X X X

The picture of Brunet[2] is fascinating. Sartre's sort of political self-consciousness is impressive – and no doubt enrages the Marxists. As does Merleau-Ponty's I expect. When next in Paris I should like to meet M-P (if he is human) and also Simone de Beauvoir.

I hope you flourish.

Je suis toujours fidèlement et affectueusement votre amie.[3]

I

1 The unexpected death of Mathieu Delarue in *La mort dans l'âme*, the third novel in Sartre's sequence *Les chemins de la liberté*. Murdoch adds here that she does not feel so strongly about two other characters, Bovis and Ivich.
2 A Communist in Sartre's novel.
3 Always your faithful and affectionate friend.

To Raymond Queneau.

St Anne's Society
Oxford
[29 October 1949]

I know you are very busy but may I nevertheless point out that I haven't had a letter from you since (I think) July. I know too that I didn't write for a long time, but I am hoping that you are not cross with me. *Vous ne m'en voulez pas?*[1]

---

1 Have you had enough of me?

I am doing quite a lot of work too – apart from teaching, I mean, which doesn't count. I hope to get this thesis organised soon. Something on *meaning*, based chez Hegel, bringing in Sartre, refuting Ryle. (Ryle is the reigning professor here. His book on Mind,[1] just published, summarises the post-Wittgensteinian empiricism which *is* British philosophy at present. I'll send you a copy.) [. . .]

What's doing in Paris about peace? I suppose the PC[2] is organising conferences and so on. But does it extend beyond Communist circles? (Does Sartre lend himself to any such organisation?) Here, regrettably, peace is regarded as a Communist racket. Everyone seems to be becoming madder and madder.

Write to me soon, dear Queneau. Ever affectionately yours

I

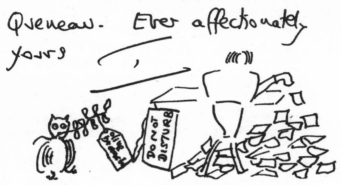

To Philippa Foot.

58 Park Town, Oxford
[autumn 1949]

Dear darling lunatic, how could you possibly lose me? We are part of each other. Forgive my not writing. Could I come and take a drink off you on Thursday of this week, 5.30 onward? Also, could you dine with me in St Anne's on Dec 1st? I think we should fix some *regular* time for meeting. I know I'm an unsatisfactory being at present to you, myself, and generally. I require your love, and send mine. My dear, no question of getting lost.

I

1 *The Concept of Mind.*
2 Le Parti Communiste Français (PCF).

To Raymond Queneau.

58 Park Town, Oxford
17 November 1949

Thank you for your very nice letter, received with much pleasure. I'm so sorry I made a fuss. Here, all goes along. I am reading at intervals *Le deux-ième sexe*, Vol. II (I'm afraid I skipped Vol. I and went straight on to the exciting part!). I think I am the only person in Oxford to have heard of this work (*j'exagère bien entendu*[1]) though there are various *personages paresseux*[2] who ask me whenever we meet to retail to them the latest of what it contains. I think it's splendid – tough, and I like the fierce warlike manner. Here one connects feminism with dear old suffragette types. This is a new voice. I feel some stuffy academic scruples about the sweep of her argument (but damn it on the whole I think this is fine). It's one-sided and tends to crudeness, I thought, at points about religion (my chief objection to date). Can any 'phenomenological description' not be *coloured* in one way or another? Anyhow the prejudices are clear and to that extent harmless. [. . .]

Have you finished the *Cosmogonie?*[3] I'll watch out for the later instalments here, where *Les temps modernes* is *trouvable*. Are you thinking of another novel??

More news from me soon. I shan't be in Paris before the spring alas. With much love to you, dear Queneau, as always

I

To Raymond Queneau, on his return from a month spent in America.

58 Park Town, Oxford
19 February 1950

Well, are you back now, full of *souvenirs de voyage*? Did you write your 'musical' successfully? What will its fate be? Write to me soon. Lucky people who go on joy rides to the USA ought to write long letters to sad humdrum people who have to stay home doing the same old job. So write and tell me all. I hope the slang came up to expectations. (I like your style in English. You don't write 100% accurately, but it's very nice.) Here, there is mainly the general election. I am doing a little work for the Labour Party. It will

1 I exaggerate of course.
2 Lazy individuals.
3 Queneau had been working on a volume of poems, *Petite cosmogonie portative*.

be a disaster if we don't get in, and I fear we may well not. (To think that the country's fate depends on a million or so silly asses who can't make up their minds –)

Also, I am giving two broadcasts (BBC 3rd programme) in the near future on Sartre, de Beauvoir, Camus, as novelists, with some talk about Hegel thrown in. All rather Merleau-Pontyesque. I'll send you the scripts when I get copies from the BBC.

I would like to see you and talk to you. Write soon, anyway.

Much love from

I

To Raymond Queneau.

4 Eastbourne Rd
16 March 1950

Cher Queneau,

I was glad to get your letter. I was beginning to worry about you, thinking about air crashes and so on. I'd like to see some of your *chansons* sometime. Don't forget.

I shan't be in Paris before June I fear, but then, *dame oui*.[1] Yes, do *communiquer* the two reviews to Merleau-Ponty. I hope he'll be around in the summer.

At present I'm in London, plunged in gloom and indecision. (*Quand même y a le printemps*).[2] Work is rather at a standstill, and success *relatif* is dust and ashes as usual. I think nothing is really worth anything except (a) being happily married, (b) being a saint, (c) writing a good novel. My chances of (a) diminish yearly, (b) is far too difficult – there remains (c) which still inspires hope. I shall abandon my archaic goddess, and try to get started on something else now and in the summer. Kant and Hegel can look after themselves for a while.

I'll look out for the Monica Baldwin you mention.[3] I've just discovered Joyce Carey – do you know his stuff? I like it, though not utterly. Am reading Conrad again now. More words soon.

Love, *comme toujours*

I

1 Definitely yes.
2 Even though it's spring.
3 *I Leap Over The Wall: A Return to the World after Twenty-eight Years in a Convent* by Monica Baldwin, who had lived in an enclosed Order.

To Raymond Queneau.

St Anne's Society, Oxford
31 May 1950

Très cher Queneau,
Forgive me for not having written for so long. (Though indeed, I think it is, strictly, *you* who owe me a letter.)
Life has been saddening and complex, as usual, though more so. I wish I could leave soon for France, but don't know when I can get away.
Did I exclaim to you how much I enjoyed your American *reportages*? The America I would have set off in search of, if it hadn't been for the State Department.
I've contracted (did I tell you?) to write a book (a very short one) on Sartre, Camus and de Beauvoir as novelists.[1] Relating them to Hegel etc. etc. Now it seems sad to write this before having seen the last volume of *Les chemins de la liberté*. (I'm supposed to produce it by January.) Have you any news of *La dernière chance*?[2] Has it appeared, or will it appear, in *Les temps modernes*? Has it been abandoned, put off, or is it likely to be published soon? I'd be glad of any news. [. . .]
I am mucking around with literary criticism at present – Richards and Leavis[3] etc. – principles of. Pure being and the synthetic a priori are getting on without me.
Au revoir alors. Je vous aime.
Toujours
I

To Raymond Queneau.

St Anne's Society, Oxford
6 June 1950

Thank you for your nice letter which crossed with mine. (Telepathy no doubt.) (Your mind is a country which I find very agreeable.) I'm delighted that you plan to come to London in the autumn. (Though I *note* that you

1 Murdoch had just signed a contract with Bowes & Bowes to write a book on the French existentialists. Although this book was never completed, the section on Sartre fed into *Sartre: Romantic Rationalist*, published in 1953.
2 The planned fourth but unfinished novel in Sartre's *Les chemins de la liberté*.
3 I. A. Richards and F. R. Leavis, influential literary critics.

are prepared to do to please Lehmann[1] what you wouldn't do to please me.) Glad too, very, that *Pierrot* will come out. I feared Maclaren Ross[2] might bury the thing. (I don't know this type, though I've often seen him in the Wheatsheaf playing a self-invented gambling game called 'spoof' whereby he rooks newcomers to pay for his drinks.)

I'm very depressed at present. I must lose someone that I'm attached to, as I can't bring myself to marry him.[3] We are simply tearing each other up.

I'm glad you want to write a novel. For Christ sake write it and don't let these bastards from the theatre and the cinema distract you any more. (I shall much hope to see your ballet in Paris, *quand même*.[4])

I'll write properly when I feel saner. You know how one's thoughts can be a pack of wolves.

I want to see you, *cher* Raymond, very very much indeed. Love to you from your faithful

I

To Hal Lidderdale, now working for the British Council in Athens.

4 Eastbourne Road
[July 1950]

My dear old thing, thank you for your letter – I was very glad to see (*enfin!*) your writing. I'm very pleased at the prospect of retaining you in England for a while – though I'm sorry about the job hunt angle.[5] Such hell it is. But the sabbatical idea is, I'm sure the right one. The thing is to relax and not fret about worldly things but just let the wings open and be oneself quietly for a bit. This never fails to renew strength. In the end, you ought to write. [. . .]

It'll be good to see you in August – I'll be in England at the Edinburgh Festival time, I think, but fear that Cash and Time considerations may keep me in the South. (I'm going to France end of July, early August, I expect.) I'll check on the time of your return – or write it to me, better still! I'm much wanting to see you, have lots to talk of.

---

1 John Lehmann, the publisher who had rejected Murdoch's translation of *Pierrot mon ami*.
2 Julian Maclaren Ross, whom Lehmann had commissioned to translate *Pierrot mon ami* instead of Murdoch.
3 Wallace Robson, fellow of Lincoln College, Oxford.
4 Even so.
5 There was a possibility that the British Council office in Athens might close, perhaps because of the unstable political situation in the city at this time.

I saw Geoffrey[1] and Lucile yesterday. G hasn't quite landed his LSE job yet,[2] but all omens are good. Meanwhile they are thinking of buying an enormous Georgian house near Caterham with 200 rose bushes, tennis court and millionaire's bathroom.

You are gloomy about politics – so am I, my God. And idle and helpless too. The search for *le vrai Marxisme* still goes on. I hope you are well, though, and full of strength, if not of joy. Dear Hal, *à bientôt. Je pense à toi, et je t'embrasse tendrement.*[3]

To Raymond Queneau, in which Murdoch refers to their having met in Paris in August.

Chez St Anne's Society, Oxford
30 October 1950

Raymond dear, how lovely – how very very nice to get those books from you. The mere sight of their covers makes me feel that *all is not lost.* (The sight of their author would make me feel this even more, but I begin to fear that he is still determined not to move beyond Neuilly.[4]) The stoical super-scription fits my present mood, which is a disposition to practise gritting the teeth in the face of almost inevitable failure.

It's bloody cold in Oxford and the yellow leaves are still falling down very very slowly. (If you delay much longer you'll miss the best of autumn here.) And I am trying to write a paper on the concept of 'consciousness' – is it any use. (Moore says that consciousness though diaphanous can be detected. What a shocking remark from a Cambridge philosopher.) I can't really think though as my head is full of cotton wool. I wish I had a mind like yours. I love and covet your mind like I never have anyone's.

What about another novel? Do write another soon. (I've met one or two fans of *Pierrot* here recently. A great bond.) Yes, I am very sad I didn't see more of you in Paris (not a reproach) – you do give me a sense of life. I love you a lot, and not as abstractly as the innumerable barriers between us (*La Manche, le langage* etc.) might lead one to expect.

Tell me if you do decide for *direction Londres.* Take care of yourself.

1 Geoffrey de Ste Croix, formerly a solicitor, studied ancient history at University College London after serving with the RAF during the war and became a historian of the classical era. Lucile was his wife. Murdoch later taught their daughter, Carolyn, at St Anne's College.
2 He was awarded the post and taught at the London School of Economics between 1950 and 1953, after which he became a fellow of New College, Oxford.
3 See you soon. I'm thinking of you, and kiss you tenderly.
4 A wealthy suburb of Paris, where Queneau lived.

More news soon from me, and maybe reactions to *Bâtons, chiffres et lettres*[1]
– always
   I

*To Michael Oakeshott, Professor of Political Science at the London School of
Economics. He and Murdoch had started a brief affair in October. Having previously
taught for a year at Nuffield College, Oakeshott still had a flat in Rose Place, St
Aldate's, Oxford, to which he had given her a key. He ended the affair in December
1950.*

Telegram dated 5 December 1950 to OAKESHOTT 20 ROSE PLACE ST
ALDATES
(FROM OXFORD)
SORRY DEAR KEY ADDRESSED YOU IN BAG STOLEN FROM ME THIS
EVENING BEWARE THIEVES
   IRIS

To Michael Oakeshott.

4 Eastbourne Road
[December 1950]

I'm so sorry about the key. One of my bags was pinched from the side door
of Musgrave House while I was putting my bicycle away – and it contained
your key in an envelope addressed to Rose Place. (It also contained the key
of my flat, labelled with the address!) I went back and left the light on;
Philippa will get the lock changed. (Fortunately I'd left a duplicate key with
her.) Maybe you'd better get the lock changed too, for your future tenant's
benefit. And meanwhile you could put down the catch on the door and use
the padlocked gate. (Thief isn't likely to be a professional burglar but he
might be!) Very sorry indeed to create all this annoyance.

I caught the 8.30 train last night and got stuck an hour at Didcot which
makes one despair at the best of times. *Don't* worry about me. I have lots
of work to do and I'll plunge into it at once. I miss you with a terrible agony,
and sense of utter loss and defeat. But I'll work hard and the pain will
decrease. Take care of yourself and don't be alone at Rose Place. [. . .]

I'm *very glad* to have known and loved you. It is *good* to love like this.
You'll be in my heart always and if ever at any time you should need me

---

1 A collection of essays by Queneau.

you know that I'll do anything or be anything for you. You've promised to remember this. Now don't be distressed about me!

Much much love to you, dearest one,

I

To *Michael Oakeshott.*

St Anne's Society, Oxford
18 January [1951]

Michael dear, this is just to send you back the Rose Place key – my bag turned up again, abandoned in north Oxford, with some things still in it including the keys. I'm very sorry about the bother this may have caused you – I hope you didn't have the lock changed.

I wonder how you are getting on at LSE – I do hope all is very well with you. You are much, and very tenderly, in my thoughts. Don't reply to this. But remember that I love you very much and would come if ever you needed me.

All's well with me except that I am trying to lecture!

With much love, as always, to you, my dear

I

To *Raymond Queneau.*

St Anne's Society, Oxford
[13 March 1951]

I notice with surprise and distress that I have owed you a letter since December 28th. Anyway, that is the date inscribed on what I take to be your last letter, now before me. I can't remember that I have written to you since then, though I did get round to sending you Auden's *Romantic Iconography*[1] which stern colleagues here say is an irresponsible and unscholarly piece of work. [. . .]

Everything has been mild hell here since I last wrote and before that too. A beastly term: I was lecturing, for the first time, an alarming experience (on 'Meanings, Descriptions and Thoughts'). Before that I was bothered about trying to marry somebody, but it didn't come off. Just as well maybe. If I could only stop thinking about marriage maybe I'd get some work done.

1 *The Enchafèd Flood: or, The Romantic Iconography of the Sea*, a book of three lectures by W. H. Auden.

If I could see a means of doing it I'd slip over from philosophy into English literature – but this is difficult, probably impossible. (I might take a chair of philosophy at Bloemfontein or Tasmania and there I could do *anything* I suppose.) Next year I shall console myself by lecturing on *imagination*. (I'd like to work on Marxism too, particularly as no one here seems to understand this or care.) When I shall write a novel again I don't know and this after all is the only important thing.

I doubt if I'll get across the Channel this year. Short of cash. I'd love to see you (this is always a large part of the point of going abroad). But when I do see you I usually come away with the sad feeling that I haven't communicated with you as I would have wished. However I don't resign myself to non-communication, here or anywhere.

I'll write again sooner I hope than last time. Raymond dear, as always, much love
from
Iris

To Hal Lidderdale.

4 Eastbourne Road
29 June [1951]

Hal, Hal – hello there. It seems to me that I haven't heard from you (or, *franchement*,[1] written to you) for very long. This is not as it should be – and is odd too, considering how very often indeed I've thought about you and wondered about your happiness and your plans for the future. I haven't even heard the latest news from Jane[2] and your mother – but I'll catch up on that very soon. I want a word from you. The only news I've had lately was from Lucile [de Ste Croix], that you would stay on in Athens if the British Council job folded up. What news of all that? Most of all, what are you feeling, thinking, wanting? Are you happy? Do you love and are you loved in Athens? I know that compared with this jobs are as nothing. Please write.

There's little news of me. Term has ended. I am at Chiswick, trying to finish a trivial thing on Sartre. Next week I go to Edinburgh to read a paper to an Aristotelian Society[3] gathering. After that I'll stay in Newcastle with

---

1 Frankly.
2 Hal's sister.
3 A society which invites speakers to give papers in London on any philosophical topic. Its annual conference is hosted by different university departments in July each year. In July 1951 the conference was held in Edinburgh and Murdoch's paper was entitled 'Thinking and Language'.

my old pal Mary Scrutton, now married to a philosopher there.[1] Then, I hope, if beastly complications about letting my Oxford flat and moving furniture don't catch me, I'll away to Devon, to stay with a nice pair called John and Jean Jones[2] (whom you must meet). I shall probably stay there some time and work. Lectures for next term, the horrid Sartre thing, perhaps a novel I abandoned eighteen months ago. No money, so no France this year. Drink some mavrodaphne[3] for me.

I was out at Caterham last Sunday and found all Croixes well. The garden is a joy. They've instituted a game called padder tennis (half size, with wooden bats) on the lower lawn, so Geoffrey is able to extend his powers of domination. I thought Lucile seemed very well, better than she's been for ages.

There is a midsummer melancholy upon me. Odd how these hot days can put the meaning of life in question! Whatever do you do in the heat and the dust? Work goes slowly, people are rare, brandy is too expensive to drink every day.

This bad letter, which doesn't really seem to speak with my voice, is just to reach out to you, very affectionately and with deep concern. Will you be home this summer? Write to me soon and tell me how you are, how the world is. Much love to you, dear Hal,

from

I

To Wallace Robson, fellow of Lincoln College, Oxford, whom Murdoch had met in February 1950 and with whom she quickly became involved. After the end of the affair between Murdoch and Michael Oakeshott in December 1950, which caused Robson much misery, the relationship between Murdoch and Robson intensified and by early 1952 they had become unofficially engaged.[xvi] Peter Ady, a female friend and fellow in economics at St Anne's, mentioned briefly here, was to become very close to Murdoch during the summer of 1952.

Cedar House
Chubb Tor
Yelverton
South Devon
18 September [1951]

1 Mary Scrutton had married Geoffrey Midgley in the summer of 1950 and Murdoch was bridesmaid.
2 John Jones, fellow in law who was to become an English don at Merton College and Oxford Professor of Poetry from 1978–83. He and his wife Jean knew Murdoch in the late 1940s and they remained friends for many years.
3 A sweet fortified wine.

Dear, this is just a quick note to say how very sorry I am to have missed your 'phone call and the lovely gladioli. My parents have sent a *glowing* account of these; and they give me almost as much pleasure as if I could see them. *Thank you*, dear Wallace.

I went a bit sooner to Devon than I'd expected, as Peter Ady offered me a lift in her car as far as Dunster, and I hitch-hiked on from there the next day. More news soon. I hope you'll be letting me have your Siena address. Much love to you, you warm sunny Chianti-drinking fellow,

　From I

To Hal Lidderdale, who had been sent by the British Council to Salonika in Greece where he was to remain for several years.

4 Eastbourne Road
6 December [1951]

Hal darling, thank you for your letter. I was *so sorry* to hear that. I thought Anna[1] was charming, so lovely and so intelligent – and had hoped to find a chance to talk about her with you. However – one must be bloody objective about these things and any pains are better than making a mistake. Take it from an old hand like me that one does recover from being in love, though at the time the mere prospect of it seems a crime. But one must and one does. And should exploit one's friends meanwhile. Hope to see you soon. It was lovely to have you here. All my love to you, dear Hal – I

To Wallace Robson.

4 Eastbourne Road
16 December [1951]

My darling, hello, how are you, how did yesterday go? It's now Sunday morning. I'm missing you extremely, but I feel curiously happy and serene. I have unpacked and washed my hair and now I want to do nothing but sit about dreamily, thinking about you and about the great strangeness of everything, and how good it is. (I told my parents this morning what was *likely* to happen, in the strange case of you and me, and they were *very* pleased. They took it calmly, and have now forgotten about it pro tem, as they are more concerned with renovating a couple of chairs my pa bought

---

1 Anna Tsitsa, Greek girlfriend of Hal's in Salonika.

at an auction.) (I hope you don't think this was premature.) Sweetheart, I feel curiously shy of you. I wonder what you are thinking and feeling today? I hope you haven't worried any more about the damned American problem; I haven't.[1] We'll solve it together one way or another.

This house is peaceful and pleasant to be in (except that there are too many cats). You and I have lived too much in pubs, confound it. There's always been a closing time. Let it not be so in the future. My parents would like to meet you again before the vac ends. (My mother said: it's very convenient that he plays bridge!) Oh dear, how can I possibly wait so long before seeing you again? I'll come very soon after Christmas. Let me know, by the way, when Dorothy[2] will be around, I don't want to miss her.

I feel full of the mystery of life at the moment. (Odd how things sometimes seem tinkling and empty and then full, full.) An overwhelming sensation that almost makes me speechless. If you were here I could tell you things that are hard to write – not coherent things, but what can be looked at or shewn. (Transcendental, like logic!)

Take care of yourself now, silly child – don't go wandering across the High Street in a daze. Eat enough, don't drink too much, and try to think about your work. I am thinking about you at every moment. (Well, every other moment! I am starting on the last half of the Wittgenstein typescript.) I hope I shall get a letter from you tomorrow. Why have you got such a long nose and why do you never wash your hair? I love you terribly, I can't think why. I'll write to Dover[3] on Tuesday, to arrive Wednesday. Don't worry about *anything*. Don't fall into the hands of any scheming woman (other than me). Dear Wallace, here's my hand, hold on. Write to me soon, you silly ass. Make a note of this: I love you.

Dear, write soon – ever ever ever

Your I

To Wallace Robson.

4 Eastbourne Road
17 December [1951]

Dearest Wallace, no letter from you this morning! (Confound you!) But maybe it's just the Christmas posts. (I hope you got mine first thing.) (Anyway,

1 The difficulty Murdoch would still have getting a visa for the United States, given her former membership of the Communist Party; it seems likely that Wallace Robson had applied for an academic post or was soon to embark on a lecture tour there and that they hoped to travel together.
2 Possibly Robson's sister Dorothy (1929–1964) who Murdoch thought bore a 'sweet likeness' to her brother.
3 Where Robson's mother lived.

you bloody well write to me *now.*) [. . .] It seems an intolerably long time since I last saw you. *You must let me have a photo.* (Otherwise I shall forget what you look like. I want my memories of your curious head to be occurrent not dispositional.)

I can't help worrying a bit about the American problem after all. The rational thing to do would be for you to go in the summer and for us to marry after – assuming you *are* willing to take me on in this role. (My mother says she will teach me to cook!) I'd be in a cold sweat all the time you were gone – in case you met another woman, or there was a war, or your ship went down, or you decided to take a chair in New Criticism at the Ohio State University or something. All a very just punishment (for me I mean, considering what I've laid on *you*) but not very nice. Still, it would be rational. I suppose there's no doubt going to the States would be very useful to you, both in some worldly sense, and because of New Ideas and so on. My heart so much urges me to take you now, if I can – and the thought of so long a wait is pure pain. I suppose the *most* rational thing to do is to wait and see if you're asked, and then to discover if you *would* fail to get a visa if we were married. But oh dear I want the future so much now and fear to lose it. Anyhow let's wait and see, about that, and forgive these nervous cries.

Dear darling, take care of yourself, and take care of *me* in your heart. I have a sort of continual pain at the moment which comes from being apart from you. (I know it would be eased if I could touch you; so that's good enough proof that it's not indigestion!) (How long will it take me to convince you that I love you, that I *do* love you? You'll *see* it soon, if you haven't already. Hold on to me, go on loving me. We *will* achieve something together.) I know this is no passing mood, as far as I'm concerned, but rooted everywhere throughout me, and strong. (Like Stonesfield slate, which is tempered in the *frost* and in the *hot sun* and then *lasts forever.*) [. . .]

I hate not knowing what you're thinking now. Write me a long letter – 'phone calls won't be enough. And take care of yourself, dear silly neurotic precious one. And bloody well write.

My most tender and devoted love to you.

I

To Wallace Robson.

District Line
Tuesday [late December 1951]

Dear, I'm sorry if I sounded moody on the 'phone. I got frightened. Am I too Gidean?[1] I do want to be happy. I want to go on being myself. I don't want to lose all my friends. *Any* case of marriage would bring all this up. Please be patient with me. Above all, do trust me –

Excuse this glooming. The nice weather you mentioned over the white cliffs of Dover has now reached London.

Hammersmith station

I am writing in pencil because my Biro is so likely to cover me with ink. I'm just going up to town now to see an old Somerville pal who is teaching for the Workers' Educational Association in Stafford. (Stafford – heavens!)

Why do I waste time reading books which *give* me nothing? I don't think you do this. I hope your work is going well today. I *must* get down to some work soon. Two papers to write, and lectures for later. I begin to hate philosophy. But may feel better when I'm doing some.

I finished *The Scarlet Letter*[2] last night.

Piccadilly Line

I think it's *very* good – deep and strong. A bit melodramatic, but it didn't matter. You must tell me sometime why literary critics Lawrence[3] and Robson think of it as destruction of man by woman. Dimmesdale destroys himself – the fact that Hester gets stronger while he gets weaker isn't *her* fault. Or am I being naive?

I feel moody today. I wish you were here. You are my ill and its cure.

I think it is always wicked to give way to depression. This sort of thing is so absolutely under the control of the will. The least effort, moving of the glance, dispels it! See, it's gone. (The world being so full of a number of things has its point. One has just to cast the consciousness *out*, read the advertisements, speculate about the people opposite, and all is changed. Odd how one is one's own captive.)

Write to me, dear one, and cheer me up. In fact, I'm *not* melancholy! In the Black Horse, holding onto my half pint, I shall be as gay as a bird.

Darling, *toujours et toujours*,

Amoureusement,

I

1 Too wracked by inner conflict, as are the main characters in André Gide's fiction.
2 Historical novel by Nathaniel Hawthorne, set in Puritan Boston in the seventeenth century and published in 1850.
3 Murdoch is presumably referring to D. H. Lawrence's *Studies in Classical American Literature* (1923), which includes a chapter on Hawthorne.

To Wallace Robson.

[4 Eastbourne Road]
[early January 1952 ˣᵛⁱⁱ]

Oh darling, I just *can't* work this afternoon – isn't it awful? I just want to sit by the fire and read *Woman's Own*. If only I were either a lot cleverer or less clever, I'd get on better. Just now I've been trying to collect a thought or two for this bloody paper for the Classical Society on εἰκασία [1] – (don't hold the accents against me) – and on looking at Plato see he *patently* didn't mean anything like what I was proposing to talk about. I suppose I can start with an enormous apology – 'This *might* have been something that Plato meant'. I wonder what my mind would have been like if I'd never come across philosophy? Full of rank and spotty growths no doubt, and perhaps one orchid among them. As it is, it seems like a bit of waste ground outside Willesden station on a rainy evening.

Your letter still hasn't come. (You have *calming* writing.) Tonight I'm going to Hampstead to have drinks with Elizabeth Vernon and her husband who works in Lloyd's – we shall play French cabaret records and drink whisky. (*That's* the level! Hooray.) E is an old school pal of mine – we've been close friends since we were thirteen. You must meet her – you'd like her and husband a lot.

I'm sorry if I sounded nervy on the 'phone. I feel a lot better now, in spite of the rage and *désespoir* about εἰκασία. (*Avez vous rencontré une petite positiviste désespérée?*[2]) Some day you must tell me about the rules for the agreement of the past participle in French.

It's raining. I wish they'd get that business of the *Flying Enterprise* settled. It's almost incredible that with all the marvels of science etc. they can't manage to get a tow line fixed onto a ship which they can come almost alongside.[3] It shews how crazy the world is and how bloody scientists must be wasting their time on other things.

I hope *you* are working? I can't tell you how deeply it would delight me if you wrote a good novel ever. (Don't retaliate by saying you'd be pleased if I wrote a book called *Logic, Reality and Truth*, or *Language, Thinking and Meaning* or *Concepts, Images and Words*, for I shan't. What I shall do will be

---

1 The word *eikasia*, meaning 'image thinking', was used by Plato in *The Republic* Book VI to refer to the inability to perceive reality. *Eikasia* prevents us from understanding that a dream or memory or a reflection in a mirror is not reality as such.

2 Have you encountered a little despairing positivist?

3 SS *Cape Kumukaki* was built for use in the Second World War but was sold in 1947; it thereafter operated in scheduled service under the name *Flying Enterprise*. In late December 1951, it met a storm in the Western Approaches to the English Channel and sank. Murdoch's remarks refer to the fact that on 3 January 1952 the tug *Turmoil* arrived but found it impossible to take the *Flying Enterprise* in tow.

write novels rather less good than yours, so that people will be endlessly muddled in future ages.) Please send me your poems. And you've promised to shew me the beginning of your other novel. *Good.*

Ever, you exasperating creature, with deep love, bound to you.

Your I

To Wallace Robson.

In the train going to Caterham
Saturday [early 1952]

Darling creature, hello. I have just been discussing you with my old head-mistress (a great woman). I went to this old girls' gathering this afternoon. (How nice it was – women are better than men) – and she kept me for dinner afterwards. I told her I proposed to wed, and she questioned me very suspiciously (*she* is Beatrice May Baker, known as BMB) somewhat as follows:

BMB: Is he good-looking?
I: Not exactly. He has a fine head and deep intense eyes. But he looks rather tortured.
BMB: What are his vices?
I: He's bad-tempered and nervous and tends to sulk if things go wrong. He's vain, in a rather superficial way, and generally rather egocentric.
BMB: What are his virtues?
I: Honesty and lack of corruption, concern about people, seriousness.
BMB: Is he charming? What are his politics? How many cigarettes does he smoke? Did he get a first? Will he go far in his job? Is he religious? What are his people? What school did he go to? Etc. etc. etc.

I spare you my replies. (I hope this doesn't make your hair stand on end. It was all out of concern for me – and I answered, I hope, as you would have had me answer!) I enjoy discussing you anyway. So you must put up with it.

I wonder what it will be like being with you. I feel that some deep change is working in me already. (I mean a change in your direction *bien entendu.*[1]) I've always had a great sense of my destiny. (My vanity and conceit is very great though!) How fantastically far one is from being humble. How much one/I want to be admired. I noticed it in myself at this gathering this after-noon. People said to me in a humble manner how much they'd enjoyed

1 Of course.

hearing my voice on the radio,[1] although they didn't understand a word etc. and I felt pleased with myself! It's very difficult to feel even the remotest *desire* for what's right. (I'm corrupt in a hundred ways – you not, in all of them.) I connect you in my mind with goodness – I'm not sure why since after all you are full of weakness and vice (see above). You're not unselfish or imaginatively considerate about people either – though when you stumble over it, you're good to them and utterly without malice. Perhaps it's because you are so completely without guile. Yet it seems much more than this. You are religious in some deep way. Is this just emotional junk? I'm not sure. Expect me to be good – please please. I shall always expect you to be.

Enough of this. Today I went to the sales and bought a pair of black and white check slacks, very dandy. Also a blue necklace. (I am vain too, and waste money on clothes.) (Stop that moralising.) Shall I buy a white duffle coat?

See you on Tuesday. If you were here I should kick you and pull your hair. Isn't life complex?

With love, ever your complicated girl

I

To Wallace Robson.

In a train
[January 1952]

Hello there. Thank you for your *enchanting* letter. What a clever chap you are. Out of so much cleverness something must emerge. Was Tolstoy clever I wonder? It's a cold blue day here. I am going to lunch with a Luxembourgeoise called Ruth Tweller who will want to talk philosophy. How awful. *Please* send me some poems (or let me see some on Monday). I know I'm no critic but I'll try to understand, if you'll help me.

How I hate Oxford just before term starts. At such moments I want to book a passage to the South Pacific or join the Foreign Legion. (Would you follow me if I joined the Foreign Legion?)

An advertisement opposite me tells me that Britain's best drink and Britain's best friend is *Tizer*. I wonder if we are missing something superb? I suppose it's the British Coca-Cola. The *Daily Worker* says that various brewing firms, including Watneys, are going to make Coca-Cola in England. The *DW* thinks Coca-Cola is dreadful on ideological grounds, and sentimentalises about the beers of old England.

---

1 Refers to Murdoch's talk on Simone Weil's *Waiting on God*, the Third Programme, 18 October 1951, repeated on 8 December 1951.

What a peculiar chap you are. I shall never get used to you. (I am grinding my teeth. Tell me to stop whenever you notice it or I'll soon have worn them down to nothing like the Rev. Canon T. B. Scrutton.[1]) I wonder if I am *really* more nervous than you? What a pair.

Later. Have just come from lunch. Para-philosophical gossip only. Ruth tells me that the *really* cheap way to live in Paris nowadays is to live in an 'erstwhile' *maison close*,[2] giving it the required air of respectability, so that it can pose as a lodging house. One lives *pour presque rien*[3] in a luxurious room and one's name, sent in to the police, diffuses a sweet odour. Only one would have to *be* respectable (the only snag) – no boyfriends after dark. Meanwhile, on the floor below –

Are you working hard today, you virtuous creature? I am becoming idle and demoralised here. (Tonight I dine with my Coal Board pal, Saunders, whom you must meet. We shall have a drink in the Coal Board Bar. I can imagine what a gay scene *that* will be.) Darling, treat me very calmly. I adore you. (*Mais oui!*)

Much love
I

To Hal Lidderdale.

4 Eastbourne Road
4 January [1952[xviii]]

Hal, how dreadful I am to have let so long a time pass without writing. Particularly as I had that lovely brandy to inspire me. I drank your health on a number of occasions. But the wing'd words never got onto paper. Thank you too, dear Hal, for your good letter of so long ago. I was glad to have some real news of you and to hear your real authentic voice speaking! I hope things are well, well with you.

The Christmas vac is half over, I am having a feverish London time and hardly doing any work. My little book on Sartre has gone to the typist. I *ought* now to be working on a new Aristotelian paper (called 'Nostalgia for the Particular') which I have to give in the spring – and also a paper on εἰκασία for next term. But all I seem to do is go to the sales and drink with various people in various bars. (I hope to see Janie next week. I saw her, very pleasantly, in Woodstock last term, we walked in Blenheim with your mother.)

1 Mary Scrutton's father.
2 Brothel.
3 For almost nothing.

Tomorrow I go to Caterham to stay with Geoff and Lucile, for a day or two. I went to the Unity Theatre panto with them just after Christmas. (Mother Goose – the wicked baron wanting to kill the goose that lays the golden eggs of socialism!) They are very well I think, in spite of Lucile's tummy and Geoffrey's perfectly fantastic work schedule. (I've given up feeling guilty about the discrepancy between G's work time and mine.)

On the personal front, I too am in a rather intense situation – and the thought of marriage comes into my head. The other person (an English Lit. don at Oxford) is a very neurotic creature with whom I constantly quarrel. Perhaps too much of violence here on both sides. I don't know what will come of it. But I'll let you know of developments if there are any. (Don't speak of this to anyone – all is so unclear.) (How complex and unhappy-making all our human contacts seem to be –)

Let me have another letter before too long. I hope your work is well. Don't drink too much. Take care of yourself. I think of you often – you are for always in my heart.

Again, forgive me for not having written – and write thou, I shall be so glad to hear. Dearest Hal, with very much love –

Ever

I

To David Hicks. Other short notes and letters beginning in the late 1940s (not included here) indicate that Murdoch and Hicks saw each other fairly regularly after he returned to England from Czechoslovakia. His marriage to Molly Purchase in July 1946 was short-lived and he left her and his daughter Julia (born 1948), probably early in 1950, for Katharine Messenger, whom he would marry in 1953.[xix]

4 Eastbourne Road
4 January [1952]

David dear, thank you very much for the hankie. I hope all's going decently in Birmingham. I'd be glad of some news a bit later – just how you're living and how things are. I'll let you have news too if there is any. I'm sorry about the tears the other night. I enjoyed our evening immensely *quand même*, one of the best ever.

Take care of yourself up there. You are very much in my heart, always, always –

Much love

I

To Raymond Queneau.

St Anne's Society, Oxford
17 February 1952

How pleased I was to get your book; everything now looks quite different (an improvement). I shall read it *very* soon and everything will look even more different. Thank you too for your nice letter of now some time ago which I've been for weeks just going to answer. I've imagined various replies (*insouciant, désespéré*[1] etc.) and have talked to you on and off in my mind, but not on paper. I'm very moody at present, and in an emotional tangle which will have God knows what outcome. I'll let *you* know as soon as I know. Anyhow, that's mainly why I haven't written.

As for how things are at the moment they are fairly hellish. I'm not doing much thinking (what I am doing, *point de vue de la philosophie*, is somewhat Hegelian too, in a dry way – next term I lecture on Bradley. Though *that* particular venture has got as far as my taking *Appearance and Reality*[2] off the shelves and laying it on top of my desk). My current novel has been abandoned a long time now. I've taken to writing poetry again and find a great facility for producing mediocre modern-sounding stuff full of millions of echoes. My book on Sartre is done, but an argument with the publishers about its length is interminable.

Write me another letter about yourself. Are you writing poetry these days? What do you think about *Le d. de la v.*[3] – do you feel it to be your best novel? Do you love it? (This is like *L'interview de M. Queneau.*) I am so pleased to see it lying there (on top of Bradley) – good, good. What are you up to now? *De l'architecture?* How is Paris? (Ah, when shall I be in Paris again I wonder?) This letter seems like a lot of melancholy exclamations. What I most want to say is how real you are, always, for me. (What a blessed thing this sense of reality is, so long as it remains to one. And I *don't* mean the rational.) I can see your face very clearly, and hear your voice. (I have a particularly clear mental image of the way you looked the very first time I saw you, turning away in the snow down that road in Innsbruck.) Enough of this recital of mental events. You have a special sovereignty over my affections and will always have. (Why do I put this in such an eighteenth-century way?) And this somehow *isn't* abstract just because I write to you so little. Anyhow I think you know all this very well. Write to me one of these days about yourself and Paris. And I'll write to you when I've read *Le d. de la v.* and tell you how good or bad I think it is. With love to you, as ever and always,

I

1 Carefree, despairing.
2 By Francis Herbert Bradley, British idealist philosopher; the book was published in 1893. He was the brother of A. C. Bradley (1851– 1935), the literary critic and Shakespearean scholar.
3 *Le dimanche de la vie (The Sunday of Life).*

To Wallace Robson, from whom Murdoch parted soon after this letter was written. She had grown increasingly anxious about the volatile nature of their relationship and had also just begun a romantic relationship with Franz Steiner, to whom she had gradually become close after they met in May 1951.

4 Eastbourne Road
[March or early April 1952]

My dear creature, hello. The sun shines, and I am sitting in my room here, surrounded by ticking clocks, stones picked up upon sea shores, and books by chaps like Empson, Boethius, Buber and Popper.[1] I wish you were here. The damn telephone rings all the time. I am invited out to look at people's babies or to advise them about their career. I wish I were with you on a desert island. (A long philosophical tract, of Buddhistic flavour, recently sent me by the author from USA, culminates with the following message: What the distracted world needs is that we should all have sexual intercourse once in twenty-eight days. This apparently makes for *idealism*.)

Your strange face haunts me. You must have that polyfoto taken in London. (I will too if you like, posing with beret and cigarette as the spirit of the 1930s.) You have a curious poetical defenceless look sometimes which oddly reminds me of Frank. I'll shew you a photo of him sometime which shews what I mean. At other times you just look intense and suspicious. If you took more care of your complexion and washed your hair oftener you'd look like a poet. I think you are adorable. I shall never get used to you. Mind you do some work. I want you to be a great man.

How lovely those few days were! I mind much less now when you are intolerable. I just think about something else until you snap out of it. You must try to be less intense. One can't communicate 100% all the time. [. . .]

You might discover about the proprieties of marriage during Lent. Easter seems to be so soon before term. I love you, you queer fellow. *Toujours, mon type en or, amoureuse de toi,*[2]

I

---

1 William Empson (1906–84), English literary critic; Karl Popper (1902–94), Austrian-born philosopher who had settled in England.
2 Always in love with you, my golden one.

To Raymond Queneau.

The Court Hotel
Charmouth, Dorset
1 April 1952

Raymond, this is a note not a letter. *Distinction!* How are you? You owe me
a letter. (*Now* – a letter, and a note.) I loved *Le dimanche de la vie*. It filled me
with that very *special* sort of *joie de vivre* which I connect with you. The
opening – immediately – that particular sort of laughter that goes on and
on, very deep down. I still like *Pierrot* best and admire *Saint-Ginglin* most
– but *this* I liked very much indeed and it gave me great pleasure.

Enough of this, since this is a *note*. (I am living *toute seule* down here, in
a large empty hotel by the sea, trying to get some work done. Lovely walks
on the beach. Meditation. The topic, apart from love and death, is F. H.
Bradley. Also a paper for the Aristotelian Society on *particularity*.) (Are there
particulars?)

But look – I've just sent off (about time) my little book about Sartre to
the publishers – and I have to add a biographical note about that famous
person. Can you tell me – is S related to Albert Schweitzer and if so how?
This would amuse the English reader (I suspect he would find it incongruous).
I don't think I've invented this notion – do you happen to know anything
of it? If *not* don't bother, but just, in your usual dilatory fashion, refrain
from replying. When I return to civilisation I may be able to discover about
it from some well-informed source such as the Institut Français in Londres.

The sun shines, the beach is covered with shells and smooth stones. *Je
pense à Queneau.* I can't see France from here. Here is my hand tho'! Stretched
out *ulterioris amore.*[1]

Ever – I

I think this is a letter after all.

To David Hicks.

The Court Hotel
Charmouth, Dorset
1 April [1952]

---

1 Evokes a line in Virgil's *Aeneid*: '*Tendebantque manus ripae ulterioris amore*' ('[they] were stretching out
their hands, longing for the further bank').

David, how are you, and how is Birmingham? Let me have some news. News of myself is brief: the plans I mentioned to you last time we met are off, *sine die*.¹ A great deal of pain all round. The future, otherwise, unclear.

I have come down here to escape from London and Oxford and try to get some work done. This is a large, empty, hotel where I am the only guest, except for an ancient couple from Poona who live here. I work in the deserted lounge by a roaring fire. Then I walk on the beach or go to look at churches in near villages. There are five pubs in this village, all of which I now know, and the cider is very cheap and strong. Now the snow has gone it is apparent that the countryside is absolutely covered with violets and primroses. There are also little calves with their horns sprouting. *Et toujours la mer*.² It's impossible not to feel that life has possibilities.

How are you, up there? I'm sorry I cried so much when we met at Christmas. I have a good memory *quand même* of that meeting.

I'll be here for about another week I expect – I have to write lectures on Bradley (oh dear!) and an Aristotelian Society paper. All here is calming, *surtout la mer*.³

Comment va Katharine?

Dear David, with much love, as always before

I

To David Hicks.

St Anne's
[May 1952]

David, thank you exceedingly for your letter (which I haven't got by me – if I can't find your address I'll send this to Pendley⁴). I'm sorry Birmingham is such hell. A few *people* could transform it I expect, but that will need time. I hope things are less beastly now, and you are managing to see Katharine. (I do want to meet her sometime –)

How is your motor bike – and when are you going to roar down to Oxford to see me? (I shall have another shot at learning – the bike I mean – this summer – though heaven knows where the time will come from what with Bradley.) (Did I tell you I was lecturing on Bradley? I'm still on

---

1 With no expectation of being resumed.
2 And always the sea.
3 Above all the sea.
4 Pendley Manor in Hertfordshire where the Pendley Open Air Shakespeare Festival took place each summer. David Hicks acted in some productions; the next letter to him suggests that Murdoch travelled there when he was playing Feste in *Twelfth Night*.

Chapter II of *Appearance and Reality* and feeling like someone setting out to cross the Atlantic in a yacht and hearing a gale warning as he passes the Lizard.[1])

I feel a bit better than when last I wrote to you. Work is very absorbing. But still rather in a state of 'wondering what I am'. Your letter was precious. Something of me is stored up with you in a way that I can never regret. [. . .]

Dear dear David –

Much love

I

To Raymond Queneau.

St Anne's College, Oxford
3 June 1952

This is just to send you one of my tedious works. You don't have to read it.

I was delighted to hear from Canetti lately that he knew you,[2] and that you had been the chief defender of *Die Blendung* in France.[3] I admire that book very much.

Did I tell you I was making a final and serious attempt to learn German properly? Tell me what's good, and modern, to read. With much love

as always

I

To David Hicks.

4 Eastbourne Road
24 June 1952

David, I'm sorry I wrote to you tiresomely. I was momentarily rather upset by the curtness of your letter. And everything to do with you still has so many echoes and resonances in all parts of me.

This is just to say that; and that I'll be here till tomorrow, then back to Oxford, then here again on Monday, and will await your briefing about Pendley. I think either the Saturday *or* the Sunday. Maybe stay one night at most. I don't know what sort of arrangements you had in mind.

1 Lizard Point in Cornwall, historically known as the 'Graveyard of Ships'.
2 Murdoch had met Elias Canetti through Franz Steiner.
3 Elias Canetti's *Die Blendung* was published in 1935 and translated into English in 1946 with the title *Auto da Fé*.

Feeling rather tired and ragged at present; but I'll be better when I've done some work. Take my hand.

Iris

To Raymond Queneau.

4 Eastbourne Road
4 August 1952

Raymond, a short note to say that I'll be in Paris on August 15 or August 18 for a few days – I'll confirm which. Will you be there?? I hope so, and that you'll have time to see me. I'll telephone Gallimard. If you'll be elsewhere, let me know – I don't want to miss you. I go on to Italy, and back through Paris later.

I have composed in my mind letters to you about Canetti, Kojève, Hegel, and other matters, but I quite forget if I actually wrote these letters or not. If not, my apologies. For some time now I have been writing a novel, a continuation of one I started two years ago. If it turns out to be of any use (about this I still don't know) I shall dedicate it to you. But I daresay it won't ever see the light. And for this I have stopped reading Hegel's *Logic*. Is Simone de Beauvoir in Paris? Dearest Raymond,

à bientot,
ever
Iris

To Elias Canetti.

Hotel des Vosges
Passage de la Petite Boucherie
Bd St Germain
Paris VIe
[mid-August 1952]

Just to say that I am really here, and would be very glad to see you, especially on Friday or Saturday, if you had the time.

It's very dreamlike to be in a place one has thought about so much when one wasn't there. I still feel rather dazed.

I hope all is truly well with you –
Yours
Iris Murdoch

To Raymond Queneau, after having met him in Paris in August.

[24 August 1952]

I'm sorry about the scene on the bridge – or rather, I'm sorry in the sense that I ought either to have said nothing or to have said something sooner. I was in extreme pain when I came to see you chez Gallimard on Friday – but what with English habitual reticence, and your cool way of keeping me at a distance I could say nothing although I wanted desperately to take you in my arms.

On the other hand, if I had started to talk sooner I might have spent the rest of the time (such as it was) in tears, and that was to be avoided. I'm glad I said at least one word to you however. I can't tell you what extrava-gances I have uttered in my heart and you have been spared. I write this now partly (for once) to relieve my feelings – and partly because you were (or affected to be??) surprised at what I said.

Listen – I love you in the most absolute sense possible. I would do anything for you, be anything you wished me, come to you at any time or place if you wished it even for a moment. I should like to state this categorically since the moment for repeating it may not recur soon. If I thought I stood the faintest chance, *vis à vis de toi*, I would fight and struggle savagely. As it is – there are not only the barriers between us of marriage, language, *La Manche*, and doubtless others – there is also the fact that you don't need me in the way in which I need you – which is proved by the amount of time you are prepared to devote to me while I am in Paris. As far as I am concerned, this is, *d'ailleurs*, an old story – when you said to me once, *recommençons un peu plus haut,*[1] it was already too late for me to do anything of the kind.

(I wrote thus far in a somewhat proletarian joint in the Rue du Four, when a drunken female put her arm round me *et me demandait si j'écrivais à maman. J'ai dit que non. Alors elle m'a demandé à qui?*[2] and I didn't know how to reply.)

I don't want to trouble you with this – or rather, not often! I know how painful it is to receive this sort of letter, how one says to oneself oh my God! and turns over the page. I can certainly live without you – it's necessary, and what is necessary is possible, which is just as well. But what I write now expresses no momentary Parisian mood but simply where I stand. You know yourself what it is for one person to represent for another *an absolute* – and so you do for me. I don't think about you all the time. But I know that there is nothing I wouldn't give up for you if you wanted me. I'm glad to write

1 Let's start again on a higher plane.
2 And asked me if I was writing to my mother. I said no. Then she asked who was I writing to?

this (*remember it*) in case you should ever feel in need of an absolute devotion. (Though I know, again, from my own experience, how in a moment of need one is just as likely to rely on someone one met yesterday.)

Don't be distressed. To say these things takes a weight from my heart. The tone dictated to me by your letters *depuis des années me convient peu.*[1] I don't know you quite well enough to know if this is *voulu*[2] or not. Just as I wasn't sure about your 'surprise' on the bridge. To see you in this impersonal way in Paris, sitting in cafés and knowing you will be gone in an hour, is a *supplice.*[3] But I well understand and am (I suppose) prepared to digest it, that there is no alternative. If I thought that you would be pleased to see me in Siena I should come. But (especially after writing to you like this) there is very little possibility of my being able to discover whether you would be pleased or not.

I can't give you an Italian address, as I'm not sure where I shall be, *au commencement* anyway. And it's little use to give you addresses as you might feel 'bound' to ask me to come to Siena, and I wouldn't know whether you really meant it, and, and – Paris and London after all are near enough to each other. If you wanted to see me I would come *any time at a moment's notice.* Please remember this. If you want to reply write to Chiswick (4 Eastbourne Rd W4) and that will follow me in time. But in fact there's nothing to say in reply.

It's happened to me once, twice, perhaps three times in my life to feel an *unconditional* devotion to someone. The other recipients have gone on their way. You remain. There is no substitute for this sort of sentiment and no mistaking it when it occurs. If it does nothing else, it shows up the inferior imitations.

I wish I could give you something. If anything comes of this novel (or its successor), it's all yours – as is everything else I have if you would. I love you, I love you absolutely and unconditionally – thank God for being able to say this with the whole heart.

I feel reluctant to close this letter because I know that I shan't feel so frank later on. Not that my feelings will have altered, *ça ne change pas*, but I shall feel more acutely the futility of these sort of exclamations. At this moment I am, *même malgré toi*,[4] in communication with you in a way which may not be repeated.

If your letters to me could be slightly less impersonal I should be glad. *Mais ça ne se choisit pas.*[5] I have become used to writing impersonally too,

1 Over the last few years hasn't answered my needs.
2 Deliberate.
3 A torment.
4 Even in spite of you.
5 But that's not something one can choose.

and this was a mistake my dear. It happens to me so rarely to be able to write a letter so wholeheartedly – almost the last but one was a letter I wrote to you in 1946. I love you as much as then. More, because of the passage of time.

Forgive what in this letter is purely 'tiresome'. Accept what you can. If there is anything here which can give you pleasure or could in any bad moment give you comfort I should be very happy. I love you so deeply that I can't help feeling that it must 'touch' you somehow, even without your knowing it.

Again, don't be distressed. There is so much I should like to have said to you, and may one day. I don't want to stop writing – I feel I am leaving you again. My very very dear Queneau –

   I

To Raymond Queneau, posted from Italy.

[9 September 1952]

The letter I wrote you in Paris must have made a disagreeable and embarrassing impression. I have your reply which is absolutely *comme il faut*.[1] In fact *reality* never allows itself to be ignored for long; but this doesn't alter the *truth* of what I said. Never mind, you know all this. I trust we can now continue more or less as before.

I have been mainly in Rome, a bit in Florence, and later staying with friends near Como. I like Italy better than ever – particularly Rome. Last time I got the scale wrong. I imagined it was a city of large things, but it's better considered as a lot of villages. Small squares and fountains give the scale. I'd forgotten too all the *glitter* of Italy. A surface so unlike France. (And the glorious ices, and the fruit drinks, and the shops!) How is Siena? I wonder if you are finding it *too* beautiful. I felt quite ill when I was there, though that may have been from eating watermelon. Maybe one gets used to it.

I hope Italy is pleasant to you. Forgive me writing this in haste. I didn't want you to be worrying any further about that other matter. I'll write later on from England –

   ever

   I

1 As it should be.

To Hal Lidderdale in Salonika.

[early September 1952]

Hal darling, just a note. Thank you for yours, from the BEA[1] departure. I am now back from Europe (Paris, Turin, Rome, Florence, Milan, Como, Turin, Paris – oh dear). My Italian is still not presentable. All was lovely though! Especially Rome. I forget if you know this city, except for aeroplane lunch purposes? Last time I had the scale wrong and looked at all *large* objects – this time I looked at *small* objects; much better. (Pretty good either way. A small fountain in a square is about right.) Are there fountains in Salonika? Send me a picture postcard with X marking your flat. How did the Fair go? Hal – it was very very good for me to see you. Much much love – I

PS I've nearly finished *Tom Jones* – Delicious!

To Raymond Queneau.

4 Eastbourne Road
14 September [1952]

Just to say that it was very nice to find *Les enfants du limon*[2] waiting for me when I got back. I haven't had time to read it yet. I'll report later.

Here it's raining like hell, *à l'Anglaise*. I am trying to make my peace with Philosophy, after so long an absence. I shall go back to Oxford in a day or two. I hope all is well, and beautiful, in Siena. It's hard to believe that somewhere else the summer is still going on. Enjoy it.

ever

I

[*Later*]

Your letter has just come. The thought of your reading *Barrack Room Ballads*[3] in Siena charms me very much. There's nothing to report since last I wrote except that I've now got a cold, and that I've just finished reading *Tom Jones*, which I'd never read before. What a delicious book – and how good to read an author who writes so well with such *relish*. I feel more robust already.

1 British European Airways.
2 A novel Queneau published in 1938, translated as *Children of Clay*.
3 An 1892 collection of songs and poems by Rudyard Kipling mainly about the late-Victorian British Army and mostly written in a vernacular dialect.

I hope you are seeing the countryside, which though it's as beautiful as the town is at any rate made of *earth* and is that much less suffocating. How is your Italian getting on? We might solve our language problems if we talked that language in which, I guess, our proficiency is about equal.

yours

I

To Raymond Queneau, concerning the death on 27 November of Franz Steiner, with whom Murdoch had been in a romantic relationship since March 1952. By the autumn of that year they were seriously committing themselves to each other but had reached a sort of emotional impasse. Entries in Steiner's journal reveal that he loved her but was aware of her anxiety about marriage: 'But how can we belong to each other without getting married. I'm not going to talk about that to her. She is afraid of it. The wish must come from her'.ˣˣ Steiner's sudden death seems to have jolted Murdoch into a reassessment of her relationship with Queneau.

4 Eastbourne Road
13 December [1952]

Dear Queneau, I haven't written for a long time; and I think you, you wrote more lately, last wrote from Siena.

Things are not very well. Someone whom I loved very deeply, and from whom I was beginning to hope very much, has died suddenly. Everything is changed. Strange, how all wishes and interests can perish, I measure now how much tied to this one person. I regret wasted time. At the moment I can't see how to get on at all.

I'm sorry to write so sadly. I wanted to write to you sooner but felt too heavy. He was forty-three, and died of an illness of the heart. We knew this might happen – but didn't expect it, or I didn't. I couldn't believe in the possibility of death.

I wrote you a foolish letter in the summer – though it was 'sincere'. My whole existence seems to me now such a tissue of foolishnesses. My feelings where you are concerned are necessarily, through force of circumstance, 'abstract'. But this man who has died was daily bread. I knew this, of course, even at the time.

I write this because I don't want, especially at this time, to lose contact with you. I can't work at present – nor can I yet digest what has happened. Days pass full of devices for avoiding being in pain.

This is not much of a Christmas greeting. Please write to me. I send you, as ever, my love –

I

To David Hicks.

4 Eastbourne Road
16 December [1952]

David,

It's good to hear from you. I'll be here on the 21 Dec, but after that visiting people in Oxford and Surrey until late Christmas Eve. Or any time in your after-Christmas sojourn would do fine. You'd better just ring up when you want to see me, either before or after Christmas. That will be splendid.

I'm not in very good shape at present. I have lately lost, by death, the person who was closest to me, whom I loved very dearly, whom I would very probably have married, if things had gone on as they were going. I can't at the moment see how one recovers from such a loss. It was sudden and unexpected. He had been very ill (the heart) some years before, and one knew this *might* happen. But one doesn't expect that people will really die. I wasn't ready for it. We were both so full of the future. And now I simply don't know what to do.

I'm sorry to write so, but there is nothing else to write about.

I shall be very glad to see you. I hope all goes well and speedily in your affairs – that you can see out of the wood into the open country. Greet Katharine warmly from me.

Dear David, much love, as always,

I

To Raymond Queneau. In this letter Murdoch tries to reassure Queneau – who suggests she might think about undergoing psychoanalysis – that she is not 'at a loss' despite the recent death of Franz Steiner. Murdoch was in turmoil because, despite still grieving for Franz, she was becoming increasingly involved with Elias Canetti. She had spent Christmas Day evening with him in 1952 and on 12 January 1953 he presented her with a copy of his novel Auto da Fé, *which he inscribed, 'To Iris in great hopes, Elias Canetti'. By February 1953 they were lovers: an entry for that month in her journal records how Canetti 'held me savagely between his knees and grasps my hair and forces my head back. His power. He subjugates me completely. Only such a complete intellectual and moral ascendancy could hold me'. In March she was to write of their love-making: 'He takes me quickly, suddenly . . . There is no tender quiet resting, as there was with Franz . . . He is an angel-demon, terrible in his detachment and the mystery of his suffering'.[xxi]*

London
11 January [1953]

Very dear Queneau of the Académie Goncourt, thank you for your letter.
I was touched by it. And although I shan't take your advice I was none
the less moved that you should have committed yourself to giving it to
me – I can well believe that you would rarely do such a thing. The idea
has crossed my mind before, of having a *psychoanalyse*, though not lately
– indeed only once (in 1947) did it seem a real possibility – and now I am
quite certain that it is not the thing. I don't think either that this is just
blind resistance or prejudice. There is of course one *insuperable* obstacle
which is cash! Here, one needs a private income, or to write detective
stories, to afford a 'proper' analysis. I believe it's possible to have one on
the National Health Service, but to get it thus buckshee[1] one would have
to be a positive wreck; and I know that I would give the impression (and
from that point of view quite rightly!) to any sensible doctor of being the
picture of mental and physical health! (Anyhow, my God! If I had *that*
much money I'd go to Sicily or buy a Lurçat tapestry![2]) The money aspect
isn't the point though – one could *find* money to save one's life. It's that
I doubt the value of the thing to me – and rather fear its dangers in general.
You speak of *une vraie, sérieuse, sévère, orthodoxe*[3] – as if these were clear
values. Perhaps to you they are. But in practice *here* (i.e. looking round in
Oxford and London), I think I'd find it hard to discover a man about whom
I didn't have radical doubts. I know that if I were desperate I'd chance it.
But short of that – many of the people one sees or hears of in that trade
are people with whom one's disagreements of outlook are so deep – But
even that isn't the whole point. I've thought a lot about the effects of an
analysis – (several of my friends have been through this) – and it seems
such a gamble. One could hardly fail, in an enterprise like that, to gain a
lot of knowledge about one's self. But the total effect? In cases I've watched
the last state hasn't always been (so far as one could see) so clearly 'better'
than the first. Perhaps one *can't* see very far here. Yet if one is thinking
of treading a costly road one can't help looking at people who've walked
a similar one. Is it wisdom they've gained – or complacency? Balance – or
a sort of ruthlessness? I often don't know. As for the costliness of the road
(not in the money sense) I don't think that I would (consciously!) be
deterred by this if I felt on other grounds that it was the thing. But (nega-
tively) I don't think my problems and difficulties are such as to make that

1 Free.
2 Jean Lurçat, a French artist noted for reviving the art of tapestry.
3 A true, serious, rigorous, orthodoxy.

gamble necessary as a desperate measure – and (positively) there are other, more normal, means to hand. What analysts do one does, ordinarily, *in part* for oneself – and also if one is fortunate enough to have friends who are wise and critical and loving (and I have such friends) this also can help, and change, deeply. I know that nothing in the world can be like a deep analysis – but I don't feel that it's necessarily, or even often, a 'better' thing than mending one's life by the ordinary methods. (Of course anything which I may say against 'the analysed' isn't a general judgement, and in particular not against you, whom, as far as I know you, I believe to be both wise and good – and I believe you when you say that you were helped by this thing.) As to whether one *can* mend it by ordinary methods – I can only say that I think I can.

I can well imagine that I have given you an impression of unbalance and confusion. It is true that I meet you at a point where there is a sort of pivot and things rock strangely to and fro. I see you, and know you, so little – and yet you mean a great deal to me in a 'mythological' sort of way. So I behave to you with exceptional craziness – and I think it *is* exceptional, nor is it (again, I think) the symptom of any general dislocation. (I am trying to picture to myself your picture of me. Perhaps wrongly.) It is true that I am unhappy, but I am far from being 'at a loss'. As far as recent events are concerned, it is not a matter of slow poison, but of a heavy blow from which one must slowly recover.

Since I'm writing you such a long letter (page ten, forsooth!) it seems the place to tell you that (as you will have already guessed if you've thought about the matter) I have by now in effect drifted out of the Christian church. This matter causes me distress. But there it is. Not that I have 'finished' with religion. I haven't begun yet. But I could not maintain this position – which on the other hand I cannot regret having adopted.

I hope all this hasn't bored you. This is a self-centred letter. But you raised a self-centred topic. (Anyway, all letters should be at least fifty per cent self-centred or why write?) And I felt so serious about your advice that I felt I must explain (also to myself) what I felt about it.

It is sad that I shall never know you properly. It has taken me all these years to accept this truth, which I think I do now completely accept. The letter I wrote to you in the summer was my last protest against this particular decree of fate. We shall be acquainted with each other only through letters – as we are now, or I very much hope a little better. Our meetings in the flesh can only be 'strange interludes'.[1]

I must stop writing this damn letter. I've been unable to work most of

1 Evokes Nina's line at the end of Eugene O'Neill's play *Strange Interlude* (1928): 'Our lives are strange dark interludes in the electrical display of God the Father!'

this vac, and now have about four days in which to write next term's lectures! I must go and write 'em. I hold you most steadily in my affections and always will. My dear Queneau,

Ever yours

I

To Raymond Queneau.

St Anne's College, Oxford
21 April [1953]

Dear Queneau, you haven't written for very long. I hope that you weren't in any way offended by my last letter. That would be a sad thing for me. If you can, please write and reassure me.

There's something else I'd like to know too, which is what you think of Beckett's *Godeau* [sic] play. I've heard a lot of people here saying, some that it's terrible, others that it's marvellous. I'd much like to know what you think. (I haven't yet read the thing, but will have soon.)

I'm just going back to Oxford, where I shall be lecturing on the existentialists, so the learned doctors in that city will be hearing the name of Sartre for the first time. (Any news of him incidentally? Especially, *vis à vis* the *Parti Communiste?*)

Meanwhile, the spring has come, and I feel more cheerful. *Cher* Queneau, do write.

Most affectionately, as ever

I

To David Hicks; written after Murdoch had been thrown out of her Oxford lodgings twice by indignant landladies.[xxii]

St Anne's College, Oxford
[May 1953[xxiii]]

David dear,

It was very good to hear from you. I'm glad your things are straightening out. You're about due for some calm waters. I am glad! (I want to meet Katharine again before long. I *did* like her.) You might let me know when your marriage date is, when you know it yourselves. I might light a candle or two. I hope the cottage is rising up now like Carthage to the sound of music.

All here is as usual, except that my pupils seem suddenly to be *exceptionally* nice. Maybe I am giving the little wretches more attention. I am lecturing on existentialist moral philosophy to a lunatic fringe of dotty clergymen and Swedish girls who seem to have nothing to do with the university, and a few others. Oxford is dazzlingly beautiful at the moment. I *never* get used to it.

I am being chucked out of my rooms in King Edward Street, which is just as well in the light of homicidal feelings towards my landlady. She is the sort of old lady who is destined to be killed with a hatchet. Or would be if this was Russia.[1] I'm moving to a couple of rooms in Southmoor Road – with a garden that runs down to the canal. Bathing in summer and rheumatism in winter.

Things are (naturally) better than they were at Christmas. It cheered me up to see you that day.

Let me know if you'll be around these parts. (How's the bike?) – If not, see you in London in the high summer.

I'm sure getting out of Birmingham is a good idea. The Longmans' offer sounds a good thing. Trust in God and take short views.

Dear David,
Ever, much love
From
I

To Raymond Queneau.

4 Eastbourne Road
II July [1953]

Dear Raymond,

I've been for so long on the point of writing to you, and have thought about you often, but I know that hardly counts. I believe I wrote you a letter in a train. Such letters are always restless and homeless.

I've been in London now for a little while, trying to think about philosophy. There are times when all human thought seems so finite and futile. One imagines one understands what the poor beggars wanted to do – and how unsuccessful it all was. ('I see what poor Kant was at', as J. S. Mill[2] said at the age of twelve or so.)

---

1 Refers to the opening of Dostoevsky's *Crime and Punishment*, in which an impoverished young man who lives in a tiny rented room kills an old pawnbroker with a hatchet for her money.
2 John Stuart Mill (1806–73), proponent of utilitarianism and the freedom of the individual.

I shall probably go to Italy in September. My Italian has improved during the year and I want to try it out on porters and bus conductors. I shall be briefly in France too. Listen. I want to meet Simone de Beauvoir. Do you happen to know if she will be positively in another continent in September? I'd be grateful too if you would tell me an address in Paris where I could write to her if need be. Sorry to bother you with this. (I suppose chez Gallimard would find her?)

What are you doing in the summer? I hope you will go to some peaceful place and write a *novel*. What news of the opera?? Write me a letter of at *least* 300 words. That is a modest wish. Love to you, as always

I

To Norah Smallwood, Murdoch's editor at Chatto & Windus. The manuscript of Under the Net *had been delivered anonymously by hand to Gwenda David, talent scout for Viking Press (which published Murdoch's novels in the USA). She never discovered who had sent it, though Conradi has suggested that the secret posting bears all the marks of Canetti's love of intrigue.*[xxiv] *Murdoch had written the novel after abandoning* Our Lady of the Bosky Gates *and discovering that the first-person narrative, in this instance, was the right way forward.*

4 Eastbourne Road
1 October 1953

Dear Mrs Smallwood,

Thank you very much for your letter, and for sending the typescript which has just come.[1] I'm very glad to have your suggestions. I shall take the thing back to Oxford with me and see what can be done when the term has settled down a bit. I'll try to keep my pupils at bay and not keep you waiting too long!

It was very nice to meet you the other day. I'm terribly grateful to you for liking the book and giving it this kind welcome! [. . .]

I send my thanks and good wishes, and look forward to meeting you again in London.

Yours sincerely,
Iris Murdoch

---

1 Refers to the typescript of Under the Net, which was to be published in 1954. Murdoch wrote two drafts of each novel in exercise books, sending the second to be typed up when the novel was completed.

To Norah Smallwood.

St Anne's College
23 November 1953

Dear Mrs Smallwood,
   This is just to say that I shall try to send back the typescript of the novel on Wednesday or Thursday of this week. Unless otherwise instructed, I'll address it to you. You may feel, when you see it, that I've spent a long time doing very little. I've simply made cuts and minor amendments which didn't involve creating anything new. Your objections to the opening chapter and the studio chapter I'm afraid haven't been met. Quite apart from a total lack of time, I feel unclear about what to do with these bits; and conclude that it must sink or swim as it is, subject to your final approval! I hope you won't think this is uncooperative. I think and hope I've done what you wanted on the other points. I'm very grateful indeed for the detailed and useful scrutiny which you gave to the novel.
   I'm still stuck for a title. I'll send my current ideas on the subject either with the typescript, or immediately after. Sorry to be slow-moving. I hope you are very well, and not overworked just before the ordeal of Christmas! I am homesick for London.
   With good wishes,
   Yours sincerely,
   Iris Murdoch

To Norah Smallwood.

St Anne's College
4 December 1953

Dear Mrs Smallwood,
   Stop press on the title question. Enclose a further list of ideas.¹ Of the earlier ones, I now like best *Under the Net*. Sorry to create this chaos. [. . .]
   Yours sincerely,
   Iris Murdoch

---

1 Other possible titles considered for the novel were: *Still Waters*; *Let Down Your Nets*; *The Looker-On*; *Dialogue of One*; *The Song and the Words*; *The Last Word*; *The Signs Among Us*; *That's What I Said*; *The Active Voice* and *Time's Fool*.

To Raymond Queneau.

St Anne's College
14 January [1954]

Dear Raymond,
    Thank you very much for your New Year card – such a piercing reminder of Paris, oh dear! I was glad to hear from you.
    Listen. I've been meaning to ask you this for some time. Chatto & Windus will be publishing a novel of mine later this year – and in accordance with my vow and promise of long ago I should like to dedicate it to you. I had thought of keeping quiet about this and just surprising you with the dedication and the novel together – but then I decided that it's better to warn you, in case, for any strange reason, you might feel embarrassed or made in any way uneasy by this offering. I very much hope you won't be – and that you'll accept it. This would please me very much. It would bind up many things from my past life which are important to me. You are connected with nearly all my early aspirations as a writer – and this book has certain affinities with *Pierrot*. And apart from all this, I just want very much to give it to you. (Whether you'll *like* it, heaven only knows!)
    I'd meant to write at greater length now – but it's beginning of term and I'm in a frenzy of philosophy. I hope your work goes well – so, my dear friend, so – as ever, most affectionately
    Iris

To Raymond Queneau.

Glengarriff
Co. Cork
Eire
11 April [1954]

Dear Raymond,
    Thank you for the kind words about the *Sartre* – I was very glad to receive them. Your letter arrived the day after I had encountered some Breton fishermen, driven by storms to a fishing village near here, who had sold me some cigarettes, so I was able to smoke a Gauloises and think about Europe – which has been seeming very far away from this Irish paradise, where I have been trying to work, amid distractions from mountains, seals, rainbows, waterfalls, leprechauns and other such.

I shall look out for the *Knave of Hearts*[1] which I expect will be around in London soon. (I go back to that city, unfortunately, in a day or two.) My novel will be out in June or July – the timetable seems very uncertain. Anyhow, as soon as I have a copy I'll send you one.

Toujours, mon cher Queneau,

I

To Lucy Klatschko, one of Murdoch's Oxford contemporaries; the following two notes were written anticipating her entry as a novitiate nun into Stanbrook Abbey in May 1954. Murdoch was to visit her there in July.

St Anne's
[April? 1954[xxv]]

Dearest Lucy, just to send this, and very much love and all good wishes. May it be all that you hope, and more that cannot be imagined beforehand. Take me with you as much as you can. With so much concern and affection, ever and always yours

I

[April? 1954]

Dearest Lucy, I was so pleased and touched to get your note. I will indeed indeed think of you then, and do whatever unbelievers can count as praying. (I couldn't have come anyway as I'll be abroad.) I do and will think of you with *much love.* May that be a good day, and the other ones too. Will hope to see you after that before too long. With best best wishes and love

Iris

To Raymond Queneau.

St Anne's College
26 June [1954]

Dear Queneau,

Thank you for your very nice letter about *Under the Net.* The thing has had pretty good criticism here, and one or two attacks from people who

---

1 A 1954 film, directed by René Clément, about the adventures of a French philanderer in Paris and London.

couldn't stand it at any price. As for this thing of getting into other people's houses when they are away, I think this is a peculiarity of Jake Donaghue[1] and me, and indicates some nomadic insecurity no doubt; I don't think it's true of the British, who would be embarrassed usually in such a situation.

Thank you too for what you say about the possibility of a translation (dazzling vision to me, of course). I'm not very clear-headed about these things, but I believe that the translation aspect is being dealt with by my *English* publisher, which is Chatto & Windus. [. . .]

This is beginning to sound like a business letter! I'll be in Paris *conceivably* in August (when you'll be away) and *more likely* in September, late September (when I hope you'll be back). It's an infernally long time since I was in Paris. I've been falling in love with Rome in the meantime – but don't tell your city this.

I'm sorry you are burdened with the *Encyclopédie*[2] and so on. I wish very much you would write another novel. I shall look out for those poems. I hope I shall see you some time before the summer ends. Enjoy Naples and the south. Have you been to Paestum?[3] I was driven mad by that place last summer.

ever and always

Iris

It pleases me *very much* that you like *Under the Net*. I hope you really do. I should be very sad if you didn't.

To Hal Lidderdale, written soon after Murdoch had moved in August to 25 Beaumont Street, near the Ashmolean Museum in Oxford.

[mid-August 1954]

Dearest Hal, thank you so much for your lovely letter, with the recipe and the pictures! I now *see* Salonika and Lidderdale in the middle of it, and the books and the sun upon the sea. (Don't despise that sun. There's none of it here.) I enclose two pictures of you, that I'm *very* pleased with, and have had enlargements of for my own benefit. (Have also given copies to Janie and your mother.) Fast-moving, since you went, I have been to a party given by your cousin Alla, and have bought off her for 25 Beaumont St one carpet and one table (erstwhile property of Avat Ad). So you see. Party was nice

1 The first-person narrator of *Under the Net*.
2 *L'encyclopédie de la Pléiade* was an encyclopaedic series published by Gallimard. The first volume, on literary history, was assigned to Queneau and published in 1955.
3 The remains of an ancient Greek city in the Province of Salerno, Campania, Italy.

– Jane and your mother there. Hal, I hope it is nice, in some way, to be back in Greece? [. . .]

I am depressed by the autumn weather and having been to a publisher's party. I shall go briefly to France next week.¹ I feel no enthusiasm about this. But at least I may see Vézelay.² What a miracle it was to meet you at the Reine Blanche.³ But I can't hope for a repetition of that.

Work is the only cure for my gloom, and I must now return to it.

Dear Hal. Perhaps you will be in England again soon. It's not really such a bad place. One can always sit by the fire or go to the pub when it rains. I hope your work is well and you very well. Take care of yourself. I will write *again*. This with very much love

I

To Raymond Queneau.

4 Eastbourne Road
9 September [1954]

Dear Raymond,

Much thanks for your Sorrento letter, which I found waiting when I got back here. Yes, I know Sorrento a bit. I hope you went to Paestum, that very god-haunted spot.

I liked your picture of Sartre. And, indeed I shall precipitate myself to read Simone de Beauvoir's new novel⁴ – shall order it at once in fact.

I was in Italy (Ravenna and Lake Como), and in Paris for a few days before August 30. I assumed you weren't there and didn't ring Gallimard. I may *conceivably* be in Paris at the end of September, and if I'm there for more than a few hours will ring you, giving you warning beforehand too if possible. [. . .]

I wish I was still in Italy. On this damned island it rains continually. I can't think why the population hasn't migrated ages ago, unless they stay so as to develop that admirable character that Montesquieu says they have because of the climate. Italy was wonderful, especially Ravenna, where one can see mosaics all day, if one avoids being knocked down by a Lambretta, and

---

1 Murdoch travelled in Italy and France during the second half of August with John Simopoulos, her gay Greek/Jewish philosopher friend, to whom she would later dedicate *The Bell*. Murdoch's progessive sexual attitudes and deep interest in different ways of being enabled her to enjoy the company of gay men at a time when there was still widespread prejudice against them.
2 A town in Burgundy famous for its Abbey.
3 Probably Auberge de la Reine Blanche, a popular restaurant in Paris.
4 *Les mandarins.*

watch television all the evening, since every square and side street has a café with outdoor television! I wonder if this plague has hit Rome and Naples?

Now I'm trying to do philosophy, i.e. write a paper to read in Cambridge next term. It's an odd game – I wish I liked it less.

Dear Raymond, I shall *hope* that I may see you in Paris. Will let you know my movements. Affectionately,

ever,

Iris

To Raymond Queneau, written after Murdoch had returned from a holiday in France in September with Peter Ady, a female colleague at St Anne's. Ady had declared her love for Murdoch after they had kissed 'with equal passion' in Ady's car when returning from a party in June 1952, according to Murdoch's journal.[xxvi] *Although little is known about this intense relationship that seems to have lasted for two years, except that they enjoyed travelling abroad together, it is evidence of Murdoch's ability to love both men and women now with equal intensity.*

4 Eastbourne Road

29 September [1954]

Dear Raymond,

Alas, I have been away and am now back (to find your nice letter) – I was only in Paris for half a day, indeed less, during which time it rained continually, and we spent our time walking to and fro under the arcade in the Rue de Rivoli, which was in fact rather an expensive place to shelter. I'm *very* sorry not to have seen you – but the holiday worked out so, as my travelling companion (a busy economist) had suddenly to rush back to send in some earth-shaking report. And as she was driving the car, I just had to come too. (I still can't drive. Can you? I've often wondered this, and meant to ask you. I feel that for some people it is written in their destiny to be drivers of cars, for others not.)

Thank you for taking such trouble about *Under the Net*. I haven't seen the temple of Mithras,[1] and am told it's difficult to, since there are usually some 10,000 Londoners standing round it. I think I am the only person in Oxford who has not written to *The Times* to say that either it should or it shouldn't be preserved. I am in haste now to get back to Oxford and do some work. In France, by the way, we were mostly at Beaune, Nuits St Georges, Mâcon, Meursault, Volnay, etc. etc. and had a wonderful time. As ever and always

I

1 Roman temple, the ruins of which were discovered in the City of London during rebuilding work in 1954.

To Hal Lidderdale. The 'awful moment' referred to in this short letter probably relates to Murdoch's complicated love life; Canetti had told her in July that he loved her and had forbidden her to have sexual relations with John Bayley, with whom she had fallen in love during the summer. Obeying Canetti's decree, Murdoch and Bayley had stayed in separate hotels during their visit to Paris in July; by September, however, they had become lovers again.

[late September 1954]

Dearest Hal, thank you *so much* for *100 Best Philosophers*. Though addressed to 28 (not 25) they did arrive, as philosophy should, in the end. Thank you for cheering me up at this awful moment – much cheered up – will now smoke one of your comforters or turn pages of Kant. When see you in Oxford? How was *Godot*? Did you get hold of Jane? Dear Hal, lots of love, and see you soon and *Thanks*! I

PART FOUR:

Decisions

February 1955 to December 1962

During these seven years, Murdoch wrote six novels, five of which were published. As a group they established her idiosyncratic brand of mystical realism; her 'moral psychology' (the term she used to describe her exploration of the inner life); her 'neo-theology' (practical ways of living a good life without God); and the habitual accommodation of her moral philosophy into her fiction. The peculiar mixture of humour and serious idea-play, distinctive style and gripping storytelling that now characterised her fiction made for intellectually challenging and compulsive reading; her books were eagerly anticipated by the public and scholars alike.

The Flight from the Enchanter (1957) is haunted in part by Murdoch's experiences when working with UNRRA. In Austria she had seen displaced people being deported to certain death and survivors who would never be repatriated. The plot includes a number of refugee characters who are displaced and persecuted, either by mindless British bureaucracy or a sinister enchanter figure who ruthlessly exploits their disempowered status in society. The power invested in the cruel enchanter Mischa Fox in fact reflects Murdoch's own tortuous affair with Canetti, by whom she was now emotionally and sexually enthralled. The charismatic Mischa, a type who was to return in various guises in many later novels, owes much to him. Mischa is skilled at creating his own myth with which the other characters are all too ready to collude as they weave their own masochistic fantasies around him. He thrives on such adoration and is made powerful by it. As an antidote to his power, Murdoch offers a methodology of *attention*, through which obsession can be overcome and goodness made accessible. In this quest Murdoch was becoming influenced by her reading of Simone Weil's work, which is central to the moral psychology within this and all her later novels. *The Flight from the Enchanter* is significant, too, as Murdoch's first novel to include civil servants as central characters. They appear frequently thereafter as a vehicle for satirical comment on bureaucracy and officialdom and enable Murdoch to explore a particular kind of male psyche that falls prey to the corrupting influences of a different kind of political power. On a lighter note, much comedy comes out of her shrewd depiction of contemporary gender relations.

Despite her meteoric rise as a novelist, the less than enthusiastic critical reception of her third novel, *The Sandcastle* (1957), revived Murdoch's early insecurities. After the moral and intellectual seriousness of her first two books, this novel shifted into the realm of romance and was quickly dismissed by critics as slight. The plot revolves around the unhappily married minor public school teacher, Mor, who falls head over heels for the urchin-like painter, Rain Carter, commissioned to paint a portrait of the retired headmaster, Demoyte. Its tension between domestic respectability and high romance echoed elements of Murdoch's own life: although now apparently happily married to John Bayley, she was still emotionally and intellectually drawn to other men. While the book appears on the surface to champion emotional security over sexual fulfilment, it covertly damns the necessity of doing so. Dissatisfaction with the book stemmed largely from the fact that sympathy for the wife and the lover is too evenly divided. That ambivalence, though central to the book's meaning, was frustrating to readers. Stylistically it baffled critics who failed to appreciate the sophisticated formal experimentation within the conventional romantic plot. Only one perceptive critic, Ronald Bryden in the *Listener*, understood her attempt to import into fiction 'the techniques and sensibility of the great French moderns'.[i] Murdoch re-established her reputation by producing the seemingly more conventionally realist *The Bell* in 1958, a novel comprehensively regarded as one of her finest.

The Bell explores more deeply the tensions between sexuality and spirituality, and is brave in its inclusion of a central homosexual character when the practice of homosexuality was still illegal in England. One of its finest achievements is the characterisation of Michael Meade, the self-absorbed failed priest and former schoolmaster whose complex and troubling state of mind is rendered with great sensitivity. The wise abbess describes the inhabitants of Imber Court, where Michael has set up a religious lay community, as 'a kind of sick people' unable to live in or out of the world. Readers become aware of the frailty of a group of damaged and often dangerous characters, yet simultaneously experience non-judgemental fear and concern for them. Encouraging such deep engagement with the consciousness of others was to become one of the artistic imperatives of Murdoch's writing, enacting her belief in the moral force of good art. The book vacillates between realism and surrealism and incorporates Gothic settings, dreams, imagery and symbolism, all densely woven into its realist foundations; this rich narrative style was now establishing itself as a signature component of her work. *The Bell* quickly established Murdoch as an important novelist of her generation and was soon being translated into other languages.

In January 1959 Murdoch was feeling depressed at her lack of progress with *Jerusalem*, a novel she had been writing since early 1958. Eager for Canetti's opinion on her work, she arranged to meet him in London. He advised her that she should avoid sentimentality and tackle more challenging areas of human experience. She then abandoned *Jerusalem*, marking it 'Not on any account for publication ever'.[ii] As the heady liberalism of the 1960s ushered itself in, Murdoch clarified the direction she thought the novel should take. In 1961, she wrote 'Against Dryness', a seminal essay on the English novel, in which she defended 'the unfashionable naturalistic idea of character' over and above 'the consolations of form'. She defined twentieth-century novels as a contest between 'journalistic' (large, shapeless quasi-documentary objects) and 'crystalline' (small, quasi-allegorical novels) and although she thought the crystalline the better of the two, she nonetheless championed the novel of character, which was impossible to render accurately in the more universal terms of myth, symbol and image: 'Literature must always represent a battle between real people and images'. This position informed the construction of her future novels in which she attempted to marry the two styles, albeit not always successfully.

Her next novel, *A Severed Head* (1961), was more of the crystalline type, relying greatly on imagery, poetics and symbolism to convey meaning. Its plot, which includes lateral incest, in this case between half-brother and sister, portends the permissiveness of the 1960s, which both energised and concerned Murdoch. By now she was also romantically involved with the writer and activist Brigid Brophy, whom she had met in 1954. While the unconventionality of Murdoch's life more than matched that portrayed within her novels, this was not evident to most of her friends or the public. *A Severed Head* perhaps reflects the deep and confusing sexual tensions Murdoch was herself experiencing, having been torn between desire for a number of lovers of both sexes and the security of married life – by 1961 she had already had an affair with Peter Ady, was deeply involved with another colleague, Margaret Hubbard, and was now becoming increasingly involved with Brigid Brophy. The character of Honor Klein may be a veiled portrait of either Hubbard[iii] or Brophy or, more likely, an amalgam of both women. The novel certainly suggests that deep sadomasochistic impulses impact on human behaviour and it explores Oedipal desire, homosexuality, incest, violence and the irrationality that hides beneath the fragile veneer of civilisation. The book is clear evidence that Murdoch had taken Canetti's advice to heart. Moreover, its plot was not only personally significant but also prefigured the 'Profumo Affair', named after the government minister John Profumo who jeopardised national security by sharing a lover, Christine Keeler, with a Soviet naval attaché. The ensuing scandal rocked the nation during the early 1960s and probably contributed to the popularity of Murdoch's novels in those years, since the intense and sometimes reckless liaisons within them seem to reflect, rather than distort, the sexual mores of the time.

An Unofficial Rose (1962) features the unsettling and destructive attraction of a thirteen-year-old girl for her mother's suitor. It also includes the passions of a father and son who, at vulnerable points in their marriages, are each faced with the choice between ordinary dull wives and exotic exciting mistresses. The father, Hugh Peronett, chooses to desert his mistress, while the son, Randall, deserts his wife. The book explores the dullness of goodness and the charm of evil alongside a veiled representation of a lesbian relationship. Although she had achieved great success with more conventional novels, stylistically Murdoch boldly experimented in this book with new ways of illustrating sexual delusions, for example by cross-referencing Tintoretto's Susanna Bathing. The sale of Hugh's fictional study of this painting provides a moral centre because the resulting cash offers freedom to all the major characters, while the painting's philosophical investigation of the nature of erotic compulsion expands the moral psychology of the novel. Murdoch's sophisticated use of aesthetics was perceived by critics as an oddity and a failure in style; she had too innovatively challenged preconceptions about the location of meaning in the novel.

Perhaps because of the varied reception of these five novels, Murdoch's letters frequently reveal despondency about the quality of her writing and a general sense of depression. She was encouraged, however, by her editor at Chatto & Windus, Norah Smallwood, by now a firm friend. Her affection and respect for Smallwood and her editors at Viking Press in the States, however, did not prevent her from frequently rejecting their editorial suggestions.

Murdoch was now in great academic and public demand. Despite having been diagnosed as partially deaf with Ménière's disease, an incurable affliction of the inner ear, she gave many lectures and interviews, as well as visiting Yale University in October 1959. She took on the varied roles of serious philosopher, popular writer and committed public intellectual, engaging in televised and other debates with noted philosophers, including Stuart Hampshire, David Pears and Isaiah Berlin, who all became good friends. Her essays and reviews, which appeared in publications as varied as the New Statesman, the Manchester Guardian, the Sunday Times, the Spectator, the Chicago Review, the Yale Review and Encounter, included 'Vision and Choice in Morality', 'A House of Theory', 'The Sublime and the Good' and 'The Sublime and the Beautiful Revisited'.[iv] Murdoch now began to focus more sharply and critically on behaviourist and linguistic approaches to morality, arguing that moral choice cannot be adequately understood through linguistic analysis but should be perceived in relation to an individual's total vision of the world, itself influenced by historical moment, culture and life experiences. Only by giving acute attention to reality as it *is* – rather than allowing it to be obscured by our own fantasies – can we transcend prejudices and misperceptions that might lead to bad judgement. In departing from the analytical approach embedded in linguistics and behaviourism – which rooted moral action in the deed and the word and the relation between them – Murdoch also departed radically from the work of contemporaries such as Gilbert Ryle, J. L. Austin and R. M. Hare. Instead, her moral philosophy was becoming increasingly influenced by her admiration for the work of Simone Weil, whose notebooks she reviewed for the *Spectator* in November 1956.[v]

In her role as public intellectual, Murdoch not only appeared on popular radio programmes such as *Woman's Hour* but also took a strong stand on certain political issues, protesting against nuclear arms and sharing a platform in January 1962 with Judith Hart, Jacquetta Hawkes, Vanessa Redgrave and Marghanita Laski at a Campaign for Nuclear Disarmament (CND) meeting at the Central Hall, Westminster. In 'Morality and the Bomb', an essay written for that meeting and published in *Women Ask Why: An Intelligent Woman's Guide to Nuclear Disarmament* (1962), Murdoch states that 'Nuclear war is wicked and futile in a way which war has never hitherto been' and urges 'a more positive incursion of morals into politics' which will include 'the decent, sensible morality of ordinary people all over the world'. Great Britain's reluctance to take the lead on nuclear disarmament would be, she claims, 'one of our greatest moral failures as a nation'. In October 2014 files released from the National Archives revealed that MI5 'opened personal files on the popular historian A. J. P. Taylor, the writer Iris Murdoch and the moral philosopher Mary Warnock after they and [Christopher] Hill signed a letter supporting a march against the nuclear bomb in 1959'.[vi] About 500 protesters demonstrated at the RAF base at Brize Norton, Oxfordshire (from which US bombers took off) in November 1959. However, Murdoch's name corresponds not only to the H-Bomb March file; it also corresponds to a generic number that refers to a larger case of documents, suggesting that MI5 were watching her well before 1959, probably because of her Communist Party past.[vii]

Although during the mid-1950s Murdoch was growing increasingly fond of John Bayley, she was not yet ready to commit herself in the way that a conventional marriage would have demanded. In 1955 she travelled to Italy for the third time with Arnaldo Momigliano. She was also still in thrall to Canetti, a fact that upset Bayley, who was aware of Canetti's status as a rival, and who remembered him much later as 'the godmonster of Hampstead'.[viii] Murdoch's love for Canetti during 1955, together with her continued involvement with Peter Ady and her close friendships with John Simopoulos and David Pears,[ix] perhaps explain her prevarication concerning a serious commitment to Bayley. Her reservations are reflected in the strangely muted way she refers to him in some letters in this section. Nonetheless, Murdoch and Bayley were married at Oxford Registry Office in August 1956 and the marriage was to prove strong and enduring. Following the ceremony, the couple honeymooned in England and Italy for several weeks and moved into their country home in Steeple Aston, Oxfordshire in December 1956.

In March 1958, Murdoch's beloved father died of lung cancer at the age of sixty-seven and her letters illustrate how deeply involved she then became in her mother's life, helping her to sell the family home in Chiswick and search for a new home in Ireland. Later in the same year Michael Oakeshott contacted Murdoch asking her to read his work, possibly essays that were to feed into *Rationalism in Politics and Other Essays*, published in 1962. They again became close and often met in London, where Oakeshott lived. Murdoch's letters to Oakeshott, whose current affair with a married woman was a source of great anguish to him at this time, clearly express her love and sympathy. However, they also reveal a voyeuristic interest in Oakeshott's emotional life, perhaps indicating Murdoch's conscious or unconscious appropriation of such entanglements as material for her fiction. Murdoch's marriage seemed able to accommodate her 'endless capacity' for both old and new loves and brought her emotional security and contentment; she wrote to Oakeshott in November 1958 that she was 'now very happy in a world which has the simplicity which I never managed to achieve before', adding 'When I got married I was determined to stop being unhappy, and on the whole with John's help I've succeeded very well'.

In 1959 Murdoch was contacted by Philippa Foot, from whom she had been remote for some time despite their reconciliation in 1946. Murdoch felt that their friendship had been 'frozen' since 1949 and confided to her journal that on hearing that Michael had left Philippa for his secretary, she felt 'a certain sense of relief at the removal of the barrier between Philippa and me which Michael constituted'. She wrote to Philippa immediately sending her 'old love'.[x] This approach resulted in a reply from Philippa suggesting they meet, much to Murdoch's delight, and they resumed their correspondence in April 1959.

Despite telling Oakeshott that marriage had endowed her life with a new simplicity, Murdoch's personal life remained complex. By 1955 Murdoch and Brigid Brophy had become close friends. Like Queneau, Brophy was a polymath. She wrote novels, plays, librettos, articles and reviews for newspapers and magazines such as the *New Statesman*, stories for children, and studies of artists such as Mozart, Aubrey Beardsley, George Bernard Shaw and Ronald Firbank, as well as tracts on topics such as religious education in state schools and animal rights. Murdoch sympathised with many of Brophy's causes, which included the teaching of Greek in schools, a campaign against factory farming (Brophy was an early vegan) and the acceptance of bisexuality. They also shared a deep antipathy to the Vietnam War. Brophy was to become one of the five authors who, in 1972, created the Writers Action Group, which lobbied for writers to be paid for the lending of their works by libraries, a long campaign that finally resulted in the Public Lending Right programme for authors.[xi] By the late 1950s Murdoch and Brophy were frequently writing to each other; when they met it was usually on the neutral ground of London pubs and restaurants. They also influenced each other intellectually, enriching each other's life and work. Brophy's deep interest in psychoanalysis persuaded Murdoch to re-engage with Freud, and her sophisticated knowledge of music (particularly her love of Mozart and opera) broadened Murdoch's musical horizons. In turn, Murdoch's profound knowledge of literature extended Brophy's reading and she frequently answered questions concerning classical literature and civilisation. Murdoch urged Brophy to return to novel-writing after she had branched into non-fiction and would read her work before it was published, offering comments and praise. They also enjoyed a shared sense of humour: Brigid Brophy dedicated her novel *Flesh* (1962) to Murdoch, sending her a copy inscribed 'Flash, a navel by Brigid Bardot'.[xii]

The two women were physically attracted to each other but Murdoch resisted Brophy's desire for a full sexual relationship as letters written in 1960 illustrate. From the start, Murdoch made it clear that she was not prepared to sacrifice her marriage to their friendship. This stormy but exhilarating liaison greatly tested Murdoch – especially as Brophy openly expressed dislike of her novels – but brought her deep joy as well as intellectual stimulation. Whereas she had always felt slightly intimidated by and inferior to Philippa Foot, with Brophy she played the wiser older woman who knew more about life than her friend, who was ten years younger. Sadly, early letters from Brophy were destroyed: Murdoch wrote to Brophy in March 1960, 'This is a mouldy frozen-up reply to your charming letter (which I have destroyed: I'm afraid I *did* destroy the earlier ones too, which I now regret!)'. It seems likely that Brophy also destroyed early letters from Murdoch. Letters therefore date from December 1957 rather than 1955, when the relationship began. Brophy was to become an important part of Murdoch's life for twelve years and they stayed in touch, albeit sporadically, until Brophy's death in 1995.

In 1962 Murdoch resigned from her academic post at St Anne's College, Oxford, ostensibly because she wanted more time to write. In fact, her resignation resulted from an affair with her colleague Margaret Hubbard,[xiii] whom Murdoch had known since 1952. Australian by birth, Hubbard had studied at Somerville before becoming tutor in Classics at St Anne's in 1957, where she became increasingly intimate with Murdoch. Despite the fact that Murdoch's marriage allowed her a certain amount of sexual and emotional freedom, Hubbard's constant proximity and her persistent demands on Murdoch's time and emotions began to threaten her marital happiness. The affair was also threatening to become a scandal in Oxford and beyond. Murdoch now had difficult and painful choices to make that changed the direction of her life. The one constant throughout, however, was her burning desire to think well, write well and be an important author.

To Hal Lidderdale, still working in Salonika for the British Council.

St Anne's College
[late February/early March 1955]

Dearest Hal, so very glad to get your letter. I'm glad things are in order and work is going on. I envy you that warm sun. Here, a sort of intermittent warmth has melted some but not all of the frozen snow. That still adheres to the roads and pavements. I still fall off my bicycle. But little birds sing. It was *good* to see you and Janie – I shall see her tomorrow week I hope when she comes to Oxford to see aunt Hat. [. . .]

I saw the *Hippolytus* performed last night, in a new English translation, by OUDS [1] (in the Divinity Schools) – very impressive, and strange, strange. Does one bemuse oneself about those plays? *Can* we appreciate them? Anyway I was very moved and impressed. They wore masks. Dear dear one, this just to send all my love to you.
    I

To Norah Smallwood.

St Anne's College
2 May [1955]

Dear Mrs Smallwood,
    I expect by now you'll have received a nameless novel which will probably be recognisable as mine on points of style, in case I forgot to write my name

1 Oxford University Dramatic Society, which had performed the Greek tragedy by Euripides.

on it. Titles I have so far thought of for it are: *The Flight from the Enchanter,*
To the Enchanter's House, and *Fathers, Children and Gods.* I think of these I
prefer the first at present. You may not like the novel *at all* – and if you just
think it's no good *please* don't mind saying so at once. I know it has many
many shortcomings.

Sometime, if there are still any copies of *Under the Net* left in your cellars,
I should like to have two more copies sent to me, to make rather belated
presentations. Sorry to bother you with these small things.

I hope all's very well with you [. . .]

With all very good wishes,

Yours

Iris Murdoch

To Hal Lidderdale, who had heard that the British Council might send him to Africa.
In the event, he was not sent to Nigeria until 1960.

[late September 1955]

Dearest Hal, Thank you very much for the Shell *démarche*.[1] Sorry no word
yet, but thank you in any case so much for trying! Julian is back in England
now and installed at Royal Holloway College, which she finds a rather
peculiar and depressing joint. The events in Turkey about 6 September[2] were
very violent apparently (and rather underplayed in English papers) – Julian's
family were not actually hurt, but her brother's factory (which he didn't
own, but had put savings into) was burnt down.

I think the Istanbul Greeks fear a massacre on a yet larger scale (a lot of
people were killed on this occasion and women raped etc.) and J's family
want to leave. (J's brother is married to a Salonika girl, by the way.) How
bloody the Turks are, and how little they change.

It must be strange and sad for you to think of *such* packing up. I hope thoughts
of Africa are strong and are consoling. I envy you Africa too. Dearest Hal.

All here as usual, too many pupils too little time. I started another novel,
but have not been able to work at it lately.

Much love to you

I

1 'Move' or 'step'; Lidderdale had responded to the request in a previous letter from Murdoch that he
  contact Shell on behalf of Nicholas Chrysostomides in an attempt to find him work. Julian, a Greek
  female student at St Anne's and twin sister of Nicholas, was taught by Murdoch during 1954 and 1955.
  Murdoch was very kind to Julian, who felt lonely in England, and they remained friends for many
  years. She seems to have been in Murdoch's mind when she created the character of Rain Carter in
  The Sandcastle.
2 The Istanbul riots saw organised mobs attacking Istanbul's Greek minority on 6–7 September 1955.

To Raymond Queneau.

St Anne's College
[22 November 1955]

Dear Raymond,

Thank you for sending the notice of the *Encyclopédie*. If I can inspire our library to buy it, I will! I enjoyed reading the Queneauesque introduction to it. I have no doubt it is epoch-making.

All the same, rather than twenty epoch-making volumes, I would rather have had a letter from Queneau, which he withheld.

There is little news of me. I am still here, I work. It is long years since I was in Paris. I was in Rome at Easter, will be in Amsterdam at Christmas. I think now and then of getting married, but have not done so. My next novel (called *The Flight from the Enchanter*) will come out in the spring. I will send you a copy. I hope you are very well; *je ne vous oublie pas.*[1] Do write, even a word or two. I am glad to see your printed words, but I would like to see some manuscript as well. I send my very good wishes, and my love as always

Iris

To Patricia MacManus, publicity director at Viking Press, New York, which published Murdoch's novels in the United States.

St Anne's College
17 March 1956

Dear Miss MacManus,

[. . .] It was most kind of you to send the copy of Miss Welty's[2] note – I know of her work and was duly pleased. I'm sorry not to have so far managed to send a photo. I hope to have a new one ready next week and will send it at once.

I am interested to hear you are connected with Ireland. Not born there? I was myself, I'm in some ways sorry to say, not brought up there. I was born in Dublin, but my parents very soon moved to England, and I spent all my school days in England. I know Dublin well, and have many friends and relatives there, but I haven't ever really lived there. Ireland remains

1 You are always in my thoughts.
2 Eudora Welty (1909–2001), American author, who had presumably written to Viking praising Murdoch's work.

somewhat of a dream country, connected with childhood, where everything happens with a difference. I certainly wouldn't want to *live* there now, though I feel strongly connected with it. Have you been there ever? You certainly have a good sound Irish name. [. . .]

I much look forward to seeing *The Flight from the Enchanter* in its American guise. Thank you indeed for your concern. With best Saint Patrick's Day greetings,

    Yours sincerely,
    Iris Murdoch

To Norah Smallwood, postcard of the Four Courts, the Quays and River Liffey, Dublin. Murdoch had met the Anglo-Irish author Elizabeth Bowen at a dinner party given by Lord David Cecil and his wife Rachel; this card was sent in July 1956 during a trip to Ireland when Murdoch stayed with Bowen at her home, 'Bowen's Court'. Conradi speculates that she was a crucial factor in Murdoch's decision to marry John Bayley. Bowen's happy but celibate marriage to Alan Cameron (who died in 1952) had provided her with a secure emotional harbour while allowing her the freedom to have affairs with both men and women.[xiv]

[25 July 1956]

Thank you so much for your letter and for sending the typescript.[1] My father is already hard at it, correcting (as he thinks) punctuation. Could you let me know (no hurry) whether you are sending printed sheets to Viking, as last time? (In which case I needn't retrieve my other typescript from them for alterations.) I hope you don't want it all back *too* soon! I am going native in this place and may settle down forever in the bar of the Shelbourne Hotel. If not, will much hope to see you (not for business) in ten days or so.

    Love I

To Norah Smallwood.

St Anne's College
[early August 1956]

---

1 Of *The Sandcastle*.

Norah, thank you very much for your dear telegram. This just to say we shall be wed, here, next week.¹ When the hurly-burly's done I shall sigh with relief, and get on with my work for you. I was sorry not to see you – I only stayed a day in London.

Au revoir then, and love from

Iris

To Jacquetta Hawkes, archaeologist, writer and second wife of J. B. Priestley ('Jack'), with whom Murdoch later worked on the stage adaptation of A Severed Head. *The Priestleys frequently entertained guests, including the Bayleys, at their country home, Brook Hill, on the Isle of Wight.*

St Anne's College
27 September [1956]

Dear Jacquetta,

I have been for so long on the point of writing to you, which is something which always feels like an excuse at the writer's end. I believe you have not yet gone to the Andes, or so I gathered from Norah Smallwood, whom I lately saw in London. I have had a very strange summer, which included, as you may have heard, getting married. I am now married to one John Bayley, a fellow of New College – he teaches English literature and has published a novel. We are involved in the exciting and devastating business of buying a house, and have more or less acquired a very nice one between here and Banbury. It was cheap because it was near an aerodrome, but I think we have not made any mistake. It has a very beautiful garden. I hope you and Jack may come and stay sometime after we are settled in, any time when you would like to combine seclusion in the country with sallies into Oxford. I have never yet lived in the country myself, and it remains to be seen whether it will prove intolerable. John who *has* lived there, and knows how awful it is, is nevertheless prepared to try again.

I remember my weekend at Brook with very great pleasure. I hope you will not think it was churlish of me not to speak of my plans then – but it was a moment when it was hard to speak. And, indeed, I think I was very silent for the whole weekend, which I hope didn't make me a bad guest. I enjoyed myself very much all the time!

I hope you will have a lovely journey. Don't forget you promised to send me a card of the Andes. I will let you off bringing back the parrot. Please give my love to Jack. I shall much hope to see you again, in London or

1 Murdoch and John Bayley were married at the Oxford Registry Office on 14 August 1956.

Oxford, and to introduce you to John. With all very good wishes to you,
Ever,
Iris

To Marshall Best, Murdoch's editor in America.

St Anne's College
[2 October 1956]

Dear Mr Best,

I have now revised *The Sandcastle* and sent it off by surface mail. I read your criticisms with great interest and considered them with great care. As you will see, I have not been able to meet all of them – but here is my account of the matter.

1. The Gypsy. I thought a lot about the gypsy, and decided to keep him. I have made a few minor changes to blend him into the picture a bit more, and also to make his function clearer. I think you may well be right that he is a weak and inauspicious figure, but I still think it would be worse to remove him. He plays a symbolic function, of course in relation to Rain. (He is her shadow. Rain is herself a gypsy: a bird, a nomad etc.) More important, he relates to Felicity, and relates Felicity to Rain. (Felicity who supplants Rain is also to be identified with her.) I know this is not as F. R. Leavis would say, very concretely realised in the book. But the gypsy is part of the structure, and it would weaken it a little to remove him. So I hope you won't mind. After all, he doesn't appear very much.

2. I agree with your criticism of the scene where Rain jumps on Bledyard's bed, and I have made alterations accordingly.

3. Nan's speech at the banquet. I have shortened it slightly but made no other alterations. I see what you mean about it – but it seems necessary to me (and I think it would have seemed necessary to Nan) to have it so, so as to be absolutely sure that Rain would take the point. After all, Nan doesn't know how much or little Mor may already have told R about it. It must also be possible that R is overwhelmed and decided to go.

4. No meeting between N and M after banquet. Again, I have made no change. The book could have had a different ending but I think the 'falling back into ordinariness' is sufficiently indicated – and I felt it better to leave the rest to the reader's imagination. [. . .]

Miscellaneous

I have not met these points. The chief weakness is lack of emphasis on Mor's politics earlier – but I hope that the adult education scene will present Mor as a certain *type* of man with political interests. I have inserted a brief reference to Donald at the banquet. As for D and Carde in the squash courts, certainly more is implied, which may also be left to the reader. Mor embracing Rain in the wood may be implausible, but I think will pass in its context.

That's all, I think. I hope you will not feel that I have not come far enough to meet you. I was very grateful indeed for your criticisms, and I assure you that I thought them over carefully.

About the gypsy, to revert to him, the more I think about it, the more sure I feel that, for all that could be said against him, he should stay in!

I hope I haven't delayed the typsescript too long. Once again, many many thanks for your careful and sympathetic consideration of the novel. *Salutes* and good wishes to you

Yours ever

Iris Murdoch

To Norah Smallwood.

25 Beaumont St
Oxford
30 November [1956]

Dear Norah,

So sorry I missed your call today. Let the name 'Rain' stay, I think – I've got used to it now! And sorry I forgot to say this earlier.

I'm leaving Beaumont St on Dec 11 for: Cedar Lodge, Steeple Aston, Oxon. But St Anne's is best address, as there's no letter box at CL and John tells me country postmen just throw the letters on the flowerbed. See you soon in lovely Christmas London, I hope. And hope you are well [. . .].

Love from

Iris

To Norah Smallwood.

St Anne's College
13 February 1957

Dear Norah,

Of course you can have an option on my next two novels. *Mon dieu*, as if I would consider going elsewhere. I hope they materialise.

Life is so gay, perhaps I shall just sit and look out of the window instead (but I think not).

Am reading *UN CERTAIN SOURIRE*. How does she do it, at that age.[1]

Salutes and love

From Iris Murdoch

I add my surname in case you want this as a legal document.

To Simone de Beauvoir, written in French, requesting a meeting.[xv] *No meeting took place; de Beauvoir sent a note politely refusing the invitation.*

St Anne's College

13 April [1957]

Dear Madame de Beauvoir,

I have long admired your work and it would be a great privilege for me to meet you. I shall be in Paris after Easter, and I would be delighted if you could find the time to have a drink with me. I shall be there from 20th April, but I'll have two students with me during the first week. I shall be more free from the beginning of the second week, about 29th April. I shall be at my London address (4 Eastbourne Road, Chiswick, London W4) until the 20th, and after that probably at the Hôtel des Deux Portes, Rue de l'Échaudé, Paris, VIᵉ. Letters will be forwarded from Chiswick, and I shall call at the Deux Portes for my post, even if I haven't been able to get a room there.

Please forgive me for writing in this manner, giving you so little notice. I know that you are very busy, and I shall understand if you can't spare the time to meet me. If that's the case, don't bother to reply to this letter but consider it as expressing the sincere admiration of a 'fan'. And of course it's quite possible that you might not be in Paris at this time. But I'm hoping for a stroke of luck. I can speak French by the way, but not very well. With best wishes,

Yours sincerely,

Iris Murdoch

PS In order to avoid confusion, if you write to Deux Portes, it would be better to use my married name: BAYLEY

---

1 *Un certain sourire (A Certain Smile)* by Françoise Sagan was published in 1956 when she was aged twenty-two. Written over two months, it concerns a student's love affair with a middle-aged man.

To Raymond Queneau.

> Hotel des Deux Portes
> Rue de l'Échaudé
> Paris VIᵉ
> 22 April [1957]

Dear Raymond,
   I am in Paris for a little while, and would love to see you. Would lunch, dinner, or a drink before lunch or dinner, be possible on Friday, April 26th? A note to the above hotel, where I think I'll be from Tuesday, should find me OK. It would be very good to see you and talk. Inter alia, I am married now (and better write to me incidentally under my married name, BAYLEY, under which I shall be masquerading!). I suggest Friday, as I know I'm free that day, but other times would of course be possible too. I do hope you are in Paris, and aren't too busy – though if you aren't the one, or are the other, please don't worry! But I'll hope we may meet, with all affectionate wishes,
   Yours
   Iris Murdoch

To Norah Smallwood, postcard of the Eiffel Tower sent from Paris.

[April 1957]

O Rage, O Désespoir, disgusting Plon¹ (I learn from a shop window) have published *Under the Net* here as *Dans le filet.*² Surely I didn't miss this on the typescript I saw? Doesn't it occur to them that the title *means* something? They also call it *un Hellzapoppin³ Anglais! Nom de Dieu!* Don't bother them about it, as it's too late. But I am *désolée* about the title. Never mind. Otherwise, springtime in Paris absolutely OK. *Toujours,*

   I

---

1 French publishing firm based in Paris.
2 *In the Net.*
3 From the 1941 American film, *Hellzapoppin'* which was, like *Under the Net*, a fast surrealistic comedy.

To Raymond Queneau.

Cedar Lodge
Steeple Aston
[26 May 1957]

Dearest Raymond, thank you very much indeed for the Hélène Bessette[1] books – I haven't read them yet, but look forward to this pleasure. Thank you too for your most memory-shaking card of the Nordkettenbahn.[2] How could I forget such highly significant days. Strange your being there again –

It was lovely to see you in Paris. I shall hope to see you again with an interval of fewer years.

My home address is above. My Oxford address by the way is St Anne's *College* (not Society). Also my married name is Bayley (not Bailey). But these are mere details. The sun shines. I wonder if you were staying at the Golf Hotel? *Eheu fugaces.*[3] [. . .]

Altogether, it was splendid to meet you again. Love to you from
I

To Brigid Brophy, addressed to Mrs Levey, 23 Earls Court Square, London SW5.

Steeple Aston
[1 December 1957]

Dearest Queen of the Night,[4]

Six or so, yes? Will bring some drink (not yet sure what). Also your play. Excuse not sending it before. (If needed before Friday, let me know.) Much to talk of.

Lots of love
I

1 French novelist and pioneer of the *nouveau roman*. In 1952 Queneau had signed her up to write ten novels for Gallimard.
2 A mountain near Innsbruck that Murdoch and Queneau had climbed during the weekend they met in 1946.
3 From Horace's Latin Ode *Eheu fugaces, labuntur anni* meaning 'Alas, the years fly by'.
4 From Mozart's opera *The Magic Flute*.

To Brigid Brophy.

Steeple Aston
[3 June 1958]

Dearest creature, thank you so much for your vain letter. A letter written on cards has especial weight, as one expects a different *point* to be made on each side; your letters are full of points. John is still on crutches and cursing away.[1] He may not be fit in time for our putative holiday.

I should be so delighted to share the burden so long as it made you happier (or *even* happier I should say, since you are shockingly happy as it is). How I enjoyed our Stratford jaunt. I was pleased I found your glasses lens again. Have you had it fixed? Your letter was not indiscreet, but I have destroyed it. Raining here. Very much love.

I

To Michael Oakeshott, postcard of Killiney Beach and Vale of Shanganagh, Co. Dublin, with Bray Head and Wicklow Mountains, Ireland. After her father's death in March 1958, Murdoch's mother Rene had decided to move back to Ireland. This trip combined both holiday and the search for a new home for Rene. Murdoch had unexpectedly met Oakeshott again in Oxford during the summer of 1958.

Steeple Aston
6 August [1958]

Just back from this wild west of Ireland and a lot of swimming in the cold Atlantic. I hope things have gone well for your Italian holiday. Dublin is gay and full for the Horses Show, and I am feeling Irish and mad. I do hope you are well – and I send all my love.

I

To Michael Oakeshott.

Steeple Aston
14 October [1958]

Michael, I was very pleased indeed to hear from you. I've thought of you

---

1 In late March John Bayley had had an accident while trying to start their car with a starting handle when it was in gear; the car had jumped forward and crushed his leg.

so often. Thank you for sending the stuff[1] – I shall be very glad to read it, though I don't know if I shall have any sensible comments.

I should much like to see you again. When I was talking to a society at LSE not long ago I knocked on your door, but you weren't there. You were in my mind earlier this year when I was writing some socialist stuff for the *Conviction* volume.[2] I suspect you are responsible, by reaction, for a lot of my political ideas! But my thoughts of you are not at all political.

I'll write again when I've read your typescript.

Love

Iris

'In love there are no tactics, only courage'. I hope that stayed in. I'm still not sure what it means.

To Michael Oakeshott, written after meeting him in London on 30 October.

Underground
[30 October 1958]

I can't easily now express in words what it has meant to me to see you again.

This is just to say that I didn't write anything inside *The Bell* because I didn't before seeing you know what to write. I know now and will write it next time I see you.

I

To Michael Oakeshott. Married with two children, Oakeshott was in love with Rosemary,[xvi] a married woman. Rosemary's attempts to end the relationship were causing him much distress at this time.

Steeple Aston
[4 November 1958]

---

1 Oakeshott had sent Murdoch some of his recent essays for comment.
2 Murdoch contributed the essay 'A House of Theory' to *Conviction*, a volume edited by N. Mackenzie, published in 1958. In this acclaimed essay she argues that a more theorised socialism, informed by Guild socialism and Marxism, should underpin Labour Party policy. Murdoch focuses on the issue of the good life for a whole society and complains that important moral issues have been eradicated from current political statements and theory. Socialism must, she states, 'far more frankly [. . .] declare itself a morality'.

Michael, dear love, it's a great joy to write to you and a sort of miracle. I feel such a strange mixture of pain and elation – as well as the selfishness that goes with being in love. I try to picture you in your absolute separateness and in the grief that besets you now – but all I keep seeing is you in relation to me, you so entirely clear and captivating – and my love that was beside you asleep for so many years. Its awakening now is so strange, the way it joins the past to the present, and makes the past suddenly so fresh and near. I knew I would be exceedingly moved at seeing you again – but did not quite expect to find myself, where you are concerned, so positively back at square one!

I shall be in danger of wearying you with this stuff. I am wretched to think that there is so little I can do for you. I have known so much grief myself of the kind you are now in, not only because of you, though that was I think the worst, but in other cases too, I know how sunk one can be in it and how nothing else consoles or matters at all. One looks with such a dull eye on the charms of the world, and affection and love from other people are little use. I wish I could think of something to delight you. You need not speak of having little to give me. Just by existing and by letting me speak to you, you give me an immense amount. You make me want to bound about you and about the idea of you like an excited dog. You are infinitely rich where I am concerned. I love you extremely and how it eases my heart to be able to say so.

So much happened to me since I last saw you – much of it unhappy. I will tell you sometime if you wish it. I have been in love several times. And am now very happy in a world which has the simplicity which I never managed to achieve before. Yet it is true too that my love for you never died, it never got twisted and changed – I never 'got over' you, though I certainly tried to, *tried* and succeeded in loving other people. But there was for me a sort of absolute purity and intensity about the way I loved you which made it impossible for that love to alter, though it could sleep.

You may think this is a lot of nonsense and not at all what you want to hear! Oh Michael, oh dear, I do love you. Poor Michael, you asked me to come to you because you thought I might give you some help, and it looks as if you will have to help me. That can be easily done, however – or at any rate it can be done, though there's no need for you to trouble about it at the moment. When I got married I was determined to stop being unhappy, and on the whole with John's help I've succeeded very well. (By the way, J knows about you, of course.) I am resolved not to be unhappy about you. I feel that, with some small shift in the universe this can be managed. But you must help me to move it. It is as if you must make some sort of spiritual effort on my behalf – and my love for you can be all joy and no sorrow. I think this is possible. However, as I say, don't worry about it now, I'm sure

you are in no mood for spiritual efforts, and this letter is becoming intolerably self-centred.

As I said yesterday, it's hard not to believe that a great deal of love *must*
heal and console the recipient – but this is a fallacy. However I do send my
love, selfishly of course, but hoping that it will be healing. Also I do truly
hope, which is more difficult (my turn for spiritual effort) that your strange
tangle may resolve itself in a way that will make you, quite apart from me,
entirely happy. (How far I am from that 'wisdom' which you foolishly attributed to me.) Miracles do happen in such things and this may be just the
darkest time before the scene lightens and improves again. *May it be so.* Let
me know if there is anything which I can do, which it is in my means to
do, for you in this matter. I do *hope* for you, and cannot believe that a person
so entirely worthy of love can be cast down for long. In one way or in
another, life will come back. Dear Michael, may it be soon.

You needn't reply quickly to this letter, or indeed 'reply' to it at all. I
know it would be, and especially at this time, burdensome for you to do so.
It is a great joy to me to write to you, and my privilege to write, not your
duty to answer. However, I hope you will write to me not too infrequently.
You needn't say much. Something along the lines of 'Pouring rain today.
Got a cold. Lectured on Hobbes.' will do fine.

I must stop this now (very hard to stop) and get on with my work. I'm
sorry to burden you with this selfish letter, but I had to. I do do hope things
are better with you and that you will soon write more cheerfully. I embrace
you with so much love and many hopes for your happiness.

I

To Michael Oakeshott.

Steeple Aston
[6 November 1958]

Michael, dearest, it's raining; and I have just wasted half the morning in
vain at the Radcliffe Infirmary waiting for a doctor who had no time to see
me (I find I write 'you' instead of 'me' – they are indeed much mixed up
at present). Among the various disasters that have come my way since 1950
is that I have contracted 'Ménière's disease', a tedious and quite incurable
ear ailment. I wonder if you noticed how deaf I have become. It's trivial
at present however and I hope will take twenty years to get really bad, by
which time I shall with luck have succumbed to something else. Luther
suffered from this disease, and also Swift, who wrote about it in a poem.
Your enemy Rousseau had it too I suspect from his description of the

symptoms. All irritable bad-tempered men. Perhaps I shall get like that. [. . .]

I hope you weren't bothered by my letter of Tuesday. Don't be. If you knew how in spite of everything I feel so deeply calm and strong about you; only I must be allowed to love you as it is so obviously my destiny to do so.

I do hope things are not terrible or too sad for you just now. It is a grief not to know, as I find myself imagining you in despair or involved in unhappy dramas. Do not let me trouble you – only, if it may be, let me help.

All my love

I

To Elias Canetti

Steeple Aston
[early November 1958]

My dear, I don't even know if you're in England. I am paralysed about making arrangements because of the difficulty of getting in touch with you, and because I am always afraid of making a date and then having to cancel it – my comings to London last year were all rather impromptu and haphazard. Could I now suggest perhaps dinner on Tuesday Nov 11 – coming to Thurlow Rd¹ between 7 and 7.30? I enclose a stamped addressed envelope. No need to put any communication inside (though of course I would like one!!) – just seal up and send off and I will know when I receive it that Nov 11 is OK. If I *don't* get any envelope back I will try to telephone you codewise in London (it can't be done from here).² If I get your envelope, I will turn up on Nov 11 as suggested (that wd be a morning middle this coming week). If I don't hear from you, or get you by telephone, by the end of next week I'll assume you are still away. *Forgive* this rather *technical* letter. I do very much want to see you and talk. As always much love

Iris

To Michael Oakeshott.

[7 November 1958]

1 Canetti's home in Hampstead, north London.
2 Canetti's close friends were given a code – let phone ring three times, put the phone down, dial again. This enabled him to distinguish friends he wished to speak to from other callers.

Dearest, thank you with all my heart for your two letters, which arrived together this morning at Steeple Aston [. . .]

I understand what you say about not being 'distracted', but wrapping the thing round with layers of patience. It can take a long time. But *that* resolution is much – and there are moments of great strength in despair, at least I have found it so, if one does not cheat about the completeness of loss. I know what you mean too about consolation. I don't offer anything intended as a substitute or based on any calculation of compassion, but simply and because I must, love and more love.

To help you, I cannot say just what you must do. I think you are doing it anyway. I need, indeed, some sense of the indestructible where you are concerned – some sense, at last, of permanence. I will say more later perhaps. *Talking* to you is really the main thing (including in letters). I must stop this and teach. Dear dear Michael, my devoted love,

I

To Michael Oakeshott.

Radcliffe Infirmary (Outpatients)
[12 November 1958]

Dear darling, it will cheer me up a lot to write to you while waiting (probably again in vain) to see my beastly doctor. How like death these places are.

It was so wonderful to see you yesterday, I still feel quite transported by it. How rarely in one's life one has that feeling, and how splendid it is when it comes, of being intoxicated and ravished just by someone's presence, indeed their *being* – so that when with them one practically wants to cry with joy. It seemed a very short time, but lives on afterwards.

Thank you for the most charming handkerchief which had that mystery which attaches to all the objects that surround you. (Something special about your relation with objects – not at all that of a connoisseur – more like the limpets that a rock might collect. A sort of random close belongingness.) *Thank you* and also for the photograph which is so very expressive and like you. You have in the photo that air of someone acting a poetic tramp in an Irish play which delights one entirely. You also bear a strange resemblance to one of my ideals, Guy the Gorilla[1] (not your *face* dear one, but something in your attitude and bearing). I wondered why I was so moved by Guy.

I shall be going to Ireland Nov 19–22, but rushing straight to London,

1 A famous and popular resident of London Zoo at this time.

probably straight to the airport, and back both ends. In a way I'd rather not know exactly when I'll see you as it makes the time between into such an attrition. (I mean, not know a *long* time ahead.) I haven't by any means yet got (but *will* I hope) that desired sense of security about you, that sense of your being deeply *tout simplement* a part of my life, permanent, enduring in time. (How absurdly little I know you in *some* ways.) I've never in fact *seen* you except when in a state of being very much in love – I think I was even at the first moment – I had somehow prepared myself to be. I was so surprised one day when I heard someone (who was not in love with you, the foolish boy) describing your appearance – it wasn't that it was unflattering, it was just not like what I had seen at all (that was at a time when I did not think I would see you again). [. . .]

I was so moved thinking of you going along with the fireworks – your love for Rosemary suddenly seemed to me less abstract. I don't think I feel jealous at this moment. (Seemed less abstract to *me* I mean. I resist picturing Rosemary. I find it hard anyway to imagine someone who, loved by you, would not be in a permanent state of complete surrender.)

Hundreds of things to ask you. I did ask I think, but we were talking at the same time and I got no answer, whether you were writing a book. I can't in fact picture your work (or you working) very clearly either. You never seemed to *do* any work in the Rose Place[1] days! Yet I have a very strong feeling about your mind – it's odd that something about your mind captivated me through your writing before we met – although I find your point of view politically speaking so unsympathetic (indeed, dearest one, pernicious!). Yet somehow you were all *there* in your writing before I set eyes on you.

I'm so sorry I swindled you out of your supper last night (and your lunch the time before). Next time *you* anyway must eat properly. I thought of you reading the thesis. I hope you had something to eat when you came back.

I hope you don't mind these letters that just go on and on. I think I'm about to be summoned now (a scene of such misery, rows of gloomy deaf people with drooping hands. The nurses obviously *despise* us) so will stop writing and close this letter later:

Later: partly with relief, one learns that medical science can do nothing for one and is indeed indifferent to one's predicament.

I must stop this now, though the talk goes on in my mind. I do hope you slept well with no nightmares. I'll write again in two or three days. I kiss you and embrace you with much love and gratitude and devoted and faithful concern. Ever ever

I

1 Where Oakeshott had his flat in Oxford.

To Michael Oakeshott.

Steeple Aston
[16 November 1958]

Dear love, thank you so much for your sweet letter. I hope it *did* make you less sad to write it. It would please me very much to think that was so. You mustn't speak of failing me – somehow there couldn't be any question of that. You, and loving you, have always meant for me more life – and I *do* think that we can, as you say, 'belong to each other's happiness'. I certainly don't feel, except for being sad that you are sad, unhappy about you now, but so very glad that my delight in your being is renewed and that something marvellous is recaptured from the past. I do hope that perhaps you are feeling, with each day, a little less sad – I see only rather dimly into your grief over Rosemary – I mean I believe in it and feel it, but don't yet know you well enough to understand with my whole imagination. I will try to. And, oh heavens, hope to know you better and learn more of you. I think of your sadness and wish I knew the place to apply my strength to make it less. You talk, and this is so like you, of living on 'for fun, as a child or a gipsy'. Don't you imagine you will be in love again and perhaps happily? I know it seems sacrilege to say or think it at such a time. But you are a creature so eminently framed for love (and somehow for happiness) – I can't believe in your unhappy destiny. [. . .]

It's been a wonderful and very misty rainy warm Irish day here. I worked in the garden in the afternoon. The house and garden here made a sort of magic kingdom – the garden is nearly three acres, mostly with a high wall round it, and in the vacation sometimes days pass without our going outside the gate. I am really very lucky.

Do not be sad. But I know how very deep these wounds are. May your patience blunt the pain at last. I'll write from Ireland.[1] (I leave on Wednesday, back on Saturday evening.) I kiss you, dear Michael, and send you all my tenderness and love.

I

To Michael Oakeshott.

Dalkey
[21 November 1958]

---

1 Another trip to help her mother buy a house there.

Dearest M, can't write properly, all too disturbing, exciting, worrying over here. The sun shines and the sea breaks thoughtfully on the rocks which have somehow remained all the way along this otherwise so urban coast south of Dublin. The house my mother is nearly buying is charming, but indecision and comparison and trying to make up other minds than my own have reduced me to a state of exhaustion. I wish I could just be quietly here and watch the sea. Even the moon shines at night with great radiance upon Dalkey island, seen from the window of the hotel. I wonder if I could see you next Monday or Tuesday afternoon – [. . .]

I think of you, love you, embrace you, dear Michael.

I

To Michael Oakeshott.

Steeple Aston
[23 November 1958]

My dear, very little time to write today, but I want to speak to you again for a moment. I think very much of you, and of Rosemary. I hope Tuesday was not a dreadful day. I got through my silly discussion[1] all right, Stuart and I and Taylor actually went on talking for forty-five minutes without (I think) repeating ourselves though the stuff was pretty hopeless. (Don't listen to it.)

I feel despondent and in a state about my writing. I'll tell you more about that later – not that there's anything to tell really. I just have a ghastly conviction of second-rateness and *no notion* of how to *get up* from where I am. An atmosphere of facile success doesn't help. I want to be guided, criticised, *really attacked* in an invigorating way – but this is hard to arrange and in the end one has to try to be, fiercely enough, one's own critic. Nausea about all this. Will talk again later.

Forgive this rubbish. I do hope you are not sad and upset today. I was so *pleased* when you predicted that you would love me more! Do so. I love you and kiss you with all my heart sending constant thoughts of concern.

I

---

1 Murdoch had taken part in a recorded radio discussion, 'The Habit of Violence', with two other philosophers, Stuart Hampshire and Charles Taylor, both fellows of All Souls College, Oxford at this time. It was broadcast by the BBC Third Programme on 28 November 1958 at 8.15 p.m. and repeated on 15 February 1959.

To Michael Oakeshott.

Steeple Aston
[25 November 1958]

Dear love, no time to write properly today, but I just wanted to talk to you for a moment. It was so marvellous to see you yesterday – I felt so wonderfully at peace with you. It was sad, though, coming back to poor old soon-to-be-dismantled 4 Eastbourne Road. It reminds me strangely of coming home here after I left you in December 1950. My father had cut down a damson tree in the garden – and when I found he had done this I began to cry and couldn't stop. My parents were very puzzled! Such a cold air comes back suddenly from that time. But there must be no such despairings now, and you must help me to take from you only joy and happiness – which seems odd when *you* are not happy. I so much hope you *will* be. But even when you are not you can make me happy, and then I can give you some back. And you must help me not to be sad.

I hope things will be well with Rosemary. You will see her. My most loving thoughts to you in this and all things. Dear dear Michael, I love you so much, so devotedly, and kiss and embrace you with all tenderness.

I

To Michael Oakeshott.

St Anne's College
[28 November 1958]

My dear, I think very much of you and Rosemary and you going to see Rosemary. I still can't picture her clearly. But I don't think angrily about her – only with puzzlement. I'm sorry I wrote such an egotistical letter yesterday! I still feel very gloomy and casting around to find as it were a *technique* for getting right away from where I am. The trouble is everything, of *that* sort, happens so slowly and requires so much faith. [. . .]

It is very hard to *reach* another person's grief – this kind of grief, I know, is pretty well incommunicable. The prospect of final partings is something one cannot bear to look at. What is so strange is that one survives. You said you had a spring of happiness within you and I can see that to be true. One needs to use, as it were, ingenuity and fancy in finding ways to carry on until some happiness returns. And as you said a true confronting and internalising of grief is the best therapy. May it be so for you. Excuse this letter which blunders on through various metaphors and says very little. The knowledge that one survives is cold at those early moments. But one must try to *put* life and interest back, in ways that seem artificial, into the areas of one's being which obsession with one thought has deadened. All this is really picturing myself, perhaps, and not you. I reflected this morning, as I was walking along the road to St Anne's, how little in a way I knew you. You are a very odd fellow indeed. However, I love you. It may be that today you are very deep in despair, and I am terribly conscious of being far away and outside when I would wish to be otherwise. I love you very much. The impotence of one's desire to heal and to protect. I will write tomorrow. I embrace you, wanting to guard you with love and make you less sad.

I

To Michael Oakeshott

Steeple Aston
[29 November 1958ˣᵛⁱⁱ]

Darling, forgive yesterday's self-centred letter. I'm still feeling self-centred today, I'm afraid. And gloomy. I hope your visit to Rosemary was all right and that she is getting on well in hospital. I hope you are not too sad. Do not be.

I want to talk to you, but somehow can't write today, no words. I detest the book I'm writing at the moment¹ – and the things I can do now so easily seem hopelessly mediocre and not worth doing. I want to go to school again, but there are no masters for what I want to learn. Or rather there are, I suppose, but it's almost impossibly hard to get them to teach one. Perhaps I should stop writing for a year and do nothing but read Shakespeare and Homer. But I haven't the nerve. Time is too short. So I shall go on chattering. Christ. I wish you were here, you would certainly cheer me up. It's a strange misty day at Steeple Aston and the garden is very very still in a greenish brownish haze. I can see a magpie sitting on the end of a branch of a fir tree. Very Chinese.

I love you and am so very glad you exist. I do hope you are not plunged in sadness or in any way tormented.

Ever ever ever

I

---

1 *Jerusalem*, the novel about utopian socialists, which Murdoch was to abandon the following year.

To Michael Oakeshott.

Steeple Aston
[2 December 1958]

Dearest, a misty afternoon at Steeple Aston. I've just been cleaning the house. We have a *gardener*, but no help in the house. I don't mind doing ordinary housework. It's cooking I hate. Fortunately John likes it. I rather enjoy washing and sweeping etc. – the house looks very beautiful afterwards, or anyway the civilised parts do. It's a most sympathetic house. The previous owner, who was psychic, said there were no ghosts, as if there had been any she would have seen them.

I think about you, turning things you've told me (about recent events) over and over. How important it is, to me anyway – I wonder if it is to you? – how people *think* about one (and how one thinks about people). Context for idea of prayer. One should never tell anything to somebody who won't think about it right. Or is this too timid a doctrine? Of course one has to be bold because of lack of knowledge (of people). Oh dear. May it be well, somehow, together or apart, for you and Rosemary. I was so touched by your worries culminating with her 'perhaps I needn't go back'. How mad love is – one human being keeping another on tenterhooks and in a state of frantic speculation. Mad, mad. Yet making the world go round of course. I feel in a melancholy, worrying about you in too abstract a way, and stuck with all my work. I do hope things are not too bad on your front today. I won't write tomorrow unless (possibly) if I hear from you. Dear poetical old Michael, most rationalistic and romantic of beings, I put my arms round you and remind you that I love you.

I

To Michael Oakeshott.

Steeple Aston
[mid/late December 1958]

Dear love, thank you so very much for your letter and for the charming and magical present! Thank you very much indeed. I was so glad to hear from you. *Don't* for heaven's sake worry about 'boring' or 'hurting' me! I would very much rather you talked to me about what was on your mind. If I felt you were putting up a cheerful facade it would be unbearable. I do hope things are well, better, and that perhaps you are moving towards some sort of peace with Rosemary. May it be so. [. . .]

I send you very best and most affectionate Christmas and New Year wishes, loving you, dearest Michael, very much indeed.

I

To Norah Smallwood.

Steeple Aston
27 December [1958]

My dear Norah, I write in a mad moment to ask the following. I have by me a small number of poems, written at various times. They are obviously not very good. However, they exist and occasionally occupy my thought. John likes a few of them. It sometimes occurs to me that I would like to shew them to someone else, *not* necessarily with any view to publication. I wonder if you and Cecil Day Lewis would sometime or other glance at them? (As I am shy about them, I'd rather no one else saw them.) There would be no hurry about this. Anyway they aren't typed or tidied up at present.

Feel terrible after Christmas and hate my novel even more. Think I had better take up leather work or something useful. All good New Year wishes and love from

Iris

To Michael Oakeshott.

Steeple Aston
[January 1959]

Dear heart, I am so sorry that things are bad. I know how terrible such times are when one moves all the day between hope and despair and cannot kill hope and yet wants to be without it. I wish I could cheer you, sending some carrier pigeon of devotion – here it is. Dearest Michael, don't be too cast down. I hope your work will begin to go well and to interest you – work can help so much. Work, and counting of one's friends. I hope you feel a little more at peace.

My mother has at last decided *not* to have the house in Dalkey that we have been dithering about – so we are back at square one. Just as well in a way, as the house at Chiswick is still not sold. When it is, it will be best that she go over without me and look at houses with the help of our officious cousins, keeping in mind my absolute veto on bungalows and housing estates!

The snow is so beautiful – we're in a sort of diffused golden quasi-sunlight – that I can't think how I shall settle down to work at all. (It's Sunday morning and I am sitting by a big log fire in the library – this is such a nice room with a tapestry entirely covering one wall. Very peaceful and good for work so I ought to get *something* done, even if it is only this lousy paper on Kant's aesthetics.)

Dearest, I do hope you are not feeling too utterly sad – do not. There are so many things in the world – so even if not as happy as kings one should be able to make a plan to keep off despair. I kiss you, dearest Michael, with all my love

I

To Michael Oakeshott. Murdoch was by now strongly attracted to Margaret Hubbard, her colleague at St Anne's, who is mentioned in this letter. In February 1959 she was to confide to her journal, 'I have no idea whether [she] has any physical apprehension of me comparable to mine of her, and whether when our hands touch when she lights my cigarette she too trembles'.[xviii]

Steeple Aston
[January 1959]

Dear darling Michael thank you so much for your letter. I was about to write to you again. So very glad to hear from you and to know that you had a happy Christmas. I am flattered that you ask my help with the dedication![1] I can back my accuracy but not my elegance – and will *discreetly* get help from my learned colleague Margaret Hubbard who really knows Latin. Yes, I am so *glad* that things are better again with Rosemary. I shall probably never stop being jealous, but I think it is a pain which like the continual noise in my right ear one will eventually get so used to that one doesn't notice it! I am so glad too that you should tell me about Rosemary, especially when it is nice things. I hope and believe you are much happier now.

I don't know when I shall be in London. It seems very difficult to leave this place when one has been steadily here for a time. It is very beautiful and strange now in the snow. I feel in an odd frame of mind, upset and desperate and elated all at once. I have stopped writing my horrible novel. I am trying to write a paper on Kant's aesthetics for next term. Otherwise do nothing but write poetry and my diary. I have written a long poem in

1 Oakeshott was composing some sentences in Latin that would form a dedication to Rosemary in a forthcoming book.

the metre of the 'Cimetière marin'.[1] Comparing it yesterday with the CM was filled with despair! The trouble with poetry is it takes so much *time*!

I would love to see you. I would also like to come up and talk to Canetti about my work, as any talk with him always gives me energy and new thoughts. But it really seems impossible to get outside these gates, as if the place were enchanted. A lovely enchantment. The trees are covered in snow and the sun shines and sparrows and jackdaws and magpies decorate the lawn. (I ring a bell every morning when I feed them, and they all come.)

How early your term starts. Ours is looming now. I'll write again very soon and hope to see you before the end of the month, and meanwhile am thinking about you with love and joy. I embrace you, dear dear Michael

Ever

I

To Michael Oakeshott. After the meeting with Canetti mentioned in this letter, Murdoch recorded in her journal, 'Canetti said the stuff I have written so far is weak and sentimental. I avoid unpleasant things, do not "let rip" enough'. This meeting resulted in her decision to write a novel about incest ('The theme of loving one's sibling, always near to my heart') with the title A Severed Head.[xix]

St Anne's College

[30 January 1959]

Michael dear, I'm so sorry not to have written sooner. Great rush, culminating in being yesterday in London to give a talk at Birkbeck. I had lunch with Canetti, and had thought of trying to see you in the later afternoon, but such short notice again seemed unfair, and anyway I was made very late by the fog. (I've never seen anything like the scene in Hampstead.) [. . .]

We have a scholarship candidate this year called Pallas Athene Rhodes-Jenkins. (I can't actually vouch for the surname, except that it is double-barrelled.) M. Hubbard and I after making simple jests about this were struck by the idea that perhaps it would turn out *really* to be PA! We shall eye her nervously.

I do hope you are well and not sad? I think of you very much – and will write again soon. With all my love, Michael

I

---

1 'The Graveyard by the Sea', a poem by Paul Valéry, which Murdoch greatly admired and which is mentioned in three of her novels. Disheartened by her failure with *Jerusalem*, Murdoch had turned to writing poetry.

To Raymond Queneau.

St Anne's College
[30 January 1959]

Raymond, to say at once thank you very much for sending your new novel,[1] I am delighted! I knew of its existence and would indeed have been angry if you had not sent it! Its arrival resolves this tension in an agreeable manner. I'm sure I shall like it, and have already enjoyed the first page, which is all that, without a penknife, I can enjoy at the moment.[2] I recently spoke of you with another admirer, John Russell the art critic, who I believe saw you in Paris. Heaven knows when I shall be over there. I think of you, am very pleased to have your book, and send, *cher* Queneau, much love.

I

To Sister Marian at Stanbrook Abbey.

Steeple Aston
[early February 1959]

Dearest Lucy, just to say, before Lent begins thank you so very much for your most kind and moving letter. I was very touched that you should have felt like writing so. The stuff I am writing now has all gone wrong, and somehow your letter, in this connection, was cheering. Will write again later. This to send you, dear Lucy, all my love and whatever sober yet cheerful greetings the season admits of.

To Michael Oakeshott.

Steeple Aston
[19 April 1959]

My dear, I do hope all's well with you. I think of you a lot, hoping so. We've been away, last week, staying first with John's parents in Kent, and then with the (David) Cecils at Cranborne.[3] That was all very nice and easy on the

---

1 *Zazie dans le métro.*
2 Some books at this time were sold with their pages unseparated.
3 Murdoch and her husband often spent a few days with Lord David Cecil and his wife Rachel at their home in Dorset, sometimes combining it with a visit to Janet and Reynolds Stone, who lived in the same county. David Cecil, John Bayley's tutor at Oxford, became his mentor when Bayley started teaching at New College, Oxford, by which time they were already good friends.

nerves and pleasantly time-wasting, with lots of parties and excursions to visit churches and manor houses etc., interspersed with reading and charades and French cabaret and the gramophone. When with the Cecils we dined with Cecil Beaton, who has a fantastically Edwardianised eighteenth-century house nearby. The air of unreality was increased by the presence of Truman Capote.

I am still hideously stuck with my novel and correspondingly depressed. Add to that the continual rain. The cuckoo arrived last week, but has been silent since in disgust. Why ever does he come to this island, he wonders.

This nonsense is just to send my love to you and many thoughts. Do write a little note when you have time. Did I tell you my mother *may* now be buying a flat in Barons Court? It's a small but very nice flat overlooking Queen's Club. But there are snags about the lease. *On verra.*[1]

Michael, dear heart, I embrace you with the old love and the new and with hopes to hear from you soon.

I

To Philippa Foot, whose husband Michael had recently left her for his secretary.

St Anne's College
[late April 1959]

I have just heard the news about M. It may be tactless and untimely to write to you, but I feel I must and at once. I simply wanted to send you all my old love. It's been a long time in store, but I think it's scarcely diminished, and that you knew then, and know now how much it is. My dear dear darling, I kiss you with very much love and all hopes for your absolute welfare.

Ever
I

To Philippa Foot.

St Anne's College
early May 1959

Thank you for your letter. It said what I would most have wished it to say. There was of course no barrier except what was connected with Michael.

1 We shall see.

Losing you and losing you in *that* way, was one of the worst things that ever happened to me. I hope very much that we can now recapture something. I have thought of you so much in these years, and dreamed painfully of you too. I would certainly wish only to speak to you from the heart.

I'll write again directly suggesting a number of times next week. All my love to you.

I

To Michael Oakeshott.

St Anne's College
[7 May 1959]

Dear love, please write, or else I shall think (indeed I am thinking already) that I have offended you. *I know* what it's like practically to die of love. And know too the futility of cries from the sidelines. Mine was wrung from me, but all you have to do is to say for Christ's sake shut up. Forgive me if I have been obtuse, but I can't help thinking about you a lot, and so running the risk of getting things all wrong, and making untimely remarks. I kiss your hands.

Ever
I

To Philippa Foot.

Steeple Aston
[May 1959]

My dear, thank you for the shift. See you then 7.15, 7.20ish this Thursday May 16. I've written you a number of letters in my head, but doubt if I've succeeded in telepathising them. Why communication so hard? You have figured in my *thoughts* for so long, maybe this makes it harder to meet the real person – and makes a lot of reliving of the past necessary in order to correct everybody up till the present. Sometimes I feel I understand myself very little. One lumbers opaquely along. I feel rather depressed and useless at the moment and *longing* to see you.

With much love
I

To Philippa Foot.

St Anne's College
[May 1959]

My dear, thank you very much for your second letter which crossed with mine. I expect a letter about Thursday is on the way, which will probably cross with this. There is a slight snag, viz. that my mother, who was to have come another time, will be here on Wednesday, and until Thursday; and on her choice of a departure train depends whether I will be free at *one* or at *one thirty*. I would like best (if Thursday lunch does suit you) that we should meet (if that's at all convenient), at Bradmore Rd, as my room in college is a bit like a railway station. But if you'd rather not, then we can easily barricade ourselves in at St Anne's somewhere. I will bring biscuits, cheese and wine. (I don't think I could face a public place.) [. . .]

I'm terribly sorry to be a bother about the arrangements: quite other things are on my mind and in my heart, I never thought that I should be able to speak frankly to you again, and the prospect makes me quite unnerved (and almost afraid) with joy!

All my love
I

To Michael Oakeshott.

St Anne's College
15 May [1959]

Michael, I was so glad and relieved to get your letter. I was on the point of ringing you up or wiring you or something, and a combination of my telegrams and your anger would not have been pleasant. Thank you for writing. I'm very glad to hear that things are better and that you are happier – more hopeful. Let all be well now. [. . .]

I feel I need to clap eyes on you before long. This a brief note to send, dearest Michael, my devoted love
I

To Philippa Foot.

St Anne's College
[17 May 1959]

I am still rather speechless after yesterday. It is strange and overwhelming so to recover a whole area of one's being which one thought was lost. But I still feel exceedingly shy and tentative where you are concerned. [. . .]

I deeply hope that life is recovering in you, and each day is less sad; hard to speak of this too. Oh dear – just loving you very much indeed.

I

To Philippa Foot.

St Anne's College
[late May 1959]

KLAS 100 / 1/.

was lovely to see you.

To Philippa Foot.

Steeple Aston
[July 1959]

My dear, thank you very much for your letter. I'm so pleased about the Vanguard – I expect you are already becoming attached to it – and I'm sure it will exert no sinister influence. John now keeps saying what a good *touring* car it is, and perhaps we ought to have one!

My mother is staying just now, and then we are probably going to London, but I'll ring or write before long and invite myself to a drink when possible. [. . .]

It was very good – and very strange too – having you here. I have a beautiful image of you sleeping on the lawn! Bless you, and till soon, and very much love to you.

I

To Raymond Queneau.

St Anne's College
12 August [1959]

My dear Queneau, it was very good to hear from you – though I was sorry that it was some damn article in a newspaper rather than my own sentimental doggerel which jerked you into it. Never mind. I am always very glad to have the (rare) pleasure of your letters. I am interested to hear you are reading Wittgenstein. I fear I could not rise to a book about him. It would be a vast task to write a decent one. I have asked my bookseller to send you a copy of a little work on the *Tractatus* by Elizabeth Anscombe, his closest disciple and an old friend-foe of mine. I think it's good though it may not all be true.

I wonder if you are writing another novel. I do hope so. I am very stuck, very mad, at present and can't get anywhere. I *may* go to USA briefly in the autumn, and have to write lectures for that. Why do my letters to you always sound to me so stiff? It may be that, having just reread your letter, I am trying to write French. I wrote a long poem in French the other day, by the way, and it sounded suspiciously accomplished. But I am not sure that French is a good language for letters. I dislike, to begin with, the anonymity of *Chère Amie*. I will carry my criticisms no further than that. I adored your letter, and love and venerate the writer.

I fear I won't be in France this year – next year surely. With very good wishes to you

Iris

To Philippa Foot.

Steeple Aston
4 October [1959]

Dear love, just a note – I fear I won't see you before I go. *Such* a rush to get these damn lectures done, and they are so incoherent. Still, no time even to worry about them! One must just get along somehow. It was very nice to see you. Drive carefully in your fast car.

I fear I've been insufficiently 'present'. It's partly a melancholy which I shall try to explain to you (and myself). I'm very glad the future contains you, it makes a lot of difference to that tract. Be well. I do hope you are cheerful and working. Be so.

Dearest Philippa, bless you always and all my love to you –
I

To Michael Oakeshott, written during Murdoch's trip to the USA in October 1959 to give lectures at Timothy Dwight College, Yale University. She travelled alone and stayed at the rather palatial university President's House in New Haven.

Yale
21 October [1959]

Michael darling, how very dear of you to write to me. I was so glad of your letter. I'm sorry about Rome. Yet it does console one, doesn't it, that accumulated past is so consoling and the particular beauty of it all. I do hope things with Rosemary are at any rate not achingly painful – dear Michael, why does one suffer so for love? It's absurd, isn't it.

I am enjoying seeing and learning things here, though I don't 'like' the place in a way. It makes me feel such a decadent sybaritic old European. I leave Yale on Friday, go to Boston, Washington and back to New York – and sail on Nov 4. I shall be glad to leave New Haven – though everyone has been very kind. It's been *strenuous – endless* talk with undergraduates, talks to women's groups, philosophy groups, literature groups, a broadcast, and two formal lectures. Thank God mostly done now. I liked my glimpse of New York. But I feel sure by now that I shall *not* see the America I came to see. I don't know precisely what *that* is – some mixed up Jewish–Italian sort of thing I suspect. The nearest I shall get is drinking with Jewish friends in New York.

I don't want to write travel news really. I want to *reply* to your very moving letter. But there is no time to do that. There was something strange about seeing your writing there on the table in the vast pseudo-colonial hallway of the President's House where I am living in *splendour*. What an odd thing time and space is. I do love you, Michael, with lots of old and new love, and always will. May things be well with you. I very much look forward to seeing you when I'm back, and talking about America. Ever

    I

To Raymond Queneau, postcard of New York.

[30 October 1959]

Overexcited and over-entertained but at least (briefly) over here. Lots of love Iris.

To Michael Oakeshott.

Steeple Aston
[4 November 1959]

Dear, I was relieved to hear from you, even sadly, as that was better than imagining you sad without knowing anything. Thank you for talking to me about what really concerns you. I value this immensely and am glad to be trusted. Oh dear, I do want to see you again soon, but as you say, beastly term has started and I don't know when I'll be in London.

About Rosemary, forgive me for talking about it, but it has inevitably occupied my mind. To the outsider of course it seems mad. (And how well one knows the necessity from within of what seems gratuitous from without.) But I can't help reflecting that you seem to be continually asking from Rosemary something she can't give, a particular sort of singleness, and that it would be better, if you haven't the strength to clear out altogether, to be far more resigned. Seeing it from Rosemary's point of view (and knowing what it's like to be confronted by a jealous person) I can imagine your ultimatums must be desperately upsetting, and also probably engender resentment. Oh, I don't know I may be wrong – you might in the end *achieve* something by them; but it looks so much, to this outsider anyway, as if Rosemary simply isn't answerable to this sort of treatment at all.

You may feel I am damned impertinent to say this, as well as having got it wrong. And I know outsiders' comments can be horrible. But I'm an old friend and have loved you very much. And to see this sad drama going on fills me with a sort of exasperation, not only with Rosemary, but with you!

Anyhow, don't be angry with me, and don't stop talking to me because I talk back.

I think I told you my mother is taking the Barons Court flat (barring last-minute snags). She is very pleased with it and much more cheerful. Someone told her there was a knife fight once in that road, but it turns out it was down the other end! Anyhow, she is not deterred by the neighbourhood, and we encourage her to think about doing her shopping in Kensington etc.

It's cold and wet today. My work is still stuck. I look forward to seeing 'The Voice of Feeling'[1] in print. I kiss your hands and send you lots and lots of old loyal love.

I

To Marshall Best at Viking Press in New York.

St Anne's College
[29 November 1959]

Dear Marshall,

I should have written to you much sooner – but things seem not to have stopped happening for a moment since I got back. *How* I enjoyed myself, and how very much because of you. Thank you for so many nice things – it was sweet of you to send the paper to the boat, and the splendid lot of books, which cheered my journey very much. I have too such good memories of our drive, the bridge in that evening light and the dear unicorn at the Cloisters.[2] Perhaps you have been back to see him. Altogether *thank you* for taking so much trouble to give me a happy time in New York. I loved meeting the other Viking-ites too – give them my best wishes. I do hope I shall see you again before too long – come soon to Europe.

It's odd being back – though I have settled down quicker than Gwenda[3] did I think! But I feel still tremendously 'connected' with New York. Thank you again – with best wishes and love from

Iris

---

1 Oakeshott's essay 'The Voice of Poetry in the Conversation of Mankind'.
2 The Cloisters' Unicorn Tapestries at the Museum of Modern Art, New York.
3 Gwenda David, the London editorial representative and scout for Viking Press, New York.

To Hal Lidderdale, who married Maria Coumlidou from Salonika on 14 January 1960. The marriage took place in England where Maria was known as 'Mary'.

St Anne's College, Oxford
[late January 1960]

Dearest Hal, I have only just discovered (by the obvious method which it took me a long time to think of) that it was *you* who sent the lovely unexpected and welcome *roses* – and their labels have come too, so I shall actually continue to know which is which! They are lovely ones, as I already know from the books – and I thank you very much for a dear present which will always be treasured and delighted in.

I so much loved being present at your beautiful wedding, and glimpsing you and Mary afterwards. I wish the glimpse could have been bigger – but perhaps we can meet again before you go. I hope you have both enjoyed holiday and *rest* since then. I hear you are now in Cambridge! – which should look fine in this rather strange misty frosty weather. I hope too you are well in health – and that silly old Council will soon get your house etc. nicely fixed. Do give my love to Mary. I much look forward to meeting her again. My warmest good wishes to both of you for all joy and happiness and success – ever, Hal, with all my love

I

To Elias Canetti. Although Murdoch had told her husband that her affair with Canetti ended in late 1955,[xx] *she and Canetti continued to meet sporadically in London thereafter. The insistent and sometimes rather urgent tone of Murdoch's letters to Canetti also suggests that she was still in thrall to him. Having shadowed the pages of* The Flight from the Enchanter *as Mischa Fox, Canetti was to inspire other incarnations of the male enchanter figure such as Julius King in* A Fairly Honourable Defeat, Gerald Scottow in The Unicorn *and Charles Arrowby in* The Sea, The Sea. *Canetti's friendship was to remain important to Murdoch for the rest of her life.*

Steeple Aston
[late January 1960]

My dear, hello. I would love to see you. You cannot write and I cannot telephone, which makes communication rather difficult! Do you think we could have lunch on Tuesday February 2nd? I would come straight from Paddington and reach you (subject to taxis) about 12.30, or conceivably earlier. I do hope that would be OK. I enclose a card for use if *not* OK! If I hear

Iris Murdoch (centre), Ann Leech (right) and another friend at Badminton School

'I'd sell every faculty I have to paint one good picture' (to Ann Leech)

Iris Murdoch, 1936

'I find myself quite astonishingly interested in the opposite sex, and capable of being in love with about six men all at once' (to Ann Leech)

Matriculation at Somerville. Iris Murdoch is second row, fourth from the right

'My job is [. . .] not to write fine poems, it is to work for a world in which man will read and write fine poems' (to Ann Leech)

Eduard Fraenkel

'You are something very
precious and permanent
in my life'

Donald MacKinnon

'I had forgotten how
very blue his eyes are'
(to Philippa Foot)

**Lucy Klatschko
(Sister Marian)**

'Take me with you
as much as you can'

Philippa Foot

'Darling sphinx, you have been
very much in my mind and heart'

Frank Thompson

'To Irushka, whom I miss these long years' (Thompson's inscription on the back of this photograph)

Hal Lidderdale

'Since seeing you *I have met Jean Paul Sartre!*'

Leo Pliatzky

'Thank you, dear Leo, for caring about me'

Iris Murdoch in UNRRA uniform

'Even a few months in UNRRA have shewn me that universal brotherhood is not a condition that comes naturally to people' (to David Hicks)

David Hicks

'I don't seem to have a real gift for making you happy'

Raymond Queneau

'Anything I shall ever write will owe so much, so much, to you'

Wallace Robson

'I just *can't* work this afternoon – isn't it awful? I just want to sit by the fire and read *Woman's Own*'

Franz Steiner

'Someone whom I loved very deeply, and from whom I was beginning to hope very much, has died suddenly' (to Raymond Queneau)

Peter Ady

'Peter Ady offered me a lift in her car as far as Dunster, and I hitchhiked on from there the next day' (to Wallace Robson)

Margaret Hubbard

'will *discreetly* get help from my learned colleague Margaret Hubbard who really knows Latin' (to Michael Oakeshott)

Iris Murdoch studio portrait

'I think now and then of getting married, but have not done so'
(to Raymond Queneau)

nothing I will assume it is all right and I will come along. I do want to talk to you. I embrace you with much love.

Your

I

To Hal Lidderdale, in response to a witty piece of writing he had sent Murdoch about the difficulty of punting on the Cam.

Steeple Aston
February 1960

Hal, what a perfectly enchanting PUNT PIECE. I'm so glad it will be circulating here – and your remark about the *prow* very apt. It is *crazy* to try to punt standing balanced on that flat slippery platform whence you can exert *no leverage*. Your whole body *demands* a ribbed sloping surface to stand on. It all goes with Cambridge insensitivity – matters of literary criticism, food and drink and so on. (There is never enough to drink in Cambridge – stuck-up lot too. We are just *naturally* better.) It was very good to see you – must have more meeting soon – very good to see Norah.[1] Alas, about 25 March we are on present plans likely to be far away. Hope Byzantine Symposium was OK. And hope see in London. Thanks and much love

I

To Brigid Brophy.

Steeple Aston
[1960[xxi]]

My dear, your letters are so hard to *answer*. I cannot find my copy of *Interpretation of Dreams*, but that is not the only difficulty. Perhaps it is better to be resigned, *à la façon de*[2] your sports simile, to alternate sets of remarks which have little relevance to each other. I am grateful in a straight and simple way for your kindness (and generosity). And of course because I admire you (more perhaps than you realise) I am flattered. And I adore the texture of your mind; and you are a writer and a thinker and beautiful. And you are witty. These things, though they remain scattered, are good and enrich me. I loved your flowers and your sending them – I have had much

1 Hal Lidderdale's mother.
2 As in.

pleasure from them and they still bloom. (NB you must write a very good novel soon. It is time.)

I stand between the difficulty of not making even a respectable *vix satis*[1] sort of response (I know it can't be *satis* ++) and the fear of 'leading you on' in some non-admissible way. (My double entendre about sparing you I only noticed afterwards – I am not as witty as you!) I do not want to harm you, though I would perhaps have no objection to hurting you in certain respects. Anyway. You see the difficulties. I cannot prevent myself ('do not' is better) from responding to your warmth and your (in every sense) wit. Yet you know I am in some ways no use. [. . .]

With love

I

To Brigid Brophy.

St Anne's College
1960[xxii]

Thanks for your poem (Freudian) received.
I must confess I found it quite a tonic,
And hope you will not be unduly peeved
If I reply in spirit more ironic.
I doubt in fact if you will be aggrieved
At being greeted in a style Byronic,
Since mixing of the sexes, which you prize,
Dear Byron certainly exemplifies.

How cleverly you write! It's quite confusing.
You want me female, then you want me male,
Or else hermaphrodite, to suit your choosing,
While for yourself you have some other tale
Of corresponding moves. ('You are amusing!')
To understand this stuff I simply fail,
Eschewing Freud and all his patter, for I
Don't make of sex a basic category.

Of course, one *has* a sex, I can't deny it.
For purposes of passports, clothes et cetera
I am a woman, and I don't decry it.

1 Only just acceptable.

Since man has always done his best to fetter her,
A woman would be man, if she could try it,
In many cases – but this would not better her
In any deep respect, and as a spirit
Woman is man's superior in merit.

But I digress. Now turning from page one
I see you speak of locks where keys can go.
It's *most* obscure and I suspect a *pun*
Or some obscene and nasty *jeu de mots*;
And how can we be lock and key in one
And also wax? It's hardly *comme il faut*
To make your metaphors quite so inflated,
Even when urging some things complicated.

And then this talk of *lying*. No, my dear,
Since something to your purpose in me lacks,
Or rather something not so (am I clear?)
I will be neither lock nor key nor wax,
Not closed, yet not for lying on I fear
(Or lying *with*. You make us sound like sacks!)
Nor by such entry to be prised apart
As rudely searching would not move my heart.

But why should I spend time to tell you this?
Your own ingenious spirit needs no lesson.
Nature denies us a consummate bliss
But gives us much to rest some happiness on:
Too great exactitude would come amiss.
Half sundered and in darkness we must press on.
For what it darkly is, then take my love,
And in the forest lost we still shall rove.

To Brigid Brophy.

St Anne's College
[6 March 1960]

My dear, thank you very much for your letter. I loved seeing you.
    Nothing is inevitable, I think. You move me deeply, as you know. But I
cannot offer you more than I ever could, and even for that time and space

divide us. This is a mouldy frozen-up reply to your charming letter (which I have destroyed: I'm afraid I *did* destroy the earlier ones too, which I now regret!).

I cannot think that (unless you throw me out, out that is of whatever and whenever I am in) I shall ever stop wanting to see you, and when I see you, being moved and affected in deep ways by you. I love receiving letters from you (and love writing to you, which is *quelque chose* as I detest letter-writing in general). I know I am unsatisfactory and that I must just ask you (and earnestly, because this matters to me) to put up with me as I am. (After all I put up with you as you are: or is this a Jesuitical argument?) Dearest girl, just that. I embrace you. Ever,

I

To Brigid Brophy.

St Anne's College
[10 March 1960]

Dear, I should either have written at once to say I couldn't reply yet, *or* later promptly, and this is neither, i.e. it is writing later to say I can't reply yet. Not that I have anything very sensational to say, but I *will* try to *reply* to your moving and Brigidian letter. This is last week of term and I am *submerged* in my so-called part-time job in this place.[1] Also I have, God knows quite why, to make a speech this evening on Man as Artist at a church hall some-where in Cowley, and haven't written the speech yet.

I haven't destroyed your letter, but will at weekend and meanwhile it is well hidden. Dear creature, much love

I

To Brigid Brophy.

St Anne's College
[18 March 1960]

My dear, this is the unsatisfactory sequel to my other letter. I am sorry about what appears to you in effect as my bitch-like behaviour. I don't know what to say. You know I am deeply attached to you, and that attachment has

1 Murdoch had been a tutor at St Anne's from 1948 and a fellow from 1952. In 1957 she let her university lectureship lapse but kept on her college post which simply involved tutorials with students.

survived shocks, misadventures and time. I think it is pretty strong and solid, and its continuance means a lot to me. Yet I am not quite constructed as you wish – hence partly conduct which seems from your end erratic. As for 'days', I don't think in the nearer future, but maybe in the farther – I mean I can't suggest anything just now which you would regard as satisfactory. I gather you don't want to see me briefly. I feel depressed about this, and about the way we can't manage, because you are important to me and might one day help me a lot. I can't spare you, although you say I'm not exactly active. This is gloomy stuff, I'm afraid – your letter made me feel sad and ineffectual, desiring yet not finding in myself a strong full-blooded response of some sort to your fierceness.

I'll write again before long if encouraged to, and even probably if not encouraged to. My love

I

To Brigid Brophy, who had recently moved with her husband from Earls Court Square to the Old Brompton Road.

Steeple Aston
[8 May 1960]

My dear, forgive my not having written. (Your letters have been, as you wish, consumed!) I have been having one damn thing after another, first a philosophical paper to read at Keele, then a speech at a prize-giving in Peterborough (!) and now a paper for a writers' conference I rashly got tangled in, together with far too many pupils. I am a very *slow* creature by nature and cannot think why I idiotically try to do so *much*. Perhaps lovely slow times will come one day.

This will be a brief letter, since I am pestered by that paper. The spring is devastating, is it not? Your forsythia will be well over by now, and the irises will be out. I hope it is merry in the Old Brompton Road. I liked your dwelling so much – and its region.

This is a poor bird to send in return for your winged words. (Travelling to Keele I saw on Wolverhampton station boxes of carrier pigeons, addressed to the stationmasters at various places in Wales, saying 'please release clear of wire and buildings. Do not release in rain or fog'! What an odd life those silly birds must lead!)

All my love, dear creature

I

To Raymond Queneau.

St Anne's College
28 May [1960]

Dear Raymond,

How very nice to hear from you, though so damned officially. Thank you too for your interesting (and flattering) request. I think I must say no to that however. I don't know anything like enough about American philosophy – even apart from the lacunae in my English knowledge. You might try my colleagues: Patrick Gardiner (Magdalen College), David Pears (Christ Church) or Geoffrey Warnock (Magdalen College), all of Oxford, of course. For the Greek volume, you might try John Ackrill, Brasenose College, Oxford, who is a good philosopher and Greek scholar. He should do it excellently.

I wonder if you are going to a fantastical writers' conference in Copenhagen in September? It seems ages since I saw you and I should like to have that pleasure again. (Excuse this letter, which is written in a car! The only time when I seem to have time to write letters just now! Our final exams are just coming up and I am busy *jusquà en mourir.*[1]) How are you, Queneau, and are you writing a novel? I am very *stuck* just now, though trying to write. Suppose you write me a proper letter containing a few sentences about yourself? I hope you can read this one.

NB I live at St Anne's *College.* Musgrove House, where I lived once, is now full of men who keep rats in cages and know the number of voles in Oxfordshire. St Anne's College, Oxford, gets me. *Alors, mon ami,* all my love, and do write.

I

PS thanks, René Mischa[2] sent me the copy of *Critique.* A bizarre Greek friend of mine, one John Simopoulos (philosopher and logician) telephoned Gallimard nine times when he was last in Paris trying to see you (for fun merely, not business) but was foiled. I should have sent you a note, as I'd like you to have met him. He is an eccentric you would have liked. Never mind. Another time perhaps.

---

1 [Being worked] almost to death
2 Belgian poet and an influential critic of art and literature who often contributed to the journal *Critique.* He had written an article on Murdoch's novels which had been published in the journal.

To Marshall Best, answering his request that she edit an anthology of existentialism for Viking's Portable Library series.

St Anne's College
7 June 1960

Dear Marshall,

Thank you so much for your letter. Alas, no, I *don't* think I could take that on. I'm rather out of the existentialist picture at present, and such a thing would take me a lot of time – and if I were to give much time to philosophy in the near future there are other things I'd rather do. Anyway, I am not a natural editor. But thanks for asking me – the idea in itself sounds a good one. And very nice to hear from you. Do come over here soon. I'm so glad you are publishing *Thought and Action*[1] – yes, Hampshire is a pal of mine. Forgive this rushed end-of-term note. I'm sure it's time you had a European holiday.

With love from
Iris

To Brigid Brophy, written after what appears to have been a brief hiatus in their correspondence.

Steeple Aston
[18 June 1960]

My dear, not in Siam, in spite of the airmail envelope. I'm so sorry about Scandinavia. (I am supposed to be going Copenhagen for a conference in Sept. but don't quite believe it.) The summer term has just ended in the usual haze of roses and champagne. What a sad time of year it is all the same. (Why 'all the same'?)

It's funny that it's so plain that it's love that makes the world go round, although it's so very difficult to get it right. I mean odd that it's so *plain*. I'm very tired and confused as you see.

We are going Venice at the end of the month (also initially for a conference). This is even harder to believe. How is my old friend Brigid? I hope Mike and Kate[2] are very well. This rather blurred shout with all my love
I

1 Stuart Hampshire's book attracted much attention. Murdoch was later to engage strongly with it in her essay 'The Idea of Perfection', *Yale Review* (Spring 1964).
2 Kate Levey, born in 1957, daughter of Michael Levey ['Mike'] and Brigid Brophy.

To Brigid Brophy.

Steeple Aston
[26 June 1960]

My dear, thank you for your charming letter. I don't know Mr Cranfill, whose name I couldn't even read, let alone decide his sex. I thought you wouldn't mind my putting him on your trail – though perhaps that remains to be seen.

Why don't I come and see *you* sometime, 'when I get back from my holiday in Europe'? I know you warned me off this. Anyway I'll suggest it again. One day you'll realise that I'm not wise or detached enough to 'do anything about you' which would be up to much, given that I can't produce the essential goods: and then perhaps you will accept me as just a poor bastard who struggles along through life in a muddled way, and your old friend. Do not be obsessed or in pain, darling. How unnecessary it seems. Yet how much time one spends thus. I wasn't drunk, incidentally, and love (properly understood) *does* make the world go round. We fly to Venezia early Wednesday, and on Tuesday will be chez my mother at 97 Comeragh Rd, W14.

I am glad that your house number and district number now both end with a 5 so that I can remember them safely.

With much of that world-propelling stuff, Brigid, ever your unsatisfactory old
I

To Michael Oakeshott.

Pub
17 August [1960]

Dearest M, I am in London and have been trying to get in touch with you, but as telephone never answers assume you are away. Alas. I would love to see you and really must try be here oftener. Have just come reeling out of Picasso exhibition.[1] That is the way to have lived. I wonder where you are now on what (I hope) sunny beach or in what cool palazzo? I was in Venice and will be in Copenhagen. Will write and ring again. All my love
Iris

1 Roland Penrose curated a huge and very successful Picasso exhibition at the Tate Gallery that summer.

To Michael Rubinstein, the solicitor for Penguin Books, which was taken to court under the Obscene Publications Act 1959 for having published the unexpurgated edition of D. H. Lawrence's Lady Chatterley's Lover *in 1960. The trial became a major public event and a test of the new obscenity law. The Act (introduced by Roy Jenkins) had made it possible for publishers to escape conviction if they could show that a work was of literary merit. Well-known academic critics and writers, including E. M. Forster, Helen Gardner, Richard Hoggart, Raymond Williams and Norman St John Stevas, were asked to defend Penguin's decision to publish the novel by testifying to its literary integrity. The verdict, delivered on 2 November 1960, was 'not guilty'. Murdoch provided a statement in defence of Penguin but was not called to witness.*

St Anne's College
21 October [1960]

Dear Mr Rubinstein,

Thank you for your letter of 19th October about *Lady Chatterley*. I don't think, reading through my remarks, that I am unduly critical of the novel.[1] That is, I should think I do make it clear that I regard it as the work of a *great* writer, and patently so. This puts it *of course* well above the run of ordinary novels (I don't think the question of a comparison with *them* can even arise: *Lady C* is obviously 'first-class work', in a sense in which there is very little of it.) All this should be understood as a background to my remarks about the faults of the novel.[xxiii] It *has* faults, and one is perhaps the more exasperated by them because of the potential and actual remarkableness of the novel in other ways. I don't think the good parts of it are inferior to Lawrence's best work – and indeed all his work is patchy.

In judging the book in any way severely I would be thought of as doing so by the *very* highest standards (as Lawrence himself would have wished) and taking for granted that it is miles better than the 'average good' novel of the period!

I don't think I want to alter any of my words – but send this by way of explanation of the tone in which they should be read! With good wishes,

Yours sincerely,
Iris Murdoch

---

1 In a letter dated 19 October, Michael Rubinstein had suggested that Murdoch's judgement of *Lady Chatterley's Lover* had been unduly harsh.

To Michael Rubinstein.

St Anne's College
[26 October 1960]

Dear Mr Rubinstein,

Thank you very much for your letter. I don't think I shall appear 'spontaneously' at the Old Bailey, but if my presence is desired, in view of the way the case turns out, or because you want one more witness, I shall willingly turn up. I certainly appreciate the points you made in your letter, and I see that the prosecution may make much of any criticisms uttered. I don't think that an *exact* assessment of the merits of *LCL* is, or should be, a decisive matter in relation to the 'tendency to corrupt' question. That it forms part of the *oeuvre* of a great writer is in itself an argument. But I see that a general impression of its merits might *seem* relevant, and that criticisms made with the assumption that the work was 'first class' might well simply lead to its being thought mediocre. As far as my own remarks are concerned, I don't think I can offer any very specific amendments, though I would certainly keep clearly in mind what you have pointed out.[1] I would have thought *some* patent critical awareness of the faults of the book should do good not harm to the cause! But I see the matter is tricky. As I say, I'll come if called for. I'm sorry to be still vague and doubtless unsatisfactory with regard to the matters you mentioned. I do see your point though, and keep it in mind. With good wishes,
Yours sincerely,
Iris Murdoch

To Marshall Best, who had written enthusiastically about A Severed Head *to Murdoch, describing it as 'a marvellously knowing study of some of the uses and abuses of love. Nobody wants a word changed.' He also enclosed a positive report by Denver Lindley, another editor at Viking Press.*

St Anne's College
7 November 1960

Dear Marshall,

Thank you very much for your nice letter, and for sending me Denver Lindley's piece. I *liked* what he wrote about the book (how clever you all are over there) and have no comments or additions. Viking has always given

---

1 In a letter dated 22 October Rubinstein had tried to persuade Murdoch to 'limit the more critical remarks'.

me highly intelligent (not to say intellectual) blurbs and I don't think I want to say anything myself. Obviously it's a book about which various things could be said (and doubtless will be – not all complimentary!). Anyhow, I am very glad at the warm and generous welcome you've all given the book. I have funny mixed feelings about it myself, and was half prepared for: do you expect us to publish this junk?

Yes, please alter back Gyges and Candaules,[1] I just put them wrong way round by mistake! You are fast workers with these proofs. Anyhow *thanks*, Marshall, and thanks to DL too. I am really cheered by your reactions.

Affectionately yours

Iris

To Brigid Brophy.

19 November [1960[xxiv]]

Dearest creature, your recently advertised efforts to amuse me certainly reached a new high in latest letter. [. . .]

Until now I have taken the view that your odd attitude to my work was unimportant.[2] Lots of my friends don't like what I write (e.g. Professor Fraenkel) but mostly they keep quiet about it, and it doesn't matter. I don't, by the way, dislike, or don't think I do, *interesting* criticism, if devoid of spite. Interesting criticism one practically never gets, of course. My own debate about the merits of my work and how to improve it is one that I think no one else can contribute to. I believe I have a *reasonably* just estimate of my faults and virtues as a writer and know when and in what respect I am overpraised. I confess I am surprised that you *altogether* dislike my work, as I should have thought it was complex enough to have *some* things in it which would touch your heart and mind. I am beginning now to think that your total rejection of it *is* important, and I am not sure what should be done. It is not a matter of love me love my books. I feel no specially protective attachment to the completed things which recede at a great speed into the past. It is partly that I am, I think, rather *like* my books, so that it is at least odd (and a little unnerving) to find you detesting them. It is also that, more important, your dislike also touches the future, and touches any present activities, with a cold hand. In this role you seem destructive. I wonder why you so much *insist* on your feelings, instead of emulating the silence of Professor Fraenkel? You will speak here of 'honesty' etc. But I don't

1 Kings of ancient Lydia, a kingdom of Anatolia in what is now Turkey.
2 Murdoch's success as a novelist had inspired jealousy in some of her contemporaries; Olivia Manning, for example, thought Murdoch's work was overpraised and Brophy possibly shared that view.

think honesty is the same as ruthless self-expression. You want to *do* something by insisting. I wonder if we shouldn't perhaps discuss the whole matter sometime (an idea which before Sunday would have seemed to me ludicrous).

All my love

I

To Raymond Queneau. Mentioned in the first line of this letter, Georg Kreisel was a Jewish Austrian-born mathematical logician. Having been an undergraduate at Trinity College, he returned to Cambridge after the Second World War to receive his doctorate. Kreisel and Murdoch met during Murdoch's time at Cambridge in 1947 and quickly became very close. Murdoch greatly admired his intellect, writing to Brophy on 12 February 1965, 'he is one of the few people whom I regard in some quite hard mechanical sense as very much cleverer than I am'.

St Anne's College
6 January [1961]

Dearest Queneau,

Just to say happy new year to you. Also: a fantastical pal of mine called Kreisel is now living in Paris, working at the Sorbonne, and I should like to commend him to you, as he is lovely, and also I think you'd like him. He is Jewish, aged thirty-seven approx, was a friend of Wittgenstein, knows a lot about philosophy, and is (I believe) in some fairly strict sense a great mathematician. He is also, as I say, fantastical, and lonely. I have (I hope you don't mind this) suggested he might look you up. He can be found: G. Kreisel, Dept de Mathématiques, 11 Rue Pierre Curie, Paris X^e. But I expect he will try and contact you before long. I do hope you don't mind me suggesting this. Write to me, yes? I have finished a novel and started another.[1] Neither is much good I fear. I sometimes have news of *Zazie* but rarely of you.

With much love,

Iris

To Brigid Brophy.

Steeple Aston
[22 May 1961]

Dearest HG,[2] I was so glad to hear from you. I was beginning to fear that on the metaphysical level where our converse continues during intervals of silence I had somehow offended you. [. . .]

1 *An Unofficial Rose.*
2 Perhaps 'Heavenly Goddess'.

No, I won't be in Dublin alas. Pour a libation for me there. I hope you are liking Edinburgh and Glasgow. I suppose those tapestries etc. are still not on show in Glasgow? I'm glad you have been getting on with the book business and I look forward to seeing the results. I haven't written anything lately except a philosophical paper on the Inner Life. (As I have lots of Inner Life I feel it must be explained to and defended against those around here who haven't, and who have it in for the IL.) [. . .]
   With love, dear Brigid
   I

To Brigid Brophy.

                                                          Steeple Aston
                                                          [25 June 1961]

Dear. I forgot to thank you for the bookmarks which always remind one of Marvell. No one else seems to be able to get hold of them, perhaps for the reasons you mentioned. They are very useful as I am reading a lot of books at once just now. Having a great phase of reading Dickens – gosh he is good – though *so* careless. But so beautifully funny – as well as other things. Oh to achieve the purely funny! Where does it reside?
   With love to Brigid
   From
   I

To Raymond Queneau.

                                                          St Anne's College
                                                          30 June [1961]

Queneau, thank you very much for your letter and your beautiful review[xxv] of *A Severed Head*. I am delighted and touched that you should have done this. I liked your review very much. (*How* unlike most reviews it is.) And I am glad you saw there *nulle morale!*[1]
   Claud Gallimard told me of the *Cent mille milliards*[2] – the mere idea of it fills me with wild joy.

1 After pondering on the '*ballets matrimoniaux*' of the novel and the Medusa image implied by the novel's title, Queneau suggests that the novel's conclusion is all the more satisfying for having no particular moral system ('*d'autant plus satisfaisante que je ne vois là nulle morale*').
2 Queneau's *Cent mille milliards de poèmes* (*A Hundred Thousand Billion Poems*).

I may be in Paris, not sure, anyhow will let you know, and much want to see you. Again thanks – and love to you from I

To Raymond Queneau.

Cedar Lodge
Steeple Aston
12 July [1961]

Queneau, I have only just got hold of the 100,000,000,000,000 poems, which got locked in the college lodge and not sent on. I am delighted, quite drunk in fact, with it – what a beautiful book and what a sublime conception! Thank you and thank you. The trouble is it gives one too much agreeable occupation. (More than enough, according to your reckoning.) I embrace you, and enclose a sonnet you have inspired. (Which I hope at least is grammatical.) I must see you before too long – with homage and love from Iris.
    Sonnet:[xxvi]

La Chanson, toujours amateur de surprises,
Se mit à badiner avec Queneau.
Ça l'amusait fort, la petite entreprise:
Pourquoi enfin on n'a fait ça plutôt?
Elle s'admirait dans les glaces bien mises
Pour fair surgir forêts d'ombres beaux.
Petrarch n'avait si riche merchandise
Qui comptait en dizaines son boulot.

Pourtant la reine des sciences, la cocotte,
Faisant avec les mots une telle gavotte,
Pour le poète semble un presage malsain.
Chanson, que seduisent tant ces equivoques,
N'oublie pas quand la machine fait tic toc
Que c'est quand même Queneau son beau bouqin.

[The Song, always a surprise up her sleeve,
Began to fool around with Queneau.
It's such fun, this little game:
Why didn't we do this earlier?
She admired herself in the mirrors, well placed
To emerge from forests of beautiful shadows.
Not even Petrarch had such good material
As he counted out his sonnets.

Yet the queen of sciences,[1] that sweet seducer,
Made these words into such a pretty gavotte,
That it seemed to the poet an unhealthy sign.
Song, seduced by so many ambiguities,
Don't forget that when the machine goes tick tock
Queneau's beautiful book lives on.[2]]

To Brigid Brophy.

Steeple Aston
[16 July 1961]

I do hope those proofs[3] have turned up. Of course you must still have the manuscript so *all* is not lost. But how monstrous of them. Why don't you leave – or is your heart still Fred's?[4] Emulating them, I have lost your auto-biography. But I expect it will turn up, and I will then sadly do as you requested. (What would posterity say, if it knew.)
  With love from
  I

To Brigid Brophy.

Steeple Aston
[September 1961]

'Buy our plastic matchboxes and save trees'. See how one good idea leads to another. However, seriously, the way for you to make money is to *write a novel*. After all you know how. Just sit and *think about it*. A short one, they sell much better. And not the short pornographic ancient history romance, but a serious book. Just sit and *think* until some lovely glittering thing comes towards you out of the darkness. [. . .]

---

1 Metaphysics, traditionally called 'the queen of the sciences', including the philosophical sciences, as famously described in Kant's *Critique of Pure Reason*.
2 Time (the machine that goes 'tick tock') is a mathematical measurement but art transcends time. Perhaps Murdoch is here teasing Queneau about his love of mathematics and gently advising him not to subjugate his literary talent to mathematical games.
3 Of Brophy's *Black Ship to Hell*, which was to be published in January 1962 by Secker & Warburg. The book is a Freudian psychoanalytic analysis of man as 'a destructive and, more particularly, a self-destructive animal' (from Brophy's Introduction). It ranges widely across classical and European literature, history and culture and demonstrates Brophy at her most erudite.
4 Frederic Warburg (1898–1981), English publisher who, with Roger Senhouse, bought the firm of Martin Secker in 1935 and renamed it Secker & Warburg.

I shall be quickly away and then a bit longer, but plans vague and will report again soon. Be well, and take above advice.

All love

I.

To Brigid Brophy.

Steeple Aston
[early October 1961]

My dear, your lovely flowers came, borne through the night by special messenger. Thank you indeed. And for your charming letter – you are certainly the best letter-writer I have ever encountered, your words all coloured and warmed by you.

This is not an answer. (I haven't had time to look up *Interpretation of Dreams* whatever the section was.) *Will* answer. Meanwhile, entrance candidates claim attention. You *must* write a novel after the *Black Ship*. What a word-monger you are, I like that, I salute you, dear tennis player.

Much love

I

To Brigid Brophy.

[26 November 1961]

My dear girl, I was so glad to hear from you. I have been meaning to write, but have been prevented by fact that I have not yet quite finished *Black Ship* – and by feeling that I ought to write you careful reflections thereon. I don't know whether I shall ever do the latter, but I shall do the former when blessed vac starts. Term is more than usually on top of me and reading is a lovely wished-for occupation. I do think the book is exceptional and somehow marvellous – though I have disagreements.

I don't agree either quite about opening chapter of *Copperfield*. I find the anti-Murdstone stuff a little forced. Yet Mrs Copperfield is beautiful. Perhaps you are right.[1] As for Thomas Mann I have no concept of him. He seemed too symbolical in some awful way. I laboriously read *Tod in Venedig* in German, also *Tonio Kröger* (what can one do with a language which calls Venetia Venedig?) and then collapsed. All right, I will try him and let you know.

1 Brophy seems to have cut this section before publication – perhaps in response to Murdoch's criticism.

I'm sorry about the money. (You see I am answering your letter point by point.) I think the paraphysical law in question is simple, and one version of it was stated long ago in the gospels. To him that hath shall be given etc. – of which another version is, don't economise, just go on spending and the stuff, impressed by your air of confidence, will turn up from somewhere. (But then – suppose it doesn't?)

How tiresome about nursery school God business.[1] And the trouble is, one can't just say: all that stuff isn't true. (To her.) [. . .]

I must stop now, not having got on to any original observations of my own. I embrace you, sending thoughts and love

I

To Raymond Queneau.

St Anne's College
29 November [1961]

My dear Queneau,

I would have loved to see you in London, but alas it is quite impossible to get away. It is near the end of term and a hundred jobs keep me in Oxford. I am most sorry – it is far too long since I saw you and it would have been a very great pleasure to talk and even to see your face! I will be in London Dec 10th onwards – but I imagine you'll be gone by then? Let me know if not. I really must try to get to Paris *soon*. After all, it's not far. I shan't wait for the Tunnel. Why don't you come to London more? I was in Madrid this summer, mostly in the Prado[2] – so why not Paris where there is you and the Louvre? Very sorry not to see you. Have a good stay and no fogs. I embrace you. *À bientôt* I hope and love from I

To Norah Smallwood.

St Anne's College, Oxford
[early 1962]

My dear Norah,

Proofs enclosed.[3] I gather you've had a copy of the play contract,[4] which

1 Brophy's daughter Kate, now aged four, had recently started nursery school.
2 The Bayleys had holidayed in Spain in September 1961.
3 Of *An Unofficial Rose*.
4 For the stage adaptation of *A Severed Head*, written by J. B. Priestley and Murdoch.

I've now got to sign. I'll delay signing two days in case you have any questions or snags to raise – and if I don't hear, I'll sign it.

On the proofs – I hope I'm to be allowed Randall's 'fuck' at the end of Part One! I have abandoned Mildred's 'Bugger' later on!

Till soon I hope –

Love from

Iris

To Brigid Brophy.

Steeple Aston
[early February 1962]

My dear, confusion overwhelmed me, partly because John has got chicken pox, and partly because I couldn't compose such a short little work as the one needed. I've been looking at your book again, and felt rage at the reviewers[1], thinking what reception asses like Colin Wilson get.[2] Your book is hard to review of course, and reviewers made nervous by it, slip into superficial clever attitudes. I suggest (would this really be any use to Secker, for ads?) something like 'Miss Brophy has written an ambitious serious disturbing book. It is rich, original, and witty; and whether or not one agrees with its refreshingly fierce and dogmatic[3] views, a great pleasure to read'. This doesn't satisfy me, and I tried some stuff about 'the modern world' but couldn't phrase it right. *Qu'en penses tu?*[4] Much love I

To Brigid Brophy.

Steeple Aston
[11 March 1962]

My dear girl, I've been delaying writing, hoping for a calm patch, but there ain't one, so here is a hasty letter, please forgive. [. . .]

I have read your novel[5] with great delight. I *do* think it's good, a handsome lovely clever book, with excellence on every page, as proper books should

---

1 In late January Brophy had sent some published reviews of *Black Ship to Hell* to Murdoch who responded that the 'sheer richness of the book (whether one agrees or not) has been missed'.
2 Colin Wilson had published *The Outsider* to great acclaim in 1956 and *Adrift in Soho* in 1961.
3 Brophy changed this to 'uncompromising'.
4 What do you think of that?
5 The typescript of *Flesh*, published later in 1962.

have. You must be the first person who has described sexual intercourse beautifully and well in a book. I liked the fine fine sensuousness of it all, and the *characters* were so damn good too. I was for a while wishing for more 'plot' in the old-fashioned sense, but the work has so much *structure* that that aspect of form is perfectly well looked after. I think it's terribly good. Could say much more about the novel, and will later. Has Fred got his hands on it? Let me know its fate. I embrace you, you good girl, with lots of love

I

To Brigid Brophy.

[June/July 1962]

My dear girl, I do hope Kate is well has no temperature or any other complications.[1] It was nice to see her, and you.

About the odd question you asked as I was leaving (which took me by surprise, or I'd have been more rational) surely the answer must be no. What you referred to would have a beginning, a middle, and an end, and might damage our rather mysterious (and to me valuable) friendship. I need you. You also need me. As for your being bored, when have I ever bored you, for heaven's sake? See you soon. Much love

I

To Brigid Brophy.

Oxford: Christ Church Staircase Vault
[early July 1962]

Very sorry, Brigid, but as I said we *can't* make July 7 – John had got it wrong re telephone-wise. Most disappointed. It sounded as if it would be a very nice occasion! With hopes for another one, and lots of love I

And thanks for asking us.

1 Kate, now aged five, was suffering from chicken pox.

To Brigid Brophy, written after Brophy had taken offence at the above brief note.

Steeple Aston
[early July 1962]

I'm so sorry Mike has the chicken pox. I expect Kate is amused. I remember, at about her age, being very pleased when I gave my mother chicken pox.

I am sorry too that you thought I was rude. (Though I don't think I was.) Let us not quarrel stupidly. I am very attached to you indeed and one has enough pain and misery without having quite gratuitous fights with one's friends. Love

I

To Brigid Brophy.

Steeple Aston
[early July 1962]

As we are both rather stiff-necked characters let us *not* now have a long silence which will be difficult to break. That would be such a waste of spirit[1] as between you and me. I say this although I feel in some ways more inclined to beat you than to send you an olive branch. (I suppose one might in some circumstances be beaten *with* an olive branch.) I was very surprised by your original letter. Your charge of boorishness I *imagine* is concerned with that invitation business. But there was a simple misunderstanding. John thought there was an invitation for 'sometime in July'. Then your card for July 7 arrived. And when I came, as you remember, I thanked you for *two* invitations, mentioning that the July 7 one was impossible. So let us now have no more foolishness about this.

I loved your novel and hope to see you before long. I do hope M is not suffering too much from his pox. Asking you not to be an ass, I embrace you.

I

---

1 Echoes the opening of Shakespeare's Sonnet 129: 'Th'expense of spirit in a waste of shame / Is lust in action'.

To Brigid Brophy.

Steeple Aston
[mid-July 1962]

Your last letter is of the kind which is perhaps better left unanswered. However it may be worth writing once more. You ask, or wonder, why I don't lie 'more suavely'. I don't lie more suavely because as it happens I am not lying. Things occurred as I told you. There was a good deal of vagueness between J and me, and I didn't reflect on the matter precisely because I was (I hoped) shortly going to see you. J did not gather that July 7 was more than a suggestion or possibility, to be confirmed or another negotiated (he got the idea it was only us, not a big party) and he did not mention the particular date to me or that we were to ring back. I was by then, as he knew, planning to see you. John is often inefficient by telephone, never knows our arrangements, and answers vaguely on principle. He certainly did not gather anything of *urgency* from the telephone call and just assumed I would fix it all with you when we met. When your card came I did not shew it to J (or even I think mention it) and certainly did not mention the date of July 7 to him. If we had each communicated to the other the idea of 'July 7' we might have cottoned on, but we didn't. I simply noted the date and that we could not come. I think I vaguely took it at first to be an invitation to drinks, anyway some other *kind* of invitation, so little did I connect it with the earlier still unfixed notion of our coming to dinner sometime in July. By then (and this is the point) I was anyway engaged in the plan to see you, and postponed all to that, not even thinking about the social arrangements or discussing them at all with John.

This is how it happened and we have said that we are sorry to have been inefficient. What you have imagined is a total fantasy and not even a very plausible one. With what possible *motive* would I have invented all this, why should I *pretend* to think there were two invitations? What sort of 'good impression' was this supposed to make? If you recall, I said to you: thank you for the two invitations, we cannot come on July 7, let us fix the other. Why *invent* such a ridiculous clumsy notion, simulating starts of surprise etc.? Use your intelligence. Occam's razor,[1] if nothing else, shall suggest I am telling the truth. And can you not recognise the voice of truth when you hear it? And does not your knowledge of my character suggest that I am capable of inefficiency and tiresome casualness but *not* of such petty intricate (and incidentally purposeless) falsehood?

---

1 A problem-solving principle devised by William of Ockham (*c.*1287–1347) based on the idea that among competing hypotheses, the one with the fewest assumptions should be selected.

I have no taste for dramas of this sort, but I can't 'accept' your letter. Friendship between us would be poisoned, would be impossible, if you assumed and I let you assume what you there said so venomously. Imagine yourself at the receiving end of such a volley of muck – which I'm amazed you had the will to send after I had *twice* written to you gently. I trust you will, on reflection, believe the above and make a suitable withdrawal of what you said in that letter.

I

To Brigid Brophy, following a reconciliation after the above disagreement. Brophy possibly sent Murdoch the manuscript version of her novel The Finishing Touch *(published in 1963), which she described as 'a lesbian fantasy', as a peace-offering.*

Steeple Aston
[late July 1962^{xxvii}]

Cher animal, j'ai lu ton bouquin avec délices. C'est beau comme un ange.[1] It gave me absolutely continuous delight. John has read it too and thinks it smashing. Thank you for this pleasure. I hope it wasn't *this* you meant as not for publication? It would be a crime to deprive others of the experience.

I am not really I trust, so tiresomely averse to being questioned. My vagueness about my movements arises partly from a quite general unwillingness to think of the future as definite. Tell me sometime, by the way, if you are discreet.

I am going to Scotland tomorrow for a week. Communications between us have lately being flying like arrows in a battle between the Apaches and the Cherokees. I give you my address there (c/o Lady Altrincham, Guisachan, Tomich, Strathglass, near Inverness)[2] in case you want to send another *chef d'oeuvre*. Or perhaps we might have a rest, though I am by no means *épuisée* and certainly not *exceédée*.[3] Love

I

To Brigid Brophy.

[late July 1962]

1 Dear creature, I've read your book with delight. It's as beautiful as an angel.
2 John and Patsy Grigg's holiday home in Scotland. John Grigg, Lord Altrincham (who was to disclaim his title in 1963) had been at Eton and Oxford with John Bayley.
3 I am by no means exhausted and certainly not exasperated.

My dear girl, in brief reply to your letter. Thank you very much for the picture of Antonia. I had already noted it in the newspaper as an interesting face. You must tell more sometime (about that and everything). I hope Sally[1] is not too *déchirée*[2] and is sorting things out happily. I hope you are *well* and not having any more of those vapours.

I am formidably well just now, one has more or less got to be up here. I walk for *miles* over rough heather and bogs and swim in a pitch-black lochan half covered with water hawthorn. (Damn cold.) Some days fly fishin' goes on which I watch admiringly for a short while and then return to the view. It should be a good place for work, and I *have* worked here, but can't this time, there are too many demons blown up the glen from Loch Ness.

I don't know about holidaying, there may be a moment for that but not yet. But I should like to see you. I may need your help sometime (demons etc.) and you could give me a lot if you would stop bounding round me like a nervous colt. (There is something in the quality of your wit which makes it hard for me to think of you as discreet!) I embrace you.

Love

I

To Brigid Brophy, on receiving Flesh *as a published book.*

Steeple Aston
[late summer/early autumn 1962]

Dearest girl, I have never before received a novel dedicated to me wrapped up in silver paper. I am utterly delighted. The labour of love round the outside is much appreciated too and I hope represents many happy hours. The picture of you on the back rather turns my head. The hunched broad-shouldered appearance is just right. [. . .] I shall treasure it. I also liked the account of you and your Keeper; and the mysterious 'go there'. (Where?) The *dédicace* gives me enormous pleasure.[3] I feel very proud and want to go round telling everyone I know you. NB I adore the novel too. Thank you, Brigid. I embrace you, you dazzling creature. With great thanks and love, your much cheered up

I

1 Probably Sally Backhouse, one of Brophy's friends from Oxford days, to whom *Black Ship to Hell* is dedicated.
2 Cut up.
3 *Flesh* is dedicated 'To I.M.'

To Michael Oakeshott. The 'troubles' mentioned in this note probably relate to Margaret Hubbard, about whom Murdoch wrote in her journal in August 1962, 'She was very hostile and bullying when we next met, spoke contemptuously about "English homes and gardens", and generally treated me with harshness and contempt. Not unusual of course . . . I have told [her] I must resign'.[xxviii] *Hubbard, described by Philippa Foot as 'raucous',*[xxix] *had been pressing Murdoch to leave John Bayley and set up home with her since the previous summer.*

[late summer/autumn 1962]

Darling Michael [. . .] I'm sorry I haven't written. Troubles and troubles. Write me a little note about anything. I love you as always and hope for news.
   I

To Norah Smallwood, concerning The Unicorn, *which was to be published in 1963.*

Steeple Aston
20 October [1962]

Dear Norah, thank you very much for your letter. I was glad and indeed relieved to get it, and to know that for you at least the magic had not altogether failed. I feel about this book, as I did about *A Severed Head* which I was so tiresome about, fearing that it may be just a quite private thing which others will regard with surprise or dislike. (I didn't feel this about *An Unofficial Rose* of course which is a public object in the traditional sense!)
   Anyway I'm so pleased that you liked the thing, and thank you for such a nice letter. Yes, I would prefer it to be delayed a bit – especially as its successor (if any) will be a very long time breaking the surface.
   Script-writing? Pshaw! Of course not!
   Lots of love

To Brigid Brophy.

[6 November 1962]

Thank you very much for exquisite account of Nancy, especially the bears! I have passed through the town, seen *grande place*,[1] never discovered park[2]

---

1 The Place Stanislas, a large pedestrianised square in Nancy, Lorraine, France.
2 Probably Parc de Pépinière, a famous park next to the Place Stanislas.

etc. Other points: know nothing about *A Severed Head* play, it is in the hands of fantastic agent. Divided skirt: you ask if I feel M masquerading as F, or F as M (I can't use those smart signs you use as I can never remember which is which. You must tell me sometime). Not sure of the answer: I think one feels a pleasant amalgam. Sometimes skirt feels rather like plus fours. The great moment however, is when, standing talking to someone who does not know what one is wearing, one casually puts one foot on a chair. (This needs to be demonstrated.)

[. . .] At least your publisher gives you lunch. Mine never even gives me a glass of beer. Except for years ago when bad measly dinner cooked on gas ring in Chatto's attic, where was very junior guest filling place while Huxley etc. entertained. But then you make trouble and I don't. (I noted your lecture about black leggings etc. Yes, ought to, but won't.)

No time for more now. Sorry I've lost my pen. I feel rather unreal with this instrument.

Love

I

To John Symonds, English novelist, biographer, playwright and children's author. Either he or possibly Michael Hamburger, who had been a friend of Franz Steiner since the early 1950s, was thinking of writing an article on the influence of Kafka on British writers.

St Anne's College
Oxford
4 December [1962?]

Dear Mr Symonds,

Thank you very much for your letter, of long ago now I'm afraid, about the Kafka question. I'm very sorry not to have answered sooner – this answer is almost certainly too late and I'm afraid has little substance anyway. I was rather troubled by what you asked, I mean in the sense of not being at all sure what to say. Yes, I think I have been influenced by Kafka – but he is a writer (it seems to me) of whom it's very hard to say what his influence amounts to. I admire him, of course, very much indeed. I owe to him, maybe, some of the sense I have of the mystery and horror and romance of organisations; but this seems superficial in a way. What I would *like* to owe to him is something hard to define which appears in many of the short stories as well as in the novels: a sense of life as real and ordinary and yet ghastly as a way of presenting people's *thoughts* in this context. Yet this seems superficial too. What one envies, and here perhaps it is almost impossible to receive an influence, is his marvellous originality and the unspeakably concrete way in which he presents certain things about being a human being. But all this is very incoherent and hardly to your purpose and probably too late anyway. So sorry.

With good wishes

Sincerely

Iris Murdoch

To Brigid Brophy.

                                                         Nettlepole
                                                      Little Chart
                                                               Kent
                                                        [late 1962]

My dear, snowed up rather satisfactorily in Kent, I haven't yet caught up with your letter which you described rather dis-spiritingly at 97 Comeragh.[1] I wish please you would attend to the positive, not negative, part of my last letter. I'd like to have talked to you more. I have now more or less (keep under hat as not official) decided to leave St Anne's, a rather painful decision as you may imagine. I should like to go on teaching philosophy but in some other way, and with not quite so *much* of it. Anyway, much confusion of mind, sense of being *déracinée, déréglée*[2] etc. and needing friendship and the love that makes things seem rather more permanent and secure. [. . .]

Hope to see you before long. If we ever get away from here. Have been rescuing stranded motorists all the morning. A very satisfying but tiring occupation. Au revoir and lots of love.

I

1 Murdoch's mother's address in London.
2 Uprooted, unsettled.

To Lady Mary Ogilvie, principal of St Anne's College. In this formal letter Murdoch
gives the reason for her resignation as the need for more time to write. This may
have been a smokescreen, if – as John Bayley believed – she had been warned by
Lady Ogilvie that her liaison with Margaret Hubbard was inviting a scandal. The
admonition provoked Murdoch's letter of resignation.

[21 December 1962]

Dear Principal,

This is just to tell you that, sadly, I have come to the conclusion that I
must leave the college. I am very sorry, as I have so much enjoyed belonging
to St Anne's and it has been such a long and happy connection. But I have
lately – and indeed always! – been trying to do too many things at once,
and I feel now that I must simplify my life if I am to get any serious writing
done at all. It is difficult, if one is interested in one's college work, to do it
really 'half-time', and I have not usually succeeded in doing so. Therefore,
since I do very much want to go on writing, and to devote time to this, I
think I must resign.

I am sorry too that this decision coincides with my sabbatical term. It
would be difficult, because of fitting in with John's arrangements, to alter
that now. So, subject to the college's agreement, I would still like to be
absent in the Trinity term; I don't mind whether I am paid or not. So that
would mean, again subject to what the college may decide, that I would
depart *in perpetuo* at the end of next (this coming) Hilary term. I am sorry
to present this rushed timetable: since when John's sabbatical came over the
horizon I had not yet decided on my resignation. And now that I have made
the painful, but I feel very necessary, decision I naturally want to carry it
out as soon as possible. I'm sure you will understand this and forgive me.
It will not be difficult to arrange the summer's teaching – nor will it, I'm
sure, be difficult to replace me, for next Michaelmas, by someone far more
useful and competent! (I know of various 'possibles'.) But we might discuss
this, and indeed the whole matter, after Christmas. I am very sorry to land
this on you by way of a Christmas gift! Till Dec 30 I shall be c/o Mrs F. J.
Bayley, Nettlepole, Little Chart, Ashford, Kent; after that back here.

As I say, I am very sad indeed to go. But sometimes one has to choose
between different 'goods' and give up one for the sake of the other. May I
say how very much I have always valued your friendship and help. I am very
sorry indeed to land you with this problem now and sorry about the short
notice. With very very best Christmas and New Year wishes and love

Iris

PART FIVE:

The RCA Years

January 1963 to November 1967

Murdoch's resignation from St Anne's College took effect from the summer of 1963 and she was made an honorary fellow in June of that year. In October she took up a part-time post at the Royal College of Art, which committed her to tutoring one day a week on the general studies course. She was offered the work by Christopher Cornford, then dean of general studies at the RCA, whom she had met shortly after her marriage and who designed the covers for four of her novels. The RCA, a prestigious post-graduate college in central London, attracted many talented and unconventional students, some of whom, such as Bridget Riley and David Hockney, went on to become famous in the worlds of art and fashion; the designers Zandra Rhodes and Ossie Clark were roughly contemporary with Murdoch, graduating in 1963 and 1965 respectively. Murdoch, delighted at being surrounded by painters and sculptors, found the bohemian atmosphere of the college stimulating and alarming in turn. During term time, she taught on Wednesdays, spending Tuesday and Wednesday nights in a small rented flat, 59 Harcourt Terrace in Earls Court, where she frequently entertained friends and students. As well as enjoying the cultural riches of the capital, Murdoch could easily visit her mother, who was by now living in Barons Court. At the RCA she ran tutorials and supervised dissertations on Sartre, Gabriel Marcel, Kierkegaard and J. S. Mill; during 1965–6 she also gave twenty-four lectures on 'Moral and Political Pictures of Man'. In addition, she gave three lectures at University College London during the winter of 1966 under the title 'On the concepts of "Good" and "Will"'.

Having taken the decision to break free of both Margaret Hubbard and St Anne's, Murdoch returned to her writing with renewed creativity. Out of the four RCA years came four quite different novels in terms of setting, style

and form. They are very much of their time and vacillate between a celebration of new sexual freedoms and a fear of the depravity to which these
freedoms could lead without the regulatory forces of Christianity. Two are
'Irish' novels: *The Unicorn* (1963) and *The Red and the Green* (1965). *The Unicorn*
is her first book to be set in Ireland, and the location provides both the actual
and the metaphorical mists that indicate the powerful fantasies that cloud
reality. A novel 'full of Simone Weil' as Murdoch admitted,[i] *The Unicorn*
symbolically frames her early meditations on the seductiveness of erotic
servitude and how far individuals have the power to break its hold over
them. It also deals with the equally seductive power of Irish ideas of heroism,
sacrifice and martyrdom. Murdoch uses the Gothic mode again to evoke
troubling and dangerous psychological forces, thus linking Ireland to a seductive ambivalent charm that has dangerous repercussions.

   The Italian Girl (1964) directly followed *The Unicorn* and is a formulaic
Freudian family romance that, like many other Murdoch novels, denotes
multiple sexual attractions within a small cast of characters. Her editors
wanted her to do more work on the book but she refused and it received
poor reviews.[ii] For *The Red and the Green*, Murdoch returned broadly to
conventional realism, setting the story in Dublin during the Easter Rising
of 1916 when the Irish Volunteer Army rebelled against English rule in
Ireland. Murdoch tried 'to get everything right'[iii] in terms of historical and
political accuracy and thought it would provide a good textbook on the
Easter Rising. However, it appeared only four years before the outbreak of
violence in Northern Ireland in 1969, which was to endure for many years
and, with hindsight, she came to perceive the political even-handedness of
the novel as too tolerant towards the Republicans; her sympathies were
henceforth firmly with the Ulster Protestants.

   The Time of the Angels (1966) was written in response to the suffering of
two world wars and the Holocaust. The book is set in an eerie post-war
'twilight of the gods' – a metaphor for a wasteland that reflects Murdoch's
darkest fears about the dawn of a godless world where Christianity, politics,
and philosophy are impotent against the forces of evil. In this novel loss of
faith leads to cruelty, solipsism and incest between father and daughter; the
characters are unable to function spiritually or morally without a substitute
for faith. Carel Fisher, the London rector who preaches a creed of no God,
is Murdoch's first portrait of real evil. Against Carel's belief that 'all is
permitted', Murdoch pits a version of her own moral philosophy in the
words of Carel's brother, the Platonist, Marcus, and a version of contemporary theology in the ineffectual proclamations of an Anglican bishop. Both
fail: philosophy and theology are portrayed as merely consoling fictions.
Only the existence of the novel itself and its suggestion that in this age, 'a
just perception of art is one of the only modes of salvation' convey Murdoch's

belief that art is the most significant hope for moral integrity in the twilight world of the 1960s.

The publication of A. S. Byatt's *Degrees of Freedom* in 1965 – a perceptive reading of Murdoch's early fiction – marked Murdoch's rising reputation as an important novelist. Murdoch and J. B. Priestley's adaptation of *A Severed Head* opened at the Bristol Old Vic in April 1963, transferring to the Criterion Theatre in London in June 1963 where it ran for two and a half years. This successful theatre venture ushered in a period of interest in playwriting; in May 1967 Murdoch collaborated with James Saunders in adapting *The Italian Girl*, which opened at the Bristol Old Vic in November 1967.

Although no longer part of an academic philosophical community, Murdoch nonetheless continued to pursue her interest in philosophy, giving several important lectures during these years. In October 1964 she presented 'Job: Prophet of Modern Nihilism' at Trinity College, Dublin, the first woman to address their Philosophical Society. In the same year she published an important essay 'The Idea of Perfection' in the *Yale Review*.[iv] In it she bravely attacks accepted ideas about 'man' and 'moral psychology' that had dominated the moral philosophy of the 1950s and early 1960s and rejects Stuart Hampshire's view that the core of a person's existence and moral life is conscious choice and overt action. Instead, drawing again on the philosophy of Simone Weil, Murdoch asserts that to learn to see objectively, not subjectively, should be at the heart of moral philosophy. This principle leads her to emphasise the importance of 'right vision' through which we can discover a moral reality external to ourselves: 'If I attend properly I will have no choices and this is the ultimate condition to be aimed at [. . .]. The idea of a patient loving regard directed upon a person, a thing, a situation, presents the will not as unimpeded movement but as something very much more like "obedience"'.[v]

In the 'The Sovereignty of Good over other Concepts', given as the Leslie Stephen Lecture at Cambridge in 1967, Murdoch argued along Platonic lines that the idea of the Good is central to morality and moral philosophy, and sovereign over all others (as distinct from, say, existentialism where the sovereign concept is 'freedom' or 'the will'). Both this essay and 'The Idea of Perfection' were to feed into her book *The Sovereignty of Good* (1970). She continued to read widely in fiction and philosophy, re-engaging with Heidegger's *Being and Time* (this time in its English translation) in January 1965 and with Derrida's *De la grammatologie* and *L'écriture et la différence* in the original French in early 1967. She also took lessons in Russian.

Murdoch continued to be politically active, championing the decriminalisation of homosexuality and contributing an article entitled 'The Moral Decision About Homosexuality' to the magazine *Man and Society* in 1964. The Sexual Offences Act of July 1967 made homosexual acts between consenting male adults over twenty-one years of age legal in England and Wales. However, homosexual activity remained illegal in other parts of the UK and Murdoch continued to support the campaign for reform in Ireland. (The Irish law was finally changed in 1993.) America's war against Communist North Vietnam escalated sharply at this time, prompting Murdoch to contribute an article entitled 'Political Morality' to the Listener in September 1967 and, in the same year, an essay to Authors Take Sides on Vietnam edited by Cecil Woolf and John Bagguley.[vi]

Many new friends were made in the mid-1960s; they included the architect Stephen Gardiner, the philosopher Richard Wollheim and two RCA students, David Morgan and Rachel Brown, whose theses she supervised and whose lives were greatly influenced by their friendship with her. Morgan had come to the RCA after an interrupted education that included a spell in a school for maladjusted boys when he was eleven and hospitalisation in a Birmingham mental health care home when he was seventeen. Murdoch became intensely, and unwisely, emotionally involved with him, and the relationship could have easily ended in a scandal. However, her enduring kindness and patience with his volatile personality undoubtedly changed Morgan's life for the better. She encouraged him to write and teach and he went on to lecture at the Chelsea College of Art, finally becoming head of part-time studies there.[vii] His debt of gratitude to Murdoch endured, not only because of her many kindnesses and stern admonitions, but also because she confirmed to him that he had a fine mind. Morgan published a record of his friendship with Iris Murdoch in 2010.[viii]

Rachel Brown became infatuated with Murdoch, who was aware of the heartache this caused her student. Murdoch nevertheless encouraged the friendship and counselled Brown to marry, a decision that was followed by much unhappiness in Brown's life. Nonetheless, like Morgan, Rachel Fenner (as she became on marriage) went on to teach at various colleges of art, including the Wimbledon School of Art, and became a noted sculptor, painter and environmental artist. If Murdoch's friendship with both these students was to some degree unwise, she was careful to draw the line at a full sexual relationship with either.

Old friends, such as David and Rachel Cecil, and Janet and Reynolds Stone (the wood engraver, designer and typographer), remained important to her, and she and John Bayley often stayed with the two couples at their homes in Dorset, a county she loved. In August 1965, while staying with the Stones, she wrote to Brigid Brophy 'Some kinds of country affect me deeply, as if I had known these scenes in dreams. And this house and garden have that quality too. (Last night, armed with lanterns, we searched for two errant donkeys through a Chinese landscape of waterfall and bamboo.)' The Bayleys also spent time with John and Patsy Grigg, who lived in Greenwich and who owned houses in Spain and Scotland. Murdoch renewed her friendship with Leo Pliatzky (who now worked at the Treasury) and frequently met him for lunch. She also occasionally saw David Hicks, Marjorie Boulton and Hal Lidderdale when in London. In February 1964 Elias Canetti reappeared in Murdoch's life and during the mid-1960s they saw each other occasionally. Although the letters to him in this section often concern practical matters of when and where to meet, their tone is sometimes urgent and rhetorically extravagant, frequently indicating a deep frustration at being unable to see him. Clearly the relationship was still important to her; it might have gained an extra frisson by the fact that Canetti's wife Veza had died in 1963 and he was now living part-time with Hera Buschor, with whom he would move to Zurich in the early 1970s.[ix]

However, some old friends became more distant; contact with Queneau, for example, became infrequent. As someone who liked to hold onto friends and lovers, she came to regret this distance, noting in her journal in 1965 'How did I mislay Queneau?'[x] She did, however, manage to see him in Paris in the summer of 1967. A rift with Fraenkel occurred – possibly, Conradi speculates, because he recognised himself in the figure of Max Lejour in *The Unicorn*; they were reconciled through a letter Murdoch wrote to him in January 1966 and a meeting shortly thereafter.[xi] Donald MacKinnon was not so easily appeased; in 1965 he cut all ties with Murdoch, believing she had used him as a model for Barnabas Drumm in *The Red and the Green*.[xii] The suicide of Carolyn de Ste Croix, daughter of Geoffrey and Lucile de Ste Croix, who had been taught by Murdoch at St Anne's and who had become a friend, also affected her deeply. Her relationships with women friends – particularly Philippa Foot and Brigid Brophy – were of immense importance during these years. Philippa Foot was a visiting professor at the Massachusetts Institute of Technology (MIT) during 1963–4, and became visiting fellow, Society for the Humanities at Cornell University in 1966; however, she sometimes spent university vacations in Oxford. Murdoch often turned to her for comfort during difficult times: 'I am in the midst of much sorrow and desolation of the spirit, and I should like to see you, and may ask a lot of you, so you are warned' she confided to Philippa Foot in early January 1963; and 'I can't fully say, but I think you know, how immensely your love supports me at this time' she wrote a month later.[xiii] Philippa's calm rationality was no doubt a welcome antidote to the emotional turmoil often occasioned by Murdoch's continuing relationship with Brophy.

Murdoch and Brigid Brophy now wrote to each other most days,[xiv] and Murdoch warmly reviewed her friend's work, praising her novel *The Snow Ball* in the *Sunday Times* in January 1964 as bold and original, although her use of the phrase 'sheer artistic insolence' suggests that she recognised the portrait of herself in what can be read as a *roman-à-clef*. Murdoch's London flat made it much easier for the two women to see each other and they also occasionally spent a few days together, Murdoch having booked a double room in a hotel.[xv] Murdoch, feeling able to trust Brophy's discretion, often confided in her about past loves and the complications of her own sexual identity. Yet this was a stormy relationship and Murdoch was frequently hurt by Brophy's erratic behaviour. Despite their differences, the relationship remained enriching for them both. Encouraged by Brophy, a devotee of Freud, Murdoch continued reading his work and also discovered the writing of Jean Genet, the avant-garde French author who wrote provocatively about homosexuality and criminality. Genet's work interested Murdoch sufficiently for her to reject the American translation and read it in the original French. Brophy encouraged Murdoch to read musical scores and her deep love of Mozart – which inspired the Mozartian structure of novels such as *The Snow Ball* – influenced Murdoch's own fiction. *A Severed Head* (1961), *The Nice and the Good* (1968) and *A Fairly Honourable Defeat* (1970) are all marked by a Mozartian dance of couples who interchange partners in such a way as to lend these works a slightly comic and operatic air.

As well as sharing intellectual interests, the two women were fascinated by gender fluidity and adopted fictional roles that allowed them to shift between male and female personae. In these fantasies they borrowed characters from both Mozart's *The Marriage of Figaro* and popular fiction, including E. W. Hornung's crime fiction novel *Raffles: The Amateur Cracksman* (1899) and the cartoon strip *Modesty Blaise*, which appeared in the *Evening Standard* from 1963. Significantly perhaps, all three works feature adventure, disguise and transgression. In a letter written probably in January 1967, Murdoch wrote, 'Glad about your reassuring words on our fantasy life. (How could anyone imagine a woman who couldn't have as good a fantasy life as a man?)'. Such role play enabled Murdoch to express the nuances, tensions and complicated dynamic of their relationship in a manner that was light-hearted, albeit revealing. Brophy was a kind of alter ego for Murdoch, who relished and encouraged her friend's unconventionality. Although, in theory, the bond between the two women was as 'open' as their marriages, each tolerating the other having additional male and female paramours, Brophy demanded more from the relationship than Murdoch felt able to give. Despite her deep love for Brophy, Murdoch became troubled by her persistent demands for greater commitment and felt slightly oppressed by the 'rather reluctant sense of responsibility I had about B – need to see her every week etc.'[xvi] Her sadness at losing such an intimate relationship in 1967 was, then, perhaps tinged with relief when Brophy fell in love with the writer and political activist Maureen Duffy, and directed her passion elsewhere. Nevertheless the two women kept in touch until Brophy's death in 1995.

Frequent travel also characterised these years, either for work or for pleasure. Murdoch and John Bayley became speakers for the British Council and in that capacity they visited Canada in 1963 and Australia and New Zealand in 1967. Murdoch also travelled to the USA in 1966 in order to take part in a 'Study Group on Cultural Unity' held at Bowdoin College in Maine, where she gave a paper entitled 'On "God" and "Good"'; this too was to feed into *The Sovereignty of Good*.

With her reputation as an important novelist rising, Murdoch decided to devote more time to writing and left the RCA in August 1967 albeit with some regret, writing to Rachel Fenner in July 1967, 'The party on Tuesday was somehow rather sad – I feel a piece of my life is ending. Well, pieces are always ending. It was a good piece'.

To Brigid Brophy.

Steeple Aston
[January 1963?[xvii]]

Dear girl, you made for once quite a sensible suggestion, as we were walking to Earls Court, viz. that we should make each other happy. Let us do that. It may need a little care at first (like holding together two bits of cracked china: your wonderful simile in *Snow Ball*).[1]

Do not be hostile to me, dear child. Would like to see you this Monday (Jan 28) if possible, drink 5.30ish? Will telephone. Thank you for my Twelfth Night handkerchief.

And much love

I

To Brigid Brophy.

Steeple Aston
[17 February 1963]

My dear, thanks for your nice letter with educational suggestions. I possess a record of *Eine Kleine Nachtmusik* but of course no score. I am not sure that I desire to know how to read a score, though it is just possible that I desire to desire to know how to read a score. (The Good = what I desire to desire.) So in all these circumstances perhaps you might have a shot at it. [. . .]

---

1 'The two cheeks might have been two fragments of broken china, reunited, being held together for the glue to set'. Brigid Brophy, *The Snow Ball*.

I must now read a pile of exam papers. It's snowing. I look forward to seeing you this (unlikely) or next (surely) week and hearing your arguments!
Love to Mike.
Lots of love
I

To Brigid Brophy.

Steeple Aston
[19 February 1963]

Dear girl, don't write me letters like that, they frighten me and are bad for my nerves. Why are you suddenly so cross with me? As far as I can see I have done nothing bad except give you a manuscript¹ which you subsequently sold – and I think you must just try hard to forgive me for that. As for your being a pillar (role which I most earnestly asked you to fill), you seem rather to resemble the Indian rope trick – it's not clear how you stay up, and at any moment there will be a pistol shot and complete collapse.

You must forgive my last letters, my non-appearance today, and my absence of speculation about your aeroplane to Belfast (if these are things that annoy you). I'm afraid I mislaid your previous letter, which accounted for some absence of detail in my reply. (I *think* you are to go to Belfast 22nd, for three days? Please specify again.) I shall be in London 26th about and will try make arrangement earlier (will telephone soon). I nearly got up today only last minute college business hitch. You must remember that I am very naive and believe everything I am told (if I can understand it, which I can't always with you). I lived in a universe of perfect harmony until I was thirteen (and went to boarding school and found out the world was not composed purely of love, but it was too late by then). *Hinc illae lacrimae.*²

I count on your love (increasingly: alarming thought) – and the threat of its withdrawal causes much alarm. I hope you enjoyed your lunch with Mr Pope-Hennessy.³ I'll telephone you.
Love
I

1 Of *Under the Net.*
2 Hence these tears.
3 John Wyndham Pope-Hennessy, art historian and museum director.

To Brigid Brophy.

Steeple Aston
[10 March 1963]

Thanks awfully for charming letters and for blue communication from Kate (thank Kate). I am rather sunk in exam papers etc. at the moment. The blooming wind blows and the rain rains and the snowdrops have come up (snow only vanished Wednesday) and the fish (under ice for months) seem to be OK.

Number of points. David Hicks, stuck in Prague while I was stuck in Innsbruck, letters not arriving etc., met charming girl called Molly and married her. (Divorced later – but I was unlucky again.)[1]

Apropos Tories, I did do my best once to marry Michael Oakeshott, but it was no use – and I think I agree with you that it would always be a bad plan.

About Klein, no connection in my mind Melanie-Honor,[2] so far as I know. I had no M. Klein concepts prior to the ones you gave me. (A psychoanalysed friend was very cross about the name as he thought I was somehow getting at Melanie. They are very touchy.)

We look forward to the Wisdom[3] gathering. Only rather sad not see you and Mike properly. Let's hope Wisdoms go to bed early. I won't be up *next* week I think (week begin. 18th) as will be interviewing entrance candidates all week. Sad about that. [. . .]

Much love
I

To Brigid Brophy.

Steeple Aston
[15 March 1963]

1 In a letter dated 24 March 1963 to Brigid Brophy (not included here), Murdoch wrote 'About D. Hicks. No, I wasn't married on the second occasion when he was available. I might even have tried again but he fled me. I think he was only really in love with me approx. Nov. 25 to Dec. 8 1938. *Eheu fugaces* [How the years fly]'.

2 Melanie Klein, Austrian-born British psychoanalyst. Honor Klein is a character in Murdoch's novel *A Severed Head*.

3 Probably John Oulton Wisdom (not to be confused with the Cambridge-based philosopher John Wisdom), who taught logic and the philosophy of science at the London School of Economics between 1948 and 1965; like Brophy, he was very interested in psychoanalysis.

Dear girl, thank you very much for your card and letter. Have left them at Steeple Aston and can't now recall new possible Rycroft[1] date. Will *try* and telephone – it always worries me so. This is not really reply but to communicate bright idea. There are two facts I have known for some time which now in an intuitive flash characteristic of the brilliant mind I connect together. These two facts are:

(a) Recently I have been growing stouter.
(b) Recently you have been growing thinner.

Clothes: see? The trouble is you and ingenious Mike will have mucked up all those lovely garments which would now fit me so well. (I have *especially* in mind the fine blue-striped *sack* you wore some years ago.) I expect they have all been taken in (bust darts etc., weapons of love). While in my wardrobes there still hang excellent dresses which won't fit me but might fit you. I fear it could be a rather one-sided exchange. But anyway we might discuss it further don't you think? The idea rather fascinates me. [. . .]

I should have recognised your writing in eye-shadow (or whatever the hell they call that stuff). Have you got it in other colours?

I have had a letter from an American girl who says she is lesbian and as I obviously am too will I please have a spiritual friendship by letter, she is very interested in philosophy. I am composing a stern reply. Love

I

To Brigid Brophy, written from John Bayley's mother's home in Kent.

Ashford
[30 March 1963]

Dear girl,

I have worn the stripey dress with éclat and am very pleased with it. I really must find some suitable rejoinder for remainder. As I said, I'd give you ties if I thought you'd dress suitably with them. In my view you ought always to be *habillée en homme*.[2] Ah well. I wonder what Kate's headmistress *thought*? That I was really Kate's mother? Who were you supposed to be then? I liked the tale of Kate's tulip-economy. Other points. I am to *give* prize in Corfu. Must read some damn boring books before then.

1 Possibly Charles Rycroft, British psychiatrist, author and psychoanalyst who had a private practice in London.
2 Dressed as a man.

About gun: this is John's .22 rifle, which he keeps licensed although I never allow him to fire it. (He once wanted to fire it out of the window to scare birds off grass seed, but I wouldn't permit even that.) Coming of military and engineering family he has passion for engines and firearms. [. . .]

Yes, I am flattered by your sulks but also frightened. Requirements of eternal sunshine. (Religious temperament. We must discuss religion sometime.)

I think I have gastric flu but propose to be better almost at once.

Love

I

To Brigid Brophy.

Steeple Aston
[14 April 1963]

Dearest Brigid, I am very sorry I didn't write during the week. There was no moment of peace and recollection, and I am not a very robust letter-writer in hotel lounges. So forgive. Seem to have been everywhere: Wales, Dorset, Bath (adorable place). I looked for fossils on the beach at Charmouth, intending to bring you one, but like every other standard the fossil standard had fallen. However I picked up a number of *stones* and will bring you one of those.

Back here, there awaits the garden, looking more earthly-paradise-like every moment, and an awful pile of letters, including the handwritten auto-biography of a man in Greenford who feels I would be interested to know of his experiences. (I wish I still loved letters: yours are the only ones now almost that I seize on with pleasure. Well, there are a few other people I like to hear from but none of them can write *letters*.)

I hope Kate and Mike are very well. I dreamt about Kate the other night but can't recall what. Do you feel it is very *kind* of people to dream about you? I always feel rather grateful if I learn I have been in someone's dream. Metaphysical query: is one morally responsible for what one does in other people's dreams?

I have also ordered (some time ago) but not yet received the *photo* you were kind enough to desire. I will bring that together with fossil (fossil and photo of old fossil) when I next come, if it's arrived. Still not sure when I'll be around, but will telephone when know and ask if can see you.

I am quite alarmed, by the way, at the way in which Christianity now seems to be on the run! The bishop of Winchester¹ seems to have enabled

1 Falkner Allison.

a lot of people, including journalists, to say what they really think about it! I don't mind that of course: but God help our society if it thinks it can just *suddenly* drop Christianity like an old potato. Of course most people don't know what 'religion' or 'God' mean anyhow – but that goes for the jaunty journalists too.

We must sometime continue our discussion which was started chez Rycroft. I may have expressed myself stupidly: indeed I am in a muddle, though clear about some things.

Now this damn letter won't reach you for ages because of damn Easter. Please write to me soon. Be well. Lots and lots of love

    I

PS don't misunderstand me about Christianity etc. I'm not being an opium-of-the-people merchant. It just offended me to see journalists who wouldn't dare to be frank about homosexuality and who until lately treated the Church as if it were the Royal Family suddenly kicking their heels and making idiotic remarks such as 'this is not really a Christian country' etc. It's like a fish saying it doesn't believe in the sea. We are sunk in Christianity whether we like it or not, not only culturally but morally. Paganism is a privilege of a few. Also I am afraid that if organised Christianity suddenly collapses people will think there is no longer any reason to love each other. And I feel for the *fright* the ordinary simple believer may feel when bishops casually attack the idea of a personal God.

I've just received one of these RSG-6 pamphlets.[1] Have you had one? Blood-chilling. I knew vaguely this arrangement existed as Freddie Ayer[2] was asked to be one of the Chosen and refused. Good for him. (Of course if they wanted a philosopher they would choose Ayer.)

    Best wishes and love

    I

---

1 RSGs (Regional Seats of Government) were planned miniature governments, which would run regions of England immediately after a nuclear attack. In March 1963 members of a group called Spies for Peace broke into a secret government headquarter (RSG-6) and photographed some documents. They then produced 4,000 copies of a pamphlet entitled 'Danger! Official Secret RSG-6' and distributed them widely in order to expose the fact that the government saw a thermonuclear attack as a real possibility.

2 Ayer, at this time Wykeham Professor at Oxford, had been a Special Operations Executive and an MI6 agent during the Second World War which is probably why he was asked to take part in this exercise.

To Brigid Brophy, written from Canada which Murdoch and John Bayley were visiting as British Council speakers. John had been invited to teach at the Shakespeare Festival summer school in Stratford, Ontario and Murdoch had been asked to take part in a discussion about values at McMaster University in Hamilton, Ontario.

Toronto
Ontario
[26 July 1963]

I was very touched and pleased to get your letter. (It looked so official I thought it might be some grim summons or denunciation!) I liked the Teddington cutting and consider it prophetic. I imagine myself as a fat roisterous old party giver retired to one of those bogus-Tudor houses with very flowery gardens and a river frontage. Gay gatherings every night, singing and sounds of bottles being hurled into the water, while the local police click their tongues: old Dame Iris is at it again tonight . . .

It's weird and wonderful here. We are pro tem at the university at Hamilton, in a luxurious flat looking out on an enchanted wood. Within half an hour of arriving we had seen chipmunks and groundhogs from the window (latter are big slow beaver-like creatures, very nice) and this morning on waking, raccoons. (I have been promised the sight of raccoons lifting lids of dustbins with their hand-like paws – that do I long to see.) Many strange birds too. [. . .]

Lots of Love
I

To Brigid Brophy.

Hamilton
Ontario
3 August 1963

[. . .] Why don't you become a realist and wear trousers? (I don't think I have ever seen you in trousers. Now you are so slim there is *no excuse*.) Thanks for the latest on Garvin and Blaise.[1] My affection for Garvin will suffer if anyone gets seriously hurt, but it seems all right so far.

1 Willie Garvin and Modesty Blaise, characters in a cartoon strip created by Peter O'Donnell and Jim Holdaway that appeared daily in the *Evening Standard*. Garvin and Blaise are asked by the British Secret Service to help exterminate various villains. Modesty is an exceptionally talented young woman who was a child refugee during the Second World War and has a criminal past; Willie Garvin is her trusty friend and sidekick.

I am enjoying Canada quite absurdly and have learnt a lot in a week of discussions with these gentle and to some extent clueless academics. I am still at Hamilton Ontario, at McMaster University, and only go to Stratford tomorrow in fact, but your letters get through by some channel. I have seen a scarlet tanager.[1] Not yet a skunk. The extreme suburban bourgeois prettiness of the colonial style houses with their magnificent trees and swimming pools delights and appals. The scenes *are* lovely though and the strange innocence of all the people takes a load off the mind. I could even imagine living here. (No I couldn't. No pubs, no cafés, and if you buy liquor you have to get it in a government store and *sign* for it.) Back just after you leave, alas. Where are you going in Scandinavia? Lots of love I

To Michael Oakeshott, postcard from Stratford, Ontario.

[10 August 1963]

You see it happens over here all over again.[2] I have telephoned you once or twice and even called once, but in vain. I'd love to see you in the autumn. This just to send best wishes and love
    Iris

To Brigid Brophy.

Steeple Aston
[28 September 1963]

Dear dear girl, many thanks for letter of yesterday – I'm very glad you wrote. I am deeply sorry you felt 'abandoned'. Things seem different from different points of view. I don't live in London, and as I said yesterday there didn't seem point, after an absence, seeing you either with John or very briefly. We rushed through London home, exhausted. Then there was this matter of J's mother – it may not have been very 'important' but it was something that just had to be done then. By that time I (and J too) was frantic to *establish* life at Cedar Lodge again and get to work. No good arrive back from Nettlepole and set off London at once (that's the sort of thing that drives J faintly crazy, and I didn't want to do it either). Hence further (short) delay. If I lived in London all this would be different of course. But

1 A colourful bird.
2 The Shakespeare Festival.

London is quite a way off, and a night there is a two-whole-day operation. This is the 'explanation' of the eleven days you speak of. One has got to live at one's own pace – long experience tells me – and when there are differences in rhythm people must try to understand. It would have been no good my seeing you hastily – you are always 'difficult' after I've been away (there is an element of vicious circle here) – you were rather touchy and sarcastic in letters. Indeed if I'd been *really* sensible I would have delayed coming till my cousins were out of the flat and could have some privacy! But I was anxious to see you.

All this makes sense to me and I hope now it makes a little sense to you. I have *got* to work and live in an orderly way and make Steeple Aston into a *place*, for John as well as myself, and this means breathing spaces and not rushings to and fro. (The Nettlepole thing was just damned unfortunate and untimely.) Dear heart, do understand all this. I have certain kinds of almost *physical* need here.

Oh Christ, I feel bloody tired and have a mountain of work to do, things I must try to finish before term. Work is a 'rival' about time, but one that you surely can be tolerant of? Dearest girl, forgive my falling short, and just take me along as I am. I can't put it more eloquently, but I do love you. (You asked earlier: how did I know? Partly by introspection and partly by a study of my conduct.) Much love

I

To Brigid Brophy.

Steeple Aston
[September? 1963^{xviii}]

Yes, I am being prodded like mad. How did she know? I found those damn African tales very hard to review and have done a bad review. *Mea maxima culpa* for taking it on at all. It is all sentiment about a man I once loved who was an Oxford anthropologist.[1] (They, the anthropologists, are like a little tribe or composite personality, they are always together, usually in a pub.)

I was charmed by *The Finishing Touch*.[2] I hope you don't mind being my brother after all?[3] Thanks for Willie too. No, not like Wisdom. Wisdom's appeal is tentative, shrinking. I will tell you the story of my life when you want but it will take AGES. Re your other *desiderata*, or rather no. (i), I doubt

1 Franz Steiner.
2 Brophy's novel, which had by now been published.
3 In a recent letter Murdoch had written 'But the incest that really interests me is brother–sister. Be a sister to me'.

if that can be managed. I have often wanted to be beaten by people who interested me, but with you everything is the other way round. This is bewildering. Perhaps it just shews I am growing old.

I have been meaning to say, by the way, that I'm glad you got round to apologising. It was necessary, indeed essential. But what is essential doesn't always happen.

I am so glad I seem to be doing well on the happiness-maximising front. May it continue. Look forward to tutorial on Freud. (Have been investigating *Collected Papers* on own since: confused.) How do *you* telekinete?[1] I embrace you. As we used to say in the Party,

Fraternally yours

I

To Philippa Foot, now teaching at MIT, Cambridge, Massachusetts.

Steeple Aston
[2 November 1963]

Dearest Philippa, how goes it I wonder at 470 Beacon Street?[2] (What's it *like* there?) I do do hope you are not still ill. *Please write soon* and give me news. I get fits of worrying about you.

I am feeling rather peculiar having just finished a novel[3] – an odd sort of loneliness – a lot of people I've been with a long time have just gone away. It's as if they've emigrated and though I shall hear tell of them I shall never be with them again. It's very sad. I must invent some new characters quickly!

I am enjoying the London lecturing though I realise now the stuff is far too difficult for them – however, they discuss with a will, and there are a number of very very sweet creatures there. I look forward to seeing more of them when we move to the new building beside the Albert Hall in January.

I am enjoying the autumn for perhaps the first time. You said you always do. I expect you've got lots of those goddam maple trees doing their stuff over there. The Steeple Aston garden looks like a painting by Cotman.[4]

Write, write! Very much love,

Iris

---

1 Much later, Murdoch's interest in telekinesis made its way into her fiction. Moy, in *The Green Knight*, is accomplished at the skill: 'She turned away toward her stones [. . .] upon their shelf, and reached out her hand, nearer and nearer. A stone moved toward her hand'.
2 A fashionable and elegant street in Boston.
3 *The Italian Girl.*
4 John Cotman (1782–1842), English marine and landscape painter.

To Philippa Foot, concerning Donald MacKinnon, her former tutor at Oxford from whom Murdoch was now estranged.

Steeple Aston
[mid/late November 1963]

Darling, just a note to try to lure one out of you. How are you? I get fits of worrying and picturing you ill. Do hope you are lots better and full of philosophical fight. How's the flat? Beacon Street must be very grand, as some fashionable people in a Henry James story were strolling down it, I noticed with pleasure the other day.

I have finished a novel and started another one.[1] They never seem to get any better though I go on happily. I've done a term of lecturing to my beatniks, and enjoyed it – though it's all too difficult for them I'm afraid.

I went to Cambridge to see Carolyn de Ste Croix (who *still* has *her* glandular fever!) and met Donald in the street. At least I saw him emerge from Corpus, pursued him wondering what to do, crossed the road ahead of him and confronted him. He looked at me as if I were a ghost and we exchanged about four sentences of the 'How are you' kind and then he hurried away. I felt so terribly sad. I had forgotten how very blue his eyes are. Write to me forthwith!

With much love, my dear –
Iris

I miss you!

To Philippa Foot.

Steeple Aston
19 January 1964

My dear, NO STRINGS[2] has arrived! So many many thanks for remembering it! I'm very pleased. And henceforth will happily associate you with those charmingly idiotic songs.

1 *The Red and the Green.*
2 Song from the musical *No Strings* (1962), words and music by Richard Rodgers.

('No strings, no strings,
Except our own DEVOTION,
No other bonds at all –
Let the little folk
Who need the help
Depend upon vows and such,
WE are much
Too tall' etc.)

Oh darling, where *are* you and *how* are you? I wrote you a letter to the terribly improbable address 4221 Sunset Boulevard. (Do please form your *numbers* more clearly! I wasn't sure if I was reading it right. Angst!) Are you back in Boston now? I wish you were coming here – I absolutely thirst for converse with you. It was about this time last year I was walking up and down your sickroom weeping and drinking champagne, remember. Come back, and we'll have champagne and no tears.

I do hope you're feeling better in yourself – though I can't honestly hope you're loving USA more! Well, yes, I do hope it, and you may stop there so long as you have a really long *settled* period in Europe every year. It will be something to look forward to. Though I'd so much rather have you permanently around. I have a lot of special thoughts which can only be communicated to you. I am living an odd life now, mostly London and Steeple Aston. It's sad about Oxford, but there it is. WRITE TO ME. Much love, and much thanks again!

I

To Philippa Foot.

Steeple Aston
[mid-February 1964]

My dear creature, do write to me. I am so depressed. My dear young friend in Cambridge, Carolyn de Ste Croix, has killed herself with sleeping tablets.[1] (She said she would – no one took it seriously enough – and she did.) I don't know if you met her. (She had glandular fever last year, and I think you exchanged some messages about symptoms through me.) I blame myself terribly for not having looked after her better, such as apprehended the situation and taken charge of it. Oh God. I ought to have written to her every day. One sees these things so clearly afterwards. Yet all her grumblings

---

1 Carolyn de Ste Croix committed suicide on 31 January 1964 but her body was not discovered until 9 February. Murdoch spoke at her graveside.

were so curiously cheerful and rational, one was put off one's guard. What was 'the matter' God knows – she was quite sane – just became unbearably miserable, her whole consciousness a misery.

I do hope you are more cheerful now and *well*. I wish it wasn't so infernally long till you're back. Do write soon. All love
I

To Philippa Foot.

Steeple Aston
23 February [1964]

My dear, thanks so much for your letter, I was so glad to get it. Yes, I know. If only one could get across to people that one is ready and willing etc. I feel my own failure to do so here is a bad failure. Though I remember Carolyn saying to me once, '*Help* is no good because I myself am the trouble.' But in fact really serious sustained help, active *love*, might have prevented this. Anyway.

I wish I could come to your classes on Wittgenstein. I am very sorry about the fruitless pining. But perhaps your luck will turn? I am not at the moment in love with anyone, *thank God*. How much of one's time and energy is spent in such suffering. Instead I am sort of quasi in love with about ten of my friends. You are certainly one. I think I was in love with you in Seaforth days and this has never stopped. I trust you don't mind. (Given a fair field in early youth I suspect I might have become a pretty serious homosexual. However, it's too late to undo that damage now.) Yes, I do love you, and not only with my mind. This is one of many reasons why you must come home. I do hope you are not too sad about those things over there. I embrace you.
Much love
I

To Elias Canetti.

Steeple Aston
[late February 1964]

My dear, just to say will come Tuesday 12.30ish chez toi as arranged. Also, could you come drinks my new flat 6 p.m. Wednesday March 4. I am asking my mama and one or two people. I embrace you. Much love
Iris

To Brigid Brophy.

Steeple Aston
1 March [1964]

My dear, thanks very much for your nice letter. I keep fearing I will get a
note from you saying let's not meet for ten years or something. Your
conjecture may have something in it. I am conscious of shaping you in my
imagination and I do sometimes notice discrepancies. Forgive, and vice
versa. [. . .]

There was a power breakdown at Steeple Aston on Friday, 7–10 p.m. so
just when I was finishing work and thinking I might listen to *Idomeneo* and
then cook my supper (John being in Oxford that evening), I had instead to
wander round in dark looking for two or three moth-eaten candles by whose
light I read *Crime and Punishment* unfed till 10 p.m. It's fantastic how much
spiritual difference light makes. I embrace you – with much love
I

To Brigid Brophy.

Steeple Aston
15 March [1964]

Darling, so much thanks for your letter. I can't reply properly or argue now,
just time-wise. Anyway I don't really know what to say. Alas, we are not
plants, but a couple of ten stone (a little less in your case and more in mine)
incarnate girls. There would *have* to be decisions, actions, times and I could
not take this calmly. It would be utterly frivolous of me to be persuaded by
you here. I am terribly puritanical and unable to be carefree about sex, even
when I'm in love. But I'm not in love with you, and don't want be. When
I am in love I am INSANE and although a great glory shines around, the
main results are anxiety, misery, despair, destruction, inability to work etc.
Just now I feel free and happy and I want to go on feeling so. I do do love
you, maybe more than you realise, because of your conceptual prejudices
– and I do want to be closer to you and more intimate and for affection and
trust to come and go between us without those inhibitions you speak of. Is
there no way here? *Ach* – I can't believe there isn't.

Do hope OK see you tomorrow, will telephone during morning. Dear
dear angel, with much love
I

PS As far as I am concerned any day is a kissing day – but you make me feel I act wrongly if I touch you. *Quae* (the above) *cum ita sint*,[1] perhaps I do – but I do want to touch you.

To Brigid Brophy.

Steeple Aston
[March 1964]

Darling, just note. Leave here for Kent Saturday, back approx. Tues or Weds (Nettlepole, Little Chart, Pluckley, Kent). Make clear letter, if any, for me, not mother-in-law! I've meant to say for some time how very much pleasure I have got from the Mozart records you gave, especially the *Requiem*. (Verdi, whose *Requiem* I know moderately, seems to have listened with some profit to Mozart!) I love the words of the Dies Irae. '*Tantus labor non sit cassus*'[2] is such a wonderful *argument*. I've read some more of your Mozart book[3] and think it wonderful, another Golden Object (that was original title of my review of *Snow Ball*). I can't altogether agree about Beethoven – but then what do I know? Yet a cat may look at a king[4] (a very nice idea – I wonder how it originates?). Much love

    I

PS I am looking for a passage in Freud, which I may have invented myself, where he says something about thinking a man more virtuous (morally better) because he censors certain things in dreams. Can you recall this? *Collected Papers*?

To Georg Kreisel, now teaching in the department of philosophy at Stanford University, California.

Steeple Aston
March 1964

Many thanks for your quick letter, which I haven't by me now at this minute. I shall forget something which you said which I meant to answer. The person I spoke of was a girl, age about twenty-eight, whom I'd known since she

1 As (the above) is the case.
2 'May such great labour not be in vain'.
3 Brophy's *Mozart the Dramatist: A New View of Mozart, His Operas and His Age.*
4 An old adage suggesting that people should not be unduly intimidated by their social superiors.

was a small child. She loved me very much and I could easily have helped her if I'd taken more trouble. She wasn't in love with me – her speciality was falling in love with married men of fifty, who encouraged her for a time and then had guilt feelings.

Kant: (I paraphrase a little) – when we are told by the Gospels to love our neighbour we are exhorted to a love seated in *principles of action* and not tender sympathy – practical not pathological love¹ – that love can be commanded. He is wrong of course. Given luck and a situation, a little effort and one *really* loves people more. And only 'pathological' love² really *helps* in so many cases –

I wish I felt we could really communicate with each other. Sometimes it feels possible, sometimes not. There is something odd, almost uncanny, in the degree of quite contextless 'rapport' I sometimes feel with you. But what is it based on or connected with? It's just that sometimes, in certain moods of beset loneliness, one thinks of certain people as refuges, God knows why. I expect if we met we would be very awkward with each other, as we always have been – anyway, I miss you. Never mind. Oh Kreisel, what a desert life sometimes seems. But it passes. I hope you are well and working hard. I embrace you – with love

I

To Brigid Brophy.

Steeple Aston
[31 March 1964]

Thanks for Iris-card. I shall certainly not give extra Mozart³ away, but keep one in Oxford and one in London. You must inscribe second one too. Have recovered from stunned delight at *Requiem* enough to start listening to *Coronation Mass*⁴ which is of course an opera not a mass – a gorgeous one, naturally. A man I know who should be well informed about this tells me

1 Using the word 'pathological' rather idiosyncratically, Kant defines pathological love as inclination or instinctive *feeling* as opposed to practical love, which is kindness done from a sense of *duty*. Only practical love, Kant suggests, can be commanded. Murdoch takes issue with Kant's claim: for her, love as inclination or feeling can be (at least partially) moulded by us, through the processes of, for example, selecting different and better things to think about, and by paying deep and sustained attention to the reality of the other.
2 In April, Murdoch would write to Kreisel, 'I cannot agree with Kant that "pathological" love cannot be commanded. I, and many other people, could have loved more in this case if we'd only tried, and it would have been quite genuine love'.
3 Brophy's publisher had sent Murdoch another copy of her book.
4 Probably Mozart's *Krönungsmesse* composed in 1779.

that when the angels play music before God they play Bach, but when they play by themselves for their own amusement they play Mozart. There is certainly a relaxed feel at the absence of God. (Though perhaps the gods are present.)

Sorry I mixed up the sexes, have never been clear about the difference – and I identify myself so much with Willie that it never occurred to me it might be Modesty I was. Still not sure about Genet.[1] I doubt if a writer can win on that subject. [. . .]

Also I want those photos I left behind.

Much love

I

To Brigid Brophy.

Steeple Aston
[mid-April 1964?]

[. . .] It's a beautiful sunny day and the swallows arrived the day before yesterday and are now hawking about the garden, being obnoxious to the other birds and blitzing stray cats. Everything is springlike and wonderful and there are only two blots on the landscape (a) I have a sore throat, temperature, cough, congested chest and have to live on aureomycin and yeast. (b) You are angry with me.

Angel, do not be. Why do we cause each other pain in this way? I know that I am blundering, thoughtless, tactless (e.g. in this recent matter) and I am heartily sorry and do apologise. I *wasn't* just trying to put you off but just suggesting what seemed more sensible. The idea of carrying you off here in the car through the summer sunshine (or summer east winds and rain) is purely delightful and must be. I am a blunderer, but I don't intentionally cause you real pain. If I ever deliberately twist your arm it is only to occasion so much pain as will be indistinguishable from pleasure. You on the other hand when you decide to punish me (vide the letter I received this morning) emulate Modesty with her kongo[2] and nerve-centres technique. Don't do it. I am fonder of you every day and your power to hurt me grows alarmingly. You will reply that my stupidity makes you automatically recede from me. Well, inhibit that movement and believe that I cry and forgive me – *c'est ton métier.*[3]

---

1 Jean Genet (1910–86), controversial French writer and political activist.
2 Modesty Blaise's choice of weapon is a yawara stick, a Japanese weapon used in various martial arts, which she calls a 'kongo'.
3 It's what you're good at.

I am going to be in London this coming week but if so only for half a day, and would only be able to see you for a short time, which would perhaps be unwise, though I might not be able to resist the temptation to ring you. But let us (assuming you want to see me) decide how we shall celebrate the beginning of term in the following week, April 28–30. I'd like to see you *seule*,[1] which rules out an evening unless Mike is away? Could you let me know if you'd prefer lunch or dinner? And let me know too about May 27, 29.

Much love

I

To Philippa Foot.

Steeple Aston
26 April 1964

My dear, thanks for letter and Chicago card – hope paper went well and pictures were cheering – pictures can so delight and console one. I never *really* understood about Toulouse-Lautrec until I saw *La Grande Jatte* at Chicago.[2] Now his stuff in London[3] seems much clearer – and his relation to Piero.[4]

So pleased you may be coming back earlier. Let me know just when. I am sorry things have been so mouldy. Is distress about those people, or person, rather less? One doesn't seem to get any less vulnerable as the years pass – I think perhaps one gets more so – and I never get over the awful sense of surprise when somebody hurts one – or more still when you suddenly notice they have a vendetta against you, or accuse you of crimes you don't know you've committed. How little one understands other people. I wish I could create really *different* people in my novels, but they are all me. I do want to see you. You've always been very separate from me, though I love you so much – this in a good way. But I don't understand you either though trust you completely. All love

I

---

1 Alone.
2 Murdoch presumably means the famous pointillist painting *Un dimanche après-midi à La Grande Jatte* (*A Sunday afternoon at La Grande Jatte*) (1886), by Georges Seurat, held in the Art Institute of Chicago.
3 Although she mentions Toulouse-Lautrec, Murdoch is thinking of Seurat's work; there are eleven paintings by him in the National Gallery and four in the Tate Gallery, London.
4 Piero della Francesca (*c*.1415–92), one of Murdoch's favourite artists.

To Brigid Brophy.

Steeple Aston
[early May 1964]

My dearest creature, please forgive any hurt from my letter. I do love you, and that is the main point. And if I am alarmed at what seemed your vicious aspect you must appreciate that I have had cause for the alarm. Time cures these things and time *is* bringing us closer together. It seems absurd in a way how difficult it all is – maybe difficulty is of the essence. It is like a relationship between two railway engines. It would be nice to be together in one shed. But we seem to spend the time rushing about on various tracks trying to meet. Sometimes it looks as if we are going to have a head-on collision. Then one of us goes roaring away down a side track wildly whistling. Then when it seems we might come together the tracks suddenly divide –

[. . .] Yes, I do love you, do believe it.

I

Are you to be wearing a shirt and tie and nothing else, like the girl in the Tootal advertisement?[1] I like that idea. I might even provide a revolver. (Unloaded.)

To Brigid Brophy.

Steeple Aston
[early May 1964]

Thanks for today's letter. I am very glad if I can make you happy for a change. You are making me so. Can't we fix this arrangement?

I have filed your previous and most interesting letter for reference and am studying it again. I can't myself quite picture this awful identification-intimacy you say is possible between two women. A woman is a human being after all – and each one is so different from others. Anyway I don't think such a relation could possibly exist between us, whatever we did, we are so alien to each other. (Read carefully your letter is a long piece of advice against going to bed!) But it is interesting that you think it possible, I mean with someone. When I have been intimate with people I have then most of

---

1 Tootal made men's ties and in 1961 their very successful advertisement showed a woman posed seductively wearing a man's shirt and tie with the strapline 'Looks even better on a man.'

all and deliciously felt their difference. Perhaps this comes of narcissism? (I
await your explanation of that business with interest.) I note that you say
the fact I expect a long-term relationship with you shews I'm homosexual!
I should have thought it just shewed I was sensible and human! (I'm not
sure what you mean actually: it sounded rather alarming anyway, as if all
you wanted really was a sort of dénouement. Another argument against
etc.) However, you talk a lot of nonsense, though it's always interesting.

I was shocked by your remark about Beethoven opus 59. Do you equally
despise the late quartets? I suspect you just hate him. Your remarks in the
Mozart book often sounded like scarcely inhibited hate!

[. . .] Managed to see Friday's 'Modesty Blaise' and am now on tenterhooks. What will Willie do when he sees Modesty's blood-stained sweater?
Keep me in the picture.

Lots of love
I

*To David Morgan, a twenty-four-year-old student at the Royal College of Art whose
thesis on oratory and its power to sway crowds (the topic also of Canetti's* Crowds
and Power) *Murdoch was supervising. Attracted to each other, he and Murdoch
subsequently met informally, out of college, once a week during 1964.*

Steeple Aston
9 May 1964

Dear David,

If you would like to have your work torn to pieces I suggest you come
to my room in the RCA new building about 5 p.m. on Wednesday May 20.
I'll expect you then if I don't hear otherwise. [. . .]

Yours sincerely,
Iris Murdoch

To Brigid Brophy.

Steeple Aston
[May 1964]

Dearest girl, thanks for letter which gets more marks as a love letter than
any previous one, even though it is rather full of obscure theory. (Could
you sometime explain, as for someone who only knows ordinary words, the
difference between narcissism and auto-eroticism? I daresay I am narcissistic.

But do you auto-erotics really not love yourselves, in spite of your name? How do you manage?)

I've got too many business letters to write to give you an adequate commentary today, so shall talk at random. I think the only thing I am 'afraid' of where you are concerned is that you may suddenly put me in a position where I have to break off relations with you. This, as a hedonist who loves you, I should dislike. Your stuff about your pattern of valuing not being the same as my pattern of valuing myself may be true, though I would describe it in a simpler way. It often seems to me that you don't value me at all, except rather blindly as an object aimed at. You don't see me. It was not clear to me either what your conclusion was. Is this coincidence of value pattern going to take place after all? Your being so argumentative here reminds me of many men I've known who, when I said I didn't want to go to bed with them, thought there must be some special *reason* which could somehow be *dealt with*. Your description of the situation anyway makes it sound rather difficult. I don't think there is much danger of our becoming intimate or identified. Lions and pythons can't be identified. We are incredibly different. But is the hostility you adopt 'in order to keep me at a distance' really adopted just for that reason? I don't enjoy this hostility and it makes me afraid of a break. Is it really necessary? And how does that problem relate to the problem about hearing the 'chord'? I like the image of you swanning about with the cutlass. I think perhaps our difficulties are more purely physical (if this exists) than psychological. Perhaps I should fall in love with you if you dressed in a tweed suit and a tie. (Though I suppose this would not be exactly a physical difference, now I come to think of it – but you see what I mean.)

[. . .] There's more to say about what you said but it must wait. How much I wish you would keep a true woman's eye and love me still and know not why . . .¹

With love

I

I got a letter today asking me to talk at some summer school, and ending up, 'We know you are a very busy man, but etc. etc.'

---

1 'Keep, therefore, a true woman's eye, / And love me still but know not why – / So hast thou the same reason still / To doat upon me ever!' From an anonymous poem 'Love not me for comely grace' set to music as a madrigal by John Wilbye in 1608.

To Brigid Brophy.

Steeple Aston
[10 May 1964]

My letter which crossed with yours gave confirmation in writing of the point you make about lateral incest. In fact I don't want you to be my sister, I have little use for sisters. Your role is probably that of younger brother. (I am elder brother.) I suspect my ideal relationship is that between two men. Usually I play the part of the younger man – but with you of course I am the older man. (Does this shew me to be homosexual I wonder?)

I suspect that part of the difficulty with you is that you are not a true classical sadomasochist like me. You are just an abnormal perverted one. Or not one at all.

Could you on Wednesday (I should arrive 1.10) give me a lecture on the anal-oral distinction? (Does it delightfully correlate with the narcissistic-autoerotic distinction?) A mad pupil of mine at RCA has written an essay in which he connects telekinesis with 'issues from the mouth' (mediums in séances etc.) and with the importance of breath in eastern religion. OK! But it just strikes me that if I 'attempt' to telekinete (if that's the verb) I certainly don't do it in terms of anything issuing from the mouth. (I do it somehow with my whole body.) I feel something about oral types must come in here. NB I do want that Freudian reading list.

Wisdom has had a pure-Freudian, a revised-Freudian,[1] and a Kleinian analysis. Kleinian was best.

Glad you enjoyed *A Severed Head*. You didn't tell me about Aldous Huxley though. Did you ever admire him? (Do you recall a character called Al Bear? He sends his respects.)

Love from
I

To Brigid Brophy.

Steeple Aston
[May 1964]

1 John Oulton Wisdom had been analysed by Ernest Jones in the 1930s.

You faithless monster, you idle oblivious Circassian whip-worthy wench.[1] Al Bear is indeed 'this same bear' whom I did not give away to a godchild, he lives in my wardrobe. He was called Al Bear because for some very complex reason you objected to his being called Albert. You even made a joke about the Prince Regent. But I expect you dish bears out to everybody and can't really be expected to keep track of them.

To Brigid Brophy, written from the Shelbourne Hotel in Dublin.

[14 May 1964]

This hotel has gone to the dogs, but Dublin is the same magic city. I am sick with emotion in it. God. Just off to look at the dear old icy cold sea. Tuesday: I'll telephone you in the morning about the evening.
    Oh the Irish, the Irish . . . How Irish your pa is by the way.
    Much love
    I

To Brigid Brophy.

Steeple Aston
[24 May 1964]

You are getting muddled. You are the one who advocates *promiscuity* and ergo lust. I am, austere puritan, against it. No wonder Michael was shocked, and rightly. In commending homosexual practices I merely point out that the homosexual is essentially in the same position as the heterosexual (apart from details such as being unwed, officially, and childless) – and like the heterosexual may be promiscuous or serious. And of course I also commend seriousness.
    I don't think I could bear to see *Les enfants du paradis*[2] again – my memory of it is so perfect, I mean beautiful.
    Thanks for *New Statesman* message. I read the bits meant for me. If you *do* send me secret messages in the press, you had better send me the cuttings *and* underline the relevant bits as I never read newspapers or periodicals now.

1 In a letter dated 26 April 1964 (not included here), Murdoch had written 'The silver-handled Circassian whip belongs of course in chapter 80 of the *Seven Pillars of Wisdom*, a book I love.' In this chapter, T. E. Lawrence describes how such a whip was used on him when he was sexually abused by a Turkish commander in Deraa in south-west Syria.
2 French film directed by Marcel Carné and released in 1945.

The laundryman, seeing through the window that he was betrayed, has abandoned you as *unserious*. (The French use this word in just this sense.)

I was so touched and pleased to see you un-made up! I had not realised how much work had to be put in to produce the serpent of Old Nile to which I am used. (Python of course.) I suspect you really look better without the purple and the gold, but will never persuade you of this. You have a Baudelairian passion for the artificial.

I read all that I wish into your charming shorthand. Dear angel, much love
I

To Philippa Foot.

Steeple Aston
25 May [1964]

Darling, just to say HOORAY HOORAY that you'll be back soon! Good, good! Only don't try telephoning me – drop a card when you hit this shore and tell me where to telephone you. And we must meet forthwith, London or Oxford. My *London* address, by the way, is 59 Harcourt Terrace, SW10, where I am Tues–Thurs each week. (Telephone Freemantle 7347 – I answer that 'phone but am rarely in!) I do absolutely long to see you – so much love
I

To Brigid Brophy, posted from Paddington.

[5 June 1964]

My dearest, *much* thanks letters and excuse midweek-style note today: I had forgotten John goes to Brighton (and me too) to lecture. Back to Oxford tomorrow. [. . .]

I really must ask Esme Langley[1] round for a drink. When I have seen whether she is a suitable companion for you I might take you to one of those clubs. (But someone might steal you there.)

With Thursday out, next week looks really hopeless, except can have moment after lunch on Tues. Will reflect. My heart did in fact beat very hard for David.[2]

1 Founder of the lesbian magazine *Arena Three* published between 1963 and 1972.
2 David Hicks. In a letter written to Brophy two days later (not included here), Murdoch commented on a recent meeting with him, 'David H. still had the old magic after all. Odd isn't it. Something was still encapsulated from October–November 1938.'

Much love, dear girl.

I

To Brigid Brophy.

Steeple Aston

[June 1964]

My dear, hello there. Was so nice see you. You are dear clever girl. I am still admiring your book (Mozart I mean). By the way, *Snow Ball* alas cannot have Hawthornden Prize this year as it was published after the year limit, which ends I forget when. But it will be eligible next year. I think Mr Naipaul is getting the prize.[1] (I expect this is secret.)

I was charmed, touched, amused, by your commentary on your love letters. (They are most beautiful letters and I am as pleased as I should be to have them.) This makes me feel more free to behave as affectionately as I please towards you. I probably ought in some ways to have treated you more roughly. But these 'oughts' are absurd. [. . .]

The skylark-yachting cap image of you is endearing, though that is not my girl. I would adore to see you in a yachting cap, and well-creased trousers.

Will be here till weekend, then in Kent. Will write frequently.

Much love

I

I must castigate you about Plato, but that can wait. The Good is of course by definition the real object of Love. (Good and Love conceptually connected.) I will send you a dissertation on this sometime.

---

1 V. S. Naipaul was awarded the Hawthornden Prize in 1964 for *Mr Stone and the Knights Companion*.

To David Morgan, who was obsessively pursuing Emma,[xix] a female student at the RCA. This letter is Murdoch's reply to one that Morgan had written immediately after an intimate meeting in her Harcourt Terrace flat. In it he had expressed his 'confused feelings' about their relationship. In this reply Murdoch refers to the book of Piero's work that lay between them on the sofa as 'a drawn sword'; Morgan interpreted this remark as a metaphor for the barrier that 'would stop us sleeping together but wouldn't stop us touching'. Their kiss revealed to him what he has called 'the sexual subplot' of the relationship.[xx]

Steeple Aston
[20 June 1964]

Dear David,

Thank you very much for your letter. Yes, I think maybe I have underestimated your common sense. Perhaps in a way even underestimated you. On Thursday and Friday (hence my card from Cambridge) I began to wonder whether you were not by now seeing Wednesday evening as a dream or feeling alarmed or baffled by it – and whether you might not feel it beyond your ingenuity to know how to write to me. In fact you have known very well how to write; and I am impressed by your immediate ability to be, as it were, 'tough' with me. I don't mean that I expected you to be awed or flattered (I equally expected you to be resentful) – but I am pleased by the way you at once treat with me as one sovereign state treating with another. This is nothing but good.

I had intended, earlier, that we should part for the vacation on rather more formal terms. But by last Wednesday it had become impossible not to touch you, and to draw you a good deal closer – and perhaps it's surprising that we held on so long with only Piero della Francesca between us like a drawn sword. Well, no, not surprising – maybe it couldn't have happened earlier though it had to happen then. About the vacation – I'm not being masochistic in saying 'till October', nor am I wanting to make you into a 'medallion' (I'll talk about that in a minute) – I just didn't want us both to be troubled by perhaps brief and isolated meetings (where someone might say something which would be misunderstood, or where something might go wrong which couldn't then be put right face to face). I have a hell of a lot of work to do this summer – and while I wanted somehow to 'secure' things before we parted I didn't want to be in a state of being irrationally upset by you or about you during the interval (straightforward self-interest). In fact things have moved more swiftly, and also our ability to understand each other seems greater than I expected – although in many ways, and in spite of all your talk, I still don't altogether know what goes on inside that singularly good-looking head of yours. I'd like to see you sooner too, but let us leave it at 'October' and not worry about it for the present.

I would like to take away your suspicions and mistrusts, but perhaps only time and experience can altogether do that. I do want to know you and love you wholeheartedly, as one entire person dealing with another. And I want this to be 'clean-cut': I too have had so many muddled and twisted relationships, and I want ours to be steady and clear, and I think it can be. (I have, by the way, mentioned your existence in general terms to John Bayley, who trusts me absolutely and never wants to hear details. All that side of things is OK. I was touched and pleased that it occurred to you.)

I was very glad that you used the words 'safe' and 'secure' – I did want to communicate this to you and hope I've really succeeded. I think you must really know that I'm not collecting you like a 'medallion' or treating you like a 'young man', in the peculiar sense you attach to this, and you must know by now that I'm not keeping 'the saner part of my mind' untouched by this. I am all here.

Apropos the 'young man' question: you are, as you observed, not all that young – and of course I don't feel myself to be all that old. You may believe I am forty-four, but I don't. Yet of course in other ways I do apprehend you as splendidly young, often as something like a son or a child, and I shall never stop regarding you as my pupil. (You may suffer from this from time to time.)

The enclosed is a payment for painting or paintings to be specified later. If anyone else wants to buy paintings, for God's sake sell them. There will always be plenty for me. If you are later in a financial fix *please* let me know – by the method you suggested or any other method. I am so glad you feel you can go on painting this summer. I look forward to seeing the ninety-six drawings. And I very much want to see you using colour, and using the *stuff* which was (I must admit I thought rather enchantingly) entangled in your hair on Wednesday. Also for Christ's sake think soberly about the job question. In about a month I shall want a report from you on what you've *done* about it. And you must act sooner rather than later, as jobs will be filled. I am hoping you will show unexpected common sense here too.

And don't get yourself into trouble. The revenge fantasies you spoke of have nothing to do with 'virility' or 'manhood' in any admirable sense, but are connected with what's muddled and muddy in you, and represent everything that will hinder your attempt to resemble Piero.

I've thought a lot about Emma, but I don't know enough about the situation to have any wisdom. She may well feel 'hunted' and indeed 'haunted' by you at present. I'd advise not trying to make a date (assuming you haven't yet had any more success) – but rather give her a letter, loving, penitential etc., the best you can write, and say you'll be on certain days at a particular place, your digs or a public place if you think this better, and will wait there from time to time for one hour, but no longer. This will take the pressure off and also let her see you as a sane person capable of altering your tactics. This might enable her to *think* about you again – the pressure may be just too great at present. But I may be all wrong here. I very much hope things will go better.

I haven't got a copy of the photo with the white cat, but I'll try to get one. (It's not my favourite photograph of myself.) I will also send you a scarf, but not yet. And I will later on ask you for the piece of the life mask.[1]

I must stop this letter now: I won't normally write you long ones. (By the way, you won't get put into the workshops. I understand all that.) I hope the *address* I've put on the envelope is OK? Let me know if not.

Write, when you feel like it, before long. I may not reply instantly but, unless I'm away (and I'll let you know about that) I'll reply within two or three days. I hoped that before term ended I could convey to you some sense of security. What I didn't expect was that you would succeed in conveying a sense of security to me, but I think you have done that. I am very glad that you exist. Do think seriously about jobs and work well. Ever
I

I think the painter we were trying to remember who did the luminous profile portrait in the National Gallery is Baldovinetti[2] – I don't otherwise know him, do you?

To Brigid Brophy.

Steeple Aston
28 June 1964

Dearest girl, I am so very sorry not to have got a letter into post on Thursday. Failure. I rushed frantically to catch 9.45 train (caught 9.15 by skin of teeth. Train then broke down.) Late in Oxford. Bought healthy food at health-food stores. Lunchtime. Drunk in hall at All Souls, drunk in quad. To north Oxford to buy various unhealthy foods. So back to Steeple Aston after last post gone. But should have managed much better. [. . .]

I feel very tired but must work. I think I probably haven't yet recovered from the Rolling Stones.[3] (I was sorry not to *see* them: the undergraduate barrier was too thick. I gather from photos that they carry ambiguity of appearance to lengths which might satisfy even me.)

1 Morgan had cast his own face in plaster.
2 Alesso Baldovinetti (1425–99), Italian early Renaissance painter.
3 The Stones performed at Oxford University on 22 June.

I am glad the roses pleased you (and Anne!)[1] – I somehow had the idea you didn't really like flowers. Still, they are remote enough from the earth (the country, etc.).

You must do exactly what you like about Alison. Only I should like to be *told* if you go to bed with her. Naturally, I do not hold you to any reciprocal bond.

Yes, I do love you,

I

To David Morgan.

[late June 1964[xxi]]

My very dear boy, what a fuss, but there is nothing to worry about. Nothing will peter out and I am not really receding. Because we have not seen each other lately there is a little stiffness (at least perhaps I am stiff – your letters are always excellent). But what is remarkable is the great strength of this thing, though we have met so few times and in a way know each other so little. (I think I will have to be the boss of it for a lot of obvious reasons, but this too will work itself out and I don't think we shall be struggling for supremacy.) Naturally you had to talk about Emma and will want to again – and I will want you to because I am interested and concerned (I would like to meet her if you still think that feasible). It's not very clear to me from your letter *how* things are exactly, but I'm very glad you feel they are better and you are less tormented. (For God's sake think about jobs now.) Are you going to Frankfurt? Your image of me waiting in a shop doorway amused me, though it was a piece of insolence! Sometimes you are an impertinent puppy who ought to be slapped. No, I don't feel any 'jealousy' here. (It would be a sad lookout if I did. I am naturally a jealous person.) This is perhaps one thing which the age difference, which you so acutely make me feel, can do for us. I want you to be happy. And our friendship is a special and peculiar one which cannot (I think) be threatened by other ties. I love you very much too. (It's odd how one *knows* these things.) You were sceptical when I first said it, but I hope you are less so now. And I *will* talk more about myself – only most of that will have to wait until we are a good deal more *used to* each other.

I wonder if you will do some painting now? I want you to be a great painter, but will put up with it affectionately if you are not! I can't write more now, as I am just going to a Steam Fair at Twyford. I'll write about that and other matters tomorrow.

1 Probably Anne Graham Bell, Brophy's literary agent and friend.

I enclose a picture of you and me. You can see from my expression that
I am a little worried in case I am spoiling you.
    Love
    I

To David Morgan.

Steeple Aston
30 June 1964

Dear David,
    I was relieved to get your letter, though very sorry to hear about the
Emma situation. I suddenly started worrying about you at the weekend,
thought you mightn't have got my letter, and thought too that you might
be too deep in trouble or despair to be able to write.
    About Emma: you know you may just have to let go here. Only I know
you can't envisage it. Anyway for God's sake stop the pursuit tactics. Suddenly
to break off the pursuit might make her miss you. Not here today – why?
I'm sure a letter suggesting a very *limited* time during which you would wait
is the thing. Yes, I know, I know, about being insanely in love, and I have
pursued people long and with ingenuity, but never with your relentlessness
in the face of a refusal. I have also been relentlessly pursued and have hated
the pursuer – and then when I wearied him out felt sorry. I think you must
somewhere in your mind locate the possibility of total failure here – and
with that change your tactics. I know how one feels that one person can
make one be at last oneself. But there has got to be also a central point,
even if it is very very small, which knows it can and has got to survive in
the face of anything and be indestructible. Don't find this gloomy stuff. I
do *hope* very much for you and Emma – (I imagine Emma a lot). But do
change the pursuit tactics.
    Listen, I would like to see you and will be in London this coming *Friday,
July 3rd*. Could I see you at Harcourt Terrace about 6.30? [. . .]
    It's hard to say briefly what I think about a lot of the other things you
have said in your letters. Of course I will talk to you about myself and not
with reluctance when the time comes. But (although we don't seem to have
been doing badly lately) we may not get to know each other all that quickly.
This doesn't worry me, because I feel an extraordinary certainty about this
thing. I am very steady in my attachments. As for your 'warnings': I do
recognise you as somebody who could be a deliberate wrecker of something
he valued, but I'm not afraid of this here. Perhaps I imagine that I can
'manage' you, still relying on the authority which you say failed to impress

you even at our first meeting. But not just that, David. I am capable of caring for you a great deal, and that is what will have to stand whatever shocks there are. I'm not so easily jolted as your 'silver spoon' and 'rush-covered halls' line of talk suggests you think. Getting to know somebody involves the removal of romanticism, and there's probably a good deal to be removed. (And there's suffering in this too.) But here we are, and this thing plainly demands to be thought of in terms of permanence.

Your letters are very self-giving and you-like. (Even the way you cross things out is like you, and like a painter.) Yes, I will tell you if I ever think you are being hypocritical – though this is often hard to tell – we are so mixed and blended. But what mostly strikes me about you is that you are naturally, indeed involuntarily, honest.

I won't write you short replies (unless you call this short) – except maybe if I'm just going away somewhere, in which case I'll try to reply properly soon. I wish with all my heart that I could help you about Emma – It's no good saying 'Don't despair' or 'Don't suffer'. I know what this pain is like.

I hope you can manage Friday evening? If I'm not there at 6.30, I'll be there at 7.30, but more likely 6.30. Keep going and don't do anything foolish. I embrace you.

Ever,
Iris

To Brigid Brophy, written from John Bayley's mother's house, the day before Murdoch's forty-fifth birthday.

Nettlepole
Kent
[14 July 1964]

What's this about a postal strike? Your CHARMING Rembrandtian card with Osbornian enclosure, postmarked 3.15 July 13, reached here 9.15 a.m. July 14. I can only conclude that since this part of England is thoroughly feudal and totally cut off the postmen are not union members and don't know there is a strike. Anyway I'm *delighted* to get your communications and hope you get mine. Thank you for *very* nice notice of my birthday. Perhaps one day we shall work together on a Thames barge and forget the past.

About *Entf.*[1] I'd better give you one more warning and then drop the subject. Music which I can't escape from often makes me weep. (Though I

1 *Die Entführung aus dem Serail* (1782) (*The Abduction from the Seraglio*; also known as *Il Seraglio*), an opera by Mozart.

weep quietly, not like Deanna Durbin in *Christmas Holiday*.[1]) This is nothing
to do with musical appreciation, but to do with my physiology-psychology
(and a reason why I avoid concert halls – though probably not the chief
reason) – music of certain kinds tends to release my demons. However I
think *Mozart* and *opera* is fairly safe though I assume it will be what is sometimes called a 'concert performance', i.e. several chaps and girls in evening
dress (standing) facing others (sitting)? Could you by the way lend me a text
of the libretto beforehand, German text, in Loeb edition if possible, otherwise just German? Don't bother if this is very difficult. No notes, of course.

This occurred to me when I was demon-ridden in early hours of this morning.
Among the hazards of this house, apart from isolation, extreme cold (usually:
it's very hot just now) and the martial law imposed by my brother-in-law
(whom, actually, I adore) is (at this time of year) a soft-fruit anti-bird gun which
utters a loud resonant explosion *once a minute*, is situated fifty yards from the
house, and starts operating *when the birds do* (imagine what time that is) and
goes on throughout the daylight hours. (This place is surrounded by hops,
raspberries, currants, strawberries etc.) *This* gun afflicts only the Nettlepudlians
who are friends of the farmer who owns it (my brother-in-law magisterially
pronounced this morning it would be most unfair to ask him to turn it off),
but another one further down the hill (which one softly hears in *intervals* of
this one, to keep things going) is from time to time attacked by the villagers
who rush out with axes in the early morning hours. After which it is mended
again and proceeds as before. This is just, apropos of *Entf.*, to explain slightly
(bang!) feverish tone of this letter and the reminiscences about demons.

Darling, dear girl, thank you for such very sweet and characteristic and
perceptibly warm-hearted birthday greetings! I am (in spite of *awkward age*)
so pleased to be thus remembered.

Just off to swim in swimming pool of gun-owning farmer. Much much
love
      I

*To Michael Levey, Brigid Brophy's husband; postcard, portrait by Velázquez of Pope
Innocent X, sent from Rome, where the Bayleys were on holiday.*

                                                              [7 August 1964]

Stop press to announce conversion to Caravaggio. Also to request lecture,
in due course, on Perruzzi.[2] [. . .] Reeling with pictures and wine. How do

---

1 An American film made in 1944, starring Deanna Durbin and Gene Kelly.
2 Italian architect and painter (1481–1536).

pedestrians survive in this town though? *Hate motor cars*. Much undigested painting experience to discuss. Love from Iris.

J sends love.

To David Morgan.

[August 1964]

Dear David,

Thank you very much for your letter. I'm sorry I didn't write one over the weekend. The time was bedevilled with visitors. I hope by now you've had mine in answer to your first protest. Your second protest to hand. Don't worry, I am not going to let go of you. And Emma does not get 'in between' – there is no question of that. (I knew you were meeting Emma on Monday, idiot child, because you told me. I hope Monday wasn't a sad business?)

I will pursue the job enquiries – but that line may not be a good one for the reasons you suggest and anyway there may not be any such jobs. Keep on watching out for yourself. (Is there any 'trade paper' where you might see advertisements?)

I am sitting in the very front of the diesel train behind the driver, seeing the Oxford to Cambridge countryside unrolling. It's not a very gay errand however, as I am going over to see the mother of a girl, a friend of mine, who committed suicide earlier this year.

I would like to hear the Welsh record. Have you got a gramophone? If not, bring the record to Harcourt. I still can't imagine this famous Welsh noise.[1]

I hope you can read this. I'm rather subdued as I have a bad cold. Also I think I've been working too hard, at least just very lately. (Not that one's ever *over*worked if one works in one's own time.)

Don't, darling boy, worry too much about the communication difficulties. We have a lot of time ahead of us, assuming we both remain alive. And of course I don't (unicorn)[2] propose simply to offer you flattering pictures of yourself. I may offer some unflattering ones (though that, if done with love, is often the subtlest form of flattery). But I shall need you too, and I'm glad you think you are in charge of part of me. Remember we've only met about

1 Ecstatic sing-song note, or 'hwyl', in the sermons of Welsh Nonconformist preachers; Morgan devoted a section to it in his thesis on oratory and had promised to play Murdoch a recording of this sound.
2 A reference to the six 'Lady and the Unicorn' tapestries in the Musée national du Moyen Âge, Paris (previously known as the Cluny Museum); in the tapestry entitled 'Sight', the lady holds up a mirror to show the unicorn his reflection. Murdoch had recently sent David Morgan a postcard of this tapestry and the implication here is that he is the unicorn.

a dozen times, or scarcely more, and time makes so much difference in these matters. I think we both feel pretty clear about this and now it's just patience we need. You know it's inconceivable I could 'finish with' you, to use your own absurd phrase. So altogether get it squarely into your head that I love you dearly, David Morgan. [. . .]

Dear child, much much love,

I

To Rachel Brown, a student at the Royal College of Art, whose dissertation 'William Blake and the Problem of Dualism' Murdoch supervised in 1964–5.

Steeple Aston
16 August [1964]

Dear Rachel,

Thank you for your letter and excuse this late reply. I have been abroad.

I'm afraid I can't recall the exact title of M. Bulley's book on Platonism in art, but it has some extraordinarily general title like *What is Art*.[1] But I'll try to check this in the Bodleian. And also the title of the book by G. Bullough,[2] which I had in mind, and if I can identify the books I'll send you a card. I'm sorry I was vague when we last met.

Your observations seem to me to go along an interesting track – and one where others have been before, as you will see. How much one can establish in this region of speculation I don't myself know. The background problems are huge old ones, some of which have a new aspect since Jung and Freud. Obviously the appeal of much (though *not all*) art is connected with symbols and archetypes, in the sense roughly given to these ideas by Jung. (Though Jung's interpretations are not necessarily 'right'.) But how do these connect with religious or moral absolutes (in the *strict* Platonic sense). Great art obviously has a high moral content – whatever exactly that means. How does this relate to its 'symbolic' content? (Might Plato be right about *mediocre* art that it veils reality? As in fact very few people are made for sanctity, this fact need not be very important to the majority.)

I don't think you should worry about the very large problems at present. You will see them in perspective later on. Just now find out all you can about Palmer.[3] (Interesting about his Platonism. Anything more about this would be valuable.) You could also look at some Jung (e.g. *Modern Man in Search*

1 *Art and Understanding* (1937) by Margaret H. Bulley.
2 Possibly by E. Bullough (1880–1934) who wrote prolifically on art, psychology and aesthetics.
3 Samuel Palmer (1805–81), English landscape painter, etcher and printmaker.

of a Soul) and Freud (e.g. *Introductory Lectures*, and *Interpretation of Dreams* – also anything in *Collected Papers* which takes your fancy) if you're not already familiar with these chaps.

Will write again if any more tips. With all good wishes
Iris Murdoch

To Brigid Brophy.

Steeple Aston
[late summer? 1964]

My dear dear darling,

What have I done now? You do upset me so. I'm *sorry* about the short notice lunch suggestion. My moves are a bit unforeseeable because John's are. But you were already writing to liquidate me. Oh God. Why all this again? I am very very sorry. If I have been the tiniest bit tiresome in two or three recent letters do you not see that the reason for this is entirely flattering to you. You must not not not not not be angry with me. I really can't bear it.

Much love
I

I *can't cope* on the telephone – you have completely wrecked my day.

To David Morgan.

[September 1964]

My dear child, it was splendid to see you. I do love you. Thank you for shewing me the bell – that was wonderful![1] Some god must have led you to it. I was feeling so tired yesterday, but simply touching you made the tiredness go away. I was glad to find you (somehow and so evidently) 'whole' again. You have much health and strength in you. Please get us the record.[2] I enclose the £2 it will probably cost. Also, do examine your financial situation and let me know if you need anything to keep you going. I hope one of the jobs materialises. In case you have any freedom in the choice of times,

---

1 David Morgan travelled round London finding real-life motifs from Murdoch's novels to show her. In this case it was a huge bell (*The Bell*) in a crypt at Brompton Cemetery.
2 Of regional 'voices', the Welsh section featured a preacher intoning the hwyl.

keep in mind that I am in London during term from Tuesday morning till Thursday afternoon. But if you have to be absent then you have to, and we must just think our way round that. [. . .]

I'm sure you have a most remarkable painter inside you. I embrace you. Ever I

To David Morgan.

[September 1964]

Dear David, thanks for your letters. I'm so glad about the Gloucester job.[1] (As I write this, you are just starting on your first class. God knows what you are saying to those poor kids. Are you nervous I wonder?) After a week or so, when Mr Moss is eating out of your hand (conceal your wolf teeth for a while) you could suggest that the class might start at 9.30 for your convenience. As they are doubtless paying you very little, they should see the point about two nights' lodging rather than one. Behave very quietly till you've dug in (and then too if you can) – think how much you have to learn about teaching. I'm so glad you've got that sort of job, however sheepish the school, as it can lead to others.

Yes, you are a wolf, and have sent me a very wolfish letter, full of hostility (you weren't even able to end it affectionately) and all (apparently) because I made some remark about your parents watching TV etc.! I don't recall the remark at all, but I am sure I must have uttered it quite at random in the course of some quick conversation simply as an immediate lure to make you go on telling me things – 'was it like that, or that, or that –?' (I love being told things and much enjoyed your letter apart from its hostile tone.) Of course I know nothing of your world and am a hundred miles from wanting to 'label' anything or 'assume' anything. Do not bite me in this hasty way. You have a very considerable power to hurt.

I was very interested to see your mother's poems – does she write much? (They puzzled me at first, as I read them before I read the letter!) Yes, they are poems (I can imagine both her and your father enjoying Housman) – and come from somewhere that's clear and untouched and alive.

You evidently went to Liverpool via Oxford and with remarkable cleverness got hold of a card of Steeple Aston which shows (interesting evidence) a pub by the church which (unfortunately) no longer exists, some 200 yards from Cedar Lodge. (That card was slightly uncanny. Perhaps you are really a werewolf.)

---

1 Having submitted his dissertation in June, for which he was awarded a first, Morgan had successfully applied for a part-time teaching post at the Gloucester College of Art.

I enclose an envelope which you left behind with testimonials and things. On the back of the envelope is what looks like the raw material of a poem. I notice that I am *listed* among your girls. Well, well.

Do write soon and let me know what Gloucester's like. You may find they're not all that sheep-like. In my experience any class contains some fierce stuff. Describe what you did to them. (Or perhaps they did something to you.)

No time to write more. I am fiendishly busy and terribly tired. How's the financial situation? Let me know if I can help at all in the interval before you've got the Glos. situation steady.

I love you dearly, David Morgan, you exasperating wolfish boy. Keep that in mind when you feel inclined to lash out in letters. And don't put me into lists. I deserve paragraphs and poems to myself.

Write soon. I embrace you with much love

I

To David Morgan.

Steeple Aston
[September 1964]

Thank you for your excellent letters. You are so extremely, almost uncannily, present in what you write. I am so pleased with you. This seems an odd phrase as if you were again my nephew. But it is also a pleasure in you as a separate being, a splendid independent animal. About the desire to convince oneself by hurting, I think I understand as well as you. (This is one of the many similarities I felt.) Only we must be careful not to go too far. I sometimes want to cause you 'pain' but never pain. That is, it must be contained within love. But you understand all this.

Your account of Gloucester delighted me and interested me very much. You have been sleeping all the summer – well, sleeping is not the image, but bound perhaps – and now I can see you have leapt into life. The woman in the house, *yes.* Did you go back, I wonder? I have known feelings like this in London, I mean just walking about and feeling real again after some time of eclipse. And feeling ordinary and buying cigarettes and feeling a whole city as it were backing up one's incognito. I feel Gloucester has made you happy. Go easy with this Gordonson.[1] And I'd go easy too on the sexual education of your pupils till you're more settled in. [. . .] I think it is very bad that they are

---

1 A fellow student of Morgan at the RCA who had also just started teaching at Gloucester College of Art.

holding back your salary for *two* months. (I suspect it might even be illegal?) What reason do they give? As for the contract, I daresay art schools do use a lot of casual labour, and you may have to wait for that. That they know nothing about you is of course their fault. Maybe you should get advice from some well-disposed grandee in the art-school world, e.g. your principal at Birmingham? You'll probably need some dough meanwhile – *let me know* if it's urgent. Discuss when we meet anyway, and if urgent let me know at once.

I'll be in London tomorrow, but rather busy (*Magic Flute* and some Russians to see), and back home almost at once. Term at RCA doesn't begin till Oct 14, and I won't be properly in London before that. But I'll try to get up and see you in the week of Oct 7. Will let you know. It's just as well there's some more time, as I haven't got my lectures anywhere near ready. (They'll be mostly on Kierkegaard this term.) I wonder what general studies you will give those children? I would be very glad to help you with that programme if I could. (You are still somewhat in need of education yourself.) Are you going to give them English literature? Probably easiest for you and best for them. We must discuss this too.

This is Sunday, and I got back from Dorset last night after all. A few days of un-work there were a good thing. I now find on return though after less than a week away more than seventy letters waiting. A few, besides yours, are welcome, but not many. Most need answers. Hell. There's a great deal more I want to say to you, but it must wait.

About photos – people sometimes photograph me but I never bother to get copies. I will try to put my hands on one for you though.

About 'really hurting' – yes, I know, one is far from those extremities, thank God, and should say that since there is an absolute seriousness between us there is a genuine power to hurt. And we both know this can play a part. But I so very much want to do you nothing but good, and to make you happy, except that this concept (happiness) seems too weak where you are concerned. And yes, I shall certainly use you. Few people are in this sense 'of use' to me.

I was interested in what you wrote of *A Severed Head*. Must talk of this sometime when there are hours of talk to be had.

Yes, I can read your writing and hope you can mine. I'll write again on Tues or Wed. I haven't got a spare watch, but let me give you one. You can get a decent one (*not* second-hand, not worth the risk) for a few pounds. For God's sake *get it* and let me know what it cost. You obviously must have one.

Have you got the Welsh record yet? I embrace you with all my heart, dearest boy –

With much love

I

To Brigid Brophy.

Steeple Aston
4 October [1964]

My dear, I'm so sorry I shouted at you, which I can't recall, I must have been a bit drunk! Apologies! I expect I was startled to see how late it was. I really mustn't stay up so late before a teaching day. Maybe should keep off burgundy too. I felt very rocky the next morning.
   With love
   I

I certainly didn't intend you to go home by yourself, you silly ass.

PS You have telephoned. Thank you. Yes, we must try to behave better. Honestly, though, I think you may just not notice your tendency to needle me and say hurtful things. But I daresay there are things in myself I don't notice too. With much love
   I

To David Hicks.

Harcourt Terrace
[15 October 1964]

Please could you and K come drinks 59 Harcourt Terrace (off Redcliffe Square Earls Court) 6ish Wed Oct 21 to celebrate begin of term and (I hope!) Labour in power?¹ Much love
   Iris

To Elias Canetti.

Steeple Aston
[mid-October 1964]

1 The Labour Party won the general election on 15 October 1964 with a majority of four seats.

My dear, just to hail the arrival of *Masse et puissance*¹ – *thank you!* I assume you are in Paris at present.

Hooray for the Labour victory. I am tired, not working. (I wish to God I could *stop* working sometimes!)

Keep well, my love. See you next term. Very best wishes and much love, Your Iris

To David Morgan, in which Murdoch mentions how much she is enjoying teaching at the RCA.

Steeple Aston
[17 October 1964]

Thank you for your strong tea and sausage roll letter. It was very good to see you on Tuesday. People have degrees of reality, and you are very real, and real in your letters too. That's good, reality is good for one. Yes, keep me in your heart sister-wise if that has meaning for you. I feel in many different ways, but always quite harmoniously, about you – sometimes very old, sometimes young and so on. We must keep this, David, and we will.

I hope you got on all right at Gloucester this week. You have plenty of nerve. I wish I wasn't so idiotically anxious about my lectures. I quite enjoyed Weds. though – and just talking to the kids brought back all my old teaching instincts. I can't help believing I *can* teach. (Odd to think of you in the building – but don't avoid me!) (When I hear the jukebox now I think of you and your megaphone.)

I meant to say, about your Gloucester lectures, if you can let me know suitably ahead what you'll be talking on I could try to lend you books – I have quite a lot of art books. I'll probably buy some pictures of Greek stuff on Tuesday. (Let me know if there's anything else special you'd like on Tues.) I hope you get the Cocteau film. It is one of the two or three films in the world that I love – at least I love certain images from it. The face of Lee Miller² really beautiful, not like most film stars. It's years now though since I stopped going to films. Do they mean much to you?

Thanks for the waxen face³ – yes, there is some resemblance – only my friend's face was pitted, pockmarked as it were beneath the surface. Oddly

1 Canetti's *Masse und Macht* was published in 1960. It was translated into French in 1960 by Robert Rovini (this is the edition Canetti seems to have sent Murdoch) and translated by Carol Stewart into English with the title *Crowds and Power* in 1962.
2 The American photographer made her only film appearance in *Le Sang d'un poète* (*The Blood of a Poet*) (1930), directed by Jean Cocteau.
3 A photograph Morgan had sent her of a face encased in wax.

it didn't at all spoil his appearance, though he thought it did. *Spirit* so much looks out of a face (or can), one doesn't just see it as a surface.

I am so touched by your thought for your father. Yes, of course I will send him *The Italian Girl* – not at once because I won't get to the post office (I tend to stay isolated here). [. . .]

I have been reading that book for which I well believe you were responsible (*Mabinogion*[1]) – and note that you charmingly invented the bit about Rhiannon using her shoulder as a mounting block. (The printed text doesn't say that: your text is better!) I like it all very much in a weird way. Will talk about it later.

I shall see your pal Tom[xxii] on Thursday. Remind me to ask you about him on Tuesday. I should be along on Tuesday by *7.15 or 7.20* at the *Hollywood* pub, in Hollywood Road, which continues Harcourt Terrace.

David, you must paint, I terribly want you to paint. Perhaps I have some frustrated painter in me who wants to come out in you. But it's not just that, it's wanting you to *be*, more and more. You will write of course – I feel that will look after itself. But you must discipline yourself to paint. I know at the moment you lack time. But think about it. You have a beautiful imagination, but such things must be *worked* on. [. . .]

I love you very much and in a quite special way and you are there for me from head to foot – and I can talk to you which really is the case, for me, with few people. *Do eat enough*. I'm glad you've having some decent meals at Kensington Gore[2] – but don't just miss meals because you can't be bothered. I was so sorry not be able to feed you properly the other night. Keep me in the picture about your finances.

Thank God for the Labour Party being in – at least it looks as if they're in.

I must stop now and work. There's always so much work to do. I wish I were better at imagining myself on holiday – or decreeing a holiday.

My dear child, be well. I embrace you and love you.

I

1 A collection of Welsh medieval stories deriving from the Celtic oral tradition about the mythological past of Wales.
2 The new location for the RCA; Morgan continued to live in London.

To David Morgan. In relation to the possible 'severed-head tour of London' mentioned in this letter, Morgan later took Murdoch to an exhibition at the Museum of Mankind to see severed heads apropos her novel A Severed Head. *According to Morgan, she was 'excited by them but reluctant to let me turn her into one by casting her face in plaster. Then we got onto head-hunting and from that to severed heads and the rites practised with them. From there we went on to a particular tribe that cuts heads off and makes them perform fellatio'.*[xxiii]

Steeple Aston
[18 October 1964]

Dear David, thank you very much for your boy to aunt letter (though the later point wasn't quite suitable for an aunt). There is that element perhaps in our curious friendship. At Bianchi's restaurant[1] I felt a little as if I were taking somebody out from school. (That meal was *lunch* by the way. We are not U[2] enough to call it luncheon.)

Your capacity to not-write letters is about equal, but only just, to my capacity not to receive them. I meant to say to you when we met that I'd like you to write at least once a week, but I think I'll now shorten that to four days. (Write oftener *of course* if you want to.) After four days of silence I shall start to worry about you. No need to write much if you have no words (though I can scarcely imagine you without words). And, as I say, do write as often as you please, it couldn't be too often.

Yes, I am a good swimmer. (It is in character somehow that you are not.) But I am also especially terrified of suffocation. (I was nearly strangled by the umbilical cord when being born, and perhaps 'remember' that.) So I'm not sure about the life-mask trial. Do you know *why* these heads and masks interest you?

Your fellatio idea (necrofellatio) is very powerful. No, it was never in my mind. I was too dominated by the image of the head as actually used by these tribes, a very taboo subject. (Also the eye to eye relation.) There was also the Medusa-genitals-sun image, but this was less important. Yes, a supreme blasphemy. You have a more blasphemous and obscene mind than I have, which could be a gift to you as an artist. Keats and Blake, yes. And we might make that severed-head tour of London, and various other ones. We obviously have different Londons. (But so has everyone.) Your Kensal Green idea was so beautiful and felicitous.[3] [. . .]

---

1 A very popular restaurant in Frith Street, Soho until it closed in 1992.

2 The British linguist Alan Ross coined the terms 'U' and 'Non-U' in 1954 to indicate the difference between upper-class and middle-class speech and behaviour. They were made famous by Nancy Mitford's essay 'The English Aristocracy' published in *Encounter* in 1955.

3 Morgan and Murdoch had recently visited Kensal Green Cemetery, one of Morgan's favourite haunts.

I'm pleased to have seen your large cell-like room.[1] I meant to ask you about the pictures. One clearly yours (?). The other? Don't forget you are going to frame a drawing, or drawings, for me. I so very much hope you'll find you are able to work this summer. Should you draw, paint, more from life? I seem to remember your saying you hadn't done enough of that. (Aunt touch. How various one is, what with aunts, Oscar Wilde etc. I rather like the image of myself as Oscar Wilde.)

Your criticisms, implied and otherwise, on what I write are acute and such as I would make myself. (Perhaps these two phrases mean the same.) It is a matter of getting one's motive power and one's technique together. I have plenty of both, but they don't co-operate properly, one mars the other. (This isn't a strong enough image for the misery of this situation.) You are quite right that Effingham was never really in that bog.[2] It was all intellectual. Equally, in this novel that's coming out in the autumn and which I wish you wouldn't see, somebody is supposed to be burnt to death – only of course they aren't as there are no real flames.[3] These failures which envelop and *are* one's whole being can feel crushing. The answer is not 'Joyceisation' (which would be Millerisation)[4] but some kind of courage which I scarcely know the name of. [. . .]

There's a lot I'd like to say to you, only perhaps today I am not as well supplied with words as usual. (It's good that we're both pretty ready users of these things.) I have a very great goodwill towards you and your existence is a source of happiness to me. I so much hope that you'll be able to dominate, control, get through the trials of, this summer, and as it were tame and handle yourself, in a sense of 'tame' which is more like providing oneself with a steel backbone.

I do hope things with Emma will take a sudden good turn (life is surprising) or at any rate become something you can think about somebody and without maddening pain. Don't *not* talk about that to me because you think you've talked about it too much. You haven't, and if it's uppermost in your mind you must talk about it.

I've asked Parkers bookshop in Oxford to send you the Shakespeare I spoke of, and it should turn up in about a week, they are rather slow.

1 Murdoch had recently visited Morgan's room in Ladbroke Grove for the first time and, according to Morgan, assessed it approvingly as the proper sort of monastic cell for an artist, not realising how little art actually took place there.
2 Refers to Effingham Cooper who experiences a near-death epiphany in a bog in *The Unicorn*.
3 Murdoch perhaps refers here to Elsa who burns to death in *The Italian Girl*.
4 According to David Morgan, Murdoch mentioned both Henry Miller and James Joyce when they were talking about writer's block and how to overcome it. 'Millerisation' meant letting go unself-critically and autobiographically in a torrent of words, which included the Joycean 'stream of consciousness' technique. Murdoch wasn't happy with either approach and, by contrast, to get a book started, she resorted to an act of faith, 'like walking on water'.

Thanks for the life mask. It's a weird trophy, and doesn't really resemble you any more than the photo does. But I can remember your face.

Do look after yourself, David, dear David, and don't fall into despairs. You are a precious being to me. With love to you and all hopeful wishes,

I

To Elias Canetti.

19 October 1964

My dear, just to say I'll hope to see you this Wednesday Oct 21 – drinks at Harcourt Terrace circa 6.30 – where I've asked one or two people (no one very novel, I'm afraid) – and will hope to dine with you afterwards. (Should get rid of the drinkers by 8 or so.) *Don't* worry if you don't feel like coming – I'll suggest other times. But much hope see you – then or very soon. Hope all's well with you – with much love

Iris

To David Morgan.

Steeple Aston
[25 October 1964]

I hope you caught your train all right and didn't fall asleep on a bench at Paddington. You must have been fantastically tired. I am glad that business turned out to be OK and I hope Emma is better disposed to you as a result. [. . .]

Well, I must meet Emma sometime, but there'll be time for these things. No letter from you since that one, but I'll expect one on Monday. I can't write much now, as I have to get on with the speech I'm to make at Trinity College Dublin on Thursday. The paper I am answering is all about Job (Book of) which I've just been rereading. The young Irishman is of course on Job's side and thinks Jehovah is simply exposed as a witless old tyrant. I am interested to find how strongly I feel against Job and pro-God. (Though God's reply is a little, though magnificently, irrelevant. The straight reply is: you suffer, you are good. So what?) Of course it is Job's friends who incite him to these complaints. But he shouldn't complain.

On Tuesday could I see you 6.45 at the Hollywood – and *if* I'm late please wait. [. . .]

It was odd and in some way distressing to see you in that room of people on Wednesday¹ – one of whom I'd known well since before you were born. However one mustn't be too solipsistic and it was probably a good thing.

I hope you're all right, child, and that all was well in Glos. I hope you've recovered from tiredness by now. I send very much love.

I

To David Morgan.

[early November 1964]

My dear child, thank you very much for your letter. I think you could usually (though not next Weds.) be dosed with gin about Weds. 5 pm to send you to sleep. I rather like this idea too. Like coming for your fix, only innocent. And it seems jolly sensible that you *should* sleep before that journey. [. . .]

Don't worry about what you said to me – I could be hurt by you, but not by things like that. Older persons don't feel older really and I wouldn't dream of thinking myself old. Also, a slightly different point, and apropos my 'gruff and neuter' persona, you must keep in mind that I have behind me twenty-five years of being told in the most extravagant terms that I am beautiful. I know that when you touch me etc. –

I didn't press you to talk to me on Wednesday not because I didn't want to know how you were in every possible way but because I felt you were uncommunicative. And always of course there is no earthly reason why you should tell me things – I hope I haven't ever pressed you too much. But I love you in a very complete way and I would always want to know anything that you wanted to say. I hope I can be tactful with you. Love unfortunately doesn't always bring tact.

Next Tuesday I have to see an American boy at 6.15, but shd be free about 7.30. Could you please await me in the Hollywood pub, 7.30 Tuesday. The following week, 24th, I cannot manage Tuesday evening though could probably do Weds. lunch. How would you feel about a *Weds evening* meeting? I feel this would probably make you too tired for Thursday. (Anyway *that* Weds evening no good I think.)

I understand about Rupert Brooke, but I hope you have entirely got over your desire to unbeautify yourself. No more of this. I must really practise being sterner with you. Perhaps next term I will make you read things and discuss them with me. I embrace you, my very dear boy, my dear David Morgan –

I

1 Murdoch's party at Harcourt Terrace.

To David Morgan.

Steeple Aston
[6 November 1964]

Dear child, please consider enclosed list with attention. It lists some of the books which an educated person must have read.[1] I'd be very interested and pleased if you would go through it and tick in the two columns provided the ones you've read and the ones you'd like to have. Clearly you would do well to tick *every* work in the right-hand column – but this test has a practical purpose too. I want some guidance (a) about what to give you for Christmas, and (b) about things I might give you later on. So could you in the 'would like to have' column, put *two* ticks if you'd like at once, one tick if you'd like sometime, and leave blank if you are pretty indifferent or don't know about. (It will be a delicate task for you to decide how many books to give two ticks to!) There are probably lots of obvious things I've forgotten – and there may be things you want which aren't on the list. We can discuss all this on *Wednesday*.

I was touched by your last letter. (The three girls you had 'made to exist'. Clever you!) That one sometimes moves like that from one person to another is almost inevitable if one is a pretty affectionate character. (As both of us are.) And I don't think it matters at all so long as one really loves and attends to each. (I mean, leaving out questions of actual jealousies or disloyalties or concealments.) There is perhaps a certain danger of egoism – exactly the note you struck at the end in fact – you felt you had created us. It was rather Morgan writ large. [. . .]

I am worried about what seems to me your tendency to terrorise Emma – and all this talk about cutting people up. This seems to me, besides being morally wrong, a sheer failure of intelligence on your part, something dull and blunting in your mind, something that makes you 'captive'. If you could get over it I'm sure you would be more free, more sensitive, more alive. I wish [*the rest of this letter is missing*]

To David Morgan.

Steeple Aston
9 November 1964

My dear, the enclosed to reach you on Sat. just in case you are short. I wish you would spend money on *food*. It's idiotic not to.

1 David Morgan remembers that this list included *The Red and the Black* (Stendhal), *The Brothers Karamazov* (Dostoevsky), *The Tale of Genji* (Lady Murasaki), *Njal's Saga*, Collected Keats, *Ulysses* (James Joyce), *Seven Pillars of Wisdom* (T. E. Lawrence), all of Shakespeare and *Sylvie and Bruno* by Lewis Carroll.

I enjoyed our National Gallery visit. It's not easy to look at pictures with someone else, but we seemed to manage. We omitted to observe your brother once again as Richard II in the Wilton Diptych. It's odd how prevalent that type is. We must go again. [. . .]

I am a bit troubled about your lodger. Please exercise iron discretion always and tear up all communication from me, past and present, and keep your mouth shut about money. Gossip will do me no good in the college.

I will let you off for this term, but next term I shall try to make you paint. You must write too, but that can be left to you and there would be less point in beating you for not doing it. I think you will, naturally, write – and for that you have much time. I embrace you with love –

I

To Rachel Brown.

Steeple Aston
9 November 1964

Dear Rachel,

Thanks for your letter. In quick reply: – 'all is one' is of course a metaphysical or religious statement. At the 'ordinary level' all is patently not one. The metaphysical statement may be supported by (a) an argument to the effect that everything plural, accidental, evil etc. is 'mere appearance' and unreal (Plato, much Eastern religion) or (b) by an attempt to show that all things, good, bad, plural etc. somehow blend into a natural unity (Blake, other Eastern religions, etc.). This oversimplifies – there are other possibilities – but perhaps these are the main ones. Of course the manifest *reality* of the material world and of evil 'messes up' Plato's endeavour. But the same things, in my view, invalidate (b). That brings us to your second difficulty – my assumption that God and Good must connect. If they do, it is more difficult to have a monistic theology of the Blake type. (In fact, if they do, it is very difficult to have any theology at all! But it has taken the churches some 2,000 years to see this point.)

I can't go further now. I'm afraid I can't see you Wednesday before the lecture, as I have someone else then. Could you come on Thursday at 9.30, in college – there won't be much time then, but we could have a word.

All very good wishes
Iris

No, I don't think 'God' is approached *only* through reason.

To Brigid Brophy, written after a short gap in communication.

Steeple Aston
[6 December 1964]

Darling, you know that affection and good will are no use. Only love is any use. I'm glad you rang up. The poetic idiom in which you make any down to the simplest statement rings endless permutations of bells for me always. Why can we not be in love with a love which is simply *sui, nostri, generis*?[1] You have a simple reply, but think again. Oh how I do not want to clip those feathers from Cherubino's[2] hat. [. . .]

I can't write more now, I am so tired. If you were here I would just touch you and feel better. I have no eloquence at the moment with which to try to persuade you not to recede from me – but do not. *Much love.*

To Brigid Brophy.

Steeple Aston
7 December [1964]

Dearest, I don't know what to say. Some of your speculations amaze me. *Of course* I assume we shall go on writing to each other every day until the end of our (while still both alive) days. I feel, at any rate, in myself, no force, however minutely embryonic, which could prevent this. I know there are such forces in you, but it needs a great deal of against the grain reasoning to make myself fear them *really* for a second. Perhaps I am very irrational? *Why* should there be an explosion, why *can't* we go on as we are, moving as it were within the envelope, tissue, of our extreme incompatibility, to and fro in accordance with your moods, causing pain often, but never breaking the envelope surface – To hell with these bloody metaphors. Let's just carry on. I cannot honestly see any alternative, and neither can you. I am amused that you feel it wrong to ask for the heart of any (woman presumably) who is not a great writer. (This would limit your choice to . . . ?)

I am not a great writer. Neither are you. (I have never of course really

---

1 Of our own kind.
2 Adolescent amorous page in Mozart's opera *The Marriage of Figaro*; the part is usually sung by a mezzo-soprano. Cherubino adores the older countess and disguises himself in women's clothes in Act Two. In a letter written in July 1966 (not included here), Murdoch noted, 'I'm not sure that *disguised* as a page will do though. You *are* a page and I am (until Act Three) disguised as a countess. I think with pleasure of our love duet'. (In another letter, however, Murdoch writes, 'Re your Cherubinitude, of course I am the count'.)

told you what I think of your work, though what I have said is truthful. In fact I don't think critically in detail about what you write. I love it as an emanation of you, and admire what is patently admirable in it.) I certainly don't feel any inhibition about asking for your heart. I ask for it shamelessly and *need* it, complete with feathers and *écume*.[1] Honestly I feel now I couldn't possibly do without you. I don't *scream* this only because I don't really feel in danger of losing you.

I've got to go into Oxford now to see the girl who has puerperal fever. A pure case of acting from the motive of duty alone. (I do occasionally do this when cornered.)

I'll be along 7.30–8ish tomorrow to carry you off –

Much much much love.

I

To Leo Pliatzky.

Steeple Aston
24 January 1965

My dear, on Feb 2nd I think it's easier if I meet you *after* the RCA thing. It's all complicated further by my Russian lesson which I'd forgotten, so my visit to the RCA will have to be brief anyway. I suggest we meet about 8.15, 8.20 p.m. in town, say at the Three Greyhounds pub, corner of Greek St and Old Compton Street – and then eat nearby there. Not like last time, *tu comprends*. Hope OK. With much love

I

Do write if you feel like. Much look forward see.

To Elias Canetti.

Steeple Aston
29 January [1965]

My dear, John Simopoulos tells me you have been abroad and will be away for some weeks. So I am assuming next Tuesday Feb 2 is not possible. (I've tried to ring you a number of times on the one-two-three-stop principle and got no answer.) I therefore won't come to London at lunchtime after all.

1 Froth or foam.

I'm very sorry not to see you. If by any chance JS is wrong perhaps you would employ that postcard! And I will try ringing you again. But if no communication established, I'll take it that Feb 2 is off. Oh dear. I much want to see you. I embrace you with much love. Your Iris

To Elias Canetti.

Steeple Aston
31 January [1965]

My dear, I now gather from Marie-Louise[1] you *are* in England after all! But she said you were very busy. I asked her to find out if you'd like lunch with me Tuesday (Feb 2) and if I don't hear to contrary I'll come along 12.30ish Tuesday to Thurlow Rd. But don't mind saying no via ML (or postcard to me!) – in which case I'll try again later. Much love I.

I've telephoned several times again.

To Brigid Brophy, posted from Paddington station.

4 February 1965

Darling, those black tights were wonderful. If those, why not black ski pants??
    Would provide.
    We must go to bed earlier and drink less (comes to same thing) –
    Much much love
    I

To David Hicks.

Steeple Aston
4 March [1965[xxiv]]

My dear, I fear I was tiresome, dogmatic, and not fully *there* during lunch! Forgive. However, to continue lecture, I do on further reflection think I was right on the *school* issue. Intelligent children learn easily things which it's so bloody hard to learn later on (languages, maths) – and I think get bored if

1 Marie-Louise von Motesiczky, expressionist painter and Canetti's official mistress.

too little is expected of them. Anyway, if one's to go to a university one must have one's Latin etc. *ready*, and not to be scrambled for at the last moment. It is *important* to know French, Latin (Greek if poss!).

Here I go again. You can ignore it all, it's only me.

I love you very much and can't always express this. Be certain of it. Much love

I

To Rachel Brown, who was to marry Frank Fenner on 2 April.

Steeple Aston
9 March [1965]

Dear Rachel,

Thank you very much for your letter. Yes, I got the drift of your conversation. *Don't worry.* I hope you are feeling better about your great decision.[1] I know it can seem very like a leap in the dark, and most people don't feel absolutely certain beforehand. But, from my own experience, the married state has so much to recommend it – one achieves a sort of calm closeness and trust which it's not easy to find otherwise. I know it's a 'bourgeois institution' etc., but even as such it has its advantages! I hope you will find your love for Frank released and enlarged by the decision – it is often so. [. . .]

Very best wishes
Iris Murdoch

To David Morgan.

Steeple Aston
[26 March 1965]

Very dear boy, it was good to see you. Yes, we are becoming old friends. [. . .]

I was so sorry and somehow upset to hear of Emma weeping and being so hopelessly sad. You *must* mend this grief. You must make some kind of metaphysical effort, pray for grace. If you can really mend this and make all well you will have made the whole world anew. You must do this. It's not impossible.

I can't think when I can see you next week – next week is awful. I will try to fix some definite longer time for further ahead.

1 Brown had confided to Murdoch her anxieties about her forthcoming marriage.

To end on a censorious note (your conduct in Three Greyhounds) you should always rise when a woman or notably older person arrives (you did rise) *and* you should remain standing until the woman etc. is seated (unless there are special circumstances which suggest this is inappropriate). (You failed on this point.) More lessons on manners later, no doubt. I embrace you.

With love

I

To Rachel Brown, written three days before her wedding.

Steeple Aston
30 March [1965]

Dear Rachel,

Just to wish you the very best of luck and to send all my warmest wishes. I hope you will both be very happy. I enclose a little present – I had thought of buying you some particular thing, but I don't really know what you need, so perhaps this unoriginal offering is best.

I still don't, I think, know your married name, but I expect you'll write to me later on and let me know. You will be far too busy to write in the nearer future, so don't worry about acknowledging this. Very best wishes to you –

Iris

To Brigid Brophy.

Steeple Aston
[early April 1965]

My dear young creature, thank you very much for letters and enclosures, especially you as suffragette (drag forsooth!). (I didn't expect any letters today and almost didn't make the journey to the stables.) I feel rather depressed too and would love to see you. It's partly also the absolute plague of daffodils in the garden. I simply cannot share Wordsworth's feelings. (Well, I suppose his were wild ones, which might make a difference.)

I hope Tuesday will work out. Ideally I see the kid[1] in the morning and lunch with you. Only it may not work like that for a variety of reasons, such

1 David Morgan.

as you being in Ireland! I still can't recall when you're going. Would you be free for lunch? Also the wretched boy may well not want to see me. (The whole thing's so precarious at the RCA. No lictors.[1] Not like dear old Oxford.) Anyway, you may be fixed up with Barbara[xxv] even if not abroad? (Is Ireland abroad?) There's that other *huge* hotel on the way out to Kingstown – at Monkstown in fact – what's it called? That might do if hotels in town full.

I have now finished *Raffles*[2] (I had an interval) with tears in my eyes (the dear old fellow, to use Bunny's language, gets himself nobly killed in Boer War) and have returned to Genet which I am reading slowly, for pleasure, and because I want to learn the argot. The English (American) just can't quite do it for charm. I wonder why? I can't get used to 'faggot' for the *doux* French word *'tante'*.[3] Why not 'queen'? Is there a technical difference between a faggot and a queen? Ask Charles[4] some day when he's in a good mood.

Lots of love

AJ[5]

Darling, a PS about B. Do, when she turns up, feel entirely free. I can take it. NB you must be happy and gay. (I intend the ordinary meaning, but the other goes without saying.)

To Brigid Brophy.

Steeple Aston
[5 April 1965]

Angel dear, forgive a short note today. A rather worrying crisis about a student at the college has just fallen on my head, and has involved most of the morning in letters and telephone calls.

I am rather worried about you and Barbara and begin to think it might

---

1 Derives from the Latin *ligare*, 'to bind', and means people who have the authority to punish wrong-doers.

2 E. W. Hornung's *Raffles, The Amateur Cracksman* (1899). Murdoch assumed the role of the eponymous charming gentleman thief who lives in an Albany flat in London and Brophy was cast as 'Bunny', his accomplice, a younger and less confident man who had been Raffles's 'fag' at Eton. Murdoch was drawn to the character of A. J. Raffles – Oxford-educated, a brilliant cricketer, a master of disguise and a clever aesthete – who was socially respectable on the one hand and transgressive on the other. In another letter written to Brophy in April (not included here) she wrote 'Some day we must go to a fancy dress dance as R and B. All we need is *immaculate* evening dress and a string of pearls. Bags I be Raffles'.

3 For the mild French word 'aunt'.

4 Charles Osborne, assistant editor of the *London Magazine*.

5 A. J. Raffles.

be so much better if you let yourself love that child. It's not the 'affair' angle that strikes me – it's the denial of love angle. No, let things not be like end of *Snow Ball*.¹ Can't you let go on loving Barbara and let the rest look after itself? I can't feel it's good for either of you as things are – and you are already too involved and as you say too suited, too alike, really to get your-selves apart. And as things are you are just hurting her and making rather than breaking the bond between you. I think in the end you will *have* to take Barbara on, don't you think? (That she doesn't live here is a factor. Sooner or later time and posh ocean-going liner, or *very* grand aeroplane with velvet wings will whisk her back to Martha's Vineyard. Of course she might *decide* to live here. But I see her as a rover. Couldn't you have a perfectly orderly and rewarding friendship with her while she's in England?) I feel upset about this and I don't think it's good for you to say no to your-self in this *really serious* instance.

I hope I didn't sound stuffy on phone. Keep in mind I am very rarely alone when telephoning especially now that the new model Cedar Lodge² is in operation, with all rooms knocked into one. [. . .]

Sweetheart, very much love.

To Brigid Brophy.

Cranborne
Dorset
8 April 1965

My dear, I miss your letter this morning. I wish our itinerary had been clearer sooner and I could have had one. The sun shines, the rooks build and caw, and it is bloody cold here. What a beautiful county though. I think I would like to live in a large country house a little inland from Bridport (and Weymouth) to be conveyed regularly to London – in my chauffeur-driven Rolls. (Perhaps we will *never get over* that experience?) I would like to take you on Little Tour, but can't suggest one at the moment because of usual difficulty about leaving John. His chief drawback is tendency to mope like dog in kennels when I am not there, unless he is compulsorily occupied in college. At very begin of term it may be poss. I will reflect. (My ideal would be you on *very fast* west of England train, first stop e.g. Chippenham, where I would meet you with car. *On verra*.)

1 Brophy's novel finishes with the end of an affair and with a central character 'thinking about death'.
2 The Bayleys had recently had two ground-floor rooms knocked into one at their home in Steeple Aston.

I hope Barbara is much better and that you are dominating your work crisis. Don't forget to shew me the thing on Simone de Beauvoir. I am swimming along happily with Genet in French. (There are some words I don't know – but I suspect they are the words I don't know in English either!) Must stop now and do Russian prose. Au revoir, my dear Bunny – much love. And be good and happy during absence of
    Your AJR

To Brigid Brophy.

Steeple Aston
[spring 1965]

My dear girl, thanks for letter. I think Barbara's idea of going to Ireland is quite an inspired one. Of course you *must* have a car. (You could visit Ballybrophy.) Feed her on draught Guinness. It is good for her and very nice too, over there. Of course her New York licence will be OK. There'd be an international crisis otherwise. As for the temperature, I expect you will find it will rise somewhat when you get there, what with all the whiskey you'll be after drinking. NB do whatever you please.

I am still wretched about my lost sheep,[1] but there's no point in going on about it. Yes, I daresay he'll be all right. It is partly one's professional conscience that is hurt. I've dropped a catch here. This sort of failure makes one realise how much one is both inspired and duped by an image of oneself as the good shepherd.

I read that piece of journalism about those two silly girls, but still don't see why I had to. The thing about me is that I'm not interested in women. I am a *male* homosexual. (Which puts me of course in rather a difficult position.) My ideal relationship would be Raffles to some Bunny. Or if per impossible I could find one, I'd gladly be Bunny to some Raffles.[2] [. . .]

Must stop. Lots of love. I'm too depressed about that child to be Raffles today.

---

1 David Morgan, who had recently disappeared without trace.
2 The homoerotic element of the Raffles/Bunny partnership, with its hint of sadomasochism, probably appealed to both women, although Murdoch resisted Brophy's solemn Freudian interpretation of the novel, writing to her in September 1965: 'I'm not sure I approve of having dearest Raffles buggerised. (Literary criticism at its old game of tearing the butterfly's wings.) Anyway Raffles and Bunny are hardly in need of an allegory. All is declared. (Pretty well.) I hope you are enjoying the adorable book'.

To Brigid Brophy, addressed to Mrs Levey, the Inter-Continental Hotel, Dublin, Eire.

Steeple Aston
21 April 1965

Darling, thank you for your very sweet and consoling letter. I do hope you are having a super time in those marble halls. And that the streets of Dublin have that pale clear look. Coffee at Bewley's?

I'm sorry I was so tense yesterday. Not much better today. I still haven't seen the boy, and flatmate just phoned to say there's no sign of him. If flatmate phones again to say he's turned up I'll catch 12 noon train, if not not. Not good for work. [. . .]

Dear girl, I hope you are having a *beautiful* time with Barbara and are happy. Forgive short letter – I am too uneasy to write. Be well, Cherubino, and enjoy Ireland.

Much love
AJ

To Brigid Brophy.

Steeple Aston
[25 April 1965]

Darling just a note to you. I do hope Ireland was gorgeous and I look forward to your letter tomorrow telling me of it. I hope Barbara and skis got off all right to aeroplane and that it was all a happy success and was also the holiday that you needed.

I hope this afternoon's jamboree goes OK! I was very sorry not to come. The doctor has been and says he thinks I'm all right. (He suggests I lose a stone in weight!)

I am still rather under the influence of the recent lost sheep drama (which is indeed still proceeding though out of my control). It's very complicated and I have been entirely unsuccessful in dealing with it. (There are also some very disagreeable aspects.) I suppose being a middle-aged childless woman has some effect here. But I usually have a better grip on myself.

Darling girl, I'll see you soon, and it cheers me to think of you. I look forward to your letter and send much love

your AJ

To David Morgan.

Steeple Aston
May 1965

David, I just got your letter as I was leaving London and had no time to write at once. I think there is no point in my entering this situation. Emma would rightly resent it – and anyway if I started giving Emma advice it mightn't be the kind you would like. I think you should try to reflect a bit on *yourself* here, and consider what it is, what sort of weakness, that makes you act in this extraordinary way and waste your own life and poison someone else's. It is a case for self-examination (if not for treatment!). You are becoming very much out of touch with reality. For you to be able to behave so unkindly to somebody is a symptom of lack of realism – you don't seem to understand what you are *doing*, and what this must be like at Emma's end. I wish I could think of some key to this – I can't – and I wish I could think of someone else (either girl friend or older person) whom I could profitably introduce into your life. (Maybe I will.)

At the moment I can think of nothing except that you ought to criticise this whole situation more ruthlessly and *analyse* your conduct. You are living in a dream world about Emma. I am sorry not to be more constructive and I will *think* about this. You *ought not* to persecute Emma in this way – you violate the most elementary human rights by doing so. My advice is lay off Emma completely (for the present if you like) – write her the nicest and most intelligent letter you can (saying you are laying off) – and think about yourself and why you do these things – and *find good distractions* (people, art).

I'll write again.

Much love.

To Elias Canetti, an invitation extended also to David Morgan and Leo Pliatzky.

Steeple Aston
[early June 1965]

My dear, just to remind: *there will be* a party at my flat, 59 Harcourt Terrace, next Wednesday June 9 between 5.30 and 8! And it would be very good to see you there. But I won't necessarily expect you.

It was very wonderful to see you. You always communicate power to me and I do love you.

I'm jealous of Hera¹ but I do want to meet her! How beautiful she is!
With very much love to you, beloved Titan,
Your humble
Iris

To Rachel Fenner.

Steeple Aston
27 June [1965]

Dear Rachel,
   [. . .] I'm glad things seem better. A sense of security and time ahead always
helps, and I imagine by now you must feel certain that our curious friendship
(well, why curious? All friendships are odd and of their own kind) has a great
stability and every chance of permanence. I hope you will come to feel calmer
and happier about it and that the pain will diminish – (though oddly one
doesn't always *want* this). This is not to say 'love less' (it might involve 'love
more'). Of course these feelings have 'value' – but what is really valuable is
the very long-term fidelity of one person to another. (A rare enough thing
actually in the beaten way of friendship.) I hope we can achieve this. But the
immediate thing is just to get to know each other better in a quiet and ordinary
way. The barriers which concern my being older etc. will reduce in time.
Meanwhile don't worry, but try to feel some happiness in something secure.
   My next visit to the Sculpture School will have to be later on, I think.
But plans are very unclear at present. I may be going to Italy in a couple of
weeks. Anyway, I'll write again soon and will let you know movements.
Write when you will. Hope *work* goes on well.
   With much love
   I

To Brigid Brophy.

Nettlepole
[June/July 1965]

Dearest dear girl, thank you for three letters here [. . .] Oh do not feel so
sad, Brigid. I know there are such deep reasons for that sort of sadness and

---

1 Hera Buschor, who was to become Canetti's second wife in 1971 and with whom he was to have a
   daughter, Johanna, in 1972.

it's no use saying look how good *this* is, how good *that* is, which one enjoys and takes for granted. But shake it off, hew it away. (Not necessarily by crying 'hew' and having 'him' (or 'her') though if that would work for you I would set my disgraceful jealousy within bounds.) You are less good at separation than I am for all sorts of temperamental reasons. I very much take you along with me. And I *like* letter-communication – I think you do too in fact. Also I haven't so many *theories*. I wonder if I had when I was younger? I don't think so, at least after twenty-five. (Sorry this is obscure. I mean I think you are always testing things against an ideal pattern, while I am quietly grateful to find that day by day I am not in hell.) Dear sweet girl, my beautiful and clever friend for whose love I am so constantly grateful, do not be cast down.

I much enjoyed your tennis letter. I think it is *lovely* that Stolle doesn't want to beat Emerson.[1] We are still men and not machines. Did you see (well no I suppose not since you take that other rag) the letter in *The Times* today how Bunny Austin[2] (you wouldn't remember him) saying that what is the matter with tennis is what is the matter with England: hedonism and no discipline. 'Our technology improves while our morals decline.' Jolly good.

It is freezing cold here in Kent as usual. Even I shun the neighbours' swimming pool. I hope you are surviving OK in Old Brompton Road. (I picture you as *shivering* all through English summer.) I will buy you a *smart* woollie if I can find one smart enough.

After much debate have fixed on Coquerico for Friday lunch. Do you know it? It looks like a Coca-Cola joint but is a very decent French restaurant. It is I *think* 333 Brompton Road, but telephone book could check this. Suggestion is meet 12.45-ish at *pub* which is next door but two or three to Coquerico on Harrods side. It's on the corner of a crescent and I *regret* to say I can't recall its name – the word 'Toby' occurs, but that may be the name of a beer advertised on the outside. Anyway there at 12.45–50 on Friday. I will write to boys.[3]

Dear heart, don't grieve. I love you so much. Very very much thinking of you,

Your

I

---

1 The two Australian tennis players Fred Stolle and Roy Emerson were to play each other at Wimbledon. Brophy was a great tennis enthusiast.
2 Henry 'Bunny' Austin, British tennis player.
3 Charles Osborne and Ken Thompson (who was affiliated to the Arts Council).

To Brigid Brophy.

Steeple Aston
[June/July 1965]

My dear, you should know by now that you can no more get rid of me (however tiresome I am) than you can get rid of Charis.¹ So make up your mind to grin and bear it.

I went to Roberta's (dress shop in Golders Green) on Friday morning, only to find that they were sold out of the snazzy sweaters with matching stockings which I was after. I lingered to admire the thrilling dresses which I might have worn had I been size 12 instead of size 20. I suppose I've been in Golders Green before, but it seemed odd, rather an un-place.

I feel confounded tired today and reluctant to think. I suppose I am getting old. A photographer Lewinsky² (did he ever get at you?) has sent me some pix of myself which John rightly says could be used to advertise a rest home for the aged poor. 'We found this poor old lady crouching in her damp hovel –'

Must stop this nonsense and collect wits for work. I *did* like your new mackintosh. When are you speaking at Trafalgar Square? I am full of admiration. Much love

    I

To David Morgan, who had boasted about his intimacy with Murdoch to a male fellow student (Tom) and who had joked about the influence this gave him at the RCA. In a note to the editors Morgan states that he was indeed guilty of indiscretion and self-aggrandisement but innocent of the more serious accusations made in this letter.

[early July 1965]

Dear David,

I am terribly unhappy about this business, and I simply cannot understand how you can have behaved as you did. I was very reluctant to believe (even when you told me so yourself) that you had told deliberate lies about me of a very damaging kind. And I still thought when I last saw you in London that there had been a good deal of misunderstanding. I came back last Thursday to find a letter from Tom which finally convinced me that you must have lied quite deliberately and maliciously, knowing what you were

---

1 Brophy's mother.
2 Possibly Jorge Lewinski, well known at this time for his photo portraits of artists.

doing, and that over a long time you had been intentionally poisoning his mind against me. He said (and I believe him) that you had for instance told him that I had made unpleasant remarks about his accent and his appearance. You must have known this to be *totally untrue*. (In fact as you know I made no unpleasant remarks about him at all.)

It is very doubtful now whether he will ever believe me or trust me, and if he leaves the college (which he shews all signs of doing) I shall feel partly to blame. I also feel a very deep and especially tormenting grief to think that someone vulnerable like Tom, and whom I like very much, should have been led to think of me as a thoroughly odious and callous person.

I simply cannot understand your motives here. As you said, you certainly have an instinct to estrange people you are fond of. But it seems you also have a kind of cruelty which I've never met before. I suspect you must have enjoyed using your power to hurt Tom, and using him in turn to torment me.

I'm afraid this can't be overlooked or got round, and you have destroyed an innocent and happy affection for you which I valued. I care very much for my professional scrupulousness and you could not have hurt or damaged me more vitally than in making me fail (or seem to fail) one of my pupils. I have always been very careful as a teacher. But clearly the worst and most foolish thing I ever did was to make friends with you.

I'm not going to 'abandon' you (unless you wish it) but we must make another start on a different basis. I know I have a responsibility for this disastrous friendship and I stand by my mistakes. But you are a very dangerous person to have for a friend, and it would be very irresponsible of me (as well as psychologically impossible) to go on as before. (God knows what lies you have told about me in other quarters.) I don't want to see you at present. (I feel I would simply have nothing to say to you.) There had better be an interval during which the impression left by this wretched business can fade a little. I will send you a note in the second half of term and will see you then, if you want to see me.

In the meantime write if you want to (let me know about Emma) and I will reply. (I note that you had the insolence to keep a carbon copy of a letter to me and shew it to someone else.)

If you could now tell Tom the whole truth and make him understand that I *did not* make the detestable remarks you attributed to me, that would be of some service – though I expect by now he does not believe a word you say. I think there is nothing else you can say to either of us except that you are very sorry for what you have done, which I hope you are.

I wish you well.

PS I am sorry to write you this disagreeable letter and to cause you pain. I am utterly miserable about the whole thing.

To David Morgan.

[July 1965]

Dear David,

All right, I've calmed down a bit now. I still believe what Tom said, but maybe you aren't as guilty as I thought at first. I imagined some kind of systematic malice and this now doesn't seem just – though instinct can produce systems. I think you are more of a connoisseur of cruelty than you admit to being. But you are quite right that I must take the responsibility for the risk involved in befriending you. (You say defensively you are twenty-five – most other people I know of twenty-five are kind and discreet.)

Thanks for your offers of help about Tom – and thanks too for ringing up that day to let me know when he had arrived. I don't think there's anything you can do at the moment.

I didn't mean I wasn't going to see you. Having taken you on as a friend I can't go back on that. I was blindingly angry with you after I received Tom's letter, but the anger has cooled. I'll still need time to get over this though. I'll see you later, maybe sooner than I said. I'm still very upset about the whole business and very worried about Tom.

The enclosed is with best wishes for your birthday. I sent it today so that it may reach you before you got to Gloucester. Any news from Emma?

You should not keep carbon copies of personal letters.

To Elias Canetti, whose birthday was 25 July.

[early / mid-July 1965]

My dear, just to send very best of wishes for your birthday, great lion, and the mask of Agamemnon. I've been out of London for ages now, and am just going to Italy. I'll write properly later. Much thinking about you. I embrace you with much love.

Iris

To Brigid Brophy, postcard of Fra Angelico's The Annunciation *from San Marco Museum in Florence.*

[15 July 1965]

Pictures yesterday, pictures tomorrow. Today Uffizi is shut and we are having a Brunelleschi day. (Also a great Perugino experience.) I am enlarging my concept of Masaccio. Firenze if one tries to drive seems organised in small self-contained areas of one-way streets (one sees where Dante got circles of hell idea) and one can't even abandon one's car as there's nowhere to park it. Otherwise the place seems OK. Much love. Will write soon properly.

To Brigid Brophy.

Orvieto
[28 July 1965]

My dearest girl, we are lingering in Orvieto, which is really rather a heavenly place, with a few works of art (Signorelli frescoes and some jottings by Angelico and Gozzoli) and no tourists. Do you know this place I wonder? I keep forgetting which of the places we've been to you've been to too, apart from Florence. (We think nostalgically of Florence now!) All very pure Umbrian, this town, with daily market, donkeys etc. and terrific views (it really *is* a crag town) over spotted countryside. We feel we are old Orvietans by now, with our special table in the café etc. The hotel is super and mysterious (indeed the whole town is mysterious and a little sinister) being a large palazzo complete with painted ceilings and *meublé* with innumerable mediocre works of art. (I write in one of the huge deserted public rooms, surrounded by florid furnishings, John is typing upstairs in bedroom.)
Very weird Signorelli stuff in the cathedral.
I'm sorry I've been short on letters. It's psychologically difficult to write letters when travelling. It's not a good letter even now because of the blank of your non-letters which oppresses me! I'm very sorry I didn't set up any poste restante system, only it would have been difficult. It's been an ad hoc sort of journey, and full of surprises and quick decisions. (Perugia was the nastiest surprise! We pictured such a quiet beautiful place (asses) and in fact it literally took us about an hour simply to find somewhere to park! Even then it was illegal!) And this place, which we expected nothing of, is delightful. [. . .]
You very much travel with me, and I've had a number of imaginary conversations with you, including some rather learned ones about art! There's a lot I want to discuss. And I miss some physical sense of your proximity which I *have* at Steeple Aston, perhaps through the very *you* quality of your letters. Sweet girl, I love you, and much look forward to seeing you before long. Will communicate again soon. Much much love
Your I

To Brigid Brophy.

Steeple Aston
[8 August 1965]

Dearest girl, very nice to hear your voice. I'd been missing it. Write if you can, but don't worry if you can't. I didn't ring you in London as I couldn't do it alone – and scarcely can here, in fact, now that we've open-planned the house. Italy was wonderful but we became so homesick towards the end – and also were running out of masterpieces. (In fact we found the shadowy remains of some superb Gozzoli frescoes in Pisa on very last day.) I am rather dazed with art – a lot of thinking and feeling has still got to catch up with experience. One will forget about the motor cars and remember the pictures. (Even Perugia may become gilded retrospectively – there is a lovely museum, I expect you know it, full of Peruginos.)

I feel terribly tired and rather stiff. I have been bitten by some animal or animals (result no doubt of pushing through underbush to get to mountain rivers) and look like something by Grünewald.[1] We had a lot of swimming, including the lakes – Bolsena blue-black, with very fine black sandy beaches, Trasimene light emerald green and reedy.

My God it's good to be back though.

I'm very hungry for news of you – of work, Ben, people in general, and altogether how you are. Do write if possible. Recall that I love you very much.

ever
I

To David Morgan.

[summer 1965]

Dear David, thank you for your letter. You don't give any news of Yvonne.[2] I hope she is OK and reasonably recovered?

If I really had your interests at heart I would probably send no money. I cannot understand why you don't *work* part of the summer.[3] Can't you get

---

1 Matthias Grünewald (c.1470–1528), German Renaissance painter of religious subjects. Murdoch is here humorously comparing herself to Grünewald's slightly grotesque figures.

2 Morgan's new girlfriend; not her real name.

3 Morgan had been sacked from his job at Gloucester College of Art and was unemployed. He had taken part in a Christmas entertainment for the students, but the college principal and his wife found an element of Morgan's conjuring act offensive. He was asked to leave the college in July 1965.

some sort of job? You do a very easy, as far as time goes, part-time job for half the year, and you can't complain of not having time for your own work as an artist. Why don't you do a hand's turn for the human race during the summer? Or do you just detest work so much? (I note that while I am working hard at Steeple Aston earning money to give to you, you are enjoying yourself in the Isle of Skye, of which you dutifully write quite a nice account.) I think it is bad for you not to do at least a little ordinary work, such as ordinary people do. I hope things are otherwise all right with you. [. . .]

    Best wishes,

    I

To Brigid Brophy, posted from Earls Court.

[17 August 1965]

Darling, was I awful last night? (It's your fault for not drinking the Macon – I think I drank it *all*.) You were wonderful. I vaguely remember we measured the distances of our ears from *something* (I won).

    Dear girl, you are so necessary –

    V. best love from your

    I

To Brigid Brophy.

[18 August 1965]

Dearest angel-bird, how naughty you are to return that record token! (Slipping it into my wardrobe too, forsooth!) All right, I won't argue. As a mild penance though you must send me a list of suggestions of what I might buy myself with this unexpected bounty. And thank you again for the record player on which they will gloriously be played. (We are loving it.) Of course you don't know what I've already got, but you may take it I only have fairly obvious things, apart from a few eccentricities. What would be heavenly to have? I feel a pure case of Angst with the problem you've landed me with. Help!

    I felt very happy with you on Monday night and you were angelic. I'm worried about your abstaining though. I hope you haven't really given up the drink. Drinking is fun. (Drink a pinta. Have fun.) Someone in Oxford is trying to make me take up drugs instead but I am resisting. I feel pretty puritanical about marijuana etc. How do you feel? Is one just being stuffy? People are now constantly assuring me that these mild drugs are nicer than alcohol and more harmless. (Did you know the derivation of 'alcohol'? I only learnt it yesterday. Arabic 'al – Kohl' i.e. that powder one puts round one's eyes in fact was originally – maybe still is – produced by distillation. Spirits were accidentally discovered in the course of such distilling.)

Glad O's Book of Birds was a success. I'm sorry the flags weren't Japanese. Is Kate on a Japanese jug? Nice picture of Mike in *Daily Mail*. (We now get as far as a morning paper.)

NB Please could you save me a few odd Modesty and Willies so that I can see how they get out of that jam? I hope they don't shoot Delphine. Au revoir, dearest girl, and much much love to you.

To Brigid Brophy.

Steeple Aston
[6 September 1965]

My angel, in sade (my God, look what I've written)¹ sad haste as I have some goddamn self-invited visitors coming soon. ('We're just passing near you in our car – may we drop in? We won't stay long.') (Old friends of course, not strangers!) (Then they stay for hours and expect lunch too.) Thanks for your speech which I'll read when time. (Soon.) Re sexes being wrong, I thought I had explained that I am a sadomasochistic male homosexual, and ergo am not interested in boys beating girls or girls beating boys or girls beating girls.

I'll await more information about Bellini.² I feel in an expansive mood about music at present. Extravagant certainly. I have sent £20 to my Irish cousin, and am not sure if I'm a pig or a fool. Probably both. [. . .] No, no one asks me when I was born, I feel rather aggrieved. Much else to answer in your letter but must stop and change out of aged country clothes for dratted visitors. Much love to Bunny from her senior friend.

Will let know very soon re London.

I

To Leo Pliatzky, responding to a draft of his novel, which was never published.

[September 1965]

1 Meaning Murdoch is both amused and appalled that she has written 'sade' (evoking the Marquis de Sade) rather than 'sad'.
2 Vincenzo Bellini (1801–35), Italian opera composer.

Leo, I've read your novel with great interest and a good deal of pleasure. I will certainly, if you wish, say a word about it to Chatto's.

Meanwhile here are my impressions. Your novel has structure, backbone and that is important (many novels are just flabby objects with no skeleton).

I think it needs a bit more flesh on the bone, but at least it has the main thing. I like its movement – one plunges soon into the story and that's good, and the story keeps on moving. And it's exciting. The style is a bit too bare for me, but it's a good clean style.

What makes me uneasy is that I feel you haven't quite decided what *kind* of book it is – is it a detective story, a love story? These categories may seem artificial but the reader does need to know where to lodge his interest – and as a reader I felt a little led up the garden. Boy meets girl. Good, what next? They go to bed at once with a chilling air of total casualness. What I felt was that the centre of the book *for you* (and the title indicates this too) was Marilyn and Connor in bed – and yet for the reader this is just a big cold void. Their relationship (at this end) was unerotic and passionless. (I could hardly *believe* they ever touched each other though you *said* so!) Now this wouldn't matter if you were telling an adventure story and the love business was very incidental. Though I don't myself much like the casual all-conquering-male love stuff in adventure stories – J. B. Priestley's later novels e.g. very much go in for the awfully-attractive-faintly-brutal-male-dream. I think this should be avoided. I was chilled by Connor's faint resemblance to this type! Now take Le Carré (*Spy Who Came in from the Cold*) – he produces a *cold* adventure story but makes the love interest, though incidental and casual, quite credible. I am going on about this adventure business because I think that was what was *good* about your novel. I thought chapter 18 was the best in the book. You are *good* on the movement of the story and ingenious about the technical side (e.g. the later explanation of the disappearance and reappearance of the package).

You could, whatever kind of novel you go in for, do with a little more filling in of character. (And also *more characters*. I believed in the policeman, and Peter and Tom Stott – they were in fact far more *there* than M or C – only one didn't have *enough* of them.) And I'd like more decoration, more *stuff* generally. (See any page of any novel or any story by Elizabeth Bowen.) One must be able to *believe* in the people and the scene, and your picture was (for me) a little too denuded.

Things like the smell of the polish etc. were good, but not enough. I could never *see* Marilyn at all. One needn't here produce detailed descriptions. Tiny touches will do. You might, when introducing Connor, have omitted the clever quotation and said *anything* trivial about him, e.g. that he had a cold or toothache. (Cf. Vronsky's famous toothache at the end of *Anna Karenina*.) There was a slight lack of air about your characters which was

perhaps the lack of a *humorous ironic* atmosphere of the author's consciousness playing about them. (The novel is essentially a comic form. Detail.)

Where did Connor go to school? I bet you don't know.

Anyway, I did like, do like, the book and am very willing to commend it
to Chatto's! In fact, authors get read pretty carefully in any case by decent
publishers. I think I shall *remember* the novel. It has presence and, as I said,
hard structure, which is the essential thing. (I see you as a Le Carré-type
writer! Do you mind? More attention to character and detail and you could
be jolly good.) Do hope you don't mind this letter!

See you soon. Au revoir and love

I

To Rachel Fenner.

Nettlepole
Little Chart
Kent
17 September 1965

Dear Rachel, just a note – and *thank* you for yours. We are down in Kent
for a few days staying with John's mother. Always a good break, this. Just
now they're harvesting the hops – not as exciting as in the days when hordes
of East Enders and gypsies did it. Now a great big red machine does it all
(almost). But there is quite a gay vintage feeling all the same.

I know the letter difficulty – but do write about all ordinary things. Letters
should aspire to the condition of talk. Say first thing that comes into head.
I love to hear about your work or anything that you're up to. (I shall certainly
want to see what you've been making as soon as you can be persuaded to
show it!) Glad Frank well. See before long. And do write again sooner of
your work. Excuse rushed note, just off to sea! With love

I

To David Morgan.

Steeple Aston
[September 1965]

Dear David,

I'm not in much of a mood for being amused by your blunders.[1] I dislike being made to look a fool. (Also the effect of that careful letter will be entirely spoiled.) If you haven't enough sense of accuracy (or even *sense*) to check the name of someone on whom your future may depend it doesn't look as if you'll get far in the academic world. Henceforth I leave you to make your own arrangements. If and when you get a place somewhere I'm prepared to make a financial contribution – I can't say how large, since my income fluctuates considerably. Meanwhile I'd advise you to get on with the Latin, and get yourself a job that *pays* so that you can save some money. Best of luck.

To Brigid Brophy.

Steeple Aston
[autumn 1965]

Darling, quite so, and please address first paragraph of your to-hand letter to yourself, in stern tones. It's always you who starts it. Sometimes I think you and my ex-pupil Helena are neck and neck for irrationality. (*Such* letters I've had from *her* lately, and screams that she was coming home and would I send her the money at once – she's in Canada, as I think I told you, doing Russian in Ontario. All settled down again now thank God.)

Angel, I'm so glad you rang – and so sorry my letter hadn't come. I think I posted it on *Saturday*, so it's very bad of it. Yes, we are unlike. I adore the Fabric Hall at Pontings, and will be miserable when they modernise it and I'd love to feel I was in a Calcutta emporium and might buy a sari length and width at any moment. (Have you ever tried on a sari? I'm sorry to say I haven't, though I've had so many terribly attractive Indian girl pupils with hair down to their waists or below.) The big shop in Chicago, by the way, called Marshall Field's, whose fame we heard of in far-off Canada (someone there casually said 'Oh I always go to buy my clothes at Marshall Field's) turned out to be *throughout* rather like the Fabric Hall – a dear old-fashioned shop which would be at home in Leamington Spa. Most endearing.

You don't *really* want to be a man, do you? I look forward to my tie – I am a bit conventional and stuffy about ties actually – but if you give it to me it will be different.

Have you come *across* a thing called *Penthouse*? – have they sent Mike an ad? It's a new pornographic glossy magazine given over mainly to pictures

1 Murdoch had written a reference for Morgan but he had misspelt the name of the recipient.

of naked and semi-naked girls. John has received a super advance notice with lots of photos – and so did all other New College senior members of the *English* School (*only*) with the exception of David Cecil. (He was very dashed, and wondered what that meant.) Why did they pick the English School, I wonder? The thing masquerades as a 'progressive form of opinon' etc. etc. and is contributed to by Colin Wilson and Alex Comfort. I think it's extremely disgraceful!

Will telephone you tomorrow or Weds. Could you get away as early as 6 or even 5.30? Henekey's in Kingly St behind Liberty's, opening time?

Much love

I

Of course not cross darling – glad I answered the phone.

To David Morgan.

[11 October 1965]

Dear David, glad the money was OK. What drivel you talk though (about my *dragging* in your friends to spoil our relationship etc.). You say: 'Emma you demanded to know about'. Come come, David. (a) Cast your mind back to our second meeting. You quite gratuitously then sought to interest me in Emma (and succeeded) in order to borrow £100 to get her back to Africa. (Which sum was subsequently used for other purposes *connected with Emma*.) You put a great deal of energy into interesting me in your girlfriend. (b) Emma came to see me in college out of the blue and of her own accord. (She came I suspect partly at least because, as she told me later, you had been telling her girlfriend that I was 'deeply in love with you'!!) As for Yvonne, she was bloody rude to me in the Painting School for I imagine the same reason – i.e. you had been stuffing her up with stories about my attachment to you. Tom became my pupil before I even knew whether you knew him, and my connection with him was something completely separate. He got involved with our friendship again because *you* thought fit to tell him a lot of lies about me. After all this it's a bit much to suggest I brought these people into the picture! Have some sense! As it is, they are in the picture and of course they interest me.

This week's no good for a meeting I'm afraid. I go back to Oxford on Wednesday, after arriving late on Tuesday, and although I'll be up for a meeting on Friday, I'm just coming for that evening. I'll write soon with a suggestion for next week. [. . .]

To Leo Pliatzky.

[24 October 1965]

Leo dear, am I to dine you and Jean on Tuesday? (Oct 26) I hope so. I have a Russian lesson just before, so hope OK if I arrive 7.45–8ish.

I *did*, officially, have lunch with you recently, didn't I? And I *have* read your novel? Please brief – best RSVP 59 Harcourt Terrace SW10.

It was very good to see you the other day. Lunch soon again I hope. Much love, old friend,

Your I

To Elias Canetti.

[28 October 1965]

My dear, I have rung once or twice in vain (but not using The Method, since from the country) and Hans Hevesi[1] tells me you are in Germany for a new play. I wonder if you are? Anyway I am assuming you are away in nearer future. Could you however have dinner with me on Tuesday November 16?

I hope that would be OK. I do want to see you. I think of you a lot. I hope one day I'll meet (I feel her name is taboo). I'll start telephoning again nearer the time. I love you very much.

Your
Iris

To Philippa Foot written after an unexplained gap in correspondence.

Steeple Aston
[early November 1965]

My dear, so many thanks for your letter which cheered me so much. I very much want to see you and see you more. My own mode of existence at present seems to make this difficult in a practical way, I mean my being always in Steeple Aston or London. This problem must be solved – I need *extended* talk with you. There is nothing else like this. I too, here, love

---

1 Austro-Hungarian anthropologist and psychotherapist, now living in London; probably a friend of Canetti.

unconditionally. (There are still many things I want to *tell* you, only one doesn't get past the stage where this is difficult.)

I'm just now finishing a novel[1] – should be able to get rid of the damn manuscript about end of week. Will then suggest meeting time or times – may telephone from London.

I suspect you are the only person who really understands my novels or indeed me.

Have you seen the Beckmann[2] exhibition at the Tate? *Super.* Will write, 'phone, again, very soon.

I embrace you.
Much love
I

To Philippa Foot, in which Murdoch expresses her shock at Donald MacKinnon's reaction to The Red and the Green.

Steeple Aston.
[early November 1965]

Darling, PS, yes, lunch next Monday Nov 8 please. I'll come chez toi just before one o'clock (High Street) unless otherwise instructed.

I have today received one of *those* letters from Donald (Oh God!) with promise of more to follow, saying how can I have been so unkind as to portray him and his wife as Barney and Kathleen! I was stunned. But maybe I ought to have foreseen this.

Much love
I

To Elias Canetti.

Steeple Aston
[early November 1965]

My dear, I was so very sorry to miss you on Tuesday. My own silly fault. I was so sure you were in London. (No evidence, except that someone said Julius Hay[3] was meeting you – and I received a card from the Austrian

1 *The Time of the Angels.*
2 Max Beckmann (1884–1950), German experimental artist who revived figurative painting and reinvented the triptych within the milieu of modernism. His paintings figure importantly in *Henry and Cato.*
3 Gyula Háy (aka Julius Hay), a Hungarian Communist intellectual and playwright.

Institute saying you'd be there on, I think, Friday.) I should have been warned by failure to get you by telephone! Anyway, I arrived just after 7.30, tried door, shouted. Your windows were dark. Waited a bit. Then I went to the King of Bohemia[1] till just before 8 and tried again. Then tried again about 8.30, waited in pub, telephoned. I'd been building up for some time to the idea of meeting you and there was so much I wanted to say. I'm sorry. I do hope you are OK and all's well. I have been thinking about you a lot. Look after yourself. I will write, telephone, again. It's nearly end of term, alas. Forgive my inefficiency. And much love
    Your Iris

To Elias Canetti.

Steeple Aston
9 November 1965

My dear, I have not had my envelope back by post, and could not get any answer from your London number though I tried a number of times, so I assume you are still away. I do very much want to see you and will try again. With much love, yours as always,
    I

To Brigid Brophy, on hearing the news of Brophy's father's death.

Steeple Aston
14 November [1965]

My dear, you will have guessed that I didn't telephone because the damn telephone won't work. The whole village is kaput. I tried the two public telephone boxes. Very sorry child.

    I am thinking of you very much. I hope your mother is calm and strong and that grief is not too terrible. I think this shock hits one several times, by degrees as it were, as one takes it in. I will *try* to telephone tomorrow and will certainly ring when in London – I hope to have had letter from you before then. I embrace you. Very much love, dear child.
    I

---

1 A pub nearby.

To Rachel Fenner.

21 January [1966]

Rachel, my dear child, thank you very much for showing me your work – I so much enjoyed being with you in the Sculpture School, and was very moved too. [. . .]

I thought your stuff much more coherent (anyway it made more sense to me) and really good. The *mystery* of sculpture still perplexes me. How can your fibre-glass objects *resemble* the world of Samuel Palmer?[1] Of course I speak diffidently as I know so little of your art. But your things gave me much pleasure and the excitement true art gives. I liked the drawings very much too and would like to buy one or two. (Will raise this question again later!) I can't see any way through next week, and I doubt if there's much time, but I'll write again before long and suggest a meeting. Don't worry too much about your emotions – you are lucky to have some genuine ones. And there is nothing to fear. I hope Frank flourishes. Au revoir and love
      I

To Brigid Brophy, posted from Earls Court.

[January 1966]

It's snowing (big flakes) and I love you. I feel depressed. I was all yesterday at the college and got exhausted and penetrated by a sense of the futility of teaching. Who listens, who cares? Why do I do it? Why do I do anything? Have fun with all those actresses. Will write you from Steeple Aston.
      Much love

To Leo Pliatzky.

Steeple Aston
[6 February 1966]

Dearest Leo, it was very good to see you, though I'd rather have seen you alone. (It was a good evening though wasn't it? Especially because of you!)

1 English landscape painter, etcher and printmaker (1805–81) whose work was influenced by William Blake.

I rang up the Treasury the next morning, but you weren't in and I assume you were nursing your cold. Hope all better now. Will telephone you soon again to suggest lunch. This just to send much love. I.

To Eduard Fraenkel, whom she had met on 4 February.

Steeple Aston
7 February [1966]

Dearest Eduard, my dear, just to say I was so happy to see you again. It's hard to put this into words: you are something very precious and permanent in my life, and I felt this all the time, even when I idiotically didn't write to you. (Forgive that.) You have always given me, ever since the days of the Agamemnon class, a vision of excellence. More simply, I love you. I will send those books soon. (I haven't got copies by me, but have ordered them.) I embrace you. Much love
   I

To Elias Canetti.

Steeple Aston
[early February 1966]

My dear, it's too many centuries since I saw you. (I get small exasperating fragments of news of you.) *Mea culpa*. Please let us meet. I suggest dinner on Tuesday 15th – me to come to Thurlow Rd about 7.30–45. Would that be OK? I'm so sorry we missed each other last time. That was my fault too. I will try to telephone this time, but I may not get you. I would be *very grateful* if you would, if you are in England and can manage Feb 15, if you could post the enclosed. If I do not receive it, and do not get onto you by telephone, I won't come. But may it be that you can make 15th all right.
   I have a lot to talk to you about – nothing particularly dramatic or urgent but just sorts of things I can only say to you, or best say to you. And I want you to tell me – oh, marvellous things. I hope you are very well – and that Hera is well!
   Very much love,
   Your
   I

PS I had a dream last night in which you were Socrates. I've never made this identification before, but it seems a good one. (Of course you are much handsomer.) In the dream you looked like yourself except for having white hair. You made a very good Socrates.

Much love

Iris

To Elias Canetti.

[mid-February 1966]

Dear heart, just a note. I've been thinking so much about you. I hope you will be well. I feel deeply convinced that the ordeal which you see ahead is some sort of dying into life – a good *Verwandlung*¹ where one goes, as it were, open-eyed into what seems utter darkness – and then finds one has entered some other and much better world. I am pleased *the novel* is there, bearing you company. Hold onto it, and it will prove a guide.

I am sure it is a time too, if I may speak of that, for holding onto Hera and consenting to let her help you and experience with you, as she would wish. As for the other thing you spoke of, I think one must endure the visitations of the gods, being glad that one is visited! – living into it with one's whole self and finding more life and more good in what has come to one and to the other person.

I wish you would *use* that piece of paper I left with you! I am wretched to think of your being worried and preoccupied with those money matters. I am *not* short of the stuff! (Will promise to tell you if I am!)

I am terribly glad I saw you. You always give me life. I love you deeply, deeply, as you know, and *always. Look after yourself.* Au revoir. I'll write from on the journey. Much much love,

I

To Brigid Brophy.

Harcourt Terrace

[23 February 1966]

---

1 Transformation, a theme that runs through Canetti's work.

Darling, enclose *shameless* document over which I trust you will blush by the light of day! (*Can't read* the two at the bottom. O. Werner?[1] Who he?) You were super last night. I do hope you enjoyed your aubergines etc. We mustn't stay up so late though. I can feel that brain cell damage this morning. Feel rather useless and ready to climb onto rag and bone man's cart. Enjoyed seeing you teased by Charis! Must emulate. Must go college. Much love, my dear.
    I

To Raymond Queneau, in which she mentions Georg Kreisel, her friend from Cambridge days. Murdoch saw Kreisel, now teaching at Stanford University in the States as well as in Paris, whenever he visited Oxford. Conradi suggests that Murdoch drew on Kreisel when creating the character of Marcus Vallar in The Message to the Planet.[xxvi]

Steeple Aston
1 April 1966

My dear Queneau, thank you very much for *Une histoire modèle*[2] and even more for your *amitié*[3] which I have only seemed to neglect (be unworthy of) of late. (You are not sinless yourself, as you deeply know.) Our contact and messenger, Kreisel, rang up lately. I hope I'll see him before long. I hope I'll see you one day. Meanwhile thank you, especially for the *amitié*, and be assured of my old established but still subsisting
    Amour
    Iris

To Rachel Fenner.

Steeple Aston
[April 1966]

My dear child, thank you so much for your letter. I still haven't the time to write to you properly, forgive this. It's a paradox of the human situation

1 Brophy had sent Murdoch a newspaper cutting of a photo of Lou Christie, American singer and songwriter. Round the edge of the photo, Brophy had written the names of many famous people, including Ingrid Bergman, Frank Sinatra, Dean Martin, Katharine Hepburn, Jerry Lewis, Anthony Blunt, Jean-Paul Belmondo, Jeanne Moreau, Iris Murdoch and O.Werner. The last named was the Austrian actor Oskar Werner, who had co-starred with Jeanne Moreau in *Jules et Jim* (1962), and also starred in *The Spy Who Came in From the Cold*, released in January 1966.
2 Essay by Queneau, begun in 1942 and published in its incomplete form in 1966.
3 Friendship.

that love is the only road to anything that's worth anything – and yet it's such a difficult road, because love is so connected with possession and filling of self. Really detached love is hard even to conceive – though *art* gives us some hints of it.

One must be prepared to accept situations, going away, partings, as part of the human lot, that 'necessity' the Greeks knew all about. And somehow not think of it as destructive as an enemy of love. Can this be done? I don't know. This is a bit of something I've thought which needs saying to you at much greater length. I am sorry that, even at the best, I can see you so little.

I will try to write properly in the vacation. I trust you completely. See you Wed. morning as usual. With much love

I

To Brigid Brophy, following a trip to Bristol where Murdoch bought Brophy a keep-sake and also visited her old headmistress, Beatrice May Baker, now ninety years old.

Steeple Aston
[late April 1966?]

I've meant for some time to send you this. Not that you need persuading, but you might leave it in your club or something. I have had a letter from Charles,[1] asking me to write about 'leaving school'. (Did you give him this jolly idea I wonder?) I have said no – it could take me ages to write about leaving school.

I greatly dis-enjoyed seeing my old headmistress. I suppose you are a bit right about my blind reverence etc. I suddenly saw her as an awful old bully, which indeed she is. She has been bullying me since I was twelve, and only now have I really noticed it. (This doesn't stop her from being a remarkable woman etc. etc.)

The philosophical question about pain is interesting. I feel inclined to define the concept as Reik[2] does, but I'm not quite sure why. Perhaps because the sense of touch is so much less penetrable by reflection? I may look at

---

1 Charles Osborne.
2 Theodore Reik, a student of Freud, who became a prominent psychoanalyst in New York after fleeing from the Nazis in 1938. In *Masochism in Modern Man* (1941), Reik explored why and how some people derive sexual pleasure when suffering pain or humiliation, arguing that patients who engage in self-punishing or provocative behaviour do so in order to demonstrate their emotional fortitude, induce guilt in others, and achieve a sense of 'victory through defeat'. Murdoch did in fact buy the book and annotated it quite heavily; it is now housed in the Iris Murdoch Archives at Kingston University.

that book. I note what you say about Firbank,[1] but I would rather read you. I have greatly enjoyed – am enjoying – Ada Leverson's *The Little Ottleys*.[2] I expect you know it.

I am off on Monday and should be back about 21st. I look forward to seeing you whenever that will be. I embrace you. Be well.

    I

To Norah Smallwood.

Steeple Aston
26 April [1966]

Dear Norah, as I am meditating making some LOANS to various impecunious friends and relations (it's remarkable how many of these one *has*) it would help me if I could have some sort of preview of my financial situation over the next six months or so. I am very sorry to bother you with this and there is *no hurry*! I wonder if you could tell me following:

(1)   Is there anything in the kitty at the moment (i.e. to be had on demand, if I demand)? I imagine not.
(2)   Have I had any of the *Time of Angels* money yet? (Sum on signature of contract?) (Have I signed that contract??) Perhaps that was included in recent cheque? How much do I get when book published? (*When* published?)
(3)   When do you next pay me in ordinary course of events? (September? Do I get paid twice-yearly? Idiotic not to know this!) And could you *roughly* estimate how much I might receive apart from *Angels* money?

So sorry to be a nuisance and as I said no hurry.

So-called spring is going forward here. Refrigerated daffodils bloom incessantly. Swallows and cuckoos have arrived, silly asses. See before long I hope.

    Lots of love
    Iris

---

1 Brophy was later to write a book on the life and work of the novelist Ronald Firbank.
2 Ada Leverson (1862–1930), writer, novelist, was a close friend of Oscar Wilde (who called her 'Sphinx'). She was sympathetic to homosexuals and between his trials Wilde took refuge in her home. Her trilogy, *The Little Ottleys*, was published between 1908 and 1916.

To Eduard Fraenkel.

Steeple Aston
30 April [1966]

Dearest Eduard, this is just a note to ask you something. It has long been in my mind that I should like to dedicate one of my books to you, as a token of friendship and gratitude. (You don't have to like them or even read them!) If you would rather not, for whatever reason, please say so and I will not be hurt or bothered at all. (I have quite got over *that*.) But I should be glad to dedicate one to you, if it would give you any pleasure.

I have been at Steeple Aston all the vac, working like a demon. Thank God the spring seems to have come. I will write later and suggest, if I may, some possible meeting time. I hardly ever seem to get into Oxford these days. I wonder if you have been away in Italy! I am trying to think about Plato. (More of this later.)

With much love to you
Iris

To Rachel Fenner.

Steeple Aston
9 May 1966

Rachel, thanks for your letter. Feeling 'inadequate' is natural to the condition you're in. Needless to say you are not that. We don't of course yet know each other very well and we're not quite used to each other. Time will mend that. Don't worry. And of course you make no 'difficulties' for me at all, except the very general one of posing me with a moral problem! (I am afraid you can't bag all the responsibility! I am obviously responsible too for having let these things happen and continue to happen.) Naturally I am 'cautious' – it would be disgraceful not to be. The situation is largely (I think) made OK by the (I believe exceptional) degree of your integrity. That it makes you (at times) unhappy perhaps should be treated as a kind of technical problem. For the rest one must trust to the gods. (The good ones, or one, not the wild ones.)

On Wednesday (evening) I may have to ask you to drive me somewhere to see someone (you to come to see them too, of course) – will explain. See you Wednes morning anyway. Hope object assembling well. Ever, all love
I

To Georg Kreisel.

Steeple Aston
[mid-May 1966]

Dearest Kreisel (are you really so many miles off? It doesn't make any difference to my feeling for you.) Excuse a quick reply – if I leave this till I can
write a long letter it will be ages. No, my dear, don't hesitate to criticise me!
(As for discouraging me, I am discouraging myself so much at the moment . . .)
You may be right. I think I have a sort of gift for philosophy (my novels are
full of philosophy, incidentally) if I could only give the genre enough time
– which I expect I can't – a gift for making certain sorts of distinctions and
inventing concepts in fields I know well. (It was your failure to make the
right *sort* of distinctions, and my failure to make them for you, which upset
me on that previous occasion. I idolise your mind and was disturbed to find
you arguing less than perfectly!) (Also I think I was retrospectively upset by
your failure to kiss me properly, or indeed in my memory of the occasion,
which may be faulty, at all.) In fact philosophy is so very difficult – I feel a
general depression about the whole thing at the moment. I hope you are
happy with your French girl, and well in health? I hope the Oxford stay comes
off.[1] I'd like to see you in some less ephemeral and encapsulated piece of
time. I will tell my publisher to send you *Red and Green* – forgive if not coming
direct from my hand. *Write again soon.* I feel like talking to you.
　Much much love
　I

To Brigid Brophy.

Steeple Aston
22 May 1966

My dear, thanks for your excellent letter and *forgive* this brief one – back
from Manchester to redoubled pile of awful letters. Fuck the post. (Other
than yours.) No, nothing has happened, dearest ass, except in your guilt-
ridden mind. (Well – the last thing that happened as far as I'm concerned
is that you sent me a letter in which you said that because I'd been a poor
girl at a rich school I something or other something or other: + I feel I
should take this opportunity to point out that Badminton was the last place
where one would feel uneasy at being poor: it was the rich girls who felt
uneasy there.) Yes, dinner on Wednesday please. [. . .]

1　Kreisel was trying to organise a term as visiting professor at Oxford University for 1967.

Manchester was a rather melancholy business (except for the incident of the three blind men, which I'll tell you on Wednesday). I pictured myself addressing the people of Manchester – but the blighters didn't turn up. There was an audience of about 500 in the immense and *awful* Free Trade Hall[1] – and they all seemed to be middle-aged CND organisers. There was a quiet homey feeling, like the Women's Institute. There were some good speeches, actually, including a fighting one from an American Methodist minister. But the temperature remained low.

I have just somehow acquired Bruckner's 7th symphony. I don't recall having heard his music. I think *this* is super – a lovely mixture of Sibelius and Wagner. Do you like him? If so, any further recommendations?

My translation of *Phaedrus*[2] is somewhere, but God knows where. On Wednesday will also tell you How I Nearly Missed the Train at Birmingham. Dearest girl, do not worry, all is well. Much love from your old

I

To Rachel Fenner, posted from London.

[2 June 1966]

My dear, thank you for taking me to that enchanted valley. I shall not forget it – and indeed I'll hope to see it again in the autumn. The little crowsfoot, or whatever it's called (waterplant) is sitting up well in a bowl of water here, and I hope will survive its journey to Steeple Aston.

Forgive what in me is not adequate to your needs. I do love you.

I

To David Hicks.

Steeple Aston
5 June [1966]

My dear, it was marvellous to see you, bearded and all. There were so many more things to talk of than we managed, but very good meeting. The other David[3] was much impressed by you and has written a rambling letter saying

---

1 Built on the site of the Peterloo Massacre, this was a famous venue in Manchester for concerts, public meetings and political speeches.
2 One of the Platonic dialogues.
3 David Morgan.

he wanted to buy you a drink, but was too shy to, etc. etc.! What do you think on further reflection about asking him to submit some drawings for the language book??

Love and best wishes to K. I hope all will go very well. So good to see you. Ever with much love

I

To Brigid Brophy.

Steeple Aston
[June? 1966]

My dear, thanks for ringing – forgive my slightly crazed air. John was just beside me saying 'Who's that? What do they want?' No, don't write to John. He is on the brink of being jealous of you, and if it's formally stated that you and he compete for my time I think this would just annoy him. Things are much better left vague and nebulous. Of course I'll do what I can about time. But it is a *fact* that I live here and not in London, and the summer is hard to foresee and organise much ahead.

I must say I feel exhausted. It's a very crazy time of year, don't you think? All one's students are mad. (Apropos students, some wit has written in huge letters on a long hoarding in Broad Street, *Support our Semen Oxford's New Emissions Policy.*)

My post was a sorry affair without a letter from you. May there be one tomorrow. Now I must struggle with fifty letters. Oh Christ how tired I feel. I wish everything could stop for even a few days.

Forgive this note, sweetheart – it comes with much love
Your I

To Rachel Fenner.

Steeple Aston
[late June 1966]

Rachel, in haste, forgive. Mountain of stuff here. I feel no clearer in my head than yesterday. I think you should try to consider if possible that you might pull out.[1] On the other hand, I'm certainly not going to impose any

---

1 Rachel Fenner has explained to the editors that at this time she was experiencing emotional difficulties in relation to Murdoch who had set strict boundaries in the relationship.

policy! I understand what you say in your letter. One's life has got to *work* though. And maybe one should aim at harmony, satisfaction, happiness. You should consider whether you can't *see* these things as existing beyond this present so upsetting state of affairs. [. . .]

Rachel, Rachel, you *are* loved here, and you must believe it. But there are the time and space limitations too. Do try to be calmer. I am not going to disappear (except under a bus or something, which I hope won't happen too soon).

Much love, my dear child
I

To Brigid Brophy.

Steeple Aston
[early July 1966]

Darling much thanks your letter. I'm glad July 9 is OK. Will send instructions to all shortly. I hope I won't have housemaid's knee or something by then.

I am so sorry I went to sleep! I always do. (How charming of you to attribute it to drink!) Please forgive me. I am so damn tired at the conclusion of *any* day (it's this living at the double –) I fall deep into sleep at once. So I can't talk in bed unless I'm sitting up if you see what I mean! Anyway *don't* please feel affronted by my somniac propensities – I was not intending to abandon you! [. . .]

We go to Kent (Nettlepole, Little Chart) on Monday, returning Friday morning. I'll keep communicating. Much much love, dear girl. Be tolerant of your
I

To Brigid Brophy.

Steeple Aston
[12? July 1966]

Yes, I suppose Rousseau/Voltaire, Plato/Aristotle. I don't adore Voltaire actually, but I don't dislike him either. I'm a Don't Know. I'm also a Don't Know about Aristophanes. I have the impression he wrote some poetry (I seem to recall some choruses in *The Birds*). How good was Voltaire's Greek? I have never managed to like Molière, have you? I think there are people who prefer Aristophanes–Molière–Ben Jonson to Shakespeare. (I think these are generally the people who prefer Aristotle to Plato and Voltaire to Rousseau.)

I can't take the Bath Robe[1] to Brighton, actually, as it would need a suitcase all to itself. I hope the weather's decent. (It's all in the *open air* you know. With your preference of Volkswagen to lakeside dell you may find all that sea and sky a bit much.)

Yes, my mother got back safe from the Rhine, and greatly enjoyed it, I'm glad to say. Though having unwisely admitted to playing bridge, had to play every night with maniac vicar and his wife and sister. (My mother won all the time to their surprise.)

How's the old conscience today? See you tomorrow, Wednesday, my dear, picking you up chez toi circa 7.30 –

With much love

I

To Brigid Brophy, written just before they went to Brighton together for a few days.

Steeple Aston
[17 July 1966]

My dear, *thank* you for *Maltese Falcon*[2] – how very nice! Shall look forward to treat. And again *thanks* for QA which small object I must say fascinates me. You are a dear.

No, I didn't see Karl,[3] wouldn't recognise Karl. Paul J[4] wants me to write a centrepiece which I can't at present do, timewise. Glad you decided not to employ Robin Something.[5] Could you remind me who Maureen Duffy *is*? (Lot of lusty Irishwomen about this season.)

I am to meet the American Women in a hotel in the Cromwell Rd, so that is quite convenient for dropping you *off* in taxi *first*. (I am going to hog those American women.) (If you came some sort of chaos would break out.)

Yes, meet at Victoria Monday. I suggest at *entrance* to the *Brighton train platform*. (It should be possible to discover which this is.) I will come direct from Paddington, doubtless arriving Victoria (DV) circa 10.30. (It is just

1 Murdoch had just been sent a bath robe as a birthday present by a fan in Atlanta, Georgia, which much amused her.
2 Novel by Dashiell Hammett published in 1929.
3 Karl Miller, literary editor of the *New Statesman* at this time.
4 Paul Johnson, editor of the *New Statesman* at this time.
5 Probably Robert Cook, whom Brophy employed as her assistant in 1967. He is mentioned in several Writers Action Group newsletters.

possible I may have to move us onto a later train because of *transport* problems but if so I *will have telephoned you* before this arrives!) Could you buy
tickets if you arrive first. NB IOU two meals. No hanky-panky over ticket
money either. Our hotel is the Royal Crescent, by the way, in case we get
lost. Hope bloody weather picks up. Much looking forward sea view with
you in foreground.[1]
    Much love
    I

To Rachel Fenner, whom Murdoch had recently congratulated on her first-class degree.

Steeple Aston
17 July 1966

Dearest ex-pupil, just to wish you a happy time in Dorset.
    Thank you for my birthday present. I would like a Welsh landscape, but
later, when I *buy* it. You were very sweet to me on Thursday. I very much
like driving about London with you. Dearest girl, be well. I hope work will
soon come to you. And may Dorset be lovely. Write to me. After Wednesday
I'll be here. Much love, Rachel
    I

To Brigid Brophy.

Steeple Aston
[late July 1966]

No letter yesterday, and today one decorated with a picture of Miss A. What
are things coming to? Please make no sacrifices for me, sweetheart, not even
as much as a piece of your fingernail. You would resent it. I do mean, please,
do not hesitate for a second *à cause de moi* when there is anything *at all* that
you want to do. This is much the wisest course. [. . .]

---

1 In a letter sent soon after their return from Brighton, Murdoch wrote 'Darling, you were an angel in
Brighton and now are an angel in the Old Brompton Road. I love you'.

To Raymond Queneau.

Steeple Aston
[July 1966]

My dear, thanks for your anniversary card. I was touched by your thinking. I recall Innsbruck and that July in Paris with great intensity. *Au* I hope some time *revoir* – with love
Iris

To Rachel Fenner.

Steeple Aston
11 August 1966

My dearest child, just a note to send love. Thank you for your letter from the mysterious lakes, I am glad you were there. Glad things are getting organised too. Work is the thing. Try not to grieve, Rachel. Love is better than no love, though it can hurt so much. Work, and be your own complete self. And do write to me in the USA.[1] I feel very connected with you. Much love to you, my dear –
Your
I

To Brigid Brophy, sent from Maine, USA.

[27 August 1966]

My dear, your third letter safely arrived, excellent (sorry you're not going to stay Yris Hotel!). So glad you are going Reykjavik (you can't spell it yet, but that will come) – you *must* go see glaciers, volcanoes, hot springs – this is important. I wish we'd had time to! Observe Surtsey[2] as you come in – it might be performing. [. . .]

I am writing this in a meeting about phenomenology, and as I'll have to make remarks before long I may have to break off. I am enjoying it all rather disgracefully (my paper went quite well) and learning a lot. It was rather a

---

1 Murdoch was about to leave for the USA in order to present a paper in mid-August at Bowdoin College, Brunswick, Maine.
2 A volcanic island off the southern coast of Iceland.

relief however to go on an expedition to sea yesterday, lovely place with grass and trees leading down to seaweedy rocks. John and I swam and then rushed over rocks exchanging information about crabs etc. Most of the other participants walked solemnly to and fro in pairs and one overheard fragments such as '*Selbstverständlich ist es dass der Existentialismus bei Husserl . . .*' These gatherings fill people with self-satisfaction, and perhaps this is their main object.

[*Later*]

Wow! We were certainly in orbit in that meeting! Some of the Hungarians seem not to know the difference between German and English ('And ven we know wie geht's in der biology system' –) and there is a German from Jerusalem whose utterance J says must be *scrambled* by the Israeli secret service.

My dear, have good time in Iceland! Wish I were along too to see those volcanoes and glaciers!

Drink Aalborg.

Off to (sorry didn't explain) Sicily, via Rome, Sunday DV.

Went lovely swim on rocky lovely Maine coast after phenomenology meeting this afternoon and *awful* nightmare might *break ankle* and be confined in USA! Oh God!

Much love my dear child – please write to Steeple Aston – will write from Italia if ever get there! Yours yours phenomenologically

I

To Rachel Fenner.

[late summer 1966]

My dearest Rachel, thanks for your letter. I am sorry things are momentarily so lousy. (Being scratched by the cat is last straw!) No, I don't think that business gets any easier as one grows older – it remains devastating, and yet one wouldn't opt out. Sorry about work being bad – that will pass, but it does shake one's nerve. One should have *techniques* for such times, ways of keeping quiet and watching. (I read Shakespeare or something – what would be equivalent for you? Looking at things, drawing?) But I know it's hard. Just try to keep cool and calm and give yourself *treats*. (This needs a bit of thought.) I do hope Winchester will be OK.[1] You're going through a weird time in anyone's life, that first job transition period. You can't expect to feel normal! Just be cunning about it.

I wanted the other day to *buy you a dress* (you are so marvellously slim, and all those with-it dresses would fit you) but it's difficult to buy one for someone else – so please don't be cross if I send you the enclosed instead, and you buy it for yourself. (Treat.) Needn't be dress of course. Any luxury will do! [. . .]

Much love, Rachel

I

To Brigid Brophy.

Steeple Aston
[10 October 1966]

Much thanks, Bird, for your letter, the Modesty and also the charming PPS of Friday which arrived this morning. Much look forward see you tomorrow eve. Today's post brings copies of *Under the Net*, now piratically published in Russian, a work by a character called Aeris Merdok.

With much love

A[2]

To Sister Marian at Stanbrook Abbey.

Steeple Aston
24 October 1966

Dearest Lucy, thank you so much for your letter and for the medals! I was very touched and pleased and somehow happily amused at your 'rum'[3] thought – how kind of you to think it and to write it. Thank you too for the stories you tell me. We have been on far journeys this summer (a conference in America, then Italy) and are so *glad* to be back in misty autumnal England. Isn't this a beautiful time of year – and October a *wonderful* month – perhaps the most beautiful. I hope you are well – indeed I know you are, I can feel it. I am very busy – writing another of those dreadful novels! And

1 Rachel Fenner was about to start work teaching sculpture at the Winchester School of Art. She left after two terms, finding it too traditional, and went to teach at Farnham College of Art.

2 For 'A. J. Raffles'.

3 Peculiar, odd.

also some philosophy lectures which I am to give at University College London. I wrote a paper for the America conference called 'On "God" and "Good"' which I'd like to send you if I may. May I? Very best October greetings and much love.

Iris

To Michael Oakeshott.

Steeple Aston
5 November 1966

Michael, I'm so sorry not to have replied sooner to your letter. Very sorry about Oct 26. Just after that in fact I was struck down by one of the most awful flu germs I have ever met. It is indeed still with me, and I'm not sure how much of next week, if any, I'll be in town. (Sore throat, cold symptoms, nose bleeding, headache, *complete* loss of voice, *faiblesse*,[1] continual cough, temperature 101.5, abysmal melancholy etc. Eating and drinking unimpaired thank God.) Anyway I am *getting better* and no anxiety need be felt! I just want to complain. I'll write again later, and suggest another date when I begin to see the country ahead. [. . .]

With love
Iris

To Leo Pliatzky.

Steeple Aston
[December 1966]

My dear, just to send Christmas good wishes. You haven't been out of my thoughts and you must extend the usual forgiveness for non-communication. One day I must TALK to you. Next term is a bit broken up as I'll probably be abroad end of Jan. But will write or ring. [. . .] Be well, dearest Leo. *Thank you* for the Whitehall data for novel![2] Happy Christmas and New Year and much love

I

1 Weakness.
2 The murder episode in *The Nice and the Good*, which Murdoch was writing at this time, is set in Whitehall.

To Brigid Brophy.

Steeple Aston
[3 January 1967]

Dear bird, no letter from you this morning. I hope by second post – and that this doesn't portend overwork collapse or displeasure with me? I really worried at your doing so much – and begin to believe that you somehow *want* to. You are an ass. No need to see journalists, do TV for barbarous Canadians etc. (It may be something to do with the telephone – fatal tendency to say yes on.)

Have you polished off your last three masterpieces we could do without?[1] Which ones are they? Reflecting back on your remarks about *Hamlet*. There is something about *Hamlet* – something personal – though I think it is scarcely a flaw (and regard the play as alpha as poetry, rhetoric, prose, psychology and oh God *play*) but it is interesting why it should be so, and as far as I recall your piece did not suggest any *reason*? Are you not exactly the person who should know the reason?

Am working like demon, though awfully distracted by damned arrangements. Feel rather *afraid* of going, not feeling like tough globetrotter at all. (Interesting that the word 'globetrotter' exists in *French* – it seems rather dated doesn't it. Scott Fitzgerald sort of era.)

I shall by the way be in London tomorrow but only for three or four hours to see Canetti who is very ill (or thinks he's very ill – I can't make out which but must see him to discover).[2] I shall have to get 3.15 train back.

NB dinner 12th. Hoping for letter.

Much love, child.

I

To David Hicks.

Steeple Aston
8 January 1967

Dearest David, just a New Year note. Thank you for your card. I don't seem to have seen you for ages, which I know is my fault. Last term was devastated by flu and every sort of minor disaster. And now I am very shortly

---

1 Together with her husband Michael Levey and Charles Osborne, Brophy was finishing *Fifty Works of English and American Literature We Could Do Without*.

2 In a letter postmarked 5 January 1967, Murdoch wrote to Brophy 'Canetti turned out to be suffering from *depression*: not that I underestimate this. From his letter I had concluded he had cancer'.

going abroad for this coming term, mostly lecturing in Australia. I view the prospect rather gloomily at the moment I must confess! (The Australian philosophers are peculiarly ferocious.) I'll look forward very much to seeing you in the summer, if I'm not eaten by a shark. Love to Kay. I hope you are both very well. Very best New Year wishes and much love

Iris

To Brigid Brophy, written just before Murdoch and John Bayley set off for Australia and New Zealand on a lecture tour organised by the British Council.

Steeple Aston
10 January 1967

My dear creature, thanks for very nice letter. I have sent those other letters on to 'Olivia'.[1] (Inverted commas means: you seem to have got very matey with her all of a sudden.) (Maybe she *did* de-recommend me and this was what influenced David to break off the engagement four months later when I was in Innsbruck and he was in Bratislava?) (I read his letter in a snowbound mountain hotel bedroom which I was sharing with another girl. I said to her, 'I've just heard from my fiancé, breaking it off.' She said 'You don't seem to mind very much!' I broke into furious tears: in fact I *didn't* mind very much.)

Yes, I gather STW[2] is of old English country tweed dog-owning queer stock. Am trying to read *Lolly Willows* – it's great stuff – will report.

No, Indian dinner *not* enough. Westernised compromised curry. I *adore* curry, don't you? (No, I believe you don't – you seemed amazed to get a decent meal at that Gaylord place.[3] I look forward to a few decent curries at least. The only *generally* cheering thing about this bleeding journey is we shall travel first class in all aeroplanes. Have never travelled first class (believe you have). Only danger is may become addicted.

Glad Charis home safe. Give her my love. So you have been using Pat's pen all this time! I come to town tomorrow, by the way. See you Thurs. Be good meanwhile. Very much love

I

---

1 Olivia Manning (1908–80), British novelist. She was part of the London literary scene at this time and known to be jealous of Murdoch's success as a novelist.

2 Sylvia Townsend Warner, author of *Lolly Willows* (1926), in which the heroine leaves her position in her brother's house as a middle-aged 'spinster' aunt and, after making a pact with the devil, happily roams the countryside as a hedge witch.

3 A well-known Indian restaurant in Mortimer Street, London.

To Rachel Fenner, postcard of Qutb Minar,[1] Delhi, visited en route to Australia.

[late January 1967]

Almost as good as the Post Office Tower. Have been in Bombay and am now in Delhi and will shortly be in Agra. Life is wonderful but far too fast. Best love I

To Rachel Fenner, postcard of Kannappa Nayanar,[2] Madras Museum.

[early February 1967]

So sorry haven't written – we have been *rushing* from place to place and trying to see a hundred temples as well as talking to universities etc. Have just got back from most southern tip of India. Leaving now for Singapore.
    Much love I

To Rachel Fenner, postcard of Sultan Mosque, Singapore.

[early February 1967]

A short breather in Singapore. A change from India to China is rather abrupt. However, Singapore is China mixed with Surrey. Arrived in time for Chinese New Year which is very boisterous. Homesick for India.
    Much love
    I

To Brigid Brophy.

Canberra
[21 February 1967]

My dear, sorry not to write sooner – we have scarcely had a moment to *breathe* since arriving in Australia. (Any unprogrammed moments are taken up by the press.) It's all very mad and to some extent enjoyable. Many many thanks for your letters – how super of you to write so long and full and

1 A red sandstone tower built in the early thirteenth century.
2 One of the sixty-three Nayanmars or holy Saivite saints, devotees of Lord Shiva.

generally you-like. I am so glad play marches on (why against Strand? A most romantic place.)[1] We must have that box when I come back and one will drink champagne and lead the laughter. I am glad *you* are enjoying it and you are sure to be not the only one.

I am filled with *awe* at your Robin Cook achievements. I think it is really a sign of your greatness. It is unnervingly bold. I feel timid and awestruck. Is Mike jealous? (Am I jealous! I am a little *nervous*. Mike puts up with me. Will R. Cook put up with me? Perhaps after six months or so he will gently explain to you . . .) Also: I fear *postcards* may no longer be private. And how does he know which letters –?

I was shocked by the way to learn of the letter to *The Times* from Amis[2] etc. supporting Vietnam War. One is stunned by the callousness of intelligent people. *Here* of course a great many intelligent people are LBJ men.[3] Fear of the yellow hordes is deep. I got very cross at dinner last night with the British High Commissioner. (Rather too much of that sort of thing.) Could you remember to tell me sometime who else signed that letter?

Australia seems all right. There is an awful lot of it. Every city seems to despise every other city. We got rather fond of little Perth which lives all by itself over on the West Coast.

But have heard nothing but anti-Perth jokes since coming east ('In the midst of life we are in Perth' etc.). And Canberrans despise Sydney, and vice versa. Sydney actually is *super* – the harbour is exciting and lovely and full of fine ships, and the bridge is the bridge, and the opera house is the most beautiful single object I've seen since getting here (with the possible exception of a West Australian novelist called Jerry Glaskin whom I had reluctantly to leave behind in Perth). The trees actually are very beautiful too, especially the lemon-scented gums. (Eucalyptus to you.) We have been promised kanga-roos, emus, possums, but have seen none yet. (The damn things are

1 Brophy's play *The Burglar* was soon to transfer from Brighton to London's Vaudeville Theatre on the Strand.
2 Kingsley Amis (1922–95), English novelist.
3 In 1965 Lyndon B. Johnson sharply escalated the Vietnam War.

nocturnal.) Have seen a lot of splendid birds – wedge-tailed eagles, and sinister black cockatoos who go about in wailing groups and are said by the abos to be escorting the souls of the dead.

We ran into a writer's conference in Perth, which was interesting, there was a sort of doleful litany of South Australian writing going on.

'Why have we got no literature?'

'Because we are suburban.'

'Because we are prosperous.'

'Because we have no *guilt feelings*', etc. etc.

All very nice chaps however, and it was enjoyable in rather a touching way. [. . .]

We will be going on from here to Brisbane, and subsequently back to Sydney, but your letters will now be following me. Do please go on writing.

I am awfully homesick, viva the play, and very much love, my dear.

To Elias Canetti.

Queensland (Near Gt Barrier Reef)
[late February 1967]

My very dear, just a note to say hello. I think of you very often – and do hope all is well. (I have talked of you several times lately – with Gershon Weiler,[1] and with a Chinaman called Lo who sends love!)

There is no time to write a really decent letter. My present mode of existence, though delightful and exciting, is absurd – in the sense that one is *exhausted*, never left alone by people, and given no time at all to reflect! India was extraordinary and wonderful, and compelled absolute love. This place is anxious, nervy, raw, full of very sweet and unassuming people and of patches of magnificent scenery (trees especially) and lovely birds. I haven't seen a single *animal*, apart from dogs and cats and humans! (My hopes of a duck-billed platypus have faded.) I have learnt how to address large audiences on simple subjects – this at least is something. I am terribly homesick. I do hope you are all right. I have so much to tell you about India. Oh *you* should have been there. I do love you. The gods guard you, my dear. Be well. Ever with much much love

Iris

1 Jewish scholar then teaching at the Australian National University, Canberra; later professor of philosophy at Tel Aviv University.

To Brigid Brophy.

Sydney
8 March [1967]

My dear, no letter from you for several days, and I am missing a sense of communication! (Last letter was no. 9.) We are still in Sydney, leaving Sunday for Melbourne but Sydney address best till March 25 circa – then c/o R. Hollyer, British Commission office, Wellington, NZ. We are rather enjoying Sydney which is a much more beautiful city than I expected – not only in terms of the drama of the harbour but also in the domestic architecture (cast-iron balcony stuff, and charming small 1890ish houses) – and also endless small sandy coves for swimming (complete with shark nets!). I hope to go surfing. Also my crawl (a stroke used in swimming) has improved. I am getting much better at impromptu speaking – even can do impromptu dinner speeches. And at propaganda! When asked to talk about problems facing the lady novelist I talk about Vietnam and the colour bar. (These *are* after all problems facing . . .)

Dear girl, I do hope you are OK? I do want a letter. Do hope play forging strongly ahead. I am very homesick, and hope for news. Be well.

With much love.

To Brigid Brophy.

[20 March 1967]

My dear girl, just a note. We are now in Adelaide, I haven't heard from you since letter no. 10, but I hope for a letter when I get back to Melbourne on the way to Hobart. (So used to aeroplanes now we treat them like buses.) Got flu in Melbourne, and have still got it. The elan that keeps one going is just about giving out, and I am beginning to want most intensely to be home – we keep going now just on novelty, of which there is fortunately a steady supply.

Adelaide is a pretty sort of hick town among brown hills – we are just off into those hills on a tour of the wine-growing regions of South Australia and hope to do some *tasting*. We leave for New Zealand on Thursday. I've enjoyed Aussieland but I've had about enough of it now. The pubs in Adelaide shut at 6, as do *all* the pubs in NZ. I feel faintly crazy, as if I'd quietly become another person. I should have made clear in answer to your earlier question that we are working in the *universities*, though a certain amount of damn

PEN club[1] etc. gets worked in. The weather is getting cooler and more autumnal. I have not been able to do any surfing. (All set to do so in Sydney, when the cissy blighters said the waves were too big.)

I do hope all's well with you and work goes decently, and you're not too bothered by bloody press etc. (I talk to press here, conceiving it to be my duty and loathe it. Bugger press.) I hope Charles's arm reasonably better, poor fellow, lousy luck.

I feel terribly out of touch with everything including myself. You must re-educate me into being me when I return. Date of return hypothetically circa April 17 [. . .]

Do hope you are working and full of fight and not being enticed by girls in sports cars. Much much love

Your old

I

To Brigid Brophy.

Auckland
New Zealand
7 April 1967

Darling, it looks as if I won't get another letter before leaving NZ (which we do tomorrow DV) – I've just checked at the High Commission office in case anything came from Wellington by first post, but no – and we leave here at 8 tomorrow – damn. I do love you. Have realised this so especially on this journey (have felt really very in touch – you too I do hope). You are most precious to me. I *do hope things well*. I doubt if any letter would get me in Bangkok – I should have given you that address earlier only very unclear till lately how long we'd be there. I forgot to describe, as asked, wombat. Wombat is medium size (large dog size) marsupial with very short legs, long claws, and huge bear-like head – very closely furry and with friendly inquisitive snuffly personality (much resembles bear actually). Things with large heads endearing.

NB we are very connected, you and I, so do look after self. I am so glad you felt better about things when told to me – would have been idiotic not to tell. I do think about you most intensely. Much love, my sweetheart.

I

1 An association of writers founded in London in 1921 to promote networks between authors worldwide.

To Raymond Queneau.

Steeple Aston
22 April 1967

My Queneau, how very sweet of you to send your poems. They are very
beautiful. To be a poet is the best thing of all, better even than to be a
mathematician. Kreisel brings me word of you sometimes. Be well.
     Much love
     I

To Norah Smallwood.

Steeple Aston
5 May [1967]

Dearest Norah
     I seem to be raining letters on you. This one is about money. The taxman
is HELL. Could you poss. let me know (a) will I get any dough from you
next Sept.? (Last Sept. for some reason I only got £1,000.) Are any ordinary
royalties etc. normally paid only once a year?
     (b) Do I get an advance, and when, on *The Nice and the Good*?
     Do hope you are much better and that Ireland was nice and good!

To Brigid Brophy.

Steeple Aston
[20 May 1967]

My dear child, I was so touched by your lovely essay on *Antony and Cleopatra*!
(And oh dear, just as I started to read it on Gloucester Road station it started
to *rain*! I am so sorry!) I was very interested in and partly persuaded by what
you had to say especially re Cleo as 'metaphor'. I will look at the play again
and meditate on all that you say (you ought to publish something on this?).
You are probably righter than I am (actually I haven't any 'position' – what
I expressed was really an impression rather than a serious view) – and it is
clearly in some way your play. I am not quite such a *Liebestod*[1] merchant as

---

1 Literally 'love death'; when used in a literary context, '*Liebestod*' refers to the theme of erotic death
  meaning the two lovers' consummation of their love in death or after death.

you are – though I can indeed enter into this. But I still feel a cold finger in the thing and cannot really see it as an image of love. However I will try again – I found your remarks most illuminating.

I loved seeing you in the morning! It was very nice. Though I'm so awfully sorry you got wet. I hope the TV thing went OK, and will expect detailed account.

Do attend to wise remarks of T. Maschler.[1] I think the Beatles jointly ought to be Poet Laureate. Much love, little one.

To Brigid Brophy.

Steeple Aston
[28 May 1967]

I think you should stop messing around with these girls. Decide which one you want and go to bed with her.

It's raining cats and dogs here and the temperature is just above freezing point. Lousy imitation English summer. (I think any season is tolerable in England except the summer.)

Our income tax situation is getting curiouser and curiouser. John has just discovered that in return for all his hard work at New College he earns £120 per annum (i.e. we are £120 better off because J works). Rather demoralising. If only New College could pay him in kind. (There is probably something on the statutes which would permit this – so many oxen, pigs etc.) [. . .]

Best love
Your I

To Rachel Fenner.

Steeple Aston
28 May 1967

Rachel, I'm afraid I haven't anything illuminating or wise to say in answer to your outcry. You are complaining about both causality and chance (and of course they are the same things looked at two ways). Of course we are rather mechanical, and psychoanalysis can offer us some useful generalities about

1 Tom Maschler, British publisher and writer. As head of Cape, he encouraged and published many new writers, including Gabriel García Márquez, Ian McEwan and Bruce Chatwin. He also was one of the key figures responsible for creating the Booker Prize in the late 1960s.

ourselves. But everything that is important and valuable and good belongs with the little piece of us which is not mechanical and no one who is not bemused by philosophy or a youthful mood really doubts the existence of this piece.

I think the sage who saw us as naturally reaching out towards the good had got something. We know, in the best part of ourselves, to use Platonic language, that great art is good, that work is often good and love often good. And if we have any certainties in the human condition these are they, and much more *evident* certainties than semi-philosophical stuff about all is flux. Of course much is flux, perhaps most is flux – but there is the other small thing and by this and in this one lives – I think almost involuntarily. (It's very bad really to believe that certain aspects of love in one's life are meaningless or worthless.) That's all for now. Love from your old teacher.

29 May 1967

Rachel, just a PS to send love. I fear my metaphysical letter won't have been exactly cheering. One is very chemical really, and if one is depressed, words, such words anyway, may seem pretty empty. Though actually you seem to me to be elated as much as depressed at present. These winds blow to and fro when one is young and when one is an artist. Thank you for taking me to see the flowers.[1] Please ring up Wednesday morn. Much love

I

To Brigid Brophy.

Steeple Aston
[29 May 1967]

I have thought further about the Maureen[2] business. *Coups de foudre*[3] must have sequels, I imagine, and should have. I feel you miss a lot of fun because of me. As she herself said, aren't there lots of midway arrangements? It might be a good thing and you might suit. In some ways you and I (as you agreed when you admitted to rejecting me) are not each other's type, and I don't want you to have to say with Swann *'J'ai gaché ma vie pour une femme qui n'était pas mon genre'.*[4]

---

1 The Chelsea Flower Show.
2 Maureen Duffy.
3 Love at first sight.
4 'I've frittered my life away for a woman who was not really my type.' Refers to Charles Swann's relationship with Odette de Crécy in Volume 1 of Proust's *À la recherche du temps perdu* (*In Search of Lost Time*; previously translated as *Remembrance of Things Past*).

This by way of vaguely encouraging you in this area. I, after all, am a fairly rock-like presence by now.

Much love

I

To Rachel Fenner.

Steeple Aston
[early June 1967]

Dear heart, how little you know of human nature. (What a bastard business *that* is.) I am not waiting for you to fall out, I have settled down to enjoying your being in. (If I wonder: who will help me shift all that junk from college? I think straight away of you and assume it will not be a nuisance! And this is merely a symbol of the much more that I feel here. You were a *help* and *support* on Thursday.) It is much more likely that you, at last getting fed up, will give *me* the boot. (However I hope you won't. You are now curiously woven into my life. I didn't expect you and I can't classify you but I am very glad you are there.)

Could Polesden Lacey[1] be done in a 9 a.m. to 5 p.m. sort of jaunt? How far is it? I will think about this, but the immediate future not much good.

Child, dear I love you, and you must forgive me for the inadequacies of my mode of existence towards you – I mean I hope you will – I think there is something worth much here.

Much love

To Rachel Fenner.

Steeple Aston
[early June 1967]

I have thought of something we might do on Thurs morning which is an entirely selfish something. For a novel I am now writing,[2] I need a closer look at Lots Road Power Station and surrounding area where I wish to locate someone's house and a small printing works. We might snoop around there, and end up at some riverside pub? (I'd have to be dropped at some tube station circa 12.20.) Discuss further? Best love

I

1 Edwardian estate near Dorking in Surrey, owned by the National Trust.
2 *Bruno's Dream*, published in 1969.

To Georg Kreisel.

Steeple Aston
[mid-June? 1967]

My dear creature, in quick answer to yours.

(a) Yes, you have New College dining rights. Yes, I am very busy, and will be very busy next autumn, I am always very busy, but I will certainly have time to see you. Could you, in due course, let me know when you'll be in England? Will you be in London first for some time?

(b) Your accounts of *amours*. No, this does not annoy me and I feel no jealousy, which is a little odd as I am crazily jealous by nature and certainly not uninterested in you. Perhaps it is that I feel we have some sort of special relationship. (It is indeed *sui generis*.) I like you to talk of such things not because of any voyeur-like interest, but because I would like you to talk to me about whatever's in your mind. (I recall your long ago saying you were only concerned with money, sex and mathematics – and I fear money might be tedious and mathematics incomprehensible – which leaves sex, which is after all in various ways nearly the whole of life.) Well there are other topics. But I like to talk to you directly and I like to be talked to directly.

(c) I think you are sometimes excessively nasty to people and this worries me in some way which I can't get quite clear. Perhaps because I somehow condone it through some general acceptance of you. And yet how little, in some ways, I know about you, in spite of the sense of direct communication. There may be some kind of, quite innocuous I think, illusion involved here. Anyway I love you, and this comes with a sort of ontological proof.

I am trying to write some philosophy, partly about Plato, and find it depressingly difficult. Look after yourself, my dearest changeling.
   I

To Brigid Brophy who, by now in love with Maureen Duffy, was unable to write to her, perhaps because Duffy was still living with her partner Sue.[xxvii]

Steeple Aston
[9 July 1967]

Thank you for your nice long letter. You sound as if you are arguing, but there is really no argument, in the sense that what is happening to you now is quite unavoidable. You haven't really chosen anything (as I see it). I think you probably have a very long *trajet*[1] to live through with Maureen before you know how things between her and you will settle down. And I think it would be absurd to want anything less than permanence. (What is wrong with being permanent, anyway? All the best things are.) Time will also show what happens to our arrangement. (Possibly I was only filling in until Maureen arrived, but *on verra*.) Yes, I'm afraid I do rather dig diffused eroticisms that last forever. I have a number of them. Anyway, there it is and don't worry. You are in the hands of gods. I hope it won't be too long before you can start writing to Maureen – and that you'll hear from her very soon.

Have you got a needle and thread *in* stock? With love

I

To Brigid Brophy.

Steeple Aston
[July 1967]

My dear, thank you for various communications which I have probably read in non-chronological order, but getting the general idea. I think Maureen will have left by now and you must be feeling very desolate. I am so sorry. And not being able to write for so long is awful. But the time will pass, and you will very soon start to feel connected with the time of her return. It is, of course, a form of insanity, but a wonderful and life-giving one, and I am so glad that you have a mutual love. I hope poor old Sue will get fixed up somehow: she'll just have to. (Maybe she'll fall in love on the boat!) People suffering from your complaint are hard to communicate with, and you must just give me cues. I feel you are a bit touchy with me at the moment, and I know people in love are a bit inoculated against other contacts and may be nervy with old friends, because everything *else* seems dust and ashes. (Rather a mixture of metaphors here and none of 'em much good to express what I want to say.) You must just help me to be, at this time, what you want me to be, whatever would be most helpful and supporting. You may even feel that non-communication for a while is a good idea? Don't write if you don't feel like it, and don't worry about me, I am just *there*. I do hope ordinary life is beginning to touch and pull you a little and that it isn't all desolation. Soon you will be looking forward. Be well, dear child, and much love

I

1 Journey.

To Brigid Brophy.

Steeple Aston
[15 July 1967]

Thank you for your note. I hope everything has gone off reasonably OK about poor old Sue. (I think on further reflection I'd rather you didn't do any 'explaining' about me to Maureen as misunderstanding would be likely and I don't want to be known in Lesbian London as your discarded lover! Better just get me into focus as a dear old pal, which indeed I am, without any special commentary!) Also, don't feel, though of course I shall watch with interest, that you have to give me, from now on, any detailed account of how things go! This might be less than fair to Maureen, who does not reckon with an unseen spectator.

It is of course sad (thank you for your previous letter) that the feathers have now come off Cherubino's hat (and there is the sobering possibility that the dear boy may be less attractive without them). However, I shall certainly reckon to be on the scene in some manner; term is over now and I will be more irregularly in London, and I'm not yet sure about next week. I may be up for a day to see my mother. However I'll report again on that. I hope everything is going very well and happily.

With love
I

To Brigid Brophy.

Steeple Aston
[19 July 1967]

Dear child, not bitter, no (certainly not!) not even particularly sad (though there is always some sadness in the ending of an era), merely objective and occasionally faintly sardonic! [. . .]

Seriously and unsardonically I do hope that the Maureen thing can be made into something stable and permanent. It is clearly something very much worth having.

With best wishes and love
I

To Frank Paluka, Special Collections, University of Iowa, USA, who had written to Murdoch, having recently purchased the manuscript of Under the Net. *Iowa now holds the manuscripts of most of Murdoch's novels.*

Steeple Aston
26 July 1967

Dear Mr Paluka,

Thank you for your letter. Yes, I think I might be willing to part with more manuscripts to you, if we could agree upon a price. (I have no very clear idea about prices, but I suppose the market price of the *Under the Net* MS might be taken as a guide.) I have had a lot of enquiries about selling MSS, but have not hitherto made up my mind to part with any; however, I am prepared to take your acquisition of *Under the Net* as a sign! Are you also interested in philosophical MSS? I have lately looked through my archives. I seem to have retained no MS of *Sandcastle* or *Flight from the Enchanter*. However, for all the other novels I have two complete and considerably amended drafts (handwritten). I have also found another version of about a third part of *Under the Net* – I think earlier than the one you have. If you would like a representative of yours in London to look at any of this stuff, perhaps you would let me know.

With good wishes
Yours sincerely
Iris Murdoch

To Raymond Queneau.

Steeple Aston
2 August 1967

Queneau, listen, I may be in Paris in the second half of August (rather briefly with my mother). Will you be there? Not a chance, I fear. The French are never in Paris in August. You will be on some Italian shore. But let me know if by any chance you are there. I haven't seen you for a ridiculously long time for reasons which are not quite clear to me. *I would very much like to see you.* And if this August no good will come over in the autumn. I ask periodically: are you ever in London? and get no reply. I love you as much as ever, in a quiet encapsulated sort of a way.

I hope you are very well. Kreisel will be in Oxford for next term, which is good. Do write to me.

With love
Iris

To Raymond Queneau.

Steeple Aston
30 August 1967

Queneau, it was good to see you. Thank you very much for inviting me to Neuilly. I was very pleased indeed to meet your wife. (I would like to write to her: could you give me the Neuilly address?) And thanks for the drinks, and also for sending Foucault who arrived this morning.[1] I will comment, if I have any comment worth uttering. How does Thai[2] spell her name? I must come to Paris more often. With love to you

 I

My mother enormously enjoyed her visit.

To Philippa Foot, who had spent most of the summer in Oxford.

Steeple Aston
September 1967

My dear, have been away Wales/Dorset and just got your letter and am *so* sorry. I had pictured you far away beside a blue sea. I do hope you'll get away somehow before term – I mean at least to the sea or to some new place? What a rotten bloody ailment it is (John is very sympathetic – he had such a story and he says no one ever *believed* it was so bad!). I do hope you're feeling a little stronger now. Don't worry about next term – all that will look after itself when the time comes. You may well 'pick up' very fast as the spring unfolds. Be it so.

 It was very good seeing more of you last term and having you as a place to come to continually – indeed in a way you've always been that, though sometimes in a metaphysical sense. That sense will remain, but let us be realists too henceforth. I won't be around in first week of term I think – but will thereafter and will make a beeline for you. Dearest Philippa – get well soon. I embrace and love you.

 Your

 I

---

1 Michel Foucault (1926–84), influential French philosopher and historian of ideas. The book referred to was possibly *Les mots et les choses* (1966), published in English as *The Order of Things*.
2 Raymond Queneau's dog.

To Rachel Fenner.

Steeple Aston
9 September [1967]

My dear, forgive just a note in reply. Just going off for weekend chez Priestleys. Painted bricks[1] look rather good, I think. Re John, he knows you are faintly keen on me, but he's used to this sort of thing and doesn't worry! Hope you'll meet him. When applauding house I hadn't reflected on distance! (I never know where anywhere is, actually.) It *does* sound very nice – and I see Frank's point about Dudley Rd. (Living *inside one's own garden* is such a treat –) See you soon, dear child. Hope work OK. Don't fret. You are a philosophical creature really, though I know philosophy doesn't help much. Yet perhaps it helps a little. Much love

I

To Rachel Fenner.

Steeple Aston
[October 1967]

My dear child, thank you for your letter and for ringing up about it. Loving and being incarnate *is* a business. One is lucky to love, and to be loved. But I know one does want a perfect understanding, security, sense of communication, which is often (always!) lacking. One knows that anxiety and fuss is bad, yet one can't help being anxious, fussing . . . In fact I think you have been very marvellous to me and I am grateful. So do not apologise so much! We are, yes, unlike yet also like – I think I spotted the likeness when I first saw you. One day I might tell you more about it. *Have a lovely holiday* – and write to me.

Forgive this brief letter. Slave-driver Val May (who was with me when you rang) wants to start rehearsing on Monday, and has meanwhile altered the plot and demanded several new scenes![2]

Much much love,
my dear
I

---

1 Rachel Fenner had been left some money by an aunt and she and Frank were using it to buy a house. They intended to paint the brickwork.
2 Val May was directing *The Italian Girl*, which was to open in November at the Bristol Old Vic.

To Rachel Fenner

Steeple Aston
15 October [1967]

Thanks for your letter to Harcourt Terrace, and I'm glad 6 on Wednesday chez moi is OK. I have to be in SW11 over Albert Bridge at 8 p.m. so maybe you could drop me off on your way home? Thank you for kind words re asthma etc. I would indeed rely on you in all kinds of crises. Only I think there is no cause for alarm in this context: in fact the damn thing seems, in its mysterious way, to have departed again.

Try not to be exasperated with me and to feel resentment. As Wittgenstein says, things are as they are and happen as they do happen. Will can do very little here (except in terms of inhibiting cross reactions etc.!). I do feel you as 'younger' – I think one feels an age gap more with one's own sex. And it's especially easy for an older man to feel contemporary with a younger girl. I hope you're prepared to blunder on. You know that I am deeply attracted to you.

I would like to see some of your work soon. You must give me some more tutorials on space and stuff.

It's raining like hell here and the garden looks a pleasant wreck. Look after yourself, child. See you soon. Much love
I

To Brigid Brophy.

Steeple Aston
[October 1967]

Darling. Lucam 4.8. *Abscede a me, Satana.*[1] Excuse letter card. I have no stamps. Do hope all OK. Long time no hear. OK so you don't write to me. OK so I don't write to you. This could escalate. Let's make tiny effort not drift apart. [. . .]
Much love
I

1 St Luke's Gospel 4.8. Get thee behind me, Satan.

To Georg Kreisel who was soon to take up an Oxford Fellowship.

Steeple Aston
[late October 1967?]

My dear, thank you for your excellent letter. (I hope my cable also reached you OK. I never quite believe in cables. Yet how improbable the flight of letters is, when one thinks about it.) I was interested in what you said about Pamela[xxviii] (and touched by what you added to it re 'if' etc.) I think some-one's sheer confidence and grip can become a kind of grace (perhaps in both senses of this word) if one loves them. Then one can feed upon their being, without problems of communication. I suppose if one could take pleasure in God it would be of this kind.

Yes, I am very much a toucher and holder and slow savourer. This can divide people. (Though I don't think it divides us, your not being so.) I suspect this is connected with something very deep about sex. (You are possibly one of the few people I could really talk to about sex. I mean seriously.) (Remember how cross Hijab used to be because you talked about sex with Shah!) I can't divide friendship from love or love from sex – or sex from love etc. If I care for somebody I want to caress them. But, or rather and so, I am probably not at all normal sexually. I am not a lesbian, in spite of one or two unevents on that front; I am certainly strongly interested in men. But I don't think I really want normal heterosexual relations with them. (It's taken me a long time to find this out.) I think I am sexually rather odd, which is a male homosexual in female guise. (This is fairly evident from the novels where it is male queer relations which tend to carry the most force from the unconscious.) I doubt if Freud knew anything about me, though Proust knew about my male equivalent. I have never been much good at going to bed, though quite often in love. It was prob-ably these general considerations, and certainly *not* any lack of *envie*,[1] which prevented me from going to bed with you twenty years ago. (I regret this very much now.) (I have also a very strong irrational fear of pregnancy.) Indeed I desired you very much then and still do. But I am very incompe-tently organised sexually.

So I am jealous of Pamela and also perhaps envious of her. But neither jealous nor envious of your clever boy pupil (I suppose he is or was your pupil) with whom in a way I can much more easily identify myself. (Have you been, or might you go, to bed with him?) In a way, my relationship with you has always been that of a gifted pupil with a clever and admired teacher. And I fear you in the way in which a pupil might fear his teacher

1 Desire.

(though in other ways too.) (The pupil–teacher relation has always been very important to me – and I can put a good deal of emotion into either role.) (I don't think this has ever made me less efficient as either teacher or pupil.) And perhaps though this is complicated maybe to the point of being nonsensical, I love you as if I were a man. (Possible this *is* nonsensical. I'm not sure. It is something which, as Wittgenstein would put it, one feels inclined to say.)

I'm not sure why I suddenly say all this to you now. I might have said it to you any time (fairly recently) or not at all. Maybe it is matter of, something to do with, the degree of warmth in your letters. (This varies.) How very easily I can talk to you in a letter – and how spontaneously and naturally I feel towards you. And how tongue-tied and awkward I might be if you were here, especially if I could not touch you (e.g. because we were in a public place). That may be something to do with the above too.

My novel goes on.[1] The characters are now formed enough to be real and continuous company for me.

Yes, I think a holiday *would* help you and maybe more than you might expect. But not necessarily as long as six weeks. Even a week somewhere *quite else* would help. Write to me soon. Much love, dearest Kreisel.

I

To Brigid Brophy.

On train
[28 November 1967]

Dear girl thanks yours. Hope Paris was super and that you sold film to good advantage. (This train is swaying like mad – I am in the last carriage – I am not drunk.) I am very sorry Michael missed the Gallery. I am sure he will get it next time, if he still wants it.[2] I was betting on him against my old friend Hugh Scrutton.

Your last letter though very nice was a bit like one of those testimonials where you look for what is left *out*. You failed to say that Maureen liked me – perhaps she didn't. (I liked her.) Also failed to say it was super to see me (maybe it wasn't?) – that we hadn't met for ages etc. I am staggered at the speed with which that baroque monster you once spoke of has disappeared – or at any rate *apparently* dissolved as if it were made of meringue.

---

1 *The Nice and the Good.*
2 Michael Levey would become director of the National Gallery in 1973.

I am sorry about this. Time and space have always been problems, and the vacuum left by your departure has already been filled several times over (not by girls). I should be sorry if we could not try to continue, somehow, a close friendship. [. . .]

Love from

I

PART SIX:

Woman of Letters

January 1968 to December 1978

The ten years between 1968 and 1978 were extraordinarily productive. Murdoch wrote nine novels – almost a novel every year – and her letters from these years not only reveal the frantic pace at which she lived and worked but also her perpetual exhaustion. Many of the novels of this decade are set in London where Murdoch now had a small flat of her own, and the city's landmarks, its architecture and the River Thames function symbolically as powerful indicators of the inner life of her characters. Moral and philosophical concerns are creatively transformed into engaging plots that challenge her readers to understand the difficulties of negotiating sexual freedom; the ridding oneself of selfish desire and loving truthfully; the dangers of dealing with unbearable suffering; and finding the courage to confront the past and the certainty of chance and death. Because such issues were pertinent to the moral lives of readers, throughout these years her writing became increasingly self-aware, taking seriously the responsibility of the writer and the impact of her art.

The two books published at the end of the 1960s were written concurrently with her seminal philosophical essay, 'On "God" and "Good"', which was published in 1969. In it Murdoch suggests that the Good instead of God should be the object of a loving attention that will save us from the selfish egoism identified by Freud. These novels engage with the fundamental question she raises in *The Sovereignty of Good*: 'how can we make ourselves morally better?' Murdoch's answer is that the freedom we need is freedom from fantasy and the ability to *see* the world as it is, not through a cloud of egotistical delusion. She also argues in the same work that 'a moral philosophy in which the concept of love, so rarely mentioned now by philosophers, [should] once again be made central'. *The Nice and the Good* (1968) is a dazzling contrast to the darkness of its predecessor, *The Time of the Angels* (1966), but its apparent sense of liberation nonetheless harbours a caveat about the excesses of the sexual revolution. The 'nice' and the 'good' relate to Murdoch's picture of the human soul in tension between 'low Eros' and 'high Eros' – the 'nice' originates in the Freudian compulsions of the unenlightened mind; the 'good' comes from the Platonic desire for knowledge and God, and the ability to *see* that releases the prisoners from the cave. But Murdoch said that no one in *The Nice and the Good* was good and the novel tests and complicates the demands of her moral philosophy in its demonstration that love is more often than not too possessive and too driven by the mechanical, unthinking aspect of the psyche to be a place of vision.

Bruno's Dream followed in 1969 and was written when Murdoch was brooding on her own past and, in particular, grieving for her old Oxford friend, Frank Thompson. Now well over eighty, the terminally ill Bruno confronts the possibility that his entire life was lived in a fantasy world – Bruno's dream – and the book is a stern meditation on love, death, remorse and reconciliation. Water imagery saturates the book in the form of rain, the flooding Thames and copious tears, and together they are metaphors for the immersion in one's past and one's conscience that Murdoch may well have been negotiating herself at this time. Before Bruno dies he is enlightened and consoled: he realises that love 'was the only thing that existed' and that his dying has acted as a moral call to arms for the other characters, who should aspire to a consciousness that admits a sober awareness of the effects of their actions on others. Nonetheless, the book also carries a paradoxical celebration of self-interested hedonism that wisely makes the most of the present moment, indicating that self-indulgence sometimes brings virtue, rather than evil, in its wake. Moral seriousness, in this book, is both invited and gently mocked.

Critics have discerned the presence of Elias Canetti in the enchanter figure of Julius King in *A Fairly Honourable Defeat* (1970). While Murdoch's letters to Canetti reveal his enduring fascination for her, the satanic Julius displays some sinister character traits. She returns to the idea that goodness deadens while evil fascinates, and the defeat referred to in the title is the triumph of evil over good. The book appears to concur with Julius's view that any human relationship can be broken; the exception is the only homosexual relationship in the novel, which is also the only one to survive Julius's evil machinations. The character of Julius is counterbalanced by a Christ figure, Tallis Browne, an example of humility and grace. But Julius finds Tallis, who lives in muddle and squalor, ineffectual and disappointing.

If the tendency toward predictability is the distinguishing psychological trait of this book, the next, *An Accidental Man* (1971), switches focus to the counterforce of contingency and attests to the randomness of life. This is the first of Murdoch's novels not to be organised into parts or chapters and the plot is advanced by blocks of letters and anonymous cocktail-party chatter which reflect various relationships and entertain the reader with rapid-fire wit and humour. The accidental man of the title, Austin Gibson Grey, invites his own bad luck and others thrive on his discomfort; sympathy and *Schadenfreude* form a potent mix. The universality of this trait and the extremity of Austin's misfortune render the book uncanny and farcical. Contingency is the dominating force; 'bad luck', says one character, 'is a sort of wickedness in some people'. An interwoven serious theme is the political dimension of the Vietnam War, including conscription and conscientious objection, with which Murdoch's mind was much occupied at this time, and cameos of stark horror are juxtaposed against the fast-moving comedic storyline.

As they move into the 1970s the novels continue to echo Murdoch's current philosophical pursuits and her relationships with certain friends and lovers. *The Black Prince* (1973), which some critics think is Murdoch's finest novel, won the James Tait Black Memorial Prize in November of that year. Overtly intellectual in its sophisticated meditations on art, love and truth, *The Black Prince* is a metafiction that engages with the aesthetic and moral considerations of storytelling; it is also a rigorous interrogation of the status of art and of Murdoch's own ambitions as a writer. The book contains the most sustained attempt in her fiction to describe the change in consciousness occasioned by falling in love, which she saw as a significant and life-changing experience. Her first-person narrator, Bradley Pearson, himself a writer, complains that although love is 'frequently mentioned in literature, it is rarely adequately described'; Murdoch rises to the challenge by vividly describing Bradley's feelings when he falls in love with his twenty-year-old god-daughter Julian Baffin. This is still a contentious novel that challenges contemporary highly theorised approaches to reading literary works, in particular those deconstructionist and post-structuralist readings of fiction that identify literary texts as sites of plurality of meaning that render authorial intent irrelevant. While Murdoch understood and agreed that no work of art can ever fully represent truth, she did believe that it could point towards it.

The Sacred and Profane Love Machine (1974) won the Whitbread Literary Award for Fiction in that year and Murdoch's novels continued to test the demands of 'unselfing' and the renunciation of the ego that lie at the heart of her moral philosophy. Not only the nature of goodness but also the nature of courage now seem to preoccupy her, and a tension emerges between action and motive in this book, which is one of Murdoch's most bleak analyses of the human capacity for self-delusion. Moral vision can too easily be tainted by the allure of sadomasochism, and heroism is often no more than self-aggrandisement; in this novel the difference between them is very difficult to identify. *The Sacred and Profane Love Machine* is unsettling too in its moral ambivalence: mere self-aggrandisement saves others, while denial of the ego induces a dangerous repression that can be murderous.

A Word Child (1975) was written against a background of industrial unrest and political violence and the novel brings issues of underprivilege in society into unusually stark relief, enlarging the range of social classes Murdoch habitually portrays. Hilary Burde, the novel's first-person narrator, is a case in point; his wretched experiences in a children's home result in psychological damage that ultimately distorts his personality and wrecks his career. The book also draws upon the tale of Peter Pan and features the statue of 'the sinister boy' in Kensington Gardens in its plot. Both the tale and the statue suggest troubling sexualised representations of the child, and point to Murdoch's remarkably sophisticated understanding of the links between damaged childhoods and adult sexual and emotional dysfunction.

The later novels of this decade draw on Shakespeare and in 1977 Murdoch spoke of a move from the light-heartedness of her earlier novels to a greater calm that had come with age.[i] *Henry and Cato* was published in 1976, when Murdoch's status as a writer of international acclaim was recognised by the award of the CBE (Commander of the Order of the British Empire). Murdoch thought at this point that her work had become more serious and certainly her novels are marked by the deepening mysticism that accompanies her later investigations into the survival of good in a godless world. They also become longer as she worries less about the constraints of form. In *Henry and Cato* Murdoch explores ways in which the ego intensifies illusion but also, in times of persecution, enables endurance. The saintly Brendan Craddock, whose wisdom owes much to Buddhism, understands that 'our chief illusion is our conception of ourselves, of our importance which must not be violated, our dignity which must not be mocked. All our resentment follows from this illusion'. But at the same time such illusions are necessary for survival, and it can be dangerous to strip oneself of more than one is ready to do without.

These ten years ended on a high note with the award of the prestigious Booker Prize in October 1978 for *The Sea, The Sea*. Its paranoid first-person narrator, Charles Arrowby, is obsessed with his first love, Hartley, unaware that the emotion is a psychological decoy to distract him from grieving over the death of his long-time lover, Clement Makin. In what is perhaps Murdoch's most sustained attempt to extend the boundaries of language to more accurately portray the inner life, she confronts the thorny questions about human consciousness on which she brooded in her philosophy, for example, how far consciousness relates to time and how far mental concepts could be represented in sentences. She believed that novelists and poets could more easily suggest the outer edges of consciousness than philosophers because they can find suitable metaphors to make these features visible. The sea itself is the central symbol for the amorphous quality of the human mind, continuously in flux, and the entire aesthetic surface of the novel conveys information about Charles's inner life, unknown even to himself. *The Sea, The Sea* also furthers Murdoch's understanding of Buddhism as an antidote to such delusion and an alternative to Christianity as a route to morality and spirituality. Murdoch once said that there was something of her own Buddhist sympathies in James Arrowby, Charles's cousin, who is advanced on the path of enlightenment and has relinquished the ego. James is the moral centre of the novel and readers will recognise the wisdom in his sound advice to Charles. But even his moral goodness is tainted, and while the formulation of a distinctive moral philosophy is reflected in Murdoch's fiction, her novels increasingly demand that it should not be unthinkingly assimilated. The achievement of this novel lies in its humorous rendering of delusion, the poignancy of its suffering, and the sheer brilliance of its expansion of the novel form. It fully deserved the accolades it received.[ii]

Publications in philosophy included 'Existentialists and Mystics: A Note on the Novel in the New Utilitarian Age' published in *Essays and Poems Presented to Lord David Cecil* edited by Wallace Robson (1970), 'Salvation by Words' (1972) and *The Sovereignty of Good* (1970),[iii] in which Murdoch developed and refined her ideas of the last ten years. The book's central question, 'Can we make ourselves morally better?',[iv] encapsulates her conviction that moral philosophy can and should be of practical value – an approach markedly different from the mainstream thought of her time. In February 1976 Murdoch gave the Romanes Lecture in Oxford and spoke on 'Why Plato Banished the Artists'. In the published version of this lecture, *The Fire and the Sun: Why Plato Banished the Artists* (1977), Murdoch argues against Plato who, although prepared to tolerate artists, was harshly critical of them. For Murdoch art and morals were always synonymous: 'Art indeed, so far from being a playful diversion of the human race, is the place of its most fundamental insights, and the centre to which the more uncertain steps of metaphysics must constantly return'.[v] Her formulation of a distinctive moral philosophy is reflected, as we have seen, in her novels, although they increasingly reflect her fears for its efficacy.

The stage version of *The Italian Girl*, written with James Saunders, transferred from Bristol to Wyndham's Theatre, London in February 1968 where it opened to mixed reviews and ran for five months only. Having reread all of Shakespeare's plays between 1965 and 1969 and despite being unsure of her talent as a playwright, Murdoch spent the whole of 1969 writing drama, which included *Joanna, Joanna*, a play that was never performed although its plot fed into *A Word Child*.[vi] *The Servants and the Snow* ran for three weeks at the Greenwich Theatre in London in September 1970 but was poorly received. *The Three Arrows* opened at the Arts Theatre in Cambridge in October 1972 with Ian McKellen in the lead but was also poorly received and ran for less than a month. At this time Murdoch saw drama as 'a public form of poetry'[vii] in which she could explore further her philosophical interest in the concepts of freedom and sovereignty.

Her insistence on the freedom of the individual translated into political action when she became involved in the campaign for the release of Vladimir Bukovsky, a Soviet dissident who had protested against the psychiatric imprisonment of political prisoners. He was released in 1976 at which point he moved to the UK. It is possible that Murdoch was at this time trying to get back in touch with her political self which had been re-energised by the explosion of student political activism in Europe between 1968 and 1972.[viii] However, she grew increasingly ambivalent about such activism. On the one hand, along with Richard Wollheim and Frank Kermode, she publicly expressed solidarity in May 1968 with the students in Paris who were violently protesting, alongside many workers, against the values of capitalism, consumerism and traditional institutions. She also wrote to *The Times*, defending the right of the student protester Daniel Cohn-Bendit to visit England. On the other hand, she found a student sit-in at the Clarendon Building in Oxford in February 1970 disturbing and 'somehow nasty'.[ix] While in favour of the many social and legal changes enacted during the 1960s – in particular the decriminalisation of homosexuality – she was deeply concerned by the erosion of authority the decade brought about.

Murdoch's increasingly high profile as a novelist resulted in many invitations to lecture in the UK and abroad, and in requests for interviews by journals, newspapers and academics. During these ten years, often under the auspices of the British Council, she travelled to Italy, Switzerland, Mexico, Greece, Egypt, Poland, Japan, Israel, Austria and the USA. The Bayleys also continued to take holidays abroad (frequently in Italy and France) and still enjoyed staying with their old friends in Dorset and Scotland. From 1973 they spent two weeks each year in the summer with Stephen and Natasha Spender at their house near Maussane-les-Alpilles in Provence. Having given up her Harcourt Terrace flat, Murdoch rented Flat 4, 62 Cornwall Gardens, South Kensington in 1970; in 1972 she bought the top flat at no. 29 at the opposite end of the square. Murdoch would often spend three days a week in London, while John Bayley worked at home in Steeple Aston.

Two friends whom she loved and greatly admired were lost in these years: Eduard Fraenkel committed suicide following the death of his wife in February 1970, and Raymond Queneau died in 1976. This time was also darkened by the beginning of her mother's mental decline during the summer of 1975. Reconciliation with Arnaldo Momigliano in February 1977, after an estrangement of twenty years, offered some comfort. A revival of her old friendship with Leo Pliatzky led to some tension in 1968 and to a decision, on Murdoch's part, to keep the relationship strictly platonic in future. She kept in touch with David Morgan, though her growing impatience with him becomes increasingly evident in her letters. She remained fond of Rachel Fenner, although after the mid-1970s, by which time Fenner had two small children, she and Murdoch exchanged letters less frequently and communicated mainly by telephone.

Murdoch and Brigid Brophy managed to remain friends, as the cheerful notes of 1968 illustrate. However, a difficult meeting between the two women in February 1970 resulted in a period of strained silence. By 1972 they had re-established their friendship and from then on met occasionally in London, often in the autumn, and communication by letter was restored. Brophy's health began to decline in the 1970s and Murdoch often expresses concern for her well-being.

Philippa Foot was now based in the United States for much of each year, having resigned from her Oxford tutorial fellowship in 1969, although she remained a research fellow at Somerville until 1988. She taught at various institutions, including MIT, the University of California at Berkeley, Cornell University and the University of California at Los Angeles, where she finally settled as a full professor in 1976. In 1988 UCLA appointed her as the first Griffin Professor of Philosophy. However, during most spring and summer vacations she would return to Oxford where she stayed in a house in Walton Street.[x] Murdoch and Foot had a brief physical affair during the spring and summer of 1968 but by mutual agreement they soon resumed their friendship in the form of a deep and lasting bond that continued until Murdoch's death. It was perhaps the most enduring and significant friendship of her life.

Murdoch established new friendships too – some of them conducted mainly through letters – including those with Scott Dunbar and Naomi and Albert Lebowitz. She had met Dunbar, a young gay Canadian who was then writing a thesis on philosophy and religion at King's College, London when she was teaching at the RCA. His return to Canada, where he found work as a teacher in Montreal, was followed by a correspondence with Murdoch in which they explored their shared interest in art, theology and gay rights.[xi] Her continued love of painting is also evident in her letters to Harry Weinberger, an artist whose German–Jewish refugee past fascinated her and to whom she was introduced in France in 1977 by the Spenders. This friendship offered her another opportunity to become a patron of art; she wrote introductions to the catalogues for two of his exhibitions and she spent some of her Booker Prize money on his paintings.[xii] Murdoch and John Bayley met the Lebowitzes when visiting the USA in April 1972; they found they had much in common with both Albert, an attorney who wrote fiction in his spare time, and Naomi, a professor of English and comparative literature at Washington University, who had published *The Imagination of Loving: Henry James's Legacy To The Novel* (1965), *Humanism and the Absurd in the Modern Novel* (1971) and *Italo Svevo* (1978).

These ten years marked a shift in Murdoch's sensibilities. Intense interest in, or obsession with, a few individuals was gradually replaced by more relaxed relationships with a range of friends. This rather changed perspective on life is also suggested by many letters that reflect her lively and increased interest in current affairs and world events. John Bayley is often mentioned too, as if she had finally grown into the idea of being married; it would appear that she no longer needed to compartmentalise her life. In a letter to Georg Kreisel written in June 1974, she commented: 'I agree about cohabiting. I couldn't imagine before I got married how it was possible. In that if one is (happily) married the other person just becomes a part of one's being and it's as good as being alone. (Being unhappily married I should think is top-grade hell.)' Indeed, letters in this section mark Murdoch's growing affection for her husband and a compatibility that enriched both their lives.

To Rachel Fenner.

Steeple Aston
[early 1968]

My dear, thank you very much for yours. God it is super here today! Quite deep snow and sun. Saw such a lovely big fox playing in the snow. [. . .]

Re your sad prognostications I can't see quite clearly here (I mean can't see you). The degree of your prophetic sadness surprises me in a way. You are young and beautiful and talented. Why should things not be wonderful for you? (You say 'Yah!' to that I expect!) One can't foresee the *good* things too. (A queerish married friend of mine aged forty has just fallen very happily in love with a girl, and now lives in two establishments.) (She is well off enough to do that.) (Not that I'd recommend this actually. Her husband is very tolerant. But then Frank doesn't apparently mind so much about the girls either?)

I wonder if you should meet more lesbians! (This I believe is called 'making the scene'.) I could put you in touch with some of the reigning figures in the London 'scene'.[1] (There are a lot of giggling asses, but some nice people.)

---

1 Murdoch knew the London lesbian milieu and was to have a brief but important relationship with Esme Langley, one of its key figures, in 1969.

Maybe this is no solution and maybe there *isn't* a solution. *I hope* you will feel later that you want children. This needn't be a 'bourgeois' development though!

This letter is unsatisfactory. I do 'feel' your predicament and do sympathise deeply. And it is little use to talk of hypothetical joys to someone who is in pain. I think we are knowing each other better?

Much love

I

To Frank Paluka at the University of Iowa.

Steeple Aston
13 January 1968

Dear Mr Paluka,

I have sent off to you by air mail a piece of the first, and corresponding piece of the second, draft of *The Bell*. And also the bit of *Under the Net* manuscript which I have found, which I think is an earlier draft of the one you have. Three envelopes. *The Bell* first draft notebook has a unique feature – some comments and suggestions by my husband! I'm afraid he soon gave that up though. The first and second drafts of the other novels are on exactly the same pattern as *The Bell*, except that some of the later ones contain rather more rewriting at the first draft stage, and more legible variants at the second draft stage. Let me know if you would like another instalment.

All good wishes –
Iris Murdoch

To Rachel Fenner.

Steeple Aston
15 February 1968

Rachel, thanks for your letter. I am sorry about these moods but what can one do? I know of such things too. We are born to sorrow. And you are not the only one in whom things 'do not fit'. I suspect it is a general human condition. (Before writing this letter I was reading Shakespeare's sonnets: there's a chap who suffered.)

You know that I love you, and in no trivial sense. Don't feel that I could be offended – I respect and value all that you feel, and you must just try to forgive my involuntary lack of 'response' in so far as it annoys you at times. We are hopelessly muddled and imperfect animals – I mean the lot of us – even Shakespeare.

Thank God for art.

Much love

I

To Rachel Fenner.

Steeple Aston
[late February/early March 1968]

Thank you, darling girl, for your detached letter. You are super! [. . .]

I am finding the *War Requiem*[1] marvellous. I have played it over now a number of times. At first it rather bothered me to have two things I know so well – the requiem mass and those Wilfred Owen poems, suddenly joined together. But now it seems right. I can't 'understand' (whatever that means) all the music yet but I am definitely with most of it. The 'Dies Irae' (one of my favourite poems) always seems to inspire good music. (Like some objects in painting which rarely miss – *The Annunciation* and *Noli me tangere*.) *Tuba Mirum*[2] with guns and bugles is very dramatic. Altogether you have given me a marvellous present. (I think I will appoint you my musical adviser: you can recommend records to me at intervals.)

I finished the Lots Road Power Station novel[3] just before Christmas. I am toying with the beginning of another, but am rather tied up with a philosophy job.[4] [. . .]

Regards to Natasha,[5] I hope she didn't catch any birds.

See soon, dear child. Write.

Much love

I

To David Morgan.

4 March 1968

1 By Benjamin Britten.
2 Part of the Requiem Mass.
3 *Bruno's Dream.*
4 Probably essays for *The Sovereignty of Good.*
5 Rachel Fenner's cat.

David, I have had no confirming note from you, as requested by my postcard. Please turn up at Harcourt Terrace tomorrow, Tuesday March 5 at 6 p.m. when a party is being given *entirely for your benefit*!

    Love I

NB please do not get too drunk!

To David Morgan.

early March 1968

David dear, thanks for yours. I'm glad you enjoyed the party. (One of the guests stole a bottle of gin incidentally.) Generosity is over for the moment. I'm sure you needn't worry about your suit. Trust to your intelligent face. (I've written you a damn good testimonial.) *Best of luck.* [. . .]

    Very best wishes and love

    I

To Leo Pliatzky, written shortly before Murdoch set off on a British Council lecture tour of Switzerland and Italy.

Steeple Aston
[10 March 1968]

Leo, I haven't seen you all term for reasons which I will explain when I next see you. (Nothing sinister or directly to do with you.) *Forgive me.* You are such a very old and dear friend that in fact I am quite confident of being forgiven. (I hope rightly.) I would like to talk to you *at length* (I wish you were more of a *talker*!). I'm going to Zurich on Tues to give a lecture and then on to Italy to give other ones, and will be back about April 6. I will get in touch with you early next term. Be well, my dear and think kindly of me. I value your friendship and support and will call you then. *This to send love.* I

To Rachel Fenner.

Venice
31 March [1968]

[. . .] Venice is super – sunny, *empty,* and Oh God the pictures (+ churches etc. etc.). And what a damn relief not to have any more lectures. Actually it's the social life that kills one. Have met 10,000 or so Italians, all of whom propose to visit us in Oxford.

I am homesick though. (Heard English schoolmaster in square today quoting 'Oh to be in England'[1] etc. to his little charges, and nearly wept.) Still, Venice is Venice and the eating and drinking is OK too. Be seein' ya kid. Look after self. [. . .]

Much love and respects to cat

I

To Brigid Brophy.

Steeple Aston
[27? April 1968]

My dear girl, thank you so much for your motel letter and also for the splendidly chauvinistic St Patrick's day greetings! Perhaps I could celebrate the beginning of term by meeting you? Could I come in for a drink on the morning of Wednesday May 1st? I might even bring a bottle of non-vintage champagne.

With love

I

To Philippa Foot.

Steeple Aston
28 April 1968

Sorry about Tues. This coming week is not much good. I'll very shortly suggest a date in the next week. Meanwhile, I'd like a kind word by letter if you don't mind.

Not that I really imagine that after nearly thirty years' service I'm at all likely to be sacked. I attempt to be rational. (Rational? What's that?)

Much love

I

1 From Robert Browning's 'Home Thoughts, from Abroad', written in 1845.

To Philippa Foot.

Steeple Aston
[early May 1968]

Thanks for that letter, I needed it. [. . .]

I feel this too about you, that I can't link expression and emotion, and that no expression seems quite easy, adequate, right. It's odd how awkward we are with each other after all these years. The emotion is very great and very deep and the name of it is certainly love. (In a way I am afraid of you, and your sense of this may make you nervous. As I am so masochistic the fear and the love are consubstantial. There is almost a problem of *style* here.)

I'll be in London Tuesday to Thursday this week, and if replying at once could you write to 59 Harcourt Terrace SW10 and, darling, write *legibly* on the envelope! I can't think how any of your letters reach their destinations.

Yours, dear heart,
with much love
I

To Leo Pliatzky.

Steeple Aston
[early May 1968]

Leo my dear, term will shortly be in operation and I would like to see you. I hope things are OK. The Italian journey was very fantastic: will tell you of it.

Could you manage lunch on Wednesday May 15, 1 p.m. chez moi (or in town if you prefer)? Let me know (to Steeple Aston).

Much love to you
I

To Leo Pliatzky.

Steeple Aston
[mid/late May 1968]

How absolutely splendid that I have made you angry. I must devise other ways of angering you in the future. Maybe I could provoke you into beating me. (I hope your secretary isn't reading this: if she is it will make her day.)

Anyway I have received a very alive letter from you at last. Use your intelligence, Pliatzky. (You are supposed to have quite a lot.) Of course I don't want you to wear your heart on your sleeve about . . . etc. (credit me with some sensibility) and as for disingenuousness, I see no occasion for this between us. Indeed I feel and am grateful for your frankness. Surely it should be clear what I mean, in the given case, by *talk* – as opposed to, say, action. Because of various things which are muddling to the mind – well anyway to my mind – I just haven't communicated with you enough. I can't act without talking. The structure of our friendship, though age-old and I venture to feel indestructible, hasn't been enough filled in. There is not enough detail and we have not sufficiently got the 'feel' of each other. Or so I think. And I know this is partly my fault. I will try to explain more when I see you. Meanwhile, you must just try to forgive my difficultness. Could I have an answer to this letter please?

To Philippa Foot, written at the beginning of what was to be a very brief sexual relationship, apparently initiated by Murdoch, who seems to have felt that moving the relationship onto a more physical plane would remove any remaining emotional barriers between them.[xiii]

Steeple Aston
May 1968

I very much want to write to you, and yet don't find it at all easy. An unusual situation for me. In fact unique. Normally desire to communicate (in this medium) means ability to. I suppose this is lucky. Indeed you are *sui generissima*.[1] I am haunted by images of you. When was I not, but now there are new ones. How can I express what I feel. You have for me something which is almost a taboo quality, though this isn't quite it. Numinous certainly. I don't understand it myself, and feel very at sea, though not unhappily so. I am very glad about recent events. In some kinds of relationship I think I probably *want* to fear the other person, so do not be made anxious by my abjection. (Does this word exist? It is rather expressive.) Or by anything else here: and I will try not be anxious either. Time and space will never be easy. (Sorry about *space* the other day!) It's odd talking to you in a letter, as if it were some completely new and strange mode of communication, something just invented by physicists and scarcely imaginable. I'll write again soon. *Much love.*

---

1 A play on '*sui generis*', meaning 'of its own kind', i.e. unique.

To Philippa Foot.

Steeple Aston
[May 1968]

[. . .] I am an indefatigable letter-writer and you will probably get a lot of these communications. I am pretty good at conversation by letter actually. (But I think this is not one of your natural activities.) I have in fact only once corresponded with anyone (now departed from my life) who was as good at writing letters as I am. However writing to you is bloody difficult. It feels like a kind of *task*. Don't start at this word. I am glad that you should set me tasks. You bring out the Dr Masoch[1] in me to a remarkable degree, as I have already said.

Will make spatio-temporal suggestions soon. Meanwhile could you let me know to 59 Harcourt Terrace SW10 about Thursdays?
Much love
I

To Philippa Foot.

25 May 1968

Thanks yours of today. Could I stay night of Tues June 4? I think your occasionally coming to London is good idea too. It's raining and I can't work. Why am I not more like Shakespeare? Much love.
I

To Philippa Foot.

Steeple Aston
27 May 1968

[. . .] I will follow instructions re Thursday, appearing circa 1 [p.m.] I go to London tomorrow.

The novel[2] is moving a little. I am getting terribly fond of my wicked

---

1 Leopold von Sacher-Masoch (1836–95), Austrian writer whose short stories explored sexual perversions and fetishes and from whose name the term 'masochism' derives.
2 *A Fairly Honourable Defeat.*

man and find myself instinctively attenuating his wickedness.¹ There is a good man in the book too. And naturally these two have to love each other. Oh dear. Can this be right?

Much love

I

To Rachel Fenner, written after Murdoch had attended a Royal Academy dinner on 31 May.

[early June 1968]

Rachel dear, it was very kind of you to ferry me into town on Wednesday. And it was nice to be able to continue our conversation with Mr Skeaping. (I forgot to tell you I had my hand kissed by Ralph Richardson, so it was quite an evening!) (Also, flirtation with Yehudi Menuhin. My musical friends say he is no good at the fiddle, but he has such a beautiful face.)

About the other thing, try not to worry, kid. Human life is on the whole an awful muddled incomplete arrangement and it's bloody hard to communicate with other people at all. Any close association is almost certain to involve pain, and as often as not more bloody pain than pleasure. (What am I saying! This is supposed to be a letter to cheer you up! I feel in rather a grim mood this morning.) I expect by now work and the general compulsory movement of life may have made things better. I do hope so!

Next week: I'm not coming up till Thursday, which I know is not so good for you. I wonder if you would be free by 6 on Friday? Suggest drink then Harcourt – and if you could convey me after to the French Institute? (8 p.m.) I wonder if that would be possible? (I arrive Thurs afternoon and leave Saturday morning.)

I wish my own work would pick up. I feel a bloody useless member of the human race just now.

Much love

I

To Brigid Brophy, written on paper headed 'Worth Abbey, Crawley, Sussex'.

Steeple Aston
[19 June 1968]

1 Presumably Julius King. In 1976 Murdoch was to state that the 'book is a theological myth [. . .] Julius King is of course Satan and Tallis [Browne] is a Christ figure'.ˣⁱᵛ

No, have not yet taken veil. Have just been telling the Benedictines what is what. Sorry not write. Have had rather awful week complete with student's suicide attempt (unsuccessful) and repeated loss of handbag (got back OK). Feel wreck, lunatic etc. Will telephone you next week and hope soon see. [. . .]

Au revoir and best love
I

To Raymond Queneau.

Steeple Aston
[13 June 1968]

Thank you, *fidèle ami*, for the beautiful book of poems – they give intense pleasure. I admire you very much.

The sun shines on Steeple Aston (it really does for once), I try to work in an intoxicating atmosphere of honeysuckle. I grow older.

I hope your life is well, and that very enchanting little dragon masquerading as a dog. I often think of you in Paris, but somehow my feet are usually set in other directions. I hope to be in Czechoslovakia this summer, and later in Italy. If I am likely to be in Paris I'll let you know. I'd love to meet you in London one day. [. . .]

This with my thanks and many thoughts and as always, my love
Iris

To The Times.

Steeple Aston
14 June 1968

Sir, Danny Cohn-Bendit[1] is not a criminal, and what he has to say, whether we agree with it or not, is interesting and important.

Why all this undignified fuss about admitting him to our country? What has happened to the nation in whose museum reading room Karl Marx worked unmolested?

Yours faithfully,
IRIS MURDOCH

---

1 A student at the University of Nanterre who was a prominent leader of the student protests in Paris in May 1968.

To Philippa Foot.

Steeple Aston
16 June [1968]

Sometimes I feel I have to *invent* a language to talk to you in, though my heart is very full of very definite things to say. You stir some very deep part of my soul. Be patient with me and don't be angry with my peculiarities. I love you so much. I

To Philippa Foot.

Steeple Aston
[June 1968]

Thanks for your letter. You may be right that there is something really ferocious there and this is what I am *really* afraid of! The fantasy part is important however both in itself (it is a fact) and possibly because it shadows and *perhaps* mitigates whatever the other thing is. Only there is all the world of difference between being punished in fantasy and being hurt in real life. I feel deeply puzzled here in a unique way.

I know my not being around is unnerving, but this absence-existence is really inevitable because of a number of factors – living in the country, what looking after John is like, my commitments in London and partly of course your timetable. I think it is better to be resigned to this at the start (what am I saying? The start was in 1939. It's just that we are slow workers!). I very much do not want us to be made too *anxious* by this. That mustn't be. I think I am probably better at absence than you are. I have had and indeed have an awful lot of it in my life. And I can live in letters. Though letters to you are quite peculiarly difficult. I think we must not feel this as a drama. We have *had* drama. And as we have known each other so long I think we can dispense with it now. We live in some odd dimension in relation to each other I think. Or is it just that I have *thought* about you so much, and often at times when I did not conceive of any real relation to you?

I go to London tomorrow. I may ring up Wednesday. I wish I could cope with the telephone! I think of you with much love, with deep love –
    I

PS John's mother is ill again – she has cancer of the breast. (This kind *can* be cured I think.) J may come up to London this week if he can get away, and altogether movements are very uncertain at the moment and have to be left fluid. But I will communicate – and will write *regularly* though not always from London. Please write to me at Harcourt Terrace. I want to be reassured. There are terrible things in the world.

To Georg Kreisel.

Steeple Aston
23 June 1968

[. . .] Your letter interested me as always. People are enormously different from each other, and one discovers this slowly, their amazingness and one's own singularity. I used to think most people were just like me. You are right of course that it is not so simple – and one tends to dramatise and simplify in one's conception of oneself – not necessarily even for deep reasons but because this is amusing. Sex is something very very diffused for me – this is certainly true – and so any one image of how it is, is likely to be misleading. I cannot think really of any corner of the universe where it is not, for me, present. It even gets into philosophy in a general way, though not into the details. (I mean, it is connected with *what* interests me, though I think not with how I work.) I know things are different for you. But it does surprise me that you don't connect *wit* with sex. Some Frenchman, asked his idea of paradise, said '*discuter les idées générales avec les femmes supérieures*'.[1] I think, *mutatis mutandis*, that might be mine. This isn't really a letter. I am very busy, with visitors coming, and wanted to respond at once. Write to me again soon and tell me of the things that are troubling you. I like talking to you, and writing these letters is not a sexless activity either. The gods be with you. Much love, beautiful one.

PS I saw John Wisdom in Cambridge last week. He spoke warmly of you.

To Philippa Foot.

Steeple Aston
23 June [1968]

My dear, feeling rather distracted. John's mother and brother are here this weekend. The operation is probably on Wednesday and I think I must be in London for the whole of the middle of the week. (J has to go up anyway

---

1 To discuss ideas with highly intelligent women.

on Tuesday.) I will keep you posted with moves. It was slightly weird seeing you at the party.

Someone lately told me that my mode of being is diffused in time, that I am always partly in the past and the future and not here. I suppose this to some extent true of anyone. But I feel it corresponds rather specially to a lot of my sensations, and perhaps results (in your sensitive perception) in the entire absence of visual presence!

I am feeling depressed. Hope to see you soon and will write. Much much love

I

To Philippa Foot.

Steeple Aston
25 June [1968]

Just to send love. I feel rather depressed and lost at the moment. I nearly rang you on Monday and asked to see you, but decided I *must* give the day to work, as it was the only possible one for some time past and future, and if I don't work I get crazy. I'll keep you posted with moves. I'm not sure how long I'll be in London, it depends on how J's mother is. I think of you with *much love*, and wish I could see you and be reassured, as I always am, by your presence.

I

Have you been reading about Lawrence in the *Sunday Times*? My heart bleeds for him. And it shows that even being Winston Churchill's friend doesn't stop you from falling out of the bottom of our lousy society!¹
PS I believe you met Scott!² I'm so glad. I was just going to introduce you to him chez John when John Simopolous bore him off.

To Philippa Foot.

Steeple Aston
26 June 1968

1 In 1968 Philip Knightley and Colin Simpson published a series of articles on T. E. Lawrence in the *Sunday Times*. Drawing on his private papers, they suggested that, while in the ranks, Lawrence had taken part in sadomasochistic acts.
2 Scott Dunbar, Canadian student at King's College, London.

Darling, thank you for your excellent letter. This is just to say I hope I may see you sometime on this coming Friday. Have just tried to telephone you. Life fundamentally very good. Fear is morally bad.

Help! and *much* love

I

To Philippa Foot, written from John and Patsy Grigg's house in Scotland, where Murdoch and John Bayley stayed for a week at the beginning of July.

'Guisachan'
Inverness
8 July 1968

My dear, I hope this letter will somehow reach you. I had forgotten the beauty of this place. The highlands are a vast *rock garden* – hundreds of kinds of tiny things flower – and the variety of the woodland – it has no horrible Schwarzwald [1] look. Much walking has been done and a little swimming – but it's damn cold. Not a soul – in many days of walking have met no one, and seen no one over those vast hillsides. (There are about four houses within some miles of here where forestry men live.)

I've tried to work and done a little – but the novel is rather stuck. I've learnt to play *vingt-et-un*.[2] I wish I wasn't always so *anxious*. Do you suffer from chronic anxiety? I think not. It is a vice, a form of deep fear.

I'd like to talk to you about this sometime. I hope you have shaken off the shades of term.

Write to me. [. . .]

Much love

I

To David Beams, an American student.

Steeple Aston
17 September 1968

Dear Mr Beams,

Thank you very much for your kind letter and for sending me your piece on *The Bell*. I hope you will forgive me for not replying in detail. It is difficult

1 Black Forest.
2 The French name for the card game blackjack.

to read about oneself and one's judgement on such writings may not be the best one. I very much liked what you have written, and as far as I can see you seem to be on the right track. How much there is 'in' a book is something which the author, for better or worse, may simply not know, and I do not feel that I can comment except in general. About Simone Weil: I don't myself think that *The Bell* is deeply influenced by her and I'm not even *quite* sure that I had read her at that time. I had certainly not studied her, as I did later. (And later novels *are* influenced by her.)

I think the idea of coupling *Bell* and *Unicorn* and the Leslie Stephen lecture is a good one. I hope you will enjoy the study. (Though I do rather feel you ought to be studying Shakespeare or Jane Austen!) I do hope that you will write to me again later, and if there are any *specific* questions about the novels which you would like to ask I should be very happy to try to answer them. Thank you for your interest in my work –

With all good wishes

Yours sincerely

Iris Murdoch

To Philippa Foot.

Steeple Aston
6 October 1968

My dear, thank you for your letter which cheered me up quite inordinately. I will very shortly suggest an evening for soon. Indeed I will tell you anything you want to know – there has never never been enough talking time. Much love.

Your devoted

I

To Leo Pliatzky, requesting information that would help Murdoch with the detail of A Fairly Honourable Defeat.

[6 October 1968]

My dear, after careful reflection I feel I don't really want to go on meeting you on your terms and trust that you will consent to meet me on mine. However, I trust in any case that I may come and see you now in Whitehall! Could I come in a bit before 6 on Wed next (Oct 9)? [. . .]

Don't forget your homework. I want

(a) Brief description of desk and in-tray covering coloured folders etc.
(b) One or two topics, names of committees etc. – these could be fictitious so long as plausible. Some funny bureaucrat.

Hope see you soon. Your very old friend, I

To Philippa Foot.

Steeple Aston
22 October 1968

My dear, I am an absolute pig and deserve to be [. . .] – I am no better than the swinish heroine of my current novel who is so concerned with analysing her own feelings she does not notice the sufferings of others.[1] (She has oddly enough a censorious older sister of whom she is afraid: *tiens*!) [. . .]

You have been active lately in my dreams where you have acquired a somewhat Branwell-like younger brother whom you and Marion[2] (who also figures) refer to as 'the Dauphin'. Also a Françoise-like retainer called 'Edith' whose speciality is chicken stuffed with honey. How terribly odd one's mind is!

Give my love to the Dauphin if by any chance you are writing to that rather delinquent youth.

Much love to you
Your
I

To Philippa Foot.

Steeple Aston
[autumn 1968]

Darling sphinx, you have been very much in my mind and heart. Forgive me for not turning up at the moment. I am pinned to the novel [3] which I want to finish before Christmas. How beautiful you looked when we last met. I am haunted by your image.

1 Morgan Browne in *A Fairly Honourable Defeat,* who has an older sister, Hilda Foster. The '*tiens!*' (well, well) that follows possibly suggests Murdoch's anxiety about Philippa's superiority as an 'older sister' figure.
2 Branwell Brontë and Marion Bosanquet (Philippa's younger sister).
3 *A Fairly Honourable Defeat.*

Sometime (*soon*) I would like to have a photograph of you. Would you mind? The only one I have dates from 1940! Not that you have changed since then, except to become more spiritual-looking still. However, the old interior cinema is pretty good and you move and speak there in full colour. No substitute for reality, though, however interesting its possibilities. I wish you would give me tutorials on moral philosophy. Perhaps you will say I have only to present myself? These must wait till the summer I fear. Next term will be torn up by going abroad. I hope you will have a marvellous time in Paris. Let me know when you'll be *back* in Oxford.

Much love, sphinx and queen. Your admiring and obedient

I

To Georg Kreisel.

Steeple Aston
[November 1968]

My dear, thanks for yours plus the piece on Student Participation by revolutionary leader Kreisel. Very glad your back is better and hope stays so and world correspondingly changed.

I was very interested and impressed by your document, which seemed to me one of the few clear-headed things I've seen on this. In England, I think we would still say, wait a minute, let's aim at eliminating (non-academic non-professional) chaps from the universities. In USA, this wouldn't make sense. My point, which your point meets, is mostly that it is very unfair on clever or even cleverish people, for whom in an important sense universities exist, not only to be forced by fashion and the few to spend time on *some* kind of agitation but also (and this is what really gets me) to enjoy its fruits in terms of popular teachers and easy courses! (A student agitation in Oxford not long ago objected to 'dry academic lectures' on the text of Dante!) Of course young people will choose what's easier, that their as yet unexpanded imaginations and sensibilities can deal with. (The Romantic movement not the eighteenth century, Dylan Thomas not Chaucer, etc. etc.) But the *expansion* is education, and that is what hurts. Yes, I am stern and sadistic towards the young and this is what makes me a jolly good teacher! [. . .]

I meant to talk of other things, but having just reread your piece wanted to talk of that. What happened at the faculty meeting where you were going to propose popular choice of teachers and what on earth does this mean? Please reply.

I often think about you. Much love.

To Philippa Foot.

Steeple Aston
[December 1968]

[. . .] I have thought about you a great deal. You are a most frequent figure in my mental world. Isn't it odd that people can *constantly* think about other people, without the latter's permission or even knowledge? The 'victim' may not be pleased, of course. I know that there are people whom I don't think about who think about me – and this merely irritates me. (I should like to think that you thought about me – though this idea is frightening too.) What can happen to one in other people's thoughts! You are of course, for me, the Sphinx: beautiful, enigmatic, alarming and wise. I believe the Sphinx knew every man's secret but did not always know that she knew. Hence your surprise at the kind of fear which you inspire. You can answer a question for me to which no one else knows the answer. But what is the question? I don't know – though sometimes I can see its shadowy shape.

This nonsense is a love letter. I have just finished the first draft of my novel. I will write again and hope to see you before too long.

Your
I

To Rachel Fenner.

Steeple Aston
[December 1968]

My dearest girl, your *object* has come, and what a truly *lovely* object it is! [. . .]

Thank you. I am really very touched, Rachel, and deeply deeply *pleased*. You are a dear girl and your enigmatic king will be greatly treasured.[1]

My last morning in London (I am very sorry I was fussed on the telephone) was entirely devoted to the drama of the electricity at 59 Harcourt Terrace. The electricians said the fault was in the basement which is empty and locked. I rang up the agents who said the keys were with the builder. I rushed round to the builder and was told 'wait till George arrives, he'll know'. Wait ages. George arrives and says, 'Oh we finished there ages ago – we returned the keys to the agent.' Ring agent again. Agent says 'Wait till Mr Patterson comes in.' Wait ages ringing at intervals. Mr Patterson arrives,

1 Rachel Fenner had made a copy of the king in the Lewis Chessmen. Found on the Isle of Lewis in the Outer Hebrides of Scotland in 1831, the chess set dates from the twelfth century.

and says 'Go to see Mr Davidson at our Kensington office. He has a lot of *unlabelled* keys, one of which *might* fit.' Take taxi to Kensington, back to Harcourt Terrace. No key fits. Take taxi to Paddington and depart for Oxford nervous wreck. (In fact they managed to get in later on and found the electricity had just been switched off. Sinister.) [. . .]

Dear child, I am sorry (my fault) we were rushed (and surrounded by *motor cars*) at our end of term meeting. You were, as always, very sweet to me, and I do constantly appreciate this. *Have good Christmas*. Best wishes to Frank. And again *must THANK YOU* for the very exceptional *thing*. Much love

    I

To Philippa Foot.

Steeple Aston
[January 1969]

Sweetheart, have just received your charming illegible Paris postcard. I am glad you got the scarf and the postman didn't. I take it you were back circa 10th. I will by then I fear be in deep Dorset. But will ring up when I am back next week. Much love and homage from your –

    I

I have been thinking about you a lot and wanting to see you and touch you. You live in my mind with a strange independent power. I trust Tuesday lunch is OK. I'll be along about 1, possibly a trifle after.

I have had my hair permed and it is a disaster. I might have known I couldn't win out that game.

Love from your – what? What am I?

To Rachel Fenner, written before Murdoch and John Bayley travelled on 29 January to Japan on a British Council lecture tour. Murdoch was to give a talk entitled 'Freedom and Virtue in Modern Literature' at Waseda University and to repeat the lecture at another venue. The week was packed with engagements, which perhaps explains why, unusually, Murdoch appears to have sent no letters from Japan to her friends.

Steeple Aston
18 January [1969]

Rachel dear, I'm afraid I won't see you before departing (on Jan 28 to Tokyo).
Very sorry about that. Life has just been the most ferocious rush. Just finished
novel before Christmas and since then have been desperately writing lectures
to be delivered in Japan and at Hong Kong. Feel exhausted and worried.
John has had the most awful toothache and tooth troubles and has been
generally ill and as last straw I now have raging cold! (Perhaps it is the ha
ha Hong Kong flu!)

I hope you and Frank are well! How goes the Latin plan? I'd advise you
to settle down to a lot of sheer *learning* at first – learn the old *amo amas
amat* and *mensa mensa mensam* till you know them backwards – it will pay
later. It is a most marvellous language.

Steeple Aston is misty and lovely and I don't feel at all in the mood for
the mysterious East, drat it. (Student riots in Tokyo and all, sounds like a
home from home.¹) Let me know later which day it is best for you to lunch
at Harcourt. Have you read *Lord of the Rings* yet I wonder? I have just been
reading *The Hobbit* which has some very good scenes in it. (Tolkien muffs
all the big scenes in *L of R* I'm afraid – it should be much more drawn out.)

Must go write lectures. Wish everything would stop. John now announces
temperature of 100°! Much love
     I

To Brigid Brophy.

Steeple Aston
[18 February 1969]

Thank you very much for the hotel details – very helpful. I was so sorry
not to see you and the gang on Friday. I hope you had a good run at the
Union? (Was it the censorship motion?) I have had a letter from an electronics
engineer (male) in Walsall who changes his clothes every evening and
becomes Hilda. He seems to think I should do something about it. Have
written him a relaxed letter.

Hope all very well and work OK. [. . .]
     With love
     I

1 The London School of Economics was closed from the end of January to 19 February, following
  student sit-ins and protests.

*To Rachel Fenner, written just before Murdoch took part in an Arts Council Writers'
tour of schools and colleges in Lancashire; the other writers included Adrian Henri,
John McGrath and Julian Mitchell.*

Steeple Aston
[late March 1969]

Rachel, just a note. Am leaving Steeple Aston today and going north
tomorrow from London by train. Feel as if I were going to North Pole.
Sorry didn't write earlier. It's psychologically difficult to write when one has
no stamps, and somehow stamps are rather hard to come by round here.
Am rather stuck with work at the moment, so perhaps it's a good time for
a break – and it's a bit of an adventure. Odd that I've travelled to all sorts
of places but don't know the north of England. (Except for that curious
sojourn at Blackpool during the war.) I bet it'll be freezing. And terribly
foreign.
    It was very nice indeed to see you, and you were looking super, as usual.
Hope work will go well. Try to keep warm in that barn of yours. Will let
know about next London visit. Lots love
    I

To Rachel Fenner.

Steeple Aston
[April 1969]

Rachel dear, much thanks for yours. Forgive a slightly distracted note. John
has some sort of gastric flu (up all last night) and I am cancelling all this
week's arrangements, such as they were.
    I did enjoy the north, though I agree I wouldn't want to live there! Had
a super meeting in Preston (hundreds of people came) and we made it into
a political meeting. Atmosphere quite electric, and long arguments with
anarchists afterwards. Fun. Wigan was kind to us too, and we had a great
climax in *Skelmersdale*, which I'd not hitherto heard of. Of our party was
one Adrian Henri (the Liverpool Scene) who seems to be a northern pop
king. Very nice bloke and certainly looked the part! All very educational for
me anyway.
    Our garden is feebly attempting to pretend it's spring – a few daffs and
Scyllas. *Frost* last night ha ha. Hope your work goes on well. Mine is haywire.
Will communicate again soon. Lots of love
    I

To David Morgan, postcard of The Virgin and Child *by Alesso Baldovinetti.*

[April? 1969]

I hope to God you're all right. I thought about you in Mozart's *Seraglio* which is about the virtues of forgiveness and magnanimity. Don't cut your- self off from that world and from all the pictures in the Louvre by those obsessions. This Madonna is by the man who painted the golden girl in profile[1] in the National Gallery we spoke of. I hope this doesn't come under the heading of 'white tablecloths'[2] but then I don't know how you and I assume some degree of ordinariness. Do keep out of trouble.
  Love
  I

To Leo Pliatzky.

Steeple Aston
[mid-April 1969?]

My dear creature, thanks for your letter. There is nothing whatever the matter with me except the hangover (now dissipated) from our last two meetings, and flu and an overdose of acnomycin (now over too). I was rather depressed policy-wise about our (your and my) situation and partly for that reason didn't get in touch with you. I didn't want a repetition of December and when we met in Feb. or whenever it was when you were (if I may say so in the kindest way) so bloody disagreeable that I rather wondered what to do next. Anyway, I do very much want to see you and will try to fix that up very first thing next term (beginning May). Of course I feel for you something which, after all these years, must be dignified with the name of L . . E. See soon. Be well.

To Rachel Fenner.

Steeple Aston
27 April 1969

---

1 Probably Baldovinetti's *Portrait of a Lady* (1465). Morgan and Murdoch often visited the National Gallery together.
2 Morgan had been sneering at the rather genteel world in which he imagined Murdoch moved.

My dear, thanks for your immense letter to which I can't reply properly – I am sunk in work (demonically) and can hardly bear to take ten mins off. (Selfish brute.) [. . .]

About you, I don't know, and probably don't understand as much as you think. That sex and spirit come together for you seems to me a marvellous thing. (Me rather ditto.) And I think it's *separate* from your unrequited, or wrongly requited complaint. Highly organised animals like you are likely to have difficulties anyway, because so much is expected. Perfect articulate communication and all the rest as well. OK, let's expect a lot and hope for luck. (Much depends on luck.) What is important is a kind of confidence in one's own tenderness and ability to communicate which perhaps comes with time. People don't often enough love, touch, make impulsive affectionate gestures to each other. More of this. Thus runs my manifesto. Anyway: it's very difficult (impossible?) to change oneself.

I'll only be in London very briefly this week with J to see his ma, who is much better. I would like to talk to you properly – may suggest a *morning* – anyway will suggest, and this policy statement comes with much love from

I

To Philippa Foot.

Steeple Aston
6 July 1969

Thank you very much for your letter and now postcard. (Your postcard came here in four days: not bad.) I'm so glad Seattle seems OK – hope you can see *sea* as well as that romantic mountain. My Seattle pals turn out to be in Europe just now. What with one thing and another we haven't been away after all, though may go to Dorset for two days at the end of week. The weather has packed up and returned to normal with rain and gales. What a country. I have been working as usual. I keep hoping that something quite Shakespearean and astonishing will come out of my head but of course it doesn't – one is the slave of one's mind, which is in some ways such a predictable machine. Art, at my level often consists in *concealing* what the silly old mind would be at. I think of you often and you roam my dreams. Have you been swimming? I suppose Sea-ttle *is* on the sea? Are there any exotic birds in your garden? Yours in whatever it is. Much Love

I

Write.

To Georg Kreisel.

Steeple Aston
[late July 1969?]

Thank you for your letter and card and for not reproaching me more harshly for jumping to conclusions! Someone said: 'Elizabeth (Anscombe) couldn't believe the telegram sent from Cambridge (offering her the chair) and thought it was sent as a joke by Kreisel, who happens to be in England'. From this, of course, nothing followed about your actual whereabouts. I got an odd sort of shock from this, wrote to you on spur of moment, and now suitably chastened, apologise. Anyway why should you necessarily tell me if you are passing through England? I would have had enough sense not to be seriously offended if you had. A lot of the relation between you and me is in my mind.

You probably did tell me some time ago that you were coming to France and I forgot. Another suitable subject for an apology. I'm sure you did *not* tell me how you lost the flat in the Rue de Tournon.[1] (You made me lose a flat once. Remember when you and Elizabeth cooked a meal in my basement flat in Park Town and failed to clear it up? The remnants some days or weeks old, including some fish soup mess which Elizabeth had strained and left in the coal bucket, were found by my landlady on an inspection tour and I was kicked out. However that's by the way.) But you seem to have settled yourself in another pleasant spot on the left bank. I feel suddenly homesick for Paris. Give my love to Queneau. Most people I was fond of long ago I've kept a live relation with, but not so him. How did I mislay Big Q? It's his fault actually.

I enjoy the more diffused friendships of middle age with considerable intensity. But in general I am a more diffused person than you.

Much love to you, my clever and beautiful friend, be well, and may all sorts of joys and pleasures visit you.

I

Last novel was *Bruno's Dream* which I think I sent you in USA but let me know if not.

---

1 One of the most prestigious roads in Paris.

To David Morgan, who had applied to study for a degree in English at Queen Mary's College, London. He had been interviewed for a place (hence Murdoch's pleasure at this 'good news') but then rejected because he did not have a pass in Latin at ordinary level (O level) – a qualification introduced as part of British educational reform in the 1950s.

Steeple Aston
18 September 1969

Dear David, in great haste. I have some visitors coming today. It's interesting and good news that QMC were prepared to take you. I didn't entirely gather from your letter how the matter ended. Did they just say, too bad, goodbye – or was anything left open?? If the former, it's a bit hard for me to write. It's rather maddening to have such a near miss. Maybe I'll write anyway, but I can't today.

I think you would find that Latin O level *hard* to get, and it would mess up your first year's work pretty effectively. (I think these rules are pretty inflexible, though they might just let you get it after you'd come up.) Did you write to any other colleges from which you haven't yet heard?

The financial question still remains unclear. I am, to be frank, a bit dismayed that you have been either unable or unwilling to get a job this summer – and I can't help suspecting you've been drifting along, confident that I will help you if necessary. Money problems tend to wreck friendships, and ours is going to be under some strain if you do do a degree, and one must be ready for it. It looks as if you have no other financial resource except me – and it seems at this end as if you are being a trifle casual about it. If I have to finance your board, lodging and fees (also books etc.) for three years this will represent a large sum. *Possibly* I can afford it, but I can't afford it comfortably and something else will have to be cut down. This is not to discourage you, but just to ask you to be realistic. Sometimes I think you live inside such an egoistic dream world that you really imagine society and other people *owe* you the kind of literary idleness which you enjoy.

Anyway, enough of this. Please write *more details* about the present situation.

With love.

Destroy this and all letters.

And keep your mouth shut.

To Philippa Foot.

Steeple Aston
12 October 1969

Dearest girl, with you I sometimes feel like someone trailing the string for the kitten in vain, or to use a (for you) more dignified metaphor, I feel like a dog carrying a stick which no one will throw. (I suppose some people go through life eternally with sticks in their mouths.) However, don't let these images worry you, I am only teasing and, you see, I *am* talking. I need pavilions and pavilions of talk. See soon, I trust. Will write or even conceivably *telephone*. Yes, super be jobless! This with much love
   I

To Norah Smallwood.

Steeple Aston
[late 1969]

Dearest Norah, thank you for letter re Bookers.[1] I am rather relieved in a way! But if any method occurs to you whereby I can solve John's tax worries without getting divorced or emigrating or shooting myself, perhaps you would let me know.
   Au revoir and much love
   I

To Philippa Foot.

Steeple Aston
23 December 1969

Dearest girl a RING! Thank you so very much. And what a lovely one – obviously magic – a ring of power. I think it is made of mithril. (I hope you know your Tolkien.[2])
   I am so pleased. You are a good gift-giver. I hope you are Christmassing

1 The 'Author Division' of the food wholesaler Booker-McConnell acquired rights over a number of well-known authors' works during the 1950s and 1960s. The scheme allowed authors a capital sum free of income tax and surtax for their work, which would be subject only to a long-term capital gains tax. The Author Division also co-founded and sponsored the Booker Prize for literature in 1968.
2 In Tolkien's fantasy world mithril is a metal found in Middle-earth.

well? I think you said you wouldn't be away for as long as originally planned! I shall much look forward to seeing you when the festive season has run its course. Meanwhile I send much love. I am very pleased with my ring and so glad you had this thought of getting it for me. Bless you and very best thanks –
Yr
    I

To Norah Smallwood.

Steeple Aston
16 January 1970

Dearest Norah,

Thank you very much for your letter about *A Fairly Honourable Defeat* monies. I'm most grateful to you for taking so much trouble. It's most helpful.

In bed again with some sort of gastric trouble, it's maddening. I haven't, what with one thing or another, been able to eat or drink properly since sometime before Christmas!

I have, by the way, written another play,[1] and will send it to you when I am able to organise envelopes and things. This, you will be glad to hear, is my last offering to the theatre for the foreseeable future, and I am beginning a new novel![2]

With much love, Iris

To Philippa Foot.

19 March 1970

My dear, forgive no recent letter. No special reason. Sense of inertia resulting from devilish cold, sore throat, loss of voice, lasting (it seemed) weeks, very cold weather, snow, breakdown in work and general grip on life. Better now. I hope you have been OK, negotiating the mazes of the car parks and students' demos. I long to hear all about it. Oxford has had a tiny revolution with students occupying the Clarendon building (asses). John and I went in to see them and I made a small speech, but not eloquent enough to effect

1 *Joanna, Joanna.*
2 *An Accidental Man.*

communication (or ha ha 'meaningful dialogue'). I feel pretty right wing about education. An American jumped up and shouted 'Students are the negroes of our society.' Cheers. Oh God. Anyway I didn't mean to write about this. You will be home soon (when?). *Good.*

J and I are taking our two mothers to Venice and are then going on ourselves to Dubrovnik. We leave 25th. Heaven only knows what all this will be like. I suspect it will rain all the time in Venice. Back circa April 10. Let me know when you're back, darling. Maybe it will be about then. I miss you frightfully. Did I tell you I saw Michael[1] and his new girlfriend? She is Dutch and fearfully in love with him. News when I see you. Forgive my silence and write.

Much love
Ever
I

To David Morgan, concerning his father's death. On the day he received this note, Murdoch visited Morgan in his room in Ladbroke Grove holding half a bottle of whisky.[xv]

Steeple Aston
8 April 1970

David, just a note to send love. I am so sorry. These final partings are terrible and can't be consoled for. Keep in mind though that in so many ways it happened mercifully – especially that he was *himself* to the end. You will be busy today looking after the living, especially your mother, and that always remains one's duty. Don't shun help in other quarters – Yvonne[2] etc. Surrender yourself to the whole thing, including nature's efforts to lessen the shock. I am sure that his image will not be blurred in you – you will see that later. Write to me.

Much love to you
I

To Elias Canetti.

Steeple Aston
26 May [1970]

---

1 Philippa's ex-husband.
2 David Morgan's new partner, whom he later married.

My dear, just to say have telephoned a number of times code-wise, and got
no answer, and as Simopoulos says you have gone to Germany and are going
on to Zurich to see Hera, I am assuming this to be true! I hope I'll see you
before term ends. I hope all's VERY WELL. Much much love, dear one
    Iris

To Norah Smallwood.

Steeple Aston
11 June 1970

Norah, I appear to have agreed to give a set of my complete works in hardback to the winner of a village raffle. Do they all still exist in hardback and
if so could I have the set please? Au revoir and much love Iris.

*To David Morgan. In a recent letter Murdoch had written advising that he should
abandon his relationship with Emma, with whom he was still obsessed despite being
in a relationship with Yvonne, who was now pregnant by him: 'It's about time you
got out of this dungeon [. . .] It seems to the outsider fantastic that you should so
cage yourself in misery. Though I know how one can be caged by one's mind. But
you should make some effort, however abstract and half-hearted, to get out.' Despite
Murdoch's hope that he and Yvonne would have the child, Yvonne decided to have
her pregnancy terminated.*

[July 1970]

Dear David,
    I expect you know what I am likely to say. I think your chances of Emma
whatever you do or don't do, are nil. I meant to write to you earlier about
this. You seem to me to be in a sort of magical-obsessive frame of mind
about Emma, which is terribly imprisoning. I believe you are someone with
talents – but I am sure these will develop much more freely if you can get
out of that *cage* and see the world.
    Exchange pseudo-magical power for open human spiritual power. (I think
this is what *The Tempest* is about.) You now have an *occasion* for doing this.
If you and Yvonne both want the child, for heaven's sake let it live. (Later
you might indeed feel – *that* was the one.) I also think you should marry
Yvonne – you seem well suited to each other and have endured life together.
And I think children should have married parents if possible – it adds greatly
to that deeply needed sense of security.

Alarming prospect yes, but life-giving, world changing –

All this may by now however be beside the point! Let me know. Very best of luck

I

To *Philippa Foot.*

Steeple Aston
[July 1970]

[. . .] I am very sorry not to see you, I have been thinking about you a lot and dreaming about you. Communication with you remains curiously problematic and filled with a sense of danger which is sometimes thrilling and sometimes sad (never now very sad). I look forward greatly to reading your denunciation of the Categorical Imperative.[1] Should not this revelation change one's life? Or is it, I suppose, that one already lives *thus* and deludes oneself? I *will* try to get down what I think (keep me to it) but it must now be in Sept. (Back Sept 2 circa.) And see you then I hope and pray, gracious being. Your loving pupil,

I

To *David Morgan.*

Steeple Aston
13 August 1970

Dear David,

[. . .] I wonder how things went yesterday – and wonder in general how you are. Do let me know. I feel so out of touch with you I can't even admonish you – and have become indeed rather pessimistic about my capacity to help you in any way at all. But time will shew, and my goodwill remains.

---

1 Immanuel Kant identified his 'Categorical Imperative', which concerns an evaluation of motives for action, as the supreme principle of morality: 'I ought never to conduct myself except that I could also will that my maxim become a universal law'. This demand commands via pure practical reason, independently of every other possible consideration, including desire. No doubt Murdoch was looking forward to Philippa Foot's 'denunciation' of the Categorical Imperative because of her own view that it relies on an account of ethics based too heavily on rational action. For Murdoch desire was not so easily dismissed; she believed that desires transform perceptions of reality, out of which actions, rational or otherwise, emerge.

I do hope nothing very unpleasant has happened and that you are reasonably in control of things. NB destroy all my letters. (I trust you, but not your room.) And try to write one yourself, even if it's very brief. I'll write to you better when I've heard from you. You know how depressing the effect of silence is.

I have an uneasy feeling you are not at Ladbroke Grove at all, so God knows when you'll get this. And I can't recall the name of the place you said you might enter. I rather hope you decided against that. But anyway, let me hear in due course – and meanwhile all best affectionate wishes and love

I

To Georg Kreisel.

Steeple Aston
14 January 1971

Dearest K, thank you very much for your very interesting letter. I'm sorry I didn't reply sooner. Christmas flu and things have intervened. You are, actually, wrong about my alleged ignorance of the tacit assumption of yours which you mention, viz. Don't Explain at Length. This I know of, though perhaps of others not. I have even (intuitively I think, not deliberately) evolved a special style to meet this assumption. As an artist indeed I share it. The context of apparent disagreement which prompted your remark was I believe re Wittgenstein. What I meant was that as a philosopher one ought not to have any general view of how much or what kind of explanation will clarify. Obviously there is no need to write for fools. (Teaching is another matter, I mean when one confronts a class.) But one should not sacrifice truth to art. (This is the case for artists too, but they have definite formal obligations also of a special sort.) Not all great philosophers are laconic (Hume and Locke are far from being). I was expressing some irritation with Wittgenstein because I felt he cared *too* much about his stylish persona, a kind of vanity. But my devotion to him is immense.

The business about irrationality is connected but separate, and here you are probably right, i.e. that I *want* at least *certainties* of some sort, often in places where those can't be had. A religious demand I suppose. Though what the difference is between an intellectual demand for wholeness and an aesthetic one is often unclear. And I think I have *political* at least *desires* which you may also rightly feel to be misplaced. (Nothing to do with *actually* working for causes.) And Kantian Protestant *conscience* very deep in it all.

About physical illness, I am not in fact so robust! I have suffered from asthma all my life, and from Ménière's disease (unceasing head noise, giddiness, deafness) for twenty years of it so far. I also have slight arthritis in my back, and *severe* arthritis in my neck, shoulder and right arm. The future of my writing mechanism (I do everything in longhand) is unclear and very worrying. How is *your* back by the way – and are you driving as much as ever? Driving is certainly bad for these conditions – but I imagine it is an inevitable part of your life. For what do you visit the spas I wonder, and do they help you at all? I may take some mud baths one day – I find the idea of a warm mud bath very attractive!

I have finished a long novel[1] and feel a bit depressed and crazy. I cannot decide whether or not to write more for the theatre. If only one had more *time* ahead. I hope you are cheerful and thoroughly better from viruses, etc. Do write soon. With much love

I

To Brigid Brophy.

Steeple Aston
5 April [1971?]

Thank you for your mauve note. We have just been in France and are just going to Dorset. I hope you are OK, and also Mike and Kate. In France the mistral blew and it was snowing as we entered Dijon. I have, I think, no special news. Work and life goes on and seems to gather in momentum and complication. I have developed arthritis in my right arm and shoulder, which is painful and inspires fear for the future. However, I find I live increasingly in the present, an effect probably of ageing rather than of any sort of enlightenment. I have, I think, put on weight, and no longer look quite nineteen. I feel about thirty-five. The reservoir of fear and melancholy continues to fill, I suppose, as one grows older. However the consolations of art and love become greater too, more complex and more vivid. [. . .]

It seems a very long time since I had any news of your part of the world, and I never seem to meet any of our, very few actually, 'mutual' friends. I meet Ken [Thompson] occasionally in Regent Street. Olivia [Manning] has invited me to lunch.

I was glad to get your note. What does it mean however? Curiosity, a signal, an appeal, nothing? I somehow felt after our last meeting on, I think, Feb. 18 1970, that we would not communicate again. I felt sad about that

1 *An Accidental Man.*

but it also seemed inevitable. Our previous two or three meetings, and *a fortiori* that one, seemed to have brought little pleasure to either of us. I felt that was your fault for being almost aggressively switched off but I daresay you may have felt it was my fault for being awkward or something. I have felt in fact very little curiosity about your life. It is rather as if you had emigrated. But I have contrived to 'miss' you, if that is the word. You continue as a presence, in the sense e.g. that I sometimes think of something I want to tell you, or there is some joke only you would understand. Also quite in general I have felt that the demise of our friendship is a cosmic pity. Our game of multidimensional chess, as you used to call it. However, all things grow, flourish, and perish. And I have also sometimes thought that it would be sad and bad if you in any sense needed me or wanted to communicate with me and the demon of pride on both sides should prevent this. Then I have thought of writing to you, and have failed to do so because of inertia or perhaps the demon of pride. So I was pleased to hear from you and I take this opportunity to say that I am always, where you are concerned, available as a friend. This doesn't alas mean that there is much point just now in our meeting. Another meeting might be just as dead as the previous ones. And for a variety of reasons at your end it may be impossible for a while or maybe always for us to talk properly together: though oddly enough letters could be a good deal easier. Anyway, take it that my affection and concern for you remains in a suspended and encapsulated state. If anything can be done about this good, if not, not. And, it is not just inertia, it is an appraisal of the situation, which has suggested silence. Maybe we might try lunching together again in the summer or autumn. But there is no need even to have any views about that for the present. Meanwhile perhaps you would write to me a letter of news?

Give my love to Mike. I'd like to see him again sometime. I hope M and Kate are flourishing. I liked M's poems. Kate must be quite grown up by now.

I'm afraid I haven't given you much 'news', except about my thoughts about you. We have had a plague of owls down the chimney. The latest one awaited us, perched on top of our bed, when we returned from France. He had flown into every room, upstairs and downstairs, leaving a trail of droppings and smashed china. We opened the window. He gave us a keen glance and flew out. Such is life in the country.

I hope you are very OK and I send much love

I

To Philippa Foot.

Steeple Aston
5 May 1971

Darling, thank you for your SUPER card – it cheered me up so much – on
a day when all the rest of the post was from awful people I hardly know
saying would I see them, surely I could spare them one day in the year, to
be with them in a green field etc. etc. (NO, I scream I cannot spare them
etc. I'm that MEAN).

I feel tired, wish I was in Mexico or Pisa or somewhere nice. Work obsesses
me, but fruitlessly, I can't get anything clear or good out of it. The sun
shines and the scene is beautiful and heart-rending. Send note to me *as soon
as* you are back in this island –

Much much love

I

To David Hicks.

Steeple Aston
26 June [1971]

Dearest David, it was a joy to see you – thank you so much for that super
time, taken out of time, in your beautiful house and garden. We were
delighted to be with you and John was so glad to meet you and K,[1] and it
was very happy indeed. I wish you lived nearer here. Let us know if you
are travelling about in or through this region. Don't forget to let me see
that novel and let me be your agent for it! I would love to read it. I was so
interested in your biblical studies, and soon after met in Oxford a (or *the*)
man concerned with organising them! It was wonderful just to sit and talk
with you, and see you. Forgive this late letter. My mother (who recalls you
and sends her greetings) has been staying for ten days and organisation has
slipped. Keep in touch, would you. Write, about anything. I think of you
and send much love –

I

1 This letter suggests that John Bayley met David and Katherine Hicks for the first time in 1971.

To Brigid Brophy.

Steeple Aston
[July 1971?]

How kind of you to send me Maureen's poems. Thank you for your previous letter too. My ailment is certainly arthritis: but it is not, in this warm weather, troubling me too much.

I had not, actually, forgotten that you in general prefer evenings. Only the last time I asked you to dinner you had yourself called for, for removal, at 9.45 – which I took, evidently wrongly, as a sign that in this context evenings were out. I will write again later on and suggest an evening. I am not very much in London at present.

I have become a convert to Powellism (Anthony not Enoch¹). I believe I am in love with Widmerpool.² Isn't it terrible?

Our garden is very E. Onegin³ at present. Love to Mike. With love.

To Georg Kreisel.

Steeple Aston
18 July [1971]

Your letter was interesting. About your style of criticism, by the way, I don't see anything in the least irritating about it, and can't quite understand what to look for here. I think somebody might be annoyed either by *what* you say (as I was on that evening in Fulham: more of this below) because they feel e.g. that you are attacking sacred values in a rather cool and casual way – or by (and this overlaps with 'cool and casual') your *style* (which is an aspect of your particular kind and degree of intelligence). You have a very cool detached *tone*, which some people, especially if they felt you were cleverer and they were alarmed by this, might feel to be 'superior'. (I don't myself feel this, perhaps because I can to some extent talk this language too.) You might be felt to be too calm for the degree of incisiveness involved. (A matter of taste in argument styles.) I think I share your taste here, though I am *incapable* of being so calm.

---

1 Enoch Powell: English politician, classical scholar and poet. He served as a Conservative MP between 1950 and 1974.
2 The surname of a disreputable character in Anthony Powell's twelve-volume sequence of novels *A Dance to the Music of Time*.
3 A reference to the beauty of the countryside outside St Petersburg in Alexander Pushkin's verse novel *Eugene Onegin*. John Bayley had just published his book on Pushkin.

I was upset that evening in London when we argued about painting over dinner because I felt an awful lack of communication about a view of yours which I felt to be quite wrong. (And which is at least connected with what you say in this last letter.) Two quite separate issues seem to have come up. One about what people are like. The other about method of description. (Linked, but separable.) About people: I think we hold different beliefs (you and I) at a level where it would be hard to deal in empirical proofs. (Well, one could try.) Perhaps I am interested in very private sort of things which I can *find out* about people and which I enjoy being surprised by and which tend to show them as odd and special. Perhaps I enjoy exaggerating these things (actually I think they scarcely can be exaggerated: novelists are accused of caricaturing – I know I can't shew *enough* oddity to be really realistic) and so neglect *big similarities* which are important too. I find even 'droll' people very *surprising* – and think of penetrating a personality like that of Peter Geach[1] (I haven't) – would the 'generalisations', the big 'similarity' categories, not need to be *so* specially qualified that they would lose their nature? These categories are of course useful and as you say we *recognise* things by them (the debby girl, etc.). But not only what interests, but the real stuff, and that which, if you like, 'determines' (in a neutral sense) what the person is up to every day lies *beyond*.

The point about description is linked in the sense that if you find certain kinds of description 'frivolous' you may not allow that the 'interior person' I am interested in and find so various could be described at all. (But the points are separable – one might try other *kinds* of description – or one might even believe in, or intuit the presence of what one couldn't very adequately describe!) Your use of the word 'frivolous' seems to me to be frivolous. We know what waves 'look like' without having any measuring conceptions or ability, and what waves look like is, in an important and *obvious* sense, what waves are. (Cf. arguments with phenomenalists about perception – and arguments with 'central state materialists' for that matter.) Ordinary people experience waves on ordinary occasions, and the *fundamental* concepts here are 'curve', 'glitter', 'roar', etc. Fundamental because all the measurements etc. can only be *those* measurements if we can recognise the phenomenon otherwise. And (this is the point that moves one, and is a value judgement!) ordinary waves are much more important than 'measured' waves! (*That* is what is beautiful, exciting, significant, and makes being on this lousy planet to some extent worth it.) Something like this seemed to me *in danger* on that evening in Fulham. And I think I was annoyed because I felt you were speaking dogmatically about painting without really *liking* painting and ergo understanding it. I could be wrong. Great artists are great

1 British philosopher (1916–2013) married to Elizabeth Anscombe.

because they have a superior *exactness* about large important phenomena which are hard to describe. Of course they look harder at what interests them, but so do scientists.

Localisation of feelings (sensations): I write about love, not ('just') sex, and I think love involves a sort of world-diffusion of one's sense of meaning. (Sorry, bad phrase.) Also I am prudish about what I write down! More of this anon. I am going to France on Saturday and on to Italy and will be away till mid-August. I want to say something rather Russian to you but can't word it in either English or Russian. I love you and like the waves you exhilarate me.

I

To Philippa Foot.

Steeple Aston
Summer 1971

Dearest girl, just to say we are reviving a former plan and going to France [. . .], partly for a conference, and partly for a following holiday,[1] which we may cut if telephone-wise my mama seems any worse. At present she is a good deal better and far less melancholy. We won't be away long anyway, about eight to ten days at most. I must say I'll be glad to get out for a while. My mind seems absolutely seized up – the novel[2] *awful* – utter inability to think – and generally demon-ridden. A break will be, I confidently expect, instantly reviving however. [. . .]

I do hope you are OK. I much look forward to seeing you later on. I'll communicate on return. With wingèd thoughts, and as always much love,

I

To Brigid Brophy.

Steeple Aston
12 September [1971?]

Thank you for your letter. I don't know that I altogether understood it, but I am very sorry that you have been so afflicted. I am also very surprised, and could not have 'told you so' anything. People say such mental adventures

1 Arts conference at Cérisy in Normandy followed by holiday in Italy.
2 *The Black Prince.*

can be interesting and profitable, and I hope you feel something of value came to you in it all. I am very glad to know that all is well now. I would be delighted (of course) to see you and friend, and Indian food, yes, fine. I shall be away on and off during rest of September and begin of Oct, but after that I'll be in London regularly as usual and I'll write and suggest dates.

I note that you think of me as a philosopher and this is gratifying, but I am in fact *not one* (and am particularly conscious of this just now as I am trying to write some philosophy lectures which I have got to write)! (I am not sure what it means to be thought of as a philosopher.)

I always think quite a lot about you (as you). I was very sorry to (as I felt) lose, mislay, your friendship that I valued very much. I shall look forward to seeing you in October; and I cannot help hoping that we can achieve some, *mutatis mutandis*,[1] resumption of friendship. My very best wishes and love

To Philippa Foot.

Steeple Aston
16 September 1971

It was very good indeed to see you: but I feel I was No Good.

Unable to communicate. It happens sometimes. I feel the world is rather far away at the moment. Either it or I is in a glass case, I'm not sure which. I saw you as through double glazing (and so was I fear rather useless company – I *wished* to be better). But it was a jolly cheering glimpse to me at any rate.

À bientôt and much love
I

To Philippa Foot, who had suggested that Murdoch might consider giving some guest lectures at a university in Mexico where Foot had a contact.

Steeple Aston
29 November 1971

My dear, it was very specially nice to see you and I felt very cheered up and refreshed afterwards. THANK YOU very much indeed, dear girl. About Mexico, if we went, it would be roughly end March early April. If you could

---

1 The necessary changes having been made.

enquire vaguely and tactfully it would be very kind. I must see you again *soon*, it's never often enough, and will telephone. Thank you for, after a busy day, cooking for me so marvellously. Dear creature, with much love,

Your

I

To David Hicks, whom Murdoch had agreed to meet sometime in January or early February 1972, partly to discuss a novel he was writing.

Steeple Aston
[3 January 1972]

Dearest David, I was very touched and pleased (and encouraged) to get your very sweet letter. Thank you for writing it. *I* think we should meet and I hope that could be organised before long. In a moment of insanity I agreed to give some lectures in Yorkshire in the middle of this month, but late Jan early Feb when I am around Londonwise maybe we could meet for lunch, and I'll write again later about that. I do hope you are generally better. Love to K. Happy New Year. And *thanks* and love

I

On 16 February 1972 David Hicks was to write to Murdoch: 'Dearest Iris, By God, that was the happiest meeting with you I have had for years, and I wept with pleasure on the tube going back to my office. What an absolute darling you are! And how sensible of me to give myself a chance to remember it from time to time.' Murdoch replied, 'I too loved our meeting.' Later she sent him three sides of closely written foolscap, commenting on his novel and how he might improve it, offering to show it, when revised, to one of her publishing contacts.

To Norah Smallwood.

Steeple Aston
[early January 1972]

Dearest Norah, I have no sympathy with you at all! Do you imagine that I have gone potty? I have received no invitation (or communication of any sort) from Collins, and if I did I would certainly not react favourably. As if I would write a thriller anyway. (Except the ones I usually write.) And if I did of course you should have it! With much love from your faithful author.

I

To David Morgan.

[mid-January 1972]

Dear David,

[. . .] Re promiscuity and 'being onself', of course not. I disapprove of promiscuity anyway, and it's often connected with being not oneself, but in a daze. To be oneself, free, whole, is partly a matter of escape from obsession, neurosis, fear, compulsions etc.

Next (this coming) week should be poss. for a drink if you could do a morning time – could you make Thursday Jan 20 about 11.50 at Three Greyhounds, corner of Old Compton and Greek St? I *think* this should be OK – though there is faint possibility I may have to see some Danish radio people. However, as I haven't heard from them I assume it's not on. Anyway, unless you hear to contrary very soon, Thursday suggestion stands.

With love
I

To Philippa Foot, who was now setting in motion (via a contact called Ribas) a formal invitation for Murdoch to give some guest lectures at the university in Mexico; the Bayleys were also asked by the British Council to give some talks while there.

Steeple Aston.
12 February 1972

Dearest girl, thank you very much for your excellent guide to Mexico. It helps to settle the mind a lot. *Thank* you, *thank* you. No word from Ribas however – maybe he is a bit of a *mañana* man? Yes, please write to your other people there. The dates would be March 24 – April 1st (or very much thereabouts.) After that we *may* be at Davis, but this still unclear. I'm glad you're enjoying California. I envy you those flowers and spring airs. We have a miners' strike here and no heat or light.[1] (However there are snowdrops in the garden.) Our politicians' voices on the wireless have an edge of panic. I *cannot* do my philosophy and it makes me feel *awful*. The lecture for Manchester–Birmingham is a screed of half-baked jumble which would take four hours to deliver and it isn't even finished yet. Also there are a lot of village and other practical problems about which I cannot *think*. And an

---

1 Seven weeks of power shortages began in England in February 1972 following a miners' strike. Power cuts and lengthy blackouts were common throughout the 1970s, culminating in the 'Winter of Discontent' in 1978–9.

eagle sits on the back of my neck and runs its claws along my right arm. (However I am perfectly OK.) You were so kind to write that letter and have *cheered me up* very much indeed. Write soon again. The sight of your very spiritual-looking writing warms my heart at once. Much love, your

I

To Philippa Foot.

Steeple Aston
2 March 1972

Dearest girl, thank you for your excellent letter of Feb 23. (I think you are getting *better* at writing letters.) I was so pleased to get it. I'm glad things are quiet and fairly OK. I can understand your feeling about just wanting *time off* now, to let life pass quietly without making any deep impressions. I hope there are pleasant enough people there – people you look forward to seeing. There are so many degrees of this of course. Important, this looking forward. When shall I see *you*? [. . .]

I haven't yet given my North Midlands lecture. Stupidly fussed about it. Will be glad when it's over. I also have to deliver a special lecture in New York in May,[1] which must be written now or there won't be much spare time in between! I feel extraordinarily *feeble*. Isn't it odd how one's power to act and feel ebbs and flows? I have a lot of quite urgent decisions to make but cannot feel the requisite *interest*. Imagination fails too at such a time. However I was so glad of your words about Mexico, they mean something. It is very misty and frosty here, rather beautiful. One feels so tired though in England at this time of year and the thrusting daffodils appall. (Subjective.) God, I wish I could see you. Write soon soon. Much love, my dear –

I

In March 1972 the Bayleys flew to Mexico, spending a week there before going on to the USA, where they visited San Francisco, San Diego, Los Angeles and St Louis (where they met Albert and Naomi Lebowitz, who were to become good friends).

1 Murdoch had agreed to give the Blashfield Address to the American Academy of Arts and Letters; her talk was entitled 'Salvation by Words' (see *Existentialists and Mystics*, pp. 235–242).

To Brigid Brophy, postcard of the Golden Gate Bridge, San Francisco. Murdoch has written 'University poster: Lesbians for Jackson' in top left-hand corner.

Well, here is the bridge they are all so keen on. It's nice here except that we have too much work to do. The campus is beautiful, full of trees, plus 30,000 tall healthy young people jogging. The sun shines all day. I do hope you are a bit better? Best of luck with the alternative medicine project. *À bientôt.* With much love
I

To Brigid Brophy.

University of California, Berkeley
Department of English
[early April 1972]

Just to send much love, *en pensant de toi.*[1] We are run off our feet here. We were at Stanford University yesterday and will be at San Diego tomorrow. We got away a day at the weekend and went down the coast and saw migrating pelicans and migrating whales, together with a few sea lions and sea otters. Our timetable is now too full for any such joys however. We long for far-off Europe where life is dense and cool and old, and people are not so bouncy and so tall.
   I do hope you are feeling better.
   With much love
   I

To Philippa Foot, written from Davis, California.

10 April 1972

Dearest best girl, thank you so much for that marvellous and strange time in Los Angeles which now seems like a marvellous dream! Forest Lawn, Sunset Boulevard, the labyrinthine freeways, and YOU – it was great – and *beautiful.* Los Angeles, not at all like what I expected. (And just like Raymond Chandler – as one might have known.) I do wish we could have stayed longer and wandered along the OCEAN. However it was a wonderful capsule – and seeing you at the airport waiting for us so cheering and sort of miraculous.

1 Thinking of you.

Thank you for Los Angeles, and for the party and oriental dinner – all so perfect. Thank you, thank you.

We are soon leaving Davis, where we feel we have lived all our lives. God knows what it will be like at St Louis.[1] We are converted to California and indeed in my case for the first time to USA (which I feel I'm *visiting* for the first time!). I can see how people become Californian addicts – all those lovely freeways and supermarkets and the *beautiful* houses and vegetation and sun. (John says the inhabitants of Gerrards Cross go to California when they die.) I hope you had (will have had) a happy time in New Hampshire, up on mountains seeing eagles. (I glimpsed Grice[2] at Berkeley, by the way, and was curiously invigorated.) It will be very good to see you at home when and if we both get there. I miss not being able to work and think properly on this hedonistic journey but I suspect it is 'doing me good'. I am sure it has 'done you good' to be in LA.

Be happy, dear girl, and (as you get this) WELCOME HOME – and so many thanks and *au* soon in Oxford *revoir* and, ever, my darling, *much love* from

I

To Philippa Foot.

18 April 1972

Just to send much love, dearest girl. St Louis is extremely interesting and extraordinary but how very much we wish we were back in LA with you! That seems like a lost paradise.

We lead an intense caged life here with a lot of blooming *writers*. I've never seen a campus with so many writers and so many dogs upon it. The students romp with the dogs and study the manuscripts of the writers! So everyone is happy.

However we are longing to be back home. Details of this strange world later. *Thank you* for LA and for your dear self. Love

I

1 Murdoch was to give a talk entitled 'Ideas of Unity in Art and Morals' at Washington University, St Louis.
2 Paul Grice, an English philosopher of language who spent the last two decades of his career in the United States.

To Naomi Lebowitz, an academic at Washington University, St Louis.

Steeple Aston
May 1972

Dearest Nay, well, we are back – I must say we feel very peculiar – poor John has this morning gone off to New College where of course there have been all sorts of needful dramas in his absence. This is just to send a still somewhat jet-crazed note to say, putting it mildly, *thank you* so very much – you and Al have really transformed our concept of America – we love and value you very much and had real *fun* in St Louis entirely because of you! Thank you and thank you. And hooray that we shall be seeing you again soon and good old Svevo¹ who will bring you to Europe. (After Svevo I will suggest other authors. What about Hardy? You must be regularly employed over here.) We miss you exceedingly and had a most deprived journey home. The last bit was by jumbo jet, our first jumbo – very weird and H. G. Wellsish. We had forgotten the coldness of the English spring – wind-torn daffodils – and London airport soaked in rain. I hope June will welcome you and Al home kindly. Thank you, Nay, so much for your very great kindness to us, for letting us constantly turn up and relax with you – we felt so easy and happy with you from the very first evening! Will write properly when saner. NB is *Yale* Avenue best address or should I write to Washington U? With much love, Iris.

To Brigid Brophy.

Steeple Aston
[May 1972?]

[. . .] I haven't seen *Sappho* before, but have been much bothered (as I expect you have) by *Spare Rib*.² Those *galères*³ tend to be full of people eager to be one's self-educated best friends, so I am rather cool.

I was about to write to Mike to ask two questions, but maybe you could pass them on?

---

1 Naomi Lebowitz was writing a book on the Italian author Italo Svevo (1861–1928).
2 Sappho was an English lesbian social club that met every Tuesday in Notting Hill in London and where Maureen Duffy sometimes read her poetry; the club published a monthly magazine called *Sappho* between 1972 and 1981. *Spare Rib* was a second-wave feminist magazine published between 1972 and 1993.
3 Circles.

1. Where is the Vuillard of Things on A Chimneypiece[1] which is exhibited postcard-wise at the National Gallery, but which I can't find even in Reserve Collection?
2. WHY can I no longer deposit my suitcase in the Nat Gall cloakroom? (This is not just a question, but a complaint.)

Give my love to Mike.
  See in autumn I trust.
  Love
  I

To Rachel Fenner.

[mid-May 1972]

Rachel, thanks very much for your letter. I know what you mean about the 'barrage of mental pain'. Even without major tragedies in their lives, human beings have so many ways of suffering. About you though: you are young and talented and healthy and you *must* find serenity and happiness. (It's your *task.*) You don't mention Frank. Isn't he the main thing now? (Or do you – I do hope not – feel that *that* is wrecked?) Oughtn't you to have a child? You *can* be a mother and an artist too – it's hard – but it's well worth the challenge and response involved. Frank's happiness is an aim which could and should embrace your own happiness too. Excuse remarks from *ignorant* outsider. They are prompted by my feeling that you really must have some ordinary peace and joy in your life now. [. . .]

I suppose 'religious backgrounds' do help. But anyone can have a go at *calming* himself. (Even the most elementary kinds of 'meditation' can help, just aiming at quietness, by any sensible method.) You *must* get out of this wood and into the sunshine which you deserve. I do hope the show will be OK. I know how one frets about work, but even quite a short 'clear run' can soothe the mind and enable one to get a firm grip on one's stuff.

Not much news of me. Since I got back from USA I've been trying (without much success) to get started on a book.[2] Just foraging around and struggling with a miscellany of ideas. Just been in Dorset where it rained without ceasing. Nice though.

---

1 Painter Edouard Vuillard (1868–1940); either his *The Chimneypiece* (1905) held in the Granger Collection, New York, or *Flowers on a Fireplace in Clayes* (1932) held in the Musée de Lyon in France.
2 Perhaps *The Sacred and Profane Love Machine.*

Forgive all these reactions from your old teacher. They are well meant. Do write again.

With much love

I

To Elias Canetti, postcard of centre panel of Max Beckmann's triptych Departure.

July 1972

My dear, many many thoughts of you and of H and of the child[1] – I do look forward to hearing news. I have been in USA, back briefly, and now away again.[2] Back soon. With many good wishes and as always, much love.

Iris

To Brigid Brophy.

Steeple Aston
[July 1972?]

I was so glad to see you yesterday. In the autumn I'll hope to be more in London and we must have longer meetings (if you will). Thank you very much for elegant Chinese birthday card! I am so glad to have recovered you (I mean rediscovered you, been reunited with you, found you again, resumed our friendship) and am very anxious to hold on. I do hope all will be well, OK, one way or the other about A. This, just leaving, with much love, dearest Brigid

I

To Georg Kreisel.

Steeple Aston
18 September 1972

I feel foolish too. It occurred to me to suggest that your depression had some chemical cause, but I didn't because I assumed somehow that you had a pet doctor (some elderly white-haired central European Jew) to whom you talked *constantly* about your health. This part of the picture was wrong,

---

1 Canetti's daughter, Johanna, by his second wife, Hera Buschor, was born that year.
2 To holiday with Janet and Reynolds Stone in Pembrokeshire.

obviously. I am so glad that you have found the background to it, and something that can be treated, even if unpleasant in itself. To feel one is on the
way *out* of the darkness, in a rational way, is good. I didn't, honestly, know
what to 'make' of your depression feelings, largely because I simply don't
know you well enough. I am very very glad that things are better. Work on
one's teeth is awful too at the time but good to have in the past, where I
hope it is now in your case! Please write again soon and report. I am sorry
I didn't reply sooner, in fact I have only just got your letter, as we went away
rather unexpectedly to Italy for ten days (after it had begun to seem psychologically impossible to go away at all). Calabria and Apulia, where I had
never been before. No tourists, except for one or two Germans. Good
swimming and enough art. And back via Naples and the art gallery there
and some great Titians. It was exhausting rather than relaxing but (so) I feel
better. Not that I feel actually able to solve problems in my work better (I
can't work at all at the moment), but the world looks more interesting.

About Russell:[1] my sense of his personality is partly connected with having
read his short stories (have you read them?). I met him twice (pretty vaguely)
and got an impression of him as rather cold and 'grand'. Maybe quite
wrongly. Probably I find his mind uninteresting and simply don't try.
Lawrence's horrible mind interests me more. You may be right that one isn't
exactly put off a man's work by his personality: it's pretty hard, with a writer,
to separate an aesthetic response from a personal one. Most great writers
keep their personality out (and in so far as it comes in, they're slipping).
When it's in, one's objections are often to be analysed as aesthetic (Lawrence,
or, a much worse and even nastier writer, de Montherlant[2]). When I feel
Lawrence's nasty conceited spiteful being present, he's writing less well.
When he's just enjoying things impersonally (parts of *Kangaroo*, the poems,
parts of most of the novels) he's writing well. I daresay this is all very
obvious. (What sort of chap was Shakespeare? The sonnets do and don't
tell one. Outside evidence suggests he was money-grubbing, etc. etc.) (I feel
tremendous *identity* with Shakespeare – partly for general and partly for
quite special reasons.) (I don't mean the money-grubber.)

You ask where I would like to be. India, yes, the Andes, yes! (I wonder
if I shall ever see the Andes. Have you seén them?) But now having been in
improbable southern Italy and having seen those Titians I am quite happy
at present to be at Steeple Aston. A touring company who are putting on a
play of mine in October will be rehearsing in Oxford next week, so I shall
have that curious pleasure of hearing real people speaking my lines.

1 Kreisel was writing a biography of the philosopher Bertrand Russell which was to be published in the
   series 'Biographical Memoirs of Fellows of the Royal Society' in 1973.
2 Henry de Montherlant (1895–1972), French writer whose work frequently expressed reactionary and
   misogynist views.

You are absolutely right about Kraft durch Freude.[1] (It is even a deep idea.) As for spas, I have a lot of money tied up in Czechoslovakia (blocked royalties) and could go free, as it were, to Karlsbad (or whatever it's called now). I can't imagine spa life though. You like it I think? People-hunger I suffer chronically (perhaps occupationally) though not for very good reasons since I have a lot of very good people. But I can (now I don't teach) never co-operate with anyone in my work, or even talk to anyone about it (except in the theatre – hence its attraction).

I wonder what you are doing now? Are you working? Is the depression going quietly away? I do hope so. *Local* irritants (teeth etc.) may even help. Describe what you are doing.

It's odd: I talk to you (letter-wise) regularly but often feel that I don't understand – I can't 'catch' your moods or grasp the intent of your words. You elude classification for me more than anyone I know (and this is sometimes charming). You know that I value this friendship very much indeed, it is very precious to me. I love you and admire you and feel (though this is a banal word) 'proud' about it all. I mean, it gives me pleasure in a special way, promotes confidence, more good things than I could explain briefly (in spite of the 'alarming *veri*'[2]).

This is not a very good letter and hasn't said quite what I want to say. I hope you can understand though. And I do hope you are feeling much better and will write to me soon.

Ever, with much love

I

To Brigid Brophy.

Steeple Aston
21 October [1972?]

It was delightful to be with you and I loved meeting Alison,[xvi] who is a darling. Let's meet again before too long. Maybe you and A could come over for lunch at Cornwall Gardens. I'll write again re possible meet November. So glad to have seen you. All very best and love

I

And love to Mike and Darius.[3]

1 Strength through joy. Possibly a reference to the German organisation set up in 1933 to promote subsidised state-controlled leisure activities, which also advertised the advantages of National Socialism and boosted the flagging tourist economy.
2 Alarming truths.
3 Michael Levey and Brigid Brophy's much-loved Persian cat.

To Philippa Foot.

Steeple Aston
3 November 1972

My dear, thank you so much for your letter. It was so moving and extraordinary to see you there in the theatre! I'm glad you liked the play.[1] As the critics (with some exceptions) didn't, I fear no London producer is likely to prolong its life, so it will cease forever to be at the end of next week. (The company is due to 'rest' anyway.) It has all been so marvellous and so sad. Married, yes, and then instant divorce. Of course I have fallen in love with Ian[2] – (Yorimitsu is, it occurs to me, the only *purely* romantic hero I have ever created) – as I idly, little did I then know, predicted to you when they were all rehearsing at the Clarendon Press Institute – but one might as well love a monk. The theatre is another world and I don't and can't live there. One has this intensely close relationship with a group of people and then they simply vanish. It has been a wonderful experience (they are *such* a good company) – but now I feel so terribly sad. (I shall not see the play again.)

I hope I'll see you *soon*, and will write or ring about that. Yes, we would *love* that marble thing and I think I know where it could so handsomely sit! *How sweet of you!* But don't be hasty. Your lovely house[3] hasn't settled down yet and it may yet be needed? I hope the curtain problem is happily resolved. *À bientôt* and much love

I

To Albert and Naomi Lebowitz.

Steeple Aston
24 January 1973

Just to say thank God about the Vietnam ceasefire. It must be such a relief to you all over there. Even here it has been such a burden on the consciousness (and conscience). So awful and so long. [. . .]

Term has just started and John is beset by pupils. It remains uncannily warm and sunny here. I have just finished reading *Middlemarch*. How super

1 Murdoch's *The Three Arrows* had opened in Cambridge in October 1972.
2 Ian McKellen, who played Yorimitsu.
3 Refers to the house in Walton Street, Oxford, where Philippa now lived during vacations.

it is. One forgets the funniness of serious writers sooner than anything. I am struggling on with my own awful novel.[1]

With much love

I

How awful German is. I have fallen back discouraged.

To Raymond Queneau, written on return from a British Council lecture tour in Egypt.

Steeple Aston
23 April 1973

Dearest Raymond, thank you very much indeed for *Le voyage en Grèce*.[2] (Concerning Le voyage en Égypte see below.) I was so grateful and touched to receive it with your words written inside. *Thank you.* And what a remarkably interesting set of texts. I am delighted with the book.

I have just been in Athens where I gave a lecture (on Natural Rights!) and talked to a very large number of writers. Then to Egypt where after John and I had toiled for some time in the university and were about to be released for sightseeing purposes (just after one final working luncheon where a Sufi mystic with very poor English was asking my views on the many and the one) (not that I yield to anyone in my interest in Sufism) John broke his leg by catching it on the safety belt of the car, and we had to come home abruptly. (He is in plaster and OK.)

I hope *you* are OK and writing more poems, novels. Be well. With my thanks and love

Iris

To Naomi Lebowitz.

Steeple Aston
[May 1973]

Dearest Nay,

Many thanks for your very nice letter written on personalised naomic writing paper. I am very sorry not to have replied sooner. I've been trying

1 Either the final draft of *The Sacred and Profane Love Machine*, which Murdoch completed in March, or the beginning of *A Word Child*, the first draft of which she finished in November 1973.
2 Queneau's latest book.

to finish (and have now thank God finished) a novel[1] and could somehow do nothing else, not even pick up papers off the floor. My room is like a very ancient forest. [. . .]

We are going to France in about ten days and then on to Greece. I don't actually want to go anywhere. I feel so damn tired, but I suppose it will 'do one good'. It must be nearly time to hear of your Italian timetable? When will you be in (en route) England? I do hope you have not abandoned your Italian villa plan. That is very important.

I have just discovered Trollope,[2] he is super! Somehow I despised him when I was young – on the basis I think of *Framley Parsonage*. Now I am Barsetised. Do you like him? Perhaps the taste is too English-ecclesiastical. Oh when shall we see you???

Much love

I

Nay, PS, I think I never told you how *charmed* I was by your delightful quote from ME about 'vanities'.[3] So apt, and so jolly kind of you to have *read* the book – one cannot (that *would* be vanity) really assume that more than a tiny handful of people actually *read* one's books.

I have a dotty fan in Atlanta Georgia who has been writing to me for ten years or so, obviously a tiny bit crazy: she has just 'discovered' that all my novels are really secret love letters addressed to her! Her ingenuity in working out the code is remarkable! [. . .]

I

To The Times.

2 July 1973

Sir, As a Labour voter, I was a little dismayed by some of Mr Roy Hattersley's[4] recently expressed views about education (uttered, I thought, with a rather commissar-like ferocity!) to the effect that all schools must be forced to join in 'the progress of education' by becoming comprehensive and (thereby?) non-selective.

---

1 *The Sacred and Profane Love Machine.*
2 Anthony Trollope (1815 –82), prolific Victorian English author, best known for six novels about the clergy and the landed gentry collectively referred to as 'The Chronicles of Barsetshire'.
3 Possibly a reference to the essay 'On "God" and "Good"' (1969), in which Murdoch had written, apropos the role of philosophy in becoming good, 'at this point someone might say all this is very well, the only difficulty is that none of it is true. Perhaps indeed all is vanity, *all* is vanity and there is no respectable intelligent way of protecting people from despair'.
4 British Labour politician, at this time Shadow Secretary of State for Education.

What constitutes progress in education is one of those matters about which decent rational people differ a lot; which is perhaps in itself an argument for variety of schools. I do not think that the main aim of an education policy should be to remove 'unfair' academic advantages or even to make children relaxed and happy. Each child should receive a rigorous academic education which implies a selection process.

While we have selective universities (and non-selective universities are not universities) we must have selective schooling. Ultimately a general comprehensive system could operate a fairish method of selection and also reach the highest academic standards. To achieve this should not be beyond our wits and there is no need to be *resigned* to the idea that 'more' means 'worse'. But at present while comprehensive schooling is in a state of experiment and coming-to-be there are sound arguments for retaining existing schools of other types, if they have high academic standards. Of course this is 'unfair' to parents who do not live near a good grammar school or who cannot afford the fees of an independent school. But at least during the interim (and people grow up during interims) some children will be receiving a suitable education of which it would be equally unfair to deprive them.

There are two separate though related points here: (1) that, as things stand at present, academically good non-comprehensive schools should continue to exist, and (2) that education should be (by some method) selective. The latter point is the more important. 'Non-selective education' is particularly unjust to the talented poor child whose home background often cannot compensate for loss of strict academic training, and the best defence of whose rights is the examination system.

Yours faithfully,
Iris Murdoch
Steeple Aston, Oxford

To Sir Isaiah Berlin, president of Wolfson College, Oxford, and long-time friend and colleague of Murdoch. This is just one example of several letters Murdoch wrote to him asking him to help European academic dissidents find refuge in Oxford. As a champion of individual liberty he was known to be sympathetic to such cases.

Steeple Aston
summer 1973

Dear Isaiah,

Please forgive me for bothering you out of the blue and at this fantastically busy time of year with the problem of one Stefan Morawski, formerly professor of aesthetics at Warsaw (expelled for political dissidence). Briefly, he is anxious to come to England from September 1973 and is looking for some sort of post. He would need *some* money. I wonder if he is the sort of person Wolfson College could consider? John and I met him at a philosophical conference and thought him very intelligent and learned – and very nice. He is an open cheerful Pole, not a neurotic one! He speaks perfect English. He was lately teaching at Berkeley, where no doubt someone could speak for him. The enclosed curriculum vitae gives a lot of information about him. Please forgive me for troubling you with this problem – about which doubtless there will naturally be waiting and seeing.

　Au revoir, and with my love
　Iris

To Raymond Queneau.

Steeple Aston
22 July 1973

Raymond, thank you very much for sending me the splendid book full of Queneau. I was *delighted* to get it – and some of the pictures of you! Much thanks. I thought that the *dédicace*[1] was a little distant after all these years, but I begin to think that such impressions may have something to do with the weird genius of the French language – which has not (am I right?) got so many stopping places between formality and intimacy as English has. English is a better language for mere affectionate talk. (This is connected with other features of English, such as those that make it the best philosophical language.) Anyhow I don't write to lecture you but to send the enclosed with my love. I enjoy Kreisel as a link between us. Be well, ever
　Iris

To Georg Kreisel.

Steeple Aston
[early August 1973]

My dear, thank you very much for your informative letter. [. . .]
　About why you want me to be more critical of you. This is indeed interesting. I wonder if you want more criticism in general or only in relation to the Russell piece? It cannot be and certainly not in the latter case, that

---

1 Probably a personal inscription rather than a formal dedication.

you imagine that you will learn anything from me. What could you possibly learn from me about anything which could be expressed as criticism? I suppose in some instances I might usefully tell you that something was unclear – e.g. if you were writing for the layman, which you weren't in the Russell case. Do you want to be criticised by Isaiah Berlin? It cannot be (or can it) that you want me to bully you. (I am not without the instinct to do so.) This would be a delicate matter. The 'tone' of our friendship has (it seems to me) rather implied that you were the dominant partner and this has pleased me. However when in a recent case you bullied me I resented it! Sadomasochism is so enormously specialised and precise. This is why it is so dangerous to the artist. (One does not want to be beaten, but beaten with a particular instrument, etc. etc.) And of course one (we) must be in the *ordinary* sense fearfully truthful and precise and mind one's tongue. (A lack of precision in your remarks about my work upset me.) This is a random speculation and may be well off the mark. Criticism increases our sense of having a real audience and may be wished for, for this simple reason.

I am going to France next week, and will be away ten days or so, could be two weeks. Best address is here. Much love

I

To Brigid Brophy.

Steeple Aston
[summer 1973]

Thank you very much for letters and for you on Firbank.[1] I don't know that I specially need conversion. I think well of Firbank. In saying I like you better I intended a compliment. But I am sure there are many finer points etc. and I shall read you with interest and as always with pleasure. [. . .]

I am surprised you evaded *War and Peace* when young. It may be a matter of generation (I mean we old war dogs all read it, thinking it would minister to our condition, which it did). I think it is very very good. Perhaps you think this now. I am going to read *Pendennis*,[2] when I have finished *Watt*.[3] It's not the bawdy in *Watt* I don't understand, but things like why particular words get repeated seventeen times, instead of ten, or not at all. Beckett if asked would probably say there was no reason: which in the context would

---

1 Brophy's *Prancing Novelist: A Defence of Fiction in the Form of a Critical Biography in Praise of Ronald Firbank.*

2 *The History of Pendennis: His Fortunes and Misfortunes, His Friends and His Greatest Enemy* (1848–50) by William Makepeace Thackeray.

3 A novel by Samuel Beckett published in 1953.

constitute a reason. I should have spotted *formal*-e. The word *formel*-e exists, in case it's any use to you. Much love

    I

To Scott Dunbar, the young Canadian whom Murdoch had met when teaching at the RCA.

Steeple Aston
[summer 1973]

Scott dear, *lovely* pressed flower card just come, thank you so much. And Rene[1] had her one too and is delighted! She asks me to send you much love and thanks. You have a wonderful line in cards (such a good invention). How beautiful the flowers are. Thank you too for the very interesting Irish journal (rather Republican I fear!). Who is Anthony Perkins[2] I wonder. I loved your letter and fascinating (and funny) account of your friend Lorna Lombardo and her wonderful huge loft flat in *the* best district. (I saw such a flat, huge loft and warehouse, when I was last there, in Chelsea area, I visited it with Dee Wells,[3] it belongs to John Cage,[4] he wasn't there.) It would be marvellous if you could live in such a flat one day. (Gay movie houses all around. I doubt there is *one* in London.) I hope I thanked you for the instructive Gay Street postcard. You were lucky to get your specs back. Lucky too to have hot weather! Cool English summer here. However, we are just going for two weeks to France (near St Remy, Van Gogh country, stay with Stephen and Natasha Spender). I shall take the philosophy stuff with me. How I hate it and wish it was all over! It's so obsessive – especially when Wittgenstein appears on the scene as he often does. (Does Wittgenstein interest you much? He is rather a nervous craving.)

    If we live till 1985 we shall see Halley's Comet. Isn't that wonderful and worth waiting for? Not that I mind waiting anyway. I am glad New York went so well and was so full of magic. Perhaps some of it came out of your pocket. With much love

    I

---

1 Murdoch's mother.
2 Presumably the American actor whose most famous role was Norman Bates in Alfred Hitchcock's film *Psycho* (1960).
3 Journalist, broadcaster and wife of A. J. Ayer, whom she married twice. The Bayleys were to be witnesses at the second wedding in 1989.
4 American avant-garde composer, music theorist and writer.

To Georg Kreisel.

Steeple Aston
[September 1973]

Kreisel dear, thank you very much indeed for your letter. [. . .]

About the matters mentioned in your letter. You 'objectify' what I persistently want to think of as your 'motives' in a curious way, *and you may be right*. You are certainly right to apprehend that you are exceptional. *What the exceptionalness is, exactly, continues to elude me*. Your 'character' (if that is the right word) is of tremendous interest to me. About 'convictions' by the way. You suggested I failed to realise that propositions had implications. (I know you are amazingly concise – perhaps I just wanted more pictures and conversations – these are, or can be, after all forms of explanation.) But do not your *views* here have implications? Perhaps you would say – maybe they have, but I do not *want to bring about anything*. This is by the way. One of the odd (and also admirable) things about you does concern 'precision': your example of 'there are less than a hundred people in this room' (when there are two) is good. But it depends what we want to elucidate. One can of course be precise and off the mark. But with some kinds of problems the serious failure is not to be precise at all, perhaps not to know what kind of thing precision would be: e.g. if the question is, 'Is A's attempt to help B to be understood as: altruism, affection, duty, officiousness, desire for power, malicious curiosity . . .' One has to invent a language to answer this question – and the most precise answer must build in the innate ambiguity, even actually haziness, of the subject matter.

About the sadomasochistic aspect of giving and receiving criticism – this is of course not a general matter – for some people it is non-existent and for others only operates in certain cases. You, I think, oddly enough (given some of your attitudes) are not in the least sadomasochistic. Would you agree? One other point: I wonder what you mean by 'self-sufficiency'? You mention this in the context of your need for help from critics. You mean that you then *include* the criticisms, take as it were the outside reaction into the inside? Are you, or are you becoming, self-sufficient about people too? I must stop this and do something else. I have far too much that I have to do. This letter may sound cool and detached but you can of course read the affection (which is really its main point) between the lines. Much love.

To Albert and Naomi Lebowitz.

Steeple Aston
[early October 1973]

My dears, thank you very much for your letters which arrived to cheer our beginning of term (return to 'school'). What a world scene. That war is so *awful*, and so needless and unexpected just when it seemed that the Arabs were settling down to diplomacy.[1] If the Israelis had only been a little more willing to *talk* even about the occupied territories – 'We want our land back' is a respectable attitude. But the wilfulness of it all – and the destruction of people and the ruining of lives every day. And the *will* to war on both sides. In my innocent childhood I did not imagine such *will* could go on existing. What a planet. Let's hope Kissinger[2] (who will perhaps shortly be running the USA – he seems to be the last man left!) and the Russians can cook up something to stop it. (Will Nixon be impeached do you think?[3] He seems to be acting like one whom the gods want to destroy.) [. . .]

I forget if I told you we are being chucked out of our London flat? We are now trying to buy a flat on the other side of the same square. It has a lovely view which you must soon come and look at.

We think of you very much. Au revoir and ever much love
I

To Albert Lebowitz.

Steeple Aston
11 October 1973

Dearest Al, thank you very much indeed for your letter. It interested me very much. I hope you didn't mind my attempt to be objective. I am so pro-Semitic (honorary Semitic) and identify so much with your race, I can allow myself the luxury of attempted objectivity. It's quite hard actually. And in the case of *Ireland* practically impossible (for me). My next letter (with 600 others) to *The Times* (when it has been put into English, which since it is not written by me it isn't yet in) will concern a splendid plan to turn the Sinai Desert into a blooming rose garden with international money and fraternal Israel–Arab toil. I suppose it's not inconceivable.

1 The Yom Kippur War.
2 Henry Kissinger, at this time the US National Security Adviser.
3 The Watergate scandal had broken in June 1972; following revelations during the summer of 1973, Nixon resigned in August 1974, thus avoiding certain impeachment.

We hardy types here are well on into the sweater era, with general oil shortage and local variety strikes. New College was blacked out lately and we attempted a delightful candlelit dinner party – everyone was delighted except the servants. What is a *parka*, by the way?

We hope to see David and Pamela Hadas[1] soon London-wise lunch-wise, and will get a good whiff from University City. The place has become now, in my imagination and memory, a paradise of beautiful houses, *palaces*, like something in the background of an Italian picture. How is your writing life, Al? Law book, novel? I picture you at work in your tree house. I am just finishing the first draft of a novel and feel rather sad and discontented with it, yet by now sold to it and unable to get my feet out of the morass: which sounds just like life. Keep well, keep writing, not only for posterity but to me. With much love

I

To Philippa Foot.

Steeple Aston
24 October 1973

My dearest girl, just another note. I do hope things are much better now? I hear you have moved! (I was with my publisher at a party concerning public lending rights at St Ermins, Caxton St, and wandering with her toward Victoria afterward saw the light on at 5 Seaforth and visited Marion!) I do hope the new place is altogether better and that you are having good philosophy and enjoying life. (Loved Goodman's party.[2] I think he is super and *so* attractive. Harold Wilson said he looked horrible. Stupid old Harold.)

John has got an Oxford chair, the new Eng lit one at St Catherine's. He did not apply and was rather stunned when it was offered – he wasn't sure he wanted it! (Not because of St Cath's, he quite likes that, but because of more lectures – he never quite gets over the speech-impediment worry.) Now however that indecision is over he is pleased; it will certainly be a change from the great teaching load.

Thank God the Middle East war has stopped for the moment. The Nixon Show goes on though – isn't it *extraordinary*?

WRITE SOON

1 David Hadas was professor of English and of religious studies at Washington State University at this time; his wife Pamela was a poet.
2 Lord Goodman, leading London lawyer who became solicitor and adviser to several politicians, including Prime Minister Harold Wilson.

With much love
I

I do wish you were here.

To David Morgan, in response to a letter from him written under the influence of LSD 'not in my normal voice, but in a sort of echoic God-voice as God. It took a bit more than that to get elevated to one of her God figures and prompted this sharp reply'.[xvii]

21 November 1973

Dear David, thank you for your letter and impression of God. I have met another high incarnation since, rather more convincing. Could we meet on Monday Dec 3 at 12 in the Duke of Wellington Wardour St?
    Best wishes,
    Iris

To Philippa Foot.

Steeple Aston
25 November 1973

[. . .] I am so sorry to hear Dawn[1] is knocked out. Well one would be, it would all revive. How rotten that so many people are unjustly unhappy. Most of the human race no doubt. But one does notice it at one's own door.
    I have finished the first draft of a novel[2] and feel very fed up with it. There it sits, all fat and awful. I feel very tired and wish I could rest but cannot. How is it done? Rest? What is that? Russian verbs console, however. And music. And great paintings. Did you ever go to see the Titian *Diana and Actaeon*?[3]
    Much love.

---

1 Dawn Daniel (née Bosanquet) was Philippa Foot's first cousin. On the dissolution of her marriage, her husband, Peter Daniel, married Foot's sister, Marion.
2 *A Word Child*.
3 Titian's famous painting (1556–9), at this time owned by John Sutherland, 6th Duke of Sutherland, but held on long-term loan at the National Gallery of Scotland.

To Philippa Foot.

Steeple Aston
20 December 1973

[. . .] Ages since I heard from you. I hope all is very well. I dreamt about you lately (a nice dream) – you had a house in France and I counted seven people working in the kitchen. Beautiful geese were walking about outside. No special news here (except of course that the country seems to be done for) (very little oil or petrol, coal strike, rail strike electricity cuts etc. There is even talk of a coalition government!!).

We should be in London for Christmas as usual, organised military style by John's brother.[1] (I like that! I want to be *organised*.) I want to talk to you very much. Your absence is absurd. When will you be back?? We may be away in the spring, but not for long. I wish I could write a philosophical poem, or indeed a poem of any kind. WRITE. MUCH LOVE.

I

To Naomi Lebowitz.

Steeple Aston
9 February 1974

Dearest Nay, thank you for very cheering letter. We need a bit of cheering with this horrible election on when everyone will be very nasty to each other in a thoroughly unBritish manner. And the coal strike etc. – I can't see how this country can stay in business. But enough of politics. [. . .]

I have stopped reading P. G. Wodehouse[2] and am now reading *Tintin*. Do Jo and Ju[3] read *Tintin*? If not, why not?

A literary question for you: what am I supposed to think about Flannery O'Connor?[4] My mad fan in Atlanta Georgia (the one who thinks all my books are cryptic love letters written to her) went on for some time to me about one Flannery O'Connor and I (not unnaturally) thought she meant Flann O'Brien. The one was female, the other male, but who cares these days? The situation was clarified when she sent me the complete stories of this F. O'Connor. I read one or two and thought them very accomplished

1 Michael Bayley was a brigadier in the British Army.
2 In a previous letter Murdoch admitted that she had abandoned Solzhenitsyn's *Cancer Ward* for P. G. Wodehouse.
3 The Lebowitz children, Joel and Judith.
4 American writer and essayist.

but was not really moved. (I find it hard to read short stories, unless by Joyce etc.) Should I persevere, *is* she very good? I feel unable to make up my own mind. [. . .]

    With much love,
    I

To *Philippa Foot*.

Steeple Aston
14 February 1974

Darling , *je pense à toi et à ton* Michael.[1] Do write. The garden here is full of snowdrops. I am hating the general election. (A *horrid* election.) I am so frightened of the extreme left. I know you glory in them. And you think people should be allowed to do nothing. Ah well. If they could only be not only happy but *quiet* doing nothing. Enough of this elliptical argument. [. . .]

    I wish you were back in yours in Walton St. I have a lot of things I want to SAY which can only be said to you. Meanwhile – enjoy sun, sea, nice Americans – when nice *so* nice. We lately entertained an American general, opposite number of John's brother. *Sweet*– though up to what?

    Much much much love
    Your I

To *Georg Kreisel*.

Steeple Aston
14 February 1974

Dearest K, thank you very much for your letter. You tend to scold me in letters these days! This time it is for professing to be interested in Wittgenstein, and not reading about him. Well, I suppose, as in the shaggy dog story, I am not all *that* interested. I am of course interested in his *thought* and frequently read him, though I only study a very small number of things therein. He always prompts thought in me. About his life – I have read Max Black's memoir[2] – I don't really want to read about him – I think I am only interested in 'my' Wittgenstein – I would love to hear anecdotes about him

---

1 I'm thinking of you and your Michael. (Philippa Foot was in a new relationship.)
2 Murdoch might be confusing here Max Black's *A Companion to Wittgenstein's Tractatus* (1964) with Norman Malcolm's *Ludwig Wittgenstein: A Memoir* (1958).

from you or Elizabeth or Shah or Hijab – as if I were to meet someone at dinner, etc. But 'Wittgenstein as I knew him' or 'The Childhood of Wittgenstein', no. I find the same about other thinkers e.g. Simone Weil, about whom there are now endless books. I like her thought, I am interested if I come across a photo, but I would not pursue *accidental* details about her very far. If a thinker forces his life on you as *part* of his thought (e.g. Kierkegaard) that is another matter. But of course Wittgenstein never did that. So I suppose my claim to be 'interested in Wittgenstein' falls in a sense to the ground!

I was very struck too of course by your (in this case) analysis of why you were cross with me, and I think I understand it. I think one can, in personal relations certainly, and perhaps also (the question is interesting) in politics, be *too* impatient with a certain 'play' of vagueness in the human mind. Some things are (e.g.) 'clearish'. As if someone were to say 'I have no view about Solzhenitsyn because I don't know the details'. Enough of this. I have left myself no space to discuss your other striking remarks about taking enjoyment in undiluted chunks! More about that later. Meanwhile, much love

I

To Philippa Foot.

Steeple Aston
5 March 1974

Dear girl, how are you? Do write. Listening yesterday to the Seventh Symphony, I felt a great sense of your presence. Why do I connect you with the Seventh Symphony?

We have had, here, our horrible election with its horrible result.[1] I hate them all. The icy cold spring is doing its stuff. I am moving out of one London flat and into another. How is your Michael? Have you managed to see each other? Do write. And WHEN are you coming home? I have just finished a novel[2] and feel pretty dotty (I miss the characters so).

MUCH LOVE.

---

1 The general election took place on 28 February, resulting in no overall majority; Edward Heath resigned and the Labour Party was returned to power with Harold Wilson as prime minister.
2 *A Word Child.*

To Georg Kreisel.

Steeple Aston
24 March 1974

Dearest K, I had an illusion of having written to you. I sometimes 'think' letters to you, and then am not sure if they emerged on paper. One wonderful thing about you is that you put your full address on every letter. This is a kind of humility, anyway an absence of silly egoism. People whom I scarcely know (and I get lots of letters from such) send one letter with their address – then if I reply (*when* I reply – I always do unless they are mad or spiteful) the second letter has no, or a truncated, address. As I haven't kept their silly letter, they then hear from me no more, and serve them right! I have of course recorded your address, but I could lose the record.

I didn't mean to spend so much time on that point! Further about my 'strong interest' in Wittgenstein, perhaps you are not as right as you think. There are certain thinkers (and others) whom one internalises – one has one's own private one. To say I am interested in Wittgenstein puts it too mildly. I am Wittgenstein. (I am also Shakespeare and Plato. Not bad, eh?) Not the 'real' Wittgenstein of course. (But *what* is that anyway?) (I like Lenin's remark about idealism.) But the one who has inspired and (*very much*) *influenced* me. As I imagine he has influenced you? I think I would *then* have loved Wittgenstein (man) if I had known him at all – though I think *now* I would not like such a person, I would judge him more harshly as a person. (As Lord Longford judged Russell in a recent broadcast, with a free naivety which I liked.) Wittgenstein (thinker) is an endless source of delight, a piercing of dullness, an electrical impulse of pure thought. I hope you are OK. With much love

I

To Brigid Brophy.

Steeple Aston
[April 1974?]

Thanks for the exciting news. 'Frank' seems to be one of those words that set people off. I forget if I told you I met JM[1] once, I think at a party at number 10. That was the night when I overheard our PM, then Harold Wilson, saying complacently 'Everyone who makes Britain tick is here tonight'.

1 Unidentified.

I was gratified then, but cannot feel now that I am making Britain tick, can hardly tick myself, main spring broken. At least I have written a letter to *The Times* attacking Reg Prentice,[1] only I don't suppose they'll print it. Tick on thou.

Love

I

PS. Reflecting on the evident impact of 'frank'. I think I told you once (or did you tell me) that market research had shown that the most commercially attractive words in novel titles were 'doctor' and 'naked'. Recently I saw that similar research had turned up 'Tangier' as a good word. Title therefore of my next novel: *Tangier Frank, the Naked Doctor*.

To The Times.

Steeple Aston
19 April 1974

Sir, I hear on my radio Mr Reg Prentice, of the party which I support, saying to a gathering on education the following: 'The eleven plus must go, so must selection at twelve plus, at sixteen plus, and any other age.' What can this mean? How are universities to continue? Are we to have engineers without selection of those who understand mathematics, linguists without selection of those who understand grammar?

To many teachers such declarations of policy must seem obscure and astonishing, and to imply the adoption of some quite new philosophy of education which has not, so far as I know, been in this context discussed. It is certainly odd that the Labour Party should wish to promote a process of natural unplanned sorting which will favour the children of rich and educated people, leaving other children at a disadvantage.

I thought socialism was concerned with the removal of unfair disadvantages. Surely what we need is a careful reconsideration of how to select, not the radical and dangerous abandonment of the principle of selection.

Yours faithfully,
Iris Murdoch

1 Secretary of State for Education and Science between 1974 and 1975.

To Raymond Queneau.

Steeple Aston
20 May 1974

My dear, I received the poems with such pleasure – thank you for the dear inscription – and have been reading them with delight. (Or 'imbibing' them – they float into the wind by some quite special process. 'Inhaling'?) You are a marvellous poet. I wish I could write poetry. I sometimes try. You are very blessed. I wish I could see you. But could we communicate? If only you were a letter-writer (to me, anyway) as well as a poet! I hope you are well and I think of you with
    much love
    Iris

To Naomi Lebowitz.

posted from Steeple Aston
20 May 1974

Dearest Nay, splendid and cheering to get your letter. I write this in our new London pad at 29 Cornwall Gardens (across the square from the old one – better side, sun and view) waiting for Gasmen to come and change our stove etc. to North Sea Gas, which is the great British Gas, more expensive, less efficient for eating, and you can't even use it to commit suicide.

Your questions: John's book[1] is a sort of general one on character in fiction – but is really I think an 'All I know at Present' book. Everyone comes in. [. . .]

In the novel I have lately finished, *Skinker*[2] makes a modest appearance, however. I am trying to write a pamphlet on education. 'Let them all come' universities are becoming popular with our left wing. Oh dear.

I feel dismay about this anti-literary criticism drive. (What – not even *structuralist* lit crit.?) So much *thought* about *everything* appears in the form of literary criticism. But of course: thought? What's that?

A man has just produced a noise like a pipe cracking and a strong smell of old-fashioned gas pervades the flat. I think perhaps I had better go out before I become unconscious. MUCH LOVE
    I

1 Probably *The Characters of Love: A Study in the Literature of Personality.*
2 Skinker Street adjoins Washington University in St Louis. The Bayleys found the street name very droll; 'Skinker' also functioned as shorthand for their fond memories of their time spent at the university in St Louis.

To the New Fiction Society (Mr Kinler's Book Club).

Steeple Aston
11 June 1974

I really do not have favourites among my novels. They all vanish into the past with equal speed and become strangers. I choose, since I must choose one, *The Nice and the Good*, because this seems to be rather a happy book. It contains two characters I am very fond of, Edward and Henrietta; and there is general reconciliation and peace at the end. By the way, since one or two people have asked: no one in the book is good.
Iris Murdoch

To Albert Lebowitz.

Steeple Aston
14 June 1974

Dearest Al, thank you for your delightful and cheering letter! Hamlet life certainly goes forward here (it has a wholesome sound at least) but I'm not so sure about hard work. My latest way of wasting time is rearing butterflies. I buy the pupae from a butterfly farm and then release them when they are hatched. It cannot be said to be an arduous task as the butterflies do all the work. Only the blighters so far have always actually emerged when I wasn't looking, thus defeating an important part of the operation. Apart from butterfly farming, I have been trying rather unsuccessfully to plan my next novel.[1] [. . .]

We were hoping to go to Poland in July and spend some of my blocked zloties, and trust that this won't turn out to be a very Polish thing to do! I believe Krakow has some charms but I expect Warsaw to be terrible. And what can one buy except vodka? We have one Polish friend, an anti-regime philosopher who however manages to get to and from Harvard, and he will look after us. (I hope.) I feel a little anxious about the whole business. [. . .] I am longing to read your presidents book.[2] It should be a best-seller. Have you got an English publisher?? Let me know. MUCH LOVE.

---

1 *Henry and Cato.*
2 Albert Lebowitz was writing a book about law and the US presidency, which was finally published as *The Legal Mind and the Presidency* in 2013.

To Naomi Lebowtiz.

Steeple Aston
2 July 1974

Dearest N (just leaving Steeple Aston en route for Warsaw) so glad to get your letter.

The butterfly farming I fear merely varies the diet of the local swallows. Is it one of ours? John asks anxiously as some winged thing zooms by. Alas, rarely is.

God knows what Poland will be like. J thinks we shall have to push the plane to get it to take off (we are going Polish airlines). Have had one Polish experience already. I checked by letter *and* telephone that I could get our visas on a certain day. Turned up at the consulate on that day to find notice: 'Today is a Polish holiday so we are closed'. We will send you postcards.

I envy you your central European adventures, historical and linguistic. What a complex. I do look forward to reading you on Svevo. I was talking of him to someone the other night. He inspires universal love.

John sends much love. His Bellow piece is coming out soonish in *Salmagundi*.[1] Must go now and pack my bathing costume. Au revoir I *hope* and much love from

I

To Georg Kreisel.

Steeple Aston
[mid-July 1974]

Dearest K, thank you for your letter. I see what you mean about living in flats – a kind of externality and public existence. My country living is without servants (I do everything including the laundry) but of course one is *secluded*. (Nice word.)

Berryman,[2] whom you have probably looked up by now, is American – he was a great student hero, perhaps still is. A gloomy drug-addicted fellow, who kept talking about suicide and then killed himself by jumping off some famous bridge. (A dicey way to go, I should have thought.) His father committed suicide when he was a boy, and this seems to have affected him very much. Not a great poet, perhaps not even very good – not as good as

---

1 An American quarterly academic magazine.
2 John Berryman (1914–72), a key figure in the American 'Confessional' school of poetry.

Auden of course, or Robert Lowell who is now I suppose the best man writing in English. Perhaps not even as good as Philip Larkin. A careless chap, puts out unfinished stuff – but somehow delightful – turning egocentric gloomy ramblings into something beautiful. Very cheering, in a trench humour sort of way. He has a poetic voice, can just *talk* poetry. (So can Lowell.) Very enviable. Do you ever feel like committing suicide? I can scarcely conceive of this. *Thank you* for the Russell addendum. More of this later. With much love

    I

To Georg Kreisel.

Steeple Aston

15 August 1974

My dear, got back little while ago and found yours, only trying to finish novel and have not been writing letters. In fact we stayed away a long time, going from Poland to Italy (Como) and then to France (Les Baux) staying with friends and trying to work – which I find very hard when the temperature is 97F+. (I somehow imagine that you don't mind the heat. I tolerate it very ill, and am so glad to return to grey skies and low-flying cloud in England.)

I loved Poland. They had spruced it up a good deal since you were there I imagine, redoing all that eighteenth-century Wedgwood-style architecture rather well. I found Warsaw, all rebuilt, very touching somehow (and pretty). And what nationalism, what martyrology, what sense of grim identity, what a fierce grasp of history! Like Ireland, only not so stupid. My translator, host for lunch on first day, proceeded to tour of city: 'Here the ghetto used to be, here I was in prison, my cell was here, here I waited to be interrogated by the Gestapo, I sat in that seat, etc. etc.' (The Gestapo HQ kept just as it was, also prisons and every possible item of gruesome evidence – well, I expect you saw all this!) We also went to Auschwitz (did you?). It is very mysterious how rational beings could have proceeded in such a way. I feel that one thing that made it possible was the idea that the world had *utterly changed*, that something totally new was beginning, the 1,000-year Reich, etc. – and if only some ruthless clearing up could be done (cf. the liquidation of the kulaks[1]) everything would be perfect. However, all that just restates the problem.

I don't suppose you ever came across a philosopher called Stefan Morawski,

---

1 Wealthy peasant farmers in tsarist Russia who were accused by the Communists during the October Revolution of exploiting the people.

who was my main Polish host? A nice chap, notorious revisionist, chucked out of party and not allowed to teach – but draws his salary and can go abroad if he likes, perhaps they hope he'll stay away. He writes on Marxist (and other) aesthetics.

I feel quite bothered about Moody Road.[1] I can't now picture where you are. Where are you each night and are you OK? Thank you for telling me about your parents. And about how you did the other boys' homework! How *disgusting* anti-Semitism is – and how strange. I can understand about your not telling your parents. (They were lucky to survive. I suppose they got out?) I remember your telling me long ago about how you went back to Austria and were annoyed because some childhood friend recognised you and called you by some old nickname!

About the Wittgenstein-homosexual book (which *enraged* E. Anscombe as you can imagine – she won't believe it) – yes, I can quite picture this, just as you say. Why not? People's sexual preferences are often very private and have an oddity quite unconnected with their public persona and talents e.g. T. E. Lawrence. (Do you like him?)

Where and how are you? *Do write.*

Much much love,

I

To Naomi Lebowitz.

Steeple Aston
26 September 1974

Nay, dear girl, much thanks letter and so glad Svevo goes well – lack of torture surely good sign? My novel[2] very slowly begins (with vast help from Al who is practically co-author at present) and simply the task of running life seems more and more complex. Pleasantly so, I mean problems like 'Shall we transfer this sofa to London?' seem to take up inordinate time – in a world reeling with sin and misery etc. etc.

About Nixon, yes. I recall long ago a friend of ours, the one we were staying with in Scotland in fact, who is inter alia a political journalist, was in America and met both John Kennedy and Nixon when the latter was not yet in power or even near it – and said how much he disapproved of Kennedy's private life, but that Nixon was a thoroughly decent and clean-living man! Well, so he is in a way I'm sure, so oddly do people divide their lives!

1 Kreisel's previous address in Los Altos, California.
2 *Henry and Cato*.

Beginning of term looms ahead and John's spirits sink (he sends much love and *will* write – he just is not much good at often-writing, to write *any* letter is a sort of enterprise). We have just been moving his books etc. out of New College into the room about the size of a linen cupboard which they have allotted him at St Catherine's. It is rather sad though of course exciting too. St Catherine's looks like a Finnish keep-fit seminary, but it is in a very beautiful *place* beside the river and looking especially beautiful now.

I am just reading *War and Peace* for the nth time and was struck by how I tend to like the *people* less and the *book* more every time! When are you coming to Trieste via Steeple Aston?

Much love

I

To Elias Canetti.

[October 1974?]

My dearest Canetti,

Please forgive my long silence. John had sabbatical leave from Oxford all last year and this meant any visits to London were rather impossible. I rang you up on a few occasions and got no answer. (I gather from John Simopoulos you will now be in Zurich.) I do want to see you and I hope you will not be cross with me. I had rather be reproached in person than by *your* silence. I shall be around more regularly in London later this month and in Nov. and I will suggest a time beforehand and send a stamped postcard for yes/no reply. My work is rather at a standstill at the moment. I am writing poetry, which has an interlude feeling, as I am always very much at sea with this form. I want many things to be different but cannot see how this can be. I very much want to see you and to hear what you have been doing, to just *look* at you. I have thought of you a lot. I send my thoughts now, many more than can be written down, and do hope to see you before too long. With homage, *love*, ever your devoted

Iris

To Rachel Fenner, written soon after the birth of Rachel's son Nicholas, a Down's syndrome baby, on 10 December. In this letter Murdoch reassures Rachel that once she has made the decision about whether to keep the child or have him put into care, things will seem easier.

Steeple Aston
[mid-December 1974]

Dearest Rachel, I tried to ring you, but no luck, maybe you are not answering the phone. (I'm pretty hopeless on that instrument anyway.) I am so sorry. I feel that any words of comfort I may try to say are already known to you. One wishes at such times for magic, but the awful weight of reality won't be moved. I should think this is *now* the darkest time and later times will be better. Decision will immediately lighten the world. Whatever one decides one may later occasionally regret, but such is the way with decisions of this sort. It seems to me that, because of the way all things are here, whatever you decide will be right. That is, I don't see you poised between two quite different moralities, or (certainly not) between good and ill. You will decide whatever you decide in the right way, weighing the right things and attending to all things that should be attended to. I know there's little cheer in this. Whatever one does one may later sometimes think one has made a 'mistake', though that's different. There are hard fates in the world, but all kinds of graces and alleviations come unexpectedly when one has entered into them. My heart goes out so much to you, and to Frank. One so much wishes that God existed at such moments, so that one could *hurl* prayers at Him! May all enlightenment and healing come to you. It's a time of hope now, at Christmas, and there always *is* hope around. Thinking of you very much – and much love
    I

To Rachel Fenner.

Steeple Aston
December 1974

Rachel dear, just a note, leaving here for Christmas. I tried again to ring you but no luck. I am thinking about you very much. I wonder if you have any family, on either side, who are any good in such a crisis? Not that anyone can really advise you – but a sort of corporate *presence* of wise persons, or even sympathetic ones, if connected, could help. I hope that strength is coming to you and abiding with you. Much love.
    I

To Rachel Fenner.

Steeple Aston
27 December 1974

Rachel, just a note, after talking to you. I am sure you are right. Especially because of this matter of being an artist. I thought of writing to you about this earlier, but decided not to – and felt anyway I might have said too much, in view of your later feelings about keeping the child. There is a certain absoluteness, even a kind of ruthlessness, about being an artist, and one must be realistic about this. A normal child takes a lot of one's time and energy, but an abnormal child would have to be literally watched the whole time – and as you say, the services available are likely to be at best rather scrappy and unreliable. My friend who has kept her child has got a faithful full-time oriental servant living in her house! Even then the strain is terrible. You have got to consider how you can go on living as a whole person.
    Do ring Sunday. Much love
    I

To Georg Kreisel.

Steeple Aston
7 March 1975

Dearest K, thanks for your letter. [. . .]
    How interesting that Wittgenstein thought one could not imagine another in sexual ecstasy. What were his criteria of success in doing it? I think I can. But if set it as a task, one could do doubtless better with some people than with others. In some cases the imagination shies, either because of improbability or because of some *pudeur!*[1] (How dare I imagine so-and-so, etc. What an intrusion!) It always seems to me odd that one can (in some sense of 'can') dream anything about anybody. Of course there is a causal background, but I mean the liberties one takes – and how *weird* to think that one is parading about all the time, up to the strangest things, in other people's dreams!
    I know exactly what you mean about Wittgenstein understanding you *precisely* (about the war and so on) – and seeing you meant *only this* which you said and no more. He suffered a lot I imagine from people always drawing long instructive implications out of what he said. This drawing of

1 Sense of propriety.

faulty inference is a great cause of annoyance between people and can be very wounding; one *hates* to be misunderstood in certain ways. I suffer from this to some extent. Thank God for those who are *rational* enough to separate things! Really a definition of rationality.

I hope you are having a lovely time in Salzburg. I spent part of a winter there once after the war and recall it looking so marvellously beautiful in snow. Golden and white. I am just (next week) leaving to give some lectures in Japan, and will be coming back via USA (probably) though not San Francisco. I imagine you'll be away in any case. Let me know where you are. I'll be away till mid or late April. Write to me. I'd love to see your Festschrift bit on Wittgenstein.

Very very best, my dear as always, and my love,

I

PS about wildlife – yes I think I see what you mean. Do you watch animals and birds for real, I mean not in films? A quite different occupation of course and a different pleasure – I identify very much with beasts and birds, though ignorantly.

To Philippa Foot, written after the Bayleys had visited Japan for the second time on a British Council lecture tour. Murdoch gave a lecture in Kyoto entitled 'The Role of Mythology in Politics and the Novel Today'; she also visited the Daihonzan or temple of Ishiyamadera and, four days later, Hiroshima.[xviii] *The Bayleys briefly visited Philippa Foot in Los Angeles and the Lebowitzes in St Louis on their way home.*

Steeple Aston
23 April 1975

Dearest girl, we are home but our hearts are still in Santa Monica with the vole warden! We had *such* a happy time with you – it was so separated and special, and a *real* holiday, such as one rarely has. Thank you so so much. I was very touched that it reminded you of Seaforth. (And that your mother remembered that song!) I do hope we were not a nuisance and did not disturb work. Just being with you was heavenly. (And walking round those super roads and gazing at the houses and the trees! Keen Santa Monicans, we are now rereading Raymond Chandler with new eyes, identifying this and that.)

Of course, after such an interval of paradise, it's sad to be home, though the sun is shining like mad on our cold daffodils. *You* in California, that is the great thing, the great topic. I must admit it suits you, though I don't want you to stay there, in the land of the great supermarkets. You were a divinely kind host and everything was perfect and somehow huge: that wonderful drive to the desert (I hope it didn't tire you too much), the vast sand and the sea, meeting Isherwood,[1] the big trees on the campus . . .

[Continued] 24 April 1975

There was a *right place* feeling about it all.

(By the way, should I write to you at dear old 6th Street, our old home, or at UCLA?) Thank you for such a lot of happiness. And simply being relaxed in your company has done me such a lot of *good*.

I still feel tired from the journey and without will. I will send you my new novel, which has just come out.[2] I am already looking forward to your return here in June! It must be nice to *live* in two places which are so far apart (and *both* so pleasant).

I hope HUME goes on well. I would have liked to hear you on him. I feel at the moment that I shall never THINK again, but I daresay thoughts will return. Chez Blessed Santa Monica life was just a harmony. Thank you, dear darling, *so much*, and with *much* love – will write again soon – ever yours I

To Albert Lebowitz.

Steeple Aston
22 June 1975

Al my dear, thanks for your super letter. John, garbed in your blue trousers, has been busy climbing trees, digging holes, mending roofs etc. and generally performing the essential duties of an Oxford professor. A pity he was not present to help you with the *curious* drainage problem which you so eloquently and yet *obscurely* described. (There is a Kafka in every Jew?) I hope all's well on that front. (Unclear how far we are to blame, but clear we are. No guilt feelings.) Let us know in due course of Chrysler problems. (This makes *us* think of trade unions. God. This country is said to be six weeks away from being bankrupt. We still have to live the rest of our life on those St Louis dollar cheques.)

Do finish your legal book soon and write that novel. Funnier than Stan.[3] And the depths and the heights of what you *know*. Don't let it perish

---

1 Christopher Isherwood, English novelist.
2 *A Word Child.*
3 Stanley Elkin, American author and close friends of the Lebowitzes.

unrecorded. Get to work in that tree house. (How we miss it. And on last day John realised ambition of seeing a cardinal out of the top window.) [. . .]
MUCH LOVE.

To Scott Dunbar.

Steeple Aston
7 July [1975?]

My dear boy, thank you for those lovely cards – I take great pleasure in them. I love the monkeys (such touching, disturbing creatures) and your self-willed friend and your rather beautiful transvestite friend. What a gang you know! And how was New York? Dear friends there too, especially that Pole[1] we are both so fond of. And Oregon and San Francisco and the job hunt? I do hope you are having some luck. You spoke of 'La Fontaine' and then 'moving to another campus'. Does this mean Dawson or part of it is closing or has closed?[2] But your lectures on the *Republic* will go on, will happen? 'Virtue is Knowledge' (as I see it) connects Reality and Truth. (The moral aspect of really *understanding* anything. Simone Weil on 'attention'.) Perception and just understanding are the background of morals together with a love for what is good and beautiful and lucid and pure and just (etc.!), and these are indeed the great moral Forms. (And they interconnect.) The Theory of Forms also of course tries to answer other kinds of philosophical questions about universals, meaning etc.

I very much hope you will write also your book *On Visibility* (excellent title). This would be a very good and important book, and it would somehow be a moral philosophy book as well. [. . .]

I am struggling on with the philosophy stuff but find it very hard going and I cannot get things *clear*. I feel I have to write something about structuralism, but what a morass! Does structuralism bug you at all in your work, do the other dons profess it? Of course there is 'something in it' but much of that was done much better by Wittgenstein! I expect you are basking in summer heat. We have had the worst June since 1890, nothing but cold and rain (and still now). I'd like to get away to some *peaceful* warm place, but seems unlikely. Thank you for your Lowry picture and for George Herbert's words. With much love
I

1 Rembrandt's *The Polish Rider* in the Frick Collection, New York.
2 Scott Dunbar was teaching at Dawson College in Montreal. In 1975 the college had three campuses, one of which was near Parc Lafontaine.

To Georg Kreisel.

Steeple Aston
15 July 1975

Thank you for your letter with satisfactory details of Landlady. I note your desire to keep your image of 'rich' England untarnished. I think it is hard to tell how 'rich' an industrialised country is by just looking at it – and as a tourist here you would notice no changes, except perhaps a slightly greater air of affluence since people are spending their money instead of saving it. Certainly your friends in four-poster-bed land would be carrying on as usual (at least I hope so). I can't imagine they are running short of whisky and claret. The only *serious* hardship here concerns the price of house property.

As for democracy and popular votes, I certainly think this is the best available arrangement – but not referenda. Imagine one on homosexuality or hanging! City-state politics are very hazardous, and always were. A stable popular controlled oligarchy is what a good democracy is in effect. (Plato had *some* good ideas about politics – he certainly wasn't just a sort of fascist as philistines like Popper think. What did Wittgenstein think about Plato? Did he ever enter Wittgenstein's consciousness??)

I'm just going to France, but not for very long. [. . .]
Much love
I

To Albert and Naomi Lebowtiz.

Steeple Aston
9 August 1975

Your rhyming postcards are super duper
And leave us in a perfect stupor
Of admiration. Here
Everything is back to what passes as normal I fear.
No thrills or treats at present save
For an all-time record HEAT WAVE
Which while threatening to do us
In, reminds us pleasantly of St Louis.
We miss the luxuries of our French stay.
(Al's swimming trunks, by the way,
After declining the English Channel got
Into the Mediterranean like a shot.

They also floated like a *bateau*
In the mosaic pool of someone's château.
I fear they are rather upper crust
And warm water may now prove a *must*.)
We are glad you are having fun as planned
In the great clam chowder land.
(I have yet to discover what clam chowder is,
And suspect that I would give it a miss,
Not being a lover of shellfish.)
May I in closing express a wish
That next year we may in Europe forgather
And have much pleasant travelling and blather,
Our excellent foursome mopping up the wines
Of the great Provençal and Tuscan vines,
And seeing lots of lovely works of art
Before making a determined dart
For some nearby café or ristorante
To get drunk rapidly upon Chianti.

To The Times.

27 August 1975

Your review of Stowers Johnson's book[1] about Frank Thompson presents a picture of a grim and fanatical megalomaniac, trying to be 'Lawrence of Bulgaria'. The book is of course not a biography and the reviewer may be forgiven for having gained this impression of the man.

Those of us who knew and loved Frank at Oxford have different memories. He was a poet, a person of exceptional charm and sweetness, always full of jokes and fun, a lover of art and nature, a scholar, a man of the highest principles, delicate, scrupulous and tender.

When he was forced to become a soldier he became a very good one and obedience to his duty led him to a heroic role. But he was never the victim of dreams of violence or grandeur. Those who knew him will never cease to mourn the loss of this brilliant, brave and good man.

Iris Murdoch

---

1 *Agents Extraordinary.*

To Naomi Lebowitz.

Steeple Aston
14 September 1975

Dearest Nay, your excellent and up-cheering letter has just come. I do, with most interest, sympathise with the psychoanalysis withdrawing symptoms. You must notice that every day you feel *better.* You still have some illusions though: for instance that one becomes more real if one does boring and unpleasant work. (See literary critics who think that novelists who write about factory workers are more realistic than those who write about the idle carefree bourgeoisie.) (A friend of mine who was head of a teacher's training college[1] and had spent a typical week struggling with drug addicts, suicides and visits from the police said last straw was when someone said: of course you academics live such peaceful unreal sort of lives.) [. . .]

It would be so marvellous if we could meet in Italy. And of course you will come and stay here and could have London fun too (you could have our flat of course). [. . .]

LOVE
I

To Norah Smallwood.

Steeple Aston
20 November 1975

NORAH, what do you MEAN, how can you slander the bunnies that I love?[2] You obviously haven't read the book! They are *not* fascists. There are fascist bunnies in the story but they are the baddies who are defeated, after many exciting adventures by the goodie social democratic rabbits. It's a *marvellous* tale and highly moral, the hero is a *saintly* rabbit with excellent *moderate* views on how a warren should be run. I *loved* it. So did John, who particularly appreciated the Napoleonic talents of the wicked rabbit dictator, General Woundwart. You must read it at once. [. . .]

MUCH LOVE
I

1 Probably Marjorie Boulton.
2 Richard Adams's *Watership Down.*

To Raymond Queneau, possibly Murdoch's last letter to him.

Steeple Aston
27 November [1975]

Dear Raymond,
How very kind of you to send the book, and with your inscription: it gives me great pleasure. How delightful and *real* those Gallimard books look – and how splendidly *you* the contents. Thank you very much indeed. What a gorgeous language French is – and what a poet of it you are. (You are also a philosopher.)
I hope you are very well and happy. I was so pleased to have this proof of your remembrance. With very best wishes and love,
Iris

To David Hicks.

[13 January 1976]

David, thank you so much for writing. Let's meet Londonwise this term. I'll suggest dates. I note your plans. I think the most beautiful country in the world lies about twenty miles west of Evesham.[1] Au revoir and with my love, also to K.
I

To Philippa Foot.

Steeple Aston
23 March 1976

Dearest girl, I haven't heard from you for ages. You are however regularly present in my dreams, you will be glad to hear. In latest one, we were in somewhere like India, where the mountains (seen from a train at night) were made of pure gold. You asked me to dine with you at some grand place, and said that afterwards we would have a swim together in the warm midnight air in some delightful bay. I said I have no bathing costume, but you said, don't worry, no one will be there but us two. A very happy dream.
It's *freezing* cold here, in the manner of the English spring. How's Sid?[2]

1 David Hicks and his wife were planning to move to Worcestershire.
2 Sidney Trivus, a professor at California State University, Los Angeles. He and Philippa Foot were close in the 1970s.

And have you seen Michael again? I had dinner a little while ago with MRDF and his Dutch wife; they now live in Hampstead Garden Suburb. M has given up his Foreign Office training centre job (or whatever it was) which he hated, and is trying to live by writing. His wife still works at the BM.[1] Other people present, a strangely awkward evening.

Write your news and date of return. MUCH LOVE
I

PS Marion has now taken over lease of Seaforth.

To Albert Lebowitz.

Steeple Aston
2 April 1976

Dearest Al, mustn't leave you out of this distribution of comic air letters. Why celebrate Scotland?? The Scots are now practically our enemies. It's all part of a plot. Now that they have found oil off Aberdeen the Scottish Nationalist Party want an independent Scotland! They think that they could do very well as a little separate state living on oil and whisky! And hang England – they've always hated us anyway. However no one has told them that the crafty government in London has already sold all their oil to the Arabs in return for permission to go on seeming to run Britain for another few years! Much love
I

+ much love to both from John.

To Georg Kreisel.

Steeple Aston
14 April 1976

Kreisel, thank you for your letter. I feel very 'dashed', feel a particular disappointment with myself when I think how I disappoint you. Partly of course our interests diverge, and I try to follow yours when I ought perhaps to raise issues of my own. (Maybe I am *afraid* to do this in case you should think my interests absurd! I mean philosophical, or more so, quasi-philosophical

---

1 British Museum. Mirjam Foot is an expert on pictorial bookbinding and worked at the British Library then housed in the British Museum.

interests.) Partly, although I am in general a good letter-writer, I have never quite (this sounds silly) mastered the *form* of letters to you. It may be something to do with paper. (The Italian ancient historian De Sanctis[1] gave up his history of Greece during the 1914 war because he could not get the right notebooks.) I hate writing on airmail paper. I don't like these things, which impose a length. If I write extensively on ordinary paper I don't know what postage to put on, and suffer *Polizeiangst*.[2]

I know I sometimes pass over things I might pick up, but I don't always forget them, and may pick them up later, as e.g. your saying I probably have little experience of marshalling data. Reflecting on this I feel I do little else. At present actually I am writing some stuff on Plato, which involves vast arrangements, but apart from that, a long novel is a huge exercise in marshalling very heterogeneous data. Indeed, I feel the marshalling as being *the* task, since the data seem to appear of themselves. (I mean, in a way they wouldn't if I were either a scientist or a scholar.)

And apropos science/philosophy (and my recent yearning to say philosophy *is* thinking without presuppositions – or aspires to it) I was *very* interested in the page you sent of your lecture on Wittgenstein (is this part of what you said I would 'read like a novel'? What did you mean by that I wonder?) I quite like your respectful-destructive style when dealing with Wittgenstein (and with other matters)! I think Wittgenstein's later philosophy *is* revolutionary – in just the sense needed to make it a candidate for what I regard (rare) 'real philosophy' as being. Of course you agree it is revolutionary for philosophers. But I was most interested in your 'silent majority'. Of course science is in some (obvious) sense 'the principal heir'. But you are somehow suggesting that philosophy is (therefore) unimportant? I suspect one of our (yours and my) main arguments (not a quarrel) is about philosophy. Actually, rereading your enclosed page I think it is marvellous, very full of razor-sharp thought and very funny! About the *effect* of the *Tractatus*, including its effect on Wittgenstein – yes. Yet one is dazed by a sense of its greatness. (It's all in Plato of course, but philosophers have, as it were, always to discover the circulation of the blood for themselves.) Thanks for answering my (repeated) Jewish question. More on that later.

Can I now have the whole of the thing you said I would read like a novel? (Do you regard *yourself* as a philosopher?) Surely you do. [. . .]

I think I will now give up writing on these air letters and will try to get some suitable paper.

Much love

I

1 Gaetano De Sanctis (1870–1957).
2 An invented German word that humorously suggests 'fear of the police'.

To Georg Kreisel.

Steeple Aston
[May 1976]

Dearest best Kreisel: argument by letter is nice but sometimes laborious.
Let me recapitulate. (1) You said (excellently) that Wittgenstein gave one
confidence in 'thinking without theories'. (2) I said – isn't that just philosophy?
(3) You said, what about boxers, housewives and businessmen? (4) I said, *they*
are consumed with half-baked theories. (5) You said, Wittgenstein didn't
mean housewives, etc. when he said get back to scratch. True! He thought
it almost impossible *even* for philosophers. (As Plato thought too.) Most
people, inside are filled with *unexamined junk* – only (perhaps) philosophers
and (?) saints ever get rid of it. (Sorry, delete saints.) I maintain my view
about housewives, etc. I think these *are* (sort of) theories they hold.[1] As for
philosophy – of course *some* philosophy deploys theory. But much, in philosophy of mind, ethics, etc. *can* be comparatively theory-less and is better
so in my view. (And thus I interpret Wittgenstein.)

Queneau (of course) didn't come alas.[2] He is a sort of casualty in my life
(I am the victim I mean). His fault no real friendship – I have tried. I suspect
it is something to do with the French language. You, I suspect, *have* a genuine
friendship with that splendid man, which I shall now never have, and I grieve
for it. I have just got now Bartley's fascinating book[3] on how Wittgenstein
used to have love affairs with rough young men. I suppose it is true. Horrid
reading for Miss Anscombe.

Much love
I

*To Philippa Foot, mentioning Murdoch's mother's mental health problems which
had become evident by the summer of 1975 and were now worsening.*

Steeple Aston
20 September 1976

My dear, I was so glad to hear from you, I was just thinking about you.
We've been away a lot, partly in France (Provence) in August, and now in

---

1 In a previous letter Murdoch had defined the ideas of 'housewives' about nutrition as 'theories'.
2 In a previous letter Murdoch had told Kreisel that she expected to see Queneau soon at a dinner at
  All Souls in Oxford where Richard Cobb – who was to publish *Raymond Queneau* later in 1976 – was
  to give the annual Zaharoff Lecture on his work. Queneau was ill at this time and died in October.
3 *Wittgenstein* (1973) by William Warren Bartley III, American philosopher.

Sept in Dorset. My mother soldiers on, but there are more and more organisational difficulties and she has also been here on and off. I'm sorry to hear of your tiring summer, and of the news of others. I do want to see your paper on euthanasia – and I do hope you will *finally* see off ethical relativism! I am becoming more and more of an absolutist, in every way.

You will shortly receive a novel of mine called *Henry and Cato*, which I will inscribe when I see you. I hope you'll have a very nice time with Sid! God bless the Sids of this world who are just nice to have around and do not haunt one in the street! I have to go to London tomorrow to make yet further changes in my mother's jigsaw of arrangements (sometimes she seems not to know she's being looked after at all, which is splendid!).

I want to see you very much – and will telephone if I'm back in time and can make sense of trying to see you for a drink before you and Sid leave (I hope you're going somewhere nice and will have lovely *carefree* time). If not, will see you soon in Oct. I've had an uneventful summer, 'bugged' with work and the *piles* of 'business' which arrives through the post. It will be marvellous and refreshing to see you and talk. With my loving thoughts always, and with bestest wishes and much love

I

To Albert Lebowitz, expressing concern for Naomi, who had recently been treated for severe depression.

Steeple Aston
9 October 1976

Dearest Al, we were very very sorry to get your news – though it sounded as if the worst *might* be over, and Nay truly on her way home – where I do hope she is now. To see her really herself again must be a joy to you all. How crazy the world is – that marvellous girl afflicted, so clever and beautiful and utterly lovable and *loved*, with you and Joel and Judith – it's crazy. I wonder if analysis is to blame – and not just some kind of chemical roulette which might grab any of us. Such things are now eminently curable – [. . .] You must have had a terrible and dark time – and I do so urgently hope that Nay is being restored to that joyfulness which I can scarcely imagine her without. How terribly odd the human mind is, so able to make its own heaven and hell. I'm glad people have rallied round as, for Nay, of course they would. St Louis seems to me to be a place where there are *real* friends to be had, and you are both of you constructed for being loved. We are thinking about you very much. I hope the holiday at least was fairly unclouded – I liked your little glimpses of it. [. . .]

This is to catch the post with, from John and me, very much love. I'll write again soon and also to Nay. Ever –

I

To Albert Lebowitz.

Steeple Aston
27 October 1976

Dearest Al, I've been thinking about you very much, and hoping to hear from you. I do hope things are better and Nay is home. (If only prayer *could* help, only if one's father is a rabbi that might be just not the thing.)

John sends much love. He is walking around in your shirts and a dressing gown and getting much comfort therefrom. Now that winter is starting he has to get into British trousers.

We have been away in Belfast, and then in Norwich where John was examining. Belfast is tragic, the centre of the city wrecked and derelict, no pub life, no nightlife, and streets and streets of dead bricked-up houses. I am through with Mr Jimmy Carter by the way: I hear he has been photographed with a 'Britain Out' badge and, after talking to Catholic bishops, rants about human rights and American interference in Ulster! This brings aid and comfort to the IRA, just when the Women's peace movement were trying to persuade Americans not to finance guns. Carter could really have helped by praising the peace movement; but I suppose there are no Irish votes in peace.

I hope the children are OK and life goes on more normally and happily now. I do hope Nay gets steadily better. Do write. Many thoughts, much love

I

To Leo Pliatzky, who was suffering from an eye problem.

Steeple Aston
5 January 1977

Dearest Leo, I was very sorry indeed to hear your news – but glad so far things go OK and you are back at work. If you can rest, then work, then rest and get into it slowly – I know it's hard for you to rest. I sympathise very very much and think of you. I hope by now, when you get this letter, things will be even better and your mind more relieved. Give me news. I love seeing you, in spite of some disagreement, and I love you, as you know. That's forever, and of course I'll be around. I shall be in Dorset from about Friday for a while, and not effectively in town till after mid Jan, and I'll communicate then or before and hope to see you early. Will think of you, with much love

I

To Naomi Lebowitz.

Steeple Aston
7 January 1977

Dearest Nay, we were *so pleased* to get your letter. Oh good, and good. I am sure you are all *high*, in the best sense, after this. I am so glad too you held onto old Kierkegaard through it all. (Yes, let's meet in Copenhagen.) I do look forward to seeing the new you, though honestly I can't believe it will be much different from the dear old one. *Do* people change? If to calmer, happier, good – but fundamentally change? You are, *of course, not* Bella,[1] I don't portray real people (it would inhibit imagination) and I can't think of any points of similarity between you and her except that you are both clever, very wise, much loved, and Jewish! (*You* are a far more glorious object than shadowy Bella, quite apart from having the advantage of being *REAL*!) No, no you are utterly *different*. Russ and Bella can count as an act of homage to N and A simply in the sense that you two have given me the only place in America where I can as it were put my root down! You are the two just guys who save the city, as far as I am concerned.

About Laura Mae[2] – yes, I heard from Benjamin Roth. How unspeakably sad. The *presence* of death seems to become more real every day. I can imagine how this must have shaken you.

Keep letter-writing. Much love

I

To Georg Kreisel.

Steeple Aston
21 January 1977

1 Bella, wife of Russell Fischer, in *Henry and Cato*.
2 Laura Mae Gottfried, wife of Leon Gottfried, professor of English at Washington University in St Louis, who died in her fifties.

Dearest K, thank you for your letter. I do hope you are feeling better, less in pain, less afflicted. Thank God for science, working quietly away to discover painkilling drugs, as well as great cures. Are you better than you were when in England? Travel can upset one. You looked very pale and beautiful.

I was most interested in what you said, apropos Wittgenstein (yes) about a conflict between art and good sense. ('Truth'? 'Good sense' sounds a little too placid here? Maybe that is part of the point, I mean 'placidity'!) In connection with Plato I have written some stuff about art versus truth – but what I write is art too! And the 'ugliness' of experiment – and the shortness of our memories. Yes. My faith in 'reason' (probably initially much larger than yours) gets less and less with the years. (That does not mean one relaxes about truth, or *should not* mean it. Simple immediate statements of truth, as in political protest, seem to me more important than ever.)

I've been trying to write a popular newspaper article (how complicated my *style* is I realise in this context!) about 'peaceful protest'. Russia, Ireland, etc. I was on the committee (here) for the release of Vladimir Bukovsky, and I lately met him. He seemed to me a *spiritual being*. Of course that was what one wanted to feel! But what *courage*, what almost unimaginable courage, and risking one's mind as well as one's life – think of being in one of those 'mental hospitals' where they drug you and perhaps can drive you permanently mad.

I would feel too shy to invite myself chez Françoise but thank you for the idea! It is odd, having no French friends. I lately met Vercors[1] and his (English) wife and *greatly* liked them, and may visit them in Provence in the summer, staying with English people however. Italy perhaps I love more.

Look after yourself. I hope your good old doctor is soldiering on. Are you glad about Mr Carter?[2] Your letters give me much pleasure.

With much love

I

To Leo Pliatzky.

Steeple Aston
[February 1977]

Dearest Leo, I was *very relieved* to hear your eye is better. What nonsense you do talk though! Why not rely on your friends? Whom should you write

1 The pseudonym of Jean Marcel Bruller (1902–91), French novelist and artist-engraver whose *The Silence of the Sea* (1941) rallied French morale during the Nazi occupation.
2 Jimmy Carter had been sworn in as president of the United States on 20 January 1977.

to if not me? I was *glad* that you should do so. It is a mistaken pride not to appeal sometimes to dear and close friends. So please do so again if you want to and don't be so damned stiff! Anyway, love to see you soon. We are pretty well snowed up here at present. Will telephone. Do hope all continues well – and with always much love I.

Not an 'intrusion' and *of course* you have 'claims'!

To Brigid Brophy.

Steeple Aston
[1977?]

Why no hear? Why not write? What happen, what go? Thanks Cora. Letter promise, no letter. When see? To worry. Cat, Mike well? Alison well? Self well? Best all.

Lot love
I

To Philippa Foot.

Steeple Aston
4 March 1977

Dear girl, thank you very much for your card. I had just been thinking (and dreaming) about you and was just about to write. *I'm so sorry* about the troubles. I do hope Sid is better. How dreadful (and absurd) about your being nearly deported! A case for help from grandfather?[1] [. . .]

No news here. I feel tired, have been working too continuously, have just finished first draft of an unusually troublesome novel.[2] Am also writing verses. We *may* go to Israel for a week but I think are more likely to be having flu, which we have just been attending John's mother in course of. I really feel too tired to go anywhere. *I want to read your book.* I do hope things are OK now and happier. I long to see you. You will be back in April yes?? [. . .]

I have too many things to do (I scream), too many letters, too many small ludicrous tasks, too many people demanding this that and the other. And I ought to clean and tidy the house! (End of scream.) Do write to me. There

1 Grover Cleveland (1837–1908), Philippa Foot's grandfather and twice president of the United States.
2 *The Sea, The Sea.*

Cedar Lodge, Steeple Aston

'We are involved in the exciting and devastating business of buying a house'
(to Jacquetta Hawkes)

Iris Murdoch and John Bayley in the garden at Steeple Aston

'Back here, there awaits the garden, looking more earthly-paradise-like every moment'
(to Brigid Brophy)

Michael Oakeshott

'How far I am from that "wisdom" which you foolishly attributed to me'

Brigid Brophy

'Dearest Queen of the Night'

**Photograph of Iris Murdoch
taken by Brigid Brophy**

'I want those photos I left behind'

**Photograph of Brigid Brophy
taken by Iris Murdoch**

'But I'm not in love with you,
and don't want be'

David Morgan

'Yes, you are a wolf, and have sent me a
very wolfish letter, full of hostility'

Rachel Fenner

'Love is better than no love,
though it can hurt so much'

Norah Smallwood

'*Mon dieu*, as if I would consider
going elsewhere'

Elias Canetti

'Great lion, and the mask of Agamemnon…
I embrace you with much love'

Iris Murdoch, 1970

'Art is doubtlessly more important than
philosophy, and literature most important
of all' (*The Sovereignty of Good*)

Iris Murdoch taking tea at Litton Cheney

'Some kinds of country affect me deeply, as if I had known these scenes in dreams'
(to Brigid Brophy)

**Iris Murdoch accepting the Booker Prize
for *The Sea, The Sea* in 1978, with A. J. Ayer (left)
and Booker director Michael Caine (right)**

'*The Sea, The Sea* does have a shadowy connection
with *The Tempest*' (to Suguna Ramathanan)

Roly Cochrane

'Iris and Roly are *stronger* than
the dark forces'

Josephine Hart

'You really are a fighter, it's the Irish in you!'

Harry Weinberger

'Oh happy painter!
May the gods be with you'

Iris Murdoch swimming

'SWIMMING, that too is the thing, a very spiritual activity' (to Philippa Foot)

Philippa Foot in later life

'I wish one had another 50 years or so –
one might (I might) really *understand* or
clarify something'

**Peter Conradi with John Bayley, Iris Murdoch
and Cloudy (Anax in *The Green Knight*)**

'What a dear dog, so beautiful and so
strange' (to Peter Conradi)

Iris Murdoch at her writing desk in Charlbury Road

'I have a new desk and one of your big sea (harbour) pictures
hangs above it and inspires me' (to Harry Weinberger)

**Objects on table in Iris Murdoch's
study in Charlbury Road**

'The mystical Christ is with us, like the
mystical Buddha' (to Peter Conradi)

The roll-top desk in Charlbury Road

The Tolkien desk where Murdoch would
sometimes spend up to four hours a
day writing letters

are a lot of things I want to EXPLAIN and can only explain to YOU. (I mean *cosmic* things.)

   MUCH LOVE

   I

PS Talking lately to Freddie Ayer: he said he could not understand idea of the divided soul because he never had any mental conflicts!

To Georg Kreisel written after Murdoch and John Bayley visited Israel in March as part of a cultural delegation led by Lord Ted Willis and including Beryl Bainbridge, Melvyn Bragg, Bernice Rubens, William Trevor and Fay Weldon.

Steeple Aston
27 March 1977

Kreisel, my dear, thank you very much for your letter. I loved your description of your old dog – it gave me a sort of delight. Yes, yes. And I have got back from Israel. About the Russian dissenters, I see what you mean but try Bukovsky. (Perhaps my mention of him prompted you?) He is a simple good brave man (as far as I can see) with no pretensions to be a 'prophet'. Of course he is being grabbed by various preaching groups and this is sad – inevitable too. In Israel I met some intellectuals just come from Russia, touching lost souls, speaking only Russian. (I connected a little – I speak a *little* Russian, read more.) Now they are sitting in classes learning Hebrew.

Of course I am pleased to be out of Israel in the sense that I would feel anguish and fear and strain living there, but I *loved* the place. It was an extraordinary experience. The trip (as guest of the government) was a propaganda exercise of course. I went in a group of six British writers. We went to the Golan Heights, to the Lebanese border, to the Gaza Strip, the Negev (not Sinai). Met rational Arabs, visited kibbutzim, talked to endless writers, intellectuals, the foreign minister, the lot. I even visited Scholem[1] (who is rather unpopular – the militant secularism struck me). I expected to like the place, but was more carried away than I expected. I have (I think) always had a fairly clear rational view of the 'Palestinian problem' and this became more detailed and not much changed. I wish Jews were more ready to recognise, indeed *shout*, that innocent Arabs have suffered harm, indeed injustice, as a result of Israel's arrival. But as soon as one says that, the Israelis start a long explanation of how the Arab governments cynically use

---

1 Gershom Scholem (1897–1982), German-born Israeli philosopher and historian who became the first professor of Jewish mysticism at the Hebrew University of Jerusalem in 1933.

and exploit the plight of the Palestinians, etc. etc., all of which I know. I thought Jerusalem very beautiful, especially the little strange villages around about, and I was moved by the Christian places, especially the Sea of Galilee. I swam in the Dead Sea of course. And visited Masada. (That was extraordinary.)

More of this later. I am exhausted, like your dog! Much love
I

To David Hicks.

Steeple Aston
12 April 1977

David, just a note to find out where you are. Have you and Kay set off for Evesham yet? I do hope you are around in London and we could meet next term (after April 25, when my London life is more regular)? Do write.

A few nights ago I dreamt (in very detailed technicolour) that *Alastine*[1] *and I* were searching for you in *Prague*. We found you in a shabby house beside a bridge (I thought in the dream: that must be the Carlovy [*sic*] Most). You were in a miserable sort of student's room on the ground floor, in bed asleep, and we sat *waiting* for you to wake. You woke, noticed A first, then me, expressed mild surprise and pleasure and said 'Let's have lunch'.

I've just been in Israel, where in the midst of some argument I suddenly recalled a phrase from one of your old letters: 'Palestine not Alastine has taught me all I know of love'! Ah well, enough of these ramblings.

Come late-April-May let's, as you said, have lunch.

Much love
Iris

Responding to this letter later in April, Hicks replied: 'As for your dream of me in a hovel near the Karlový Most, it is not far from the truth, now that I'm jobless and can't really afford the rates of this house. I'm only sorry that you took Ali along. My own dreams of you are pretty frequent – maybe once a month or more – and I am always doing something quite absurd like helping people to climb up a vertical mud bank 2,000 feet high, or dashing to give a lecture on an unknown subject without notes, being quietly surveyed by a Beatrice-figure at the top or in the audience. [. . .] But dreams I find fallible as a guide to one's real state of mind.'

1 Alastine (Ali) Bell, a former girlfriend of Hicks.

To Leo Pliatzky.

Steeple Aston
[April 1977]

Leo, my dear, just to send you a note. I hope things are OK. You must have been intensely busy inventing Denis's[1] budget for him. I do hope you can have a bit of a rest now or sometime soon – and that the eye is fully recovered. (I recall that Kafka-like scene in the hospital that you described so vividly!)

Israel was a fantastic experience. I will tell you about it. And I want to ask you many *further* questions about your Jewishness! (Of course I am practically a Jew myself by now.) I'll be in London, come beginning of term and my usual arrangements, end of month and onward and will write again soon to suggest possible day or days. Meanwhile, my dear, much love.

Iris

To Philippa Foot.

Steeple Aston
25 June 1977

My dear girl, much thanks for your card, which arrived two or three days ago – (postcards are despised by postal services I am told). I hope you had a lovely time in Frogland. You missed persistent cold and rain here (as today). I would love to see you but am now just going away myself alas. I go to Norwich at the beginning of next/this working week, then to Durham, then (via here and London) to Belfast, then to France. I don't really want to go *anywhere*. Perhaps I am getting old. I shall like it when I am on the move, I know. Like our 'you'll like it when you get there' of return to boarding school, not in that case true. I have not yet read your two papers, but will start reading when I start travelling. (Yesterday I spent *the whole day* writing business letters.)

I haven't read any serious philosophy for ages and look forward to reading YOU! (Must read Stuart Hampshire's work too I suppose. Have you?) Not that I shall ever 'do' any more philosophy. I would like to write a long philosophical poem. That's how philosophical I am now!

1 Denis Healey, Chancellor of the Exchequer.

We won't actually be in France long,[1] not more than a fortnight, and let us meet thereafter, i.e. late July–Aug. I rather un-look forward to being in Belfast. I feel such deep sympathy with my cousins there (my nearest family) and I *admire* them, but find their company and way of life lowering! (e.g. no alcohol). And what a tragic sight that once pleasant town is. [. . .]

Much love, my dear, much love

I

To Hal Lidderdale, who had just retired.

Steeple Aston
[July 1977]

Hal dear, thank you so much for your letter, and many congratulations on your liberation – and good luck with the oily ones. I would love to take a jar (or two) with you, but we are just (Tues) off to France. See you later on. I applaud the Hammersmith idea. I do love that region. Go down North End Road toward Fulham Broadway, turn right anywhere and swan around – there are lovely and as yet decrepit and uncolonised streets of beautiful terrace houses – and the whole area has a pleasant village air. Au revoir and ever, much love

I

To Norah Smallwood.

Steeple Aston
[late August 1977]

Dearest Norah, I don't usually say anything about novels until they are *finished*, for that way madness lies. However, since you ask specially I will tell you *in confidence*, and for publication in January if it then seems likely, that the novel will actually be completed and that you will actually wish to publish it, the title of the next one which is: *The Sea, The Sea*.

I'll hope to see you in London one of these not too distant days – now much much love

Iris

1 The Bayleys visited the Spenders for a fortnight in mid-July at their home in Provence. Murdoch later used the landscape of this part of France in her novel *Nuns and Soldiers*, which she dedicated to them.

To Brigid Brophy.

Steeple Aston
29 September [1977]

My dear girl, I hope yesterday's letter didn't sound too old and weary as a reply to your beautiful one. Time and space weigh on me more and more as I age, and not being a bird one can't be in two places at the same time. I think I have to live *slowly*, as our old gardener worked slowly yet steadily (or *did*, the old blighter – now he only does it in his own garden). (The new man has cut down one of my roses while 'weeding'.) Could I have dinner with you next *Tuesday*, that is Oct 4? I do hope so. I do want to see you and talk properly. (I mean about many things.) Much love, old pal.
    Your old I

Do Write.

To Philippa Foot.

Steeple Aston
[September 1977]

[. . .] I *loved* seeing you, but I felt I couldn't talk to you properly. I store up a lot of things to say to you then I don't say them – but just seeing you is a joy and THANK YOU for the lovely photos, how beautiful you are! (I will try and find some to send, won't forget.) And even more THANK YOU for being so extremely kind as to think of that dedication!¹ It would give me the *greatest pleasure* and it makes me very happy now to think of it. YES, PLEASE! I do look forward to seeing the work. HOORAY! [. . .]
    I am just finishing a novel and feel tired and fed up because the last bit is so finicky and hard though entirely uncreative and dull. I feel I need a holiday just as term approaches. I ought to be able to make a HOLIDAY IN MY SOUL. I will try. Write to me *soon*. And I'm sorry I didn't *talk better*. MUCH LOVE as ever and always,
    Your I

1 Philippa Foot was to dedicate her book *Virtues and Vices and Other Essays in Moral Philosophy* to Murdoch.

To Harry Weinberger, a German–Jewish refugee who had lived in England since
1939 and whom Murdoch had met while staying with the Spenders in August. He
was an artist and was at this time head of painting at Lanchester Polytechnic (now
Coventry University).

Steeple Aston
[September 1977]

Dear Harry,

Thank you very much for your letter and please forgive my late reply to
it. You have been in my thoughts but I should have written sooner! We have
had my mother staying again and I have been rather obsessed with her
problems. I was very glad to hear from you – and I do understand how
difficult it is to write at length about painful things, and especially when
such things are in process of change. I do hope that the scene is better,
clearer. I feel the greatest sympathy but cannot yet *see*, which is not surprising!
I would love to talk to you, and for such a talk the easiest place is now
probably London in October. During Oxford term I am in London every
week, and we have a pad there. So maybe you could come up, and we could
see the gallery you mention, and we could have lunch? (And you could bring
the icon: THANKS about that!) Would that be OK? I will suggest date or
dates a bit later. I *greatly* look forward to seeing you and talking of many
things – and I'll hope to see more of your paintings. And of course we must
meet in the country later too. Please give my love to Barbara.[1] And I do
hope things are well. Au revoir and with love to you.

Iris

To Scott Dunbar.

Steeple Aston
19 October [1977]

Scott, I am so delighted by your last two communications, thank you so
much! I love those pictures of your life – where you go walking, how the
cat comes – bless you, may all be well. And *thank you* for the charming
Thanksgiving card, and for the remarkable and beautiful introduction to
1978 – I shall treasure it – what an interesting painter, I had never come
across him. A disciple of Paul Klee surely – all that wit and tender happy
vitality. I am very pleased. God bless you in 1978.

1 Harry Weinberger's wife.

I have just finished a novel, and feel rather odd and loose-endish. I have an enormous number of put-off things to do, but cannot concentrate *or* rest. I think I find it harder and harder to rest in an ordinary way, though I find rest in my work and in certain kinds of study (e.g. languages, grammar). How is your French by the way? I expect you are fairly fluent by now. I shall be 'visiting Canada' in a little while when we dine with Charles (Chuck) Taylor[1] and his wife. I hope your work goes well – it sounds well, in your occasional mentions of it. Did I tell you that, since reading *The Myth of God Incarnate*,[2] by various theologians, which has just caused a stir here, I have discovered that I am a Christian? As far as I can see, I believe what they (Maurice Wiles, John Hick etc.) believe about Christ. However, they still credit God the Father, which I can't. (They are very unpopular with various other Christians, who feel very let down.) They see the historical Christ as a man who occasioned a God-revealing myth. (Pure heresy!)

Thank you, dear Scott, again for your card and for your lovely present. I am very pleased to have it – and wish you all good things – and send much love

I x

Note otter on stamp

Re *Myth of God Incarnate* – Shall I send you a copy? Has it emerged in Canada?

much love

I x

To Scott Dunbar.

Steeple Aston
31 December 1977

Dearest Scott, thank you so much for two letters. I hope you had a very happy Christmas, and you are *really* better. Have you a good doctor? Will you be teaching again from Jan? Teaching is hard work, there is no doubt about it – but it does constantly stir up one's thoughts! I have sent your letter to Plato along one of my telepathic thought lines. The trouble is, I know so little about the other end. I am *sure* Plato would approve of your chair, especially as you sit and *think* in it! God bless philosophy in all its forms. (Well, not structuralism. Are you much bugged by structuralism down your way?)

---

1 Canadian philosopher who divided his career between McGill University in Montreal, and Oxford University where he was the Chichele Professor of Social and Political Theory.

2 A collection of essays edited by John Hick.

I was so pleased to hear of the 'sexual orientation' clause in the new Human Rights bill.¹ Well done you. Is Quebec now ahead of other parts of Canada in this matter?

Best best new year wishes, Scott my dear, and do *be well* in the new year, and with much love

I

To Harry Weinberger.

Steeple Aston
[10 January 1978]

Harry, just a note to say that I will write more at length later. I am absolutely, to use an excellent American word, *bugged* by a lecture I am trying to write and which must be done soon. I had hoped to finish it before Christmas and it goes on and is *difficult* and prevents me from working on other things and I am desperately trying to complete it. Then I have to go to Cambridge, then of all places to Caen for an Irish and French literary conference.² Thank you for your last – in 1977 – letter. You *couldn't possibly* lose my friendship and interest. Such things become established forever in some very mysterious way. I trust we can meet in London in February. Anyway I will write again. And I wish you and Barbara a very happy new year.

With much love
Iris

To Philippa Foot.

Steeple Aston.
11 January 1978

My dear, how goes it? Do write. It is terribly cold here, snow, gales, the Thames almost overflowing, elm trees falling right and left on power lines (we have been without electricity for thirty hours) and other such (so far)

1 On 16 December 1977 Quebec included sexual orientation in its Human Rights Code, making it the first province in Canada to pass a gay civil rights law. The law made it illegal to discriminate against gays in housing, public accommodation and employment. (In the UK regulations for protection against discrimination on the grounds of sexual orientation in employment were not introduced until 2003.)
2 At the University of Caen. Murdoch opened the conference with a paper entitled 'L'art est l'imitation de la nature'.

fairly minor ills. I am reconciled with Nelson Goodman,[1] though I do not agree with him about truth and merit questions in art. I cannot understand half of his book of course. I am still reading *La Chartreuse de Parme*[2] and though less bored cannot feel affection for Fabrice. We *may* be briefly in LA (on the way back from Denver–Santa Barbara in earlyish to mid-April) and wonder if you will still be there? Maybe you will be in England by then. I do look forward to your philosophy book. [. . .]

I feel terribly unable to think, it is perhaps the cold. (I am shuddering with cold as I write. I recall how you said people in USA regarded it as shocking to allow the weather inside the house!) I have forgotten some interesting things I had to say to you. MUCH LOVE and happy new year, and do write. Will write more rationally later. *Toujours* –

I

To Scott Dunbar.

Steeple Aston
[January 1978]

Scott dear, thank you so much for your letter and enclosures. I like the Plato-worthy chair pattern very much! I would love to see Paolo Vitrate's book. I am so glad you have sane learned friends. That Anita Bryant[3] sounds awful, and her logic is odd too: the Bible condemns homosexuality *and* bestiality so the Bible is right to condemn homosexuality! The lavender-cream-pie-throwing girl was surely right to say the *most* violent and dangerous people around are male heterosexuals! (What is a *lavender* cream pie I wonder?)[4]

I have been in France at a *Franco-Irish* literary conference. The French are sentimental about the Irish. The Irish ambassador, a genial figure was there. No one mentioned the IRA. No one, except me, mentioned the troubles in Ulster. It was all charm and W. B. Yeats. (Not enough to drink, though.)

1 Murdoch had been reading his *Languages of Art: An Approach to a Theory of Symbols.*
2 A novel by Stendhal published in 1839.
3 Anita Bryant, former Miss Oklahoma and a successful American pop singer during the 1950s and 1960s, was an outspoken critic of homosexuality and an anti-gay rights activist.
4 In 1977 a gay rights activist had thrown a lavender cream pie – a custard cream or cheesecake-like pie infused with the flavour of lavender – at Anita Bryant during a TV press conference held in Des Moines, Iowa.

I hope work goes on well. I feel tired and have a streaming cold.
Much love
I

To Norah Smallwood.

Steeple Aston
25 February 1978

Dearest Norah,
     Thank you very much for your letter of 23 Feb. I enclose another from
Peggy[1] to Oxford University Press (please return). I am *sorry to bother you
with this*. I have not the strength to understand it fully at present. I don't
mind their having 40% and the marvellous composer[2] deserves MUCH
MORE, the main point is just to see that original play receives my copyright.
     I had a good talk with Toni[3] yesterday. I think the novel[4] is *very good*, the
whole thing will be a major achievement. I wouldn't myself want anything
cut, as I enjoyed it *all*, Marcus's visions, all the literary stuff, the lot. I think
the Grecian Urn is essential. The thing is so full of 'internal relations' that
it is difficult to cut without real loss. And the outsider simply cannot advise
without knowing *this* work very well and also knowing what from here is
connected with what in later volumes.
     I think the time jumps, when the author suddenly speaks from the future,
are very good too and give a sense of the larger texture. Toni says she will
cut a little of the 'theology', but otherwise is disinclined to shorten it and
I would agree with her, as a reader. This just is, by its nature, a *long novel*,
and I am sure will in the long run pay you well! I feel it must be just accepted
as a long novel and part of a major work. And I hope the Americans can
be persuaded to see this too! (Could try Viking if Knopf not?) Hope all this
not unhelpful!
     How marvellous you were in Orkney – and that you got safely back!
Much love
I

1 Peggy Ramsay, British theatrical agent.
2 William Mathias, who composed the opera *The Servants* for which Murdoch wrote the libretto (adapted
   from her play *The Servants and the Snow*). The opera was to be performed in Cardiff by the Welsh
   National Opera.
3 Antonia Byatt (A. S. Byatt).
4 *The Virgin in the Garden*.

To Scott Dunbar, written before Murdoch and John Bayley travelled to the USA in mid-March on a brief British Council lecture tour.

Steeple Aston
[11 March 1978]

My dear, thank you for your letter just come and, yes, thank you so much for the St Patrick's card! (It's a pity he left so many snakes in Ireland, but I'm sure he did the best he could.) (Connolly[1] said that all the snakes swam the Atlantic and became Irish Americans.) I look forward to your article.[2] This in haste, just leaving. We shall be moving about a lot, St Louis, Oklahoma, Denver and finally Santa Barbara. [. . .] It's a crazy trip. I would rather stay and watch the English. I hope your daffodils have come. And that you often meditate in your Plato chair. Will write later about US journey. All bestest and much love

I

To Albert and Naomi Lebowitz, written after a brief stay with them in St Louis

Steeple Aston
20 March 1978

My dears, please forgive hasty anxious self-centred departure! The difficulty of propelling John as well as myself sometimes overwhelms me! I wish I had prolonged our goodbye. There were so many thanks to give you. We were severed by that piece of security machinery and I turned to find you gone. Forgive me and receive so much gratitude for our fabulous magical god-determined visit to you. We cannot help bowing to the tree house. I'm sorry we couldn't have stayed longer (interrupting your lives, depriving you of your study) and continued many talks which were just beginning. I feel that I was only just starting to *talk* when it was time to go. The visit was a solid gold asset, and proof that we can and must meet. Next year, anyway, in Greece-Italy-Spain year, and who knows where else. 743 Yale is the centre of America, the *ompholos*. We loved the party too, the connections and continuations and memories. We believe in your world (one doesn't all that often credit other people, to say nothing of their worlds!) and you illuminating it! We hope we were not riotous guests and were not too 'tiresome'.

---

1 James Connolly (1868–1916), Marxist and Irish Republican leader who was shot by a British firing squad for his role in the Easter Rising.

2 Dunbar published 'On art, morals, and religion: some reflections on the work of Iris Murdoch' in the journal *Religious Studies* later in 1978.

The battered caravanserai is now on the road. Norman[1] is wonderful –
everything is huge and flat – the largest longest flattest most lurid garages
and shopping centres and *immense* houses built in Japanese style for oil
tycoons (these latter more in Oklahoma city). And we have seen some oil
wells. It is all weird and desolate and fascinating and inhuman. [. . .]
    To be continued in our next.
    MUCH LOVE
    I

PS Someone looked up 'pratfall' and says derivation is from 'prate'. *Most*
implausible.

To Philippa Foot.

> Steeple Aston.
> 20 April 1978

Dearest girl, it seems a miracle that I can write to you at Walton Street and
that we shall both have traversed half the world into *another* world when
you get this! What a wonderful significant beautiful time you gave us in LA
– your lovely house, the trees, the desert, *people*, so many marvels, and the
basic general fun of being with you.
    Thank you so much! And I'm so pleased that I talked to your mother on
the telephone! And that we saw dear Sid. I hope he was reasonably well
when you left. There's quite a feeling of home about LA for us now. You
are lucky to live in two *absolute* worlds. Did you manage a good 'house'
arrangement before you left? If I recall, Sid had some promising house-sitters
who might turn into tenants.
    Thank you for so kindly helping us to see all our pictures and so on. We
had nothing but treats. (NB if there's a next time I shall *again* struggle to
get to that forbidden paradise, Disneyland! Perhaps by then you will be a
convert, who knows?) It was all super, and seeing Rosalind[2] too, that merry
girl.
    It's very good to be home (damn cold) but we have an extraordinary
degree of jet lag, cannot even now make sense of day and night. And a
hundred problems waiting of course. I must fetch my mother in a day or
two for a longish sojourn here. She is rather batty, but cheerful and so good.

1 A city in Oklahoma.
2 Rosalind Hursthouse, a young New Zealand moral philosopher working on virtue ethics who was
  being mentored by Foot and who was later to edit *Virtues and Reasons: Philippa Foot and Moral Theory:
  Essays in Honour of Philippa Foot* (1995).

Let's meet soon. There's an awful lot I want to say, discuss. It was a great *tonic* to see with the whole USA as your background (you are indeed its *raison d'être*) – it was, for us a good journey with climax of 612 Midvale. (I feel there are two of you and one *must* be still there: how could America continue to exist otherwise?) I hope your paper went well in New Orleans, and that you found your mama full of fight, she sounded wonderful on the telephone.

I cannot work, think, do my novel[1] or reflect on other things I might do. Madly, we are going to Austria on May 15, and on I hope to Hungary, Budapest anyway. And we have other obligations later. It's a tearing-about year (I have to lecture in Austria). *En pensant à toi, chérie, chérie,*[2] with so many thanks and with, ever,

Much love,

I

To Harry Weinberger.

Steeple Aston
2 May 1978

Harry dear, I was so glad to get your letter. Your writing looks like your pictures. And I am imagining your ship picture, and what you used to see in the river when you were a child. (Have you been back to that place I wonder.) I loved the ship pictures you showed me when I was in your studio. I connect you with great blue *spaces*. Yes, you are lucky to be a painter.

I feel tired and cannot write. But a painter could always do *something*– or just look.

This is a rather dotty summer as John has sabbatical leave and we keep going away. USA was good, more real – I begin to believe in it. But it is all so raw and unworked, and I hate not walking, and absence of urban life. (Cars to supermarkets, and no pub or café existence.) We are going to Austria in May to lecture.

I *will* see you and talk, the time will come. And meanwhile I certainly believe in *you*. Work well. With much love

I

My mother is staying at present. She is very helpless and confused – it is so sad.

1 Probably *Nuns and Soldiers.*
2 Thinking of you, dear darling.

To Harry Weinberger.

Steeple Aston
[8 May 1978]

Dear Harry, I am *so pleased* with the drawing – it is so absolutely you, your signature, your being is there, and so beautiful, and so Portuguese, and carries one, as art does, away and away – thank you so much! (I would have liked to have the letter on the nature of creativity *too*, so maybe you will write another version of that later!) I am so touched – and by your imaginative consideration in sending the apparatus for hanging it as well! I have put it near my desk where it radiates light. I shall have to see the painting too (and many others, ships, and blue seas, and white clouds and space and space) one day. Thank you, indeed, so much for your *telegram*! We are just off on Monday to Austria, back early June. As I said, this is not a very typical summer but we usually can't travel at this time of year because of Oxford term. (Did I say summer? It is grey and raining here and the wind is bashing the daffodils. The daffodils have been in flower for about six weeks because they are *refrigerated*, so there are some advantages!) Give love to Barbara. We shall hope for meeting, later, and meanwhile, paint on. I wish I could. With thanks, dear Harry, and with love *toujours*
      Iris

To Naomi Lebowitz.

Steeple Aston
26 July 1978

Nay, much thanks for your letter. I can see the signs. Next thing will be your *conversion*. May I be a godmother when you are baptised? (Peter Alscher[1] could be a godfather?) And how do you know Jesus isn't running with you?[2] (Would Al mind?) Whether or not Jesus, you are lucky to be living with Søren Kierkegaard.

I don't know much about Daudet[3] but it would be hard to beat the Dane. He is one of the few writers (Simone Weil is another) who is I think *guaranteed* to do one good.

---

1 A friend of the Lebowitzes who had noisily converted from orthodox Jewry to Christianity.
2 Murdoch had recently begun the first draft of *Nuns and Soldiers* in which the former nun, Anne Cavidge, has a vision of Christ in her kitchen; Murdoch was clearly dwelling at this time on the idea of Christ showing himself to ordinary people and travelling with them.
3 Probably Alphonse Daudet, the French novelist.

We have been in France (Provence, Van Gogh country). The mistral blew. Here it is coldish, wettish, windy, in fact English summer. [. . .]

Dearest Nay, all bestest. So glad all well and plenty of chicken and spaghetti. Keep cool. Much love

I

To Philippa Foot

Steeple Aston
28 July 1978

My dearest girl, I have rung your telephone number some fifteen times lately at various moments of the day to ask you to come over here and sadly conclude that you are AWAY! That is indeed where I have been too much this year: we have been in France, Austria, Hungary, Spain and USA (so *far*) – partly in honour of John's sabbatical term and partly by accident (honouring old pledges etc.). In August, similarly by accident, we will, if God wills, be in Italy.[1] I have arranged to do quite a lot of work nevertheless, taking my stuff to people's houses where possible (on a novel). I wish time wasn't fleeting away so fast, there's so much I want to do. Philosophy won't go away. I read in proof by the way, Mary Midgley (Scrutton)'s book *Beast and Man*[2] and I think it's good, quite a large operation.

No special news. My mother gets iller, so sad and increasingly difficult. She is here quite a lot, very confused, thinks she's in Ireland etc. I wonder where you are? I hope it's nice wherever it is, sunny, with plenty of wine, churches, pictures, the necessities of life. Could you alert me (best by letter, 'phone may be switched off) when you are back? We shall be away *about* Aug 12–30. Then here indefinitely I hope. I am *longing* to see your philosophy book and I keep thinking about the dedication and feeling oh *good good*! And I think of you – you were in a dream I had lately about Frank. Much love, my dearest,

I

1 The Bayleys holidayed with Janet and Reynolds Stone in August.
2 In which Midgley argued that human beings are more similar to animals than many social scientists then acknowledged.

To David Hicks (now living in Hopesay, Shropshire) whose son Barney, aged twenty-two, had recently committed suicide.

Steeple Aston
28 July 1978

David, my dear, Hal has rung up and told me the terrible news and I am so very sorry. I had no idea that Barney was suffering from 'depression', that dreadful mysterious soul-ailment that so many seem to have now, with a will to die. I have known of several cases lately, when talented apparently lucky young people have decided to go. Hal told me too of his music which BBC are broadcasting in September. Oh my God, I am sorry – I had been thinking about you, and guessed you would have moved by now, and was hoping that a letter would be forwarded from Ealing. What can one say. A desire to die is very hard to understand, but many people have it, a deep desire. And those who choose sleep in this way have carried out a deep desire and come to peace. Perhaps one must respect this. And one has got to live on and console those who remain. Give my love to Katharine. I think of you very much and send much love.
     Iris

To David Hicks.

Steeple Aston
5 August 1978

David, my dear, thank you very much indeed for your letter. I have no doubt that your view of the matter is right, that this thing would have gone on and on. I have known quite well three young people who became seriously 'depressed' and killed themselves at just about Barney's age. One of them was Caspar Fleming, Ian Fleming's son – handsome, clever, rich etc. etc. but just *did not want to live*. He tried twice, then succeeded. The determination to go was, in all the three cases, very very deep and not touched by what would ordinarily seem to be consolations or help. (Caspar had every sort of treatment.) I don't think the medical profession understand this thing at all. Perhaps there is some brain condition which will one day be discovered, or perhaps the causes are infinitely tangled, complex, various, although they produce something which is (perhaps for some superficial reason) recognisable as 'the same disease' in different cases. Oh God, I am sorry, and I do well understand how K feels in that rat trap, although you are surely right about the matter. Much love to K. We must meet later. We are going to

Italy next week, back end of month. Keep in touch. Ever, my dear, with so much love

I

To Philippa Foot.

Steeple Aston
5 September 1978

Dearest girl, I have rung your number several times and conclude you are away. Could you let me know when you are back? Oh let you not have departed to USA!! We spent most of August in Italy, at a friend of friend's villa near Assisi. Very nice, because I could work there. Not so nice for John driving parties of us up into hill towns and endeavouring to park the car! ('Oh look, there's a space – no there isn't!' 'I think that man's going!' 'Go right', 'Go left' etc. etc.) We saw a lot of jolly frescoes and things. And ate a lot of jolly pasta. It was fun, but one is *so glad* to be back! Our garden is ragged and autumnal and (at the moment) it is beautifully raining. I have been thinking of you a lot. Do communicate (best by 9p letter) when you get this.

Much love, ever your,

I

To Sister Marian at Stanbrook Abbey.

Steeple Aston
[October 1978]

Dearest Lucy, so glad to get your letter, though sorry Honor¹ is not there, imbibing spirituality! Could you forward my two unimportant letters to Ireland. I was trying to find out where she was! Maybe we shall see her at Christmas. Yes, I am delighted with your new pope!² So good to see an honest northern face after all those foxy Italians! And a formidable man. Perhaps he will lead a new Crusade. Much love to you, my dear, and with many thoughts of you

Iris

---

1 Honor Tracy, English journalist, novelist and travel writer who first met Murdoch and John Bayley in Ireland in 1958 and thereafter became a friend. Tracy lived on the edge of the community at Stanbrook Abbey and knew Sister Marian.
2 Karol Józef Wojtyła became Pope John Paul II on 16 October 1978.

To Harry Weinberger.

Steeple Aston
[15 November 1978]

Harry, I was so relieved to get your letter. I had been wondering how you were and what the docs said. I am so glad you are OK. But what about those art school snakes? How *can* anybody attack you, I feel very indignant! (I know a little about the art school atmosphere from RCA. Yes!) I hope it may all now blow over? I really cannot imagine what anyone could say against you, but of course less talented people are often envious alas, and thus spiteful. I hope it's all been blown away, and that it isn't worrying you. Thank you very much for sending lovely photo of Joanna[1] – how pretty she is, and like you in some subtle way. Thanks too for the interesting picture of those two touching animals! If you would still like to lend them to me later on I should be glad. You are a very kind chap. I loved being with you – that was a much memorable and delightful encounter, and I did enjoy the icon palace. I can understand how they must inspire you. I hope you are generally much better and doing what your doctor tells you and resting and not worrying. Au revoir, my dear, and ever with much love
  Iris

To Naomi Lebowitz.

Steeple Aston
20 December 1978

Nay, thank you so much for your letter and kind words. Too bad about Aristotle on short people! But he had mixed feelings about Plato, so his judgement must have been pretty rocky. So glad you are living with Kierkegaard. Pleased to get very nice letter from Howard.[2]

I gather there are some Jews who are not Christians but accept Jesus as the Messiah. Perhaps you could join them? I am reading a lot of stuff about JC at the moment (*not* going to write book about him, just beavering for some lectures on morality / religion). It's all so incredible, it suggests divine intervention!

I gather the Oxford Union invited Nixon so as to make fortune and pay

---

1 Weinberger's daughter.
2 Howard Nemerov, American poet, who lived near the Lebowitzes and who was one of their close friends.

off their overdraft. (Union is a sort of intellectual debating club, not like an ordinary representative students' union.) Nixon's rewriting of the past is fascinating.

I hope you get your sabbatical term to deal with those old scholars. Good girl.

The great task of Christmas is coming up. I hope you will have a lovely one with good New Year. I'm so glad Al's book nears completion. I much look forward to it.

All best and with season's greetings and much love.

I

To Albert Lebowitz.

Steeple Aston
28 December 1978

Al, a genuine letter from genuine you, thank you so much!! I'm glad you liked the book. And I'm glad to hear from Nay that yours is near done, *excellent.* I won a prize for the novel[1] (£10,000) but now I have to pay income tax on it at 83%.[2] I receive £1,700! (You might tell Howard when you see him – he kindly enquired if the booty was tax free!) Such are the joys of living in England (well worth it of course).

Our Christmas was as follows, water started pouring through the wall of our London pad on Christmas Day (we eventually got a plumber who mended the leak two days later – water turned off in interim). And our car broke down and we had to *push* it all the way down King's Road, Chelsea and leave it at a garage and come home by train! Enough of our festive doings. MUCH LOVE and all New Year best.

I

---

1 Murdoch had won the Booker Prize in October for *The Sea, The Sea.*
2 This figure proved to be wildly exaggerated.

PART SEVEN:

Dame Iris

January 1979 to December 1989

These years brought fame and further accolades: Tom Phillips was commissioned to paint Murdoch's portrait for the National Portrait Gallery in 1984 and it was exhibited in 1987, the year in which she was made a dame of the British Empire. A symposium on her work at the Free University, Amsterdam in 1986 confirmed her status as one of Britain's most important writers and in the same year the Iris Murdoch Society was inaugurated at the Modern Languages Association Convention in New York. In 1982 *The Bell* was adapted for BBC Television and proved popular with viewers; in 1983 *The Unicorn* became a set text for the French *agrégation* examination.

Although Murdoch's literary career continued to flourish with the publication of five novels in these ten years, doubts about her philosophy fed doubts about her novels. She still saw herself in the second league of writers, despite two books from these years being shortlisted for the Booker Prize. As the end of a millennium and the end of her publishing career approached, the novels became longer, more densely philosophical and mystical, and certain themes and types haunt their pages. In interview she said that her books were now about battles between 'magic' (the compulsion towards consolation and obsession) and freedom or goodness, which she thought of as 'holiness'.[i] 'Magic' manifests itself in her characters' desire for gurus who will provide absolution from sin and the conferment of grace, or texts that will provide answers to society's problems in the form of overarching theories. The novels illustrate the strengths and limitations of various competing ideologies and offer a poignant rebuttal of what Murdoch increasingly came to fear as her own role as a guru or 'magical' figure.

Yet 'magic' in her novels is both spurned and invoked; she understood religious experience as omnipresent and accessible through the power of storytelling and imagery, and that human beings could move with ease through such imagery to what lies behind it. She became increasingly preoccupied with her search for a workable neo-theology, a fresh kind of reflection or moral philosophy that would explain fundamental things about humanity and the human soul.[ii] She found much to interest her in the work of the radical theologian Don Cupitt, describing him in a letter to Margaret Lintott, an old Badminton school friend, as 'my hero'.[iii] The books of these years also reflect her enduring commitment to Platonism, the pilgrimage from illusion to reality that destroys false images and enables the emergence of the pilgrim out of the darkness into the sun. At the same time her art provided fresh spiritual images that could point to this truth beyond. She retained her fondness for the Buddha, still seeing him as a mystical figure and a vehicle for grace and spiritual power. The figure of Christ becomes increasingly important – she liked St Paul because he was not concerned with the details of Christ's life but with the mystical Christ, the Christ within the soul; this sense of 'otherness' within us connects us not with magic but with what is real and true. Christ makes an appearance to deliver this message in *Nuns and Soldiers* (1980), in what is one of the most remarkable religious encounters in Murdoch's *oeuvre*. The former nun, Anne Cavidge, meets Christ in her kitchen in the form of a veridical vision. The reality of his presence is confirmed when Anne wakes the next morning, having in her vision touched the sleeve of Christ's shirt, and finds that a finger on her right hand is raw and the skin abrased, 'as if she had been burnt'. In their conversation Anne and Christ discuss suffering, salvation, death, morality and love, but his main purpose is to resist humanity's superstitious dependence upon him. When Anne asks Christ what she must do to be saved he tells her that she must relinquish all perceptions of him as her saviour: 'You must do it all yourself'; 'I am not a magician. I never was. Do right, refrain from wrong'.

The *Philosopher's Pupil* (1983) with its mysterious composite narrator, 'N' and 'a certain lady', on the one hand echoes the narrative style of Victorian novels in the meticulous recounting of setting and inner life, and on the other is a self-conscious experiment in metafiction. This vastly complex book is Murdoch's bravest since *The Bell* in its confrontation of sexual taboos, recounting the incestuous attraction of a grandfather for his granddaughter, and presenting a depraved psychopathic character who is identified with Hitler. It alludes to William Blake's *Songs of Innocence and of Experience* in showing the two contrary states of the human soul, as characters superficially form bands of innocents and demons. But innocence is shown to be naive and degenerate, and evil has energy and a powerful charismatic charm. The Quaker faith provides a truly good man in William Eastcote, whose wisdom counterpoints the wickedness of the two central characters, the morally bankrupt George and the vindictive analytic philosopher Rozanov, George's former tutor who cruelly spurns him. Rozanov fears that the great thinkers who have held that good and evil should be absolute and separate were in error. Privately he speculates that 'the holy must know the demonic', but if so, one becomes 'the demon who is god', and the only answer to evil is murder or suicide. The boundaries between innocence and experience, good and evil, are so blurred in this novel that readers can find themselves angered and perplexed. The book's unusually sustained philosophical debate between Rozanov and the priest, Father Bernard, cuts deep to the heart of Murdoch's own terror that philosophy may be 'all rubble, jumble. Not even muck, but jumble', and is key to understanding all her late novels.

The Good Apprentice (1985; shortlisted for the Booker Prize) confronts the biting pain of remorse when the young student Edward Baltram realises he is solely responsible for the death of his much-loved friend, Mark Wilsden, who jumped from a window to his death after Edward fed him a drug-laced sandwich. Help in healing his dangerously damaged self-image comes from characters who range from a crazed vampiric painter who foreshadows the demon that Edward could become, and the saintly Brownie Wilsden, Mark's sister, who blesses him with the words, 'life is full of terrible things and one must look into the future and think about what happiness one can create for oneself and others'. These two characters lie at the extremes of good and evil that the book presents and each has a part to play in Edward's healing. The book bears the emotional effects of Murdoch's visit to Auschwitz in 1974 and she ascribes them to the eponymous 'good apprentice', Stuart Cuno, who is haunted by the memory of a young girl's shorn plaits that he saw at Auschwitz. This memory becomes the book's central image of evil. The existence of negative spiritual power and the nature of goodness are the two dominant themes and again Murdoch acknowledges the ambiguous powers of 'magic' and how it must necessarily and sometimes dangerously be used in the pursuit of goodness. Art itself participates in this magic and in the dangerous battle between good and evil. Her own role in this process is reflected in the good psychotherapist, Thomas McCaskerville, who manipulates and engineers Edward's recovery. Thomas reveals the ambiguous nature of his power when he says, 'I'm a calculator, a manipulator'. Such tactics belong also to Murdoch's own role as a writer, and Thomas, like his creator, understands most fully the danger of the 'conflict between holiness and magic, so alike, so utterly different'. Murdoch here places herself and her philosophy under the microscope of her own art.

The Book and the Brotherhood (1987; also shortlisted for the Booker Prize) focuses on a group of friends who are funding one of their number to write a book. Her main character, the charismatic, obsessive and destructive David Crimond, finds writing philosophy extremely difficult and has moments of despair but remains convinced that liberal democracy is on the point of collapse and that his Marxist diagnosis of what needs to be done is right, even if it involves a period of cruelty and an authoritarian government. On one level, 'The Book' is Crimond's analysis of society but on another it represents all ideologies that offer the vision of a better society; similarly, the 'Brotherhood' is not just the group of friends but the whole of humanity. The novel also exposes the dangerous seduction of intellectual ambition; Rose rightly describes Crimond's book as a vanity project. Her belief that 'there can never be a perfectly good society – there can only be a decent society, and that depends on freedom and order and circumstances and an endless tinkering which can't be programmed from a distance. It's all accidental, but the values are absolute' reflects Murdoch's own belief in an inevitable tension between the absolute and the contingent. Dickensian in its capacious form and moral agenda, the novel is not entirely dark, however, offering hope in individual acts of kindness and love. It ends with Lily Boyne speculating that, like her grandmother, she might be a witch, but that 'if I ever have any magic it will only work through love'. Thus the novel explores the tension between abstract, theorised concepts of morality as embodied in political theory and philosophy and the small acts of kindness and empathy that actually make up the 'good' society.

The plot of *The Message to the Planet* (1989) is dominated by another false prophet figure and a group of London-based friends. However, Marcus Vallar is not egoistic and destructive, like Crimond, but mild and muddled. A once brilliant mathematician and a gifted painter, Marcus has turned to philosophy later in life. His visit to the desperately sick and comatose Patrick, a young Irish poet, seems, miraculously, to raise him from the dead, and from then on Marcus acquires, for some, the status of guru. Alfred Ludens, a historian, becomes obsessed with the idea that Marcus has a valuable message for humanity and that he should write a book expounding his 'universal language' through which the evils of humanity might be confronted. News of Marcus's supposed supernatural powers soon spreads and he becomes a cult figure worshipped by New Agers, pagans and ordinary people who make pilgrimages to see him. The reality of the situation remains elusive. Patrick's recovery is seen differently by different characters – as a miracle, as a natural event, as the end of a psychosomatic illness. Similarly, Marcus is variously regarded as a healer, a saint, 'an incarnate god', a magician, a megalomaniac, a 'monster', 'a holy monster' and as suffering from Asperger's. The narrator gives no answers, leaving readers to decipher these multiple voices and narratives of projection. Marcus, well aware that he has no 'message for the planet', finally rejects his role and dismisses his followers. The debate between 'magic' and 'holiness' deeply informs this novel which is pervaded by images of light and dark and constant echoes of *The Tempest*. The novel gradually intimates that true enlightenment lies in confronting the darkest spaces in history and within ourselves.

These last two books of the 1980s illuminate how the spiritual vacuum of the late twentieth century inspired fundamentalism and cult worship only to dismantle any possibility of a great overarching philosophy that can teach us, or a great leader who can save us. The only magic is love and the only message is that love is the one hope for the salvation of the soul and thereby the planet. Father Bernard, at the close of *The Philosopher's Pupil*, most articulately expresses Murdoch's antidote to the problems of the age: 'There is no beyond, there is only here, the infinitely small, infinitely great and utterly demanding present. This too I tell my flock, demolishing their dreams of a supernatural elsewhere. So you see, I have abandoned every kind of magic and preach a charmless holiness. This and only this can be the religion of the future, this and only this can save the planet'.

Murdoch remained interested in drama, and after reading *The Fire and the Sun*, Michael Kustow – an associate director at the National Theatre – asked her if she would write Platonic dialogues for actors, and she agreed. The resulting two dialogues, *Art and Eros: A Dialogue About Art* and *Above the Gods: A Dialogue About Religion* were published as *Acastos: Two Platonic Dialogues* in 1986. The first dialogue, *Art and Eros*, was performed at the National Theatre in February 1980. The performance was well received and Conradi suggests that 'Nowhere else are her ideas brought so alive as in these two dialogues'.[iv] She also wrote the libretto for *The Servants*, an opera based on her play *The Servants and the Snow*, for which William Mathias composed the music and which opened at the New Theatre Cardiff in 1980. A political play for radio, *The One Alone*, was broadcast on BBC Radio 3 in 1987 and Murdoch's stage adaptation of *The Black Prince* opened at the Aldwych Theatre in April 1989. The latter was not a success, however, and closed in September.

Honorary doctorates abounded and scholarly and mainstream articles, both by and about her, appeared, as well as interviews in broadsheet newspapers, including the *Guardian*, *Telegraph*, *The Times* and the *Independent*. Murdoch spoke frequently on the radio, was often interviewed on television and was profiled in BBC2's *The Book Programme*. Her celebrity status was by now international: interviews also appeared in the *Washington Post* and the American edition of *Vogue*; in 1981 she spoke at a conference at the Pompidou Centre in Paris in French and gave a short talk in Russian on the BBC World Service. In 1982 she was made an honorary member of the American Academy of Arts and Sciences.

However, there was little public engagement with philosophy in these years, possibly because the decade began with a bitter disappointment. In 1982 Murdoch gave the Gifford Lectures in Edinburgh, discussing Kant, Plato, Schopenhauer and Wittgenstein but found it difficult to articulate her philosophical thoughts. She did not perform well and the audience shrank during the two weeks the lectures were delivered. It is perhaps not surprising that the novels of these ten years feature many failed thinkers and dispirited philosophers. Her conversations and thinking became more mystical and she experienced epiphanic moments that were to influence her writing. One of these occurred in 1983 when she visited 'The Genius of Venice' exhibition at the Royal Academy and was deeply affected by Titian's *The Flaying of Marsyas*, a painting that had always intrigued her but that now came to have iconic meaning for her. As the decade progressed, Murdoch did return to philosophy, writing on Heidegger and gradually reworking the Gifford Lectures, which eventually fed into *Metaphysics as a Guide to Morals* (1992).

Murdoch remained politically engaged in these years, as the letters in this section illustrate. She became increasingly concerned about Labour's move to the left and, despite her dislike of the Tories, shifted her political allegiance, voting Conservative in the general election in June 1983. By the end of the decade she had come to think that the Thatcher government had achieved some good, despite her concern about its erosion of the independence of universities. She also continued to campaign for gay rights, expressing her delight to Scott Dunbar in 1982 that 'San Francisco is in process of setting up legal homosexual marriage!'[v] Her fears about Ireland intensified during this decade which saw an escalation of the IRA bombing campaign in mainland Britain.

Her frantically busy lifestyle often left her exhausted. Occasionally she feared she was losing her grip, writing to Naomi Lebowitz in 1986, 'my memory is going – I sometimes can't find *words* – they're there, but blacked out'.[vi] Occasional fragmentation of thought in some letters suggests the beginning of Murdoch's mental decline. Nevertheless, she juggled a gruelling, self-imposed work schedule with the necessity and desire to travel, mostly with her husband but sometimes alone. Despite Norah Smallwood's concern that she was doing too much, during this decade Murdoch spoke at many institutions in the UK and often travelled abroad, visiting Romania, France, Germany, China, Iceland, India, the USA, Switzerland, Korea, Spain, the Netherlands, Italy and Norway. Even brief visits could leave vivid impressions: of an otherwise enjoyable trip to Berlin in 1979 Murdoch wrote to Scott Dunbar: 'One cannot forget the *wall* however, which is pale and terrible. I went into East Berlin – melancholy and frightening (Kafka)'.[vii] Her weekly routine involved frequent travel between her London flat and the marital home in Oxford, yet this period saw a strengthening of her marriage. In 1986 Murdoch and her husband moved from their beloved home of thirty years, Cedar Lodge in Steeple Aston, to a much smaller house in Summertown, Oxford. By 1989 they were on the move again, this time to a quieter but slightly larger home at 30 Charlbury Road, Oxford, where they were to remain until Murdoch's death.

Close friendships continued to play an important role in Murdoch's private life, and these years brought both losses and gains. In 1979 one of her dearest friends, the wood-engraver Reynolds Stone, died at seventy of a massive stroke and Murdoch gave the eulogy at his memorial service at St James's Piccadilly. Both J. B. Priestley and Norah Smallwood died in 1984; in the same year Brigid Brophy was finally diagnosed with multiple sclerosis after having been ill for some time; and Murdoch's friend Indira Gandhi, who had been educated with her at Badminton and Somerville, was assassinated. In 1985 Murdoch's beloved mother Rene, whose mental state had become increasingly problematic, died of a stroke. Arnaldo Momigliano died in 1987 and Honor Tracy, her journalist and travel writer friend, in 1989. Other deaths, unrelated to her personally, also touched her: 'What very sad news, just this morning, about John Lennon – I feel the Beatles planted *some sort* of spiritual banner' she wrote to Scott Dunbar in 1980 .[viii]

Consolation came from new friends, who included Suguna Ramanathan, head of the English department and dean of the arts faculty at St Xavier's College, Ahmedabad, India, and Peter Conradi, whom she met at Norwich in 1981. Conradi had written his doctoral thesis on Murdoch's work[ix] and was later to become professor of English at Kingston University. Murdoch introduced him to Buddhism which had a profound effect on his life. In 1983 the Bayleys stayed for the first time with other new friends, Borys and Audhild ('Audi') Villers, on Lanzarote in the Canary Islands. In 1984 Ed Victor, who was also to become a good friend, became her literary agent and took control of financial arrangements with her publishers. In 1985 she began a correspondence with a mysterious American fan, Roly Cochrane, whom she was to meet only once but corresponded with until she was no longer able to communicate. During this year she also met Josephine Hart, writer, television presenter and theatrical producer, who suggested to Murdoch that she should adapt *The Black Prince* for the stage. This liaison marked the start of a warm friendship with Hart and her husband Maurice Saatchi. Murdoch gained much pleasure from frequent trips to art exhibitions with Harry Weinberger and often wrote to gallery owners promoting his work. She also still kept in touch with her former students David Morgan and Rachel Fenner, occasionally alerting the latter to artist-in-residence opportunities.

Dame Iris reached her seventieth birthday on 15 July 1989. Newspapers and magazines carried many celebratory articles, including 'Iris Murdoch at Seventy' in the *Telegraph Weekend Magazine*, and the BBC produced a *Bookmark* programme entitled 'A Certain Lady' in her honour, broadcast in December 1989.

To Philippa Foot.

Steeple Aston
29 January 1979

My dearest girl, your book[1] has come – and the dedication – I am so glad, so pleased, so thrilled – thank you *very much indeed. I much* look forward to reading the book, I know I will find it deeply interesting. Thank you and thank you!

Life goes on here, humorously, tolerantly, in spite of all reported in my last letter. (The lorry drivers' strike *may* be ending.) There's enough to eat. (We are OK apart from running out of central heating oil. The snow goes on and on.) But I think there is a different mood. God knows what will come of it. Schools and hospitals here and there have had to close or restrict activity. No ambulances, no porters, no laundry etc. etc. mean no operations, no medical care, some people die. Violent pickets isolate the docks. Firms go bankrupt. *What can be done?* The public and the government are *frightened.* The stupid menacing voices of trade union leaders resound upon the air. (To be continued in my next.)

HOORAY for the book, and with much love
I

To Walter Redfern of Reading University, who was writing on Raymond Queneau.

Steeple Aston
14 March 1979

Dear Mr Redfern
Thank you for your letter. You have an interesting subject! I knew Queneau well, he was a friend. No, I have never written or published anything about him. I think he (especially *Pierrot*) influenced *Under the Net*. (Not later works.) I once made a translation of *Pierrot*, but it isn't published (it was not a complete success). On the philosophy, *yes*, he was a natural, absolute philosopher. The 'playing' with Hegel was very serious. He was a very reflective man and in many ways, I think, a melancholy, unhappy man. What *joie de vivre* in his work though! A mathematician who knew him (who might or might not answer a letter about him) is Prof. G. Kreisel, Dept of Philosophy, Stanford University, California. All best wishes – hope these brief remarks help –
Iris Murdoch

1 *Virtues and Vices and Other Essays.*

To Philippa Foot.

Steeple Aston
24 March 1979

My dear girl, so glad to get your card. I am glad you got to Arizona and saw some flowers and felt some sun. Our garden here is still full of *snowdrops* and two days ago there was so much snow we could hardly get the car out. The country is in a bad state. There may be an election soon, and about time. I hate the Labour Party and cannot love the Tories. The bullying tactics of the unions is an awful now unforgettable *fact*. But what can be done? The closed shop[1] is one of the villains of the piece, but what to do about it?

I am *so tired* and overwhelmed with too much work. Interesting work mostly (well, not answering twenty letters a day) but *too much*. The house is in chaos and I have *no time* to clean it up, tidy it, hoover it. I can just about wash clothes and dishes.

I would like an interval but this is *impossible*. I go away to give some *lectures* in April (ten days). Let me know when you are HERE.

MUCH LOVE,

I

To Naomi Lebowitz.

Steeple Aston
31 May 1979

Dearest Nay, much thanks for your letter and forgive this fearfully late reply. We survived Romania,[2] a melancholy place cheered by the patriotic spirit (they are very pleased with themselves for being descended from the Romans). You are right, their language is a sort of Balkan Esperanto, all mixed up French, Italian and Latin. We spent most of our money on a trip to the Danube Delta where we saw the pelicans arriving from Africa. Otherwise, there were rather too many meetings with writers. (Talking to writers through an interpreter, not jolly fun.) [. . .]

I have a terrible lot of heterogeneous work to do – I am somehow bugged by it more than usual. (And a hundred Romanians write asking for books or testimonials to say they must come to Oxford or something.)

---

1 The 'closed shop' system, agreed in 1976, allowed organisations the right to employ only people who were members of a trade union. Murdoch blamed Labour Party policies for the rise in union power which had brought about the strikes of the 1970s.
2 A British Council trip.

It *rains* here continually. We have a jolly woman prime minister.[1] I am quite glad, I am so afraid of left-wing Labour, and the Tories may as well *try*, and won't do anything irreparably awful one hopes. John sends love. Love to Al. Work is a great blessing but can become an addiction. [. . .] Much love
 I

To Harry Weinberger.

Steeple Aston
18 August [1979]

Dearest Harry, just to say I'm back and when reading this you will be. I hope Crete was *wonderful* and I long to see the new sheaf of drawings. Yes, I should be very pleased for you to draw me one day, subject to the usual time and space problems! I hope Joanna continues well. My mother is staying now and I am tied here, and in general I won't be around much this month. But later we'll meet, God willing, and I do want to see the paintings again. We had a lovely holiday, partly in our old haunts (Carcassonne, Cévennes, St Remy – so beautiful and so *nice* –) and then in Spain with other friends, lots of swimming and I stepped on a sea urchin – (no lasting damage, even I think to the sea urchin). This just to greet you – love to Barbara. Paint well, be well – ever with love to you
 I

To Scott Dunbar.

Steeple Aston
[September 1979[x]]

Dearest Scott, much thanks yours. Yes, I get it about the racism. God. How ingeniously human beings can arrange to stir up hate. (The Pope has just left Ireland. A great man, but God would be needed for that island.) I'm glad you are reading Simone Weil now partly to improve your French. That would please her. And I'm glad the first part of your book is done. I feel sure it will be a *good book*. As for those 'pop' non-philosophers – alas too much of the world belongs to them.

    I wonder about jobs?? I wish I could help – let me know if I can. I wish I were more God-like, or even more Pope-like. [. . .]

---

1 On 3 May Conservative Margaret Thatcher became Britain's first woman prime minister.

Yes I like street-haunting too, pub crawling or just wandering. Montreal sounds a nice place for that – and would be OK without the French, as Ireland would be without the Irish. (If only one could import some nice Scandinavians or Dutch.)

I shall be away now for two weeks, but do write for my return.

Much love

I

To Harry Weinberger.

Steeple Aston
3 October 1979

Harry, thanks very much for your letter and for sending that interesting messy stuff by John Berger.[1] Certain political dogmas do stop people from thinking – he is trying to think, but prevents himself from saying anything deep about the timeless/ephemeral/time business. Art (and religion) are about these matters, absolutely. Recent art history (as summarised by Berger) distracts attention from the permanence of these questions (as if one were in this respect moving somewhere fast!). Of course modern physics is moving fast. But a problem about human nature is at stake. Of course you are right to say that artists are more deeply moved, and more mysteriously. [. . .]

Au revoir, but I'll be away now for two to three weeks. Work well. With best love –

I

To Naomi Lebowitz.

Steeple Aston
[3 October 1979]

My dear girl, thanks so much for letter. You seem deep in the Germanic world, well done. Get to the bottom of it. (Ah, what is there?) God bless Søren Kierkegaard. The Pope has survived Ireland and is now with you, bringing his message of peace (also of no divorce, contraception or abortion). What a perfectly wonderful man, surely the most attractive public human being on the planet. [. . .]

---

1 Probably *Ways of Seeing*.

I have just finished a novel.¹ You and Al have *tiny* (very flattering) walk-on parts! (I'm sure you won't mind. There is a sort of chorus of Jews.) [. . .]
With much love
Iris

*To Brigid Brophy, written probably just before leaving for a three-week trip to China on a cultural visit arranged by the Society for Anglo-Chinese Understanding (SACU).*ˣⁱ

Steeple Aston
[early October 1979]

It was super to see you. I'll be back, God willing, 24th and will communicate thereafter. Alison's call was mostly her saying that she loved you absolutely, you were the love of her life. There can be no doubt about that.
Much love to you, my dear
I

To Scott Dunbar.

Steeple Aston
15 November [1979]

Dearest Scott, I'm sorry not to have written sooner – I've been away almost all of October, in China, see below. Thank you *very much* for letters I find on return. Such lovely cards from the Frick, such joyful Fragonards² and that lovely calm Turner – and the Berthe Morisot³ from National Gallery in [Washington] (who says women can't paint? See Germaine Greer on that subject!⁴) [. . .] I'm especially pleased H.D. Lewis⁵ liked your 'Self and Immortality' piece (well he may). And I picture you with Simone Weil and the *Iliad*. (She is very interesting on Homer, on Greeks generally.) And home with your plants. (Good that you have a Quaker base in NY. I recall your

---

1 *Nuns and Soldiers.*
2 Jean-Honoré Fragonard (1732–1806), French painter and printmaker.
3 Painter (1841–95) and member of the Impressionist group in Paris.
4 *The Obstacle Race: The Fortunes of Women Painters and Their Work*, in which Greer explores why there have been no women painters with the stature of Leonardo da Vinci or Titian and gives many examples of the work of neglected women artists. Brigid Brophy's review of Greer's book was published in the *London Review of Books* on 22 November 1979.
5 Hywel David Lewis, Welsh theologian and philosopher, founding editor of the journal *Religious Studies*.

Quaker connection from earlier days.) I hope you are writing *Plato and the Beautiful Boy*! I am glad to know of your doings, large and small.

I was asked rather suddenly to join a delegation going to China, early October (alas John couldn't come because of Oxford term). (Another member was David Attenborough, the very nice animal TV man.)¹ We were in Peking, then various places south and back through Hong Kong, and met all sorts of people, writers, farmers, factory workers, the universities, politicians (including Deng Xiao Ping² with whom we had a TV interview). We didn't talk to anyone really freely – but to a lot quite spontaneously. I mean, the Party is everywhere, a 'cadre'³ could always be assumed to be on the horizon. Of course it is a very different scene from the terrible Gang of Four⁴ days (everyone blames that quartet now for everything) – but still it is a remark-able sort of repressed society – the Party, like the medieval church, has its tentacles right down into the remotest corners. Of course one must also say, in every sentence as it were, what a miracle – how is it possible to govern 1,000,000,000 people – *unify* such a state (persuade them all to dress alike, for instance!). All fed, clothed, housed, not lying about in the street as in India. Another contrast – absolute absence of religion in China – a few shadowy old Buddhists, odd Christian centres in Peking, and *quite flourishing* Islam in places where a national minority is Muslim – but generally utter loss of this dimension and *ignorance* of the past. But there we are – we saw very few police and only about two or three armed men – though the (unarmed) army are around everywhere. How is it done? It was all very somehow touching, moving – such a desire for contact with the West, to talk English. And a *poor* people living with equal sacrifices – everyone in two-room flats, including the manager of factories etc. And EXAMS back again – to find engineers, physicists – for them a career open to talent. (But literary matters and more reflection not so popular.) As you probably know, some chaps who were encouraged by the new atmosphere to shout for 'democracy' are now in jug. Poor old human race – so much good, and then the old repercussions. The writers seemed to me to have swallowed so much 'self-censorship' they didn't even notice it any more!

Lovely to be back in misty autumn Oxfordshire. All for now – do write – Lots of love

I

---

1 Other members of the group included Michael Young, the sociologist and author of *The Rise of the Meritocracy*, and Brian Aldiss, the science-fiction writer.
2 Reformist leader who, after Mao's death, led China towards a market economy.
3 Member of an activist group.
4 The name given to a group of four Chinese Communist Party officials that became powerful during the Cultural Revolution. The gang's leading figure was Jiang Qing (Mao Zedong's last wife); the other members were Zhang Chunqiao, Yao Wenyan and Wang Hongwen.

PS re the Prayer Book: I signed, with many others, a great petition for its restoration, partial at least. The synod of Church of England rejected this with sneers and saying many signatories were atheists!

To Philippa Foot.

Steeple Aston
8 December 1979

My dearest girl, how are things, I think of you so much. I hope you are OK, and Sid¹ is OK. It's silly to worry. You are surrounded by loving friends I know. I'd just like to see your writing, for selfish reasons! Here, Christmas looms up. Laser beams in Oxford Street. It's still miraculously warm. I have finished the first draft of a novel² and feel for the moment let off from the demons that usually organise me. The TASK of Christmas itself is of course considerable. I like the dark days and days getting up in the dark and seeing the light break.

I do hope you are well and I *long* for news, just a word.

Very best Christmas and New Year wishes, my dear, and Much Love

I

To Albert and Naomi Lebowitz.

Steeple Aston
December 1979

Just to send you one of these almost frivolously pretty air letters. Thank God something is. This country seems to be descending into some sort of chaos. 'London is grinding to a halt' has been a curious joke. We have got our ration books and are *praying* for petrol rationing (ten miles a day).³ It will soon be the only way to get petrol. It is fantastic what a set of white-robed medieval tyrants who ought to have been assassinated years ago can do to the world. [. . .]

---

1 Sidney Trivus, with whom Philippa Foot had been in a relationship since the mid-1970s, had recently become ill.
2 *Nuns and Soldiers.*
3 The energy crisis had been triggered by the Iranian Revolution which culminated in 1979 with the then shah of Iran leaving the country. This political crisis severely disrupted the oil industry in Iran, leading to decreased production, the suspension of exports and oil rationing in various countries, including Britain.

The IRA have blown up the Slieve Donard hotel¹ where John and I have had many a merry drink. What a planet. I am glad Christmas is coming, which we usually manage to enjoy. Hope you will too. Will probably write again before that. [. . .]

With much love

I

To Scott Dunbar.

Steeple Aston
25 January [1980]

Dearest Scott, thanks very much for letters and cards – I was glad to see that button again! – and the Pro Musica² programme – wish I'd been there, I'm glad you liked the Beatrix Potter mouse pillow fight³ – I thought that was utterly enchanting and special. And your memories of Ian Ramsey⁴ – alas the new archbishop of Canterbury (Runcie)⁵ seems as big an ass as the last one! Duds, they seem. (I may be wrong about Runcie.) I too have been considering Bultmann,⁶ MacKinnon etc. (in a shadowy way, I can't *grip* the stuff). I agree very much with what you say – theology must be bolder – the trouble is, the *Faith* holds these people. They don't want to *scandalise* others (whom they might, they feel, harm) – or themselves! I wonder what will happen to Christianity? If only it could be *changed* more quickly – but dropping, and *how* to drop, the historical-religious divinity of Christ, without destroying the whole thing – [. . .]

I am idiotically busy with too much and too many various things to do. One should rest more. Potter around. Admire one's Chinese plates. Much love

I

---

1 In County Down, Ireland.
2 London Pro Musica, a mixed-voice choir based in London, Ontario, Canada.
3 From *The Tale of Two Bad Mice* (1904).
4 Professor of the philosophy of religion at the University of Oxford and bishop of Durham from 1966 until his death in 1972.
5 Robert Runcie, archbishop of Canterbury from 1980 to 1991.
6 Rudolph Bultmann, German Lutheran theologian who argued for an existential interpretation of the mythological elements in the New Testament.

To Naomi Lebowitz, written after the Bayleys had made a British Council visit to Iceland which Murdoch much enjoyed. In a letter to Albert Lebowitz dated 22 April (not included here), she mentioned the 'Tall enthusiastic stone-eyed blonds of both sexes wanting to discuss Kant and Shakespeare. I loved it'.

Steeple Aston
24 April 1980

Dearest Nay, just to say that we survived the Iceland experience which included the Halldór (Nobel Literature Prize) Laxness[1] experience. HL is a very nice old bean who lives in a solitary white concrete house beside a raging stream in the middle of absolutely nowhere. Lots to eat and drink. There are no trees in Iceland except a few unhappy dwarfs which people have made, very rarely, to survive. I forget if you've been there? I wanted to see huge plumes of scalding hot springs shooting into the air, but in the Reykjavik area they are all in pipes warming houses, greenhouses and pools. (It was interesting to cross the *snow* in one's bathing costume and plunge into a very hot swimming pool completely obscured by steam!) [. . .]
    Much love
    I

26 April: PS I wrote to you just before the attempt to free the hostages.[2] What anguish, and very much felt over here, and with sympathy for Carter (although of course etc. . . .). What a scene. I hope this won't get Kennedy or Reagan in. If only Carter could have some *luck*. This just an exclamation and to send much love. I

To Brigid Brophy, written when Bjorn Borg played John McEnroe at Wimbledon.

Steeple Aston
[July 1980]

[. . .] As I write you are I trust watching Borg (or whatever his name is) defeating that rude American, accompanied by Alison, cherries, Chablis etc. I am sure you will produce a most elegant account of the sporting activity.
    Will you let me see your *Spectator* solution to the problem of Ireland? Almost everything said or written about Ireland annoys (or infuriates) me

---

1 Halldór Laxness, Icelandic author who won the Nobel Prize in Literature in 1955.
2 The Iran Hostage Crisis, which culminated in a secret military mission to rescue fifty-two American hostages held in Teheran on 25 April 1980. The mission failed, leaving eight American servicemen dead and no hostages rescued.

these days; dare I hope your piece will be an exception? Thanks for your
cryptic explanation of ISBNs. I'm glad to learn I have one.

As for Esperanto did I tell you of my controversy (the one I actually
started in the Esperanto world) about '*patrimo*' which is the Esperanto word
for 'mother'!! (I spent a little time learning that language, as a friend of mine
is a member of the Esperanto Academy.) I will explain this saga when I see
you – which I hope will be soon – [. . .]

Much love

I

To David Morgan.

Steeple Aston
[11 August 1980]

I am much enjoying that bit of Irish Flannery[1] you lent me. I note, in the
so-called blurb, the names of J. Joyce and J. Stephens[2] (mentioned as influences). To this duality add the holy ghost of S. Beckett. I, too, in my youth,
was moved to write a pastiche of Joyce-Stephens-Beckett. Title of pastiche:
Under the Net. Sale of pastiche: moderate to good (including paperback).
Comparison of Murdoch's pastiche (*qua* pastiche) with that of Mr O'Brien:
in the latter's favour. Reason for superiority (*qua* pastiche) of that of Mr
O'B: greater flow of original genius in Murdoch. Or some other reason.

You see it is catching and quite easy really. Why don't you try it? After
all a Welshman is a junior honorary Irishman.

I

To Brigid Brophy.

Steeple Aston
[December 1980]

Thanks very much for letter and Alison's address. I have sent her a card. I'm
sorry you don't like the Christmas festival. I love it. Doesn't it *symbolise*
something wonderful? There's no need to be *personal* about Jesus Christ.
Treat him like Buddha. (But, well, how would you treat Buddha!) As I write
dawn is breaking and an owl is crying – or is it an owl or a *parrot* who lives

1 *At Swim-Two-Birds* (1939), Flann O'Brien.
2 James Stephens, Irish novelist and poet.

nearby and can perfectly imitate an owl? I imagine the unfortunate parrot endlessly kept awake by those tedious repetitive owl-birds. I *will* be in London but not yet – I have to get rid of a cold and collect an honorary degree at Bristol.[1] (Since I went to school there that town has a permanent black cloud over it.) Au revoir, my dear, and much love

   I

PS Talking of going to Bristol, I vividly recall our pleasant meeting at *Swindon* station on the way to (I think) *Bath*.

To Brigid Brophy.

Steeple Aston
[17 December 1980]

Just to reiterate letter-wise thanks for that very pleasant (with such short notice for us) evening with you and Mike and Darius and the champers. It began the festive season very felicitously for us. Thank you for that heart-warming celebration. Talking of which, thanks for two postcards with commentary. The earlier one (with reference to 'favoured' London) is probably Yorkshire propaganda engineered by Lord Scargill.[2] (When Scarborough is the capital city, they won't even have to change the name.) We'll be in town just over Christmas but rather tied up with Bayley arrangements organised by John's military brother. (I rather enjoy it all, actually! There is a pleasant helpless-victim feeling. I am tired of willpower.) Be well and have a happy Christmas. I look forward to meetings in the New Year. All very Christmas and 1981 best and with love

   I

To Brigid Brophy.

Steeple Aston
[8 January 1981]

---

1 In January 1981.
2 Arthur Scargill, socialist activist who was president of the Yorkshire branch of the National Union of Mineworkers at this time. In 1974 he had helped organise the miners' strike that brought down Edward Heath's government.

My dear, how splendid and delightful!¹ Sorry we didn't know and thank you for telling us, it might have become more and more difficult to do it as the years walked by. Well done indeed! It *is* odd that at the shake of a pen 'Mrs Levey' no longer exists. I think name-changing is fun and a *good thing* especially if it happens by decree as a felicitous gift. It is very picturesque and decorative and we do congratulate you both so much. We know a lot of fine people now, knights and ladies and lords and a duke and *lots* of bishops. I doubt I shall be Lady Bayley. I wouldn't mind being St Iris B, or Cardinal B (my friend who was our candidate for *Pope* some fifteen years ago but got nowhere, is mouldering in a parish outside Rome, after having been a star in the Vatican hierarchy. Being very queer has not I think harmed him. I cannot think what has gone wrong). With many cheers and cries of pleasure and throwing of hats in the air – and much love and see you soon I trust.

To Philippa Foot.

Steeple Aston
14 February 1981

Dearest girl, hooray for your letter. So glad to hear from you. I hope you are not working too hard. I am pleased to hear you are having philosophical thoughts and making plans for WRITING. I wish I were a philosopher. I wish I was a painter. (Well, I'd rather be a painter actually.) I suppose the Reagan scene must be alarming. But perhaps, he has *some* good rational people to advise him? I suppose he will, with a name like that, support the IRA. I'm glad too that you watch television. I'm sure it is good for relaxation: which in my case I scarcely have. I am *too* busy, it's *absurd*. We *may* be briefly in USA in late April but I expect you'll be here by then? [. . .]

As for the Labour Party – splendid news. That increasingly leftward bound organisation is in process of splitting, and Shirley Williams,² Roy Jenkins³ etc. will found a new Social Democratic Party⁴ (this oddly repeats events in Oxford circa 1940 when I was chairman of the leftward bound Labour Club and Roy Jenkins led a group to found a new Social Democratic Club. How right he was!). It's a pity about the Labour Party but given the whole scene

---

1 In the New Year's Honours list Michael Levey had been awarded a knighthood; he and Brigid Brophy therefore became Sir Michael and Lady Levey.

2 Politician and academic, Labour Member of Parliament and Cabinet minister.

3 Politician and writer; in 1981 he was about to finish a four-year term as president of the European Commission.

4 The Social Democratic Party, a centrist political party founded by four senior Labour Party 'moderates' known as the 'Gang of Four' (Shirley Williams, Roy Jenkins, David Owen and Bill Rodgers).

the split is best. It is now official *Labour policy* to leave the Common Market
and NATO! And unofficially are likely to abolish the House of Lords instantly
and have no second chamber, abolish private schooling etc. And of course
(this is perhaps the main point) to have the leadership under the control of
the executive committee (and Labour activists in the constituencies) substi-
tuting party 'democracy' for parliamentary democracy. I blame Denis Healey
and others very much for not reacting firmly earlier against the left. A crucial
move was when the parliamentary party elected Michael Foot, that wet
crypto-left snake, as leader instead of Denis. Now Denis and co. are left
behind, complaining bitterly, to fight the crazy left. Shirley still hasn't resigned
from the party so it's all a bit odd! 'On your bike, Shirl,' the lefty trade
unionists shout at her!

So go things in England, we live in stirring times. I am on the whole very
glad about this development. [. . .]

Write again,

Ever,

Much love

I

To Naomi Lebowitz.

Steeple Aston
April 1981

Dearest Nay, thanks for a super letter. We all felt your and our anxiety-shock
over the Reagan-shot business.[1] What an extraordinary scene and what *luck*
for all, excluding that one poor fellow[2] (and even he 'makes progress'), and
including USA, world etc. It's not a moment for muddles and weakness.
What a time though. I imagine Polish jokes are *out*.[3] (I will tell an Irish joke:
did you hear about the Irish harpoonist who entered the 'Miss Wales' competition?) [. . .]

I'm glad you saw the Snowdon photo in *Vogue* – S suddenly saw me as a
refugee sitting in a sort of nowhere place. (He has imagination.) I liked that.
As for other royal stiffs, I doubt if we shall specially hang around for Charles's
wedding[4] (though indeed we have no summer plans). I think the girl is nice,

1 On 30 March 1981 John Hinckley Jr tried to assassinate President Reagan in Washington.
2 James Brady, press officer, who was left permanently disabled.
3 On 27 March 1981 the Polish trade union Solidarność (Solidarity) went on a nationwide strike in protest
  at the violent beatings of three of their members by the security services. In December 1981 the new
  prime minister began to crack down on Solidarity and by the end of the year it had been broken.
4 Prince Charles was to marry Lady Diana Spencer on 29 July 1981.

modest and beautiful, and probably has some sense. But it's sad in a way that he is to marry inside the old English Debbie¹ circle, and not have some interesting foreign bride! (Preferably black.) The Luxembourg princess² was fine only *Roman Catholic*, which our law forbids. (Bloody Pope doesn't have *everything* his own way!) [. . .]

We are it seems (I can hardly believe it) actually visiting your country shortly but *alas* briefly and not St Louis-wise. John is involved in a Shakespearean seminar somewhere in the inner vastness of New York State, but whether the journey will *happen* or not has been unclear for a long while. I am, I confess, rather reluctant to go there (or *anywhere*) at the moment, but it may have consolations. I will report on this.

Ever,

I

To Harry Weinberger.

[14 April 1981]

Harry, in absolute haste, just leaving for USA, back mid-May – so glad to get your letter saying peace of mind (my God, how important that is). Paint well, be well – see in summer, God willing. (Two references to God; now three.)

Much love

I

To Philippa Foot, written on return from a cruise holiday.

20 September 1981

My dearest girl, I'm so sorry I didn't talk or telephone before your departure. We came back on 16th to the usual muddle and maddening minor crises of our two mothers and after a day in London arrived back here bringing my mother with us. I telephoned, but alas must have been just too late. I'm sorry not to report viva voce and at length! It was very interesting, exciting and tiring. I loved it, but experience was marred by John's having periodic claustrophobia – though he mostly enjoyed it too. We saw, though briefly,

---

1 A debutante or 'deb'. In England, the presentation of debutantes to the king or queen at court marked the start of the British social season.
2 Princess Marie-Astrid of Luxembourg.

magical places – and such as one would be unlikely otherwise to see, such as Samothrace, *Troy*, Patmos, Ephesus, Delos – also (necessarily from the boat) the fantastical monasteries of Athos. We had been to some of the places before (Olympia, Athens, Istanbul) but had renewed visions: I have an old crazy mythological obsession with Greece (not scholarship) and it was wonderful to stir up all these old images. Of course the pace was ridiculous, and our fellow travellers, though of the greatest *variety* and *interest* and niceness, were something wished away! I enjoyed just being on the ship launch after first day, outside on often beautiful bits of land, misty islands etc.

I loved to see ancient derelict shrines, with one or two marble pillars standing, in green overgrown places though would have preferred not to see our fellow tourists in the picture too! Lots of jolly lectures of course! Many people were on cruise who scarcely knew who the Greeks were, gallant fellows! Lots of (good) eating and drinking. Of course one gets back exhausted, head full of visions, but deprived of usual daily hourly inner life.

Write to me soon about *how* was your return to USA, what news, people, work etc. You are like Persephone, spending both the year in the light and both in the dark (I cannot say which is which in this case). Here winds and storms. *Write*. Much love

I

To Naomi Lebowitz.

Steeple Aston
3 December [1981]

Dearest Nay, many thanks for two communications. I note your French phase, what with *Balzac* and Diderot. Lucky your pupils! And *Bleak House* – thank God for Dickens. I must re-read *Great Expectations*, but it's so *distressing*. Haven't read Ricoeur[1] on Freud, perhaps will. I'm reading Zola at the moment, *Germinal*, my *first* Zola! *Terrific*! [. . .]

I am very *bugged* by work, *ghastly philosophy* and bits of novel – feel very tired – and the house is in chaos and I have no time to clean it – books and papers and clothes and spiders *everywhere*. Fortunately John (who sends much love, doesn't mind). [. . .]

Things here are at least interesting politically with this entirely *new* party

---

1 Paul Ricoeur, French philosopher who argued, like Heidegger, that every form of human awareness is interpretive. Ricoeur examined how human understanding is deposited and mediated through myth, religion, art and language. He was particularly interested in the narrative function of language and in how narrativity and temporality interact.

(run by two friends of mine, Shirley Williams and Roy Jenkins) looking as if it might actually win the next election, and crush the Labour Party, now increasingly run by lightly disguised Communists, out of existence. They (the Social Democrats) haven't actually got a *policy* yet, but they are very wise people with high ideals! The opinion polls put them top (they've only *existed* for about eighteen months so it shows what can happen in a democracy if you try). I am watching them anxiously to see that they do things right (e.g. about things that matter most to me such as education, trade union reform and Ireland). They are sound on Common Market (Europe) i.e. want to stay in. I wonder if any of this far-off stuff ever gets mentioned in your papers?

I shall be glad when my philosophy lectures are over. Has Joel decided on his university yet? Strange to think of ranging over that *huge* map, thinking of possible places. God bless America. God bless Lebowitzism. *Do wish* we could drop over for a drink and dinner and a *jolly good* talk. Do come to Europe soon! Much love to Al, and much, my dear, love to you.

I

PS Royal news is brief. I am sure you are longing to know how Lady Di, now Princess of Wales, is getting on. She became very unpopular in the autumn because she (how can they have let her do it?) shot a stag. However she is now popular again because she is pregnant. (She and the prince are both descended from Henry VII so it must be OK.)

PPS Some aide of your president has stated in Dublin that 'all Americans are praying for a United Ireland'. As this presumably includes you and Al, could I ask you please to *stop* praying at once!

To Suguna Ramanathan, an Indian academic and admirer of Murdoch's work.

Steeple Aston
8 December [1981]

Dear Mrs Ramanathan,

Thank you for your touching and interesting letter. I am glad that you have enjoyed my books and found in them images of reconciliation. Thank you too for speaking of your own life. I am interested to know you work in a Jesuit college. (I have had many and highly intelligent Jesuit pupils.) And about what English literature and the King James Bible means to you. You are fortunate to be able to see both into Christianity and into the great Hindu tradition of religion and philosophy. (In the West only the *greatest* philoso-phers can tentatively join religion and philosophy together.) I think I understand what you say about reality and goodness (humility) being the ordinary not the 'high'. Yes. Life has many modes and mansions and levels, or whatever metaphor one chooses here. Ordinary duty. I think the best people I have known have been quiet schoolteachers, not at all 'demonic'. You thought of writing about Larkin? A poet I much admire. (Though perhaps not a truly *great* poet like W. H. Auden.) It is kind of you to think of writing about my work, and I will be glad to try to help if so. But should you not think seriously of *writing a novel* yourself? You know and have experienced many things which would provide marvellous material for a novelist.

I have visited India once and I *love*, and feel a deep affinity with, your country. I hope I'll come again one day, but I have no plan to do so at the moment. Let me know if you come to England. Thank you for writing to me. Let me know about your novel! All very best wishes

Iris Murdoch

To Naomi Lebowitz.

Steeple Aston
14 December 1981

Dearest Nay, things at Cedar Lodge are not quite like the pictures on the outside of this ridiculous air letter.[1] I wrote you a LONG letter full of wise saws and elegant jesting, and gave it in open envelope to JB to add his epistle. He then promptly, when dancing in the snow by moonlight, fell and broke his ankle and is in hospital. The letter has, in this crisis, been lost (not in the snow), he says it is in his study on the table but it isn't. I expect it *will* turn up and *will* be posted, but this meanwhile is a rather mouldy substitute to send you and Al our very best festive season greetings and love.

We have had most unusual snow blizzards here (would be nothing to you) and I have been alone and snowed up at Cedar Lodge, unable to get to see John who is in Banbury. Hope to be able to get through today perhaps. I *think* he'll be out by Christmas – he may have to have pins and bits of string etc. put in to mend the ankle. [. . .]

All very picturesque with snow and full moon. I suppose *your* pipes never freeze? Electricity off at intervals doesn't help. I have a *battery* of candlesticks. Enough of these complaints. I hope you are all flourishing and *enjoying* your snow, complete with cardinals.[2] Much love

I.

1 Dickensian scenes of joviality and celebration.
2 Brightly coloured birds indigenous to North and South America.

To Philippa Foot.

Steeple Aston
7 January 1982

Dearest girl, so glad to get your letter. I hope you got mine vaguely addressed to Institute of Advanced Study, Stanford and to Midvale Ave (earlier). I hear you have been having terrible storms, and hope you are OK. We had long beautiful snows before Christmas, in which John broke his ankle admiring the effects of the moonlight, and this rather blighted Christmas and New Year arrangements, and since he will probably be in plaster till March, next term's arrangements too, so I have had to postpone *sine die* the lectures I was to have given in Scotland,[1] since I cannot leave helpless J. (We were to have spent New Year *by the sea*! Lucky you, with all that sea to look at! I average about four days a year!)

What a scene in Poland and how deeply sad it all is. I feel very tired and have been working like a demon for two years and see no way of stopping this! Not to much effect philosophy-wise either. I am just *not a philosopher* – it is all too difficult for me and the result is a sort of superficial muddle. I am also trying to write a novel and two librettos, also no good. When will you, on present plans, be in England? See our green hills for a change! Write and tell me more of your life and what you are doing. How do you EAT?

Much much love –

I

To Philippa Foot.

Steeple Aston
20 April 1982

Dearest girl, I am so glad to get your letter. I hope you got mine some time ago addressed to Centre of Humane Studies or something. I am very sorry you have been depressed, glad it has passed. A disinclination to work doesn't seem an unusual ailment – and that Cobbe's house nightmare[2] and sadness about Sid[3] – these are all quite rational things in a way – I mean not like a *determination* to be depressed. Time and the beauty of the world tend to

1 The Gifford Lectures, to be given in Edinburgh.
2 Refers to the house in Walton Street, formerly owned by Anne Cobbe, in which Foot stayed on her return trips to Oxford. Through Cobbe's will, Foot held life-tenure of the property. Presumably there was a problem either with the house or the tenure agreement.
3 Sidney Trivus had died in 1980.

remove. I am so pleased to hear of the China trip and look forward to talking with you about that marvellous terrible country. I felt great sympathy, great interest, much enjoyed being there, but also it all *chilled the blood* very much. The power of the Communist Party in Russia is as nothing to its power in China. The 'Cultural Revolution' horrors not so long ago.

I don't see either why you need worry about philosophy being central in your life – it is not likely to be *the* (only) centre because of your strong connection with people. Why shouldn't it be central? I'd like to see your (very basic, I suspect) piece on the colour business. I'm glad that goes on well – you see you are working. As to those Giffords I am very pessimistic, and also *pressed* about the whole thing. If it hadn't been for John's mishap, the whole beastly thing would be over, I would have done it in a crazy impetuous way! Now I see, as I laboriously rewrite, how *hopelessly* bad, indeed partly *senseless* it is! And it is taking away time which I need for other things which I *can* do! I've just finished a novel¹ and want to start another. I am also tired with something else which I *can't* do, two librettos one (sort of) a longish poem (only of course it *isn't* a poem) and other things I said I'd do . . . but can't . . . I'm bedevilled by letters too, arriving up to twelve a day, *piling up* into *accusing piles*.

The garden is a paradise, the sun shines but (to continue complaining) the *terrible* winter weather has killed so much. I hope I haven't already bored you with this litany. We lost earlier the mulberry tree and all the wisteria. Then in December and January a large pine tree, our eucalyptus tree, a very tall acacia (I think), a great many of the *roses*, including noble old climbers on the house, and on walls, worst of all two fine, one huge, *ilexes* (oh my God), a lot of laurels, of course all the rosemary, lavender etc. a big blue ceanothus, a vast yellow clematis, a myrtle (this is becoming tedious, I will knock off). However as I say paradise reigns with many many flowers and the green grass again (and the dear nettles for snake). As John's leg is still not mended – the *wound* of the third operation not healed, the foot utterly stiff, he is still on crutches – we have *no* plans to go *anywhere* and will certainly be here in July and much looking forward to seeing *YOU*. Keep in touch, let know when.

BON VOYAGE to Chinaland. About John's mother, by the way, I don't think he was *deeply* upset.² But he does *miss* her, so do I! [. . .]

MUCH LOVE – see in July – write – ever your

I

---

1 *The Philosopher's Pupil.*
2 John's mother had died suddenly in February.

PS About the Falklands¹ – it is a *nightmare* and I feel very miserable about it – divided between *intense* chauvinism and a pacifist horror of the idea of anybody being in the least hurt over such an issue. But it is one of those *traps* where people really (and even not unreasonably) feel they have no alternative but to do something awful!

To Philippa Foot.

Steeple Aston
30 May 1982

Dearest girl, thank you so much for your letter from China. Yes, I've been there, and I share a lot of your impressions, such as the many little work-shops and being followed about in amazement! I went as a guest of the government in a small (six) 'Distinguished Persons Delegation'. We heard all about the Long March² all right, and were indeed constantly lectured to (and saw some terrible propaganda films) – and saw *the best* farms, factories and so on.

Very interesting, very touching, *awful* too. My main impressions were the *absolute power* of the Party (much more than Russia – cadres everywhere and no cynicism *visible*), and the (alarming to me) total disappearance of religion. (Ignorance of Buddhism complete.) Also, the 'Cultural Revolution' obviously much more terrible *even* than I imagined (and I imagined horrors). An extraordinary people. A few *elderly* writers (not alone with me – that they could never be – a party cadre present) took their hair down about it. They didn't care. Younger writers, laughing nervously (and ditto) said, 'Oh we are all dissidents these days' (i.e. producing only rather mild propaganda or work on harmless subjects). It was a terrible vision – yet so moving – such touching people – and what a contrast with India! No religion (which is *everywhere* in India) – but also no starvation! No one lying in the street. Oh yes – and NO SEX! Sex *abolished*. Amazing. No holding hands in public (may be changed now). Late marriages – one child – very sensible of course.

I asked about homosexuality. Our excellent interpreter didn't know the word. I explained. 'No, we don't have that!' Illegitimate children? 'Oh hardly

---

1 The Falklands War, the culmination of a long-standing dispute over the sovereignty of the Falkland Islands, was fought between Argentina and the United Kingdom, from 2 April 1982 to 14 June 1982, when the islands were returned to British control.

2 The Long March (October 1934–October 1935) – actually a series of marches which covered 6,000 miles in just over 370 days – was a military retreat by the Red Army to evade pursuit by the Chinese Nationalist Party Army. It initiated Mao Zedong's ascent to power.

ever' – but if *so* the *mother* and the *child* are persecuted. Enough of this. We'll TALK when, God willing, you ARRIVE. Let me know.

Much love,

I

To Brigid Brophy.

Steeple Aston
[July 1982[xii]]

My dear girl, thank you very much for your letter with enclosures and for the elegant and charming clerihew[1] which will cast its light upon my birthday. I liked your Falklands piece and feel no urge to dispute it. A crazy (and awful) business. I think I am more simply patriotic than you are, whatever that means. (Of course actually it is perfectly clear what it means, only I know you will say 'What does that mean?') Breakfast, no. (Except for treats in hotels, in the north bacon and eggs, in the south and east mangoes, in Israel avocados.) [. . .] I am working like crazy, doing philosophy which is just too bloody difficult for me and trying to start a novel. I wish I saw you oftener. One day I will stop work and begin to PLAY. By the way: *IMPORTANT.* I think I saw in a newspaper that Mike has published a novel.[2] Is this so? (Hooray.) I cannot find the newspaper which I had to drop to rush into Oxford or down the garden and later could not find it. I think it was drowned in the rain which floods into our back passage and kitchen when it rains hard. I am sorry to be so ill-informed and beg you to send me a report on this matter. Much love

I

To Scott Dunbar.

Steeple Aston
27 August [1982[xiii]]

Scott, my dear, I've just got your letter and am very upset by the news. I do hope you weren't hurt by that mugger – and did he steal anything? Such things happen in London now and one lives probably in a fool's paradise if one goes about at night. [. . .]

---

1 A whimsical, four-line biographical poetical form invented by Edmund Clerihew Bentley.
2 *Tempting Fate*, Michael Levey's first novel.

I hear today on news that French is to be official language in Quebec Province. How will that affect you? People are mad – like the Welsh nationalists wanting all teaching in Wales to be in Welsh. (Welsh! At least French is a civilised language.) I was very sad to hear some people persecute you – how *wicked* people can be too. I wish you could move to some better place – keep searching – elsewhere in Canada could be much better. I keep an eye on things here of course. That you earn far more and pay less tax than top English academics must be small consolation, but perhaps it's some! I have become a sponsor of Irish Gay Lib, which is getting organised at last. Their laws are pre-Wolfenden.[1] What an *awful* country, and all that bogus charm!
MUCH LOVE, dear Scott
I

To the Sunday Times.

29 August 1982

Your article[2] (page 3, August 15) suggests that Elias Canetti is not allowing publication of his autobiography in Britain because he resents neglect of his work in this country. This is not his motive; he wishes simply to avoid hurting the feelings of certain people who live here.
Iris Murdoch, Steeple Aston, Oxford

To Brigid Brophy.

Steeple Aston
30 August 1982

My dear, how absolutely thrilling about your becoming a grandmother – Mike – grandfather! I can't see why a shock should be involved as, quite apart from the delightfulness thereof, it was surely a development capable of being foreseen. I think it's splendid and will be a joy to all concerned – I do congratulate you all, and am with Alison on this. Well done! I see the name problem: Levey-Gurney. Brophy would be rather smart. I *quite* like

1 The 1957 Wolfenden Report recommended decriminalisation of homosexual behaviour between consenting adults in private.
2 By Norman Lebrecht, in which he suggested that *Die Fackel im Ohr: Lebensgeschichte 1921–1931* (1980) (translated as *The Torch in My Ear* in 1982) was withheld by Canetti because of resentment at the way he had been neglected in England until the award of the Nobel Prize in 1981.

Diamanté but would prefer *Diamond*, a good solid name for either sex.[1] (I am not clear whether Diamanté means fake-diamond?) What fun and how good. (I think Diamond should be combined with a more conventional name – Richard Diamond Gurney-Levey sounds well – and when he becomes a pop star he can be Dickie Diamond.) I imagine you want a boy?? [. . .]

In France the mistral blew all the time, while I gather England had decent hot weather. I had intended to read Alison's novel at once on return, but have not, and am now going away again for probably two weeks. *Sorry* about this. I am not usually so mobile. I came back here to various urgent *ennuis* letter-wise, and also the increasingly usual problems of our two mothers which must be sorted out promptly. So, *apologies*, and I *will* attentively read on (DV) next return, when I will report generally on life etc. I hope you are very OK and I much look forward to seeing you in the (by then) autumn. [. . .]

Much love to you

I

To Brigid Brophy, written just before Murdoch travelled to Edinburgh to give the Gifford Lectures.

Steeple Aston
28.9.1982
(note palindrome)

I have just returned from (a) Cambridge (b) Hampshire (by the sea).[2] At Cambridge I took minor (John major) part in a Virginia Woolf centenary conference. As I hadn't read any VW since school (possibly college) days, I felt bound to reread at least all the novels. It's super to wake up now in the morning and realise I don't have to read a Virginia Woolf novel today. I am prepared to admire some of the stuff but do not *like* either it or her [. . .]

I go to Scotland about Oct 24.[3] I dread the whole business. (The ten lectures will occupy most of my baggage, together with large woollen sweaters.) I forgot to mention that there was a very large and good Raeburn[4] (of an ancestor) at the 'hunting lodge' place. I like him very much, that

---

1 George MacDonald's book for children entitled *At the Back of the North Wind* (1871) features a boy named Diamond and his adventures with the wind. In the event, the grandchild was called Roland Matthew.

2 Lady Diana Avebury, who occasionally acted as Murdoch's agent in theatrical matters, and her husband, the Hon. Maurice Patrick Guy Lubbock, owned a flat in Hampshire which overlooked the Solent and had views of the Isle of Wight.

3 To give the postponed Gifford Lectures.

4 Sir Henry Raeburn (1756–1823), Scottish artist who served as portrait painter to King George IV in Scotland.

dreamy spiritual look. I saw two lovely ones at the Fitzwilliam too (main picture gallery closed at Louvre). So Mike is Jewish after all?[1] My Jewish friends will be very pleased. It is rather gratifying, isn't it? I cannot get any enjoyment about being Irish these days. Write. Much love
   I

To Naomi Lebowitz.

Steeple Aston
[early October 1982]

Dearest Nay, thank you very much for your letters [. . .]

I had to read all Virginia Woolf's novels for the conference and am glad *that's* over. I admire her but I can't feel at home. I just somehow don't *like* the stuff, or her. We were surrounded by enthusiasts of course (and had to keep our heads down). There was a ceremonial dinner with *boeuf en daube* (see *To the Lighthouse*). Of course in some sense she's a marvellous writer and original – but I can't be very interested in her thoughts. (Wonderful images, *bits* of writing.)

I have to go to Edinburgh (to lecture) in two weeks and *hate* the idea – I just have to keep thinking that it will be a relief when it's over.
   We were delighted to find you *and Al* on the last page (a treat deferred) of Washington University magazine doing a favour to one Jarvis Thurston, lucky man. No one in Oxford would take so much trouble for a colleague. I think you love each other more in St Louis. It was delightful to read the list of familiar names! (Nice drawings of Howard, Stanley, Bill and John Morris[2] also earlier in mag. You see we *do* read it.) What wonderful *names* you Americans have. I wish I'd invented URDANG. I could *never* have invented IMWINKELRIED. (Urdang is clearly some ancient curse.) [. . .]
   I

Am reading B. *Karamazov*,[3] with great relief.

---

1 Michael Levey had been brought up as a Catholic; perhaps some family history research had uncovered a Jewish ancestry.
2 Howard Nemerov, the well-known poet, Stanley Elkin, novelist and essay writer, and William H. Gass (Bill), a philosophy professor and writer at Washington University, were all good friends of the Lebowitzes. John Morris was presumably also a colleague and friend.
3 *The Brothers Karamazov* (1880), Dostoevsky's final novel.

To Philippa Foot.

Steeple Aston
17 October 1982.

Dearest girl, I'm so sorry we missed each other. I was on that 'Bayley holiday' in Scotland (and then with Michael Bayley in Yorkshire). It all turned out quite well, though John was a bit nervous beforehand at being with both his brothers! [. . .]

We were in my favourite sort of country (except not quite by the sea) with rivers bounding over boulders and descending in waterfalls. I wish you were *more here*! You were scarcely here at all this year because of China etc. I was lately in London and met Michael F[1]. at a literary party. He is handsomer *than ever*, quite the best-looking man in a large room which also contained Enoch Powell, who is rather good-looking in an intense way. Silver-haired laughing M was surrounded by young girls (his wife was away, restoring some pictures, I think).

I go to Edinburgh next week, curse it, except that the sooner it starts the sooner it will be over. I look forward to seeing the stunning room of Poussins in the Art Gallery. Are you installed at Midvale Ave? And how are all 'the gang', do write news of them all. Best address here – I am staying at the 'Staff Club' (or something) at the university and do not quite believe in it – except that it is sure to be in cold and gloomy spot.

As for your spiritual life, what are you fussing about? The fact you think you haven't any shows it is in a very healthy state! You are *radiant* with spiritual life! (What do you mean, actually?) Be well, be philosophical, pray for me. MUCH LOVE
   I
Tell me what philosophy you are doing now?

To Philippa Foot.

Steeple Aston
15 December 1982

Dearest girl, to send you much love on one of these gaudy things. How are you? Do write. Christmas, that vast (delightful I must say) time-consuming operation is going on here. I love London at this time of the year, dark, a little foggy, full of lights and nonsense. *You* of course have eternal springtime.

---

1 Philippa's ex-husband.

I hope you will have a happy excursion for the festive time – and that in general you are not working too hard. I am still experiencing *relief* that the Gifford Lectures are over, and that I don't have to think about philosophy. I might even get round to cleaning the house. I was in France last week for a conference (in Normandy) and got to Cabourg (Baalbec) and saw Proust's Grande Hotel and the beach where Albertine, Andrée and company disported themselves.[1]

All bestest New Year wishes and *toujours* much love.

Write.

I

To Naomi Lebowitz.

Steeple Aston
15 March [1983]

Dearest Nay, much thanks your letter [. . .]

Yes, writers and 'the pain of exclusion' (twice in *Portrait of a Lady*, interesting) – art must be a sort of defensive gesture, a safe place, in some sort of way always maybe. I think it can't help feeling like that! That's something modern art wants to stop perhaps. Can one imagine a world without art? It would *have* to be invented. As for philosophy – I haven't looked at the *beastly* Gifford Lectures since I stopped giving the blighters – I want to get a novel started, and then it might be safe to dig them out of the cupboard. But I can't start the novel – only rubbish is sent along by those who organise these things. [. . .]

Surely you don't *seriously* think about suicide? It's immoral. And you have *such* a *joie de vivre* capacity, more than most people. Irrelevant points of course! But my imagination can't get *inside*. I'm reading, actually, *Suicide and the Soul*[2] just now, with much interest, and will write to you about it later when I've finished. His view alarms me in some way; I suppose I am just having the reaction which he deplores! Has he a streak of romanticism? More on this subject later.

Even without a term of teaching I am ridiculously tired. I'd like to swim in warm sulphurous waters. My SPA book, it's also a DOG BOOK,[3] will arrive to you in due course. However did I write it? I can't write anything

1 In *À la recherche du temps perdu*.
2 By James Hillman.
3 *The Philosopher's Pupil*.

now. John sends much love. (He also told me about CLEATS.[1]) Much love, my dear,

Toujours,

   I

To Brigid Brophy.

Steeple Aston
[late March 1983]

My dear, *sorry* not to have communicated – I had *hoped* to ring suggesting meeting soon, but haven't been able to get to London. How fascinating about the Observer Literary Festival – the first I have heard of this weird event! Thanks for the 'writers against nuclear weapons' piece. I don't think I want to join in. I find it very difficult to know what to do about such matters or even how to find out what I think. But on the whole I feel that we should continue to arm Europe, which will otherwise be reasonably handed over to Russia by the Americans. One must *hope* that the hideous Russian empire will not last forever – things *could* change one day in Eastern Europe, and meanwhile we must not tempt the Soviet Union by becoming helpless. It is all awful however. I haven't forgotten my squirrelled away bottle in your cocktail cabinet and *will* come for it. This coming week however we appear to be going (though briefly) to the Canary Islands.[2] (I will explain this strange move later.) I'm not *quite* sure where they are. [. . .]
  Be well. Much love
  I

To Brigid Brophy.

Steeple Aston
5 April 1983

1 Studs on the sole of a shoe that provide extra traction on a slippery surface; Naomi Lebowitz had referred to them in an earlier letter (not included here).
2 To see Borys and Audi Villers in Lanzarote.

Dear girl, well, we survived the Canary experience and indeed enjoyed it. I imagined canaries, but the place is called after *dogs* actually. These are very handsome rather large tawny animals some of which, we were vaguely told, are still wild and may be seen roaming in groups (packs?). Our informant added there was no rabies on the island. All the same when we met two large beasts doing a Greenham Common act on the road[1] we were rather glad we were in a car. There are some canary-like birds, and also (very rewarding) hoopoes. We swam variously in the sea, off sand, off rocks, from a boat, all that excellent, as also was the (very considerable) eating and drinking in (one of my ideas of paradise) small restaurants in small coves beside waves. I knew the islands were volcanic but didn't realise how utterly volcanic, anyway on *our* island, Lanzarote, one of the smaller ones, which is *crammed* with volcanoes and also very barren (like Iceland) and with areas of chaotic lava where nothing grows. Nothing is also helped to grow by a pretty persistent wind and a rainfall of about three or four inches a year. (It rained when we were there, great excitement. We always seem to carry rain with us.) Sun mostly shone however, and it was *fairly* warm. It's all much further south than I imagined, well south of Spain and off the coast of Africa. We went to no mandatory conferences but to stay with some friends who live in Lanzarote, and who have often suggested we come and this time insisted. He is Russian, she is Norwegian. (She suffers from chronic asthma, that is why they live there, though are often in England.) The unclothed volcanic hills, classically shaped, are very beautiful. The volcanoes are dormant rather than extinct I gather, and some hot smoking hillsides added to the fun. [. . .]

I hope you, Mike, Darius are all very well, and had a happy Easter. Also Kate and family. Does Easter move you at all via the Christian story? It moves me. I wish more people who reject dogma and supernatural religion (as I do) could 'enter into' these symbolic rituals and stop them from fading. I'll communicate again soon and hope to see you, drink that *vin rosé*. Be well. Much love to you

I

To Peter Conradi, who submitted his doctoral thesis on Iris Murdoch's work in 1983.

Steeple Aston
[April 1983]

---

1 Blocking the road – after the 'Greenham Common women' who formed a blockade around the RAF Greenham Common base in the early 1980s to protest against the siting of cruise missiles there.

Dear Peter, thank you so much for all those thoughts. I'm sorry Elizabeth Dipple seems to have presented such a gloomy absolutist view! I didn't really read her book,[1] I can't read books about myself. OK to your (very kind) queries, except to the two points overleaf (the dialogue[2] wasn't 'commissioned', it was suggested in a friendly way by Michael Kustow without reference to the theatre). I like what you write, which seems to me on the right lines, only don't overdo the Platonism, dear boy. Critics love to think, oh *that's* the key! A previous book prompted someone to say, 'I *see*, it's all a cipher for Simone Weil'. These are works of fiction in the Anglo-Russian tradition and full of heterogeneous stuff. However you know all that, and indeed say so in one or two places. [. . .]

I would love to see you, and Jim,[3] when next term starts and I shall be more regularly in London. Let us make a date sometime in May. I would like that very much. As for the interview, I am not keen on these things, but you are a special case. Could we consider the matter? [. . .]

Many thanks and au revoir and with love

I

To Naomi Lebowitz.

Steeple Aston
[May 1983]

Dearest Nay, thank you so much for letter and so-like-life Feiffer[4] cartoon. I'm glad you went out in your cleats to cheer the Cardinals.[5] I wish I could come to your Joyce classes. I tried to get going on *Ulysses* the other day but felt sick at the first page. This is a purely *Irish* reaction in fact. (That Martello tower[6] was a place where I played often in childhood on that heavenly coast, but that's a yet further point.) I couldn't get going either on a novel by Ford Madox Ford, being put off by a sentimental RC priest. My God these writers go deep. Do you like FMF? I feel I may be missing something. [. . .]

Isn't it splendid that a *Belfast man* is now president of Israel?[7] How I would

1 *Iris Murdoch: Work for the Spirit.*
2 *Art and Eros* and *Above the Gods.*
3 Peter Conradi's partner, Jim O'Neill.
4 Jules Feiffer, American cartoonist, best known for his long-running satirical cartoon strip titled *Feiffer.*
5 Baseball team of St Louis, Missouri.
6 A Martello tower (a small defensive fort) in Sandycove, Dublin where James Joyce spent six nights in 1904 and which is featured in the opening of *Ulysses.* The building is now the James Joyce Tower and Museum.
7 Chaim Herzog, Irish-born Israeli politician.

like to hear that well-known accent pealing out. (Is he a Protestant or a Roman Catholic Jew??)

Did I tell you my crazy Atlanta fan has surfaced again? She has started ringing me up at 3 a.m. Atlanta, 8 a.m. here (I'm glad it's not the other way round). Yesterday she said would I *please* have a blood test to determine whether I am male or female? (She thinks I am male, only no one knows this but her.) She also thinks I wrote all Agatha Christie's later novels. In spite of such delusions she managed, till lately retiring, to hold down a regular job in an insurance office. Dottiness sure is selective.

Much love, dearest Nay. Write. Be well.

Toujours yours with much love

I

To Peter Conradi, giving advice on books about Buddhism. Conradi has since suggested that John Blofeld's The Way of Power *was a useful source for Murdoch when she was researching for* The Sea, The Sea.[xiv]

Steeple Aston
[June 1983]

Dear Peter, so good to hear from you. There are piles of books on Buddhism around, mostly on Zen, and the thing is to read a lot of them and find the little bits in each that strike you. I like Suzuki,[1] *Zen Studies*, and John Blofeld, *The Way of Power*.[2] Blofeld's book is on Tibetan Buddhism but has a lot of good things, as well as much picturesque information.

About seeing, interview etc., forgive can't yet. My mother is here at present and needs a lot of attention – and I have a lot of *jobs* and *tasks* after she returns to London, and generally feel rather pressed. I shall be in a better state to make plans a little later on I hope. I did so enjoy that evening with you and Jim. Au revoir. Love to Jim. And all very best and love to you. Be well,

I

1 Daisetsu Teitaro Suzuki (1870–1966), Japanese author of many books on Buddhism, Zen and Shin.
2 Blofeld's *Tantric Mysticism of Tibet: A Practical Guide* was reprinted as *The Way of Power* in 1970.

To Philippa Foot.

Steeple Aston
[June 1983]

Thanks for your lovely letter, my dear girl – I wish we could have talked longer – but we will – I have to go to St Andrews, to get an honorary degree and that together with visit to Dorset, carries me on to July 9–10. I'll write after that. St Andrews is a fearful waste of time but I am told the *sea* is there, and there is also a *Graduation Ball* which I certainly shan't miss; though if there are lots of Highland Flings I shall sulk in the bar.

Be well – and au revoir and much love

ever

I

To Brigid Brophy, who had complained to her doctor about her loss of mobility and was being tested for arthritis at a local hospital.[xv]

Steeple Aston
[July 1983]

Dearest Brigid, I'm glad the hospital scene was brief and not too unpleasant. I hope that now you have an interval you can return to some sort of ordinary routine. (Good old ordinariness.) I hope you'll be able to read and write – don't let the novel go, hang on, continue. Writing, if you can get the right subject, mood, style, tone, language (etc. etc. which makes it sound difficult which I don't mean) is a great relief and (for us) a natural function. (How odd it is actually, turning thoughts and feelings into words – how do we do it?) I wonder if you keep a journal? I don't recall ever asking you. Do get rid of the remains of your PLR tasks,[1] and don't take on too many reviews. Create things out of your metamorphosis. And if you feel rotten, go to bed. Can you work in bed? John can, I can't. I think it's probably a good idea, promoting relaxation and thereby thought. A chaise longue not. I have never imagined anyone being comfortable on such a thing for *any* purpose.

I hope the birds sing suitably round your place, but not too loudly early in the morning. We are now wakened at 4.30 by *swallows* who have deafening pointless song.

It's good to hear birds and see trees. I'm glad Darius is better and so

---

1 Refers probably to Brophy's book *A Guide to Public Lending Rights* and her continued public work in this area.

much himself, though I could not interview him very satisfactorily on my last visit. What are you reading? Is reading still OK, absorbing etc., pleasurable (and everything structuralists say it should be)? (Looking through the page into another world etc.) I'm still reading Proust. The narrator has just spotted Albertine out of Elstir's window. (He's seen her before of course on the beach.) Elstir is a bit of a bore actually. Is he supposed to be Whistler?[1] He speaks with awed reverence of Odilon Redon[2] (whom I like very much, but such admiration, with so many others to admire, seems odd). I'll hope to be along before too long and will meanwhile communicate. Do write to me – with much love to you –

    I

To Scott Dunbar, following his visit to England in the summer.

Steeple Aston
12 August 1983

Dearest Scott, I'm sorry I didn't write at once to Penn to say how glad I was to see you! It was a delight and increase of being! Very soon after you saw her Rene became very mentally unbalanced – this failure in the form of loss of memory, mild delusions etc. had been coming on for some time, though, as you saw, she was able to respond to individual people, and was very glad to see you. We finally decided to have her admitted to a mental hospital at Northampton[3] (no National Health Service, or even private Oxford, place could be found). After she had been there a short time she had a stroke (not a severe one they say) and is now in the General Hospital in Northampton.

Her limbs are not paralysed, but she cannot speak. And she is generally 'astray'. They say the speech function is likely to come back. This is all terribly sad and unhappy-making, as you can imagine. Do write to me. [. . .]

    Ever with much love

    I

1 James Whistler (1834–1903), American-born artist based in London. An articulate theorist about art, he did much to introduce modern French painting into England.
2 French symbolist painter (1840–1916), printmaker and pastellist.
3 St Andrew's Hospital.

To Brigid Brophy.

Steeple Aston
23 August 1983

My dear, thanks for letter. Your excellent queen mother ground-floor neigh-bour must be a great blessing. As of course *you* are *to her*, and to her *cat*. I hope the loony workmen have done their work conscientiously and *gone away* leaving you and Darius and the pigeons in peace.

No, I have not read the political novels of Trollope[1] but *will*. I can't find anything right to read just now (and don't think these would be yet). I can only desire to reread books it seems. But I know them by heart! (Dostoevsky, Dickens, Tolstoy etc.)

My mother is still in the Northampton hospital, there is a chance they plan to discharge her to a Northampton nursing home in September. She is a good deal better, so far as living in the present is concerned, and no longer hostile, manic etc. – and we are thinking of 'trying her out' in an old people's home in Oxford. Meanwhile, for one week, we plan a short 'holiday' if nothing dramatic happens in the next day or two! One lives in perpetual anxiety, dreading telephone calls.

I wonder if you are feeling at all better – and whether anything has been said with authority about 'the neurological problem'. Do keep acupuncture in mind. It must be an anxious interim – [. . .]

En pensant à toi – with much love

I

To Suguna Ramanathan.

Steeple Aston
15 September [1983]

Dear Mrs Ramanathan,

Thank you very much for your kind and encouraging letter. I am glad you have liked the books, including the most recent one[2] which you are kind enough to read slowly! No connection there with Jane Austen, or of *Nuns and Soldiers* with *Hamlet*, *Tempest*, so far as I know. I am touched by your desire to write about my work. Perhaps you ought rather to be writing your own novels? Your questions are large and difficult so forgive brief tentative

---

1 Six books known collectively as 'The Palliser novels'.
2 *The Philosopher's Pupil.*

replies to them. I think selfless love is very rare, though the *idea* of it is an inspiration. Love runs through the self. Calm objective humble people, such as teachers and helpers, often seem to come near a selfless loving. It is harder for mothers etc. But it's an attractive idea. Christ is one such *idea*. One would *start* there. Duty, also essential. It has no particular special connection with the social order. There are 'conventional duties' – but *duty* is to see beyond or test those. Kant. Yes. If with love, good. But with duty, also good. *Necessary*.

Good – learnt through *everything*, as Plato thought. A light shining everywhere. But to be *learnt*, through all learning. That's what I think anyway. You are very lucky to have Jesuits *and* the wisdom of the east in your life. I have known splendid Jesuits here. You have, quite evidently, your own wisdom. All very best wishes

Iris Murdoch

To Brigid Brophy, who had recently been diagnosed with thyroid deficiency. This diagnosis prompted a letter from Brophy to Murdoch in which she attributed her recent vulnerability to ill health to the painful break-up in 1979 of her fourteen-year relationship with Maureen Duffy. Brophy was finally diagnosed with multiple sclerosis in 1984.

Steeple Aston
[October 1983[xvi]]

I am so sorry, and indeed dismayed, about how things are, or were, as you may by now feel better. I can't very clearly or eloquently say what I think. You know my affection for you and will I trust forgive blundering. Hatred is a terrible thing which can darken the world and perhaps affect the body too. How to *cure* jealous hate and obsession – this isn't easy at all – but some positive *move* away from it is necessary I believe. A religious person would pray! There are secular equivalents: *Concentration* upon something grasped as good, for instance – the positive *love* of other people, Mike, Alison, Kate – yours for them, theirs for you. Even the existence of some works of art, or beautiful indifferent things (I mean indifferent to you, but *existing, being*) – or Darius – I'm not quite sure how to class him! One must *turn away* from obsession and *see* the whole *other* world, grasped as good, beautiful, vital, full of energy, which can enter you. Don't give in to this bad force. It's as if some bad magician were sending rays at you. You can defeat them and be free. Some *movement* may help. (I hope you understand this and don't feel it's impertinent.)

I also feel you should soonish try another doctor – but this is a specialised question and I can't think of any brighter idea – and I'm worried about your diet, which you don't even seem to be *eating*. You admitted no breakfast, no lunch! Your vegan regime may be the healthiest diet in the world but you've got to eat *lots* of it! Who could you ask? Your GP seems an oaf.

This is just a sketch of what I think. Excuse. I'm going to be away mostly till next Monday (I mean Monday 24th) dealing with my mother's arrangements, and then going (indeed flying) to DUNDEE where John is giving a lecture. I've never seen bonny Dundee. Will report. This with *much* love

I

To Brigid Brophy.

Steeple Aston
[late October 1983]

Dearest girl, please excuse, I don't know why I worked in otiose 'jealous'. After all, not a necessary component. But pure hate, just as bad for one. Oh dear. My letter chiefly expressed my extreme concern. Also I suppose I just can't accept your 'mad' label. You don't *seem* so in the least. Obsession, obsessed fantasy, I can imagine here. It seems to be a disease (illness, ailment) you could do something about getting over. Madness (very ambiguous term of course) suggests a degree of psychological compulsion which I simply cannot attribute to you. Though I know neurotic obsessions can be very strong and such rat-runs hard to get out of. You must know a bit why it is. Excuse exclamations, please.

Dundee was delightful. We saw the huge Silvery Tay (and the new railway bridge) and a lot of fine stone-built houses, once resided in by jute merchants, and we saw the SEA and the River Esk (containing we were told salmon, but not on show) racing through romantic gorges and over waterfalls. We also met a lot of *very nice* academics and drank a great deal of malt whisky. Keiller's marmalade has been taken over by Indians (perhaps left behind with the jute). When op? I will communicate, write, ring, hope see. Send much love

I

To Harry Weinberger.

Steeple Aston
[November 1983]

Harry dear, how silly you are! How could I possibly be cross or offended, ever, where you are concerned? Dismiss that *entirely* from your mind! If I don't write it is just for ordinary reasons, being away or pressure of work, or 'work letters', things that must be answered instantly etc. *You* overburden me with kindness, offering to drive over etc. and I'm very grateful indeed. My mother's arrangements continue to be unclear and very difficult to *think* about, and take up London time to not much avail – I sit in some office, social security, nursing service, etc. for forty minutes and see someone for eight minutes who says she can't help me (etc. etc.). I can't at the moment *plan* anything nice, such as seeing you (or taking delivery of pictures) – but I soon will. We are just going for the weekend to David Cecil, and that will be a good change. I am of course also working like a demon on those two books. I loved to hear about the accordion and the SONGS – I hope you will give me a private concert sometime! Having childhood roots for one's art is surely not a lack of purpose! The unconscious mind is unaware of time (one is told) – it continually *works* however. I look forward to choosing another picture – you must guide me. *Routine*: good, isn't it? Hope painting goes very well. Will write again. With much love

I

To Philippa Foot.

Steeple Aston
22 November 1983

Dearest girl, so very glad to hear from you. Briefly re my ma, since early July she has been in a mental hospital in Northampton, a general hospital in Northampton, a nursing home in Northampton, an old people's home in Oxford, a mental hospital in Surrey, and is now in an old people's home in London. The latter costs about £7,500 a year. However her first port of call cost £125 a day. The place she's in now is *good* but she won't settle down because she wants to go back to her flat and cannot think why wicked people, chiefly me, stop her. Return to flat would be hopelessly impractical and risky – she is now incontinent apart from other (mental) ailments. She would probably start drinking again, be left alone too much, the whole saga would start again, and she'd lose her place at the present establishment. Meanwhile Jack[1] (you remember Jack) occupies her flat – and would be incapable of looking after her properly now. He'll be there forever, also supported by us, incidentally. So it goes on. (He's a nice chap but clueless.) [. . .]

We've had a superb autumn, sunny, with marvellous leaves – and now the trees are bare and there is glittering frost and the landscape looks different

1 Murdoch's mother's companion after she was widowed.

and the mess of late summer cleared away. I love mists and fogs and the approach of *Christmas*. I'm glad you have Rosalind Hursthouse with you, give her my best wishes. Where will you be at Christmas? I'm so glad all is well and you flourish. I hope philosophy goes well too. Did I tell you I had been in Korea in October? They seem less remote than the Japanese. I'm going to a Thanksgiving dinner on Thursday – I'm never quite clear what the thanks is for, but I expect I will find out – it'll be my first one.

Write again, and *much* love, my dear –

Ever

I

To Philippa Foot.

Steeple Aston
9 January 1984

Dearest, thank you so much for the card with that super get-up for lucky Ida Rubinstein![1] Yes, I wouldn't mind having that. Sorry I didn't write sooner. I don't know what happened to Xmas and New Year (I adore these festivities) – much looked forward to, have passed in a flash. At New Year we stayed with friends at the SEA, not far off, near Southampton (nearest sea to Oxford, eighty miles!) and saw some magnificent storms. You are lucky to live beside the sea.

I am working, and feel it very burdensome at present. The house gets untidier and dustier, and we have mice which I keep trying to trap (alive of course and then we carry them off and stray them!) but the little blighters are too clever. They are dangerous mice who eat *paper*. [. . .]

Asinine aspect of my life, I don't see my friends enough. I hope you haven't had any of the American bad weather? I imagine it eternal summer in your lotus-eating land. It's been remarkably warm here, snowdrops soon. *Write*. Much love

I

To Harry Weinberger.

Steeple Aston
20 February [1984]

---

1 Russian actress and dancer (1895–1960).

Dear Harry

[. . .] I'm sorry I didn't write sooner – I've just been overwhelmed with work and sense of pressure and by an increasing quantity of mail (*your* letter very welcome but most *not*!) and by a mild virus infection (or something), permanent cough and sense of being frozen. It's very difficult to plan or think. I look forward to seeing my / your pictures, and will think of a meeting. I am obsessed with the Titian Apollo and Marsyas[1] at the Royal Academy. I suspect it's the greatest picture in the world. I hope painting goes on well with you – oh happy painter! May the gods be with you. I'll write again. With much love

I

To Brigid Brophy.

Steeple Aston
[March 1984]

Dearest girl, thank you for your letter, with aggressive vegetarian poster! I expect you have stocks of these to stick onto all sorts of things. I trust Mike is back by now, having swindled the Americans out of something. (I forget if I told you we are to be in USA for much of April – I never believe really in the future and am only just taking it in as possible.) I am very sorry to hear of persisting symptoms, Yes, you must now try the less orthodox healers. I wish I could advise you – I don't know any of those magicians, but there must be pals of yours who do. Homeopaths, yes, chiropractors perhaps (some of these are full of animal magnetism – I knew one here in Oxford, alas dead, he couldn't evade *that* complaint), and acupuncture might be worth trying. I do believe there is a lot of old wisdom about to be made use of. *Ask* everybody. No harm in going on taking the pills meanwhile!

It's fearfully cold here and has just been *snowing*. I hope you and Darius are curled up and warm. I wish I could send some thought-cure to you – I am trying.

Much love

I

PS[xvii] I SAY I THINK I HAVE DISCOVERED A GREAT WRITER WHOM I HAVE NEVER READ BEFORE. HIS NAME IS JOHN COWPER POWYS.[2]

---

1 Titian's *The Flaying of Marsyas* (c.1575)
2 British novelist (1872–1963) and poet who became famous in 1929 with the publication of *Wolf Solent*, the first in his series of 'Wessex novels'.

To Philippa Foot, written from the USA where the Bayleys had travelled to take up a joint fellowship at the University of California, Berkeley.

5 April 1984

My dearest girl, *thank you* for your welcoming letter! I have been, and to some extent still am, rather prostrate with an unusual case of jet lag. This place is *beautiful* but rather a strain – (perhaps the air? Like Mexico) – and I have a scattering of appointments which rather preclude making any arrangements of my own. We shall I hope and pray see each other soon in *OXFORD*, and I'll tell you of my adventures. I hope to see Larry Blum[1] next week. He sounds nice. How exhausting USA is! Great – but it is so hard to get a drink! We picnic in our room with Californian wine, but can only buy it miles from the campus. The place (Women's Faculty Club) is *very* nice. And the *TREES* are wonderful. This is to send *much* love to you and au soon revoir. *Sempre, siempre*[2]
    I

To Scott Dunbar.

Women's Faculty Club
12 April [1984]

Dear Scott,
    Just to say you would be very welcome here if you felt like coming down to discuss those philosophical questions. The philosophers are a good lot here, as you know. John Searle is having an interesting feud with Derrida.[3] (Derrida himself was here last week.) Hans Sluga,[4] whom I also knew in London, is head of the department. We have had discussions. The weather, also, is very good! With all best wishes and affectionate greetings
    Iris

---

1 Lawrence Blum, American philosopher.
2 Respectively the Italian and Spanish for 'always'.
3 In the mid-1970s a hostile debate regarding speech-act theory (made famous by J. L. Austin) occurred between Searle and Derrida, and continued into the 1980s. Austin argued that speech acts have a performative function in language and include such acts as promising, ordering, warning, inviting and congratulating. An essay by Derrida both praised and criticised Austin's *How to Do Things with Words* and Searle replied by accusing Derrida of misunderstanding basic elements of the philosophy of language. Derrida wrote a rather condescending reply defending his position.
4 Professor of philosophy at the University of California, Berkeley.

To Scott Dunbar.

Women's Faculty Club
14 April [1984]

Dearest Scott
[. . .] The pressure here is considerable and constant though (or because) everyone is so nice! I have a full programme but if you did turn up (any time) we could fit in some talk. [. . .]

I am rather looking forward to getting home! There is too much of everything here – too many people, too many engagements, too many (and too large) oranges, apples, etc. etc. in the huge supermarkets, though I must say the *asparagus* is excellent. And, as I say, everyone is very kind to us. My dear, sorry not to be able to say just *come* – but I know your own life and timetable must be pretty full too. Derrida, as I say, was here – a very nice man, but what a mystagogue! It's all based on philosophical mistakes. (And he's regarded as God.) Dearest Scott, with much love –

I

If you wanted to come England in summer I would help with fare too [. . .]

To Naomi Lebowitz.

Berkeley, Department of English
[April 1984]

My dears, excuse not sooner write USA wise, we have been in rather a daze since we arrived, partly through the natural causes of the frenetic nature of California (oh for the rational calm of St Louis) and partly because of the unremitting strains and pressure of our JOB which though it doesn't seem too extensive on paper, somehow proliferates into all kinds of side- and sub-tasks. Everyone is very kind and the *trees* on the Berkeley campus are beautiful and very spiritual. We have seen pelicans and sea otters and sea lions and grey whales. We have seen Big Sur where big Miller[1] lived. We've had one swim in the sea (the waves are pretty big too, too big), and lots in (heated) pools. I've talked to the philosophers and we have talked to the English lot.

America is extraordinary. We haven't however come across the kind of close-knit intellectual society you enjoy in University City. There's a distinct lack of calm. (Of course such a society must exist here, we just feel outside

1 Henry Miller, whose *Big Sur and the Oranges of Hieronymus Bosch* was published in 1957.

it.) The Women's Faculty Club where we are staying is delightful, except there is no *bar*. (There is a good bar next door in the Men's Club however.) There is a communal kitchenette on our floor which John has taken over, and we buy the huge goodies (huge fruits, huge wine bottles etc.) in the huge supermarkets and have feasts in our room but it's not as nice as our memorable FLAT (apartment) chez vous. (When we arrived here we kept looking for SKINKER¹ and never finding it.) We look forward to going home next week, and will write from there. *See you this summer? Come.* Much love, ever, dearest Nay and Al. Hope all Book systems go.

I

To Naomi Lebowitz.

Steeple Aston
[late April/early May 1984]

Dearest Nay,

We are back from northern California. It was nice there, there were lots of trees on the campus and they even arranged a 6.2 earthquake shock. But there was no Skinker, and worse still no Al and Nay. It wasn't like our US home. But we saw some whales, and people were very kind, and there were 30,000 students all very good-looking.

We saw, heard and even *met* Derrida. We listened to him talk, in French, for *two hours*, the most terrible tosh. But, I must say, when I met him I thought he was charming! (His audience of course was spellbound with raptured awe.)

I came back to some bad news from a friend of mine, a writer,² who has just been diagnosed as having multiple sclerosis. Also, by coincidence, there was the Washington University magazine with the delightful and touching piece by Bill Gass, Stanley gassing so well, lovely picture of Stanley, etc. I told my friend about Stanley and will show her the mag in a little while – she's still rather overwhelmed by the news. Don't bother S himself, but do you from general knowledge know whether there are any new good treatments for that thing – can it be arrested?³ (Is S in a wheelchair or can he walk fairly well? In the picture he looked as if he were flying!) Should one

---

1 The name of the street in St Louis which reminded the Bayleys of happy times spent in the city.
2 Brigid Brophy.
3 Stanley Elkin suffered from multiple sclerosis.

take second opinions about treatment? (The doctors here diagnosed thyroid deficiency, even when the symptoms became extreme! They've only just changed their minds.) Please excuse these rather incoherent questions. [. . .]

Here, everything is heavenly springtime, bluebells, cherry blossom etc. – only it's rather *cold* and *raining*. The birds sing however.

Much love. Communicate.

I

To Carmen Callil, manager director of Chatto & Windus.

Steeple Aston
4 May 1984

Dear Carmen,

Just to say I'm back from sunny hedonistic California. I wonder if I could now have a typescript of the bird poems,[1] to check in case whoever typed them couldn't read my writing? Much thanks.

A thought: could not Virago (or Chatto) republish the works of Brigid Brophy, most of which I think have been out of print?? (My idea, not Brigid's.)

I'll be in London in a week or two, will ring up, would be very nice see you lunch. I hope you are well and not *too* busy. Au revoir and with love

Iris

To Harry Weinberger.

Steeple Aston
27 June 1984

Harry dear, just leaving for Scotland, probably missing any letter from you by today's post if any, just to say THANK YOU for the unique touching Tibetan relic, so beautiful, so full of (utterly mysterious) past, which lies, looking like a little sword on my desk, near to its other Tibetan friends! I am so touched – and I thank you very much, *and* for the pictures – so pleased to have them, they are so full of joy – and for so kindly driving me home! Sorry to miss Barbara, and hope to meet Joanna and Jacob[2] one day. Will communicate. With much love

I

---

1 *A Year of Birds* (1978; revised edition, 1984).
2 Joanna's son.

To Philippa Foot.

Steeple Aston
28 July 1984

Your letter just came. How extraordinary and splendid that you saw Donald[1] and *talked*! I'm glad he was well, and it's good that you did talk. That old language again – it seems so remote. In some ways time stands still. (In good ways too.) You communicated at once. I'd *love* to hear all about it.
    Au revoir, just leaving, with much love, darling, from
    I

To Naomi Lebowitz.

Steeple Aston
4 August 1984

Dearest Nay, thanks for your splendid letter. I'm glad you approve of, and feel some twinge of hope re Ferraro[2] and Jackson.[3] There are always places of renewal, springs of better life etc. etc. in our situations of great variety. [. . .]
    I haven't ever *got* Ibsen however. I'll reflect on what you say about him[4] and James. I'm glad Al is writing on the nineteenth century and on such a good topic! I very much see Al as novelist. (A friend of ours, who is an art historian and the director of the National Gallery,[5] has just published his second novel, set 100 AD in Rome, the narrating character, himself of course, being a Vestal Virgin!) (Good old novel, can do something for everybody.) [. . .]
    About psychoanalysis. I'm very interested – but disturbed by your 'torture chamber'. Must that continue? I agree very much, if I understand it, with what you say about 'content' not mattering so much as the magic atmosphere which produces (though exactly how . . .) the *quantitative* intensity of suffering. Is the idea of *paying* really important here? The notion that

---

1 MacKinnon.
2 Geraldine Ferraro, attorney, was selected by Democrat Walter Mondale as his running mate in the 1984 US presidential election. She was admired as a strong advocate on behalf of abused children and for her support for the elderly and equal rights for women.
3 Henry Jackson, US congressman and senator from the state of Washington, who had strongly supported the Civil Rights Movement, was posthumously awarded the Presidential Medal of Freedom in 1984.
4 Naomi Lebowitz's book *Ibsen and the Great World* would be published in 1990.
5 Michael Levey.

'neurosis' is somehow (scientifically quasi-medically) dispelled by a going over of crucial events in detail, getting it right etc., seems to me a sort of myth which people just thoughtlessly swallow on Sigmund Freud's authority. (Maybe word 'neurosis' should be dropped, describe conditions without it.) And about the moral model, *yes*, I suppose 'scientific' analysts would try to avoid it – but as in art or philosophy which professes some sort of neutrality or objectivity, the morality soaks in for better or worse. The good analyst would do it well by instinct. Why don't they *say* this? (This ends up in metaphysics about the soul and the ground of being and *OK by me*!) I didn't get any feeling of how *your* analyst made the moral point? Perhaps he just put you in a position to make it yourself? Of course one *imbibes* a moral vision from another without being 'told'.

  We have just come back from France and just going to Spain – an unusual amount of such activity. Do write. [. . .]

  With much love always and from John

  I

John managed to fall into a wishing well (well, it wasn't a *deep* well, more like a swamp), but missed a great wishing opportunity, since he only wished to get out again, which he would probably have been able to do anyway.

  Much love, my dear, and to Al – be well – ever, and from John,

  I

To Harry Weinberger.

Steeple Aston
26 September 1984

Dear Harry,

  [. . .] I'm glad the gods are with you and guiding your hand! May it be so. I look forward to seeing the results. I'm glad too that we have no TV and cannot *see* Scargill![1] [. . .]

  My conference in Ireland was about theology. Thirty priests, two ex-priests, three nuns and me! I was the only Protestant. All went well except for row, initiated by me, about Ulster! *Lot* of whisky was drunk. I liked seeing a bit of Dublin and having a *pleasant* (on the whole) visit to my native land.

  Send news. Au revoir and much love

  I

---

1 By this time Arthur Scargill had become president of the National Union of Mineworkers. He led the union through the 1984–5 miners' strike.

To Philippa Foot.

Steeple Aston
14 October 1984

Darling girl, so very glad to hear from you. I wish we could meet more. I've been in this summer, especially later summer, ridiculously preoccupied and pressed with work. I've just finished a novel[1] and in later stages want so passionately to get rid of it, I just go on and on working in a frenetic manner! I've left the philosophy stuff entirely for the present, however, because whatever happens feel I will have lost faith in it entirely when I look at it again!

I'm very sorry to hear about Rogers. One's old friends mean so much, more and more. My publisher, Norah Smallwood, has just died and I shall miss her terribly.

I think of you among all those beautiful Californian trees. Here it is beautiful too with mists and yellow leaves. Term just beginning. Donald, yes. What a phenomenon. Of course religion means so many things. I 'got' it in childhood, which I think you didn't. I feel at home with Christ and the Anglican Church! (Not with God however.) Donald's agonisings are another matter. We could never explain to him. I still dream of a long talk however! I'll write again – this to send very much love – be well – I

To Naomi Lebowitz.

Steeple Aston
20 October 1984

Dearest Lebowitz, thank you so much for Ibsenite etc. letter. I'm so glad you've discovered the Arch[2] at last though I imagine (infer) you haven't been *up* it. I loved it at first sight. Yes, inspiration, imagination, among the city fathers. And I'm pleased to hear of Joel's and Judith's adventures, he in France, she in art history, two wonderful regions full of marvels. And you and Al will come to Europe, you'll *have* to, *often* (not least to accompany Judith to all those galleries). I greatly envy you the Beckmann show – thanks for the envy-making reviews. I find I feel that I own some of those pictures.

I am very interested by what you say about psychoanalysis – and of course (like mysticism etc.) it (psychoanalysis) defeats the outsider. There are, I

---

1 *The Good Apprentice.*
2 Gateway Arch in St Louis and the world's tallest arch.

expect, an increasing number of people whose families 'wash out value' and who are attracted to (some) analysts by the smell of it. We both belong to value-rich families, though of different kinds. Did you feel, yourself, that there was 'too much morality'? I suppose one escape from guilt is through 'relaxing' (and retrieving it later – perhaps) but no doubt another is in 'going on'. It might be difficult to decide, in either case, when to use the word 'neurosis' (and of course whether to use it). Yes, one can certainly see the 'mechanical' aspect of many distressed states. [. . .]

I've just been visiting (second visit) a chap called Krishnamurti,[1] who used to be very famous (and beautiful – he's still beautiful age ninety-one) some time ago. He is an Indian sage, discovered as a child by the theosophists (as the 'destined one' etc.) and transported to Europe. In India he is a god. He teaches a kind of anti-religious quasi-mystical good way of life. I was asked to have a (videotaped for the faithful) discussion with him, which though producing little clarity interested me a lot. How very very serious human beings are in their deep assumptions about morals, mind etc. etc. (Obvious idea, but I find I lose it from time to time!) I think he is a remarkable *being*, though I don't like all his talk. [. . .]

I hope Al's presidents book[2] has found a home and that his NOVEL progresses well.

MUCH LOVE

I

J sends MUCH LOVE.

---

1 Jiddu Krishnamurti, speaker and writer on philosophical and spiritual subjects.
2 *The Legal Mind and the Presidency* was finally published in 2013.

VICTORIA AND ALBERT MUSEUM   KUAS80 /30

THOMAS GAINSBOROUGH R.A.
(1727-1788)
The Painter's Two Daughters.
Oil on canvas. 16 x 23 in.
Forster Bequest.

When we went to the V&A

Harry and Iris.

Ⓘ

Sketch by Weinberger, not part of letter, but posted by him to Murdoch. It features them
recently visiting the Victoria & Albert Museum together.

To Harry Weinberger.

Steeple Aston
20 November 1984

Dear Harry, what a charming picture of us going to the V and A! I loved
that day too – and I'm so glad some pictures were sold. I hope you got off
to Vienna and that it has been, as it should be, marvellous. I have been in
Germany (Cologne) then in Sweden (Stockholm). I had been to both cities
before, Cologne wrecked after the war and Stockholm briefly en route for
USSR, when I was too excited (about USSR) to see it! What a beautiful city
Stockholm is – and how well you would paint it! I was doing a job for the
British Council in Cologne and for my publisher in Stockholm.

I love the photo of your Tower Bridge painting, so blazing with light, it's
superb. [. . .]

Send news. With much love
I

To Naomi Lebowitz.

Steeple Aston
3 December [1984]

Dearest Nay, the *wonderful Beckmann book* has COME – oh we are so *pleased* – THANK YOU both very very MUCH INDEED – it is the greatest treat, full of things which are near to us, and other things we know but have no experience of and altogether a perfect joy to have. I'm quite overwhelmed and delighted. I get madder and madder about Max Beckmann. (Lately in Cologne art gallery I found *seven* Beckmanns, three first class.) [. . .] Did I tell you I actually once got a letter from Quappi?[1] I found she was still around and living in New York and I sent her a copy of *Henry and Cato*, with the acrobat picture on the cover, and she replied so nicely. From the book you sent I learn I have another bond with him – he knew the Motesiczky family in Vienna, and a drawing by him is reproduced by Marie-Louise Motesiczky, a painter who later lived in London and whom I met via Canetti, and who painted a portrait of me for St Anne's College when I left that institution. It is a marvellous picture, but the barbarians of St Anne's didn't like it – anyway there it still is. (They daren't destroy it!) Hooray for Beckmann, and what a super present.

[. . .] To return to Canetti, I haven't read his autobiography. I met chez lui in London one of his brothers, who lived in Paris and was a music impresario. I have the book and *will* read it but feel rather paralysed about reading at the moment. A friend has at last forced me to read *L'éducation sentimentale*[2] which I don't much care for so far, have only read half. My heart does not beat for that chap and his love. I cannot like Flaubert, or Stendhal. [. . .]

A friend of mine has died, my publisher (she had retired) Norah Smallwood, and I miss her awfully. I also 'miss', though she could not in the circumstances be a close friend, Indira Gandhi, with whom I was at school, and also at college. We corresponded, met occasionally in London, and also when John and I were in India, and we met Rajiv,[3] then a quiet chap who was leaving public life to Sanjay.[4] I was looking forward to seeing her again.

1 Beckmann's second wife, Mathilde von Kaulbach, whom he married in 1925. Her nickname, 'Quappi', derived from the similarity of her surname to the German word *Kaulquappe*, meaning 'tadpole'. Beckmann painted many portraits of her.

2 1869 novel by Gustave Flaubert.

3 Rajiv Gandhi, who became prime minister of India after the assassination of his mother Indira Gandhi in 1984. He was himself assassinated in 1991.

4 It was assumed that Sanjay Gandhi would follow in the footsteps of his mother Indira as head of the Indian National Congress, but his death in a plane crash at the age of thirty-four resulted in his elder brother Rajiv becoming their mother's political heir instead.

The scene is emptier and I feel tired. I've finished a novel and am fiddling with starting another¹ and I have a lot of other things on hand. This year I've been to Scotland, and Ireland, and France, and Spain, and USA, and Germany, and Sweden. Sweden (Stockholm that is) was fun, although the country has some alarming (political) features. I think you've been there on your Scandinavian wanderings? [. . .]

I GLOAT over my lovely Beckmann book and I *thank* you with all my heart for such a wonderful and *right* present! Write again soon. Think about that novel. You are so full of thoughts.

Dearest Nay, with much much thanks and lots and lots of love, and also to dear Al, Your
I

To Philippa Foot.

Steeple Aston.
4 December 1984

Dearest girl, much thanks yours. Yes, it's awful about Norah. I can't stop looking forward to seeing her. After going to her memorial service at St Martin's-in-the-Fields I thought, I'll tell Norah about that. Well, things go on. [. . .]

I reflect sometimes about our conversations about Donald! Real life is so much odder than any book. Don't work too hard. Go and look at the SEA, you lucky dog. I'm glad you are *well. Be* well. *Be.* I miss you and want to tell you things (not particular things, just things).

Very much love,
ever,
I

To Josephine Hart, with whom Murdoch was to collaborate in adapting The Black Prince *for the stage.*

Steeple Aston
28 December [1984]

---

1 Murdoch had finished *The Good Apprentice* and was starting on *The Book and the Brotherhood*.

Dear Josephine,

Thank you so much for sending *Flaubert's Parrot!*[1] I am delighted to have it and much look forward to reading it. Thank you for such a nice idea, following on our wide-ranging and so pleasant talk! I am very grateful for your interest in the novel, perhaps play. It remains to be seen whether I can actually do it! As I explained, I cannot start at once, I have to do final finishings to the latest novel, and also in a hurry to rewrite a philosophical paper for publication by May next. But I will be keeping the thing in mind and reflecting. I look forward to *trying* and we would love to visit you and make the acquaintance of Maurice.[2] (I was so touched by his anxious note sent in during lunch!) Au revoir and all very best wishes and love, and hopes for 1985,

Iris

To Philippa Foot.

Steeple Aston
25 January 1985

Darling, thank you very much for your card. I have been thinking about you and dreaming about you. I imagine you now in the sun, surrounded by those magic trees, in a garden of flowers, looking out upon the glittering dolphin-crowded sea. Here it has been snowy, windless, with dark yellow light, rather beautiful. How is philosophy? I hope you have not too much work, and only pleasant travels to places like Arizona. We shall be in New York in February but only for four days (John is giving a lecture). It seems impossible to *go* anywhere at present.

I am OK but have too much to do – crazy things I said I'd do long ago (like writing a preface for someone's book) seem to be crowding around, little things for BBC, I can't get at those long calm necessary pieces of time and people send their bloody poems and so on. I don't see much of Oxford. I go to London to see my mother. She is OK, still in that 'home', getting more out of touch, but fairly quiet thank God. It's sad to see the person disappearing. [. . .]

I feel (effect of the snow I expect) that I have not stirred from my cell for years (nice cell) but I was (perhaps I told you) in Germany and in Sweden before Christmas. I think I have stopped hating being in Germany. Dear old

1 Novel by Julian Barnes.
2 Maurice Saatchi, Josephine Hart's husband, and founder of the advertising firm Saatchi & Saatchi with his brother Charles in 1970.

Europe, poor old Europe. (Dear old planet, poor old planet.) Mainly to say I think of you – be well – do write – much love –

I

I forgot to mention that I have finished a novel and started another. I suppose that's news. It all seems to be happening (only) inside my head.

To Philippa Foot, written just before Foot was to leave for Japan.

Steeple Aston
9 March 1985

My dear, thanks for your welcome letter full of the feeling of spring in deserts and canyons! It's spring here too, misty, wet, not yet entirely recovered from the blanket of cold. [. . .]

I am reading Wollheim's book *The Thread of Life*, which I seized on with joyful anticipation, thinking it would really interest me and teach me something. I've read only a third of it so far, but it seems to me thoroughly wrong-headed. How can he, and *mutatis mutandis* J. Searle, resurrect all that Husserl-style stuff for describing the mind? (Intentions, mental states etc.) In Richard Wollheim's case I suppose it's more Freudian and *Kleinian*, but the machinery seems so stiff. Still, I'll read the rest of it and hope for the best. Have happy happy journeys – much much love, my darling, my thoughts go with you always – and I do so much look forward to seeing you later. Take care of yourself.

I

To Roly Cochrane, an American fan of Murdoch's work who lived in Amsterdam.

Steeple Aston
18 March [1985]

Dear Roly

Thank you for your letter. I certainly remember your cards, usually, as I recall, with pictures of marshes or fenlands (or perhaps they were abstract pictures), bearing encouraging messages. I thought somehow that you would eventually add your address. Perhaps now you will also divulge your surname. I imagine you to be American. I'm interested to hear you are a writer, I thought you might be. I hope you're a happy and successful one. I wonder if you do another job as well. What is this drug thing you speak of? I am touched by your letter and glad to hear from the writer of the postcards. Perhaps you will communicate again.

All my very best wishes to you,
Iris

To Carmen Callil.

Steeple Aston
[1985^{xviii}]

My dear Carmen, thanks so much for your letter, I was just about to write to thank you VERY MUCH for the altogether delightful and *special* lunch chez Groucho. It was a most happy occasion, and I do thank you. About the Booker, I think it's a nice gesture.[1] I assume and hope Doris will get it. I don't know anything about the others, but Doris must have it. Again, thanks immensely, and with lots of love
Iris

To Naomi Lebowitz.

Steeple Aston
5 May 1985

Nay, I am, we are, absolutely delighted to have the Kierkie book,[2] looking as splendid and magisterial on the outside as it also is on the inside [. . .] I hope it will be dropped by helicopters all over the USA – well striven. Thank you so much.

This can scarcely pose as an answer to your excellent and deep letter of a month ago which gives me so much pleasure and interest – particularly about your James/Conrad/deconstruction point. The deconstructionist argument leads does it not out of the moral tension of both (differently) James and Conrad and into a relaxed area where authority is not just eclipsed but obliterated? Will think. The whole structuralist scene is such a *mess* – clever old Derrida, stupid messy critics, each man for himself. Motives, motives.

I like you on Ibsen too. I am very ambivalent about ambivalence – it's certainly a deep matter. I suspect I'm with Plato, as against the pure Socratics,

---

1 *The Good Apprentice* had been shortlisted for the Booker Prize, as had *The Good Terrorist* by Doris Lessing. In the event, Keri Hulme won it with *The Bone People*.
2 Naomi Lebowitz's *Kierkegaard: A Life of Allegory.*

Jung etc. (In fact I'm sure I am – tolerance etc. is another matter.) [. . .]

I am more than usually bugged with work. I must try to stop sometime for, say, one hour. [. . .]

Give much love to Al – I will answer his letter – this chiefly to say to you hurray for you and SK and the foundering of metaphysics on sin – both much love my dears

Your

I

John sends much love and cheers.

To Roly Cochrane.

Steeple Aston
[20 June 1985]

Dear Roly,

Your letter is so long and filled with things that it is difficult to answer, and I shall not attempt to do so systematically. I am interested in the information about yourself – the early death of your mother, your father being a preacher. Have you (yes, you imply you have, as recipients of your father's gifts) brothers, sisters? I think of you as an only child, but you can't have said you were, I can't spot it in the letter. So you grew up in Los Angeles – where? I know the bit around the university quite well. What was your first university – Stanford, which I fleetingly visited and where I know people – being the second.

No, I never did a degree in French – I just know French, and Proust, and parts of France, fairly well. I did what's called 'Greats' at Oxford. Greek and Latin, ancient history, philosophy. When did you move to Europe? I note you have had a happy, presumably harmless, relationship with drugs. You are lucky. I have never touched them and feel hostile.

I work out that your father must have died when you were youngish too. I won't try to work out your age. I assumed that the writer of the postcards was about thirty. I hope you earn money from your real books too, and not just for translating? I hope the translating gives some pleasure. If you have published novels, poems, perhaps send.

Your man who hates the church must be in a novel, so you are writing a novel (or I suppose he could be in a long poem. Do you write poetry?). Zen evidently connects with you and with your work. Have you been to Japan? No need to have, of course, there's plenty in California, perhaps in Holland. This is not a terribly interesting commentary on your letter, I just want to elicit more information. I'm interested that you regard *An Accidental Man* as a turning point. (I would say *Unofficial Rose.*) *The Bell* is one of first four, *A Severed Head* five and *Italian Girl* six (I think). I have another novel (successor to *Philosopher's Pupil*) coming out in Sept–Oct, called *The Good Apprentice.* I don't think you will like it, or the one I'm writing now, so much. Perhaps I am going into another phase. I always have something to write with in my pocket of course, and I don't see any difference between men and women. I assume you are not only unmarried, but have not been married. Do you play an instrument, e.g. piano? There are more important questions to ask, but they can wait. The question must arise sometime of whether and when (and where) we eventually meet. It may be a mistake to meet a writer whose work you like. Write again anyway (about anything) – [. . .]

Be well, and thank you for that letter and all those postcards.

Iris

To Harry Weinberger.

Steeple Aston
26 June 1985

Dear Harry,

[. . .] I was glad to get your cheerful letter with Tate news. I went to the Bacon exhibition[1] and liked it more than I expected. It's high obsession – and indeed impressive. I wish there had been more monkeys and landscapes. I was faintly reminded of Sidney Nolan[2] here and there. But the electric light bulbs and keys were good too. This is just to say I met another gallery owner at a party, Angela Flowers [. . .] I spoke of you, and she said do send some photos. I'm sorry these ideas usually come to so little, but could try!

Write again when you are back (France, Wales?). I'll be in Ireland, but briefly, mid-July.

This to send much love.

I

To Suguna Ramanathan

Steeple Aston
28 June [1985]

1 The Tate Gallery held a second retrospective exhibition of Francis Bacon's work in 1985.
2 Australian painter and printmaker, much celebrated for his Ned Kelly series.

Dear Mrs Ramanathan, thank you so much for sending your piece on *Nuns and Soldiers*. The novel has, as far as I am concerned, nothing to do with *Hamlet*. (Whereas *The Sea, The Sea* does have a shadowy connection with *The Tempest*.) I can't see your picture. It is true that the count could be seen as regarding Gertrude and Guy as father and mother – but the deep drama is not Hamlet-like. ('Gertrude' is an accidental name, and the 'Prince of Denmark' a passing convenient jest.) However, it does not matter much, as your ingenious idea has enabled you to think about and comment on the book! I should add that, as far as I am concerned, Anne is the genuinely unselfish disciplined person, and Gertrude's desire to love and be loved, though endearing is an exercised natural selfishness. (I am with Anne, not Gertrude.) And I am, I believe, *asserting* the certainties of the humanist literature of the past, and am, I trust, humbly in the tradition of nine-teenth-century English and Russian novels. There's a lot of certainty in the book. But as I say, the work has stirred you to thoughts of your own and that is important.

Thank you very much for your interest, and for sending the essay. I hope all your plans and work will go well. I send all very best wishes

yours
Iris Murdoch

To Naomi Lebowitz.

Steeple Aston
22 July 1985

Dearest Nay, so pleased to get your splendid letter. How lucky you are to have family – I wish I had some more *relations* – I have no one except my mother who is a sadness and grief, such a wonderful person, in good health, mentally fading away. I have Irish cousins and quasi-cousins (lately saw some on Dublin visit) but they are strangers. Horrid weird feeling being in Ireland. (I went to get honorary degree at Trinity College Dublin – I have one from Belfast.) [. . .]

We are just going to Scotland, as did last two years, to stay at a nice house of friends in Galloway. Loch to swim in. Will be cold, rainy etc. [. . .]

I read a bit of Paul de Man[1] once and thought it tosh. Don't feel too lonely – I think literary criticism thing will pass – but some deep awful (determinist) sort of doom may be upon our whole race. I note that books are now written, and reviewed in *New York Times*, to say that ethics is over.

1 Belgian-born literary theorist and critic who emigrated to the USA in 1948 and made an academic career there, finally becoming Sterling Professor of the Humanities at Yale University, where he was part of the Yale School of Deconstruction.

If religion is over that's important too. What can one do but go on talking against every form of despair and deterministic *pseudo*-scientific absolutism? Connection and comradeship between humane people, and writings of all kinds help. No better idea re world's evil. *You* are fighting good fight. [. . .]
   Love to Al. Be well. John sends love. Much love – *Avanti – sempre* –
   I

Good old eighteenth-century moralists! Good old moralists!

To David Morgan.

Steeple Aston
6 August 1985

Thanks for your letter. Your cone of sizes¹ is a nice idea and the problem is not absurd or easy. It has troubled many philosophers. Kant discusses it in the *Critique of Pure Reason* – in relation to space, and also *time*, where there are analogous questions. (Interesting that space and time are a *pair*.) (Kant concludes measurement is, to use your, and also his, language connected with phenomena not noumena,² and involves certain unavoidable and insoluble paradoxes. Consider the question 'Has Time a beginning?')
   We could discuss this, if we meet next week. Ring me Thurs. morn. I enclose a contribution. Why the hell don't you do some *work* during the summer?
   Love
   I

To Philippa Foot.

Steeple Aston
9 September 1985

1 Murdoch could see that Morgan's idea of a 'cone of sizes' – which for him denoted scale, that is, the sizes of things in ascending and descending order – was similar to Kant's thoughts on causality. In his *Critique of Pure Reason* (1781), Kant tried to demonstrate that the principle of causality – namely, 'everything that happens, that is, begins to be, presupposes something upon which it follows by rule' – is a necessary condition for the possibility of objective experience. Morgan had explained to Murdoch that his 'cone of sizes' connected with his interest in infinite regression, a sequence of reasoning that can never come to an end.

2 Kant argued that it was important to distinguish between phenomena and noumena. Phenomena are the appearances of things, which constitute our experience; noumena are the (presumed) things themselves, which constitute reality.

My dear, thank you very much for your letter. Just to say that my dear mother has died – she never regained consciousness.[1] I expect it is 'all for the best' as she went quietly, and would have been awfully reduced if she'd lived – and never had any pain or fear. But it's a terrible blow and a terrible *absence*.

I'll ring up later and hope to see you soon –
With *much* love
I

To Naomi Lebowitz.

Steeple Aston
14 October 1985

Dearest Nay,

Thank you so much for your very kind letter about my mother, and for your other previous letter. It is good to hear you talking. You have a happy fortune in having a loving twin – with only minor competition feelings! I always wanted to be a twin myself, and did my best to make myself one!

My mother's absence is very strange. I keep finding myself making *plans* about seeing her, sending her something, thinking about Christmas together etc. I was with her every week, and that pattern has gone too. I have a whole store of postcards of *cats* which I kept for sending to her – I sent her a picture postcard every other day, sometimes every day – she especially loved cats. I have in fact lived her death, in a way, over some years, seeing her gradually losing parts of her mind.

I hope the 'anxiety' that you speak of, and the avalanche-climbing, is giving way to calmer climes. And work goes well. I note you are on, far post Ibsen, into Strindberg! And I trust the Cardinals are still at the top. (I *stunned* an American here recently by casually referring to the Cardinals. I let him get the impression that I was an expert on baseball!)

With much love, ever
I

To Naomi Lebowitz.

Steeple Aston
30 November 1985

1 Rene had suffered a massive stroke on 30 August.

Dearest Nay, I knew about the sad fate of the Cardinals (over which I hope you have now got) even before you told me, because an American pal in London, amazed that I know *anything* about this scene, now keeps me informed in detail which suggests that I am an expert! (I gather rotten old Kansas City pitched some mean ball and the referee sided with them, quite unjustly of course.)

As for Rousseau, I rather like him too, for all the evil results (well, there were good ones too) of the *Social Contract* – it's ages since I read the *Confessions* – I think it was that work that made me side with him. (Who wouldn't be against Voltaire anyway – though actually a lot of people care for that horrid Frog.) I don't at all, then, mind you identifying with Rousseau – but D. H. Lawrence . . . well . . . the genius OK, but . . .

I don't think I *identify* much with writers – except Shakespeare perhaps – who sort of 'isn't there' – but I identify with some first characters, like Achilles and Hamlet and Mr Knightley and Frodo. (Lots of others too actually.)

I'm so fed up with work just now – I think the interminable philosophy still is *no good*, and the novel I'm writing is *dull*.[1] I can't find anything to read either. I've read *The Possessed* with the usual glee, and am now reading *A Glastonbury Romance*, which I like (do you read J. C. Powys, I forget) and after that – there's nothing – I know all my favourite books by heart.

It's cold and misty and rather beautiful here. Have you snow? Much love to you and to Al. John sends love.

Ever
I

[. . .] Be well. Onward, onward. (But pleasant pubs and restaurants to stop at on the way.)
Much love
I

To Philippa Foot.

Steeple Aston
16 December 1985

Dearest girl, thank you so much for letter and *so* glad to hear from you. It's been a rather a melancholy autumn here and I miss my mother awfully. I am glad philosophy goes well for you – I hope you are *writing* a lot and will

1 *The Book and the Brotherhood.*

have a MERRY Christmas – and will be able too to read and cogitate dreamily. (What's that? Maybe I could do it too? Can't remember what it's like!)

[. . .] I am tired too but rather stupidly – when I'm not working here I'm doing *jobs* in London and racing about. I should do exactly that you speak of – read, muse etc. etc.

Darling, be well – see you before long – with many thanks – much love

I

I fear I am becoming a *recluse*! It seems natural however and probably suits me. There are lots of things I'd like to talk about with *you*. I am writing too much, and should look out of the window more at mist (very nice mist).

To Roly Cochrane.

Steeple Aston
14 January 1986

Dear Roly,

Thanks for letters and for one of your splendidly murky cards. I was moved by the story about your father and how you were sure he was right, and how you met again by accident and are good friends. Good. I'm glad you like *The Red and the Green* – no one has cared much about it, generally least successful – people don't want to hear about Ireland. Yes, I am 100% Irish – Protestant of course. But I left at a very early age. I hope you had a cheerful Christmas. Send me some more news in due course. All very best New Year wishes and love

I

Do you see your half-brother, sisters?

To Albert and Naomi Lebowitz, concerning the recent move in March to Hamilton Road in Oxford.

68 Hamilton Road
17 May 1986

Dearest Nay and Al,

A wonderful case of delicious wine has come! How very very kind. 68 HR is very grateful too. We are so touched and moved by your house-warming thought. We are already drinking it in. We wish you could be here too – but you will be, God willing, before long we hope and ask. Dear good friends, *thank you so much*!

It's amazing actually how quickly we have fitted into this small (and it really is small) house with its drawing-room-size garden.[xix] We feel we've been here for years. We must have known it was waiting for us. We couldn't quite imagine beforehand what it would be like to be *surrounded* by other people, houses, gardens, neighbours. Now we look out with pleasure on flowery gardens and trees not our own. It's a quiet region and we are on a *corner*, and have effectively only one real next-door neighbour: very nice, keep rabbits, their children sometimes scream, but on the whole very OK. We are in a 'garden suburb' and need a bus to reach (in five mins, but you have to wait for it) central Oxford. One of the great reliefs is not having the fifteen-mile drive to get there.

The river Cherwell, a mile away at Steeple Aston, is a quarter-mile away here. Some of the elegant residences and roads round about remind us very much of America, and we have pleasant walks inspecting houses and gardens. It's on a small scale compared with your sort of scene, but the *variety* of domestic dwellings and garden-styles is a special urban pleasure. We feel *relief* at having left Cedar Lodge – though it is distressing to have to go there *still* to sort out the seemingly endless debris of our thirty years. Destruction of old manuscripts and letters is a major part of this task! [. . .]
  MUCH LOVE
  I

To Brigid Brophy.

68 Hamilton Road
[22 June 1986]

Much thanks for card, also for Labour Party slip with hijacked rose.[1] Nothing pleases me at present on the political scene. I think Maggie has done her job and become purely destructive and should go. Perhaps we *need* a Labour government having a try. I can't feel enthusiastic. I used to be certain that if Labour won T. Benn[2] and E. Heffer[3] would quickly throw Kinnock[4] out.

---

1 The Labour Party had recently adopted a red rose as its logo; presumably Murdoch uses the word 'hijacked' because the red rose is traditionally thought of as the flower of love.
2 Anthony Wedgwood 'Tony' Benn, British Labour politician and Cabinet minister known for his very left-wing views.
3 Eric Heffer, Labour Member of Parliament from 1964 until his death in 1991.
4 Neil Kinnock, Welsh politician and leader of the Labour Party from 1983 until 1992.

Now I fear that J. Smith,[1] B. Gould[2] et al. will *not* be able to throw Kinnock out. Ah well. Sorry your relation failed to be elected. It's *cold* here today. No more swims in the Thames for the present. Au revoir and much love

I

To Roly Cochrane.

68 Hamilton Road

22 July [1986]

Roly, thank you so much for beautiful card of girl looking out of window, and also for your letter of 17 July just come. How awful to have to RECEIVE on one's birthday. I can't recall how I spent mine – just working as usual I think, nothing special happening. I can't decide whether or not you ought to go to Ireland. I am very disaffected from the Republic, but that won't matter to you. The west of Ireland is probably the most beautiful place in the world (if you don't mind rain) and its small area can easily be visited in a hired car, pilgrimage to Yeats's grave included, if you care about Yeats. Japan is more important (though harder to get to). I adopted Japan after (ages ago) first reading (which I've read again often since) Murasaki's wonderful novel *The Tale of Genji* which you probably know. I've been to Japan twice and found it remarkably like Murasaki (born circa 976 AD). I hope you will have a good time with the collies (nice docile friendly dogs usually) and with the nice people. I wonder if you often go to France, Italy, England? I hope this mafia business is not too serious – I wasn't sure how to take it. Thank you for writing and sending cards. Please continue to do so.

With love

I

To David Morgan.

68 Hamilton Road

4 October [1986]

Dear David,

Thanks for your letter. I do hope you are feeling better and no longer plagued by stomach pains? If they go on, see your doctor.

---

1 John Smith, Shadow Secretary for Trade and Industry between 1984 and 1987.
2 Bryan Gould, British MP and member of the Labour Party's Shadow Cabinet between 1986 and 1994.

I expect Angharad has begun to settle into Putney High.[1] I don't care for those children who boast about their bathrooms and visits abroad! It's very *bad form*, and was absolutely *out* at my boarding school where children who had *ponies* (which of course I hadn't) didn't dare to mention them! As for going abroad – shouldn't you take Angharad and Y on a cheap weekend visit to Paris? I could make a contribution to the Travel Fund.

As I expect he told you, I met your brother at the unveiling of a plaque to T. S. Eliot in Kensington. What a nice chap, good-looking too, marked resemblance to you!

Keep in touch. I hope we can meet before too long.

With love from

I

To Roly Cochrane; postcard written prior to a British Council visit to the Netherlands.

II October 1986

I gather you have been invited to a party by Julian Andrews (British Council) on Sunday Oct 19 evening. Please come, since it looks as if the gods too have arranged this.

I

I'll be at Hotel Ambassade from Sat morning.

To Roly Cochrane, written after their only meeting.

68 Hamilton Road
26 October 1986

[. . .] I'm so glad we've met, it was for me wholly good and delightful. I think our (important) letter-writing personae are not thoroughly damaged, rather enriched. You remain suitably mysterious. You caused pleasure and interest to others too, who asked me about you (I could tell little), especially dear good James Brockway[2] whom I've known for a great many years. It was a good party, wasn't it? And the storm was *magnificent*.

---

1 Morgan's daughter, Angharad, now aged eleven, had won an assisted place (i.e. subsidised by the local authority) at this fee-paying school. Murdoch had paid for private coaching to help Angharad get through the entrance examination.
2 English poet and translator who lived in the Netherlands.

Altogether Amsterdam was very good indeed. John too was delighted to meet you.

I loved the way you said 'Roly' when you lifted the telephone.

With love to you, dear Roly,

I

To Brigid Brophy, after it was announced in the New Year's Honours list that Murdoch had been made a dame.

68 Hamilton Road
[January? 1987]

Dearest creature, thank you, and Mike, very much for your communications. I have received a lot of jests referring to *South Pacific* (a musical containing a song which says there's nothing like a dame), also queries as to whether I have a lame tame crane, and mentions of Julian of Norwich. As for that comb matter, I'm so sorry Alison was troubled, I found a shop open in the Gloucester Road where I purchased one.[1] (Vanity, vanity.) I'm afraid that I did not send those daffodils. I'm sure I should have but I didn't.

Much love to you

I

To Suguna Ramanathan, written after a visit in January to New Delhi where Murdoch gave a keynote address at a conference held to commemorate Indira Gandhi.

68 Hamilton Road
[26 January 1987]

Dear Suguna,

I was delighted to hear your voice and talk to you on the telephone. Thank you very much for telephoning! I spoke with your friend Mrinalini Sarabhai[2] briefly at the conference. It was a wonderful visit for me, and a *marvellous* experience to see India again. I look forward to seeing you in England. You should ask the college principal (I forget which college you are to be attached to) about accommodation. If no ideas there, we must

1 Murdoch had arrived from Oxford without a comb so Alison lent her one but wished afterwards she had given it to Murdoch.
2 Celebrated Indian classical dancer, choreographer and instructor.

look elsewhere. But the convent hostel project is certainly promising. Keep in touch. With love and best wishes

Iris

To Tapan Kumar Mukherjee, a student who, with his teacher, had attended the conference on Indira Gandhi in New Delhi.[xx]

68 Hamilton Road
26 January 1987

Dear Mr Mukherjee,

Thank you for your kind letter. I will try to answer some of your questions. I have never been an existentialist and do not think I have been influenced by Sartre. The philosophers who have most influenced me, in order of importance, are Plato, Kant, and Wittgenstein, but especially Plato. No, I do not intend to write any autobiography. My publisher might supply you with a rough outline of my life. I do not think its details are relevant for understanding of my work. I think linguistic philosophy is still the dominant force, but it has become considerably more sophisticated in recent years. I regret I do not read many modern novels and therefore cannot advise you. (I constantly read non-modern novels, especially the English nineteenth century, the Russians and Proust.) I love India and greatly enjoyed being in the Delhi conference. I have some small knowledge of Indian philosophy – my approach is mainly through Buddhism, though I have some acquaintance with Hindu philosophy and religion.

All my best wishes for your studies.

Yours
Iris Murdoch

To Sister Marian at Stanbrook Abbey.

68 Hamilton Road
24 February [1987]

Dearest Lucy,

It was marvellous to see you – altogether a special gathering! I do hope you can come often to see Honor (+ me). I have read out your letter to her and she was much cheered by it – you will have heard from her. She will also have told you that at last she has an appointment at the hospital for Friday 26. I have written to the parish priest (a Father

Paschal – not O'Connor eh!) about visiting her – I hope that machinery will work.

Do send any other letters to Honor by the system and via me if need be! I hope *you* are OK – you look so young and beautiful, the spirit is with you! I'm glad Honor is remembered in prayers by the community at Stanbrook! Be well, my dear creature – with much love.

    I

To Brigid Brophy, written after Murdoch had attended the ceremony at Buckingham Palace where she was formally made a dame of the British Empire.

68 Hamilton Road
[10 March?] 1987

Dearest girl, it was fun at the palace and quite moving (see below) but disappointing, and even shocking, in certain respects. Disappointing: I wasn't allowed to kneel down (gracefully on one knee) like the men. Also I didn't get the lovely red and gold medallion which Mike has, but a rather nasty sort of diamanté star brooch – much less distinguished. Second-class citizen. Shocking: the military band instead of playing Gilbert and Sullivan, played Moore's Irish melodies! I assume it was Moore – I distinctly heard The Rose of Tralee, Kathleen Mavourneen (Good luck to Erin[1]) and one or two others of those soppy pieces – when I was listening, that is, which wasn't all the time. Fancy! The music of a country that hates us and with which we are practically at war! But the ceremony moved me more than last time, and the Queen, escorted by tall beefeaters and small Gurkhas, and surrounded by tall soldiers, sailors and airmen with medals, was, in canary yellow, quite numinous. I had a royalty feeling. (I am royalist of course, but don't always have that feeling.) The Queen asked me if I was still writing, to which I replied that I was, and then it was time to go. It all *moved* very well, like a slow-motion ballet. Still, I think dames are less real than knights, and I suspect it will all blow over – it's been fun being a dame, and now I shall return to the ordinary life of Miss and Mrs. It was very good to see you. I will write or ring again soon. John was so pleased to hear from you. Much love *toujours*

    I

---

1 A romantic name for Ireland.

To Brigid Brophy, written just before the Bayleys travelled to Tulane University in New Orleans where they were to discuss the role of the novel in front of a large audience. Murdoch was also to conduct an hour-long seminar on A Fairly Honourable Defeat *and* The Black Prince.[xxi]

68 Hamilton Road
[mid-March 1987]

My dear girl, thank you very much for your letter. Talking of bended knees, the elegant bending of one knee, on a velvet stool put there for that purpose, is incredibly touching, and combines homage with an air of elegant independence.

I (we) are just now going away to America (New Orleans) to give (sort of) lecture, and hope to see the local sights, such as Mississippi (s's p's?) delta and alligators (or are they elsewhere?), something anyway. Why on earth does one take on such jobs? I hope Scott Joplin is still around, but I fear not. It all disturbs one's work dreadfully. I hope you are less snow-drifted by letters, and that the word processor is happy. I know these creatures are much loved by their owners.

I would like to talk to you about lots and lots of things, and will hope to do so later on. I love you very much, and will communicate on these and other matters. Be well. God be with you. *Semper.*

I

Love to Mike.

To Naomi Lebowitz.

68 Hamilton Road
[April 1987]

My dearest girl, much thanks for your lovely letter, so full of thoughts and you. I think seeing your book on TV[1] is a *marvel!* It's a good sign, omen, act of gods. I do look forward to next volume, Ibsen as Søren Kierkegaard. You are deep, deep, and yes, in the *highest sense* also simple, and so is Al, to whom I send much love. We've just got back from New Orleans and are just off to Italy. I note your point about Scott Joplin. We saw a bit of the picturesque city and the *great river* – though my vision of the delta as innumerable

---

1 Naomi Lebowitz's book on Kierkegaard had been held by an actor pretending to be an intellectual in a recent film.

streams (all full of alligators) turned out to be (as far as N.O. is concerned) wrong. I've met though don't know, John Castle,[1] and am pretty sure I met *his wife*. Not that that proves anything.

I can't resist sending you the enclosed. The *great* picture by Titian is in the unpronounceable place (a monastery) in Czechoslovakia.[2] The other picture[3] is in the National Portrait Gallery London. The painter of the latter shared my absolute passion for the former, so kindly placed it on the wall behind me. Titian painted that picture when he was over ninety. I saw it on its very rare, first, I do hope not last, journey outside Czechoslovakia when it was exhibited here not long ago. The green spray in the picture of me is of a gingko tree, a tree I love and hold holy.

Much love, excuse haste – [. . .].

I

+ J sends love.

To Philippa Foot.

> 68 Hamilton Road
> April 1987

My dearest, I am so glad to hear from you – I wrote to both addresses asking when you will be HERE. I'm so glad you've been in Venice (we have sometimes stayed near where you have stayed) and are now at Serbelloni[4] (where we once spent a short pleasant time). I hope you are relaxing and thinking and looking at the blue lake. I am sorry the ankle continues to be a trouble.

I picture you sitting in the garden. You lead a strenuous life – I expect you still are doing so now – but with *differences* which this change of scene must bring. (I mean you don't *have* to talk to the German professors who throng around you!) Oh be well – and, later, do come home here. A candle for Donald. I have never lit one, but I think about him very much. I feel sure he thinks of us. I don't suppose I shall ever meet him again.

I am very tired with work, trying to comb over those old lectures, so *bad* in parts.

---

1 Possibly John Castle the English actor.
2 *The Flaying of Marsyas* is housed in the National Museum in Kroměříž in the Czech Republic.
3 Tom Phillips's portrait of Iris Murdoch, the background of which features part of Titian's *The Flaying of Marsyas*.
4 On the shore of Lake Como.

I have abandoned my present novel[1] meanwhile. I hope your Italian flourishes. Mine, once not so bad, now rusts and fades (as does my Russian). Words *go*. [. . .]

I hope you are resting and quietly thinking and seeing many new things in your mind. I want lots more news of you; and do want to see you here. Write again. *Pensant à toi*, much love ever

I

To Maurice Saatchi, following the general election on 11 June which saw the Conservative Party returned to power.

68 Hamilton Road
[June 1987]

Dearest Maurice, We saw such a lovely photo of you in the paper, smiling because you had piloted Maggie to victory![2] Well done! (So say I, a lifelong Labour voter, but now no more.) We are just going to Wales, where I gather there is rain and nothing to drink. But do hope see you soon. Be well – with much love

Iris

To Naomi Lebowitz.

68 Hamilton Road
16 June 1987

My dearest Nay, thanks so much for letter, I like Judith's passion for pretty rubble at 5 a.m. This is truly spiritual. And shopping is good too. I enjoyed short trips to Italy and Paris where I saw many great pictures and ate, in Paris, many good meals. I am shortly going on the Bayley Family Holiday to WALES where it is cold and wet and the pubs are shut all the time and there are no pictures. Still, I hope to see the sea. I am working like crazy, can't stop, and will take my work with me, as a house is booked – or cottage; that doesn't sound too good.

So IBBIE is for the press.[3] Well done. And that you enjoyed it too. I can't understand your Isabel Archer[4] point. (A book, and character I can't get on

1 *The Message to the Planet.*
2 Saatchi and Saatchi were the Conservative Party's advertising campaigners.
3 *Ibsen and the Great World.*
4 The heroine of Henry James's *The Portrait of a Lady* (1881).

with.) And I cannot love William James[1] more than Henry! Perhaps you could expand? [. . .]

Although we disagree with her on many points, we are relieved that Margaret Thatcher is still with us and *not* the disastrous Labour Party. The British public, when it came to it, was *not* for Yanks Go Home! If only Maggie can get Selection back into Education – the Labour Party thinks it's jolly unfair if anyone at school is ever said to be better than anyone else (except of course at football). [. . .]

I've got a new pen. Is my writing more legible? Montblanc, very expensive. I am tired and not at all clever at present. My novel is in a sad way. I hope you *do* come later in summer. Give much love to Al. John sends love. He has invented a spicy fish dish which he says is 'Siamese' and people are impressed. Much love, dear Nay, ever

I

To Josephine Hart, in response to her invitation to comment on the production of the play The Black Prince.

68 Hamilton Road
21 August 1987

Dearest Josephine,

Thanks so much for your letter, of which I have read *every word*! I am always delighted to see your writing, which I like so much, upon an envelope! I am longing to see Ron.[2] He has been away in Yorkshire and other places I gather. I had a very brief word on the telephone and have talked to his answering machine. I cannot do anything about Christian[3] until I see Ron properly and find out what he wants. I have already altered and curtailed her, poor girl, and *I* think her dotty well-meaning presence floating through the play, and offering another facet of Bradley – and 'supporting' him at the end – opens a kind of space and air which does the play good and no harm. It is a *large* change to make her bitter shrewish vindictive, just come to despise him etc. (which would also mean that her friendly role at the end would have to vanish). I think such a change would make less of Bradley and I can't see this character except as a sour and standard caricature. I've got to see more *point* in the new Christian before I can invent her! So I must talk with Ron. I'm not too sure about his other change which removes one

1 Philosopher and psychologist (1842–1910), Henry James's older brother.
2 Ronald Eyre, English theatre director, actor and writer.
3 A female character in *The Black Prince*.

of the moments when B can appear as a figure of dignity and authority – which is needed – audiences must not see him as a pathetic buffoon. But I feel less anxious about that – R may even be right!

To Hal Lidderdale, concerning Murdoch's being made a Companion of Literature.

68 Hamilton Road
[mid-October 1987]

Dearest Hal, just to say you will receive an invitation – from the Royal Society of Literature, 1 Hyde Park Gardens W2, to a gathering (*drinks*) on Thursday Oct 29 and I hope you and Mary can come, if it's convenient to you (6.30 to 8). It's a sort of celebration where various people will be handed scrolls or something, but I think speeches won't be too long! Just to warn you – and come if you feel like it. With much love
   I

To Peter Conradi, who was preparing to spend eleven weeks in a group retreat in tents high in the Colorado Rockies, a sojourn required in order to receive permission to study the 'secret' Vajrayana teachings peculiar to Tibetans.[xxii]

68 Hamilton Road
22 January 1988

Peter dear, thanks very much for your letter, I am very pleased to hear from you – and am most impressed by your summer programme. The vow backed up by threats[1] sounds rather dangerous – and you must keep in mind that the aim is supreme goodness not supreme power! However you are already experienced and wise and will know what to do. I like about 'not getting worse'.

I'm glad to hear Jim is settled and has a new trade[2] where he will do much good. I hope that you will now write a novel. I think I'll see you before too long – I'll be in London occasionally, though not immediately. Be well, dear boy – with all bestest wishes to Cloudy[3] and Jim and with much love
   I

1 So-called Samaya in Sanskrit, the sacred bond between teacher and student, neither to be entered into, nor broken, lightly.
2 Jim had recently given up being a schoolteacher in order to train as a psychotherapist.
3 Peter and Jim's Welsh Border collie.

To Philippa Foot.

68 Hamilton Road
19 February 1988

My dearest girl, so very glad to hear from you – [. . .] The weather has been *fantastic*, warm days, sunshine, no rain, cloudless blue skies and there has been *no winter* (yet everyone says we shall pay for it – but why? Maybe we'll just get away with it). Daffodils almost out.

Yes, I was sorry about Marghanita[1] and somehow shocked, though people do die, and why should one have warning. But of course I didn't know her as you did, and I can imagine that you feel very bereft. The houses which have gone, yes, the places of refuge. For us the house of Reynolds Stone in Dorset.

I'm glad your work goes well, and that you think of *home* over here – when will you come? Let me know. Warm sun and flowers and SEA must be hard to leave all the same – and your close LA friends. Sea, sea, yes.

I'm not happy with my work, or with the other thoughts I am struggling with (I mean the abstract ones)! I am not *thinking* well. And *j'ai lu tous les livres*[2] – can't find a work I'd like to read which I don't know by heart! Pictures console (though *not* those of Lucien Freud, now on show at the Hayward Gallery!). I was about to write to you. Write again soon. Ever, much love,

your
I

To Naomi Lebowitz.

68 Hamilton Road
[early March 1988?]

Nay, dear, enclosed with love from John (and from me). I met Todorov[3] yesterday. He gave an absolutely traditional non-structuralist non-Barthes[4] lecture to a large Oxford audience. He is a darling. (I think the young Turks were disappointed!)

---

1 Probably Marghanita Laski, author and journalist.
2 And I've read all the books.
3 Tzvetan Todorov, Franco-Bulgarian historian and essayist.
4 Roland Barthes (1915–80), French philosopher and semiotician whose work was very influential in the development of structuralism.

Any news about the McCarran Act?[1] I also hear that we (English) won't need visas for tourist and business (and I assume academic) visits. Of course this doesn't apply to *me*. I got a dusty answer from the US Embassy. So you must come over here. Be well.

Much love, and from J

I

Todorov said *the* excitement *à Paris* is about further revelations of the degree of Heidegger's Nazism.

To Sue Summers, journalist, in response to a request for information about Frank Thompson and Franz Steiner.[xxiii]

68 Hamilton Road
12 April 1988

Dear Miss Summers,

Thank you for your letter. I don't think Frank resembled T. E. Lawrence (though it's difficult to know what exactly Lawrence was like). Frank was a remarkably good classical scholar and if left alone might well have stayed in Oxford pursuing classical studies and writing learned books. He was particularly attached to Pindar and could have become an expert on that poet. When he was captured, there was a copy of the poems of Catullus in his pocket. He also wrote poetry himself. Equally, he might not have done these things. He was very clever and versatile and a good linguist – he knew Russian before the war. He was a gentle quiet man who loved animals and knew a great deal about flowers and birds. He had no desire for worldly power, had a horror of violence, and would never have dreamt of himself as a soldier or a war hero. When the war came and soldiering was his job he did it well, and just was a hero. That is, he was good and unselfish and brave and ready to use his talents for soldiering. But he was *forced* to become a fighter, and was not seeking glory. I have the impression that I did somehow hear from him after he left Cairo, because there was a letter which mentioned seeing some flowers. I got to know Frank in the autumn of 1938, so there was one year before the war. The details of what happened to him emerged gradually from various sources.

About Franz – I got to know him in Oxford, when I returned there in

---

1 The McCarran Internal Security Act, introduced in 1950 during the McCarthy era, required the registration of anyone belonging to or affiliated with the Communist Party and made it possible to deny individual Communists entry to the United States. Each entry required a new waiver.

1948, via a network of friends, some of whom were anthropologists. He was certainly one of Hitler's victims. But, though so terribly sad and wounded, he was one of the wittiest, merriest, sweetest people I ever met, with a remarkable capacity for enjoyment. He was gentle and good and full of spirit and imagination. He was, as you know, a very good poet.
   With best wishes,
   Yours
   Iris Murdoch

They were both of them full of truth and pure in heart.

To Kenneth Baker, Secretary of State for Education, concerning the Education Reform Act which, if implemented, would change the face of higher education and restrict academic freedom.

68 Hamilton Road
25 April [1988]

Dear Mr Baker
   I have been asked by colleagues in Oxford to express to you our acute anxiety about the future of our universities. I hope you will excuse another letter on this subject; I'm sure you have had many! The new proposals alarm us very much. The abolition of the University Grants Committee in favour of the new Universities Funding Council[1] virtually gives *any* government complete control of the area of higher education. This at least appears to be the intention of the proposed legislation. The freedom of its universities, and so of its intelligentsia, is essential to a democracy; and we have hitherto enjoyed this privilege to an enviable degree. Now, by a step which it would be very difficult to reverse, this freedom is threatened. It is no comfort to say that extreme powers would probably not be used. If such powers exist some government will find reasons for using them. Academics are regularly used by philistines, bureaucrats, politicians and ignorant citizens as an expendable luxury. Our liberty is fragile. Equally distressing are recent suggestions that what is taught in higher education should 'take account of the economic requirements of society'. Of course this may be understood in a reasonable sense; but may also imply an enforced preference for technological subjects,

1 The University Grants Committee, an independent body that advised the government on the distribution of funding to British universities, came to act as a buffer between government and the interests of the universities. The Universities Funding Council, established under the Education Reform Act 1988, distributed funds provided by central government to universities and was directly answerable to Parliament.

economics, business studies, at the expense of ('useless') history, literature, and philosophy, and of languages except as a tool for commerce. In fact a rigorous training in *thinking*, gained from whatever subject, has generally been valued by commerce and industry, and the Civil Service has seemed happy with 'firsts' in arts subjects, and indeed once favoured Greats in the days when Greek and Latin were widely taught. This strict disciplined training in *how to think*, which involves a sophisticated mastery of language, and has traditionally been offered by a study of history, literature or philosophy, is I believe one of the most valuable gifts which the universities can offer to the individual and to society, in every field of endeavour. University education should offer an open scene for the pursuit of excellence and, by teaching of the highest quality, the most refined and the most highly toned development of talent. This is now also threatened by the proposed removal of the established understanding of 'tenure'. Real thinking, arduous imaginative scholarship and truth seeking, demands open time, the absence of petty constraints and 'deadlines', and the damaging necessity of having to prove one's 'value' by scurrying hastily into print. Here the most scrupulous people are most likely to suffer. A friend in another university told me that some of her colleagues are neglecting their pupils in order to produce books quickly as an insurance against future interrogation! Many of the most valuable and influential university teachers, remembered by their pupils with lifelong gratitude and who have inspired and enabled generations of students, have published little or nothing. Plans for frequent 'testing' and 'scrutiny' and counting of publications by external judges are likely to operate also against those who study obscure ('useless') subjects. Down that road too, one may fear, lies the testing of opinions. Of course universities must live with the problems of the times, especially financial ones; and of course traditional arrangements such as 'tenure' are open to abuse. But the precious independence of the universities must, as we see it, include the ability to put their own houses in order.

I also personally (to allude to another matter) grieve about the absence of Greek and Latin on the list of possible (state) school subjects. This removes a lifelong benefit from many clever children, and evokes the sad picture of future historians and literary scholars who do not know either of the classical languages. Of course, 'one cannot have everything' but one might hope for some pathway to those languages on the road back to the essential principle of 'selection'. I need hardly add that I greatly favour, and rejoice at, many of the impending reforms in school education, for instance in the matter of core curriculum. I have misgivings about 'opting out' but I won't pursue that subject. I was and remain very grateful to you for your kind suggestion concerning the 'teaching of English' committee, and was sorry that I had to decide to refuse.

I hope you will excuse this letter expressing the very strong feelings which exist here concerning what we see as damage to our universities. I trust you will be patient with those arguments, which you will have heard before, and will doubtless hear again! I send very best wishes for your plans for better, more selective, school education which will change the fates of clever children from poor bookless homes. With all cordial greeting to you,

Yours sincerely

Iris Murdoch

I look forward to the Kingman report.[1]

I hope grammar will be saved!

To Peter Conradi.

68 Hamilton Road
29 April [1988]

Dearest Peter, thanks for your very good and welcome letter, it was a great pleasure to see you. Yes of course David-Néel's fascinating (thrilling) accounts must be taken soberly.[2] I am sure you will be OK. I feel inclined to make a sign of the cross over you, but will not suggest that you wear a crucifix. (Someone I know wears one when he goes climbing in the Cairngorms – and your part of the Rockies might be rather full of ambiguous electricity – but you will walk unscathed among demons, without such extra aids.) Yes, I'd love to see you with Jim and Cloudy, those good creatures. You are also a good creature. I'll reflect more about the things you said, and wrote, and I'd also be glad to see the other books you spoke of.

About magic – what indeed – I think it's everywhere just over a certain borderline – when a kind of will-to-power radiation takes possession of up till then innocent or harmless or spiritual images or activities or states of being. [. . .]

Be in communication, with much love

I

---

1 The Report of the Committee of Inquiry into the Teaching of English Language, chaired by John Kingman.

2 Alexandra David-Néel (1868–1969), Belgian–French explorer, Buddhist, anarchist and writer, best known for her visit to Lhasa, Tibet, in 1924, when it was forbidden to foreigners. Her most famous work is *Mystiques et magiciens du Tibet* (*Magic and Mystery in Tibet*) (1929).

To Peter Conradi. In a previous letter, Conradi had 'mentioned that the journey described in Trungpa's[1] Shambhala training teachings – from the "cocoon" of the ego towards the vastness of "Great Eastern Sun" vision – sounded like Plato's "great myth" of the Cave and the Sun from The Republic'. *In response to Murdoch's comment in this letter that her demons 'are all male', Conradi was later to note that she 'could not understand the fact that Tibetans "visualise" in deity-practice, and that the visualisation might be female'.[xxiv]*

68 Hamilton Road
[9 May 1988]

My dear, thanks for your very interesting and helpful letter, and for the piece about John Welwood,[2] I'd also like to see more about Trungpa some day. I'm all for leaving the cocoon and making for the Great Eastern sun, but not so sure about my ability for cheerful tolerance. (That problem is worth reflection of course.) About 'visualising' – I cannot understand this. Not like meditation on Christ's passion. Seems dangerous. (David-Néel tells us she visualised into 'separate being' a familiar who then became exceedingly tiresome, and started expending a lot of time and spiritual energy destroying him!) I'm glad to think you won't bring one of *these* back from Colorado, since you say such feats lie ten years ahead!

Interesting about the female deity. The sex of one's god must be a very deep matter. I think my demons are all male.

Sitting quiet, yes, yes.

Thanks for writing about those matters. I'd like to understand more about it all. [. . .]

With much love

I

To Naomi Lebowitz.

68 Hamilton Road
21 May 1988

Chère dearest Nay, thank you for your spring letter about reading Adorno, Benjamin, Lukács etc. – yes, yes. (Brecht I have never been able to like. And I am through with Beckett.) Frankfurt School, yes, most endearing,

1 Chögyam Trungpa Rinpoche, Tibetan Buddhist meditation master who developed Shambhala training, a secular approach to meditation, and whom Conradi had met in London in 1986.
2 American clinical psychologist and author, known for integrating psychological and spiritual concepts and a prominent figure in transpersonal psychology.

true voices. (Not so keen on Marcuse.[1]) I saw Ruth Marcus[2] from Yale yesterday (do you know name?) and we had a jolly time slanging Derrida and co. Have you read Julia Kristeva?[3] And is it true that she is anti-Semitic? She is endlessly quoted by poor wretches who are entangled in revolting women's studies. Oxford now has a ghastly (optional) women's studies paper in final exam.

Elizabeth Bowen I like very much – especially *Eva Trout* and *The Little Girls*, and the short stories. I knew her quite well, as a *friend*, and I stayed two or three times at Bowen's Court. Elizabeth sold that big fine house with a legal agreement that it should be preserved etc. A few months later it had been totally destroyed and the plough had passed over it. *Nothing* remaining except open fields. That's Ireland. I was very fond of her. She should have been queen.

As for Quine,[4] I don't understand him either (and have scarcely tried – no point waste time on *not* one's cup of tea).

I'm glad you saw that star between the tips of the moon, as noted in *Ancient Mariner*.[5] I've never seen that. A good omen.

To Peter Conradi.

68 Hamilton Road
26 July [1988]

Dearest Peter, thank you very much for postcard (safely arrived) and letter. I like to hear of the tame animals and birds enjoying the spiritual atmosphere. And so it was thus in Tibet in the old days. The place sounds beautiful, and I imagine golden weather, not too hot at that altitude, and no rain. And good (delicious, healthful) food too! I am of course most interested in your studies and can, of course, make little of your general description (and look forward to talking of it with you later when you, I hope, return). I'm interested that outsiders can evidently visit (drinks and parties). Tell me more about the Tulkus.[6] *Will* there be a next Dalai Lama?

1 Herbert Marcuse (1898–1979), German–American philosopher, sociologist, and political theorist who, like Theodor Adorno, Walter Benjamin and Gyorgy Lukács, was associated with the Frankfurt School of critical theory.
2 Halleck Professor of Philosophy, Yale University.
3 Bulgarian–French philosopher, professor at the University of Paris Diderot, well known for her writings in structuralist linguistics, psychoanalysis, semiotics and philosophical feminism. Kristeva is internationally regarded as a key structuralist and post-structuralist thinker.
4 Willard Van Orman Quine, American philosopher and logician in the analytic tradition.
5 'The hornèd moon, with one bright star / Within the nether tip'.
6 An honorary title given to a lama recognised in Tibetan Buddhism as reincarnate.

And I feel the greatest curiosity, likely to be unrewarded, about the secret teachings! I'm sorry to hear other (theistic) religions are positively condemned. (As for Freud, he can look after himself – but this special hate is interesting too.) What I can, I think, a little imagine is your not-knowing-what-one-is-feeling. I feel this may be, in that context, a 'good thing'. After all, what is one?

I note your timetable. I shall be away mostly now (rather on and off) till end of August, and away again in *later* September. But do write here, if you feel like writing, as I will be passing by to pick up post. I wonder a lot of things, such as how much this scene depends on veneration of certain *obviously holy* figures (I mean real present people!). I note you admire the kitchen staff best.[1] Do you very much admire any of your teachers? Do you feel they are *good*? Where is 'good' in all this?

Much love and good be with you, ever

I

To Naomi Lebowitz.

68 Hamilton Road
9 October [1988?]

Dearest Nay, forgive interval – I was demoralised by our *postal strike* which occupied at least half of September. I hope you heard about it? It was in many ways (not all ways) marvellous. Just after that we went to Italy[2] where we looked, in various places, at large numbers of pictures, especially by Signorelli and Crivelli. Now the leaves are falling and it is beginning of term. Am I right in thinking you have finished a book on Zola, Manzoni[3] etc.? I hope so. [. . .]

I have finished a novel[4] which no one will like, I fear. I am back, for the moment, struggling with Heidegger – or rather just trying to decide: what's in it for me? I gather a lot of stuff about how Nazi he was is now appearing.

I hope Eliot, Yeats, Brecht and Strindberg are getting on OK. I have a prejudice against Brecht based on little knowledge. Nay, I have at last read Milan Kundera's novel *The Unbearable Lightness of Being*, and, assuming I would not, liked it very much. Not the endless sex scenes, but the *dog*, and a lot of *tendresse*, and the horrors of the cage. Do you like it?

1 Because they cooked three meals a day for 400 people.
2 The Bayleys travelled in Italy with Borys and Audi Villers; an evening parade in the small town of Ascoli Piceno and other incidents were later to feed into *The Green Knight*.
3 Alessandro Manzoni (1785–1873), Italian poet and novelist.
4 *The Message to the Planet.*

I hope your weather is now more rational. One can be frightened of the weather these days. (Nothing extreme here of course.)

I am delighted to hear about *your* DOG, I mean the dachshund. *Sad* about Sophie – but she had a long happy life. Somehow she grew up with the children. More details about new dog please. Do write soon – and do come over next summer.

John is still wearing Al's shirts. He sends much love.

Much love, my dear, and to Al, ever

I

To Naomi Lebowitz.

68 Hamilton Road
8 December 1988

Dearest Nay, Al's book[1] just come, looking so strong and beautiful, we are very pleased! We shall read it again and hope it will be much read everywhere. Hope its successor is flourishing. [. . .]

An English friend of mine, gone to live in Paris, finds her seventeen-year-old daughter, who knows French well, struggling with a book called *Philosophie comme débat entre les textes.*[2] She, the mother, writes to me asking for an explanation! Of course schoolchildren should *never* be allowed to come *near* philosophy. The survival of philosophy as real free thinking is more and more important – while here universities are closing their philosophy departments.

How good, how moving, your twin book, with such an appetising title.[3] I much look forward to it. (Have much to learn about Manzoni.)

I'm glad to hear Howard Nemerov is top poet[4] and will be interested in his view of Maggie. Maggie is a lot of good, and a lot of bad too, e.g. cutting money to universities, and being discreetly anti-gay – this latter is obscure, actually. Some London district councils idiotically circulated to all schools a jolly book (story) about two chaps bringing up a baby – this resulted in an outcry and so legislation against the *promotion* of homosexuality by

1 Probably *A Matter of Days*, a collection of short stories for which Murdoch had written the blurb.
2 By José Médina, Claude Morali, André Sénik and Jean Bernhart (1985).
3 *Dickens, Manzoni, Zola and James: The Impossible Romance*, written by Naomi Lebowitz with her twin sister, Ruth Newton.
4 Howard Nemerov had been made Poet Laureate Consultant in Poetry to the Library of Congress for the second time.

councils (who control education)![1] That means of course, legislation against homosexuality! We joined massive protest, no good. Of course a referendum about homosexuality here, as I imagine in your country, could produce a large anti-gay vote! But that's another matter. So bad marks to Maggie. But she's very brave, and has introduced sensible rules for trade unions (they ran riot before), not bad on improving school education (a general curriculum), brought inflation down, and is in many ways rational and well intentioned. I've met her briefly a few times and *like* her quite a lot, as well as, selectively, admiring her. [. . .]

The old Christian business is upon us and I feel more than usually helpless about it. Since finishing that last novel I *cannot* get started on the new one – or *a* new one, since it scarcely exists. I struggle weakly with some philosophy and feel generally *feeble*, unable to conjure much 'passion, depth, the universal, the mysterious' which you so rightly invoke. I've finished reading *Buddenbrooks* and am now reading *Dr Faustus*.[2] That's OK. Even my pen won't write properly. Come to beautiful Britain next year. I love to hear of your delightful DOG. Thank heavens for dogs. Very best Christmas and New Year wishes.

Au revoir and much love

Ever your

I

To Carmel Callil, regarding Murdoch's request that Michael Kustow, one of Murdoch's Jewish friends who had previously worked at the National Theatre and was now a commissioning editor for Channel 4 television, be asked to check for any errors concerning Jews and Judaism in The Message to the Planet.

68 Hamilton Road

30 January [1989]

Dearest Carmen, thanks for your letter. It's very kind of you to pay Michael.

I don't think he will send you a formal report – I mean he's not asked

---

1 Section 28 of the Local Government Act 1988 resulted in an amendment to the Local Government Act 1986 stating that a local authority 'shall not intentionally promote homosexuality or publish material with the intention of promoting homosexuality' or 'promote the teaching in any maintained school of the acceptability of homosexuality as a pretended family relationship'. It was repealed in June 2000 in Scotland as one of the first pieces of legislation enacted by the new Scottish Parliament, and in November 2003 in the rest of the United Kingdom by section 122 of the Local Government Act 2003.

2 Thomas Mann's *Buddenbrooks* was published in 1901 and his *Dr Faustus* in 1947.

to assess the quality of the work or anything – just to spot any awful errors about the Jewish world! He has already before reading it told me of one, since I asked him: if you give someone a prayer shawl you don't just wrap it up in brown paper, you put it in a *special* velvet bag!¹ That's the sort of thing I need to know. I talked to M lately by phone, when he had not yet finished the book, but he said he hadn't found any more mistakes! I will ring him again and see if there are any more points – I'm sure he will write to you too when he's finished his task! Be well. Thanks and with lots of love

Iris

To Naomi Lebowitz.

68 Hamilton Road
26 February [1989]

Nay dear, very glad letter, pleased hear Chair ascended² with help of crew (you have a *jolly nice* crew). [. . .]

The Rushdie business is terrible.³ The Muslims in this country (quite a substantial number of them) speak like savage madmen – I mean *some* of them do, and keep it up. All *men* speaking out and being photographed of course, no women. They are constantly demanding Muslim schools, compulsory separation of women, teaching the Koran etc. They are quite unlike other persons from elsewhere. Perhaps Islam will conquer the whole planet in the next century. To think that the *wicked* old priest can condemn someone to death just by pointing at him – it's a nightmare. 'Protests' are going ahead, talk of sanctions etc., but nothing effective can be done as far as I can see. So one goes on helplessly in fury and amazement. It is a pity that Islam will now be hated in this country – including nice perhaps *innocent* shopkeepers etc. who just want to go on with their lives. But I exaggerate I daresay. Anyway it's a rotten religion which owes much of its popularity to its absolute and fundamental degradation of women. Or expresses what (a large number of) men feel in their hearts. Sorry, all this is not amusing and not even informative. [. . .]

1 The rabbi Daniel Most, in *The Message to the Planet*, sends Marcus Vallar a prayer shawl in a velvet bag.
2 Naomi Lebowitz had been professor of English and comparative literature, Washington University since 1972 and had recently been awarded an endowed chair as Hortense and Tobias Lewin Professor in the Humanities.
3 Salman Rushdie's *The Satanic Verses* (1988) had caused a major controversy and the Ayatollah Ruhollah Khomeini, the supreme leader of Iran, issued a fatwa against him on 14 February 1989.

John loved his Valentine – I loved mine from Al. I can't think of anything funny to tell you and must stop rambling on.

Much love

ever

I

To Carmen Callil.

1 June 1989

Carmen dear, just to ask if you can confirm that a loose-leaf book full of typescript poems or music which I confided to Norah long ago is still around in Chatto safe? I feel an impulse to 'collect' some poems (there aren't perhaps a good many I want to publish) before they are lost.[1]

With much love

I

To Josephine Hart.

68 Hamilton Road

9 June [1989]

Dearest Josephine, thanks so much for your letter and for your gallant fight for the play! You really are a fighter, it's the Irish in you! I am very glad it will go on till September. Maybe the rescue party will arrive in time. *Thank you* for your support which I do hope will not prove too hard a gamble. You are an ace!

I have arranged (or am arranging – dates not yet confirmed) to see the *Evening Standard* man and also Terry Wogan. (How Irish he looks, the divil!) [. . .]

By the way, we are (at the end of June) moving house again. New address: 30 Charlbury Road, Oxford. In the chaotic moving period (circa 28 June–5 July) best address is St Anne's College.

I'd love to see you and Maurice soon – and hope you are very OK – with much love

I

1 These poems, which Murdoch had sent to Norah Smallwood in January 1963, can be found in Smallwood's papers in the Brotherton Library, Leeds University; the collection is entitled 'Conversations with a Prince'.

To Sister Marian at Stanbrook Abbey.

68 Hamilton Road
[late June 1989]

Address after July 31st: 30 Charlbury Road Oxford OX2
Lucy my dear, I should have written sooner but have felt rather overwhelmed
by Honor's death.[1] I suppose I expected it, and she spoke so often and so
constantly of that 'light beyond' and of 'going home'. But when she went
it was a shock, one wasn't ready, there were plans, you were to come, and
so on. I shall miss her very much, with her warm heart and her funniness
and her splendid courage and her *reality*. She was a noble person. As you
know, you were her greatest support and shone with brightness in her life
and enlivened her faith. I wish we had once more been together with her.
I remember that time clearly! I hope you are well, I think of you and see
you as good and beautiful as ever! With much love, Iris

To Sister Marian at Stanbrook Abbey.

30 Charlbury Road
[November 1989]

Dearest girl, thank you so much for your letter, with the sad dream and the
strange funny dream. As for 'where do you come from', where *do* you come
from? I know it is – I think it is – the Baltic – but where were you born? Do
tell me, if you feel like it! [. . .]
    Such wonderful news from Eastern Europe[2] – and sad and bad news too
of course. What of your homeland – or is it very remote from you – ?
    Much love
    Ever
    I

To Sister Marian at Stanbrook Abbey.

30 Charlbury Road
[November 1989?]

---

1 Honor Tracy died on 13 June.
2 The fall of the Berlin Wall on 9 November 1989.

Dearest Lucy,

Thank you very much for your interesting letter. I am touched by what you say about your own difficulties; not doubts, and about the mysteries of windows. I hope you have now fewer difficulties. The concepts (experiences) of mysteries might help (save) us in the next century. Love might say: what else can. [. . .]

semper
I

To Josephine Hart.

30 Charlbury Road
[December? 1989]

Dearest Josephine, thanks for your letter, so glad to hear from you! With good news of tall Adam doing well, and of super-cool Edward[1] – and super-cool Maurice. I can imagine how *good* he was in every way. (I saw mainly reports of his calm and *charm*!) And you had a lovely sea-time at Fadarello.[2] (Sea always good for the soul.) And your NOVEL – I long to see it!

I am rather overwhelmed with work and *letters* and so on at present, writing to all my friends in Poland, Czechoslovakia and Romania[3] to make sure they are all right. A Romanian friend got a letter to me by handing it to a journalist in the crowd when they were fighting at the TV station in Bucharest! Friends here are joyful because their friends are now in the government, instead of in the prison! It's all so amazing and wonderful. 'Bliss was it in that Dawn to be alive!'[4]

We'd love to see you both, we *miss* you. I have to go to New York next month[5] (I don't want to but must) and although it is not imminent and not for long it blots the future and I find it hard to make plans. We will see you before long though, God willing, and will be in touch – ever with much love
I

and much love from John.

1 Adam is Josephine Hart's son by her first husband, Paul Buckley; Edward is her son by Maurice Saatchi.
2 The Saatchi family's holiday home at Saint-Jean-Cap-Ferrat in the south of France.
3 The end of 1989 saw the collapse of Communism in all three countries, with much upheaval and some conflict.
4 From Wordsworth's *Prelude*, Book XI.
5 To receive the National Arts Club's Medal of Honor for Literature.

To Philippa Foot.

30 Charlbury Road
13 December 1989

Dearest, thanks so much for your letter. I should be sorry to be suspected of approving of *God*. I believe heartily in his non-existence and indeed regard him as an obstacle to the spiritual life. I suppose an interest in religion is regarded as suspect. Anyway, Good is the point. Never mind. Platonism must look after itself. I am so glad you are (I hope you really *are*) feeling and being much better. SWIMMING, that too is the thing, a very spiritual activity.

I think of you under those palm trees. It's still quite (by English standards) warm here. It's pouring with rain at present. I have just been to memorial service for Freddie Ayer. Hundreds of people, not all philosophers. Peter O'Toole read Tennyson's *Ulysses* poem (very moving). Be well, be well – Happy Christmas and the Nineties – I miss you – dear dear, with so much love,

I

PART EIGHT:
Last Letters

February 1990 to September 1995

Murdoch's popularity continued to flourish during her late years. A play version of *The Sea, The Sea* was broadcast on Radio 4 in 1992 and her two last novels, *The Green Knight* and *Jackson's Dilemma*, were published in 1993 and 1995 respectively. In a poll in the *Sunday Times* in 1994 Murdoch was voted the 'greatest living novelist writing in English', and in 1995 Malcolm Williamson's song-cycle adaptation of her book of poems, *A Year of Birds*, premiered at the Proms Festival in the Royal Albert Hall, where Murdoch made a now rare public appearance on stage with the composer himself. Her last two novels are even more enigmatic and mystical, each with a central ethereal character who carries a knowledge and understanding not vouchsafed to the other characters, who flounder in their attempts to comprehend him. Readers can flounder too, as these otherworldly novels exuberantly disregard realist conventions and unapologetically embrace the supernatural. They fascinate and frustrate in equal measure.

The Green Knight provides a startling contrast to the novels of the 1980s in its Shakespearean disregard for plausibility (like Hermione in *A Winter's Tale*, the eponymous green knight, Peter Mir, is miraculously restored to life), and the book surprised and puzzled reviewers. Nonetheless, its sparkling narrative, its engaging characters and its Shakespearean attempt to harness myth and magic into the truth-telling capacity of art has led a number of critics to situate *The Green Knight* amongst her finest novels. The story revolves around the three Anderson sisters, Aleph, Sefton and Moy, who each share certain aspects of Murdoch's personality, and suggests she was undertaking an uncompromising self-examination of her own strengths and failings as a writer and a human being. Such soul-searching results in the book's concern with the dangers of idolatry; idols may themselves be culpable and are too easily manipulated to serve personal fantasy. An irritated priest, Father Damien, quotes Dante to the spiritual seeker Bellamy James: 'Do not expect any word or sign from me. Your will is free, upright and sound, it would be wrong not to be ruled by its good sense. And so, master of yourself, I crown you and I mitre you'.[i] Related preoccupations regarding the nature of, and necessity for, courage feature strongly in the novel, and for the last time Murdoch includes a much-loved painting as a secular spiritual icon: *The Polish Rider* (attributed to Rembrandt), which she had often visited at the Frick Gallery in New York, becomes the central image of ideal courage, 'steadfast, calm and temperate'.[ii] But this vision is poignantly dismantled, as courage in this book is compromised by a compassion that appeases evil, and a willingness to accept second best. The book seems to articulate Murdoch's fears that ultimately, as with the philosophers of her late novels, her own philosophy might be impotent or flawed.

Reviews of Murdoch's final novel *Jackson's Dilemma*, though generally duly respectful, were mixed; her work was now more clearly faltering. The book begins with a wedding being unceremoniously cancelled by the bride, and ends magically in Shakespearean fashion with the characters having been matched to unforeseen partners. There are familiar figures, each articulating the preoccupations of Murdoch's final years: a would-be philosopher, Benet, who like Murdoch is attempting to write a book on Heidegger; a spiritual seeker, Tuan, who is haunted by the Holocaust; and Mildred, who practises Christian and Eastern faiths and draws strength from images of Shiva and Parvati, and the Parthenon Frieze in the British Museum. The central character, the eponymous Jackson, is an enigma, another of her Christ figures who also has some of the gifts of a bodhisattva (an individual on the path to awakening or enlightenment) and a guardian angel. He may be what had by now become a somewhat sentimentalised image of Murdoch herself and her art. As a natural healer and helper Jackson intuits those in need, appearing in an uncanny way when and where he can be of use. Most significantly, he is a working servant of great practical as well as spiritual help. Jackson indeed executes many of the functions of his creator and her art, and knows that now his powers are diminished: 'at the end of what is necessary, I have come to the place where there is no road'.[iii] Jackson's farewell to the world is Murdoch's own.

In the world of academia, now heavily engaged in promoting postmodernism and postcolonialism, Murdoch's novels were perceived as old-fashioned and her thinking outmoded. Wary of totalising theories, she had repeatedly attacked deconstruction, which, if carried too far, she believed would kill the novel and thereby destroy the valuable social function of storytelling. In these years Murdoch's attitude towards Derrida in particular hardened, and in a letter to Suguna Ramanathan dated 27 November 1992, she expressed concern about his elaborate language: 'One thing (among many) which worried me about Derrida and co. is the loss, in the elaborate language, of plain truth. There is also the evident dualism between those who *know* (the jargon, made of discourse etc.) and those who *do not*, who are not really using language but being used by it. (These are as it were the illiterate workers as compared with the aristocrats!)' Her insistence on the ethical dimension of literature, and her demand that literary theorists and philosophers should not abandon rigorous discussions of morality, rendered her out of kilter with mainstream critical thinking. Nonetheless, she bravely defied this trend by reaffirming morality to be at the centre of both the writing and reading of fiction and validated the study of literature as 'the most essential and fundamental aspect of culture [. . .] since this is an education in how to picture and to understand human situations'.[iv] Her commitment to the humanist tradition of the past never wavered.

1992 was a landmark year in terms of Murdoch's status as a moral philosopher: *Metaphysics as a Guide to Morals*, a volume based on her 1982 Gifford Lectures, was published by Chatto & Windus. She had found this work much more difficult to write than her novels, admitting in an interview in 1992 that it had imperfections, but confirming that it adequately conveyed her beliefs. Criticised in some quarters as meandering, incoherent and unfinished, in the twenty-first century *Metaphysics as a Guide to Morals* has been reassessed as bravely dialectical.[v] A disquisition on the reality of Good, and how it relates to God, religion, art, consciousness and morality, *Metaphysics as a Guide to Morals* focuses throughout on the tensions between metaphysics and empiricism, and between overarching theories and the particularity of moral decisions in everyday life. In this respect, it explores in philosophical language concerns already rehearsed metaphorically in novels such as *The Book and the Brotherhood* and *The Message to the Planet*.

After six years of work on a manuscript entitled *Heidegger*,[vi] which she envisaged as a book, Murdoch abandoned it at the proof stage in 1993. While she believed Heidegger to be one of the most influential philosophers of the twentieth century, she mistrusted his later work which ignored the concept of goodness and which had become remote from the problems and concerns of ordinary life.[vii] Despite having written in the spring of that year to Jonathan Burnham, publishing director at Chatto & Windus, that she thought the manuscript needed 'scarcely any tidying up' and that she did 'not want [the work] to vanish', she later judged it not coherent enough for publication. Part One, 'Heidegger: The Pursuit of Being' is included in *Iris Murdoch, Philosopher*, edited by Justin Broackes; however, the rest of the manuscript (now held in Kingston University's Iris Murdoch Archives[viii]), though praised by many readers, currently carries a ban on direct quotations.

These years brought no slowing down in terms of travel and public appearances. The Bayleys made lecture tours to Spain several times and in 1993 Murdoch was awarded an honorary doctorate from the University of Alcalá. The couple travelled twice to Moscow in the early 1990s and in May 1993 they made their third and last trip to Japan with the British Council. In 1994 Murdoch flew to the USA for a conference at the University of Chicago Divinity School where she appeared alongside other prestigious speakers such as Charles Taylor, Cora Diamond and Martha Nussbaum. The couple were also in demand at literary festivals and spoke at the Charleston Festival and the Hay Festival in 1995 before travelling to Thailand in the summer of that year. They were back on the festival trail again in October when Murdoch appeared at the Cheltenham Literary Festival where she seemed pleased with the reception of *Jackson's Dilemma*.

In 1992 Murdoch admitted spending up to four hours each day writing letters to friends, acquaintances and fans of her work. These late letters reflect two major separate concerns that are clearly evident in the novels of these years: the realm of the mystical ('we are surrounded by magic', she wrote to Jane Turner, then her editor at Chatto & Windus, in 1993) and the political world, especially as it affected the future of the planet. Deeply absorbed in spiritual and political matters, she nevertheless eschewed extremism of any kind: 'The inwardness of some kinds of Buddhism has its terrible aspects. (It's dangerous – as I suppose any religion is at a certain degree of intensity)'.[ix] The politics of Ireland equally preoccupied her; she expressed horror at the atrocities committed by the IRA in the name of freedom. Nevertheless, her Irish nationality remained important to her and she continued to define herself as Irish both as a woman and a writer. More generally she remained politically conservative, believing that the Tories would handle three issues very important to her – the unions, education and the Irish problem – better than the Labour Party. In the early 1990s she actively supported the Irish Peace Movement and became exercised about the Maastricht Treaty[x] which came into force in November 1993; she also signed a petition organised by the *Guardian* demanding justice for Tibet, which was under threat from China. She remained delighted about the liberation of Eastern Europe from Communism but was increasingly depressed by world events, which she followed with a keen eye. At a more local level, she protested against men being admitted to Somerville College, Oxford, where she had studied as an undergraduate.

Now settled in their new home at 30 Charlbury Road, Oxford, Murdoch and her husband enjoyed seeing friends old and new, particularly after John Bayley retired as Warton Professor of English in July 1992. Old attachments remained strong; in August 1992 Murdoch made plans to fly to Zurich to see Canetti, but he cancelled the visit, telling her that he was unwell.[xi] Other, newer friendships flourished. The Bayleys were frequent guests of Maurice Saatchi and his wife Josephine Hart, of whom Murdoch had become very fond. Murdoch remained unfailingly kind and supportive to her friends, writing, for example, a well-informed introduction to the catalogue for an exhibition of paintings by Harry Weinberger at the Duncan Campbell Gallery in Kensington in 1994. The Bayleys' friendship with Peter Conradi and his partner Jim O'Neill also deepened and the couple spent many happy times with them at 'Cascob', Conradi's home in Radnorshire. Losses that would have cut deep included the deaths of Michael Oakeshott in December 1990, Borys Villers and David Hicks in 1991, Hal Lidderdale in 1992, Elias Canetti in 1994 and Brigid Brophy in 1995.

These later years were marked by biting self-reflection: Murdoch began editing her old diaries in 1990 and confessed to A. N. Wilson that the only book she was ashamed of was *The Red and the Green*.[xii] She had come to feel that this novel, about Irish patriotism and set in Dublin at the time of the Easter Rising in 1916, seemed to glorify Irish Nationalism. In 1991, thinking back to her time at Badminton, she suggested that the school had encouraged a dreamlike and unrealistic view of the world that had contributed to her belief in the Soviet Union as a model society. In 1992 she reflected in an interview that the two great sources of happiness in her life had been her marriage and the opportunity to use her mind creatively. She began discussions with Wilson about the possibility of his writing her biography but by 1993 the idea had been abandoned.[xiii] Peter Conradi would later publish *Iris Murdoch: A Life* in 2001.

By 1993 Murdoch was becoming reluctant to engage in public activities and dreaded giving interviews. These late letters increasingly evidence the language difficulties and amnesia that, in retrospect, suggest the progression of Alzheimer's disease, although the condition remained undiagnosed until 1997. The *desire* for epistolary contact movingly remained with Murdoch long after the capacity for it had left her. She would begin writing with the customary 'Dear . . .', 'My very dear . . .' but her letters fade away unfinished. Towards the end John Bayley wrote on her behalf. In 1993 she wrote to Naomi Lebowitz about preparations for Christmas, 'I *must* buy a lot of things, but just can't get on to doing it, them. I have just *lost my grip*'. In the summer of 1995 she wrote to Roly Cochrane, 'Iris and Roly are *stronger* than the dark forces. The sun is decently shining. I have been rather exhausted and knocked down', adding in another letter 'I feel under a burden. What is it?'[xiv] A small selection of such letters are included here because they demonstrate most poignantly, in the face of growing exhaustion and confusion, the survival of Murdoch's characteristic gentleness and loving kindness, which her illness could not destroy.

To Philippa Foot.

30 Charlbury Road
[early February 1990]

Dearest girl, so glad to have your letter. *Sorry* you are so low – I can understand worry about Michael T. (*Can* one be too eccentric in California? Of course philosophy is so much divided by sections?? and sects and deep prejudice – it's as bad as religion.) I hope there may be better news. And the shadow of AIDS must be upon your students more than most. I hope by now you are feeling less depressed. As you say, we can always think about Eastern Europe! I have had wonderful letters from friends in Czechoslovakia and Poland and Romania (one of them was actually fighting in Bucharest). *Dear* Europe.

I hope you have got intentional actions on a lead by now. [. . .]

I am just going to New York, but only for five days to receive some sort of little award at the National Arts Club.[1] I don't want to go but feel I have to.

Ed Victor, my wonderful agent (American) is going to 'show me New York'. Most necessary as I don't really know anything except Chelsea and Greenwich Village and the Met Museum. I want to see *The Polish Rider* again, I don't know who painted it (Frick). I think this will be my last visit to USA. I hope I get back. Quite apart from other considerations I am fed up with the McCarran Act.

Do write to me again *soon*, and tell me how you are. I want to feel *in touch* with you. I have been working on my sort of para–philosophy. My novel[2] is paralysed (well in eclipse). I wish one had another fifty years or so – one might (I might) really *understand* or *clarify* something.

Be well, be better, be happy – much much love, my dear, ever
I

To Josephine Hart, after reading Hart's novel, Damage, *in manuscript form.*

30 Charlbury Road
[February/March 1990]

Josephine, I think your book is marvellous, absolutely *splendid*, I was *spellbound* and had to go on and on reading it. It is so beautifully written and

1 Her acceptance speech was to include an attack on Derrida.
2 *The Green Knight.*

full of *thoughts* – and the intensity of the evil and the doom is maintained with a sort of ruthless logic. It is a tour de force, and will make a very good play, film etc. too! At intervals one positively shuddered, and felt so sorry for the innocent characters. I kept wondering how you would *do it* at the end, and that was very good, and clean and neat and awful! Well done! Who is to publish it? It will be much read. And *the next one* – going on well I hope. Thanks for sending *Damage* (excellent title and a most interesting concept, about the one who survives). We would love to see you and Maurice and will *hope* to – I am *overwhelmed* with letters and people at present – and demands and jobs. But I will clarify it all (well, some of it) fairly soon I hope and anyway will communicate again before long. Hooray and much love

    I

To Harry Weinberger.

30 Charlbury Road
[29 March 1990]

Harry my dear I'm sorry not to have communicated, I have been working on philosophy and have had to be away and am now going away again (to Madrid to lecture) for a week.[1] I *will* get in touch. I have a new desk and one of your big sea (harbour) pictures hangs above it and inspires me.

    Much love ever

    I

To Suguna Ramanathan, whose critical study, Iris Murdoch: Figures of Good, *would be published in 1991.*

30 Charlbury Road
9 April 1990

Suguna, my dear, I am *delighted* to receive your resourceful merciful auspicious clever (and literary) god – he is a most felicitous helpful presence, sitting near my desk! I thank you very much indeed. Yes, with Hinduism, less need to demythologise, it is built in. Thanks for your snatch of words! You have available the whole moral and spiritual universe. We struggle with problems about the Resurrection. I take Christ as a mystical figure – I wish this, which I think many Christians now believe, would take charge of all

---

1 The Bayleys were to visit Madrid and the University of Castille with the British Council.

the awkward dogma. Thank you for your very kind thought, I am very grateful – be happy, and gods be with you!

    With much love

    I

To Philippa Foot.

14 April 1990

Darling, where are you? Isn't it time to be in England? (No snowy boots now.) I do so much want to see you. I am in Hampshire at present and will then be abroad till about April 25. Please communicate! *Much love*

    I

To Naomi Lebowitz.

30 Charlbury Road
24 May 1990

Dearest best Nay, hooray, your *wonderful* book[1] has arrived – it came two days before your letter – I started to read it, but John has snatched it and loves it, and I shall have it next. I see that it is, as a great book should be, *about everything*. I value it very much and it's so luscious to read and full of light. Thank you so very much. You are a real scholar and thinker, thou rare bird. Oh how much I seek enlightenment. Thank you so much for this everything-book. And now you are I hope happy browsing and digging chez [Robert] Frost, William James et al. [. . .]

    Yes, you understand about religion. I hope you are writing another book. I am not writing a novel at present, but trying to finish a version of some old mouldy philosophy lectures (*no good*).[2]

    Our garden is beautiful, the freakish sunny weather continues – I hope you are not too hot, and that the Cardinals are winning. I do hope *Al* is getting on with *his* novel – and riding the waves of the law. We are glad to think that you will be in Europe next summer. Ever, much love – wish you were nearer –

    I

1 *Ibsen and the Great World.*
2 The revised Gifford Lectures which would later be published as *Metaphysics as a Guide to Morals.*

To Philippa Foot.

30 Charlbury Road
19 November 1990

Dearest girl, I am so *pleased* to get your letter with its *back-to-England* news! Perhaps even the winters won't be too bad. (Though a *severe* winter this year is now forecast – perhaps just on the basis of the number of berries on the holly trees.) Houses less warm than those you are used to, east winds, snows. But you will be happier and it is *home*, and I do applaud your decision to retire and be *free*– and thank God you'll be around the place *here* – I keep thinking of things I want to tell you, and ask you. I am so much cheered up by your letter!

The autumn here has been more beautiful than any I can remember. It still continues with vast shows of red and golden leaves and marvellous skies and little birds singing very loudly. The weather is calm and warm, as I write the sun shines from a cloudless sky! (However all will soon be over I fear.) Christmas decorations are already going up in Oxford Street and Regent Street! How *very much* people in LA will miss you. (Thinking of Christmas and your Christmas dinner party!) Moscow must have been strange. I feel such a strong strange love for Russia, and for India. May the gods protect them. [. . .]

With much love to you
ever
I

To Sister Marian at Stanbrook Abbey.

30 Charlbury Road
[December 1990]

Dearest Lucy,

Thank you for your beautiful card. Yes, I miss Honor terribly – she was some sort of holy being. Her company was always both comforting and surprising – a source of life. I loved her very much. And I was surprised that she died.

God filling empty spaces, like in Eckhart,[1] yes. We are keeping warm

---

1 Eckhart von Hochheim (*c*.1260 –*c*.1327), commonly known as 'Meister Eckhart', German theologian, philosopher and mystic. Murdoch's reading of Eckhart's work, Buddhist texts and *The Cloud of Unknowing* (an anonymous work of Christian mysticism written in the second half of the fourteenth century) fed into *Jackson's Dilemma*.

here, and I hope *you* are. (Honor worried about this too!) And I hope you
have a happy Christmas (I think this will arrive after) and will have a happy
1991. (I mean happy in *your* sense, which is *really* happy.) Much love to you
Dearest Lucy
   I

*To Peter Conradi, who taught at Jagiellonian University in Krakow between the
summer of 1990 and the summer of 1992.*

30 Charlbury Road
[mid-December 1990?]

Peter dear, so glad to hear from you, and thank you for sending me your
paper! (Let me know if you want it back.) I am most grateful to you for
these thoughts, wherein I can often see what I meant! Indeed enlightening,
your light. Just two comments.

   Page 1, you say ready to 'learn from Buddhism, though Christ not Buddha
is . . . to save us'. I certainly don't think Christ is to save us/everyone – I
guess that Buddha will save more (and what about Krishna), and I would
be glad to be saved by Buddha! (Or by Christ – I'm not so well acquainted
with Krishna.) I have learnt more from Buddhism.

   Page 4 re Julius[1] – in the theology of that novel Julius actually is the Prince
of Darkness, Morgan is the human soul, and Tallis's father is God the Father
('It all went wrong from the start!'). Tallis himself is of course a high avatar,
though rather shaggy and invisible. (And this 'theology' is scarcely visible too!)

   All best wishes for MLA[2] – do hope you'll be back before long – I look
forward to more Polish news – be well, my dear, much love
   I

To Marjorie Boulton.

30 Charlbury Road
[late December 1990]

Marjorie, you are a darling! I am quite overwhelmed by the wonderful
necklace, each bead a marvel, such beautiful stones – I have it on my desk

---

1 Julius King in *A Fairly Honourable Defeat*.
2 Modern Language Association convention, held annually in North America; in December 1990 it took
   place in Chicago.

and *study* it. You are very kind (to me and to many *others*, such as your Russian Esperantist). I hope you both had a riotously joyous Christmas, eating and drinking and chattering in Esperanto. The Esperanto world is a *great thing*, you are one of its great pillars. It must be rather like a family too, a happy family. I fear this letter may miss Christmas (if not, happy Christmas!) – and anyway I wish you a VERY HAPPY NEW YEAR. Au revoir and all my love to you, be well, and so many many thanks, my dear – be happy – ever

  I

I enclose earrings I bought long ago I think in Venice. I don't wear earrings so much now – I don't know if you do?

Give my love to the pussy cats too.

To Naomi Lebowitz.

30 Charlbury Road
[March 1991]

Nay dear, v. *much thanks letter*. I am feeling rather done over by heterogeneous tasks (which I cannot seem to decide to refuse) such as judging a children's poetry competition (about fifty of the *best* entries, of which I had to choose two – *extremely* difficult!)

 I'm so glad you have (we have) Jimmy Carter[1] – I intuit what you say. It was a terrible alternative (the Gulf business) – I can't say anything intelligent about it. I am involved with Buddhists crying 'What about Tibet?'

 About the vile McCarran Act, nothing has changed. I have to get a visa (latest eighteen-month visa just expired) – either I send my passport to the embassy and they keep it for six weeks (once they *lost* it and I had get another passport) *or*, I thought it might be better, I *go* to the embassy, queue for entry, eventually get into a large room full of various nationalities longing to emigrate to America – wait a long time, then am called to a clerk (in a row of desks) where a fluttering damsel of twenty-five or so says 'wouldn't I like to apply for defector status?' I only have to be interrogated and find some persons of standing to vouch for me! I now have no visa and have no intention of applying for another one. I *now* sometimes mention the McCarran Act to the various people who invite me to USA, and they never

---

1 After his term as president of the United States, Jimmy Carter travelled widely in order to conduct peace negotiations and was awarded the Nobel Peace Prize in 2002.

(though replying) say anything about this! I think they think the Act was repealed long ago and I am dotty!

Anyway never mind. The latest theory here is that Wittgenstein was mad (some doctor says). One newspaper had headline *Loopy Ludwig*.[1] At least they'd heard of him.

I must brush up my William James. I read him some time ago and have by now lost that book. [. . .]

Excuse slightly dotty letter (loopy too). I'm so glad to hear from you. Do come over here. [. . .]

Be well, my dear, carry the flag, by you and Al America is saved. Much love ever

I

To Philippa Foot.

30 Charlbury Road
18 April 1991

Dearest girl, *so glad* to hear from you and wonderful that you'll really be back here and so soon! *See* you soon! Yes, John is retiring in 1992. (And is being succeeded by *Terry Eagleton!*[2]) Thanks for lovely card, picture in London, museum in Westwood, and printed in Korea! I like it very much.

Spring here is lovely with the usual procession of aconites, snowdrops, scillas, primroses, violets, daffodils, bluebells etc. etc. and rain and wind and mud (wellington boots) etc. etc. I feel tired. Your advent is such good news. Much love ever

I

To Naomi Lebowitz.

30 Charlbury Road
12 August [1991]

Dearest Nay I am very sorry to hear about Howard Nemerov[3] – expected etc., but one is so grieved by the sheer terrible *absence* when the time comes. We are glad we met him. The sadness of waiting. [. . .]

1 The *Sun*, 12 March 1991.
2 Literary scholar, cultural theorist and public intellectual.
3 Who had recently died of cancer of the oesophagus.

I love the picture of you with the great baseball player[1] – how privileged the fellow is. You look splendid. I like his positive tie. (John says he looks like a French intellectual!) Your graph paper Ampad letter reminds me of the only letter I ever got from Simone de Beauvoir which was also on graph paper (and said that she was leaving Paris and could not see me). [. . .]

News of psychoanalysis has reached Oxford, but I don't think it is put in practice yet, though that may soon come. I was saddened to receive a letter lately from a Buddhist friend of mine (whom I love and respect) sending a paper by one David Loy,[2] proving that deconstruction and Buddhism were one and the same. And my friend seemed to be *persuaded* by this rot! I am rather close to Buddhism, perhaps it is the only religion which can save the world. (Or have I been mistaken all along?) Thanks for the Henry James wisdom. I have been messing around with a novel and a bit of philosophy and feel rather defeated by both.

We were briefly in France (Provence) and will be briefly in Italy (Naples for the pictures and then two Greek temples). Just now we are going away even more briefly to our friends in Hampshire by the *sea*, where I shall swim whatever the weather. I'm glad you are pro-Schopenhauer. He says a lot of deep things and prefigures much that is OK in Wittgenstein. And he loves animals. Give our lots of love to Al, who is doing much legal good. We wish you'd come to Europe – why not come and *live* over here, London or Paris? John sends much love. You and Al are the great light-sources of America. How lucky we were to find you.

Much love ever

I

To Josephine Hart.

30 Charlbury Road
10 September [1991]

Dearest Josephine,

Thank you so much for your lovely letter – I am delighted by the *Damage* news, it's so splendid, and just what I expected, that the book is *whizzing*

---

1 Stanisław Franciszek Musiał, affectionately nicknamed 'Stan the Man', was first baseman on the St Louis Cardinals between 1941 and 1963.

2 American author and authorised teacher in the Sanbo Kyodan lineage of Japanese Zen Buddhism.

into orbit!¹ Oh well done, and onward with *the next one*! You are a good and brave girl and will succeed!

I (not John alas) will see you (DV etc. as they say in Ireland) on September 24 at Ed's party for you², and I look forward to that very much – and also to the both of us seeing you later in the autumn. (When the rains come. Will they ever come?) I'm so glad to hear the Adam and Edward news too – what a pair – they will conquer the world!

I'm longing to see you and Maurice and to have lots of talk. See soon anyway – John sends much love, with much love to you and Maurice

I

To Peter Conradi.

30 Charlbury Road
15 November [1991]

Peter dear, thank you very much for your card. I'm glad you are settling down in Poland and finding it nicer – it possibly *is* getting nicer and I hope there is more in the shops and *warmth* in the houses. I get such gloomy letters from friends in Romania. Fancy having peasants, and they doffing their caps. On our only visit to Poland we found the unspoilt countryside so beautiful with poppies in the corn – though maybe the market economy has by now removed those poppies. So you can see the Tatras. Maria sent me a book of pictures of them. I've never really lived with mountains and wish I had seen a few more.

I am trying to write about this and that. I expect you have seen Andrew Harvey's book.³ I know *your* field is different. I wish I really *knew* something about something, such as Buddhism.⁴ You are really inside. I worry about England which I love. Christianity, said to be always changing itself into something people can believe, is not changing fast enough. Actually TV is probably the most sinister thing! Perhaps the Poles haven't been enslaved by it yet. A row is always going on about education but little is achieved – I feel sad about small children not taught to read, or to learn grammar or

1 Hart's novel, published that year, was critically well received and quickly became a best-seller. In 1992 it was made into a film directed by Louis Malle, starring Jeremy Irons, Miranda Richardson and Juliette Binoche.

2 Ed Victor was literary agent for both Murdoch and Josephine Hart.

3 *Hidden Journey: A Spiritual Awakening*. Harvey had been taught by John Bayley and became the youngest ever fellow of All Souls College, Oxford. He stopped teaching in 1977 to pursue his interest in spirituality and mysticism. He had dedicated *Journey in Ladakh*, which describes a spiritual pilgrimage, to Murdoch.

4 In fact Murdoch had been reading about Buddhism since the 1940s.

how to get things right or to stop watching TV! And the poor students reading the new literary criticism instead of reading Shakespeare and Milton. These are suddenly to be seen as *old* sayings, *like* people said when things were falling down.

Write again and tell me some mundane things about your day. Who do you teach and what? Much love to you as ever

I

Please excuse pessimistic letter. Actually it is a sunny day and the trees still have golden leaves!

To Brigid Brophy, who had moved to a care home in Louth, Lincolnshire in May 1991, where her daughter, Kate, had lived for some years. Brophy's husband, Michael Levey, had bought a house in Louth in the late 1980s and he also moved there in 1991.

30 Charlbury Road
21 November 1991

Dearest Brigid, please forgive a gap in communication. No excuse, except that I have been very tired and somehow 'paralysed' by trying to write some philosophy. Why do I want to write philosophy, why can't I just forget it, what use is it anyway? I suppose it is a sort of addiction. *Is* it philosophy, am I any good at it? Probably not. I must try to write a story. I am so sorry not to have been in touch, I think about you very much – and I hope that, if that could be convenient and wished for, to visit you in 1992. How the years flash past. I believe you have been writing poems. I sometimes used to try. It is very hard.

I am very glad about Terry Waite.[1] I expect you heard his *remarkable* speech. (And you probably saw him on TV. John and I remain the only people in the south of England not to have one.)

We have now at least got a cassette player. John looks forward to retiring next June. This, to be in touch – with much love

Iris

1 Waite, who had travelled to the Lebanon as an envoy for the Church of England in order to negotiate the release of hostages, had himself been held hostage in Lebanon by the Islamic Jihad Organization between January 1987 and 18 November 1991.

To Katharine Hicks, in response to news of David Hicks's death. Earlier in 1991 Hicks had written to Murdoch, 'These novels of yours, some of which I used to detest because I hated the people in them, I now read with growing wonder. Thanked be fortune that once I knew you, and therefore have the privilege of saying what I think. You are writing some of the most beautiful fiction of our age, and the best.' His letter concluded: 'I don't want to meet: my nervous system is not too firm since my illness last spring, and you will have noticed I always make a gauche idiot of myself. But I do want to send you homage and love'.

30 Charlbury Road
[30 December 1991]

Dearest Katharine, I am so moved by your letter – I have so many memories of David – how good he was, how brave, how clever, how joyful, and full of imagination and invention. So lovable. He had a quiet swift departure surrounded by love. I shall think of you all on January 1st.
  With much love
  Iris

To Peter Conradi.

30 Charlbury Road
[13 January 1992]

Dearest Peter, thank you for your card. I don't know whether I can give you clear answers to all the questions. I must have taught Plato and Aristotle at St Anne's, but I suspect 'Plato' was mostly *Theaetetus*[1] with the Line[2] and the Cave. There was no wide consideration of him, he was simply misunderstood. I learnt nothing of value about him as an undergraduate (he was regarded as 'literature'!). Yes, Simone Weil helped me very much. I can't recall just when I discovered her – probably in the late 1950s. My copy of *La source grecque* is dated by me January 1961. She came to me somehow through France, I have almost all of her works in French. I have always been close to Plato in Greek since I have all of his works in the helpful Loeb edition – without the crib I would be less close! Everything

1 One of Plato's dialogues concerning the nature of knowledge, dating from 369 BC.
2 Plato's Analogy of the Divided Line comprises four unequal parts: segments A to C represent the visible world and segments C to E represent the intelligible world. Socrates explains that the four segments also represent four separate 'affections' of the psyche. These affections are described in succession as corresponding to increasing levels of reality and truth from conjecture to belief, to thought, and finally to understanding.

important I heard of course in the Greek as well as the English – his voice *sounds* in Greek. I started reading Derrida quite early too. I first read *L'écriture et la différence*, judging from my annotations, soon after it was published in 1967. I did not (judging from my annotations) 'buy' it. ('Hubris!' 'Literary idealism!' 'Revelation rather than truth' etc.) I have read or 'read' other books since – *De la grammatologie*, which I think has had most influence, also *Marges, Dissémination, Glas, Psyché*. I feel deep hostility to Derrida, he is a *pharmakeus*,[1] an outrageous player, a great scholar, but not a philosopher. A wonderful phenomenon. (I met him once and liked him very much!) He has so much to say, and *knows* so much, one can learn from him. But truth, and the individual, seem lost. Loss of the individual is an ambiguous idea. Loss of egoism good, but one must hold on to the contingent, the individual, truth. I regard 'ἀπορία',[2] and rhetoric, with suspicion. Please *tell me* more about shunyata[3] and is it a good thing to be driven through that narrow funnel?

I hope you are *well*– you speak of a clinic. Let us meet in Oxford or London – write to me soon.

Much love ever

I

To Peter Conradi.

30 Charlbury Road
[17 February 1992]

Dearest Peter, thank you so much for your letter and for coming here – I'm so glad that you came! *And* brought Cloudy! She is already in my novel,[4] and now I have gained a welcome amount of valuable detail. What a dear dog, and so beautiful and so strange. Well, that applies to you too, *mutatis mutandis*. No, nothing found out now about Christ would dismay me or harm the teachings: the mystical Christ is with us, like the mystical Buddha. Teachers who exist now as ordinary humans and have not yet achieved this status are perhaps another matter, since we can still detach the teaching from the person! Anyway none of this can touch you and your faith and your judgement of what's there, which has my entire confidence! I think you are well on along the way – look after yourself and *be happy*. I hope

---

1 Sorcerer, magician.
2 Doubt or perplexity.
3 The Buddhist term shunyata – or sunnata – carries various meanings including 'emptiness' and 'openness' but it can also refer to a meditative state or experience.
4 As the dog Anax in *The Green Knight*.

you are feeling much better, and now 100 percent recovered. Let me always have news. My dear, much love ever

    I

To Naomi Lebowitz.

30 Charlbury Road
10 March 1992

Dearest Nay, thanks for lovely letter. No, I am *not* voting for Glenda Jackson,[1] *or* grieving for Fergie.[2] I think dear John Major[3] is cute – but is he acute? I think Bush[4] is *quite* cute, and he did some good jobs on foreign affairs (which evidently did not please those at home).

Our election has produced the most *disgraceful bad manners* on the part of Labour and Tories. The Liberal Democrats are going round with a halo, which may even win them some votes. I don't know who can possibly rescue our economy. I won't vote Labour because of their *awful* education policy – abolition of 'assisted places' (how clever poor children can get to fee-paying schools), abolition also of any sort of 'streaming' (finding the clever poor children and helping them on). Equality = keep everyone *down*, abolition of all the new hospital schemes (which may be good, not even time to have tried them), elevation of Kinnock etc. etc. I suspect too that Labour have a foul policy on Northern Ireland, sell all those Protestants down the river.

I hope your Clinton[5] will be OK and a good president, he has a good press here. (So did Tsongas.[6]) [. . .]

Glad you are 'doing' Hardy. John has been lecturing on him. John looks forward to his liberation next June. He sends much love. I send much love and to dear Al. *Yes*, what about that plan for the *house in Europe*? [. . .]

    Much love, *toujours*,

    I

1 Glenda Jackson retired from acting to stand in the 1992 general election, subsequently becoming the Labour Member of Parliament for Hampstead and Highgate.
2 Sarah, Duchess of York, née Ferguson, wife of Prince Andrew, second son of Queen Elizabeth II. The couple announced their separation in March 1992.
3 Tory politician and prime minister of the UK from 1990 to 1997.
4 George H. W. Bush, president of the USA from 1989 to 1993.
5 Bill Clinton, president of the USA from 1993 to 2001.
6 Paul Tsongas was an unsuccessful candidate for the Democratic nomination in the 1992 USA presidential election.

To Harry Weinberger.

30 Charlbury Road
[1 May 1992]

[. . .] I'm glad Whitby was so beautiful, and you and Matty looked for fossils. (One of my ideas of heaven – picking up stones beside the sea.) [. . .]

I used to meet Francis Bacon a bit with some other London people. He once said he'd take a woman friend, me, round the gambling clubs, but it never happened! I liked him very much, but never *knew* him. I look forward to Whitby pic photos.

Much love
I

To Naomi Lebowitz.

30 Charlbury Road
4 June 1992

Dearest Nay, thanks for super letter. I love your writing paper. No, I'm afraid I don't (having no TV) know the Morse fellow with blue eyes[1]. I'm glad he makes an impression. And yes, there is a serious drought here, our rivers are drying up. Water is scarce.

I'm glad also that you saw that peacock. Plenty of them wander about here, quite tame, in the gardens of grand houses (they know where the grub is). Ordinary people don't usually keep them. They are rather special. They survive our winters with ease. I recall our headmistress (at my enlightened left-wing boarding school) publicly condemning some poor rich girl for going about boasting of the peacocks on her terraces.

Buddhism – yes – a good thing, don't you think. I have been peripherally involved in it for some time. I have some quite far and varied Buddhist friends. (I have been blessed, but in a rather momentary encounter, by the Dalai Lama.[2]) Have you long been a Buddhist?[3] I am interested in your William James connection. I hope one can be a partial Buddhist – or (I think I am) a perpetual Buddhist beginner. I think it is the greatest religion. Do write to me more about this. Meditation must take the place of all those Christian prayers. But can it come in time? [. . .]

1 John Thaw played the character of Morse in the British detective TV series *Inspector Morse*, which was popular in both the UK and the US.
2 During a trip to Paris in October 1990, Andrew Harvey had introduced Murdoch to the Dalai Lama, who blessed her in Tibetan.
3 Naomi Lebowitz was never a Buddhist, although she was quite attracted to Buddhism.

I am very unhappy about Europe, I am very anti-federal. France and Germany want to run the whole show together. The little children (Greece, Portugal, Italy etc.) long to be taken over and have their states run for them, and their peasant populations given lots of money. But we (never conquered) have had a parliament for a long long time and value our sovereignty very much. This sovereignty is being quietly removed. (Jacques Delors[1] is king.) It's a difficult choice. (Denmark has just opted out.) But it's heart-rending to find details of our way of life now being ordered from Brussels! Not enough people are *noticing* this!

I agree about Virginia Woolf. I hope Al is very happy and writing. We are watching your USA political adventures too. Much love, and from John

I

To Michael Hamburger, poet and academic whose translations of work by Friedrich Hölderlin, Paul Celan and W. G. Sebald were highly praised. He had also been one of Franz Steiner's close friends.

30 Charlbury Road
[1992?[XV]]

Dear Michael

Thank you very much indeed for your letter about Franz and please forgive a late reply. I have been away, I have also been having the local Oxford flu and have felt rather in eclipse. Your letter went to a previous address. I'm sorry I missed you at Holywell Manor[2] – I hope you got to Prague. I'm so glad you are translating Franz – what about your earlier translation, which you speak of – could there not be a book here of those poems and translations – can I help at all? Some publisher should be interested. I hope and believe Franz's poems *will* become known. I am sorry Jeremy[3] was let down by that publishing house, and hope he may succeed with another. Franz's presence, his being, is very alive for me. It is hard to believe it is forty years since he went. I'm glad you will speak of him at the University of East Anglia. I have lost my German (or much of it). Never was very good. Franz enlivened it. If only one could live to be 200 or so.

I have beside me now your book of translations of Hölderlin. Inside I see I have written 'Iris Murdoch, Oxford, September 1943' and at the foot of the

---

1 French economist and politician who was president of the European Commission between 1985 and 1995.

2 An Oxford building which houses postgraduates; presumably Michael Hamburger had given a talk there.

3 Jeremy Adler, academic, poet and journalist who was at this time a professor at Queen Mary and Westfield College London; also the son of Günther Adler, one of Franz Steiner's close friends.

page 'HM Treasury'. In fact I left Oxford in 1942 but evidently felt I still belonged there! I entered the Civil Service (conscripted, war on) at once after my final exams. I have treasured your book ever since! *Sorry* not to have written sooner. Do keep in touch, and let me know of any Oxford visits. I hope your poems flow on well – with all my best wishes to you

    Yours
    Iris

To Sister Marian at Stanbrook Abbey.

30 Charlbury Road
[1992]

Dear Lucy,

    Thank you very much for your letter – yes, the loss of Christianity is terrible – young people (young students I know, children of friends etc.) *know nothing* about it. I think that Buddhism, Hinduism, Judaism find it easier to handle what is holy, what is good – to *keep* it in a changing scene. I mean, the *literalistic* pictures of God as Person, and that Christ rose and so on are too crudely taken – there must be some *transition*. (We, who are not Jews[1] etc. suffer from the awful crude clarities of the technological age.) I am writing this rather crudely but perhaps you see what I mean.

    The Cloud of Unknowing – I have the book in my hand this moment, with, inside the cover 'Iris Murdoch June 1957'.

    I have read, at various times – will now read again!

    Excuse a hasty letter – I hope not too crude and muddled.

    Much love
    I

Christ must never be absent.

To Josephine Hart.

30 Charlbury Road
[summer/autumn 1992]

Dearest Josephine. I have READ the BOOK[2] – sorry, I didn't write sooner, have been briefly away.[3] I think it is terrific and horrific. It has less detail

---

1 Possibly an echo of 'We who are Jews by nature and not sinners from among the Gentiles'. Galatians 2:15.
2 *Sin*, Hart's second novel.
3 The Bayleys had holidayed in Sorrento and Capri with Audi Villers.

than the earlier one, but it has a poetic quality and mode of presentation. It is certainly a picture of evil – which is a thing not easy to present. It is remarkable and very mesmerising. For instance the scene in Scotland with the strange boy – but indeed so many scenes are awfully memorable! The subject is splendid. I am writing a novel at present with a similar subject![1] This in confidence! (The *elder* brother, adopted, detests his, preferred by parents, younger brother who is the 'real' child.) Such hatred is indeed a reality and something terrible. I hope you are already far on in your *third* novel. You have such strong sincerity and insight, it's the truth which is rarely so well told.

All best best wishes and much love, and to M and Boys,
     ever
     I

To Albert Lebowitz.

30 Charlbury Road
[October 1992]

Al dear, I didn't say (absorbed in my own affairs) in my last letter how moving I found your afterword.[2] Yes, you must miss Howard very much, with his ironic wit and his profound and vital Russian gloom. We scarcely knew him but we have vividly remembered him – and, whether I actually saw it or not, I saw or 'saw' you and him sitting by the pool. (The chess game I can only 'see'.) A poet, yes.

We have just been breathing Russian air in Moscow (where there is a new Russian Booker Prize,[3] and John is on the jury). Moscow so beautiful, with its golden domes and its amazingly wide streets covered with snow, along which orderly and not all that many motor cars parade. Well, that's Europe too. And the Underground is as fantastic as ever. I expect you have been there. We were there years ago.

Much love, dear Al, and to dear Nay, and with hopes to see you – and from John,
     Ever
     I

1 *The Green Knight.*
2 Albert Lebowitz had written an afterword for Howard Nemerov's *The Homecoming Game.*
3 Russian literary award modelled after the Booker Prize and inaugurated by English Booker chief executive, Sir Michael Harris Caine, in 1992.

To Naomi Lebowitz.

30 Charlbury Road
[November 1992]

Dearest Nay, thank you so much for your letter and badge¹ – I am so glad of your joy! And I gather from other Americans that America is happy and has the *right man* and that Clinton will be a far better and wiser leader. Congratulations!

There is one slight shadow here. In the *Sunday Times* on 8 November we are told that Clinton, 'in an official letter to a prominent Irish American', has called for the British government to safeguard against the 'wanton use of lethal force' in Northern Ireland. The letter makes no mention of the IRA and calls for 'the appointment of an American peace envoy to the province'. He has, it is said, during his campaign, pledged that he would allow Gerry Adams, leader of Sinn Fein, the political wing of the IRA, to visit America on a fund-raising tour. He complains of 'wanton killing by British Troops' and seems to indicate that he would not allow the extradition from America of suspected terrorists. Of course there is no 'wanton killing'; the British Army is kept on a close lead (watching their comrades murdered daily and weekly) and very rarely behaves improperly on that awful scene. The money raised by Gerry Adams would go straight to terrorists who are in league with other terrorists all over Europe who supply the material of their bombs, and devices such as brought down the American plane at Lockerbie.² Meanwhile, the destruction of Ulster goes on, the town centre of Coleraine was blown up last week. The IRA become increasingly expert at creating larger bombs. The City of London is a recent target where already several very large buildings have been destroyed, costing millions (billions) of pounds and (of course) killing people.

I'm sorry, I mustn't go on about this. It would be wonderful if some Americans could come over here and *solve the Irish Question* – maybe it could be done by some magic! Of course there are now Protestant terrorists too (partly a religious war). Only they are amateurs fortunately. It is a scene of such evil, and such tragic grief. And people get used to it, as they must do in a war. My relations in Belfast, for instance.

Forgive this tirade. I wonder if you have seen anything about Ireland in the American papers? I think many Americans think Britain is holding Ulster by force. But one cannot *give away* part of one's territory against the will

---

1 Bill Clinton 1992 presidential portrait pinback button.
2 The town in south-west Scotland where, on 21 December 1988, the wreckage of Pan Am Flight 103 crashed after a terrorist bomb on board detonated. All 259 people on the flight and eleven residents of the town were killed.

of the majority of its citizens! Oh dear, as if we didn't have enough troubles, with the Maastricht Treaty for instance. I may hold forth about that another time. Sorry to send you such a gloomy letter. Much love to you both, and from John, [. . .] do write soon and cheer me up,

Ever

I

Speaking of religion, the Church of England is now going to ordain women priests. Hooray, hooray! This has caused quite a lot of misery however, and a lot of clergy and laity who abominate the idea are thinking of *going over to Rome*! (There really is a good deal of pain about it.)

To Sister Marian at Stanbrook Abbey.

30 Charlbury Road
[Christmas 1992]

Dearest Lucy,

Thank you so much for your card and letter and your references to *malheur* (Simone de Beauvoir and Simone Weil). 'Affliction' does not properly translate it, even 'grief' might be better, though less precise.

I hope you are keeping warm in this sudden winter weather, I think of you, and that you are a spiritual being. ('Spiritual' is also a difficult word, but you know what I mean.) How selfish the life of the world is in which *we* are so deep. Christmas thoughts. I also think of Honor! And I remember you at Somerville. (The JCR¹ voted for *women only*, but it seems that it will soon be male as well as female!)

Much love, dear girl, Christmas, and New Year – and oh let 1993 be a *better* year –

semper

I

PS my libretto alas has rather faded away. I'm glad you mentioned my mother. And what you say about Eckhart, and Simone Weil – and also Buddhism – do go on about this – Nirvana, as happy move to death – you know so much and I nothing! (But mainly Eckhart.)

Much love dear dear girl

Iris

---

1 The Junior Common Room at Somerville College, which was to admit male students from 1994.

To Naomi Lebowitz.

30 Charlbury Road
12 January 1993

Dearest girl, much thanks your letter – I am relieved to hear what you say re the IRA. I spoke of the matter earlier to an American who said casually, 'Oh, Clinton's Sinn Fein connection is well known.'

I had a jolly experience in London, Oxford Street, just before Christmas – suddenly barriers, police, booming commands, 'Get out of Oxford Street, get out of Oxford Street.' Of course the street was absolutely crowded with Christmas shoppers, people ran about in various directions. Oxford Street and Regent Street were *emptied*, all the shops also emptied and closed. IRA rings up, saying 'bombs planted in Oxford Street area' (they have a special code so the police know it's them!). I had a British Council appointment and stupidly got into a taxi which was then stuck for an hour in a traffic jam, since Oxford Street had been emptied of persons except for police, ambulances etc. One of the bombs was located in John Lewis's (big store) and went off about half an hour later destroying much of the store, then another went off in a nearby square. Unfortunately the bombs had not been found in time to get everybody out – a number of people were injured, some seriously, and of course the police and first aid and doctors etc. were among the injured, fortunately no one was killed.

A similar Christmas joke was played at Harrods a couple of years ago, killing a number of people including American tourists. This is happening now all over the place, they are used to it in Ulster, but now Manchester and Birmingham are targets as well as London. The bombs become bigger and more efficient. I imagine these incidents are not mentioned in the American press – indeed they are not much mentioned in the English press, if not in central London! Perhaps it is better kept quiet since the vastly greater amount of damage (quite apart from *persons killed*) has meant that buildings *cannot be insured* except at phenomenal rates, and this not good for trade and investment!

Perhaps after all the American Army might well come and take charge of Ireland – they are doing pretty well elsewhere! I wish they could arrest the Dublin government, who tolerate the IRA so long as they stay north of the border! (They know who and where they are.) It is all a very grievous tragic mess.

Other news – we have been twice in Moscow where John has been on the jury of the new Russian Booker Prize. (He knows Russian – I used to but it has mostly gone.) Moscow is so beautiful. Come to beautiful Europe. Excuse passion. Much love

Ever and ever

I

To Jane Turner, editor at Chatto & Windus, concerning an episode in The Green Knight.

30 Charlbury Road
24 February 1993

Jane dear, Much thanks letter and about Moy. Of course she would be unlikely to be able to run after nearly drowning. But fictionally, she can. The runic stone, being near suddenly to its old home, sends out warm rays, felt first of course by Anax. Well, we are surrounded by magic. I think the order of events should remain. But thanks very much for your so kind and careful command of detail! With lots of love, Iris

To Harry Weinberger

30 Charlbury Road
March 1993

Harry dear,
    Thank you *ever so much* for my visit to you, such a lovely time among your pictures and in that really gorgeous hotel, it was all a great treat. I love the pictures – your present picture is *magnificent*– your work is noble and beautiful. Thank you very much for your Scottish boat painting, it's delightful. And the *mask* – we love it, John loves it, it is full of mystery and of a good mysticism. Thank you. I wish I could think of some magic (a magic picture show of *all* your pictures).
    Give my love to Barbara. How lucky your child and grandchildren are to be visiting you! Much love, will communicate, ever
    I

To Sister Marian at Stanbrook Abbey.

30 Charlbury Road
[spring 1993]

Dearest Lucy,
    Thank you so much for your letter. No, not exactly ill, but submerged by things people want me to do for them! Anyway, that's another matter. I am *so glad* to hear from you. I am not sure what the 'excellent retreat' was – or 'his charm': I sympathise much about the destruction of Honor's tulips. Would she were here. I think of you and remember when we were in that

field and you asked for a cigarette! A hundred years ago. Actually I gave up smoking soon after, inspired by Stanbrook. Do tell me more of what you do. I am trying to write a novel,[1] but am not getting on well. One of the difficulties is that my hero is, though recognised only by a few, a very spiritual person, possibly from Tibet, and of, perhaps, considerable age. However I do not know how to *end* his activities. Never mind. I have still a very long way to go! What do I know of such persons? (*Mutatis mutandis* like you. Only you are still much younger.) I am attached to Buddhism, but am not 'practising'. I am still with Julian of Norwich and *Cloud of Unknowing* etc., but only in a feeble way. What will the next century bring? A pal (A. N. Wilson actually) said to me that Christianity (in the next century) will be *only* in the Roman church. (This can seem plausible.)

Much much love to you, my *dear* girl,
Iris

To Peter Conradi.

30 Charlbury Road
[March 1993]

Dearest Peter,

Thanks so much for letter. I am very glad to hear of your advancement – I revere your wonderful pure experiences. You describe a wonderful state of being. Are you also a bodhisattva? I am so pleased for you both and happy to be near you! *May there be more of you* to save the next century! I am rereading the 'Cimetière marin' and will compose a *short* thought.[2] Will write you soon, much love, and to Jim and Cloudy,
I

To Jonathan Burnham, publishing director at Chatto & Windus.

30 Charlbury Road
[spring 1993?]

Dear Jonathan, a thought. When I decided to finish *Metaphysics as a Guide to Morals* I set aside a considerable amount of writing about Heidegger, which I thought would make the book too hopelessly long. I put this stuff

---

1 *Jackson's Dilemma.*
2 Paul Valéry's 'Le cimetière marin' ('The Graveyard by the Sea') (1920) was one of Murdoch's favourite poems, and is alluded to in *The Unicorn*, *The Time of the Angels* and *The Nice and the Good*.

aside and have now looked at it, and I think it would make a book – not of course to be tagged on to *MGM*, but set up separately – in fact a complete book, with indeed scarcely any tidying up. I would not like it to vanish – would you mind looking at it? It is more dense and generally difficult, in many parts, than *MGM* and thus 'duller'. I doubt if it would sell very many. Anyhow I feel unwilling to throw it aside. Would you, and Ed, consider it? Love and best wishes,

I

I am writing to Ed too.

To Naomi Lebowitz.

30 Charlbury Road
10 March 1993

Dearest Nay,

I hope you are not fed up with me and my miseries about Ireland (which I will now close down).

We here all admire Clinton (and Hillary[1]) – there is real leadership and getting necessary things done and being human. Our so-called leaders are just not strong or clever enough.

John is enjoying retired life. He is writing a novel![2] I am trying to write one. I feel rather like the juggler who suddenly wonders, but how do I do it? I am rather tired and this house fills with unanswered letters and old newspapers and books. We haven't got into Europe, even as far as Paris. The French fishermen are fighting with our fishermen.

I hope you are very well and teaching and writing many things. Much love as ever

I

To Carmen Callil, written in response to her letter of April 1993 suggesting publicity interviews for The Green Knight.

30 Charlbury Road
[April 1993]

1 Hillary Clinton, wife of Bill Clinton and First Lady of the United States, who went on to become Secretary of State within the administration of Barack Obama.
2 Probably *Alice* (1994).

Dearest Carmen, Thanks so much for your letter about the horrors of publicity! I would not like, but I would agree to, signing books in Waterstones Charing Cross Road, and one more place in London. I'd rather not Blackwell's, there would be too many people I knew around! I'd rather not go to Dublin, Manchester or Scotland. I would not like the *Woman's Hour* or *Late Show* or any TV or radio. OK interviews are *Times* or *Independent*. I can't think of any bright, personal idea, though one *might* arise. I am so sorry to be so withdrawn! I *am most grateful* to you for looking after me!

Much love ever,

I

It's partly a matter of *time*.

To Cloudy, Peter Conradi's dog, in response to a letter in which Conradi had corrected Murdoch's description of the colour of Cloudy's coat in a draft of The Green Knight *and offered a number of unrelated textual corrections.*

30 Charlbury Road
[14 April 1993]

Dearest Cloudy,

Thank you so much for your letter, I am so glad to hear from you. I will pay careful attention to what you say, and make suitable alterations! Tell Peter I am going away for several days, but will write again. Gratefully and with much love

Iris

To Simon Kusseff, author and journalist, who was working on a biography of Frank Thompson.

30 Charlbury Road
[1993?[xvi]]

Dear Simon Kusseff,

Thank you, I am very moved by yours about Frank. I have nothing 'mysterious' to say about him. His last letters, coming from Bulgaria, were about flowers and general remarks about how he felt he was changing etc. Of course he could not write other than a bland letter. I recall him in various ways – three of us, me, him and Leo in a punt. Also at Labour Club gatherings and someone pointing him out, 'we must get that chap into the

Communist Party'. Also he used to come (as I did) to Eduard Fraenkel's class (a very small intense class). His letters, more open, from Egypt were rather expressions of change, how our earlier days (Communist Party etc. etc. not mentioned of course) were childish and how we (generally) had grown up and seen the world differently. No details of course. He talked merrily about girls! Then came the terrible move into Bulgaria (soon after deemed useless in high quarters). If he *had loved* and wanted to *marry* me when he returned of course I would have married him. I can't imagine in detail what he would have wanted to do. The Greeks etc., an academic life probably (politics?). I don't quite imagine the 'new Communist ethic'. *Not* the CP. Something different. Thank you very much for your deep concern, I am glad you cared. Thank you!

    With all best wishes to you,

    Yours,

    Iris

To Josephine Hart.

30 Charlbury Road

[June 1993^{xvii}]

Dearest Josephine,

    I am so glad to hear from you, and about the house. So sorry about Adam, but pleased he has had the operation successfully. He is indeed a remarkable boy and will be a remarkable man, full of power and calm.

    We have just been in Japan (our third visit) and seen the latest marvels, and talked at universities. They are all amazing. Didn't see Fuji however, he was wreathed in mist. I'm so pleased to hear of your intimations of the next novel! Just sit calmly and wait. I look forward to see the new house, and see you and Maurice and Adam and Edward again. You are *all* so grown-up and full of knowledge and talent and loving kindness. Excuse this brief letter, I have to go to *Ireland* (Coleraine) to receive hon. degree of university, and make a speech. A tricky matter! Will communicate.

    Much love and to M

    ever –

    I

To Naomi Lebowitz.

30 Charlbury Road
29 July 1993

Dearest Nay, please forgive my very late letter, I have been so overcome by urgent correspondence and travel and honorary degrees (the St Louis one is absolutely the best). I have in the last two or three months, received a degree in Spain (Alcalá University, very grand), in Cambridge (Cam. University) and in Ireland, University of Coleraine (Ulster). I have also been with John to Japan (visiting various universities and enjoying the Japanese). This year, I begin to feel terribly tired, and I keep forgetting things – and I have had to make speeches which I don't like. (I have another hon. degree, Kingston University, a *new* university, coming up in the autumn (or fall).)

I also have a novel coming out in the autumn (fall) called *The Green Knight*, you will be acquainted with those chaps, the story i.e. *Sir Gawain and . . .*; (my story) is loosely, and *up to date*, connected with them. I hope to fiddle with another novel, but anxiety about speeches and degrees and Japan has disturbed my state of mind to an unusual degree.

Ulster goes on with remarkable calmness. I met (after some time) two of my cousins and we (briefly) toured the north coast where we used to swim together when we were sort of twelve to sixteen. It is surely one of the most beautiful places in the world – utterly unspoilt. Oh how lucky *they* are to live within sight of the sea. (Well, they live in Belfast, but they spend their (retired) summers by the sea and are a short car drive away from it.) Oxford is eighty miles from the sea – and the nearest sea is *unsatisfactory*. Oh for those breaking waves and those sunsets and that horizon, in the north.

I'm glad you are still pleased with Clinton – he is good and brave – and I forgive him (re Ireland) – and he works very hard and is a pragmatic idealist. Our political leaders here are nice but unable to lead. I cannot but love however our small House of Commons where they shout and contradict each other 'The honourable member for such and such', just like in the last centuries. (Like in Trollope – I forget if you like Trollope? I rather do.) But not first class. I am reading *War and Peace* at the moment, a rather higher, indeed highest, matter. I don't like Natasha and I love Sonja, poor Sonja.

Please excuse my having lost your letter, do write again before long. I don't *touch* a word processor. I hope your two powerful children are flourishing. John is OK, retired, but of course still tied to the college (especially his PhD students). Much love dear Nay, and much love to dear Al, and much love to you both from John,
Iris

To Peter Conradi.

30 Charlbury Road
[28 September 1993]

Peter dear, thank you so much for your card – I am so sorry to hear about your father – it must be a terrible loss – and your poor stepmother – I miss my parents dreadfully, they were so full of love. I'm glad you got to the Hebrides and saw those seals and otters. We have never been there! 'Anax'[1] is Greek for 'Lord' – Apollo is the Anax who lives at Delphi. I'm glad you liked the book. Yes, indeed, see soon. Much love always
    I

and love to Jim and lovely dog!

(Hope she doesn't mind!)

To Michael Levey.

30 Charlbury Road
25 February 1994

Michael dear,
    I am sorry I haven't written for so long. Now this first of all. Jon Wynne-Tyson[2] (whom you probably know) has written to me saying he would like to send two of his books to Brigid – if she would like to receive them, read them, etc. – and would I find out. Could you tell me, also for myself, how she is now? I do apologise for so much silence, and not visit. I wish you were both nearer! If a visit would still be welcome I must attempt one in the summer! And how are you, and Kate. Do write anyway – I think of Brigid and most vividly remember her. Give her my love if she remembers me, and if this is appropriate. And love to you, my dear,
    Your
    Iris

1 The dog in *The Green Knight*.
2 British author, independent publisher and pacifist.

To Naomi Lebowitz.

30 Charlbury Road
1 April 1994

Dearest Nay,

Please excuse late reply to your letter. Somehow I am weighed down and suffer all sorts of demands. I must get over this! I'm glad your flu is now in the past. I applaud your Indian and Buddhist studies. I studied Buddhism once but have not persevered. In fact I am rather tired. We still have no TV and don't go to the cinema (movies). The radio is descending into such vulgar depths (well not *too* bad, but bad enough). Maybe we shall be driven to take up TV.

I am delighted and impressed by your cartooning career, I trust it is going on well. And your essays being published? Maybe you would let us see. John is involved in the Booker Prize business[1] and even more books are arriving.

You mention Adorno whom I like very much. He was once long ago in Oxford, on some musical matter. (Before my time!) I am driven back on Dostoevsky, I mean I'm *enjoying* it – except for *The Idiot* which rambles so dreadfully. I have laid aside Proust whom I keep on reading. I also love John Cowper Powys. You have probably read him? I do wish you would come to Europe. Do not the young people go there? They must be going there?

Thanks also for your evaluation of modern criticism.

We have spring and birds and all that, they start up at 5 a.m. I expect yours are deafening too. I hope Miss Marple is well, and that soon you will be swimming in your pool. I hope dear Al is well, and can enjoy the tax work. John sends lots and lots of love. Lots and lots of love from me to you and Al. Forgive late communication. Ever

I

I am very upset about Ireland – sorry that swine Gerry Adams got loose in USA.

To Michael Hamburger.

30 Charlbury Road
[1994]

Dear Michael, thank you so much for your letter, please excuse late reply, have been away (not far!). I am so sorry you have been ill (also teeth etc.)

---

1 He was chair of the Booker Prize judging panel that year.

and trust you are now better. About Franz. *Message to Planet* not connected with him. But Franz was absolute goodness, absolute being, absolute love – his loss was terrible. Beyond words. I loved him so much. He loved Canetti very much, and admired him. I am sad to hear of Canetti being unpleasant to him (hurtful jokes). Franz introduced me to Canetti. Canetti is not anywhere in my novels, by the way! I would not want to 'copy' people, I invent them.

I love your Hölderlin translations[1] and your preface. I mention Hölderlin in a novel I am writing.[2] My German was once fairly good but is now *not* so good! I am very grateful to you – do keep in touch. With thanks and love –

Iris

To Simon Kusseff, concerning a fiftieth anniversary service held in Bulgaria marking the death of Frank Thompson.

30 Charlbury Road
[1994[xviii]]

Dear Simon,

Thank you very much for your letter – I was very moved indeed to know of the gathering in memory of Frank. I had not heard about it. I am so glad to see your text. (I expect you have seen my poems.) It is all so moving and so near, all this memory of Frank. *Thank you* so much – all my very best wishes, to you

Yours
Iris

To Harry Weinberger.

30 Charlbury Road
[30 August 1994]

Dearest Harry, thank you very much for your letter which expresses so explicitly my own feelings about the situation of art. Sometimes one may feel quite *dazed* – is one moving into a new era? It makes one sick. There are still exhibitions of Bonnard etc. etc. etc. – Cannot people *see* – I mean the people

---

1 *Friedrich Hölderlin: Selected Poems and Fragments*, published that year.
2 *Jackson's Dilemma.*

are making money etc. – and feeling original and grand, smart with it – by presenting *junk, and,* as you say, those who ought to be setting up standards, intellect, respect for the past, learning from it etc. It is alarming. Even now in *schools* standards are falling. It is easier to get honours etc. – (at my dear old boarding school, where I leant Greek and Latin, there is no Greek, Latin is optional, technology is compulsory). Every girl has a word processor – well, I suppose it has to be! Anyway – all one can do is try in one's own space. [. . .]

Au revoir and much love

I

To Jeremy Adler, who had recently been appointed as professor of German and head of department at King's College, London and who had phoned Murdoch in August to tell her of Canetti's death on 19 August 1994. He later co-edited Franz Steiner's work and two books by Canetti.

30 Charlbury Road
[September? 1994]

Dear Jeremy,

Thank you very much for your letter about Canetti. I can imagine your grief – I was so glad that Johanna has carried it so well – and that he went so calmly.

How good that you are getting this *Chair* – these things are not easy to acquire! Well done, and onward!

I would be very glad to see you for lunch in London. I trust there can be an Oct–Nov date.

With love to you,

yours,

Iris

To Naomi Lebowitz.

30 Charlbury Road
[November 1994]

Dearest Nay, thank you so much for your most distinguished picture of the most distinguished Miss Marple. You are indeed a versatile girl. I love your usual graph paper. This always reminds me of (ages ago) in Paris with Raymond Queneau, he pointed me out Simone de Beauvoir in a restaurant. I composed a letter to her, after that. She replied, alas she could not see me, on graph paper. And I then never saw her. (Sartre I met in Brussels and had one long talk with.) [. . .]

I have not touched a computer. I don't even get to a typewriter. I am trying to write another novel but it has become very difficult and I may give it up. It is perhaps, in this respect, the end of the road. I love *Dombey and Son* (not read recently though). I've read and reread Tolstoy, Dostoevsky etc. Have I asked you if you know John Cowper Powys? I must return to Dickens. I've been reading Japanese novels (my Jap language is nil alas). I have tried and given up. Have you read Mishima?[1] [. . .]

MUCH LOVE TO YOU AND AL
from JOHN AND ME

To David Morgan, probably Murdoch's last letter to him.

30 Charlbury Road
[13 February 1995]

David dear, so glad see you after long time. The Turbo[2] took me briskly back to Oxford. I am glad that you are a *head of department*[3] – and that you work beside the dear Thames. There was much to talk about, for instance about Wales, and that you lived at Shirley, Birmingham. And the Battersea Shield.[4] (Red coral.) Hope you were well returning and on your bike. I like Proust versus the horse's foot.[5] (Also Shirley.) Poem:[6]

Said Tweed to Till,[7]
'What gars ye rin sae still',
Said Till to Tweed,
'Though ye rin wi speed, and I rin slaw,
For aye man ye kill, I kill twa'.

I do hope Angharad recovers and wants to go to the university. It is a very precious time. She *must* go.

1 Yukio Mishima (1925–70), Japanese author.
2 A fast diesel train running out of Paddington.
3 David Morgan had become head of part-time studies at Chelsea College of Art.
4 The Battersea Shield (*c.*350 – 50 BC), an ornate bronze shield not made for warfare but for spectacle, apparently entranced Murdoch when she and Morgan saw it together at the British Museum.
5 A hollow hoof in a stream near Birmingham that used to conjure up childhood memories for Morgan and that echoed Proust's involuntary memories of his past triggered by biting into a madeleine.
6 Morgan had asked her to recount the Northumbrian folk poem in which rivers boast of their drowning powers.
7 The Till is a tributary of the river Tweed.

Be well. You seem to be very well and full of power.
With love
Iris

So glad meet again!

To Naomi Lebowitz.

30 Charlbury Road
[February? 1995]

Dearest Nay,
   Please forgive this late Valentinish letter – we are so glad to have that *book,*[1]
many *thanks.* I began a letter and then *lost* it. I don't know where I am. I
am trying to *think.* And I believe I have got in on Oscar Wilde somehow, it
was about time.
   I am having trouble with my present novel – I fear that my power may
be failing. We are having amazing weather, blazing sunshine, storms, violent
rain, beautiful stars. (Recently the Thames flooded as never before, here too,
not at our doorstep however.) (The Thames has been having a lovely time.)
I hope you and Al are well – Al writing another novel – and you are still
busy in the university and other books. John still works in the college, though
he is supposed to be retired, they won't let him go. He enjoys teaching the
younger chaps, and fighting Derrida. (I expect *he* is getting on well in
USA.) [. . .]
   Why am I so tired? I hope I am not 'giving up'. I have still scarcely touched
my Christmas mail. Never mind. I hope you are having a beautiful springtime
– perhaps storms too? Much love to you, dear dear Nay – we wish you were
here – and to Al – ever
   Iris

To Sister Marian at Stanbrook Abbey.

30 Charlbury Road
[spring? 1995]

Dearest Lucy, please forgive late reply to your very interesting letter – I do
hope you are now physically better (you are of course spiritually well as

---

1 Naomi Lebowitz's *The Philosophy of Literary Amateurism.*

ever). Thank you for your mention of Franz Steiner, whom I loved so much
– such a sweet good man, but died so early.

I wish I had got to Tibet, when this would have been easier. Evidently
there are still monasteries! (The Chinese are devils.) 'And dogs!' Yes, anyway
it is better to be in England!

I am afraid I am not 'up to' ashes on rose-bed![1] Maybe you will tell me.
Do tell me also how really better you are – I hope you are not working too
hard. I have just finished a novel[2] (will be out Oct. Nov I think). I think I
don't really know what it is like! Much love to you my dear – ever Iris

To Jeremy Adler.

30 Charlbury Road
[spring 1995?]

Dear Jeremy,

I am so glad to hear from you and with the splendid news about Franz's
poems. I would be pleased to talk to you about Franz – alas how brief a
time I knew him. I did not think he would die, I could not believe it. I shall
be away on and off in the near future – later May would be good – perhaps
you could telephone me. Anyway we'll keep in touch, and we must have a
London meeting.

Thank you and with love,
dear Jeremy,
Iris

To Marjorie Boulton.

30 Charlbury Road
[29 July 1995]

Dearest Marjorie

Thank you so much for remembering my birthday and for the delightful
spotty jaguars, I love them *and* you! I expect you have been away in many
far lands, being Queen of Esperanto. I admire your *energy* and your *care* for
others. I feel there is some *magic* in Esperanto, it belongs to the whole world.
I have so occasionally heard you speaking it. (Not understanding of course.)

---

1 Probably refers to the memorial service held for Honor Tracy.
2 *Jackson's Dilemma.*

Alas, I have lost languages that I once knew. (Never knew them well anyway.) I wish I could start it all again. Thank you for your darling jaguars. Be *very* well and happy – au revoir and much love

    Iris

To Arthur Green, former undersecretary in the Northern Ireland Department of Education who served on the council of the British Council and who wrote nineteen entries for the new Oxford Dictionary of National Biography. *An Irish Protestant from County Down in Northern Ireland, he had a particular interest in Murdoch's genealogy.*[1]

30 Charlbury Road

9 August [1995?]

Dear Mr Green,

    Thank you for your interesting account of my family background, not all of which I knew about. On page 9, yes, *The Sea, The Sea* does not derive from an Irish background. And yes, *The Unicorn* is certainly set in County Clare (Burren Cliffs in Moher)! I note that on page 10 you say my mother and father were married in a Dublin registry office. I was long ago shown, by a connection of the family, the church in Dublin where they were married. Page 14, no derivation from a Robert Richardson, or from Ennis, Co. Clare.

    On page 15 you suggest that any identification with the Anglo-Irish is 'romanticism'. This not so. My mother's family tree, going back to 1619, and containing the record of the birth of Irene and Gertrude, names the house Crayhalloch, later called Oaklands, later called Drum Manor near Cookstown, Co. Tyrone, as the original family house. The coat of arms is described, also the family crest (a lion in a wreath of oak leaves) and the family motto, *Virtuti paret robur*. My mother showed me this document long ago and quoted the family motto, translating it as 'Virtue overcometh strength' (rather than the, I think, more beautiful, literal translation, 'Strength obeys virtue'). Effinghams and Coopers and Nolans appear in this genealogy and I used all these names in *The Red and the Green*.[2] I cannot now find my copy of the family tree, I think I gave it for safekeeping to my literary agents, and I think A. N. Wilson has seen it. It may be found in O'Hart's *Old Irish Families*.[xix] The latest, recent, fate of the family

---

1 Green sent his research into Murdoch's genealogy to Chatto & Windus, who passed it to the editors of the *Iris Murdoch News Letter* in which a slightly shorter version was published as 'The Worlds of Iris Murdoch' (Issue 10, December 1996).

2 Murdoch has misremembered here. The Effinghams, Coopers and Nolans appear in *The Unicorn*. 'Crayhalloch' becomes 'Grayhallock' in *An Unofficial Rose* and the family motto on Iris's mother's side is used in *The Green Knight*.

is certainly wrapped in mystery, especially the matter of the missing Effingham!
Thank you for your interesting researches – with all my best wishes to you,
    Yours
    Iris Murdoch

To Michael Levey, who had recently written with the news that Brigid Brophy had died on 7 August 1995.

> 30 Charlbury Road
> [mid-August 1995]

Dear dear Michael, thank you for your very moving letter – it was all so sudden, that she was gone – so beautiful, so brilliant, so loving, so witty, so brave. I am very sorry that I did not see her more often – I was thinking, I will see her – then I saw her lovely photograph in the paper. And so recently you were in Oxford bringing your brilliance and your greatness. We thought to see you in London, but will hope for later – I can imagine, and for *Kate*, give her love. I am involved briefly this week in some unusual radio and TV, and then we go to France for two to three weeks. After that I shall look for you – *I am very sorry* I have lost your home address –
    Much love and from John
    Iris

To Suguna Ramanathan.

> 30 Charlbury Road
> [24 August? 1995]

My dear girl, thank you for your wonderful letter – it is so full of the huge reality of India. India the largest and greatest of all – even though full of violence etc. etc. But it is full of civilisation, goodness, courage, nobility – I would go on and on! I have known Indian friends. Thank you for your descriptions of Ahmedabad and what goes on it. And Gandhi was there – he was from Gujurat. Talk Gujurati. And you teach at St Xavier's College, next door to the Jesuits. (How *tiny* England seems!) Campus of Indian Institute – only 250 out of 50,000. And you are on the Tropic of Cancer – a spiritual place. Summer 110–120, winter lovely cold with bright sun. And the cattle who own the roads. (I pause here in my joyful reflections about the cattle. In Delhi, in some of the more shabby quarters, in a street packed with people rushing about, an immense black bull was sitting calmly in the middle of the road.) Resume: you speak Tamil and Hindi – a bit of Gujurati – please excuse my excited imagination. You must be a queen there, many will come to you. I am very sorry about the vindictive girl – I hope she may change – or *disappear*. How interesting that your daughter is working in America – with baby in October – and you will go there. I am sure all will be very well.

Oxford is a quiet little town surrounded by calm countryside! (Have you huge mountains nearby –) I hope you will soon come to England. I *love* India, but I know so little – I am really imagining. It is a unique place in the whole world. The spirit is there. Of course religions can bring about catastrophe and evil. But there is a *steady spirituality*. What will happen to Europe, America, in the next century? What will happen to Christ? Christianity must change.

Be well in America. Come home.

Much love to you, my dear –

ever Iris

PS About Anne[1]

Her meeting with Christ connects with Julian of Norwich, whom you probably know about. [. . .]

Excuse in haste

I

To Michael Levey.

30 Charlbury Road
[early September 1995]

Michael dear, thank you very much for your letter. I was away in France and have only just read it. How much I wish I had come to see her in the later time – well –

About the books – how such a deep kind remembrance – Yes, I would like you to give me back the Latin Primer on long loan, and and [*sic*] the old Oxford edition of Aeschylus. I am glad that Kate and her family are so helpful. And I *thank you* for memories of the times with Brigid in the "Fulham area restaurants" – [. . .]

I grieve about those old times and about that has [*sic*] come up to the present. I saw you so briefly in Oxford. Oh so much – with much love to you

Your

Iris

1 The character of Anne Cavidge in *Nuns and Soldiers*.

To Michael Levey.

30 Charlbury Road
[September 1995]

Michael dear, thank you very much for sending those two books. I am glad of them and they are precious. How long ago. I am sorry I imagined you lived also in London – why should you! I do hope there are times when we can meet, and/or talk. I hope you may have times in London – you must be doing all sorts of things! I was so glad to see you in Oxford, perhaps you will be back here. I hope Kate and the children are flourishing, so much time has passed, yes the time – Be well, my dear –
 With much love
 Iris

To Sister Marian at Stanbrook Abbey.

30 Charlbury Road
[September? 1995]

Dearest Lucy,
 Please forgive my *blanc* pages, I mean just not the writing. I have been away etc. etc.[1] The autumn comes. I do hope that you are *better.* I picture you in hope. Indeed I have always been picturing you. (I think you are the greatest.) Tell me something. I have just finished a novel (called *Jackson's Dilemma*) which may come out soon. Would it be in order if I were to send you a copy? Are things changing, and how? (With you I mean.) I am tired and desiring another novel, which does not appear to me yet – perhaps it will now never appear. I think of the past, and you and me in the past.
 So much love
 I
 Please forgive all this stumbling –

---

1 The Bayleys visited Thailand in August 1995.

Iris Murdoch died on 8 February 1999. During her illness she was cared for at home by John Bayley, with the help and support of good friends including Philippa Foot, Marjorie Boulton, Peter Conradi, Jim O'Neill, Audi Villers and Julian Chrysostomides. During her last days at Charlbury Road, Philippa Foot was the only person with whom Murdoch could be left in John Bayley's absence. She spent her final days in Vale House, a nursing home for dementia sufferers in Oxford where, according to a letter written by John Bayley to Murdoch's childhood friend Ann Leech, she died peacefully in his arms. In accordance with her wishes, no one attended her cremation or was present at the scattering of her ashes at Oxford Crematorium. There was no memorial service.[xx]

DIRECTORY OF NAMES AND TERMS

Ady, Peter Honorine (1914–2004)
Peter Ady was a student at Lady Margaret Hall, Oxford, later becoming tutor and then fellow in economics at St Anne's. Murdoch met the bisexual and unconventional Ady when she took up her post as a philosophy tutor at St Anne's in 1948 and they became close over the next few years, occasionally taking holidays together in France. The relationship developed and in 1952 Ady declared her love for Murdoch. Although during the late 1950s Murdoch's involvement with Margaret Hubbard and Brigid Brophy displaced her love for Ady, they remained friends and Murdoch was a great comfort to her following the death of two nieces. Ady went on to become an important consultant and adviser to several major banks and government bodies.

Anscombe, Elizabeth (1919–2001)
Anscombe – known professionally as G. E. M. Anscombe – read Mods and Greats at St Hugh's College, Oxford, graduating in 1941. She was then awarded a research fellowship for postgraduate study at Newnham College, Cambridge, where Wittgenstein, whose work had inspired her as an undergraduate, was teaching. She became one of his closest friends and a translator of and an authority on his work. In 1953 she gave Murdoch a copy of her translation of his *Investigations*. After Anscombe's fellowship at Cambridge ended, she was awarded a research fellowship at Somerville College, Oxford, where she taught until 1970, at which point she became professor of philosophy at Cambridge University. Other than her seminal translations of Wittgenstein's writings into English, her most important philosophical work was her monograph *Intention* (1957) which was described by the analytical philosopher Donald Davidson as the best treatment of the subject since Aristotle. Murdoch's relationship with Anscombe was rather uneasy; while admiring her intellect and her seriousness, she was not drawn to her personality. There was also an element of emotional tension between the two women, Murdoch describing Anscombe as 'an old friend-foe of mine' in a letter to Queneau in 1959. Their friendship survived, however, and in 1993 Murdoch dedicated *Metaphysics as a Guide to Morals* to Anscombe.

Balogh, Thomas (1905–85)

Thomas Balogh was born in Budapest and educated in law at the Péter Pázmány University of Sciences, Budapest. He went on to study economics at the University of Berlin and spent 1927–8 as a Rockefeller fellow at Harvard University. From 1931 he lived in England, becoming a lecturer in economics at University College London between 1934 and 1940, then a tutor at Balliol College, Oxford. A fierce and brilliant man, he taught Philippa Bosanquet from 1942 and soon became her lover. By 1943, however, Murdoch was in thrall to Balogh and had taken Philippa's place, leaving the latter with a sense of betrayal. Cruel and cavalier, Balogh caused Murdoch much pain and she ended the relationship in 1944. Fiercely anti-Communist, he might have influenced Murdoch's decision to leave the Communist Party. He went on to become a senior adviser to all six of the post-war Labour governments and was economic adviser to his close friend Harold Wilson. He was made a life peer in 1968, taking the title Baron Balogh of Hampstead.

Bayley, John (1926–2015)

Born in India and educated at Eton, John Bayley won a scholarship to read history at New College, Oxford. However, the Second World War intervened and he joined his father's regiment, serving until 1947. Returning to England he read English at New College and, after further postgraduate study at Magdalen College, was elected English fellow at New College in 1954. In 1974 he became the first Warton Professor of English at Oxford, a post he held until his retirement in 1992. His books of literary criticism – which included *The Characters of Love* (1960), *Tolstoy* (1968), *Pushkin* (1971), *Hardy* (1978), *Shakespeare and Tragedy* (1981) and *The Short Story* (1988) – were aimed at the general reader and are clearly and elegantly written. Like Murdoch, whom he married in 1956, he was committed to what he saw as the moral purpose of fiction and deeply distrusted structuralism and post-structuralism. Having published the well-regarded novel *In Another Country* in 1955, he abandoned writing fiction for many years but returned to it later in life. His book *Iris: A Memoir* (1998), which documented Murdoch's decline into Alzheimer's disease, became a best-seller and was made into a film, *Iris*, directed by Richard Eyre. After Murdoch's death in 1999, he married Audi Villers and spent a great deal of time during the last fifteen years of his life on the island of Lanzarote.

Beauvoir, Simone de (1908–86)

Novelist, existentialist philosopher, feminist and partner of Jean-Paul Sartre, Simone de Beauvoir had a great impact on the young Murdoch who discovered her work in 1945 and admired both her intellect and her unorthodox lifestyle. After studying philosophy at the Sorbonne, de Beauvoir went on to establish herself as a freelance writer and as one of France's foremost intellectuals. The emphasis on freedom, responsibility and ambiguity that permeates most of de Beauvoir's work reflects the core themes of existential philosophy. Her novels *L'invitée* (1943) and *Les mandarins* (1954) were well received but it was *Le deuxième sexe* (1949) that brought her international fame. This book, which contains the famous line 'One is not born, but rather becomes, a woman', adapts Hegel's concept of the Other in order to explore the oppression suffered by women. *Le deuxième sexe* was not translated into English (as *The Second Sex*) until 1953 but Murdoch read the book in French in its year of publication and introduced it into her teaching at St Anne's. She was also very taken during the late 1940s with the existentialist notion of *mauvaise foi* or 'bad faith' – i.e. acting inauthentically due to the pressures of society and conformism – promulgated by both de Beauvoir and Sartre. In April 1957 she wrote to de Beauvoir in Paris, asking to meet her, but the French author politely refused.

Behaviourism

A movement in psychology that flourished during the 1950s, behaviourism included proponents such as B. F. Skinner, who focused on external behaviour and believed that the inner world of the mind was of no importance. For behaviourists, human beings were merely conditioned into their behaviours by environmental stimuli. Murdoch, who argued that the inner life and emotions (such as desire and jealousy) affect the way we see the world and impact on our moral decisions and our actions, rejected what she saw as the behavourists' limited and mechanical approach to understanding human interactions. In her first academic papers presented in the early 1950s she questioned behaviourism and challenged the way it had been used by philosophers such as Wittgenstein and Gilbert Ryle.

Bosanquet, Philippa: see Foot, Philippa

Boulton, Marjorie (1924–)

Marjorie Boulton went up to Somerville in 1941 where she read English and met Murdoch. She went on to become an author, poet and teacher of English literature, publishing a widely used series of introductory texts on literary studies. She was principal for twenty-four years at Charlotte Mason College at Ambleside in the Lake District before turning to full-time research and writing. She became an expert in Esperanto and was president of two Esperanto organisations. Murdoch was intrigued by Esperanto and learnt it well enough to be able to discuss its merits and failings with her friend, although it slipped from her mind as she grew older. Marjorie Boulton was one of the lifelong friends who helped provide John Bayley with respite from caring for Murdoch during her last years, and she devoted much affection and time to her.

Brophy, Brigid (1929–95)

Brigid Brophy was a novelist, critic and campaigner for social reform. She attended St Paul's Girls' School and won a scholarship to read Classics at St Hugh's College, Oxford, from which she was sent down for drunkenness and raucous behaviour. She was acting, she later wrote, 'in the belief that I had more to learn by pursuing my personal life than from textual emendation, with the result that the authorities could put up with me for only just over a year'. A brilliant, unconventional and experimental author of fiction she also wrote non-fiction in which she expressed her strong political views. From a young age, she spoke openly about her own bisexuality; a dynamic campaigner, she fought on a number of issues ranging from public lending rights for authors, to vivisection, which she strongly opposed. She was passionately fond of music, especially opera and Mozart, and published the very successful *Mozart the Dramatist* in 1964. Her first novel, *Hackenfeller's Ape* (1953), won the Cheltenham Literary Prize in 1954; Iris Murdoch's debut novel *Under the Net* was runner-up. In 1954 Brophy married the art historian Michael Levey (later director of the National Gallery 1973–86) and they had a daughter, Kate, born in 1957. Brophy and Murdoch became very close during the 1960s and their love affair had a strong intellectual and emotional impact on Murdoch's life. Brophy's *Flesh* (1962) was dedicated to Murdoch, who encouraged her writing. In *Baroque 'n' Roll* (1987), Brophy wrote about her struggle with multiple sclerosis, diagnosed in 1984.

Brown, Rachel: see Fenner, Rachel

Camus, Albert (1913–60)

Born and educated in Algeria, the French journalist, author and philosopher's deep concern with questions of individual freedom contributed to the development of existentialism in France. However, he denied that he was an existentialist even though he was frequently described as such during his lifetime. Previously Communist, then anarchist, and then a member of the French Resistance during the Second World War, Camus became a pacifist in the 1950s and devoted himself to human rights. His best-known works include *L'Étranger* (1942; translated as *The Outsider*) and *La peste* (1947; translated as *The Plague*). In these and many other works he expresses his idea of the absurd – the result of our desire for clarity and meaning in a world that offers neither. He was awarded the Nobel Prize in Literature in 1957. Murdoch discovered Camus's work in the mid-1940s and read it with admiration. Although her enthusiasm for *La peste* was contested by Queneau's criticisms of both the man and the novel, she continued to engage with Camus's fiction and philosophy, including him in her talks on French existentialist authors for the BBC Third Programme in 1950.

Canetti, Elias (1905–94)

Born into a Sephardic Jewish family in Bulgaria, Canetti moved with his family to Manchester in England when he was six years old so that his father could join his brothers-in-law's business. After his father's unexpected death a year later, Canetti and his two brothers were taken by their mother to live in Austria; subsequently the family moved to Zurich, where they lived from 1916 to 1921, and then to Frankfurt. Canetti went back to university in Vienna and graduated in 1929 with a degree in chemistry. However, his primary interests during his student years became philosophy and literature, and he began to write. In 1938 Canetti moved to London with his wife, Veza (Venetiana) Taubner-Calderon, where he stayed until the 1970s. Canetti spent the last twenty years of his life mostly in Zurich with his second wife, Hera Buschor. His mature works include *Masse und Macht* (1960, translated as *Crowds and Power* in 1962), a novel, *Die Blendung* (1935, translated as *Auto da Fé* in 1946), and a memoir, *Party im Blitz; Die englischen Jahre* (published posthumously in 2003 and translated as *Party in the Blitz* in 2005). Canetti was awarded many prizes, including the Nobel Prize in Literature in 1981. A brilliant, volatile and possessive man, Canetti had a huge influence on Murdoch, both intellectually and emotionally, and for many years she was in thrall to him. Through her relationship with him she learnt much about power and obsession and she drew on his character and her feelings for him when creating the many male enchanter figures who haunt her novels. Appropriately, she dedicated *The Flight from the Enchanter* to him in 1956.

Cochrane, Roly (Rollin) (1939–2002)

A graduate of Seattle Pacific University and Stanford University, Roly Cochrane then moved to Europe to continue his language studies. He first wrote to Iris Murdoch in the mid-1980s and they began a correspondence that lasted until she was no longer able to write letters. He settled in Amsterdam where he worked as a translator and wrote a novel, *Facing Reality*, which was never published, but Murdoch admired the book and discussed it with him in her letters. Murdoch met Cochrane only once, in Amsterdam in October 1986; this was a romantically charged friendship sustained almost entirely by 'living on paper'. In 1991 Cochrane was hit by a lorry and suffered irreparable damage to his hips and legs, as well as loss of long-term memory.

Conradi, Peter J. (1945–)

Peter J. Conradi wrote his doctoral thesis on Iris Murdoch's fiction and philosophy and is now one of the foremost authorities on her life and work. He is author of *Iris Murdoch: The Saint and the Artist* (1986) and editor of *Existentialists and Mystics: Writings on Philosophy and Literature* (1997). He is also author of *Iris Murdoch: A Life*, the authorised biography of Iris Murdoch, published in 2001. He edited and introduced *Iris Murdoch: A Writer at War, Letters & Diaries 1938–46* (2010) and is adviser to the *Iris Murdoch Review* to which he contributes articles and reviews. Conradi shared with Murdoch a deep interest in Buddhism and his *Going Buddhist: Panic and Emptiness, the Buddha and Me* was published in 2004. His most recent book is *A Very English Hero: The Making of Frank Thompson* (2012). He is an emeritus professor of English at Kingston University and is adviser to the Iris Murdoch Archive Project. He is also honorary research fellow at University College London and was made a fellow of the Royal Society of Literature in 2011. Conradi and his partner, Jim O'Neill, became close friends with Murdoch and John Bayley and in her last years they spent many happy times with them at Conradi's home in Radnorshire.

Deconstruction

Deconstruction is a form of philosophical and literary analysis that is derived from structuralism and is linked to post-structuralism and postmodernism: it challenges the attempt to establish any absolute meaning in a literary text. Basing itself in language analysis, it seeks to 'deconstruct' the ideological biases (gender, racial, economic, political, cultural) and traditional assumptions that deconstructionists believe infect all histories, as well as philosophical and religious 'truths'. Deconstruction is based on the premise that much of human history, in trying to understand and then define reality, has led to various forms of domination – of nature, of women, of the poor, of homosexuals, etc. It is also a method of interpretation whereby a constant deferral of meaning is granted to the signifier or linguistic unit, which therefore cannot be finally and fully stated or grasped. This position was seen as a liberation, but in turn led to accusations of relativism and danger from the idea of there being 'nothing outside the text'. In philosophy deconstruction was associated with Jacques Derrida, and in literary theory with Paul de Man. Deconstruction gained ascendancy in some university literature and continental philosophy departments in the USA and Europe, predominantly in the 1980s.

Derrida, Jacques (1930–2004)

Derrida was one of the leading figures in the field of twentieth-century continental philosophy. He taught at some of the finest academic institutions in France including the Sorbonne, the École Normale Supérieure, the École des Hautes Études en Sciences Sociales, as well as at the University of California, Irvine, and was visiting professor at many other European and American institutions. His famous early works, particularly *Of Grammatology* (1967), were highly influential in establishing contemporary continental philosophy as a significant force in the fields of literature, philosophy and cultural studies. While liking the man, Murdoch was deeply suspicious of work that, in theory, undermines the unity of language and consciousness and reduces the self to a cipher in a linguistic network that 'speaks' the individual. As in her criticism of Wittgenstein, Murdoch felt Derrida was in danger of propounding a linguistic idealism that diminished the inner moral life.

Dickens, Charles (1812–70)

Murdoch greatly enjoyed reading Dickens and shared his love of London. She returned frequently to his novels throughout her life, admiring his ability to combine humour with darkness and his use of fiction as an instrument of moral purpose. By the time she was in her sixties and rereading his work, he shared a pedestal with Dostoevsky and Tolstoy as one of her favourite writers. Her late long novels in particular, such as *The Philosopher's Pupil* (1983), *The Book and the Brotherhood* (1987) and *The Message to the Planet* (1989), which carry clear moral agendas and which are capacious and amusing but also serious and profound, indicate his influence on her work.

Dostoevsky, Fyodor (1821–81)

Like Dickens and Tolstoy, Dostoevsky was one of Murdoch's favourite novelists and she often returned to his work. As a young woman she was no doubt attracted to the element of existentialism and the evocation of demonic powers in the Russian writer's work; later she was perhaps drawn more to his focus on suffering and his concern about the loss of faith in God in the modern world. She included *The Brothers Karamazov* (1880), a novel rich in philosophical ideas, in the list of 'books which an educated person must have read' that she sent to David Morgan in November 1964. Peter J. Conradi has suggested in *Iris Murdoch, A Life* that her best novels, with their fantastic realism, concentrated time-schemes and their interest in sadomasochism and moral anarchy, owe much to Dostoevsky.

Dunbar, Scott (1934–2006)

Scott Dunbar met Iris Murdoch in 1966 when she was teaching at the Royal College of Art and he was a postgraduate student at King's College, London where he was writing a thesis on philosophy and religion. He returned to Canada on completion of his studies, where he found work in Montreal as a teacher. Dunbar occasionally published articles in theological journals and was also very interested in, and published on, bioethics. He later moved to Toronto in 1997, only to return to Montreal unemployed. A profound thinker and skilled writer, Scott became one of a group of gay male friends who were important to Murdoch and who included John Simopoulos, Roly Cochrane, Andrew Harvey and Peter Conradi. Although they met only infrequently when Dunbar visited England on vacation, Murdoch was very fond of him and particularly appreciated his kindnesses to her mother.

Ethics

Ethics, also known as moral philosophy, is a branch of philosophy that concerns itself with what is good for the individual and for society and with decisions that are important in everyday life. It covers: how to live a good life; the rights and responsibilities of the individual and of a society; the language of right and wrong; and how to make moral decisions in certain situations. Our concepts of ethics derive from various religions, philosophies (in the West, the work of Plato and Aristotle, for example) and cultural practices. They underpin judgements and debates on topics such as abortion, civil rights and euthanasia. There are various moral systems within the philosophical study of ethics, including Kantian 'deontology', that judges the morality of an action on how far it adheres to a set of rules; 'consequentialism' (for example the utilitarianism of Jeremy Bentham that judges moral action on its consequences, including pleasure, economic well-being and the lack of suffering); and 'virtue ethics', which develops the idea of good actions by looking at the way virtuous people express their inner goodness in the things that they do. The last system greatly interested Murdoch. In the field of ethics tensions exist between moral absolutists, who argue that there are universal moral rules that apply to everyone, and moral relativists who point out that different cultures and different periods in history have produced different moral rules. The study of ethics does not provide right answers but it can clarify the bases on which we make decisions in response to difficult moral dilemmas.

Existentialism

A philosophical movement that emphasises the existence of the individual as a free responsible agent who determines development through acts of will. It tends to be atheistic (although there is a strand of Christian existentialism deriving from Kierkegaard), to disparage scientific knowledge, and to deny the existence of objective values, stressing instead the reality and significance of human freedom and experience. Existentialism was developed mainly in the twentieth century by philosophers such as Martin Heidegger, Jean-Paul Sartre, Albert Camus and Simone de Beauvoir although the work of some earlier writers, such as Dostoevsky, Nietzsche and Kierkegaard, can be described as existentialist. When Murdoch first heard Sartre speak in Brussels in 1945 she was excited by his ideas and swept away by his charisma but became critical and suspicious of what she saw as his over-reliance on will. Her first book, *Sartre: Romantic Rationalist*, a pioneering study of his novels, was published in 1953. By the time she wrote *The Sovereignty of Good* in 1970 her criticism had become stringent: 'we are not isolated free choosers, monarchs of all we survey, but benighted creatures sunk in a reality whose nature we are constantly and overwhelmingly tempted to deform by fantasy'.

Fenner, Rachel (née Brown) (1939–)
Rachel Brown was born in Scarborough and studied for her first degree at the Wimbledon School of Art. She was awarded a place at the Royal College of Art in London in 1962 where Iris Murdoch was her supervisor for a dissertation entitled 'William Blake and the Problem of Dualism'. Despite the difference in years, Murdoch and Brown became close friends although Murdoch made it clear that she could not reciprocate her student's desire for a more intimate, physical relationship. After her marriage to Frank Fenner in 1965, Rachel often turned to Murdoch for advice and emotional support; in turn, she provided Murdoch with practical help, often driving her about London. Her correspondence with Iris Murdoch began in May 1964 and lasted until the mid-1970s by which time Fenner was preoccupied by her work and bringing up two young sons, although she and Murdoch continued to keep in touch by telephone. She went on to become a noted sculptor, painter and environmental artist. Her paintings are largely inspired by the coastal landscapes of Pembrokeshire and Dorset.

Foot, M. R. D. (1919–2012)
Michael Richard Daniell Foot was educated at Winchester College and New College, Oxford, where he read PPE and met Murdoch. He joined the Royal Artillery when the Second World War was declared. He fell in love with Murdoch during the early 1940s, recalling in later life that she was 'absolutely captivating: she had personality and that wonderful Irish voice. Practically everyone who was up with Iris fell for her'. He pursued her for months before she agreed to become his lover in 1943. However, she soon became besotted with Thomas Balogh and treated Michael Foot badly, ending their relationship in early 1944. In June 1944 Foot was transferred to the staff of the Special Air Services brigade, an international unit containing battalions of soldiers from the countries of occupied Europe. Sent abroad in August 1944 to track down a notorious Gestapo officer, he was quickly captured by the Germans but soon returned to England, weak and wounded, in a prisoner-of-war exchange; by the end of the war he was a major. He married Philippa Foot (née Bosanquet) in June 1945. After the war he taught at Oxford for eight years and then became professor of modern history at Manchester University, leaving in 1975 to become director of studies at the European Discussion Centre. He also became the official historian of SOE. He and Philippa Foot separated in 1959 and divorced soon after. After what Murdoch described as 'the quadrilateral tale' of sexual intrigue between herself,

Philippa Bosanquet, Foot and Thomas Balogh, her relationship with Foot became difficult and was to remain strained.

Foot, Philippa (née Bosanquet) (1920–2010)
Philippa Foot graduated in 1942 from Somerville College, Oxford where she had been a contemporary of Iris Murdoch. It was here the two women established a friendship that was to endure – despite a few difficult patches – for the rest of their lives. Murdoch, unsure of her own ability, often felt slightly intimidated by Philippa's brilliance and thought of her as an older sister in whom she could confide. After graduating, Philippa Bosanquet took up a post in London as an economics research assistant and for two years she shared a flat in Buckingham Gate with Murdoch. In 1945, after marrying M. R. D. Foot, she was awarded a graduate scholarship at Somerville. In 1949, Philippa Foot became a fellow at Oxford and held the post of vice principal of Somerville College from 1967 for two years. From the mid-1960s onwards she often spent her winters in America as a visiting professor, while remaining a resident fellow at Somerville. In the late 1960s and 1970s she held visiting professorships at Cornell, MIT, UCLA, Berkeley and the City University of New York, before settling at the University of California in Los Angeles in 1976, where she became Griffin Professor of Philosophy in 1988. Throughout these years Murdoch and Foot kept in close contact by letter and managed to see each other fairly regularly. Murdoch and John Bayley sometimes visited her on their trips to the United States and Foot re-established contact when she returned to Oxford for spring or summer vacations. Murdoch dedicated her novel *The Red and the Green* (1965) to Foot, who in turn dedicated her book *Virtues and Vices* (1978) to Murdoch. Foot published *Natural Goodness* in 2001, after fifty years of reflection on the topic, and an important collection of papers, *Moral Dilemmas*, in 2002. Murdoch may well have had Philippa Foot in mind when she created the character of Paula Biranne in *The Nice and the Good*. In the more advanced stages of her illness, when care from anyone other than her husband troubled and embarrassed Murdoch, John Bayley noted gratefully that she could still go out alone to lunch 'with such an old friend as Philippa Foot'.

Fraenkel, Eduard (1888–1970)
Born and educated in Germany and having lost his post at Göttingen University under the anti-Semitic laws passed in 1933, Fraenkel emigrated to Britain. He settled first in Cambridge but in 1934 took up the chair in Latin at Corpus Christi College, Oxford, where he became well known for his lectures on Horace and his influential seminars on Aeschylus's *Agamemnon*. These seminars had a powerful effect on those present, particularly Murdoch who attended whilst an undergraduate. She also had private tuition from

him; Fraenkel adored Murdoch and he was for her, though terrifying, 'a vision of excellence' and his scholarship was a profound influence. She later noted that 'the best teachers are a little sadistic'. She seems to have drawn on Fraenkel when creating the classical scholar, Levquist, in *The Book and the Brotherhood*.

Hart, Josephine (1942–2011)

Josephine Hart, Lady Saatchi, was born in Mullingar, County Westmeath, Ireland. She moved to London in 1964 and became a director of Haymarket Publishing. She was a theatrical producer and initiated the friendship with Murdoch by suggesting that *The Black Prince* should be adapted for the stage. She was a founder of Gallery Poets and ran the Josephine Hart Poetry Hour, delivering weekly poetry readings at various locations in the West End. She also organised highly successful poetry readings at the British Library. She married Maurice Saatchi, co-founder of the advertising agency Saatchi & Saatchi, in 1984. She wrote six novels and is best remembered for *Damage* (1991), which was made into a film in 1992. Murdoch read the drafts of both *Damage* and *Sin* and, recognising Hart's talent, encouraged her to continue writing fiction.

Hegel, Georg (1770–1831)

A German philosopher and a major figure in German idealism, Hegel's historicist and idealist account of reality revolutionised European philosophy. Maurice Merleau-Ponty, the French philosopher, claimed that 'All the great philosophical ideas of the past century – the philosophies of Marx and Nietzsche, phenomenology, German existentialism, and psychoanalysis – had their beginnings in Hegel'. Initially baffled by Hegel's philosophy, Murdoch came to see its importance, writing in 1952 that his work, which 'contains possibly more truth than any other, is unread and unstudied here' and lamenting the fact that his investigation of human consciousness was a topic no longer considered valid in British philosophical circles. According to Hegel, concepts do not remain fixed in our minds but alter and develop as we mature. Murdoch's sense that our understanding of the world and of words (such as 'love') changes as we age because our moral concepts change owes much to Hegel's work.

Heidegger, Martin (1889–1976)

The German philosopher Heidegger, who worked in the tradition of Husserl and Kierkegaard, is widely recognised as a key thinker in the fields of existential phenomenology (which looks at the individual as a dynamic responsive phenomenon in organic relationships with others) and philosophical hermeneutics (the theory of textual interpretation in the area of philosophy).

His *Sein und Zeit* (1927, published as *Being and Time* in 1962), which so excited Murdoch in 1949, opens with a quotation from Plato's *Sophis*, which states that philosophy had neglected 'being' because it had been considered as obvious, rather than as worthy of question. Here Heidegger concentrates on the kind of existence peculiar to human beings. His 'Dasein' is what differentiates humanity from the material surroundings within which individuals find themselves; it is a condition characterised by anxious awareness of the future, contains the necessity of both choice and death, and has ethical consequences: authentic life is possible only if death is resolutely confronted and freedom exercised with a sense of its essentially creative nature. Initially excited by Heidegger's emphasis on consciousness, Murdoch became critical of his later work which ignored the concept of goodness and was remote from the concerns of ordinary life. However, she returned often to Heidegger and over six years during the 1980s spent much time writing a book on his work which she decided not to publish, feeling unsure of its coherence. The Heidegger manuscript, part of which has been published in Justin Broackes's *Iris Murdoch, Philosopher* (2012), is held in the Peter Conradi Archive at Kingston University. In *The Time of the Angels*, written just after Murdoch had read *Being and Time*, Carel Fisher is reading the book; in *The Sovereignty of Good* she refers to Heidegger as 'possibly Lucifer [. . .] in disguise'. In her last novel, *Jackson's Dilemma*, Edward Lannion is struggling to write a book on Heidegger. One of the issues Murdoch wished to explore philosophically was the question of why Plato and Heidegger (whose relationship with Nazism has been widely debated) were attracted to tyrants.

Hicks, David (1916–91)

David Hicks graduated in PPE from Worcester College, Oxford, in 1938. He and Murdoch had a brief flirtatious relationship that year which was curtailed by Hicks's rejection of her in early 1939 and his decision to study for a Diploma of Education at Birmingham, after which he joined the British Council. He was posted to Egypt for six months during the war and from Egypt was sent to Cyprus, Iran and Czechoslovakia. During these years he and Murdoch corresponded frequently, her letters gradually changing from affectionate interest to declarations of love; they spent ten days in London together in November 1945, at which point they decided to marry. However, soon after this decision Hicks met and fell in love with Molly Purchase; Murdoch responded generously to the letter that abruptly ended their engagement. Hicks married Molly in 1946 and they returned to England where, shortly after the subsequent collapse of their marriage, he became a pioneer of Teaching English as a Foreign Language. In 1953 he married Katharine Messenger and they had two children, Barney and Tom. Unable to continue travelling with the British Council because of poor health, he began work for the BBC and became editor of *English by Radio* on the World Service, ending his career with a highly successful listeners' queries show. Hicks and Murdoch kept in touch throughout his life, remained good friends and met fairly frequently in London.

Husserl, Edmund (1859–1938)

The German philosopher asserted that in order to study the structure of consciousness, one has to distinguish between the act of consciousness and the phenomena at which it is directed (consciousness is always consciousness of *something*). This proposition is a key element in the method of phenomenology – the philosophical study of the structures of experience and consciousness – which Husserl helped to establish in the early twentieth century. From the *Ideen* (1913) onward, Husserl concentrated on the ideal, essential structures of consciousness, a topic that greatly attracted Murdoch who had read the *Ideen* and who initially intended to write her thesis at Cambridge on Husserl's work. In his later writings Husserl abandoned the realistic distinction between the mind and its independent objects and leaned towards a view of consciousness as all-embracing. By the mid-1980s Murdoch had come to see his ideas as outdated and criticised the philosopher Richard Wollheim for drawing on it in his own work.

James, Henry (1843–1916)

An American author who spent much of his life in England, James was an early modernist whose work greatly influenced the modernists who followed him, especially Virginia Woolf. Many of his novels, including *The Portrait of a Lady* (1881), *The Wings of the Dove* (1902) and *The Ambassadors* (1903), examine the impact of Europe and corrupt Europeans (the Old World) on innocent Americans (the New World). His method of writing from the point of view of a character allowed him to explore issues related to consciousness and perception and it was no doubt this aspect of his style that first attracted Murdoch, who absorbed his novels during the 1940s. A letter to Frank Thompson, written in November 1943, reveals her enormous admiration for James; reading his work undoubtedly taught her much about how to represent in fiction the workings of the mind. In particular she was greatly influenced by his commitment to the idea of the 'sister arts' – that the writer and painter should 'explain and sustain each other'. The literary, philosophical and painterly analogies that are interwoven in James's writing became the paradigm for her own experimentation in using the visual arts to expand the representation of consciousness in her novels. By the 1960s the English novelist Angus Wilson was describing Murdoch as a neo-Jamesian, and Conradi suggests that *Nuns and Soldiers* (1980) draws on the plot of James's *The Wings of the Dove*, pointing out that it twice echoes the final line of that novel, 'We shall never be again as we were'. Murdoch once said that 'the only person I know [who] has influenced me is Henry James'.

Kant, Immanuel (1724–1804)

Kant's work in metaphysics, ethics and aesthetics influenced all subsequent philosophy. In his *Critique of Pure Reason* (1781) Kant argued that our experience is not of things as they are in themselves (or noumena); but only of things as they appear (or phenomena). Other important works included *Critique of Practical Reason* (1781), *Critique of Judgement* (1790), and *Metaphysics of Morals* (1797). Having found Kant's work 'a complete mystery' when a student at Oxford, Murdoch reread his *Metaphysics of Morals* in 1946 and taught his work at St Anne's. In 1959 she wrote a paper on Kant's aesthetics entitled 'The Sublime and the Good', calling for a revision of the Kantian sublime. Much later she re-engaged with Kant in her 1982 Gifford Lectures. While recognising his importance, she argued that his work, like that of Hume, had left philosophy with 'too shallow and flimsy an idea of personality' and that 'One may regret or deplore the way in which Kant's dualism seems to deny to human passion any access to the spiritual'. In January 1987 she was to tell a young Indian admirer that the three philosophers who had influenced her most were Plato, Kant and Wittgenstein.

Kierkegaard, Søren (1813–55)

Danish philosopher, theologian and poet, Kierkegaard – often claimed to be the first existentialist thinker – stressed the importance of choice and commitment to the idea of a 'constant self', that is a self maintained by a belief or pursuit that gives unity and continuity to one's life. Using various pseudonyms, he wrote a great deal on Christian ethics and the nature of faith but was fiercely critical of the practice of Christianity as a state religion. Believing that God comes to each individual mysteriously, he focused on the inner life and the spiritual world, declaring that although they cannot be observed empirically, they are vital aspects of being: 'Christianity teaches that the way is to become subjective, to become a subject'. The phrase 'leap of faith' is attributed to him, by which he meant the act of believing in or accepting something intangible or unprovable without empirical evidence. Kierkegaard's main publications on religion include *Fear and Trembling* and *Either/Or*, both published in 1843. His work had a strong influence on later theologians, philosophers and writers, including Ludwig Wittgenstein, Karl Barth, Jean-Paul Sartre, Franz Kafka, Rainer Maria Rilke and W. H. Auden. Murdoch started reading Kierkegaard's work in 1944 and later drew on it when formulating her ideas about individual choice. In 1946 she considered writing a thesis on him, lamenting that 'no one reads Kierkegaard' in England. She introduced his work to her students at St Anne's and lectured on it in a course entitled 'Moral and Political Pictures of Man' during her years at the Royal College of Art. She took much pleasure in the late 1970s and early 1980s from the fact that her American friend, Naomi Lebowitz, was writing a book entitled *Kierkegaard: A Life of Allegory* (1985).

Klatschko, Lucy (1918–2001)
Lucy Maria Klatschko, the youngest child of a Russian emigré father and a Latvian mother, was born in Zurich and brought up as a Protestant. Her father's death in 1920 left the family penniless and thereafter she was cared for by relatives in Vienna, Paris and London. Her guardian was Dr René Paresce, a half-Italian, half-Russian emigré, who was the London correspondent of *La Stampa*, the Italian daily newspaper published in Turin. Under his care, Lucy attended South Hampstead High School and in 1935 won a scholarship to read French and German at Somerville College, Oxford, where she met Murdoch. After graduation in 1939 she did numerous jobs, including working in a munitions factory, schoolteaching, the Civil Service and then becoming a sales assistant in a bookshop. She converted to Catholicism in 1952 and eighteen months later entered Stanbrook Abbey, Worcester, as Sister Marian. She there became an 'extern sister', liaising between the abbey and the outside world; her life as a nun is briefly portrayed by Honor Tracy in *The Heart of England* (1983). Murdoch was deeply interested in Lucy Klatschko's life as Sister Marian, feeling a certain envy of the cloistered life, and the two women corresponded until Murdoch's death in 1999.

Kreisel, Georg (1923–2015)
An Austrian-born mathematical logician, Kreisel came from a Jewish background. Just before the annexation of Austria by Nazi Germany in March 1938 his family sent him to England where he studied mathematics at Trinity College, Cambridge, receiving his degree in 1944. During the war he also worked for the Admiralty, studying the effects of waves on the harbours designated for the Normandy landings. After the war he returned to Cambridge and received his doctorate in mathematical logic. Kreisel and Murdoch became close friends, having met at Cambridge in 1947 during Murdoch's year of study there. Murdoch recognised him as having a brilliant mind, and Wittgenstein, who was then teaching at Cambridge, declared Kreisel to be the most able mathematician-philosopher he had ever met. He went on to teach at Reading University and the Institute for Advanced Study in New Jersey; later he worked at the University of Paris and at Stanford University where he was appointed a professor in 1962, remaining on the faculty until he retired in 1985 as professor emeritus of logic and the foundations of mathematics. He and Murdoch stayed in touch for many years and they would meet in Oxford or London when he visited England. Murdoch

dedicated her 1971 novel *An Accidental Man* to Kreisel and drew on his ideas about philosophy when creating Guy Openshaw in *Nuns and Soldiers* and Marcus Vallar in *The Message to the Planet*.

Lebowitz, Albert (1922–)

Having attended Washington University in the 1940s, Albert Lebowitz received his law degree from Harvard University in 1948 and then practised as an attorney in St Louis. He was an editor of *Perspective* magazine from 1961 until 1975. He is the author of two novels, *Laban's Will* (1966) and *The Man Who Wouldn't Say No* (1969) as well as a number of short stories, including a collection entitled *A Matter of Days* (1989) for which Murdoch provided a jacket endorsement: 'These elegant and moving stories, which are really one story, compose a very beautiful, very funny, very frightening picture. The animals add their silent, surreal commentary upon the sad absurdity of human things.' His most recent book is a work of non-fiction entitled *The Legal Mind and the Presidency* (2013). Murdoch and John Bayley met him and his wife Naomi when visiting the USA in April 1972; they found they had much in common and a lively friendship developed. Although they stayed with the Lebowitzes several times in St Louis, the friendship was sustained mainly through letters.

Lebowitz, Naomi (1932–)

Until she retired Naomi Lebowitz was Hortense and Tobias Lewin Professor in English and Comparative Literature at Washington University, St Louis, and is now an emeritus professor there. Her books include *The Imagination of Loving: Henry James's Legacy to the Novel* (1965), *Humanism and the Absurd in the Modern Novel* (1971), *Italo Svevo* (1978), *Kierkegaard: A Life of Allegory* (1985), *Ibsen and the Great World* (1990), *Dickens, Manzoni, Zola and James: The Impossible Romance* (with Ruth Newton) (1990), *The Philosophy of Literary Amateurism* (1994), and an English translation from the Danish of *Lucky Per* by Henrik Pontoppidan (2010). Murdoch's letters convey her pleasure that Naomi Lebowitz wrote on authors and philosophers she much admired, such as Henry James, Kierkegaard and Dickens, and the two women clearly enjoyed exchanging views on art, literature and politics.

Leech, Ann (1919–2009)

The youngest daughter of a Manchester doctor, Ernest Leech, and his wife Mary, Ann Leech started at Badminton school on the same day as Murdoch, each girl having gained one of the first two open scholarships to Badminton in 1932. They remained friends for the rest of their lives. Leech went up to Girton College, Cambridge. She closely followed the political career of Indira Gandhi, who was also a contemporary at Badminton school, collecting many articles and cuttings about her. She devoted the greater part of her adult life to a career in housing, with a special interest in homeless mothers and children.

Levey, Michael (1927–2008)

After reading English at Exeter College, Oxford, Michael Levey became an English art historian, joining the National Gallery in 1951. In 1954 he married the novelist Brigid Brophy, and their daughter Kate was born in 1957. His publications include *A Concise History of Painting: From Giotto to Cézanne* (1962), *From Rococo to Revolution* (1966), *Early Renaissance* (1967) and *Painting at Court* (1971). From 1963 to 1964 he was Slade Professor of Fine Art at Cambridge University; he then became deputy keeper of the National Gallery in 1966, keeper in 1968, and director from 1973 to 1986. He was knighted in 1981. He relinquished his directorship to care for his wife who had been diagnosed with multiple sclerosis in 1984.

Lidderdale, Henry ('Hal') (1917–92)

Murdoch met Hal Lidderdale while he was reading Greats at Magdalen College, Oxford. After graduation he joined the Royal Scots Fusiliers and was based in Egypt during the Second World War, achieving the rank of captain. After the war, he joined the British Council and became a lecturer in English. He was posted to Afghanistan and then to Athens; he later worked in Salonika in Greece where he taught his wife-to-be, Maria ('Mary') Coumlidou. They married in 1960 and, after a brief spell in London, moved to Port Harcourt in Nigeria and later to Uganda. They had two children, Norah and Demetrius. In 1971 they returned to London, where Lidderdale worked at the British Council headquarters. Throughout his postings, Lidderdale kept in touch with Murdoch by letter and, as one of her Oxford friends with whom she was not romantically embroiled, she often confided in him about her emotional turmoils; their friendship lasted until he died.

Logical Positivism

A philosophical movement that arose in Vienna in the 1920s and asserted the primacy of scientific observation and knowledge in assessing the truth of statements of fact. It rejected metaphysical and subjective argument as meaningless because its propositions are not demonstrable. Logical positivism differs from earlier forms of empiricism and positivism in holding that the ultimate basis of knowledge rests upon public experimental verification rather than personal experience. It suggests that the 'great unanswerable questions' about substance, causality, freedom and God are unanswerable because they are not genuine questions at all. All genuine philosophy is a critique of language and its result is to show the unity of science, meaning that all genuine knowledge about nature can be expressed in a single language common to all the sciences.

MacKinnon, Donald (1913–94)

Donald Mackenzie MacKinnon was assistant in moral philosophy, Edinburgh University 1936–7; fellow and tutor in philosophy, Keble College, Oxford 1937–47 (during which time he taught Murdoch); Regius Professor of Moral Philosophy, Aberdeen University 1947–60; and Norris-Hulse Professor of Divinity, Cambridge University 1960–78. His books include *Christian Faith and Communist Faith* (1953), *Borderlands of Theology* (1968), *The Problem of Metaphysics* (1974) and *Explorations in Theology* (1979). A rather eccentric individual, he would sometimes give male undergraduates tutorials from his bath. He was a charismatic figure who inspired many students, including Philippa Foot (then Bosanquet) and Murdoch, who thought he was a brilliant teacher and who admired and loved him. He profoundly influenced Murdoch's thoughts on moral philosophy, particularly through his insistence that philosophy should be central to how one lives one's life. However, in the mid-1940s the relationship became tense and difficult, probably because MacKinnon's wife thought he had become too intimate with one of his favourite students. In 1965 Murdoch and MacKinnon became completely estranged when he took exception to the character of Barnabas Drum in *The Red and the Green*, in whom he recognised elements of himself. Murdoch was deeply upset by the rift. The marriage between Bill and Nan Mor in *The Sandcastle* may owe something to the MacKinnons' marriage, and the character of the philosopher Rozanov, in *The Philosopher's Pupil*, was perhaps based partly on MacKinnon.

Marcel, Gabriel (1889–1973)

French philosopher, playwright, critic and leading Christian existentialist, Marcel's work focuses on the modern individual's struggle in a technologically dehumanising society, a topic of great interest to Murdoch. She found his *Journal métaphysique* – which comprised his philosophical notebooks – 'full of gems' and in February 1947 described his work as 'profound and suggestive'. Murdoch met Marcel in London in 1947 when they took part in the same lecture series on modern philosophy. Her reservations concerning Sartre's philosophy, expressed in *Sartre: Romantic Rationalist* (1953), owed much to Marcel's attack on Sartre. She shared Marcel's optimism in finding contingency an occasion for grace rather than horror and agreed with his objections to existentialism, which included the criticism that it was excessively individualistic and failed to place enough value on either the Other, or on love.

Midgley, Mary (née Scrutton) (1919–)
Educated at Downe House School in Berkshire, Mary Scrutton went on to
Somerville College, Oxford, where she studied Mods and Greats between
1938 and 1942 and became good friends with Murdoch. After leaving Oxford
she worked first for the Civil Service and then as a schoolteacher before
returning to Oxford in 1947 to pursue postgraduate study. She taught briefly
at Reading University before marrying Geoffrey Midgley in 1950, then moved
north to teach philosophy at Newcastle University. On the publication of
her first book *Beast and Man* in 1978, for which Murdoch wrote the cover
recommendation, she became regarded as an important moral philosopher.
Her publications also include *Animals and Why They Matter* (1983), *Evolution
as a Religion* (1985), *Science as a Salvation* (1992), *The Ethical Primate* (1994) and
a memoir, *The Owl of Minerva* (2005).

Merleau-Ponty, Maurice (1908–61)
Strongly influenced by Husserl and Heidegger, the French phenomenological
philosopher Merleau-Ponty argued that perception plays a vital part in our
understanding *of* the world as well as engaging *with* the world. He thus
emphasised the role of the body in acquiring knowledge, thereby departing
from the long philosophical tradition of seeing consciousness as the source
of knowledge, and concluding that the body and that which it perceived
could not be disentangled. Less celebrated than Sartre during his lifetime,
Merleau-Ponty's work has had a significant impact on the fields of contemporary cognitive science, psychology and medical ethics because of its
emphasis on embodied consciousness. Merleau-Ponty was on the editorial
board of *Les temps modernes* to which Queneau often contributed and which
Murdoch enjoyed reading in the late 1940s. In 1948 Murdoch read his
Phénoménologie de la perception (1945) with enthusiasm, and the following year
wrote to Queneau saying how much she would like to meet the French
philosopher. There may well be an echo of Merleau-Ponty's work in *The
Nice and the Good* in the narrator's comment: 'We think with our body and
its ghostly yearnings and its shrinkings and its ghostly walkings'.

Morgan, David (1939–)
The eldest of three brothers, David Morgan enjoyed a childhood filled with
books and won places at a public school and a grammar school. However,
he had a troubled and rebellious boyhood and adolescence that resulted in
expulsion from school and a spell in a home for maladjusted boys at age
eleven, followed by hospitalisation for psychiatric problems in Birmingham
at the age of seventeen. Rejected as unfit for National Service, he devoted
his time to writing and drawing. He then became a student at Birmingham
School of Art and in 1961 won a place at the Royal College of Art where,

in 1964, he met Iris Murdoch, who supervised his dissertation. Their friendship lasted for thirty years and Murdoch was a strong and positive influence on Morgan, helping him to educate himself and giving him confidence in his abilities. He went on to publish concrete poetry – in which the typographical arrangement of words is as important in conveying meaning as the words, rhythm and rhyme – and made discoveries in the field of 3D fractals. From 1974 to 2010 he taught at the Chelsea College of Art; his final post was director of part-time studies at the University of the Arts (Chelsea). In 2010 Kingston University Press published his memoir of Iris Murdoch, *With Love and Rage: A Friendship with Iris Murdoch*.

Oakeshott, Michael (1901–90)

Having been educated at Gonville and Caius College, Cambridge, Michael Oakeshott went on to become a philosopher and political theorist who wrote on the philosophies of law, aesthetics, education and religion. He became a fellow of Gonville and Caius in 1925 and, having published a number of books on political theory, is now regarded as one of the most important conservative thinkers of the twentieth century. He joined the British Army in 1941 and was on active service in Europe with the intelligence unit Phantom, which had SAS connections, but did not fight on the front line. In 1945, he returned to Cambridge and then went on to Nuffield College, Oxford, in 1947. In 1948 he became professor of political science at the London School of Economics where he stayed until his retirement in 1969. Although she did not share his political views, Murdoch admired Oakeshott because he valued experience over rationalism and this informed his definition of conservatism and his view of the state. Indeed, she introduced his theory of the state, alongside the work of Thomas More and Rousseau, to her students at St Anne's when exploring concepts of Utopia with them. On a personal level, she was very close to him in 1950 and then between 1958 and 1963.

Plato

A philosopher and mathematician in classical Greece, Plato is considered a central figure in the development of philosophy in the Western tradition. Murdoch first came into contact with his philosophy at Oxford but rejected what she saw as his dialectical tricks. She next encountered him through reading Simone Weil in 1947, and her engagement with his ideas became a seminal influence on her philosophy and novels. She engaged most significantly with his suspicion of art; his allegory of the cave; and his definition of Eros. Murdoch directly addresses Plato's and her own ambivalences about the nature of art in *The Fire and the Sun*, defending art against Plato's claim that it misleads by conducting a rigorous and convincing defence of it and finally granting art, and herself, a qualified victory. Plato's myth of the cave in the *Republic* provides her with an image through which to explore the pilgrimage from illusion to reality, and the novels abound with imagery of darkness and light that evokes the allegory of the cave. The two erotic dialogues *Phaedrus* and *Symposium* provide the terminology to describe Eros, the inner energy field that is a tension between two opposing forces, low Eros (blind, obsessive, mechanical desire) and high Eros (love of the highest good, and desire that is educated and refined so that it becomes dispassionate). Murdoch's concept of Até is derived from Simone Weil's view of Plato and is best explained by the Platonist Max Lejour in *The Unicorn*: 'Até is the name of the almost automatic transfer of suffering. The victims of power, and any power has its victims, are themselves infected. They have then to pass it on, to use power on others. This is evil'. Murdoch wrote two Platonic dialogues – *Art and Eros: A Dialogue About Art* and *Above the Gods: A Dialogue About Religion* (later published together as *Acastos*) – which debate all these ideas, the first of which was performed at the National Theatre in 1980.

Pliatzky, Leo (1919–99)
Educated at Manchester Grammar School and Corpus Christi College, Oxford, where he met Murdoch, Leo Pliatzky was one of her early admirers. In 1939, after receiving a first in Classical Mods at Corpus Christi, he served with the Royal Army Ordnance Corps and the Royal Electrical and Mechanical Engineers for five years. He returned to Oxford after the war and was awarded a first in PPE. He then spent some time working for the Fabian Society before joining the Civil Service in 1947. He spent 27 years in the Treasury from 1950–1977 when he left to take over as Permanent Secretary of State at the Department of Trade. He and Murdoch wrote to each other during the war, kept in touch afterwards and renewed their friendship much later when Murdoch was working at the RCA. He provided Murdoch with much useful information about the Civil Service which fed into several of her novels. He was knighted in 1977.

Proust, Marcel (1871–1922)
French novelist and essayist best known for his long novel in seven volumes, *À la recherche du temps perdu* (*In Search of Lost Time*, previously translated as *Remembrance of Things Past*), published between 1913 and 1927 and critically acclaimed as the definitive modern novel. Murdoch first read *À la recherche* in her early twenties and returned to it constantly, remarking in 1994 that 'I have laid aside Proust whom I keep on reading'. As a young writer, she would no doubt have been deeply interested in Proust's use of symbolism and in how a character's memory or inner contemplation of an event becomes more important in the novel than the event itself. In particular,

Proust's emphasis on the involuntary nature of memory – as encapsulated in the famous 'madeleine' episode, in which eating the small cake prompts vivid flashbacks to his childhood in the narrator's mind – would have intrigued an author who wished to find new ways of representing human consciousness in fiction.

Queneau, Raymond (1903–76)

French poet, novelist, artist and lyricist, Raymond Queneau earned his living by working for the Gallimard publishing house, where he began as a reader in 1938, rising eventually to become director of *L'encyclopédie de la Pléiade* in 1956. A precursor of the New Novelists in France, he wrote the novel *Le chiendent* (*The Bark Tree*) (1933) and twenty other books of poetry and prose, including *Zazie dans le métro* (1959), an experimental novel, much of which is written in colloquial language as opposed to 'standard' written French. The book was made into a film by Louis Malle in 1960. One of his most influential works, *Exercices de style* (1947), tells the same story in ninety-nine different ways, and Murdoch's letters record her great excitement on reading it. He was a member of the surrealist group in Paris for a few years in the 1920s, and in 1960 co-founded with François le Lionnais the Oulipo movement (**Ou**voir de **Li**ttérature **Po**tentielle – The Workshop for Potential Literature). The main aim of this experimental group was to trigger innovative writing through the imposition of certain formal constraints, for example, by replacing every noun in a text by the seventh noun after it in the dictionary. He met Iris Murdoch in February 1946 when he gave a lecture in Innsbruck, where she was stationed with UNRRA. His experiments with language and novel-writing had a profound influence on Murdoch's first novel, *Under the Net*, which is dedicated to Queneau. She visited him several times in Paris, declaring her love for him more than once, but Queneau, married with a wife and child, managed to keep the friendship platonic. Their correspondence ran for over thirty years and Queneau kept her letters, in their envelopes, neatly filed in several shoeboxes.

Ramanathan, Suguna

Murdoch's correspondence with Suguna Ramanathan began in the 1980s. Ramanathan retired as head of the English department and dean of the arts faculty, St Xavier's College, Ahmedabad, India, in 2002. She greatly admired Murdoch's work and contacted her by letter in the early 1980s, at which point the two women began a correspondence. Her publications include *Iris Murdoch: Figures of Good* (1990) and *The Novels of C. P. Snow: A Critical Introduction* (1978).

Robson, William Wallace (1923–93)

A noted literary scholar and critic, Wallace Robson, went up to New College, Oxford, to read English in 1941. After graduation, he taught for a short time at King's College, London, before returning to Oxford in 1946 as lecturer and then fellow of Lincoln College. In the early 1950s he and Murdoch became lovers and at one point were unofficially engaged. His volatile character, however, and Murdoch's increasing interest in Franz Steiner, led her to end the relationship in 1952. He left Oxford in 1970 to become Professor of English at Sussex University and in 1972 moved to Edinburgh as Masson Professor of English Literature. In the early 1950s he helped F. W. Bateson found the Oxford journal *Essays in Criticism*, and he was a founding editor of *The Cambridge Quarterly*. His published work includes *Critical Essays* (1966), *Modern English Literature* (1970), *The Defence of Literature* (1982) and *Critical Enquiries* (1993).

Sartre, Jean-Paul (1905–80)

French philosopher, novelist and literary critic, Sartre was one of the key proponents of existentialism and phenomenology and a leading figure in the French Communist Party and Marxist thought. He studied for a degree in philosophy at the École Normale Supérieure where he met Simone de Beauvoir, who was to become his lifelong companion. Central to Sartre's philosophy is the idea that individuals are 'condemned to be free' and that, because there is no God, we are each responsible for our actions: there is no higher authority to which we should answer. Individual 'authenticity' can only be earned through lived experience and by rejecting the influences of society and conformism; failure to do so results in *mauvaise foi*, or bad faith. His novel *La nausée* (1938) presented his philosophy of existentialism in fictional form and was followed by *The Road to Freedom*, envisaged as a series of novels written in response to the Second World War, the Nazi occupation of France, and the concept of *engagement* or political commitment. *L'age de raison (Age of Reason)* and *Le sursis (The Reprieve)* were published in 1945 and *La mort dans l'âme* in 1949. Sartre never completed the fourth novel, *La dernière chance (The Last Chance)*. Murdoch met Sartre in Brussels in 1945 and was excited by his emphasis on consciousness and value. However, she soon had reservations about his work and by the autumn of 1947, when she gave two lectures on Sartre in London, was able to present a more balanced overview of his fiction and philosophy, noting that he diminished both the inner life and the importance of the 'Other' and that he overprivileged individual will. She finally came to see existentialism as excessively individualistic and its promise of freedom as false. She nonetheless recognised Sartre as an important thinker, introducing his work to her students at St Anne's and later at the Royal College of Art, and speaking on Sartre on the BBC Third

Programme in 1950. By April 1952 she had finished her book *Sartre: Romantic Rationalist* (1953) and her quarrel with his philosophical ideas fed into her writing of *Under the Net*. In 1987 Murdoch wrote a revised introduction to the second edition of *Sartre: Romantic Rationalist*, for which she re-read all his publications.

Scrutton, Mary: see Midgley, Mary

Sister Marian of Stanbrook Abbey: see Klatschko, Lucy

Smallwood, Norah (1904–84)
Murdoch's editor at Chatto & Windus for many years, Norah Smallwood joined the publishing company as a secretary in 1936 and quickly worked her way up, becoming a partner in 1945. She was appointed to the board of Chatto & Windus when it became a limited company in 1953, and became chairman and managing director in 1975. She retired in 1982. As she was Murdoch's editor for her first novel in 1954, Smallwood saw most of her subsequent work through the press, and became a close friend whom Murdoch trusted and respected.

Steiner, Franz (1909–52)
Born in a suburb of Prague, Steiner studied at several universities, could speak many languages and obtained his doctorate on the history of Arabic language roots from the Charles University of Prague in 1935. With the rise of Nazi anti-Semitism, he moved to London in 1936 to study at the London School of Economics. In 1938 he moved to Oxford where he registered for a research degree at Magdalen College. At this time he became good friends with Elias Canetti, to whom he had been introduced in Vienna. He was appointed a lecturer in social anthropology at Oxford in 1949, a position he held until his premature death. His main publication was a collection of essays entitled *Taboo*, based on lectures he had delivered at Oxford. Murdoch had briefly met Steiner in 1941 and they became friends in 1951. They had much in common, including a love of Kafka, with whom Steiner strongly identified. By March 1952 they were in a romantic relationship and it is possible that they would have married had it not been for his sudden death from heart failure later that year. Like another of her lovers who died young, Frank Thompson, Steiner was to become idealised in Murdoch's memory. She recalled him in 1988 as 'one of Hitler's victims' (his parents had died in the concentration camp at Treblinka) and as 'gentle and good'. Conradi has suggested that Steiner inspired the creation of Peter Saward, in *The Flight from the Enchanter*, the Dachau survivor Willy Kost in *The Nice and the Good*, and the Christ-like Tallis Browne in *A Fairly Honourable Defeat*.

Thompson, Frank (1920–44)

Frank Thompson was educated at Winchester College and New College, Oxford, where he read Mods and Greats. There he met Iris Murdoch, whom he described as his 'dream-girl', and who persuaded him to join the Communist Party. In 1939 he left Oxford in order to volunteer for the army. On becoming a member of Phantom and then SOE, he served in North Africa, Syria, Iraq, Sicily, Serbia and Bulgaria. In charge of an SOE mission in 1944, he was executed in Bulgaria with some partisans and villagers who had helped them. His younger brother, E. P. Thompson (1924–93) – who became the distinguished socialist historian and writer best known for his *The Making of the English Working Class* (1963) – published two books in memory of Frank: *There is a Spirit in Europe* (1947) and *Beyond the Frontier* (1977). Like Franz Steiner, who also died prematurely, Thompson became idealised in Murdoch's mind; in a letter to the journalist Sue Summers in 1988, she described both of them as 'full of truth and pure in heart'.

Virtue Ethics

The discipline of virtue ethics emerged within the landscape of moral philosophy in the second half of the twentieth century and challenged the dominance of two traditions: Kantian 'deontology', that judges the morality of an action on how far it adheres to a rule or rules (Kant's Categorical Imperative), and the utilitarianism of Bentham that judges moral action on its consequences, including pleasure, economic well-being and the reduction of suffering. In 1958 Elizabeth Anscombe critiqued these two dominant ethical discourses because both were founded in the idea of 'obligation'. Virtue, she claimed, should be understood as part of what Aristotle called 'human flourishing' – that is, what constitutes human goodness – independently of obligation. Anscombe turned philosophy in the direction of psychology, claiming that psychology had to be right before philosophy could be right and referred back to the Aristotelian idea that the best life for an individual consists of the exercise of the virtues. Thus virtue-ethics philosophers provide theories according to which one should act virtuously by referring to the rationality of virtue itself and debating *why* one should live a virtuous life. The consideration of character, virtue ethicists argued, should be taken into account as well as, or even instead of, one's actions when morality is considered. Murdoch's contribution to virtue ethics is succinctly summarised in *The Sovereignty of Good* (1970) and is the work most frequently referenced in this field. Murdoch set out to extend Anscombe's position by giving a broad account of the virtues against a Platonic background. She went further in dislodging the Kantian ideal of the rational person and introduced her own critique of Sartrean existentialism in the process. Murdoch's picture of a virtuous person is someone who pays sustained attention to the Other. Such attention results in behaviour that is not chosen or willed but comes out of a natural respect for the Good. Murdoch refused to separate ethics from real lived experience: she argued that it should inform our whole mode of being.

Weil, Simone (1909–43)

French Jewish philosopher, teacher, Christian mystic and political activist, Weil was deeply afflicted by the suffering of others, and her death from tuberculosis during the Second World War was hastened by malnutrition because she refused to eat more than the minimal rations given to soldiers fighting at the front line. She became attracted to the Christian faith in 1935 and experienced a spiritual ecstasy in the Basilica of Santa Maria degli Angeli in Assisi in 1937, and another in 1938 on reading George Herbert's 'Love III'. Her love of Christ did not preclude respect for other religious traditions including Buddhism and Hinduism, which she also believed contained elements of revelation. Weil was the only female amongst Murdoch's philosophical teachers and her work is fundamental to Murdoch's moral philosophy. She first came across Weil's work at Cambridge in 1947 where she read *The Need for Roots* and *Gravity and Grace*. Murdoch was compelled by Weil's idea of the moral life as a task that demands the slow destruction of the ego and later adopted the idea of 'attention' to the 'Other' as a path to goodness. Weil's claim that the moral task is to perceive reality as it is, and expel 'obsession, prejudice envy, anxiety, ignorance, greed, neurosis', moved her deeply. In the margin of her copy of Weil's *Intuitions pré-Chrétiennes* Murdoch has written 'Virtue is knowledge/is attention'. Weil also speaks of moral levels above which the moral pilgrim cannot proceed without danger, a fact amply demonstrated by many characters in Murdoch's novels. Murdoch thought that Weil's account of 'afflictions' (*malheur*), that were passed on by all but the saintly, were more relevant to the horrors of the age than Sartre's questioning of the 'authenticity' of suffering. Weil's idea that it is beauty, by means of love, that liberates the soul from being captive in the cave, articulated in Weil's *Notebooks*, worked its way directly into the heart of Murdoch's moral philosophy.

Weinberger, Harry (1924–2009)

Born in Berlin into an affluent Jewish family, Harry Weinberger left Germany when the rise of Nazism prompted the family's move to Czechoslovakia in 1933. This relocation brought only temporary safety and Weinberger escaped to England on the last Kindertransport leaving Czechoslovakia in 1939. Following a spell boarding at Amersham College in Buckinghamshire, he became an apprentice toolmaker. He joined the Queen's Own Royal West Kent Regiment in 1944 and transferred to the Jewish Brigade with which he served in Italy. After the war his ambition to become a painter took him to Chelsea School of Art in London and then to Goldsmiths College. However, the main influence on his work, as he acknowledged, was a fellow émigré, the painter Martin Bloch, who gave him private lessons. Weinberger taught art in schools before becoming a lecturer at Didsbury Teacher Training College in Manchester, eventually becoming head of painting at Lanchester Polytechnic in Coventry (now Coventry University). He became an accomplished and successful painter with many one-man exhibitions in Germany and the UK to his credit. He was introduced to Murdoch by Stephen and Natasha Spender in France in 1977. As he was both an artist and Jewish, Murdoch found him interesting immediately and they became firm friends, often visiting London galleries together. Murdoch was passionate about Weinberger's art and worked hard to get his paintings exhibited; she also wrote forewords for two of his exhibition catalogues (in 1988 and 1994). She owned several of his paintings, one of which she kept above her desk in her study at her last Oxford home.

Wittgenstein, Ludwig (1889–1951)

Austrian-born Ludwig Wittgenstein worked mainly in logic, the philosophy of mathematics, the philosophy of mind and the philosophy of language, and taught at the University of Cambridge from 1929 until 1947, succeeding G. E. Moore as professor of philosophy in 1939. In 1921 he published the *Tractatus Logico-Philosophicus* which was translated into English the following year; his *Philosophical Investigations* (translated by Elizabeth Anscombe), now regarded as a classic text, was published posthumously in 1953. Having rejected traditional metaphysical philosophy, in his early work Wittgenstein focused on the logical relationship between propositions and the world, believing that in providing an account of the logic underlying this relationship, he had solved all philosophical problems. In his later work, he rejected many of the ideas in the *Tractatus*, proposing instead that language gains its meaning through its embedded use in a social context. Murdoch was reading Wittgenstein's early work during the 1940s and focused on it during her postgraduate year at Cambridge. Much to her disappointment, Wittgenstein left Cambridge shortly after she arrived there in October 1947, although she did meet him. However, her tutor, John Wisdom, had been greatly influenced by Wittgenstein and she was also able to discuss his ideas with Elizabeth Anscombe, who was translating Wittgenstein's writings, and Yorick Smithies, one of his pupils. By the early 1950s Murdoch had engaged deeply with Wittgenstein's work, finding herself 'more and more astonished at the *Tractatus*', and was writing philosophical papers on his theories. Her first novel, *Under the Net*, takes its title from the *Tractatus* and echoes Wittgenstein's sense of language as the net of discourse that can separate us from the

world but that also connects us to it. Much later, she became more ambivalent about both the man and his work, seeing the latter as potentially
dangerous. In particular, she rejected his suspicion of the inner life and of
imagination, concerned that such a view of the individual can lead to a
mechanistic view of human behaviour. In this respect, she saw a relationship
between Wittgenstein's work and structuralism. Two of her later novels
directly reference Wittgenstein: Nigel in *Bruno's Dream* quotes from the
Tractatus, and *Nuns and Soldiers* opens with a conversation about him.

MURDOCH'S NOVELS AND
THEIR DEDICATEES

1954	*Under the Net*	Raymond Queneau
1956	*The Flight from the Enchanter*	Elias Canetti
1957	*The Sandcastle*	John Bayley
1958	*The Bell*	John Simopoulos
1961	*A Severed Head*	Undedicated
1962	*An Unofficial Rose*	Margaret Hubbard
1963	*The Unicorn*	David Pears
1964	*The Italian Girl*	Patsy and John Grigg
1965	*The Red and the Green*	Philippa Foot
1966	*The Time of the Angels*	Eduard Fraenkel
1968	*The Nice and the Good*	Rachel and David Cecil
1969	*Bruno's Dream*	Scott Dunbar
1970	*A Fairly Honourable Defeat*	Reynolds and Janet Stone
1971	*An Accidental Man*	Georg Kreisel
1973	*The Black Prince*	Ernesto de Marchi
1974	*The Sacred and Profane Love Machine*	Norah Smallwood
1975	*A Word Child*	Peter Ady
1976	*Henry and Cato*	Stephen Gardiner
1978	*The Sea, The Sea*	Rosemary Cramp
1980	*Nuns and Soldiers*	Natasha and Stephen Spender
1983	*The Philosopher's Pupil*	Arnoldo Momigliano
1985	*The Good Apprentice*	Brigid Brophy
1987	*The Book and the Brotherhood*	Diana Avebury
1989	*The Message to the Planet*	Audhild and Borys Villers
1993	*The Green Knight*	Ed Victor
1995	*Jackson's Dilemma*	Undedicated

See Valerie Purton, 'Iris Murdoch and the Art of Dedication' in the *Iris Murdoch Review* Vol. 1 No. 1 (28–37) for a discussion of the significance of Murdoch's dedications.

SOURCES OF LETTERS

Letters written by Iris Murdoch to the following individuals are held by the Iris Murdoch Archives at Kingston University Special Collections:
Marjorie Boulton
Brigid Brophy
Jonathan Burnham (as part of the Peter Conradi Archive)
Elias Canetti (as part of the Peter Conradi Archive)
Roly Cochrane
Peter Conradi (as part of the Peter Conradi Archive)
Scott Dunbar
Rachel Fenner
Philippa Foot
Arthur Green (as part of the Peter Conradi Archive)
Michael Hamburger (as part of the Peter Conradi Archive)
Simon Kusseff (as part of the Peter Conradi Archive)
Michael Levey
Hal Lidderdale
Margaret Lintott (née Orpen) (as part of the Peter Conradi Archive)
Lady Mary Ogilvie (as part of the Peter Conradi Archive)
Leo Pliatzky
Raymond Queneau
Wallace Robson
Sister Marian (Lucy Klatschko) (as part of the Peter Conradi Archive)
John Symonds (as part of the Peter Conradi Archive)
E. P. Thompson (as part of the Peter Conradi Archive)
Harry Weinberger

Letters written by Iris Murdoch to the following individuals are held by Special Collections and University Archives at Iowa University:
David Beams
Marshall Best
Frank Paluka

Letters written by Iris Murdoch to the following individuals are held by Special Collections, Reading University:
Jonathan Burnham
Carmen Callil
Norah Smallwood (and Leeds University Special Collections)
Jane Turner

Letters written by Iris Murdoch to Eduard Fraenkel *are held by the Library of Corpus Christi College, Oxford University.*

Letters written by Iris Murdoch to Josephine Hart *are held by Howard Gotlieb Archival Research Center at Boston University (copies kindly provided by Lord Saatchi).*

Letters written by Iris Murdoch to Jacquetta Hawkes *are held by the Special Collections, J. B. Priestley Library, Bradford University.*

Letters written by Iris Murdoch to the following individuals are held by the Bodleian Library Special Collections, Oxford University:
Isaiah Berlin
David Hicks
Katharine Hicks
Frank Thompson

Letters written by Iris Murdoch to the following individuals are held by the Special Collections, Washington University, St Louis:
Albert Lebowitz
Naomi Lebowitz

Letters written by Iris Murdoch to Ann Leech *are held by the Leech Family Archive, Chetham's Library, Manchester.*

Letters written by Iris Murdoch to David Morgan *are held by David Morgan. In addition, some letters have been reproduced, with David Morgan's permission, from* With Love and Rage: A Friendship with Iris Murdoch *(Kingston University Press, 2010).*

Letters written by Iris Murdoch to Michael Oakeshott *are held by the Archive Collections, London School of Economics and Political Science.*

Letters written by Iris Murdoch to Michael Rubinstein *are held by the Special Collections, Bristol University.*

Letter written by Iris Murdoch to Maurice Saatchi: *copy kindly provided by Lord Saatchi.*

Letters written by Iris Murdoch to The Times *are held by the British Library Newspaper Archive, the British Library, London.*

Letters written by Iris Murdoch to Georg Kreisel *are held by Special Collections, Stanford University, California.*

ABBREVIATIONS

References in the Notes to the following texts refer to the editions indicated and are abbreviated as follows:

Peter J. Conradi, *The Saint and the Artist: A Study of the Fiction of Iris Murdoch*, 3rd Edition (HarperCollins, 2001): **The Saint and the Artist**

Peter J. Conradi, *Iris Murdoch: A Life* (HarperCollins, 2001): **A Life**

Peter J. Conradi (ed.), *Iris Murdoch: A Writer at War, Letters & Diaries 1938–46* (Short Books, 2010): **A Writer at War**

Peter J. Conradi, *A Very English Hero: The Making of Frank Thompson* (Bloomsbury, 2012): **A Very English Hero**

Gillian Dooley (ed.), *From a Tiny Corner in the House of Fiction: Conversations with Iris Murdoch* (University of South Carolina Press, 2003): **Conversations**

Iris Murdoch, *Existentialists and Mystics: Writings on Philosophy and Literature*, ed. Peter J. Conradi (Chatto & Windus, 1997): **Existentialists and Mystics**

Iris Murdoch, *Metaphysics as a Guide to Morals* (Chatto & Windus, 1992): **Metaphysics as a Guide to Morals**

Iris Murdoch, *The Sovereignty of Good* (Routledge, 1970): **Sovereignty of Good**

Valerie Purton, *An Iris Murdoch Chronology* (Palgrave Macmillan, 2007): **Chronology**

NOTES

INTRODUCTION

i *Iris Murdoch News Letter*, No. 19, 21.

ii Murdoch, *Sovereignty of Good*, 76.

iii Don Cupitt, 'Iris Murdoch: A Case of Star Friendship' in Anne Rowe and Avril Horner (eds), *Iris Murdoch: Texts and Contexts* (Palgrave Macmillan, 2012), 11.

iv Interview with Biles in Dooley (ed.), *Conversations*, 64.

v Interview with Bellamy in Dooley (ed.), *Conversations*, 47.

vi Bran Nicol, *Iris Murdoch: The Retrospective Fiction* (Palgrave Macmillan, 1999 and 2004), 167–8.

vii Conradi, *A Very English Hero*, 224, 259, 312, 360.

viii Martha Nussbaum, 'When She Was Good' (review of Conradi, *A Life*), *New Republic*, 17 January 2002.

ix Maria Antonaccio, *A Philosophy to Live By: Engaging Iris Murdoch* (Oxford University Press, 2012).

x Murdoch, *Existentialists and Mystics*, 215.

xi A phrase used by Murdoch in a letter to Brigid Brophy dated 9 July 1967.

xii Murdoch, *Existentialists and Mystics*, 216.

xiii Biographical sources so far include: John Bayley, *Iris: A Memoir of Iris Murdoch* (Duckworth, 1998); John Bayley, *Iris and Her Friends* (Duckworth, 1999); John Bayley, *Widower's House* (Duckworth, 2001); Conradi, *A Life*; Jeffrey Meyers, *Remembering Iris Murdoch: Letters and Interviews* (Palgrave Macmillan, 2013); David Morgan, *With Love and Rage: A Friendship with Iris Murdoch* (Kingston University Press, 2010); Conradi (ed.), *A Writer at War*; Frances White, *Becoming Iris Murdoch* (Kingston University Press, 2014); A. N. Wilson, *Iris Murdoch As I Knew Her* (Hutchinson, 2003); *Iris*, directed by Richard Eyre (Miramax, 2001).

xiv Bayley, *Iris: A Memoir*, 40–1.

xv Whereas Murdoch's letters to David Hicks stop in February 1946 in *A Writer at War*, we have included a selection of her letters to him written up until his death in 1991.

xvi The Conradi Archive comprises the material amassed by Peter J. Conradi, while he was writing *Iris Murdoch: A Life,* and subsequent donations.

xvii There are thirty-one letters from Iris Murdoch to Canetti in the Zentralbibliothek Zurich, but Canetti's papers are closed until 2024.

xviii Published by Palgrave Macmillan (2014) and Cambridge Scholars Publishing (2014) respectively.

PART ONE

i Interview with Haffenden in Dooley (ed.), *Conversations*, 129.

ii From Murdoch's reminiscences of her time at the Froebel School (written in 1992), held in the Conradi Archive, Kingston University Special Collections, KUAS6/9/8.

iii Conradi, *A Life*, 57.

iv Conradi, *A Life*, 92.

v Conradi, *A Life*, 96, 612. For more letters to David Hicks written during the war years see Conradi (ed.), *A Writer at War*.

vi Conradi (ed.), *A Writer at War*, 177.

vii The 'Festival of Music for the People', described in this undated letter to Ann Leech, was held at the Albert Hall on 1 April 1939, which suggests that it was written during the first week of April 1939.

viii See Conradi (ed.), *A Writer at War*, 31–79 for a fuller account of this venture.

ix Conradi, *A Life*, 87, 141, 619.

x Conradi, *A Life*, 91, 147, 78. For more letters to Frank Thompson written up to his death in 1944 see Conradi (ed.), *A Writer at War*.

PART TWO

i Peter J. Conradi, '"The Guises of Love": The Friendship of Professor Philippa Foot and Dame Iris Murdoch', *Iris Murdoch Review*, No. 5 (2014), 17–28, 18.

ii Conradi, *A Life*, 138.

iii Letter (not included here) dated 26 September 1946.

iv Letter (not included here) dated 15 October 1946.

v Conradi, *A Life*, 170–1.

vi Raymond Queneau, *Journaux 1914–1965* (Éditions Gallimard, 1996), 585.

vii Letter (not included here) dated 21 April 1946.

viii Letter (not included here) dated 13 November 1943.

ix Letter (not included here) dated 8 January 1947.

x Conradi, *A Life*, 618.

xi Murdoch was being taught Russian at this time by a White Russian émigrée, Malvina Steen (Conradi (ed.), *A Writer at War*, 121). Frank Thompson had taken lessons in Russian while at Winchester College and continued to teach himself when at Oxford and during his war service (Conradi, *A Very English Hero*, 86–7, 227–8).

xii As Conradi points out, Lawrence 'was the man of action most admired by Iris's future philosophic heroines Simone Weil and Simone de Beauvoir' (*A Very English Hero*, 224).

xiii Conradi, *A Very English Hero*, 254–6.

xiv Conradi (ed.), *A Writer at War*, 14, and Conradi, *A Very English Hero*, 312.

xv This letter can be found in Conradi (ed.), *A Writer at War*, 161–3.

xvi See Conradi, *A Very English Hero*, for a full description of these events.

xvii Extract from a letter in the Bodleian Library written by David Hicks; all extracts from David Hicks's letters are reproduced with the kind permission of Tom Hicks.

xviii Søren Kierkegaard, *Concluding Unscientific Postscript* (1846), translated D. F. Swenson (Princeton University Press, 1941), 462n.

xix Letter undated, but written after Philippa Foot had visited Murdoch in London; *Les mouches* was broadcast on the Third Programme on Tuesday 29 July of that year.

xx Conradi, *A Life*, 254.

PART THREE

i   Letter (not included here) dated 29 October 1947.

ii   Letter to Queneau (not included here) dated 14 October 1947.

iii Letter (not included here) dated 29 October 1947.

iv   Conradi speculates that Canetti's 'radical atheism probably played its part in her leaving the Anglo-Catholic Metaphysicals in 1953', and an entry for January 1953 in Murdoch's journal reads: 'I shall have to remake my attitude to religion. (Am I excessively "open to influence"? Franz influenced me very much. Now C's influence operates in a rather different way.)' (*A Life*, 372.)

v   Conradi, *A Life*, 301.

vi   Conradi, *A Life*, 289.

vii Conradi, *A Life*, 310–12.

viii Conradi, *A Life*, 317–40.

ix   Conradi, *A Life*, 313–14.

x   Conradi, *A Life*, 314.

xi   Conradi, *A Life*, 344.

xii Julian Preece, *Guardian*, 7 February 2004.

xiii Conradi, *A Life*, 346.

xiv Conradi, *A Life*, 379, 377, 378.

xv   Conradi, *A Life*, 378.

xvi Eleven poems from Murdoch to Wallace Robson, written during these years, were published in *Iris Murdoch Review* 5 (2014), 8–16.

xvii Letter undated, but the remarks about the *Flying Enterprise* suggest it was written in early January 1952.

xviii Letter undated, but as Murdoch has just sent her 'little book on Sartre' (which was published in 1953) to the typist and is working on a paper entitled 'Nostalgia for the Particular', published in *Proceedings of the Aristotelian Society*, LII (1952), it was probably written in 1952.

xix Conradi (ed.), *A Writer at War*, 171.

xx   Conradi, *A Life*, 333.

xxi Conradi, *A Life*, 357–8.

xxii Conradi, *A Life*, 293.

xxiii Letter undated, but Murdoch's anticipated move from King Edward Street to 48 Southmoor Road in June 1953 suggests it was probably written in May of that year.

xxiv Conradi, *A Life*, 368.

xxv Both letters to Lucy Klatschko are undated but Conradi has suggested that they were written close together, probably in April 1954.

xxvi Conradi, *A Life*, 295.

PART FOUR

i   *Listener*, 16 May 1957, 80.

ii   Conradi, *A Life*, 427.

iii A. N. Wilson notes that 'Honor Klein was seen by many of [the Bayleys'] friends to resemble IM's friend Margaret Hubbard' (*Iris Murdoch As I Knew Her*, 93).

iv   Several of these essays were later collected together in Murdoch, *Existentialists and Mystics*.

v   See Justin Broackes's introduction to his *Iris Murdoch, Philosopher: A Collection of Essays* (Oxford University Press, 2012) for a good overview of Murdoch's development and career as a philosopher.

vi   *Guardian*, 24 October 2014.

vii   This larger case of documents is not yet in the public domain. Thanks to Kevin Sawar-Polley, who visited the National Archives on 27 October 2014, for this information.

viii Bayley, *Iris: A Memoir*, 106.

ix   Conradi, *A Life*, 399.

x   Conradi, *A Life*, 430.

xi   See Brigid Brophy, *Baroque 'n' Roll* (Hamish Hamilton, 1987), 6–7. The Authors' Lending and Copyright Society was incorporated on 23 March 1977 with its first Council of Management consisting of Brigid Brophy, Maureen Duffy, Ted Willis, Colin Spencer, Michael Levey, Elizabeth Jane Howard and Joyce Marlow. The Public Lending Right Act was passed by Parliament in 1979.

xii   Conradi, *A Life*, 486–7.

xiii Hubbard was often referred to by the Bayleys as 'the Chumman', a nickname deriving from '*Cumann na mBan*', Irish for 'Club of Women' (Conradi, *A Life*, 457). Conradi did not reveal the identity of the 'Chumman' in his biography of Murdoch but confirmed it as Margaret Hubbard in 2014 in '"The Guises of Love"', *Iris Murdoch Review* 5 17–28.

xiv See Conradi, '"The Guises of Love"', *Iris Murdoch Review* 5., 19.

xv   This letter can be read in its original French in Éliane Lecarme-Tabone and Jean-Louis Jeannelle (eds), *Simone de Beauvoir* (Éditions de L'Herne, 2012), 375. Thanks to Ursula Tidd for drawing it to our attention.

xvi Not her real name.

xvii Letter undated but '29.11.58?' written in another hand, probably Oakeshott's, on the envelope. Several other letters to Oakeshott included in this section are dated in this hand.

xviii Conradi, *A Life*, 457.

xix   Conradi, *A Life*, 429, 430.

xx   Conradi, *A Life*, 640.

xxi   Envelope postmarked 1960 but day and month illegible.

xxii Undated, but given the tenor of recent letters to Brophy, probably 1960.

xxiii According to Murdoch's 'Proof of Evidence' statement, these faults included Lawrence's tendency to theorise about sex in such a way as to interfere with his development of character and to render the novel 'occasionally absurd'. She also described *Lady Chatterley's Lover* as 'a propaganda novel: a fact which in this case does tend to diminish its literary value'. However, she praised the book as 'a serious attempt to deal with an important aspect of personality' and Lawrence's wish to 'purify the vocabulary of sex' as a 'worthy aim, especially at this time when all our values, including those relating to sexual behaviour, seem to be in a state of flux'.

xxiv Letter undated, postmarked 19 November but year illegible; possibly 1960.

xxv Raymond Queneau, 'A Severed Head par Iris Murdoch' (*inédit*), *Manuscrits et notes de Raymond Queneau (1903–1976): Articles, préface, textes publiés* <http://www.queneau.fr/> (D20_108) [accessed 21 September 2014].

xxvi Thanks to Alison Scott-Baumann, Justin Broackes and Ursula Tidd for help with interpreting this sonnet, and particular thanks to the last for helping us to understand its meaning.

xxvii Letter undated, but the Bayleys first went to the Griggs' holiday home in Scotland in July 1962.

xxviii Conradi, *A Life*, 458. Conradi notes that six pages of Murdoch's journal have been excised prior to this sentence.

xxix Conradi, '"The Guises of Love"', *Iris Murdoch Review* 5, 28.

PART FIVE

i   Conradi, *A Life*, 456.

ii   Priscilla Martin and Anne Rowe, *Iris Murdoch: A Literary Life* (Palgrave Macmillan, 2010), 73.

iii   Interview with Chevalier in Dooley (ed.), *Conversations*, 94. See also Martin and Rowe, *Iris Murdoch: A Literary Life*, 65–70.

iv   First given as a lecture at the University of Wales in 1962 and written up that year.

v   Murdoch, 'The Idea of Perfection', in *Sovereignty of Good*, 40.

vi   Conradi, *A Life*, 497, 650.

vii The college became a constituent college of the London Institute in 1986 and was renamed Chelsea College of Art and Design in 1989. The London Institute was granted university status and was renamed University of the Arts London in 2004. In 2013, the college was renamed Chelsea College of Arts.

viii David Morgan, *With Love and Rage: A Friendship with Iris Murdoch* (Kingston University Press, 2010).

ix   Conradi, *A Life*, 355.

x   Conradi, *A Life*, 289.

xi   Conradi, *A Life*, 483.

xii Conradi, *A Life*, 440.

xiii Letters (not included here) dated 4 January 1963 and 10 February 1963 respectively.

xiv Kingston University holds over 1,000 letters written by Iris Murdoch to Brigid Brophy in its Iris Murdoch Archives of which only a small fraction are included here.

xv   Before one trip in 1965 Murdoch wrote 'Proceed to Bath, go to Francis Hotel where Mrs B has booked room, then on to Hole in Wall where Mrs B has booked table (1.15), have lunch. (Suggest *soupe aux cresson, omelette fines herbes, crème brûlée*) and Mrs B will doubtless turn up at hotel later in day. (Do not wait in, go sightseeing.) (Wear shoes for *walking*.)'

xvi Journal entry, Conradi, *A Life*, 490.

xvii Letter undated, but 28 January fell on a Monday in 1963 and although *The Snow Ball* was not published until 1964, Brophy might well have sent Murdoch the novel to read in manuscript form.

xviii Letter undated, and postmark illegible, but *The Finishing Touch* was published in 1963 so probably written that year.

xix Not her real name.

xx   Morgan, *With Love and Rage*, 40, 88, and note to the editors.

xxi Where Murdoch's letters to David Morgan do not carry a precise date, as in this case, Morgan has dated them himself either by postmark or from memory.

xxii Not his real name.

xxiii David Morgan, *With Love and Rage*, 76, and note to editors.

xxiv Year date suggested by Bodleian Library archivist.

NOTES

xxvi   Conradi, *A Life*, 559.
xxvii Not her real name.
xxviii Not her real name.

PART SIX

i   Dooley (ed.), *Conversations*, 44–55.
ii   The analyses of novels here and elsewhere in *Living on Paper* are necessarily brief. For fuller discussions of them, see Martin and Rowe, *Iris Murdoch: A Literary Life*.
iii The book comprises three essays: 'The Idea of Perfection'; 'On "God" and "Good"'; 'The Sovereignty of Good Over Other Concepts'.
iv   Murdoch, *Sovereignty of Good*, 52.
v   Murdoch, *Sovereignty of Good*, 73.
vi   The play was finally published by Colophon Press with Old Town Books in 1994.
vii 'A Note on Drama', *Cue: The Greenwich Theatre Magazine* (September 1970), 13–14.
viii This observation was made by the theatre director Bill Alexander in an email to the editors dated 3 October 2014.
ix   Conradi, *A Life*, 495.
x   Anne Cobbe, an old Somerville friend, who had become a lecturer in mathematics at Lady Margaret Hall and who died in 1971, gifted her house in Walton Street through her will to Somerville College, on the condition that Philippa Foot would be granted life tenure. This gift provided Foot with a home in Oxford, leaving the college responsible for its maintenance and repair during her lifetime, including those periods when she was teaching in the United States.
xi   There may well be other letters which pre-date those included here but these seem to have been lost.
xii Conradi, *A Life*, 557.
xiii Conradi, *A Life*, 485.
xiv Dooley (ed.), *Conversations*, 51.
xv   Morgan, note to the editors.
xvi Not her real name. A close friend of Brophy who was to replace Maureen Duffy in her affections.
xvii Morgan, note to the editors.
xviii Purton, *Chronology*, 133–4.

PART SEVEN

i   Interview with William Slaymaker in Dooley (ed.), *Conversations*, 139–47.
ii   See interview with Jonathan Miller in Dooley (ed.), *Conversations*, 209–17.
iii Letter (not included here) dated 18 May 1981.
iv   Conradi, *A Life*, 548.
v   Letter (not included here) dated November 1982.
vi   Letter (not included here) dated 3 October 1986.
vii Letter (not included here) dated 18 June 1979.
viii Letter (not included here) dated 9 December 1980. John Lennon was murdered in New York on 8 December 1980.

ix   A revised version of Conradi's thesis was published in 1986 as *The Saint and the Artist*.

x   Letter undated, but probably written during or soon after September 1979 when Pope
        John Paul II visited Ireland.

xi   Following the visit, Murdoch drafted a letter to the chairman of the Chinese People's
        Association for Friendship with Foreign Countries – their host in China – raising ques-
        tions about 'the problem of individual freedom' in his country. The letter, which she
        and three other group members were to sign, was not sent (on the advice of Derek
        Bryan, Sinologist and founding member of SACU).

xii   Letter undated, but references to the Falklands War and to Michael Levey's first novel
        suggest 1982.

xiii   Letter undated, but probably written in 1982, the year during which the Canadian Charter
        of Rights and Freedoms (which contained much about the use of English and French
        in Canada) was passed.

xiv   Peter J. Conradi, *Going Buddhist: Panic and Emptiness, the Buddha and Me* (Short Books,
        2004), 141.

xv   See Brigid Brophy, 'A Case-Historical Fragment of Autobiography' in *Baroque 'n' Roll* for
        a fuller picture of her health problems during the early 1980s.

xvi   Letter undated, but John Bayley gave his lecture at Dundee University in late October
        1983.

xvii   This postscript, written on a separate piece of paper, is not attached to any letter to
        Brophy and is undated. We have guessed that it was written sometime in the mid-1980s.
        If so, it is possible that the odd figure of Irina Vallar in *The Message to the Planet* owes
        something to the strange Christie Malakite in *Wolf Solent* and that, more generally,
        Murdoch's late novels may have been influenced by the work of John Cowper Powys.

xviii   Letter undated, but Doris Lessing's *The Good Terrorist* was shortlisted for the Booker
        Prize in 1985.

xix   In a letter dated 4 May 1986 (not included here), Murdoch described this house as 'small,
        narrow, made of red brick, with a high pitched roof and Edwardian style windows (tall,
        unsashed), date disputed, either 1913 or 1919. It's not pretty, but it has a little character
        and repose. There is a gaudy little pink cherry in the tiny front garden and a birch tree
        and an apple tree in the extremely small back garden'.

xx   Our thanks to Mr Tapan Kumar Mukherjee, West Bengal, India, who sent us a copy of
        this letter in November 2014.

xxi   Purton, *Chronology*, 181.

xxii   Conradi, *Going Buddhist*.

xxiii   Sue Summers was collecting information for an article, 'The Lost Loves of Iris Murdoch',
        which was published in *You* magazine, *Mail on Sunday*, 5 June 1988, 16–22.

xxiv   Conradi, *Going Buddhist*, 144, 153.

PART EIGHT

i   *The Green Knight* (Chatto & Windus, 1993), 269.

ii   Interview with Murdoch, *New York Times*, 22 February 1990, 20.

iii   *Jackson's Dilemma* (Chatto & Windus, 1995), 249.

iv   Murdoch, *Existentialists and Mystics*, 326.

v   See, for example, Maria Antonaccio, who asserts that 'the experience of reading it is
        actually dialogical and intertextual' in her essay 'The Virtues of Metaphysics: A Review

of Iris Murdoch's Philosophical Writings' in Broackes (ed.), *Iris Murdoch, Philosopher*, 169. See also her *A Philosophy to Live By: Engaging Iris Murdoch* (Oxford University Press, 2012).

vi   This book was to be dedicated to Stanley Rosen, the American philosopher (1929–2014). One of the central themes of Rosen's work is the claim that the specialist discourses of philosophy have no other basis than the intelligent understanding of aspects of ordinary life and human existence. Murdoch and Rosen admired each other's work and they became friends (see Conradi, *A Life*, 586, 658).

vii Conradi, *A Life*, 586.

viii Iris Murdoch, *Heidegger* (1993), unpublished typescript held in the Conradi Archive, Kingston University Special Collections, KUAS6/5/1/4.

ix   Letter to Naomi Lebowitz (not included here) dated 12 January 1992.

x   A treaty undertaken to integrate Europe, signed on 7 February 1992 by the members of the European Community in Maastricht, the Netherlands.

xi   In his memoir *Party im Blitz* (written 1991–4 but published posthumously in 2003), Canetti was scathing about Murdoch, claiming that she was the embodiment of everything he hated about England, accusing her of self-interest and emotional coldness.

xii Conradi, *A Life*, 465.

xiii However, A. N. Wilson went on to publish *Iris Murdoch As I Knew Her* in 2003.

xiv Letters (not included here) to Naomi Lebowitz dated 7 December 1993 and to Roly Cochrane, one undated, the other dated by the editors June/July 1995.

xv   Letter undated, but Murdoch's statement that 'It is forty years since he went' indicates that the letter was written in 1992.

xvi Letter undated, but probably written during 1993 as Kusseff 'was given permission to write a life of Frank [Thompson] about 1993' (Conradi, *A Very English Hero*, 6).

xvii Letter undated, but written after the Bayleys had returned from their last visit to Japan in May/June 1993.

xviii Letter undated, but the reference to a 'gathering' in memory of Frank Thompson suggests it was written sometime in 1994, the year in which Colonel Robert Pearson, the British defence attaché in Sofia, Bulgaria, 'arranged a fiftieth anniversary service near the Litakovo monument to Frank and his colleagues' (Conradi, *A Very English Hero*, 367).

xix In a letter (not included here) to Jane Turner, editor at Chatto & Windus, written later in May 1993, Murdoch mentions that her mother's family were 'Richardsons, squires who were planted in Ireland in 1616 to control the wild Irish. I have the family tree since then, wherein I gladly note that I am related to another novelist, Henry Handel Richardson!'

xx   A celebration of the life of Iris Murdoch, organised by Chatto & Windus, her literary agent Ed Victor, and her friend Josephine Hart, took place at the Royal Society of Literature, 1 Hyde Park Gardens, London, on 17 March 1999.

ACKNOWLEDGEMENTS

We are deeply grateful to Katie Giles, Kingston University archivist, for her efficiency and for her unfailing co-operation, often at short notice, in helping us locate letters, books and documents. Her overview of the material held in the Iris Murdoch Archives in Kingston University's Special Collections and her knowledge of Murdoch's life have been invaluable. Katie is also now adept at deciphering Murdoch's handwriting, which became less legible as she grew older, and this expertise has been crucial for those transcribing Murdoch's letters in the Kingston archives. Thanks are also due to Frances White, honorary assistant director of the Iris Murdoch Archive Project and writer in residence at Kingston University, for her interest, support and comments on the final draft of the book, to Katrina Clifford, senior information adviser (bibliographic and metadata), Kingston University for useful information and for her unfailing kindness, and to Pamela Osborn for research help and her skill in proofreading.

Peter Conradi's biography, *Iris Murdoch: A Life*, was an essential resource during the compilation of *Living on Paper*, providing illuminating factual information that enabled us to flesh out many of the people and relationships mentioned in Murdoch's letters, date particular letters, and link others with Murdoch's novels. It is also invisibly present in innumerable facts and observations provided throughout this volume. In addition, we found Conradi's *Iris Murdoch: A Writer at War, Letters and Diaries 1938–46* and *A Very English Hero: The Making of Frank Thompson* extremely useful. Our debt to Conradi's scholarship is huge. *Iris Murdoch: A Literary Life* (2010), co-authored by Priscilla Martin, and Conradi's *The Saint and the Artist: A Study of the Fiction of Iris Murdoch* (2001), were extremely useful when writing the introductory sections of this book. Valerie Purton's *An Iris Murdoch Chronology* made checking dates and events easier than it would otherwise have been. Special thanks are also due to John Bayley, who ceded copyright of all Iris Murdoch's letters to Kingston University when the Iris Murdoch Centre (now the Iris Murdoch Archive Project) was inaugurated in 2004.

We have also drawn on the goodwill of many archivists and librarians who accessed letters and material for us or who provided information about

Murdoch's life and friends. These include: Gemma Cook, Churchill Archives Centre, Churchill College, Cambridge; Alison Cullingford, Special Collections, J. B. Priestley Library, Bradford University; Nancy Fulford, Special Collections, Reading University; Sean Gledhill, Leeds University Special Collections; Colin Harris, Helen Langley, Judith Priestman and Rebecca Wall of the Bodleian Library Special Collections, Oxford University; Kathryn Hodson and Kalmia Strong, Special Collections & University Archives, Iowa University; Alison Marshall, Felicity Crentsil and Damien McManus of Bristol University Library; Anne Manuel and Kate O'Donnell of Somerville College, Oxford University; Hannah Lowery, Special Collections, Bristol University; Michael R. Powell and Kathy Whelan, librarians, Chetham's Library, Manchester; Catherine McIntyre, Elinor Robinson and Sinead Wheeler, Archives Services Group, London School of Economics and Political Science; Jean Rose, archivist, Random House Group Archive and Library, Northamptonshire; David Smith, Kate Davey and Sally Speirs, St Anne's College, Oxford; Sarah Schnuriger, Special Collections, Washington University, St Louis, Missouri; David Plant, Oxford Brookes University; Tim Noakes and Nan Mehan, Stanford University, California; Eric Legendre, Éditions Gallimard, Paris; William Swainger, Tate Images.

For financial contributions that have enabled purchase of letter runs for the Iris Murdoch Archives at Kingston University over the last ten years we are grateful to the Victoria and Albert Museum Purchase Grant Fund; the National Heritage Memorial Fund; the National Lottery through the Heritage Lottery Fund; the Friends of the National Libraries; the Breslauer Foundation; the Alumni Fund, Kingston University; members of the Iris Murdoch Society; several anonymous donors; members of the general public and various social media sites. Avril Horner wishes to thank the Leverhulme Trust for an Emeritus Fellowship award of £5,248 in 2012 that enabled her to undertake research in various archives in the UK and the USA.

We are particularly grateful to David Morgan for access to letters not already published in his book *With Love and Rage: A Friendship with Iris Murdoch* (2010) and for his helpful commentaries on them. We wish to thank Christopher Stray for sending us images of Murdoch's letters to Eduard Fraenkel (held at Corpus Christi College, Oxford) and also Kate Thompson for special permission to read Iris Murdoch's letters to Frank Thompson, held in the Bodleian Library and closed at the time of requested access. We would like to thank Lord Maurice Saatchi for allowing us access to photocopies of letters from Iris Murdoch to Josephine Hart, the originals of which are held in the Howard Gotlieb Archival Research Center at Boston University. Thanks also to Mary Lidderdale for providing contextual information and help with dating letters from Iris Murdoch to Hal Lidderdale. We are grateful to Harry Smith for reading through Murdoch's letters to Albert and Naomi

Lebowitz held in Special Collections, Washington University in St Louis, and for liaising with the archivist there who kindly photocopied a selection for us. Enormous gratitude is due to Joanna, Matt and Jake Garber for gifting Murdoch's letters to Henry Weinberger to the Iris Murdoch Archives.

Many people offered us support in various ways and generously gave time to answer questions about Murdoch's correspondents, including solving puzzles concerning dates, events and the contents of letters. They include: Bill Alexander; Janet Beer and David Woodman; Cheryl Bove; Justin Broackes; Janet Dance; Mark Doran; Maureen Duffy; Rachel Fenner; Andrew and Becky Gardiner; Paul Girard; Judith Harris; Laurence Horner; Monique Henry; Meg Jensen; Gavin Lawrence; Mary Lawson; Albert Lebowitz; Kate Levey; David Mackintosh; Priscilla Martin; Marie Mulvey-Roberts; Hugh Robson; Joan Scotson; Alison Samuel; Kevin Sarwar-Polley; Judy Shane; Ursula Tidd; Susan Mary Walters; and Stephen White. Although they are not included in *Living on Paper*, we would like to thank John Chrysostomides for the loan of letters to Julian Chrysostomides, and Barabara Dorf and Joan Scotson for donating letters to the Iris Murdoch Archive. Thanks to Paul Girard for permission to quote from the letters of Scott Dunbar, and to Tom Hicks for permission to quote from the letters of David Hicks. For help with the translation of certain passages and phrases we owe a particular debt to: Alison Scott-Baumann, Barbara Servant and Ursula Tidd (French); Justin Broackes (Latin and French); Ellena Bassil-Morozow (Russian); and Korina Giaxoglou (ancient Greek).

Our task of transcription was made considerably lighter by the many volunteers who helped transcribe letters held in the Iris Murdoch Archives at Kingston University. These included: Abigail Adeusi, Shivani Bhargava, Maire Bounds, Paul and Patricia Brudenell, Emily Clifton, Sam Coles-Rogers, Peter Ely, Jade Harvey, Charlotte Meredith, Vanessa Palmer, Charlotte Perks, John Spearman, Liam Sprod, Kalee Stegehuis, Clare Watson, Frances White, Charles White, Samuel White, Jane Whitfield and Janet Wilkinson. Special mention must be made, however, of a small dedicated group who, as well as working on other runs, stepped in at the last moment to transcribe Murdoch's letters to Brigid Brophy, which arrived in the Murdoch archives in July 2014. This group worked hard and fast, enabling us to include a sele-lction of these letters in the book before it went to press; it comprised Penny D'Souza, Pat Garth, Jenny Matthew, Jill Speed and Sally Wood and Rachel Hirschler, who led and oversaw their work.

We are grateful to Williams Music, A Division of Rodgers & Hammerstein: An Imagem Company, for allowing us to quote from Richard Rodgers's song 'No Strings' and to Penguin Random House for allowing us to quote from Don Marquis's poem 'Poets' from his *The Lives and Times of Archy & Mehitabel*.

We owe a special debt of gratitude to Peter Conradi, Justin Broackes and Mark Luprecht, who all read through *Living on Paper* before it went to press and spotted numerous omissions and small errors. Any errors that remain are our responsibility alone. Above all, we are deeply grateful to Becky Hardie, our editor at Chatto & Windus, for her encouragement and her expert eye. Thanks are also due to Susannah Otter and Natalie Wall for overseeing the production of *Living on Paper*, and to David Milner, whose copy-editing was meticulous. Last but not least, we would like to thank our husbands, Nigel Rowe and Howard Horner, for their patience, support and practical help over the four years we worked on this book.

INDEX

All works are by Iris Murdoch (IM) unless otherwise stated.

Green Knight, The (1993) xvi, 248n1, 549n2, 557–8, 562, 573, 578, 582, 584, 585, 587, 588, 595n2
'Greenham Common women' 499n1
Greer, Germaine: *The Obstacle Race* 476
Greeves, Tom 89
Grice, Paul 400
Grigg, John and Patsy 226, 236–7, 371
Grünewald, Matthias 302
Guardian (newspaper) 469, 560
Guy the Gorilla 185

Hadas, David 415
Hadas, Pamela 415
Hamburger, Michael 229, 576n2, 589; *Friedrich Hölderlin...* 576–7, 590; IM's letters to 576–7, 589–90
Hammett, Dashiell: *The Maltese Falcon* 323
Hampshire, Stuart 166, 188, 211, 235, 447; *Thought and Action* 211
Hardy, Thomas 401, 574
Hare, R. M. 167
Hart, Josephine (Lady Saatchi) 471, 561, 610; *Damage* 562–3, 569–70; *Sin* 577–8; *see also Black Prince, The*
    IM's letters to 520–21, 540–41, 553, 555, 562–3, 569–70, 577–8, 586
Hart, Judith 167
Harvey, Andrew 575n2, 606; *Hidden Journey...* 570; *Journey in Ladakh* 570n3
Hattersley, Roy 408
Hawkes, Jacquetta (Priestley) 167, 345; IM's letter to 174–5
Hawthorne, Nathaniel: *The Scarlet Letter* 133
Hay, Julius 310
Healey, Denis 15, 44, 49, 447, 484
Heath, Edward 419n1, 482n2
Heffer, Eric 531
Hegel, Georg W. F. 23, 76, 77, 82, 87, 106, 115, 116, 120, 123, 144, 472, 602, 610; *Logic* 144
Heidegger, Martin 23, 50, 72, 82, 106n3, 109, 470, 543, 549, 558, 559, 583–4, 607, 610–11, 618; *Sein und Zeit (Being and Time)* 109, 117, 235
Henderson, Isobel 96
Henri, Adrian 378
Henry and Cato (1976) 354, 423, 426, 440, 442n1, 519
Hepburn, Katharine 315n1
Hepworth, Barbara 4n1
Herbert, George 432; 'Love III' 625
Herzog, Chaim, President of Israel 500–1
Hevesi, Hans 309
Hick, John (ed.): *The Myth of God Incarnate* 451
Hicks, Barney 460, 611

Hicks, David 611–12; meets IM 1, 7; brief relationship with her xvi, 9, 54, 611; works for British Council in Egypt 14, 32n1, and Teheran 37; sent *The Brothers Karamazov* by IM 42; in Prague 42; in Scotland 48, 49; spends ten days in London with IM 55, 65; they decide to marry 55, 56, 65; breaks off the engagement 63, 64, 81, 330; meets Molly Purchase 63, 65, 70; tries to 're-establish relations' with IM 70–71; marriage 81–2, 138, 241; regular meetings with IM 95, 138, 142, 150; acts at Shakespeare Festival 142n4, 143; second marriage to Katharine Messenger 138, 153; occasional meetings with IM 237, 277, 288; still has 'the old magic' for IM 262n2; impresses David Morgan 320–21; meets John Bayley 391; is writing a novel 396; has happy meeting with IM 396; plans to move to Worcestershire 436n1; jobless 446; dreams of IM 446; son commits suicide 460; letter to IM 572; death 561, 572
    IM's letters to vi, xviii, 7–9, 14–16, 22, 23, 24, 37–40, 41–6, 48–9, 51–4, 55–9, 60–64, 81–2, 138, 141–3, 143–4, 150, 153–4, 277, 288–9, 320–21, 329–30, 391, 396, 436, 446, 460–61
Hicks, Julia 138
Hicks, Katharine (*née* Messenger) 138, 142, 153, 276, 391, 611; IM's letter to 572
Hicks, Molly (*née* Purchase) 63, 65, 70, 81, 82, 138, 241, 611
Hicks, Tom 611
Hijab, Wasfi 103, 108, 110, 112, 347, 419
Hill, Christopher 167
Hillman, James: *Suicide and the Soul* 497
Hinckley Jr, John 484n1
Hippolyte, Jean: *Genèse et structure de la phénoménologie de l'esprit de Hegel* 106
Hitler, Adolf 12, 58
Hobbema, Meindert 43
Hobbes, Thomas 93
Hockney, David 233
Hodges, Professor H. A. 82
Hoggart, Richard 213
Holdaway, Jim *see* O'Donnell, Peter
Hölderlin, Friedrich 576, 590
Holland, William 19
Homer 190
Horizon 29, 76
Hornung, E. W.: *Raffles: The Amateur Cracksman* 238, 291, 293
'House of Theory, A' (1958) 167, 181n2
Howard, Elizabeth Jane 636nxi
Hubbard, Margaret xviii, 165, 170, 193, 194, 228, 231, 233, 600

entries) 236, 258, 272; has 45th birthday at
Nettlepole, Kent 269, 270; in Rome 270–71;
enjoys teaching at RCA 278; gives party at
Harcourt Terrace 277, 282–3; lectures at Trinity
College, Dublin 235, 282; publishes 'The Idea of
Perfection' 235; reputation rises 235; another
party 295; at Nettlepole 297, 306; in Italy 300–1,
302; depressed by the futility of teaching 312;
visits Beatrice May Baker 316; plans to lend
money to friends and relations 317; lectures in
Manchester 319, 320; exhausted by students 321,
322; receives bath robe from fan in Atlanta 323;
presents paper at Bowdoin College, Maine 239,
325–6; lectures at UCL 233, 328; illness 328; in
India and Singapore 331; in Australia and New
Zealand 239, 330, 331–5; and income tax 336, 337;
sells her manuscripts to University of Iowa 343,
359; leaves RCA 239; sees Queneau and wife in
France 237, 343–4; and stage production of *The
Italian Girl* 345; gives Leslie Stephen Lecture 235,
372; politically active 235–6

1968–75 begins a productive ten years 351 (*see The
Nice and the Good, Bruno's Dream, A Fairly
Honourable Defeat, An Accidental Man, The Black
Prince, The Sacred and Profane Love Machine, A
Word Child, Henry and Cato* and *The Sea, The
Sea*); gives another party 361; on British Council
lecture tour in Switzerland and Italy 361, 362,
363; at Royal Academy dinner 366; at Worth
Abbey 3667; and student protests 356, 374, 377,
384–5; defends Cohn-Bendit in *The Times* 356,
367; in Scotland with the Griggs 371; on British
Council lecture tour in Japan 376, 377; takes part
in Arts Council Writers' tour in Lancashire 378;
writes dramas 355–6; receives money from
Booker-McConnell 383; illnesses 384; in Venice
with husband and their mothers 385; donates
complete set of works to village raffle 386;
illness and arthritis 388, 389, 392; in France 389;
has owls down the chimney 390; in France again
and Italy 394; plans North Midlands lecture 397,
398; lectures in Mexico 395–6, 397, 398; visits
USA 357–8, 398–401; meets Albert and Naomi
Lebowitz (*see entries*) 357–8, 398; lectures in Italy
404; and production of *The Three Arrows* 406;
lectures in Athens 407; has to return from Egypt
after Bayley breaks leg 407; further letters from
her mad Atlanta fan 408, 417; tries to help
Morawski 409–10; stays with the Spenders 412;
wins James Tait Black Memorial Prize 353; at
parties 415; her Christmas organised by
brother-in-law 417; hates the General Election

417, 418, 419; rears butterflies 423, 424; visits
Poland 423, 424, 425–6, 574; goes to Auschwitz
425, 467; in Italy and France 425; buys flat at 29
Cornwall Gardens 356; lectures in Japan 430; in
USA 430; struggling with philosophy 432; and
beginning of mother's mental decline 356–7, 439
(*see* Murdoch, Rene)

1976–82 awarded CBE 354; gives Romanes Lecture
(Oxford) 355; campaigns for release of Bukovsky
356, 443, 445; in France 439; in Belfast 441, 448;
has too much to do 444; visits Israel as part of
cultural delegation 444, 445–6, 447; visits
Spenders again 448*n1*, 450; introduced to Harry
Weinberger (*see entry*) 357, 450; 'bugged' by a
lecture 452; without electricity and frozen 452,
453; at Franco-Irish literary conference 452, 453;
on US British Council lecture tour 455–6, 457;
lectures in Europe 457, 458, 459; in Italy 459, 461;
wins Booker Prize 354, 463; Christmas 463; and
strikes 472; overwhelmed by work 473; in
Romania 473; pleased with Mrs Thatcher 474; in
France and Spain 474; in Berlin 470; gives eulogy
at Reynolds Stone's memorial service 471; in
China 476, 477; and petrol rationing 478; enjoys
lecture tour in Iceland 480; and Iran Hostage
Crisis 480; learns about ISBNs 481; awarded
honorary degree by Bristol University 482;
Snowdon photo 484; in US 485; speaks in French
at Pompidou Centre conference 469; gives talk
in Russian on World Service 469; on Prince
Charles and Diana 484–5, 487; meets Conradi
(*see entry*) 471; on Greek cruise 485–6; 'bugged'
by work 486; and creation of Social Democrat
Party 486–7; and further power cuts 488; enjoys
her garden 490; and Falklands War 491, 492;
made honorary member of American Academy
of Arts and Sciences 469; in France 494; at
Virginia Woolf centenary conference 494, 495;
meets M. R. D. Foot 496; on holiday in Scotland
and Yorkshire 496; gives Gifford Lectures
469–70, 489, 490, 494, 495, 496, 497, 559, 564, 613;
in France 497

1983–8 stays on Lanzarote with the Villers 471, 498,
499; her crazy fan 'surfaces' again 501; votes
Conservative 470; awarded honorary degree by
St Andrews University 502; finds swallows deafening 502; in Korea 508; in Dundee 506;
publishes *The Philosopher's Pupil* 466 (*see entry*);
stays near the sea 508; troubled by paper-eating
mice 508; overwhelmed with work 508, 509;
illness 509; obsessed by Titian's *The Flaying of
Marsyas* 509; takes up six-month fellowship at

penguin.co.uk/vintage